INTERNATIONAL LAW AND TRANSNATIONAL ORGANISED CRIME

International Law and Transnational Organised Crime

Edited by
PIERRE HAUCK
and
SVEN PETERKE

OXFORD
UNIVERSITY PRESS

OXFORD
UNIVERSITY PRESS

Great Clarendon Street, Oxford, OX2 6DP,
United Kingdom

Oxford University Press is a department of the University of Oxford. It furthers the University's objective of excellence in research, scholarship, and education by publishing worldwide. Oxford is a registered trade mark of Oxford University Press in the UK and in certain other countries

First Edition published in 2016

Published in the United States of America by Oxford University Press
198 Madison Avenue, New York, NY 10016, United States of America

British Library Cataloguing in Publication Data
Data available

Library of Congress Control Number: 2016944982

ISBN 978–0–19–873373–7

Preface

The purpose of this book is to supply the academic need for a thorough account of the key concepts of international law to transnational organised crime (TOC).

Having been disregarded by international legal doctrine for a long time, TOC has more and more become an important subject matter in state practice. As a matter of fact, the United Nations have categorized TOC and international terrorism as a 'new threat' to international peace that has the potential to undermine not only democratic institutions and the rule of law but also sustainable development and regional stability. In this way, TOC and its combat pose enormous challenges to the theory and practice of international law.

By contrast, however, TOC still plays a marginal role in academic writing and there are only few systematic publications offering profound insights into the various international treaties and documents dealing with the suppression of this complex phenomenon.

The reasons for this unsatisfying state of affairs are multifaceted. With all due caution, it still appears that the issue of TOC is neither very inviting nor very accessible to international lawyers. Especially compared to international criminal law *stricto sensu*, which is commonly defined as encompassing exclusively those norms that entail individual responsibility directly under public international law, TOC is widely seen as part of so-called transnational criminal law: an area of law placed at the outer limits of international criminal law *lato sensu*, forming part of a new area of interest with novel empirical and theoretical features. Last but not least it follows a crime control model to comprehend which requires multidisciplinary knowledge of both international relations and criminological concepts in particular. These concepts have indeed been incorporated into international law, but their adequacy and universality have been compromised by academics all the time.

The mere existence of the UN Convention against Transnational Organised Crime and its Protocols gives yet another reason. It demonstrates the need to approach this subject in a more comprehensive way than by simply looking only at the content of the numerous international treaties and initiatives that complement them. Over the last decades and under the impression of a 'globalization' of TOC states have set up an international framework that affects virtually every corner of our societies, be it in a negative or in a positive sense. To understand this better, however, requires insights into the basic concepts and controversies that surround the numerous documents that define this area of study. This also implies the necessity to analyse the effectiveness of these instruments.

Furthermore, many international lawyers have a conservative background in public and administrative law and therefore possess only rudimentary knowledge of the conceptual fundaments of the debate on organised crime and its transnational manifestations. Thanks to the emergence of international criminal law this profile has indeed begun to change. But there is still growing awareness today of the need to go beyond these traditional limitations of international legal doctrine and theory. In the special case of TOC, it seems that many scholars even find it difficult, or simply have too little time, to build this bridge by noticing appropriate publications.

Our book is meant to provide this necessary, multidisciplinary 'backpack'. It contains systematic contributions to the pertinent universal conventions and other relevant international regimes and issues, such as money laundering, cybercrime, or cultural property. In addition, it inimitably analyses TOC from the perspective of those branches of international law in which non-state actors and their activities deserve special attention, namely international security law (the use of force and its exemptions), the international law of armed conflict, international human rights law, international criminal law, and the law of the sea.

This book is based on an innovative approach that takes into account (1) the criminological fundamentals without which a more critical understanding of the topic is almost impossible, (2) the demand for a systematic compilation of the various international regimes that set standards for national legislators, and (3) the increasing fragmentation of international law, which necessitates special reflection on the subject from the perspective of its relevant sub-areas.

Corresponding to this multidisciplinary approach to content, our team of thirty authors likewise comes from a public international and/or criminal law background. It mostly consists of academics but also contains practitioners, and it spans Africa, Australia, Europe, North America, and South America in global experience.

It is our hope that this book will prove to be a useful tool for both practitioners and academics of all disciplines dealing with TOC who are seeking an easy access to this complex area of law.

We would like to thank OUP, notably Emma Endean, Nicole Leyland, and Louise Summerling, for their continuous support throughout this project and our team in Trier, Monique Schmidt for supervising the editing process, Johanna Horsthemke and Lina Kahlert for preparatory works, and Kim Eifel, Matthew Langford, Maximilian Metzen, and Julia Schmidt for proofreading services.

Pierre Hauck and Sven Peterke

Trier/Germany and João Pessoa/Brazil
May 2016

Table of Contents

III. OTHER RELEVANT INTERNATIONAL REGIMES AND ISSUES

V. PROCEDURAL AND TECHNOLOGICAL CHALLENGES FOR THE INVESTIGATION OF TOC—POLICING, TECHNOLOGICAL ASPECTS, EFFICIENCY, EXCHANGE OF INFORMATION, ABUSE OF POWER, AND TACTICS FOR CONDUCTING INVESTIGATIONS

Table of Cases and Other Decisions

I. INTERNATIONAL JURISDICTION

1. International law

2. International criminal law

II. NATIONAL JURISDICTION

1. United States

2. SBiH

Table of Legislation

I. INTERNATIONAL LEGISLATION

1. United Nations

2. Other international jurisdiction

3. European Legislation

4. African Union

II. NATIONAL LEGISLATION

1. Southeast Asian Nations

2. American

3. Australia

4. Bahamas

5. Brazil

6. Canada

7. France

8. Germany

List of Abbreviations

ACHPR	African Charter on Human and Peoples' Rights
ACLU	American Civil Liberties Union
ACTA	Anti-Counterfeiting Trade Agreement
AIDP	International Association of Penal Law
AJIL	*American Journal of International Law*
AML	anti-money laundering
AnwK-StGB	AnwaltKommentar StGB (Heidelberger Kommentar)
ANZUS	Australia, New Zealand, United States Security Treaty
AP	Additional Protocols
APEG	Asia-Pacific Economic Cooperation
APG	Asia/Pacific Group on Money Laundering
APuZ	*Aus Politik und Zeitgeschichte* (quoted by year and page)
AQIM	Al-Qaeda in the Islamic Maghreb
Arab ITO Convention	Arab Convention on Combating Information Technology Offences (Cairo, 21 December 2010)
Art.	Article
ASEAN	Association of South-East Asian Nations
ASEAN-WEN	ASEAN Wildlife Enforcement Network
ATM	automatic teller machine
ATT	UN Arms Trade Treaty
AU	African Union
AU-CS	African Union Convention on Cyber Security and Personal Data Protection (Malobo, 27 June 2014)
Aust ILJ	*Australian International Law Journal*
BeNeLux	Belgium Netherlands Luxembourg
BGBl.	*Bundesgesetzblatt* (German Federal Law Gazette)
BGHSt	Entscheidungen des Bundesgerichtshofs in Strafsachen (Germany)
BKA	Bundeskriminalamt, German Federal Police Office
Boston College Intl Comp L Rev	*Boston College International and Comparative Law Review*
BSA	Bank Secrecy Act
BVerfG	Bundesverfassungsgericht, Federal Constitutional Court
BYBIL	*British Yearbook of International Law*
C	communications et informations
CAC	Convention against Corruption
CAH	crimes against humanity
CAR	Central African Republic
CARICOM	Caribbean Community
CARSI	Regional Security Initiative for Central America
CAT	The Committee Against Torture
CBD	Convention on Biological Diversity

CCALMR	Commission for the Conservation of Antarctic Living Marine Resources
ccBH	criminal code of Bosnia and Herzegovina
CCC	(Council of Europe) Convention on Cybercrime
CCE	continuing criminal enterprise
CCPCJ	(UN) Commission on Crime Prevention and Criminal Justice
CCTV	closed circuit television
CCW	Convention on the Prohibition or Restriction on the Use of Certain Conventional Weapons Which May Be Deemed to Be Excessively Injurious or to Have Indiscriminate Effects (also known as 'Convention on Conventional Weapons')
CDD	customer due diligence
CDPC	(Council of Europe) Committee on Crime Problems
CEO	Chief Executive Officer
CEPOL	European Police College
CETS	Council of Europe Treaty Series
CFR	United States Code of Federal Regulations
CFATF	Caribbean Financial Action Task Force
CFT	combating of financing of terrorism
CGPCS	Contact Group on Piracy off the Coast of Somalia
Ch	Chapter
Chinese JIL	*Chinese Journal of International Law*
CI	confidential informant
CIA	Central Intelligence Agency
CIA-offences	offences against the confidentiality, integrity, and availability of information systems and/or data
CICAD	Inter-American Drug Abuse Control Commission
CINOA	Confédération Internationale des Négociants en Oeuvres d'Art (International Confederation of Art and Antique Dealers' Associations)
CIS	Commonwealth of Independent States
CIS-CI	Agreement on cooperation among the Member States of the Commonwealth of Independent States (CIS) in combating offences relating to computer information
CITES	Convention on International Trade in Endangered Species of Wild Fauna and Flora
CJEU	Court of Justice of the European Union
CJS	criminal justice system
CJTL	*Columbia Journal of Transnational Law*
CLPRC	Criminal Law of the People's Republic of China
CNCP	Commonwealth Network of Contact Persons
CND	(UN) Commission on Narcotic Drugs
CoCom	Coordinating Committee on Multilateral Export Controls
CoE	Council of Europe
Com	(European) Commission
COMESA	Common Market for Eastern and Southern Africa
COMM	Communication
CoP	conference of the parties
CoPU	Conference of the Parties to the UNTOC
COSP	Conference of States Parties

CP	(France) Code Pénal; (Italy) Codice Penal
CPI	(Transparency International) Corruption Perceptions Index
CRC	United Nations Convention on the Rights of the Child
CSEC	commercial sexual exploitation of children
CSI	crime scene investigation
CTC	Counter Terrorist Committee
Cth	Commonwealth of Australia Consolidated Acts
CTOC	Convention on Transnational Organised Crime
CTRs	currency transaction reports
CTS	Consolidated Treaty Series
CTU	Caribbean Telecommunications Union
CUP	Cambridge University Press
DEA	Drug Enforcement Administration
DIA	(US) Defense Intelligence Agency
DNA	deoxyribonucleic acid
Doc.	Document
DPF	Brazil's Federal Police
DRC	Democratic Republic of Congo
EAG	Eurasian Group (on money laundering)
EAW	European Arrest Warrant
EC	European Community, European Communities
ECHR	Convention for the Protection of Human Rights and Fundamental Freedoms
ECtHR Ser A	European Court of Human Rights, Series A, Judgments and Decisions
ECJ	European Court of Justice (now CJEU)
ECOSOC	UN Economic and Social Council
ECOWAS	Economic Community of West African States
ECOWAS-Cybercrime	ECOWAS Directive C/DIR. 1/08/11 on Fighting Cyber Crime within ECOWAS of 19 August 2011
ECRIS	European Criminal Record Information Centre
ECtHR	European Court of Human Rights
ed.	edited by/ editor(s)
EEZ	exclusive economic zone
e.g.	exempli gratia, example given
EIA	Environmental Investigation Agency
EIO	European Investigation Order; Directive 2014/41/EU of the European Parliament and of the Council of 3 April 2014 regarding the European Investigation Order in criminal matters
EJCCLCJ	*European Journal of Crime, Criminal Law and Criminal Justice*
EJIL	*European Journal of International Law*
EJN	European Judicial Network
EP	European Parliament
ESAAMLG	Eastern and Southern Africa Anti-Money Laundering Group
ESCWA	Economic and Social Commission for Western Asia
ETA	Euskadi Ta Askatasuna, the Basque separatist movement

ETS	European Treaty Series
EU	European Union
Eurojust	European Prosecutors Office
Europol	European Police Agency
FAO	(UN) Food and Agriculture Organization
FARC	Fuerzas Armadas Revolucionarias de Colombia
FATF	Financial Action Task Force
FBI	Federal Bureau of Investigation
FBN	(US) Federal Bureau of Narcotics
FCPA	(US) Foreign Corrupt Practices Act
FD	Framework Decision
FD OC	Framework Decision on Organized Crime, Council Framework Decision 2008/841/JHA on the fight against organized crime
f./ff.	following page(s)
FinCEN	(US) Financial Crimes Enforcement Network
FIU	financial intelligence unit
FLEG	forest law enforcement and governance
FLEGT	forest law enforcement, governance, and trade
Fordham Intl LJ	*Fordham International Law Journal*
FRAP	Frente Revolucionario Antfascista y Patriota
Frontex	European Agency for the Management of Operational Cooperation at the External Borders of the Member States of the European Union
FSRBs	FATF-style regional anti-money laundering bodies
G-7	Group of Seven Industrialized Nations (Canada, France, Germany, Italy, Japan, United Kingdom, United States, and European Union)
G-8	Group of Eight Industrialized Nations (Canada, France, Germany, Italy, Japan, Russia, United Kingdom, United States, and European Union)
GA	(United Nations) General Assembly
GABAAC	Groupe d'Action Contre le Blanchiment d'Argent en Afrique Centrale
GABAC	Central African Group on Money Laundering
GAFISUD	The Financial Action Task Force on Money Laundering in South America
GC	Geneva Convention of 12 August 1949
GCDP	Global Commission on Drug Policy
GDP	gross domestic product
GDS	gunshot detection systems
GIABA	Inter-Governmental Action Group against Money Laundering in West Africa
GIFCS	Group of International Finance Centre Supervisors
GIS	geographical information systems
GPAT	Global Programme against Trafficking
GPS	global positioning systems
GRAPO	Grupos de Resistencia Antifascista Primero de Octubre
GRECO	Group of States against Corruption
GRETA	Group of Experts on Action against Trafficking in Human Beings

Harv Intl LJ	*Harvard International Law Journal*
Houston J Intl L	*Houston Journal of International Law*
HR	human rights
HRA	Human Rights Act
HRLR	*Human Rights Law Review*
Hum Rts & Intl Legal Discourse	*Human Rights and International Legal Discourse*
IAC	international armed conflict
IAIS	International Association of Insurance Supervisors
ICAC	Hong Kong Independent Commission against Corruption
ICAI	International Civil Aviation Organization
ICC	International Criminal Court
ICCPR	International Covenant on Civil and Political Rights
ICCSt	ICC Statute: Rome Statute of the International Criminal Court
ICCWC	International Consortium on Combating Wildlife Crime
ICE	(US) Immigration and Customs Enforcement
ICESCR	International Covenant on Economic, Social and Cultural Rights
ICJ	International Court of Justice
ICJ Rep	International Court of Justice Reports of Judgments, Advisory Opinions and Orders
ICLQ	*International & Comparative Law Quarterly*
ICOM	International Council of Museums
ICPC	International Criminal Police Commission (precursor of Interpol)
ICPO	International Criminal Police Organization
ICRC	International Committee of the Red Cross
ICRG	(FATF) International Cooperation Review Group
ICT	information and communication technology
ICTR	(UN) International Criminal Tribunal for Rwanda
ICTY	(UN) International Criminal Tribunal for the former Yogoslavia
i.e.	id est, that is
IFAW	International Fund for Animal Welfare
IFRC	International Federation of Red Cross
IG	Interessen-Gemeinschaft, interests community
IGCI	Interpol Global Complex for Innovation
IGO	intergovernmental organisation
IHL	international humanitarian law
IHRL	international human rights law
ILC	International Law Commission
ILLICID	Project: 'Verfahren zur Erhellung des Dunkelfeldes als Grundlage für Kriminalitätsbekämpfung und -prävention an Beispiel antiker Kulturgüter' (Procedure for illuminating the unknown as the basis for fighting and preventing crime, using the example of antique cultural objects)
ILM	*International Legal Materials*
ILO	International Labour Organization
IMB	International Maritime Bureau
IMF	International Monetary Fund

IMO	International Maritime Organization
IMoLIN	International Monetary Laundering Information Network
IMT	International Military Tribunal
INCB	International Narcotics Control Board
Indian J Intl L	*Indian Journal of International Law*
INR	Interpretative Note to FATF Recommendation
Interpol	International Criminal Police Organization
Intl Organizations LR	*International Organizations Law Review*
iOCTA	internet organised crime threat assessment
IOM	International Organisation for Migration
IOSC	International Organisation of Securities Commissioners
IP	internet protocol
IRA	Irish Republican Army
IRC	International Red Cross
IRMCT	International Residual Mechanism for Criminal Tribunals
IRRC	*International Review of the Red Cross*
IS	Islamic State
ISIL	Islamic State of Iraq and the Levant
ISP	internet service provider
ISPAC	International Scientific and Professional Advisory Council
IT	information technology
ITI	International Tracing Instrument, International Instrument to Enable States to Identify and Trace, in a Timely and Reliable Manner, Illicit SALW
ITLOS	International Tribunal for the Law of the Sea
ITU	International Telecommunication Union
IUCN	International Union for the Conservation of Nature
IUU	illegal, unregulated, and unreported (fishing)
JCLC	*Journal of Criminal Law & Criminology*
JCLEC	Jakarta Centre for Law Enforcement Cooperation
JCSL	*Journal of Conflict and Security Law*
JHA	cooperation in the fields of justice and home affairs
JICJ	*Journal of International Criminal Justice*
JIHLS	*Journal of International Humanitarian Legal Studies*
JIT	joint investigation team
JLEA	(Department of) Justice Law Enforcement Agencies
KEK	Kosovo Electricity Company
KYC	know your customer
L	*Législation*
Legat	Legal Attache
LJIL	*Leiden Journal of International Law*
LNTS	League of Nations Treaty Series
MANAFATF	Middle East and North Africa Financial Action Task Force
MANGO	mafia-non-governmental organisation
MARPOL	International Convention for the Prevention of Pollution from Ships

Max Planck Ybk UN L	*Max Planck Yearbook of United Nations Law*
MLA	mutual legal assistance
MLAAs	mutual legal assistance agreements
MLAT	mutual legal assistance treaty
MLCA	Money Laundering Control Act
MONEYVAL	The Council of Europe Committee of Experts on the Evaluation of Anti-Money Laundering Measures and the Financing Terrorism
MoU	memorandum of understanding
MUJAO	Mouvement pour l'unicité et le jihad en Afrique de l'Ouest (Movement for Oneness and Jihad in West Africa)
NAFTA	North American Free Trade Agreement
NATO	North Atlantic Treaty Organization
NCBs	National Central Bureaus
NCCTs	non-cooperative countries or territories
NGO	non-governmental organisation
NIAC	non-international armed conflict
NITs	network investigative techniques
NJIL	*Nordic Journal of International Law*
NJW	*Neue Juristische Wochenschrift*
nm	nautical miles
NPS	novel psychoactive substance
NRC	*NRC Handelsblatt*
NYL School L Rev	*New York Law School Law Review*
NYULR	*New York University Law Review*
OAS	Organization of American States
OCCA	Organized Crime Control Act of 1970 (US), also known as RICO
OCG	organised criminal group
OCTA	organised crime threat assessment
OECD	Organisation for Economic Co-operation and Development
OFCs	offshore financial centres
OFFP	UN Oil for Food Programme
OGBS	Offshore Group of Banking Supervisors
OHCHR	Office of the High Commissioner for Human Rights
OJ	Official Journal of the European Union
OLAF	European Anti-Fraud Office
OLG	Oberlandesgericht, higher regional court (Germany)
OPSC	Optional Protocol to the Convention on the Rights of the Child on the Sale of Children, Child Prostitution, and Child Pornography
OSCE	Organization for Security and Cooperation in Europe
OUP	Oxford University Press
Palermo Convention	United Nations Convention Against Transnational Organized Crime (Palermo Convention) (also UNTOC)
PCIJ	Permanent Court of International Justice

PJCC	police and judicial cooperation in criminal matters
PKK	Partiya Karkerên Kurdistan (Kurdish Workers Party)
PLO	Palestine Liberation Organization
PoW	prisoner of war
PSI	Proliferation Security Initiative
RAF	Rote Armee Fraktion, Red Army Fraction
RBA	risk-based approach
RdC	*Recueil de Cours*
Rec	FATF Recommendation
REFCO	Network of Prosecutors against Organized Crime
RFMOs	Regional Fishing Management Organisations
RIAA	Reports of International Arbitral Awards
RICO	(US) Racketeer Influenced and Corrupt Organizations Act
RSC	Revised Statutes Canada
S.Ct	Supreme Court Reporter
SAARC	South Asian Association for Regional Cooperation
SADC	Southern African Development Community
SALW	small arms and light weapons
SAR	suspicious activity reporting
SBiH	Sud Bosne i Herzigovine
SCO	Shanghai Cooperation Organisation
SCR	Security Council Resolution
SDNY	Southern District of New York
SEC	Securities and Exchange Commission
SFO	(UK) Serious Fraud Office
SIS	Sehengen Information System
SMS	short message service
Smsid	*Studies and Materials on the Settlement of International Disputes*
SOCTA	(EU) Serious and Organised Crime Threat Assessment
SOFAs	Status of Forces Agreements
StAR	stolen asset recovery
StGB	Strafgesetzbuch (German Criminal Code)
STL	Special Tribunal for Lebanon
STR	suspicious transaction reporting
SUA Convention	Convention for the Suppression of Unlawful Acts Against the Safety of Maritime Navigation and the Protocol for the Suppression of Unlawful Acts Against the Safety of Fixed Platforms on the Continental Shelf Transparency International
SVG	Serb Volunteer Guard
Syracuse J Intl L & Com	*Syracuse Journal of International Law & Commerce*
TC	transnational corporation
TCO	transnational criminal organisations
T-CY	Cybercrime Convention Committee

TEU	Treaty on European Union
TFEU	Treaty on the Function of the European Union
TI	Transparency International
TIP	trafficking in persons
TOC	transnational organised crime
TRIPS	Treaty on Trade-Related Aspects of Intellectual Property Rights
TSETT	Australian Federal Police Force's Transnational Sexual Exploitation and Trafficking Teams
UAV	unmanned aerial vehicle ('drone')
UK	United Kingdom
UKHL	United Kingdom House of Lords
UKTS	United Kingdom Treaty Series
UNC	United Nations Charter
UNCAC	UN Convention against Corruption
UNCITRAL	UN Commission on International Trade Law
UNCLOS	UN Convention on the Law of the Sea
UNCTAD	UN Conference on Trade and Development
UNDIR	UN Institute for Disarmament Research
UNDP	UN Development Programme
UNEP	UN Environmental Programme
UNESCO	UN Educational, Scientific and Cultural Organization
UN GA	UN General Assembly
UN GAOR	UNGA Official Records
UNGASS	UNGA Special Session
UN GIFT	UN Global Initiative to Fight Human Trafficking
UNHCR	UN High Commissioner for Refugees
UNICEF	UN Children's Fund
UNICRI	UN Interregional Crime and Justice Research Institute
UNIDROIT	International Institute for the Unification of Private Law
UNMIK	UN Interim Administration Mission in Kosovo
UNODC	UN Office on Drugs and Crime
UNODCCP	UN Office for Drug Control and Crime Prevention (forerunner of UNODC)
UNPOL	UN Police
UN SC	UN Security Council
UNTOC	UN Convention Against Transnational Organised Crime (also UNCTOC; also Palermo Convention)
UNTS	UN Treaty Series
USAID	US Agency for International Development
US	US Reports
USC	US Code
Utrecht J Intl Eur L	*Utrecht Journal of International and European Law*
VAT	(Europe) value added tax
VCLT	Vienna Convention on the Law of Treaties
Vienna Convention	United Nations Convention against Illicit Traffic in Narcotic Drugs and Psychotropic Substances

WCO	World Customs Organization
WEOG	(World Ministerial Conference) Western Europe and other group
WHO	World Health Organization
WMD	weapon of mass destruction
Yale J Intl L	*Yale Journal of International Law*
ZStW	*Zeitschrift für die gesamte Strafrechtswissenschaft*

List of Contributors

Neil Boister is Professor of Constitutional and Administrative Law, Criminal Law, International Law at the University of Waikato.

Sheelagh Brady is Co-founder and Senior Analyst with SAR Consultancy in Ireland, former Senior Security Information Analyst with the UN Department of Safety and Security in Abuja, Nigeria, and a former police officer in Ireland.

Dominik Brodowski is Senior Research Assistant at the University of Frankfurt am Main.

Aaron X. Fellmeth is Professor of Public International Law is Professor of Public International Law at the Arizona State University College of Law.

Thomas Feltes is Professor of Criminology, Criminal Policy, and Police Science at the University of Bochum.

Shahrzad Fouladvand is Lecturer in Human Rights Law and Staff Development Co-ordinator at the University of Hull.

Pierre Hauck is Professor of Criminal Law, Criminal Procedure, and the Philosophy of Law at the University of Trier.

Bernd Hecker is Professor of German and European Criminal Law and Criminal Procedure at the University of Trier.

Hans-Joachim Heintze is Senior Researcher at the Institute for the Law of Peace and Armed Conflict at Ruhr-University Bochum.

Robin Hofmann is Research Associate and PhD Student of Criminal Law, Criminal Policy, and Police Science at Ruhr-University Bochum.

Tobias Hofmann is Research Associate and PhD Student at the Department of Law of Trier University.

Louis de Koker is Professor of Law, Deakin Law School, Deakin University.

Bernhard Kretschmer is Professor of Criminal Law and Criminal Procedure at the University of Giessen.

Michael Kubiciel is Professor of Criminal Law, Criminal Procedure, and Comparative Criminal Law at the University of Cologne.

Charlotte Lülf is a research associate and PhD student at the Institute for International Law of Peace and Armed Conflict (IFHV) and Chair for Public Law and International Law at Ruhr University Bochum.

Frank G. Madsen is Affiliated Lecturer at the University of Cambridge and Research Associate at the Von Hügel Institute at Saint Edmund's College, Cambridge.

Thorsten Müller is Chief Officer of the Regulatory Authority and a specialist in international child law in Balingen.

Math Noortmann is Professor of Transnational Law and Non-State Actors at Coventry University.

Sven Peterke is Professor of Public International Law at the Federal University of Paraíba.

Alexander Proelss is Professor of Public Law, Public International Law, and European Community Law at the Department of Law of Trier University.

Anna Cornelia Rink is a research associate at the Institute for Criminal Law, Theory of Criminal Law, and Comparative Criminal Law in Cologne.

Andreas Schloenhardt is Professor of Criminal Law at the the University of Queensland and Professorial Research Fellow at the University of Vienna.

Dawn Sedman is Senior Lecturer in Law at Oxford Brookes University.

Arndt Sinn is Professor of German and European Criminal Law and Procedure, International Criminal Law, and Comparative Criminal Law at the University of Osnabrück.

Hennie Strydom is Professor for International Law and holds the National Research Foundation Chair for International Law at the University of Johannesburg.

Pierre Thielbörger is Professor of German Public Law and Public International Law and Executive Director of the Institute for International Law of Peace and Armed Conflict at Ruhr University Bochum.

Mark Turkington is the HSBC UK Head of Sanctions and Senior Compliance Officer in London.

Richard Vogler is Professor of Comparative Criminal Law and Criminal Justice and Director of Postgraduate Law Courses in the School of Law, Politics, and Sociology at the University of Sussex.

Bettina Weißer is Professor of Criminal Law, Criminal Procedure, and International Criminal Law at the University of Münster.

Joachim Wolf is Professor emeritus of Environmental Law, Administrative Law, and Administrative Studies and former Executive Director of the IFHV at the University of Bochum.

PART I

GENERAL QUESTIONS

1

The Historical Evolution of the International Cooperation against Transnational Organised Crime

An Overview

Frank G. Madsen

1.1 Introduction

Transnational cooperation in the fight against organised crime is an inextricable part of the development of international criminal police cooperation as such. Its theoretical particularity arises from the definitional opaqueness of the subject matter, organised crime, while its empirical difficulty is linked to the complexity inherent in law enforcement and judicial cooperation on an international level. Academically, the subject is located in the intersection of two disciplines, international relations and criminology.[1]

After brief theoretical considerations of the concept of organised crime, this chapter surveys one of the earliest transnational crimes, piracy. It is observed that from the outset the crimes now making up the international prohibition regime were either sponsored or at least tacitly allowed by governments. Apart from piracy, examples are also provided by trafficking in narcotics and in humans. In the 1880s the overlapping spheres of local politics and prostitution led a New York judge to describe the governance of New York City as 'a noctivagous strumpetocracy'.[2] A final section of the chapter considers harmonization within the framework of World Society Theory and notes that its core concept of rationalization in the form of technological development remains crucial for the development of law enforcement cooperation.[3]

A number of scholars see the development of international criminal police cooperation as a worrying lack of governance accountability. It is worth recalling Joseph Fouché, who in 1824 wrote that the power of the police lies in the general belief in its omnipotence and omnipresence.[4] It is only too clear, at least to practitioners, that the police is neither omnipotent nor omnipresent.

[1] Peter Andreas and Ethan Nadelmann, *Policing the Globe: Criminalization and Crime Control in International Relations*, Oxford and New York, Oxford University Press, 2006, p. viii.

[2] Timothy J. Gilfoyle, *City of Eros: New York City, Prostitution, and the Commercialization of Vice 1790–1920*, New York, W. W. Norton, 1992.

[3] Anja P. Jakobi, *Common Goods and Evils? The Formation of Global Crime Governance*, Oxford, Oxford University Press, 2013.

[4] Joseph Fouché, *Mémoires de Joseph Fouché, Duc d'Otrante, Ministre de la Police Générale*, Paris, Jean de Bonnot, 1986 (1824), p. 373.

1.1.1 Organised crime: theoretical considerations

Organised crime has one and only one motive, namely profit. Proper conceptualization in academia has been severely hampered by a misunderstanding of this point. The purpose of organised crime is neither violence nor power. Violence may be used and a position of power may be reached, but solely as a means of obtaining or securing revenue streams. Nor is organised crime—in its majority—ethnic or territorial in nature. It consists of often ad hoc groups, as shown as early as 1974 in the pertinent analysis of organised crime by the then Secretary-General of Interpol, Jean Népote.[5]

Functionally, the activities of these crime groups are the protection racket (i.e. extortion), fraud, and the satisfaction of denied demand, or coercive, predatory, and market crimes. Most organised criminals obtain part of their funding from extortion of business owners and others. Likewise, they have always been involved in various fraudulent schemes, a trend that seems to increase with the opportunities offered by the cyber environment. But the most important part of their revenue-generating activities is market crimes, i.e. the satisfaction of denied demand. In this respect, organised crime can be seen as the *arbitrage of borders*; geographical, certainly, but not solely.[6] This explains the curious fact that organised crime needs the state, because this creates borders both between itself and other states, and also inside itself, between licit and illicit drugs, licit and illicit gambling, citizens likely to receive organ donations and those not, individuals who are citizens and those who are not.[7]

1.2 Early Beginnings

International policing cooperation may be said to have commenced with the fight against piracy, if one takes 'policing' in a very large sense. This crime is also an example of the criminalization of activities that had hitherto been accepted, condoned, and often encouraged.

1.2.1 Piracy and privateering

The early beginnings of cooperation against transnational organised crime are coextensive with the process, whereby control over extra-territorial violence was centralized and monopolized. This entailed the creation by nation-states of a legal order and of the states establishing themselves as defenders of that order.[8]

Maritime piracy is one of the oldest crimes on record in the Western world. The crime typically involves robbery or criminal violence committed at sea, but includes

[5] Jean Népote, 'Interpol et le crime organisé', (1974) 282 *Revue Internationale de Police Criminelle* (November), 230–6. For a so-called 4:3:2:1 configuration, see Frank G. Madsen, 'Trafficking crimes', in Barry A. K. Rider (ed.), *Research Handbook on International Financial Crimes*, Cheltenham, Gloucestershire, UK, Edward Elgar Publishing, 2015.

[6] See—for the matter of definition—Ch. 2, sections 2.1.1 and 2.3.2, and Ch. 21 of this book.

[7] Alexander C. Diener and Joshua Hagen, *Borders*, Oxford, Oxford University Press, 2012.

[8] Janice E. Thomson, *Mercenaries, Pirates, and Sovereigns. State-building and Extra-territorial Violence in Early Modern Europe*, Princeton, New Jersey, Princeton University Press, 1994, p. 3.

similar acts on land by seafaring gangs. Raids by sea-borne criminals (pirates) of seaside communities for looting and slave-taking have been more detrimental than piracy at sea. Piracy has always been linked to slave-taking; examples are the slavery raids of the Moors along the coast of Italy and of the Moro along the coasts of Mindanao and Luzon.

The 'classic' period of piracy, however, was the so-called Caribbean piracy. From about 1630, buccaneers, i.e. pirates, sometimes acting as privateers, were active in the Caribbean. The English Crown issued letters of marque and reprisal, seeing this activity basically as a low-cost option for warfare against Spain. The practice ended in the 1690s, when it became clear that the buccaneers were difficult to control. Piracy has been considered an offence against the law of nations from the time of Grotius, who called pirates enemies of the human race: *hostes humani generis*.[9] Therefore, the public vessels of any state have been permitted to seize a pirate ship, bring it into port, try the crew (regardless of their nationality or domicile) then, if found guilty, punish them, and confiscate the ship.

In the late twentieth century, the practice of hijacking ships or airplanes developed into a new form of piracy and nautical piracy once again became prevalent in east and south-east Asia and in the waters off eastern and southern Africa.[10] Coordinated patrolling in the Strait of Malacca, however, by the navies from the three jurisdictions concerned has had an appreciable effect on this crime in what had become a bottleneck for international trade.

Privateering was carried out by all nations until the 1856 Declaration of Paris, in which Great Britain and the other major European countries except Spain declared privateering illegal. The US government refused to accede, holding that the small size of its navy made reliance on privateering necessary in time of war. The USA finally abolished privateering at the end of the nineteenth century once the US navy grew to a concomitant size, while Spain only agreed to the ban in 1908.[11]

The Hague Peace Conference in 1907 stipulated—and this has become part of international law—that armed merchant ships must be listed as warships. There have, however, been various interpretations of the term 'armed'.[12]

1.3 Institutionalization in the Early Years of the Twentieth Century

The formal roots of criminal police cooperation, however, are to be found in the second half of the nineteenth century, with the convergence of four characteristics: identification technology, the creation of investigative bureaux, professionalism, and the slow but successful liberation of police agencies from high police duties.

[9] Jody Green, 'Hostis humani generis', (2008) 34 *Critical Inquiry* (4), 673–705.

[10] Andreas and Nadelmann, *Policing the Globe*, cited in note 1 above, p. 264; Gal Luft and Anne Korin, 'Terrorism goes to sea', (2004) *Foreign Affairs* (November/December), 62.

[11] Thomson, *Mercenaries, Pirates, and Sovereigns*, cited in note 8 above, p. 72.

[12] *Maritime Alert: Protecting Crews and Ships from Piracy by Arming Merchant Vessels for Self Defense.* Squire Patton Boggs Online (May 2009), available at: http://www.squiresanders.com.

During the mid-to-late nineteenth century, ten-finger fingerprinting was perfected for use by the colonial authorities in India for identification purposes in the civil administration, in order to re-employ in one part of the British colonial administration a person who had not been dismissed by another.[13] The technique was introduced into Europe, where its use was extended to the criminal administration, in order to identify arrestees who were known in another part of the country, albeit under a different name. In France, for example, this very quickly led to the realization that a number of professional criminals existed in the country, that they travelled around the country to commit crime, and that they operated under multiple identities. Likewise, the use of the photograph; in 1886, in New York, the chief of police, Thomas Byrnes, published a photo album, *Professional Criminals of America*, which discloses the important fact that the majority of the professional (later 'organised') criminals were forgers and confidence tricksters, not murderers. The discovery of the existence of professional criminals may very well explain the preoccupation with or sudden discovery of so-called organised crime.

While street police had existed at least from the Bow Street Runners (1749) and the 'Peelers' (1829) in London, only in 1849 was a dedicated detective bureau established in that city. In the second half of the same century, two major crimes threatened the very existence of states and therefore led to the creation of specialized police offices in many countries, partly to deal with these crimes, partly to cooperate with foreign counterparts: the assassination of heads of state and the counterfeiting of currency. The former is typically exemplified by the murder of Sisi (Empress Elizabeth of Austria, 1898), the latter by a case at the British High Court of Chancery, *The Emperor of Austria v. Day and Kossuth* 1861, concerning Austrian nationals residing in England who had counterfeited Hungarian currency with the political aim of destabilizing the regime in Hungary by undermining the value of its currency.

1.3.1 Slave trade and human traffic

This section surveys the very broad area of slavery and human trafficking, including illicit traffic in organs for transplantation and commercial sexual exploitation of children. Since the subject matter is extensive, a certain level of selection is, *par force*, involved.

It is to be deplored, from a purely academic point of view, that the term *slavery* is now used to cover a series of crimes that, although serious, are fundamentally different from slavery; these disparate offences are believed to have in common that human beings are in some sense being sold. Slavery, however, is not the description or definition of a crime or of human behaviour; rather, slavery designates a legal status, namely that one human being is legally the property of another. 'Slavery does not include other forced labour systems: historical forced labour by prisoners, labour camps, or other forms of unfree labour, in which the labourers are not considered property.'[14]

[13] Simon A. Cole, *Suspect Identities: A History of Fingerprints and Criminal Identification*, Cambridge, Massachusetts, Harvard University Press, 2001, p. 65.

[14] Seymour Drescher, *Abolition: A History of Slavery and Antislavery*, Cambridge, Cambridge University Press, 2009.

The point here is that it is not the view of the domineering person (industry owner, pimp, etc.) that determines whether a person is considered property; rather, it is the law. Slave owners, if necessary, could appeal to law enforcement and the judicial system to enforce their rights; this is not the case for so-called modern slavery, which is therefore a misnomer. Human beings do terrible things to each other; what distinguishes slavery, and makes it particularly odious, must surely be its legal character.

The traffic in slaves from *c.* 1500 is traditionally divided into four parts. In the so-called *eastern slave traffic* from the seventh to the nineteenth centuries, between 7 and 12 million slaves are estimated to have been taken out of Africa and into slavery in the Arab empires. The *intra-African slave trade* began well before the arrival of the first European explorers and both slavery and the traffic in slaves were practised in Africa independently of overseas slave traffic.[15]

Concurrently, from the sixteenth to the eighteenth centuries, the weakening of the Turkish grip over the Maghreb resulted in the virtual independence of the so-called *Barbary States* Morocco, Algeria, Tunisia and Tripoli, whose pirates are estimated to have brought approximately 1 million individuals into slavery, caught mainly in the western Mediterranean.[16]

The *European colonial slave traffic* was the object of detailed tax, administrative, commercial, and health legislation. The traffic is generally estimated to have transported between 12 and 13 million individuals out of Africa, of which approximately one-third were women.[17]

A large number of slaves died in the process of being captured and transported. Schematically, for the period 1501–1853, the deaths occurred thus: 50 per cent died *in Africa* as a result of slave-catching wars between native kingdoms, including those who died during forced marches towards the coast, to the so-called *factories*.[18] A further 4.5 per cent died *in* the factories and 12.5 per cent *during transport* to the Caribbean, and 33 per cent died in the seasoning camps in the Caribbean, i.e. camps where the slaves were 'broken in' before being moved on to the Americas.[19]

The abolition of the slave trade was a process. The main steps were the abolition by France in 1794, although Napoleon reintroduced it in 1802; the next country to abolish the trade was Denmark in 1803; and finally Great Britain did so in 1807.

The campaign in Britain had lasted twenty years and, to a large degree, had been driven by non-governmental entities and, indeed, individuals. For instance, as early as 1761 the Society of Friends declared a ban on slave-holding among Quakers on both sides of the Atlantic. A tangible—and touching—relic of the debate is Josiah Wedgwood's medallions with their cameos of a kneeling Negro slave and the inscription 'Am I not a Man and a Brother?'

[15] Some Africa scholars deny the existence of an intra-African slave trade.

[16] Robert C. Davis, *Christian Slaves, Muslim Masters: White Slavery in the Mediterranean, the Barbary Coast, and Italy 1500–1800*, New York, Palgrave, 2003.

[17] In 1501 occurred the first transatlantic transport of black slaves, to Hispaniola, now known as Haiti and the Dominican Republic. The first slave was transported to North America (South Carolina) in 1526.

[18] David Stannard, *American Holocaust: The Conquest of the Modern World*, Oxford, Oxford University Press, 1992.

[19] Milton Melzer, *Slavery: A World History*, Boston, Massachusetts, Da Capo Press, 1993.

1.3.2 Trafficking in humans

This crime is of increasing import in the consideration of organised crime for which it generates substantial revenues. According to the US government, 600–800,000 persons are coerced into forced labour every year, of whom 80 per cent are female and 50 per cent are under the age of 18. The UN calculates the annual income to human traffickers at approximately $10 billion and notes that each trafficked human is worth an average price of $12,500, of which $3,000 represents costs. Kapstein emphasizes that the cost of a slave today is much less than that of an African slave during the Atlantic slave trade; the deflated price is explainable by the less onerous transportation now available.[20]

Trafficking in persons is defined in Article 3(a) of the United Nations Protocol to Prevent, Suppress, and Punish Trafficking in Persons, especially Women and Children, supplementing the 2000 United Nations Convention Against Transnational Organized Crime (UNTOC).[21] It is probable that in absolute terms the traffic in persons is larger than was the Atlantic slave trade in the eighteenth and nineteenth centuries.[22] The comparison, however, is deeply flawed because the majority of the individuals trafficked have expressed at least some consent to the transport; none of the African slaves did so.

Over the last couple of decades human trafficking has probably been the third-largest source of income for criminal organisations of various kinds, beside the illicit traffic in narcotics and illicit arms sales; it is most certainly the fastest-growing.[23] Trafficking in humans shares certain dynamics with alien or people smuggling, but is different in having the additional element of coercive exploitation. Alien smuggling creates a one-time profit when the smuggling of the alien has been paid for, whereas trafficking in humans may and often does include long-term exploitation and thus continuous profits.[24]

Along with central offices dealing with political agitators and counterfeiting of currency, international prostitution (called 'the White Slave Trade') soon became a crime that has prompted international police cooperation. As a result of a 1902 police conference in Paris on Suppression of the White Slave Trade, bureaux were established in each of sixteen participating countries. More offices, similar to these, were created as countries became aware of the existential threat to their sovereignty from the counterfeiting of their currencies; these became models for the later National Central Bureaux of Interpol.

[20] Ethan B. Kapstein, 'The new global slave trade', (2006) *Foreign Affairs* (November–December), 103–15.

[21] Adopted 15 November 2000 as Annexe II to United Nations General Assembly Resolution A/RES/55/25.

[22] Kapstein, 'The new global slave trade', cited in note 20 above.

[23] Francis T. Miko, 'Trafficking in women and children: the US and international response', in Anna M. Troubnikoff (eds), *Trafficking in Women and Children: Current Issues and Developments*, New York, Nova Science Publishers, 2003, p. 1.

[24] James O. Finckenauer and Jennifer Schrock, 'Human trafficking: a growing criminal market in the US', in Troubnikoff, ibid, p. 32.

In general, commercial sexual exploitation of children (CSEC) will meet the definition of organised crime in (the 2000) UNTOC and the provisions in the Trafficking Protocol will therefore be applicable. Since the Convention and its Protocol are the subjects of extensive treatment in separate chapters in this book, in the rest of this chapter I will, instead, consider mutual bilateral instruments, exemplified by a Thai-Cambodian memorandum of understanding (MoU) and municipal legislation with transnational reach in two countries, the USA and France.

There are in total roughly eighty international instruments that concern, in one way or another, the situation of children. The most important international instrument in the fight against CSEC remains the United Nations Convention on the Rights of the Child (CRC), which supplemented the 1959 Declaration on the Rights of the Child.[25] It was supplemented by an Optional Protocol to the Convention on the Rights of the Child on the Sale of Children, Child Prostitution and Child Pornography.[26] The CRC has 192 states parties, of which only two have not ratified it (Somalia and the USA).[27] Articles 34 and 35 impose a duty on states parties to take all appropriate national, bilateral, and multinational measures to prevent sexual exploitation of children, commercial sexual exploitation of children, and child pornography; and the traffic in children.

Apart from municipal law and multilateral treaties, there also exist a number of bilateral instruments, often in the form of memoranda of understanding. An example is the MoU of 31 May 2003 between Cambodia and Thailand referred to above.[28] After noting that trafficking in children and women is an infringement of human rights and that it impacts negatively on 'the social fabric and value of society', the MoU observes 'that transnational criminal groups and organizations are actively involved in trafficking in children and women and that such transnational organized crimes have affected not only Thailand and Cambodia but also the region and the global community at large'. The MoU deals with prostitution, forced or exploitative domestic labour, and bonded labour, as one might expect, but also, in Article 3, with issues often neglected, such as false adoption, sex tourism, and slavery by the use of drugs on children and women. It is worth noting that the MoU explicitly includes *sex tourism* as one of the purposes for the traffic in women and children. This, undoubtedly, is related to the important traffic in women and children from Cambodia and Burma (or Myanmar) to houses of pleasure in Thailand partly, and perhaps mostly, to cover the demand from so-called sex tourists. A number of countries have passed legislation criminalizing overseas travel for the purpose of engaging in sexual activity with minors.[29]

[25] Adopted by GA Res. 44/25 on 20 November 1989; it entered into force on 2 September 1990.

[26] GA Res. A/RES/54/2003.

[27] Status at 23 June 2015. United Nations Treaty Collection. Human Rights, Ch. IV, Section 11.

[28] Memorandum of Understanding between the Royal Government of the Kingdom of Cambodia and the Royal Government of the Kingdom of Thailand on Bilateral Cooperation For Eliminating Trafficking in Children and Women and Assisting Victims of Trafficking, signed in Siem Reap, Cambodia, on 31 May 2003.

[29] June Kane, *Sold for Sex*, Brookfield, Vermont, Arena, 1998, p. 107. Margaret A. Healy, 'Prosecuting child sex tourists at home: do laws in Sweden, Australia, and the United States safeguard the rights of children as mandated by international law?', (1995) 18 *Fordham International Law Journal*, 1887–8.

1.3.2.1 France

The French Penal Code has a general provision that extends its reach to *crimes* and *offences* committed abroad by French nationals; offences, however, only if they are also punishable under the legislation of the country in which they were committed. The French legislation, which extended the offence of 'sexual assault' outside France if such acts are committed by French nationals or persons having their customary residence in France, was enacted on 2 January 1994. In the ten-year period, however, from the enactment of the law to 2004, only five cases were brought.[30]

1.3.2.2 United States of America

The White Slave Traffic Act, also called the Mann Act, treats the subject of transportation for illegal sexual activity and related crimes.[31]

The United States delegation was highly influential in the elaboration of the Yokohama Global Commitment 2001, which encouraged new laws to criminalize child prostitution, 'including provisions with extra-territorial effect'.[32] Although because of jurisdictional and enforcement problems the legislation on illicit sexual activities by US nationals or US residents outside the United States has not met with the success one could have expected, some cases have been brought in the United States. A common factor in all of them is an unsuccessful attempt by the defence to challenge the sentencing (district) court's extra-territorial jurisdiction.

1.3.3 Trafficking in organs for transplantation

The demand for organ transplants increases and will likely increase at an even faster pace in the future. At the moment, health-care systems in the world do not have access to enough organs to satisfy the demand, giving rise to a typical situation of *denied demand*. In response, the black market for organs is rapidly expanding.[33] According to the World Health Organization (WHO), each year at least 10 per cent of kidney operations performed in the world involve kidneys trafficked on the black market.[34] Moreover, and without exception, no grey market has ever been defeated from the supply side, if we take 'grey' as referring to both illegal and illicit market activities. Therefore, at best legislation and law enforcement will only marginally influence the satisfaction of the marketplace.

Most jurisdictions in the world, with the exception of Iran, have legislation prohibiting the sale of organs or most other body tissue. Typically excluded from this interdiction are renewable body parts, e.g. hair, nails, sperm, and eggs.

[30] Aurélie Sobocinski, 'En dépit des lois, les condamnations pour tourisme sexuel restent rares', *Le Monde*, 10 September 2004.

[31] Ch. 395, 36 Stat. 826 (1910); codified, 1998, as amended at 18 USC paras 2421–7, Ch. 117.

[32] See www.unicef.org/events/yokohama/outcome.html.

[33] *Jane's Intelligence Digest*, 'Organ-trafficking: a fast-expanding black market', 7 March 2008.

[34] Denis Campbell and Nicola Davison, 'Illegal kidney trade booms as new organ is "sold every hour"', *The Guardian*, 27 May 2012, based on information from Luc Noel of the WHO.

On the international level, a host of hortative declarations has issued from various international bodies, UNESCO, the WHO, the so-called Istanbul Declaration, the Council of Europe, as well as the 2000 United Nations Protocol to Prevent, Suppress, and Punish Trafficking in Persons. Since the Protocol is a supplement to UNTOC, its text must be read in conjunction and interpreted together with the Convention, cf. Articles 1 and 2. The Protocol, as part of an international convention on transnational crime, only applies to *transnational* trafficking in persons; less obvious, but logical in view of the scope of the Convention to which it is a protocol, is the requirement that the traffic in question must be effectuated by organised crime.[35]

Although a transplant of an organ of illicit origin is performed every hour, twenty-four hours a day, somewhere in the world, our knowledge of the traffic is very limited, partly because studies of organised crime by their very nature suffer from a lack of robust quantitative information, and partly because illicit traffic in organs is considered a crime without victims.[36]

Case studies point to the conclusions that the compensation paid to the donor is risible and often not even paid in full; that there is no appropriate post-surgery follow-up of the donor; and, except for India, that the cases are transnational (in India often, but far from always, donor, surgeon, and recipient are all Indian nationals). Donors in Moldova, Pakistan, and Turkey, for instance, receive from $1,000 to $8,000 for one kidney—although this amount increases if the operation is performed in a developed country—while wealthy patients pay up to $200,000 for a kidney transfer. By way of comparison, in jurisdictions considered medically less advanced, a kidney transplant could be obtained in India and Pakistan for $50,000 (US equivalent); in January 2011, the black market price for a kidney transfer in Bangkok, Thailand, was $30,000 (all figures US equivalent).[37]

Illicit organ transplants from living donors are increasing: this may be related to geopolitical instability in certain areas, which increases the pool of potential donors.[38] An example is Egypt, where traffickers target Sudanese refugees and other asylum-seekers.[39] Organs are excised 'either by inducing consent, coercion, or outright theft'. In Egypt, between 500 and 1,000 licensed transplants are performed annually, with an additional 100–200 unlicensed.[40] Likewise, refugees from Eritrea may be victims of a crime organisation that engages in criminal abductions partly for extortion and partly for organ removal, depending on the circumstances of the victim. Organised

[35] Leslie P. Francis and John G. Francis, 'Stateless crimes, legitimacy, and international criminal law: the case of organ trafficking', (2010) 4 *Criminal Law and Philosophy*, 283–95. Antonio Cassese, *International Criminal Law*, 2nd edn, Oxford, Oxford University Press, 2008, pp. 11–12. Calinka Watson, 'The organised crime of organ trafficking', *Magister Legum* dissertation, University of the Free State, Bloemfontein, South Africa, 2006.

[36] Dominick Tao, 'Worldwide markets fuel illegal traffic in organs', *New York Times*, 29 July 2009. Campbell and Davison, 'Illegal kidney trade booms', cited in note 34 above.

[37] Personal communication from non-Thai patient seeking treatment in Bangkok. Chinese kidney; Chinese surgeon.

[38] James Cockayne, 'Chasing shadows. Strategic responses to organised crime in conflict-afflicted situations', (2013) 158 *RUSI Journal* (2), 10–24.

[39] United Press International, 'Illegal organ trafficking up in Egypt', 12 December 2011.

[40] Coalition for Organ-Failure Solutions, *Sudanese Victims of Organ Trafficking in Egypt. A Preliminary Evidence-Based, Victim-Centred Report*, Bethesda, Maryland, UNODC, December 2011.

crime finds a lucrative *vivarium* in fragile post-conflict states. The United Nations High Commissioner for Refugees (UNHCR) claims that some of the victims end up in the Sinai, where they, ultimately, are killed for their organs.[41]

1.3.4 Opium

Law enforcement against the misuse of opiates can be seen in retrospect as the driver of a very large part of the intensification of international law enforcement directed against organised crime. From the vantage point of, say, 1900 this would not have been immediately obvious. There certainly was a misuse of opiates, both acknowledged (Chinese opium dens) and not (widespread use of opiates during the American Civil War, 1861–5). The sufferings on both sides during this war were indescribable; they were somewhat appeased by the use of opiates in various forms (laudanum, Dover powder, etc.) provided both by army surgeons and by merchants following the armies. Although the major problem clearly was in the general population in the USA after the Civil War, the wrath of the law was concentrated on the Chinese population, in particular in the northern part of California.[42]

Driven by the United States, the narcotics problem was defined as a law enforcement, rather than as a medical, issue. This categorization was undoubtedly influenced by the very strong British and American Missionary Prohibition Movement, which a little later also was responsible for the equally misguided alcohol prohibition. Two individuals were allowed to play an excessive role in the creation of the narcotics prohibition scheme: bishop Charles Brent and the world's first narcocrat, Henry Anslinger.

Brent had introduced opium prohibition in the Philippines in approximately 1905 and was then appointed to sit on the 1909 Shanghai Opium Commission, which in part had been convened on his recommendation. He used this platform to extend his inefficient Philippine opium prohibition regime to the world. Also in 1909, at his recommendation, the US Senate enacted the Opium Exclusion Act, with the rather foreseeable result that opium smokers turned to morphine, heroin, and other drugs. As a result of the work of the Shanghai Opium Commission in 1912, a number of countries signed the first of what was to become a series of narcotics treaties. This first treaty was very much driven by the United States, which has also been the main proponent for the narcotics treaties concluded in the century following the 1912 Shanghai Opium Treaty, namely those of 1961, 1971, and 1988.

Henry Anslinger in the United States became the most vociferous opponent of any view of drug abuse as a medical problem. Instead, he worked on an American and international programme of criminalizing production, trafficking, and possession, and on the creation of the first US specialized federal anti-narcotics law enforcement unit, the Federal Bureau of Narcotics (FBN).

In the meantime, however, in 1926 the Opium Board of the League of Nations had analysed the results of Brent's prohibition regime in the Philippines. They found

[41] Agence France-Presse, 'Eritrean refugees kidnapped, killed: UNHCR chief', 12 January 2012.

[42] Frank G. Madsen, 'International narcotics law enforcement: a study in irrationality', (2012) 66 *Journal of International Affairs* (1), 1–19.

that, notwithstanding the prohibition, opium was cheap and plenty, and enforcement corrupt. Indeed, one might argue that this early analysis already identified the apparently causal relationship between narcotics prohibition schemes, increasing drug availability, falling drug prices, and corruption; quite symptomatically and ironically, Anslinger's FBN was closed down in 1968, in part because of problems of corruption.

Alfred McCoy has somewhat ironically summed up that, over the period 1970–2005, the United States fought five drug wars at a cost of $150 billion with the following successes: first, an increase of world opium supply from 1,000 tons in 1970 to between 5 and 6,000 in 2005; second, an increase in US heroin users from 68,000 in 1970 to 1 million in 2005; third, an increase in Andean coca production from 300 tons in 1985 to 600 tons in 2000; and finally a difficult-to-measure increase in drug traffickers' political influence in a number of jurisdictions such as Colombia, Burma, Afghanistan, and Pakistan.[43]

1.3.5 Interpol

Continuous cooperation between national criminal police organisations commenced in the late nineteenth century and is linked to the so-called high or political police. In particular, the assassination of Empress Elizabeth of Austria (Sisi) led to international law enforcement action at the Rome Conference 1898, which agreed on extradition of individuals who had attacked heads of state or their families. While twenty-one countries had sent delegates to the Rome Conference, only eleven participated in the London Conference the following year on the Suppression of White Slave Trade, which was followed by conferences on the same subject in Paris in 1902 and 1904, leading to the 1910 International Convention for the Suppression of the 'White Slave Traffic'.[44] One might argue that in a modest way the Paris Conference 1902 developed the blueprint for what would become Interpol.

These specialized, thematic, international police conferences were soon followed by general international police conferences in Madrid in 1909, Sao Paolo in 1912, and Washington DC in 1913. In the following year, 1914, consolidated, international criminal police cooperation was (almost) born at the First International Congress of Judicial Police in Monte Carlo, but the commencement of the First World War cut short the process. Only in 1923 in Vienna, Austria, at the International Police Congress (seven participants: Germany, Austria, Denmark, Egypt, France, Greece, and Hungary), was the International Criminal Police Commission (ICPC), 'Interpol', created with headquarters in Vienna, Austria, and a fingerprint department in Copenhagen, Denmark. Deflem rightly observes that the *professionalism* of the police played a more decisive

[43] McCoy at conference 6 October 2005 at CERI, SciencePo, Paris, France. See Steve Hirsh, 'Experts question global counternarcotics strategies', *Jane's Intelligence Review* (1 November 2005). The US National Institute of Drug Abuse, however, estimates heroin users in the US at some 400,000. A recent report puts the number at 900,000: Associated Press, 'Number of US heroin users rose 300,000 over a decade', 7 July 2015.

[44] The Convention was amended in 1949. See UNTS 23.

role in developing structural cooperation than political or legal guidance, i.e. an operational logic based on a shared system of knowledge.[45]

The organisation grew slowly and in 1938 encompassed thirty-four countries. From 1938, however, its activities were severely inhibited by the political events of that year—Austria's loss of independence—and in 1942 the ICPC, which by then was almost no longer functioning, was transferred to Berlin. Only one year after the end of the Second World War, at the 1946 Brussels Conference, the ICPC was re-installed under the name 'the International Criminal Police Organization' (ICPO) with headquarters in Paris.[46]

1.4 Modern Era

The major developments in criminal police cooperation in the modern era are the 1994 Naples Declaration followed by the 2000 UN Convention against Transnational Organized Crime and its three protocols. Since these international instruments are dealt with in later chapters in this work, they will not be analysed here.

It is worth noting, though, that the origin of most of the legal provisions in the 2000 UN Convention against Transnational Organized Crime can be found in the innovative 1988 Drug Trafficking Convention, for example the provision that the treaty itself can be used as an extradition treaty between states parties that do not have mutual extradition treaties.[47] The modern era, however, saw an important innovation, namely the realization of the importance of the economics of transnational organised crime.

1.4.1 Transnational organised crime and the financial markets

The US Racketeer Influenced and Corrupt Organizations Act (RICO), also known as the Organized Crime Control Act of 1970 (OCCA), is the precursor and the model for later national and transnational law against organised crime.[48] One of the major preoccupations of the American legislator was not so much a concern that criminals succeed in obtaining, concealing, and safeguarding their ill-gotten gains, but rather the use to which such funds are put. The act attempts to prevent organised crime from engaging in interstate or foreign commerce or from taking a controlling interest in a securities-issuing corporation.[49]

At least for the last thirty years, the United States has used 'economic statecraft' in its fight against transnational organised crime. For example, the US Foreign Assistance

[45] Mathieu Deflem, 'International police cooperation, history of', in Richard A. Wright and J. Mitchell Miller (eds), *The Encyclopedia of Criminology*, New York, Routledge, 2005, p. 796. Matthieu Deflem, *Policing World Society: Historical Foundations of International Police Cooperation*, New York, Oxford University Press, 2003, p. 62.

[46] For the history of Interpol, see 'Spécial Cinquantenaire (1923–1973)', (1973) 267 *Revue Internationale de Police Criminelle*, 98–102.

[47] The 1988 United Nations Convention against Illicit Traffic in Narcotic Drugs and Psychotropic Substances—commonly known as the Drug Trafficking Convention.

[48] RICO statute, 1970, 18 USCA para. 1961ff. Analysed in Gerard E. Lynch, 'The crime of being a criminal. Parts I and II', (1987) 87 *Columbia Law Review*, 661–764.

[49] 18 USC para. 1962(a).

Act of 1961 as amended, section 490, requires the US executive to consider the extent to which major drug-producing and transit countries have met the goals and objectives of the 1988 Drug Trafficking Convention. If it decides they have not, the Act requires the executive to decertify the country in question, which results in the suspension of most forms of assistance by the USA together with the application of optional trade sanctions.[50]

1.4.2 Organised crime control and global crime governance

Interpol is the only world-wide criminal police organization, but complementary to it is the United Nations Office on Drugs and Crime, UNODC, with headquarters in Vienna, Austria. The UNODC was created in 1997 through the merger of two existing programmes, the United Nations Drug Control Programme and the Centre for International Crime Prevention. The Office operates on three main levels: by offering field-based technical cooperation programmes, by research and analysis, and by normative work, in particular to assist countries in the process of ratifying treaties and by creating model national legislation regarding drugs, crime, and terrorism.[51]

1.5 Regional Arrangements

A number of regional arrangements have been created, in particular after the adoption of the UNTOC and the 2003 United Nations Convention against Corruption (UNCAC), to assist in the fight against crime, the best known of which is Europol, the police office of the European Union, and its judicial sister organisation, Eurojust.

There are, however, a series of relevant regional organisations, world-wide, apart from strictly law enforcement such as Interpol and Europol, of which only a few examples can be mentioned here. The Network of Prosecutors against Organized Crime (REFCO) is an initiative of the UNODC funded by the Government of Canada. It was launched in 2011 and consists of ten prosecution offices from Central and Latin America. The aim of the Network is to facilitate regional and international cooperation in the investigation and prosecution of serious and organised crime; it is closely coordinated with the offices of the Attorneys-General of Central America.

Likewise, in 2007 the Commonwealth Secretariat (with headquarters in London) created an interesting, pragmatic organisation called the Commonwealth Network of Contact Persons (CNCP). It facilitates cooperation in criminal cases between Commonwealth member states, including on mutual legal assistance and extradition, and provides legal and practical information through a network consisting of at least one contact person from each of the jurisdictions of the Commonwealth. It is clear that the results of the work of the CNCP are only as good as the contact persons, but contrariwise, there is no limit to the possible successes of cooperation if these persons are high-quality and energized.

[50] Neil Boister, 'Transnational criminal law?', (2003) 14 *European Journal of International Law* (5), 953–76.

[51] See www.unodc.org.

The CNCP is inspired by the European Judicial Network (EJN), which is a network of national contact points for the facilitation of judicial cooperation in criminal matters between the member states of the European Union. The EJN is composed of more than 300 national contact points throughout the 27 member states, the European Commission, and a Secretariat based in The Hague.[52] The EJN promotes judicial cooperation between the competent local authorities, for example over the dispatch and implementation of requests for judicial assistance.

It is of the utmost importance that such prosecutorial cooperative devices exist in order to counter the difficulties inherent in judicial cooperation in criminal matters. In itself, an indication of the weak point in international criminal cases, namely the obtaining of evidence from one jurisdiction in such a form that it is useable in another, is the fact that several of these organisations—or indeed most of them—consist in networks of prosecutors, who are particularly knowledgeable about and interested in overcoming the differences between legal systems. Both the 1988 Drug Trafficking Convention and UNTOC (2000) allow the conventions themselves to be used to facilitate mutual legal assistance (MLA), extradition, etc. One should keep in mind the rather pragmatic problem in international judicial cooperation in criminal cases, that, if necessary, witnesses from one jurisdiction must be brought to another to testify, which is administratively and economically onerous—apart from the fact that witnesses cannot be coerced to testify in a foreign as they can in a domestic jurisdiction.

1.6 Harmonization

This section postulates that international police cooperation in general, and in particular cooperative efforts against organised crime, repose on an international moral, institutional, and conceptual framework that began timidly; this is best analysed in academic form as World Society Theory. A main tenet of that theory is rationalization, which is seen as one of the founding pillars of modern policing.[53]

1.6.1 Transnational vs international crimes

Organised crime may and often does have an international aspect. The definitional question of international *versus* transnational crimes has not, as yet, been fully settled. The term 'transnational crime'—a criminological rather than juridical term—was coined by the Executive Secretary of the Fifth United Nations Congress on the Prevention of Crime and the Treatment of Offenders, Geneva, 1975, Gerhard O. W. Mueller, and has since gained general acceptance.[54]

[52] Established by EU Council Decision of 17 June 1997. The Network's Secretariat forms part of Eurojust but functions as a separate unit. It enjoys autonomy, as stated in para. 20 of Council Decision 2008/426/JHA of 16 December 2008 on the strengthening of Eurojust.

[53] Mathieu Deflem, 'Technology and the internationalization of policing', (2002) 19 *Justice Quarterly* (3), 457.

[54] M. Cherif Bassiouni (ed.), *International Criminal Law*, 2nd edn, Vols 1–3, Ardsley, New York, Transaction Publishing, 1999, p. 887, n. 19.

By way of a shorthand expression one could posit that international crimes—also called core crimes or *stricto sensu* international crimes—are subject to international jurisdiction but do not necessarily entail the implication of more than one national jurisdiction; genocide is an example of this. They are characterized by universal jurisdiction, i.e. an alleged perpetrator of one of these crimes can be prosecuted in any country, even if neither he or she, nor the victim, nor the *locus* has a link to the prosecuting country, and they are customary international crimes.[55] On the other hand, transnational crimes—also called 'crimes of international concern' or treaty crimes—involve more than one national jurisdiction and are subject to municipal, not international jurisdiction.[56] Only limited extraterritoriality obtains in these treaty crimes that all originate in municipal legislation, which have been formulated 'in normative terms for the purpose of binding states'.[57]

1.6.2 World Society Theory

Theoretical and methodological issues in transnational criminal police cooperation should be examined against the background of the wider concept of *global crime governance*.[58] The development of global cooperation against organised crime has passed through a spiral of institutionalization. This view, which is coherent and perhaps represents the majority view in academia today, is based on World Society Theory, a strand of sociological institutionalism. Global criminal governance follows two vectors, the development of common criminalization and of global law enforcement cooperation.

1.6.3 Rationalization

The development of modern policing is intimately linked to that of rationalization, an important facet of which certainly is that of risk. Jakobi claims that a major trigger of global crime governance is the preoccupation of modern society with avoiding risk.[59] Indeed, one may term modern Western society a *risk society*, in which governance is preoccupied with risk anticipation. On this view, risks and their perception become more and more indistinguishable.[60]

55 Stephen Macedo (ed.), *The Princeton Principles on Universal Jurisdiction*, Princeton, New Jersey, Princeton University Press, 2001. Note the important exception by Lord Browne-Wilkinson.

56 A more substantive treatment of this fascinating subject would be inappropriate for the present chapter, but see Boister, 'Transnational criminal law?', cited in note 50 above, and Cassese, *International Criminal Law*, cited in note 35 above, p. 11.

57 Boister, ibid, p. 963.

58 Jakobi, *Common Goods and Evils?*, cited in note 3 above.

59 Ibid, pp. 4 and 10. Kenneth W. Abbott, Robert O. Keohane, Andrew Moravcsik, Anne-Marie Slaughter, and Duncan Snidal, 'The concept of legalization', (2000) 54 *International Organization* (3), 401–19. Ulrich Beck, *World at Risk*, Bristol, UK, Polity Press, 2009.

60 Giorgio Agamben suggests that the security concerns are created by governments as a way of exercising power while undermining the democratic process. Giorgio Agamben, 'For a theory of destituent power', public lecture, Athens, 16 November 2013, available at: http://www.chronosmag.eu/index.php/g-agamben-for-a-theory-of-destituent-power.html.

1.6.4 Police and technology

Technology in policing is a constituent part of rationalization and is, as such, at the very core of the creation of modern policing. Development of such technology, however, raises questions of justice and right, as it influences both the means and the objectives of international policing activities and thereby leads to developments that are independent of law and politics.[61]

In 1843 in Brussels, Belgium, the first photograph was taken of a convict in prison. This led in the 1880s to the creation of the first collection of photographs of international criminals and to exchange of information with forces in Europe by the New York Police Department. Of particular concern to the authorities regarding international criminals was the rapid development of the railway network in Europe: in 1840, there were 4,000 km and twenty years later, 50,000 km.[62] Likewise, the rapid development in communications via the telegraph profited the criminal world and law enforcement, alike.[63]

It is difficult, at any given moment, to evaluate whether the criminal world or law enforcement is ahead in the exploitation of available technology. Some of the major steps include the development of dactyloscopy and the more recent digitalization of same, a technology that remains crucial for the immediate identification of arrestees.[64] The development and use by law enforcement of DNA technology are of import, nationally and internationally, now that the DNA code can be digitalized. One might think that law enforcement has the technological upper hand. But this view must be modified when one considers that the same information technology that allows for analysis and transmission of fingerprints and DNA codes, and interrogation of very large and diverse data bases, gives the criminals an important advantage in, for example, online fraud and dissemination of child pornography, not to mention currency counterfeiting, market manipulation, and the production of counterfeit credit cards and identity documents. Also, a very recent development is the use of drones, unmanned aerial vehicles (UAV), by law enforcement for surveillance; simultaneously, however, criminals are using drones to transport narcotic drugs across borders.[65]

The efficiency vs rights debate is exemplified by a US Supreme Court ruling of 2001.[66] Law enforcement had used a distance heat-measuring device to determine that the outside of one side of the home of a person suspected of growing marijuana, was hotter than the rest. Based on this expertise, a federal judge issued a search warrant,

[61] Deflem, 'Technology and internationalization', cited in note 53 above, pp. 454 and 456.

[62] Norman J. G. Pounds, *An Historical Geography of Europe*, Cambridge, Cambridge University Press, 1985.

[63] More often than not, telegraph lines followed the rail lines.

[64] The fascinating history of the development of the *portrait parlé* (a development of Bertillonage, numerically expressed and therefore transmissible by telegraph, adopted by the Rome 1898 conference) and dactyloscopy would consume too much space, but see Cole, *Suspect Identities*, cited in note 13 above; Deflem, 'Technology and internationalization', cited in note 53 above, pp. 460–61.

[65] On 20 January 2015, one such drone crashed in Tijuana, Mexico, on its way to the USA carrying six pounds of methamphetamine. In April 2014, a drone was found outside a prison in South Carolina, USA; it had been used to carry mobile telephones, marijuana, and tobacco into the prison. Associated Press release, 21 January 2015.

[66] *Kyllo v United States*, 533 US 27 (2001).

which was executed and the suspicions substantiated. The Supreme Court held that the search was unlawful as the search warrant had been issued on the basis of a law enforcement act that violated the right of the accused to privacy.

An amazing development, with hitherto unimaginable consequences for the cooperation between developing and developed countries, very recently occurred in the surveillance and control of wildlife depletion. Poaching of wildlife in Africa has developed into a major source of income for organised crime and threatens the extinction of, for instance, the rhinoceros and the African elephant, of which respectively 1,215 and 30,000 were killed in 2014. The trade is highly organised—contrary to the initial perception—by middlemen, who on one side finance and direct the poaching operations and on the other organise the transport and sale of tusk products in South-East Asia. Even though increased funding has been made available, in particular for the hiring of wildlife rangers, the sheer size of the areas to be patrolled makes efficient control an unobtainable ideal.[67]

Recently, however, an important and promising development in the use of technology, crime mapping, and intelligence may provide law enforcement with a much-needed advantage—the *anti-poaching UAV intel programme*, based at University of Maryland in the United States. The programme has deployed UAVs over wildlife areas in Africa since May 2013. Concurrently, an intensive geographical information systems (GIS) intelligence programme was carried out over the same area, whereby the position of rhinoceros was plotted, by season, time, and weather conditions. Likewise, the known locations for the killing of rhinoceros were plotted. As a result, the GIS intelligence programme predicts, with approximately 90 per cent accuracy, the exact location of rhinoceros on a given night between 6.30 and 8.00 pm, the preferred killing time. It can likewise predetermine the most likely killing grounds, based on a number of vectors: the location of the rhinoceros, weather, and time.[68] The drones are therefore concentrated on areas of high risk, as determined by the GIS intelligence algorithm.

The results are cautiously positive. When drones are deployed, a certain number of arrests are executed in a given area and all further poaching activity ceases. It is quite obvious that poachers—at this stage—are capable of continuing in a non-surveyed area; this opportunity will obviously be inversely proportional to the number of drones the programme is capable of deploying. Second, the intelligence algorithm must be constantly updated—or self-correct—by taking into account behaviour changes in animals and poachers.

The programme prompts a number of important observations. First, only relatively recently did local authorities take the—perhaps courageous—step of admitting that poaching and trade were directly by 'powerful' individuals, residing in the major cities in Africa, rather than being a cottage industry inspired by Chinese traders. This clearly lifts the problem into the sphere of organised crime, and this category change must lead also to a fundamental law enforcement change. Second, the proposed solution

[67] For example, in the Virunga National Park, DRC, more than 150 rangers were killed between 1995 and 2014.

[68] Most killings take place on nights with a full moon and within 160 metres from a vehicular road.

calls for a close cooperation between technology, intelligence, and the human factor, represented by the rangers.

1.6.5 Random collection

The major—to some very worrying—shift in the investigation of organised crime, and indeed of crime *tout court*, came, however, in the 1970s with the development of intrusive surveillance techniques that were not based on nor justified by the suspicion that a crime had been or was being committed, or, indeed, was being planned by the individuals, who were the subjects of such surveillance. In popular language such techniques are known as 'fishing expeditions'. They have hitherto met with opprobrium from the judiciary in democratic countries, as well as from public opinion.

The first, highly organised, international random-collection technique was the Echelon Programme, conceived in the 1960s, fully operational, including for US law enforcement, *c.* 1980. It is an electronic listening system operated on communication transiting communication satellites. Although all information concerning the system is secret, nevertheless it would seem that the system originally only involved the UK and the USA; later it was expanded to include the other three Anglo-Saxon countries, Canada, Australia, and New Zealand. The system confronts the stream of international, digitalized telephone traffic with a pre-established, digitalized list of key terms.

Concurrently, a number of countries installed CCTV surveillance cameras in public places; indeed, a simple walk in the streets of any town or city in England will lead to the walker being observed and the images of his or her walk recorded and filed. The ultimate, but presumably not final development of random routine surveillance of citizens without the classic 'probable cause' is the anti-money laundering legislation.

1.6.6 Cryptography

The most worrying issue faced by modern law enforcement remains *cryptography*.[69] Law enforcement and the security services rely on the collection and evaluation of information from and by technological means. If such collection is possible, but evaluation is not because of unbreakable encryption, a major—and in many respects *the* major—area of law enforcement information collection becomes non-productive.[70]

The dichotomy between the undisputed advantages to society in using information technology and the potential misuse of the same means by criminals and terrorists has given rise to a series of spirited debates about the concept of encryption and in particular of two connected issues: first, whether encryption should be considered a

[69] For reasons of space this sub-section has been kept somewhat shorter than the subject matter deserves. For a fuller treatment, see Madsen, 'International organization and crime, and corruption', cited in note 63 above.

[70] The term 'unbreakable' is used in the context of encryption to mean that an encrypted message (written or spoken) cannot be deciphered at all, or cannot be deciphered within such time limit that the information contained in it still remains of importance to those attempting to understand it.

munition and as such be subjected to the limitations established in various transfer-of-technology agreements and, second, if limitations were imposed, at what strength of encryption should governments draw the limit. What used to be a rather obtuse, technical discussion between military and arms control experts grew into a heated public debate in the early 1990s. The commercial potential of the internet, however, was soon recognized, in particular so-called *e-commerce*, the sale and purchase of merchandise via the internet with its unconditional need for secure communication. One of the many problems highlighted by the debate was the fact that the 'virtual' nature of the internet blurred the traditional line between domestic and overseas intelligence collection, since the latter, directly or via friendly foreign services, can collect on behalf of the former.

1.6.7 Extradition

A main tool and perhaps *the* measure of success or failure in international cooperation against organised crime is constituted by extradition. Countries have entered into bi- or multilateral extraditions agreements and some international instruments; for example UNTOC and the 1988 Narcotics Convention can themselves act as extradition treaties, when necessary. Nevertheless, *extradition remains a question of discretion*. In the UK, the element of discretion 'remains with the Secretary of State in current practice'.[71]

1.7 Fragmentation?

Fragmentation in the global crime governance system is incrementing, partly in the form of slowly emerging resistance in developing countries against crime governance measures that are imposed by the developed world on, and often not adequate or suited for, the developing world, and partly as the re-emergence of a number of phenomena discontinued in the past. These two issues will be considered separately in the following.

The submission of an ill-prepared developing country to policies and regulatory mechanisms imposed by developed countries, also known as *coercive policy transfer*, is best illustrated by the anti-money laundering (AML) regime. Research indicates that not only do these regulations cost approximately five times more than the funds forfeited under them, but they also might have pernicious effects in developing countries: for example the Know Your Customer requirement for opening a bank account may pose severe problems to some who have neither an acceptable address, nor receipts for gas or electricity.[72] They are therefore forced into the arms of underground banking.

[71] Ivor Stanbrook and Clive Stanbrook, *Extradition*, 2nd edn, Oxford, Oxford University Press, 2000, paras 8.05 and 9.43.

[72] A thorough treatment of this theme would exceed the limits of this chapter. See Hlophe Zakhele, 'Regulating money laundering in developing countries', PhD thesis, King's College London, 2012. *Contra*: Brent L. Bartlett, *The Negative Effects of Money Laundering on Economic Development*, The Asian Development Bank. Regional Technical Assistance Project No. 5967, 2002.

The reappearance of a number of enforcement phenomena that most would have thought discontinued in the past is illustrated by the development of a new species of law enforcement personnel, the so-called modern mercenary,[73] and with the usurpation by multinational enterprises of the state monopoly on violence. The use of private armies—modern mercenaries—commenced in 1994 when the first private military company was created. But the market for private military companies strongly increased under the US President George W. Bush, who wanted to find support troops for the occupation by the United States of Afghanistan and Iraq. Although private military companies are now mostly used by the United States, some scholars expect their use to spread to the protection of humanitarian organisations, for example. Obviously, the services of such companies may also be retained by entities that are not under political control.

1.7.1 Waste: present and future opportunity and risk

Waste and in particular toxic waste is increasingly attracting the attention of transnational organised crime. This includes the voluntary sinking in the Mediterranean of cargo ships carrying toxic waste and the dumping of dangerous waste in developing countries. Recently, according to the United Nations, organised crime has moved into the discharge of electronics—so-called *e-waste*—in African and Asian countries, where the United Nations Environmental Programme (UNEP) estimates that 90 per cent of all e-waste in the developed world is dumped in illegal discharges for destruction and reuse. Shipments are falsely labelled and are transported to Ghana and Nigeria (and to a lesser degree to the Ivory Coast and Congo-Brazzaville) in Africa and to China, Hong Kong, Pakistan, India, Bangladesh, and Vietnam in Asia. The sheer volume of this traffic makes it improbable that law enforcement will have much effect.

1.8 Final Observations

In the developed world, the health sector is increasingly important. As the populations of the richest developed countries grow older, their health-care requirements increase and private individuals and governments heavily invest in the sector. In 2010, the average OECD-country's private and public expenditure on health was 9.5 per cent of GDP.[74] A US court of appeal has determined that improving the health of its citizens is an interest central to the state's core police powers.[75] The sheer quantities of funds

[73] Sean McFate, *The Modern Mercenary: Private Armies and What They Mean for World Order*, Oxford, Oxford University Press, 2015. 'Return of the hired gun', *The Economist*, 10 January 2015, 75–6.

[74] OECD, 'Health Expenditure', in *OECD Factbook 2013: Economic, Environmental and Social Statistics*, Paris, France, OECD Publishing, 2013, p. 249.

[75] *Newman v Sathyavaglswaran*, USCA, 9th Circuit, argued 17 October 2001, with reference to *Cruzan*, 497 US at 262, 110 S.Ct. 2841, that states have an 'unqualified interest in the preservation of human life'. *Police power* describes the basic right of governments to make laws and regulations for the benefit of their communities. In the United States, the Tenth Amendment to the US Constitution describes police powers as those necessary to preserve and protect the safety, health, welfare, and morals of the community.

involved in the sector attract criminal organisations as does the *de facto* creation of *denied demand*, such as access to cutting-edge pharmaceutical products, organs for transplantation, and care and cure homes for the elderly and long-term ill. Also, using health in a broader sense, the safe disposal of toxic, including electronic, waste will increasingly pose a problem in developed countries. Organised crime will play an increasing role here as well, with severe threats to public health, be it by clandestine disposal in developed countries or more or less transparent disposal in developing countries.

The typical marketing crimes will continue unabated and the law enforcement efforts to counter them will remain gallant and inefficient. In the meantime, however, other crimes threaten society, linked with health in a broad sense. Indeed, the Italian quip that 'health makes a rime with crime' will, undoubtedly, prove itself only too prescient.[76]

[76] The expression was coined by the Italian daily *La Repubblica*.

2

Transnational Organised Crime: Concepts and Critics

*Arndt Sinn**

2.1 Transnational Organised Crime as a Linguistic and Social Construct

The forward pace of globalization is greatly influencing the phenomenon of organised crime (OC). Transnational organised crime takes advantage of market liberalization, relaxed border controls, and the internet. The result is criminal groups with international membership and activities and connections to multiple countries.[1] The term 'transnational organised crime' is already used to discuss and explain the international elements and connections of organised crime, but the terminological and sociological questions it raises cannot be ignored.

The term 'transnational organised crime' has both a denotation and a connotation, though it has been said to exclude certain important sociological issues.[2] It has been criticized for lacking consensus even around the core idea of 'organisation', around which there is room for much discussion and which few legal systems explicitly define. It could certainly be treated as an extra-legal concept, given that the term is not a list of definitional elements but rather a criminological phenomenon.[3] The addition of 'transnational' is no help to definitional certainty, not least because there is no proper differentiation between the adjectives 'transnational' and 'international'.[4]

2.1.1 What does transnational organised crime denote?

The core meaning of 'organised crime' is not an easy thing to identify: OC is not an especially visible phenomenon, and it is one that is understood very differently in various countries because of their diverse historical and cultural experiences with such crime.

* I would like to thank my assistant Ass. iur. Johanna Siebert for her constructive discussion and cooperation in the preparation of this chapter.

[1] Cf. SOCTA, EU Serious and Organised Crime Threat Assessment, 2013, p. 16, http://www.europol.europa.eu/content/eu-serious-and-organised-crime-threat-assessment-socta, accessed 7 September 2015; cf. Arndt Sinn, Organisierte Kriminalität 3.0, Berlin, Springer, 2016, due June 3, 2016.

[2] Frank G. Madsen, *Transnational Organized Crime*, London and New York, Routledge, 2009, p. 9.

[3] Mark A. Zöller, 'Verschwimmende Grenzen zwischen Terrorismus und Organisierter Kriminalität', in Arndt Sinn and Mark A. Zöller (eds), *Neujustierung des Strafrechts durch Terrorismus und Organisierte Kriminalität*, Heidelberg, C. F. Müller, 2013, p. 2.

[4] Madsen, *Transnational Organized Crime*, cited in note 2 above.

It is possible to identify more than 100 definitions worldwide[5]—and even the value of having a definition at all is not uncontroversial. Some attempts at a model definition have been rejected for lack of a basis in scholarship, accused of being too far removed from reality and of not focusing on criminal enterprises and their economic activities.[6] This objection can be answered with the rejoinder that the definition of organised crime plays a decisive role in national and international criminal law, in the design of investigative powers and prosecutorial instruments, in the distribution of police resources, and as a motor for legal harmonization. If one is prepared to accept that position, then clarity about the definition of organised crime is required, for only then can the definition and its elements serve as a check on state power and its arbitrary exercise. This important limiting function of the definition is often neglected in such discussions. Definitions allow proposed changes to the law or anticrime strategy to be scrutinized and resources to be reallocated: they serve not only to increase the visibility of the phenomenon, but also as a yardstick by which to examine any initiative that is directed against organised crime. There can be no evaluation of anti-OC initiatives without a definition, nor any adjustment or recalibration. Definitions must of course be adapted to changing phenomena, since they should describe reality. The legislator can then react to the description and take appropriate measures. Thus the normative is reconnected to the phenomenon and the law becomes able to be evaluated against its stated purpose. This is not a naturalistic short-circuit, but rather a mechanism for ensuring transparency in a liberal society under the rule of law.

The 1995 working definition of the Council of the European Union was an attempt on the level of European police practice to give the phenomenon of transnational organised crime a tactically and criminologically useful face. The EU treaties even mention cross-border organised crime by name, and a number of supranational competencies assume the existence of such a phenomenon (see section 3.2 of this chapter).

Organised crime is deemed to consist of conduct that meets criteria 1, 3, 5 and 11 in the following list, plus at least two more:

1. an association of more than two people …
2. who each perform individual tasks assigned to them …
3. *for a long or undefined period of time (an indication of stability and potential permanence) …*
4. using specific methods of discipline and control,
5. *where the persons are suspected of having committed serious crimes …*
6. at the international level …
7. using violence and other means of intimidation,
8. using commercial or commerce-like structures,

[5] Cf. collection by Klaus von Lampe, 'Definitions of organized crime', available at: http://www.organized-crime.de/organizedcrimedefinitions.htm, accessed 7 September 2015.

[6] Cf. Ulrich Sieber, 'Organisierte Kriminalität in der Bundesrepublik Deutschland', in Ulrich Sieber (ed.), *Internationale Organisierte Kriminalität*, Cologne, Springer, 1997, p. 85; Cyrille Fijnaut, 'Organisierte Kriminalität in Nordwesteuropa' in the same volume, p. 15.

9. committing money laundering,
10. influencing politics, the media, public administration, the justice system, or the economy and/or
11. *motivated by the accumulation of money or power.*[7]

The European Union and the United Nations have incorporated the question into their laws in various ways without settling on a single definition. Instead, the instruments speak of 'criminal associations', an 'organised grouping', or 'organised criminal groups'. The first official proposal for a definition of a 'criminal association' at the international level was made by the Council of the European Union as part of the Joint Action of 21 December 1998 (98/733/JHA) on the basis of Article K.3 Treaty on European Union (TEU). The definition is as follows:

> Within the meaning of this joint action, a criminal organisation shall mean a structured association, established over a period of time, of more than two persons, acting in concert with a view to committing offences which are punishable by deprivation of liberty or a detention order of a maximum of at least four years or a more serious penalty, whether such offences are an end in themselves or a means of obtaining material benefits and, where appropriate, of improperly influencing the operation of public authorities.[8]

In 1994, at the worldwide ministerial conference of the UN on organised crime in Naples, comprehensive strategies for combatting organised crime were developed, and through the UN Convention against Transnational Organized Crime (the 'Palermo Convention') of 15 November 2000 the UN General Assembly created a working definition that treats organised criminal groups as a phenomenon with the following characteristics:

> Organized criminal group shall mean a structured group of three or more persons, existing for a period of time and acting in concert with the aim of committing one or more serious crimes or offences established in accordance with this Convention, in order to obtain, directly or indirectly, a financial or other material benefit.[9]

Framework Decision 2008/841/JHA of the Council of the European Union of 24 October 2008 on Combatting Organized Crime is the third instrument of international law that contains a definition of a criminal association. For the purposes of the framework decision, the term is stated to mean:

1. Criminal organisation means a structured association, established over a period of time, of more than two persons acting in concert with a view to committing offences which are punishable by deprivation of liberty or a detention order of a

[7] EU/12247/1/Rev. 1; European Council, Organised crime situation report 2005, p. 21.
[8] Francesco Calderoni, *Organized Crime Legislation in the European Union*, Berlin, Heidelberg, Springer, 2010, p. 27.
[9] Cf. United Nations Office on Drugs and Crime (UNODC), *Legislative Guides for the Implementation of the United Nations Convention Against Transnational Organized Crime and Protocols Thereto*, New York, UNODC, 2004, pp. 12, 14.

maximum of at least four years or a more serious penalty, to obtain, directly or indirectly, a financial or other material benefit;

2. Structured association means an association that is not randomly formed for the immediate commission of an offence, nor does it need to have formally defined roles for its members, continuity of its membership, or a developed structure.[10]

But even these definitions are only descriptions of the phenomenon consisting of elements requiring interpretation. National legislators have to complete and concretize them. Most member states of the European Union punish the offence of forming a criminal association (e.g. Germany's §129 Strafgesetzbuch [StGB]; Article 450-01 of the French Code Pénal [CP]; Article 416 of the Italian Codice Penal [CP]). The design of the individual norms differs from country to country, as do details such as the minimum number of members required or the elements that must be present for the group to be considered structured.[11]

One possibility for unifying the various definitions would be to draw on the various criminological models as a greater unified concept. The result would be a model of organised crime on a spectrum between a hierarchically structured, discrete organisation on one hand and a structured, flexible network on the other.[12] But regardless of where one puts organised crime in the end, its existence is beyond doubt.

2.1.2 What does transnational organised crime connote?

Apart from the term's purely definitional content, there is the question of value statements contained in the definitional penumbra of the term transnational organised crime. One could claim, for example, that the word 'crime' automatically divides society into Good and Evil.[13] Here, Jakobs's concept of 'enemy justice' becomes relevant, especially as it relates to questions of legitimacy and the shifting of criminal liability. In the context of certain offences, Jakobs explains, the offender is treated by the state not as a citizen but as an enemy. 'Enemy justice' preserves the integrity of certain protected legal rights at the expense of constitutionally guaranteed individual liberty. As an example, Jacobs gives §129 of the German StGB, which codifies the offence of forming a criminal association. He also includes the manifestations of organised crime around drug and financial crimes.[14] The term transnational organised crime, goes the argument, carries a whiff of a foreign conspiracy,[15] and thus of xenophobia and racism, defying clear evidence that the majority of organised crime offenders come from within the country in which they operate.[16] Language has made a separate criminal class out of organised crime, a threat to the peace and safety of the law-abiding

[10] Calderoni, *EU Organized Crime Legislation*, cited in note 8 above, p. 36.

[11] Ibid, p. 55.

[12] James Sheptycki, 'Against transnational organized crime' in Margaret E. Beare (ed.), *Critical Reflection on Transnational Organized Crime, Money Laundering, and Corruption*, Toronto, University of Toronto Press, 2003, p. 124.

[13] Ibid, p. 126.

[14] Günther Jakobs, 'Bürgerstrafrecht und Feindstrafrecht', (2004) *HRRS* (3), 88, 92; Günther Jakobs, 'Kriminalisierung im Vorfeld einer Rechtsgutsverletzung', (1985) 97 *ZStW*, 751, 757.

[15] Sheptycki, 'Against transnational organized crime', cited in note 12 above, p. 126.

[16] Madsen, *Transnational Organized Crime*, cited in note 2 above.

citizen that is constructed out of racism and cultural differences.[17] Moreover, the term contains phenomena that are difficult to subsume within one of the many definitions of organised crime but must still be included in any description of the phenomenon ('pre-OC').

2.1.3 The exclusion of certain sociological issues

It has been argued further that current definitions of transnational organised crime take insufficient account of financial crimes and criminal enterprises. The argument runs as follows: the initial assumption must always be that an enterprise has a legitimate purpose,[18] but that this assumption has been shaken by the financial crisis and is changing.[19] The number of accusations against commercial enterprises of criminal energy in the false reporting of mortgage-backed securities, interest-rate manipulation, and tax evasion, is increasing. If one assumes that organised crime uses business-like structures to return criminal profits and reinvests these via money laundering in the legitimate economy, then it is obvious that the realm of financial crimes is not free from organised crime. It will thus be even more important in the future to include these types of organised crime in any definition.[20] Taking Germany as an example, it might be harder and harder to ignore the idea that the financial crisis was not simply the result of a systematic failure but that there is a certain likelihood that it was also the result of massive, objectively criminal conduct by people in positions of responsibility within the financial sector. Banks invested in risky and ultimately worthless American securities—in economic terms, they subsidized the spending of American consumers at the expense of German taxpayers.[21] The traditional faith in a trustworthy and responsible financial sector has been permanently damaged, raising the question of whether 'mafia' is not just a metaphor for pathological abuse of power. Organised crime is not just a hallmark of structurally weak societies: it has spread to all political systems in one form or another.[22] If one takes these new societal developments into account, individual states must adapt their definitions accordingly. In Germany, there is an element beyond the cumulative criteria: 'the use of commercial or quasi-commercial structures'. In order to avoid doubly subsuming a given situation within both the general cumulative criteria and the alternative criterion, it may be necessary to eliminate this alternative criterion, given that it has anyway been the subject of comprehensive criticism.[23]

[17] Sheptycki, 'Against transnational organized crime', cited in note 12 above, p. 126.

[18] Ibid, p. 134.

[19] Cf. Madsen, *Transnational Organized Crime*, cited in note 2 above, p. 10.

[20] Cf. ibid, p. 10; Europol, *Exploring Tomorrow's Organised Crime*, available at: http://www.europol.europa.eu/content/exploring-tomorrow's-organised-crime, accessed 7 September 2015.

[21] Bernd Schünemann, 'Die sog. Finanzkrise- Systemversagen oder global organisierte Kriminalität?' in Bernd Schünemann (ed.), *Die sogenannte Finanzkrise – Systemversagen oder global organisierte Kriminalität*, Berlin, Berliner Wissenschafts-Verlag, 2010, p. 102.

[22] Wolfgang Hetzer, 'Finanzindustrie oder Organisierte Kriminalität?', *Aus Politik und Zeitgeschichte* (38–9), 16 September 2013, available at: http://www.bpb.de/apuz/168914/finanzindustrie-oder-organisierte-kriminalitaet, accessed 7 September 2015.

[23] Cf. Jörg Kinzig, *Die rechtliche Bewältigung von Erscheinungsformen organisierter Kriminalität*, Berlin, Duncker & Humblot, 2004, pp. 58, 777.

2.2 Conceptions of Organised Crime: A Phenomenology

The recognition of organised crime as a discrete type of criminality probably dates from the 1920s and 1930s in the United States. The term 'organised crime' was born as a criticism of societal structures that obviously shaped life in the large cities of the north-eastern United States. Industrialization, migration to the cities, and immigration had come together in a crisis that society did not seem to be capable of handling.[24] Prohibition, designed to reduce crime, led to the opposite. 'Organized crime' referred to 'gangsters' and 'racketeers', 'gangs' and 'syndicates', and powerful individuals in the underworld such as Al Capone.[25] These American developments are difficult to separate from the phenomenon of the Italian mafia, given that the late nineteenth century saw mass migration of Italians into the large cities of the United States, where they organised themselves as an ethnic minority and expanded existing community structures.[26]

2.2.1 Two meanings

Engaging with the term organised crime requires looking at the various theoretical approaches and structural analyses surrounding it.

2.2.1.1 A set of actors

The first sees organised crime as tied to traditional subcultures of the modern city. This model orients the structures of organised crime in the underworld, from which they only occasionally participate in normal society.[27] It thus corresponds to the model of organised crime that they operate out of sight.[28] Under this approach, a distinction is made between two types of structure.

2.2.1.1.1 Mafia-type structures

The mafia-type structure consists of independently operating groups of offenders. The organised crime within these structures is a form of offending organised within closed, strictly hierarchical, ethnic, international syndicates.[29] Typical examples are usually given as the Italian mafia ('Sicilian syndrome'), the Chinese triads, or the Japanese yakuza ('alien conspiracy').[30]

[24] Klaus von Lampe, *Organized Crime*, Frankfurt am Main, Peter Lang, 1999, p. 54.

[25] Cf. Madsen, *Transnational Organized Crime*, cited in note 2 above, p. 13; Lampe, ibid, p. 55.

[26] Cf. Madsen, ibid, p. 13; Heinz-Josef Möhn, *Organisierte Kriminalität—Terminologische Darstellung und Begriffsbestimmung*, Trier, Verlag Dr Kovac, 2006, p. 36.

[27] Hans-Jörg Albrecht, 'The UN Transnational Crime Convention', in Hans-Jörg Albrecht and Cyrille Fijnaut (eds), *The Containment of Transnational Organized Crime*, Freiburg, Edition Iuscrim, 2002, p. 10.

[28] Oliver Bossert and Guido Korte, *Organisierte Kriminalität und Ausländerextremismus/Terrorismus*, Bonn, Brühl, 2004, p. 21.

[29] Andreas Kohl, Peter Krevert, and Gerhard W. Wittkämper, *Europa und die innere Sicherheit* Wiesbaden, BKA, 1996, p. 50.

[30] Ibid; Letizia Paoli, 'Implementation: concepts and actors', in Albrecht and Fijnaut, *The Containment of Transnational Organized Crime*, cited in note 27 above, p. 209; Jan Rolf Sulk, 'Internationalisierung Innerer Sicherheit auf völkerrechtlicher Ebene', (2010) *JURA*, 683, 687.

2.2.1.1.2 Network-type structures

The network-type structure is characterized by multifaceted horizontal connections among the offenders, which traverse regional or multiregional networks and operate on a national or international scale.[31] Within the networks exist groups of offenders of different sizes: small, loose associations of two to five offenders without an internal hierarchy; core groups of five to ten offenders divided into planning and operational levels and closed to the outside, and large groups of twenty to fifty offenders with a high level of organisation, a multilevel structure, and a chain of command among the various operational levels.[32] These groupings work together occasionally, and maintain informal contact.[33] This type of structure is more common in Germany, according to empirical studies.[34]

2.2.1.2 The enterprise theory

The second theoretical approach deals with crime as a reasonable, well-organised enterprise. We encounter organised crime in the form of everyday, conventional economic activities.[35] In this approach, less emphasis is placed on the relationships between offenders and their environment and between subculture and underworld. What remains is transactional crime, profit as a driving motivator, and a rationality that seeks to reduce opportunity costs (in the form of the risk of criminal prosecution)[36] using the division of labour, corruption, and violence. Under this approach, organised crime can hardly be distinguished from a legitimate commercial enterprise. It is described as an open system, one that adapts quickly to political, legal, and economic developments.[37] One example of this is money laundering in which neither the offender nor the offence itself can be traced back to a single criminal act.

By way of summary, it probably has to be admitted that organised crime is a phenomenon that is difficult to squeeze into the structure of a particular definition, since its manifestations can be so various depending on its ethnic origin and type of criminal activity.

2.2.2 Recent developments

More and more frequently, law enforcement authorities discover groups of offenders that do not qualify as organised crime under any extant definition, but who show a

[31] Madsen, *Transnational Organized Crime*, cited in note 2 above, p. 14; Kohl *et al.*, *Europa und die innere Sicherheit*, cited in note 29 above, p. 50.

[32] Eugen Weschke and Karla Heine-Heiß, *Organisierte Kriminalität als Netzstrukturkriminalität*, Berlin, Fachhochschule für Verwaltung und Rechtspflege, 1990, p. 18.

[33] Ibid, p. 43.

[34] Cf. Sieber, 'Organisierte Kriminalität in der Bundesrepublik Deutschland', cited in note 6 above, p. 54.

[35] Albrecht, 'The UN Transnational Crime Convention', cited in note 27 above, p. 11.

[36] Hans-Jörg Albrecht, 'Terrorismus und organisierte Kriminalität—Beziehungen, Zusammenhänge und Konvergenz', in Arnold, Harald *et al.* (eds), *Terrorismus und organisierte Kriminalität*, Berlin, 2014, p. 23.

[37] Sulk, 'Internationalisierung Innerer Sicherheit', cited in note 30 above, pp. 683, 687.

high degree of potential organisation. Networks for the distribution of child pornography are not motivated primarily by profit, but they operate in the same way as e.g. groups that sell stolen credit card information over the internet. For many motorcycle gangs, criminal conduct is part of their group identity, but cybercrime offences often only involve one or two offenders. Overall, a hybridization of organised crime groups is definitely noticeable.[38] So what should the implications be for extant definitions and instruments of crime prevention and prosecution?

2.2.3 Distinguishing organised crime from other phenomena

2.2.3.1 Terrorism

Terrorism is another concept for which there is no universally agreed definition, and since 11 September 2001 it has become harder and harder to distinguish terrorism from organised crime in a meaningful way, since terrorist networks have resorted to the traditional activities of organised crime such as illegal drugs, human trafficking, and money laundering in order to finance their activities. This leads to hybrid groups:[39] the Taliban and Al-Qaeda earned millions through the cultivation and preparation of poppies and opium.[40] The so-called 'Islamic State' is not just in the business of destroying cultural property: it also sells it to finance its purposes. The classic differentiation between types of criminal group according to the purpose of the criminal activity also collapses here. At least theoretically, terrorist groups pursue radical changes to the social order by means of violence or threats. It can be seen as a communications strategy for one's own ideological agenda, whereas organised crime is about making a profit.[41] But with hybrid groups, this distinction can no longer be drawn, which has consequences for the legal treatment of this phenomenon. Prosecution, at least, will be greatly affected in practice, both structurally and tactically.

2.2.3.2 Gangs

As with terrorism, as a matter of criminology and law organised crime must be distinguished from gangs, but here, too, a clear separation is quite difficult, since there is considerable overlap among the characteristics and the two types of group might even form alliances with one another. As can be expected, there is no single definition here, either. German case law requires a minimum number of participants (three) as one criterion; they must have formed the intention to commit several independent

[38] Europol, *Exploring Tomorrow's Organised Crime*, cited in note 20 above, p. 60; SOCTA 2013, cited in note 1 above, p. 45.
[39] EUROPOL, *Exploring Tomorrow's Organised Crime*, cited in note 20 above, p. 60; SOCTA 2013, cited in note 1 above, p. 45.
[40] Bossert and Korte, *Organisierte Kriminalität und Ausländerextremismus/Terrorismus*, cited in note 28 above, pp. 282, 285.
[41] Cf. Madsen, *Transnational Organized Crime*, cited in note 2 above, p. 63; Frank Bovenkerk and Bashir Abou Chakra, 'Terrorism and organised crime', in Leslie Holmes (ed.), *Terrorism, Organised Crime and Corruption*, Camberley, Edward Elgar, 2007, p. 29; Zöller, 'Verschwimmende Grenzen', cited in note 3 above, p. 11.

but as yet undetermined criminal offences laid out in statute over a certain period of time. A fully-formed 'gang intent' or 'activities in the higher interest of the gang' are not necessary.[42] From a criminological point of view, a gang is a special group structure characterized by individual role allocation and division of labour, and a gang generally has an internal system of norms with hierarchical rituals and sanctions. It generally has an externally identifiable leader and a name, often with a specific or fixed territory.[43] But unlike organised crime, no particular organisational form or hierarchical system is required, and financial profit is not necessarily a primary motivation. At the same time, motorcycle gangs such as the 'Hell's Angels' are squarely within the realm of organised crime.

2.2.3.3 White-collar crime

The example of white-collar crime vividly illustrates the role of organised crime as a kind of surrogate concept—a surrogate for substructures of the economy and society perceived as threatening, difficult for political interference to access, and thus capable of destabilizing the political order itself.[44] The offences of subsidy and investment fraud, money laundering, tax evasion, corruption, and insider trading are examples of the criminalization of economic conduct. The actions they cover are complex and difficult to supervise. The boundaries between compliant and deviant behaviour are blurry. There is little discussion of organised crime in these areas within the criminal justice system itself;[45] instead, it is referred to as corporate crime or white-collar crime. But where is the line? As mentioned above, there is some hesitation to compare bankers with mafia bosses, but we now know that mafia is not the same thing as organised crime and is itself often indistinguishable from legitimate enterprises, so there can be no final distinction drawn between corporate crime and organised crime. The focus is on power: the power to make decisions, the power of a position, of contacts, or over resources and influence.[46] Even if there is no physical violence, the power over money and other people can often have a similar effect.

2.2.3.4 Organised crime as a model of 'crime as a service'

With the expansion of communications channels, the spread of IT into every area of life, and the accompanying opportunities for misuse, organised crime will change as well. 'Crime as a service' is the idea that traditional criminal networks will also move towards the model of individual service providers. Hackers will join together for individual jobs rather than form permanent hierarchical networks. A criminal offence will be offered as a service, allowing a consortium of many people to come together

[42] BGHSt 46, 321, BGH-Bundesgerichtshof (Federal Court of Justice), 22.03.2001—GSSt 1/00.

[43] Bossert and Korte, *Organisierte Kriminalität und Ausländerextremismus/Terrorismus*, cited in note 28 above, pp. 25, 26.

[44] Peter-Alexis Albrecht, *Kriminologie*, 3rd edn, Munich, C. H. Beck, 2005, p. 346.

[45] Ibid.

[46] Cf. Arndt Sinn, 'The influence of power on the criminal justice system', in Arndt Sinn, *Straffreistellung aufgrund von Drittverhalten*, Tübingen, Mohr Siebeck, 2007, p. 54.

for one 'big job' and go their separate ways afterwards.[47] Prosecution must thus adapt, too. Europol will need smaller-scale operational powers in order to support investigations on the internet. IT will have to be developed. Web-based crawlers and tools can be extremely valuable investigative approaches, collecting publicly available data over the internet. Academia, practice, and the private sector must all work together.

2.3 Conceptions of Transnational Organised Crime

2.3.1 The phenomenology of transnational and international crime

Considered closely enough, all criminal conduct takes place somewhere and is thus bound to a territory and a jurisdiction. Laws governing jurisdiction deal with every case conclusively if they apply the territoriality principle to both the location of the conduct and the location where the offence is committed, as the ubiquity doctrine suggests should be done.[48] So what does 'transnational' mean? Transnationalization can refer to the process through which, over a period of time, groups form stable networks that span individual states but do not directly involve state actors. This development is a sign of the liberation of society from comprehensive state control, as both multinational corporations and civil society organisations begin to form their own relationships parallel to international relations among states.[49] This process has also changed organised crime, and this has adapted to other developments and changes in its environment. Thus the question arises: what conditions or factors drive the development of transnational organised crime?[50]

The first that should be mentioned is the ever-increasing digitalization of society and the creation of virtual identities, globalization in the transportation and logistics sectors,[51] and the most recent developments around nanotechnology and robotics. A second is the increasing number of international crises, whether in the financial sector or involving natural resources, that open up whole new fields of criminality. Alongside these developments, demographic change not only ages society but also contributes to these types of crime. Economic inequality contributes to human trafficking, exploitation, and illegal migration.[52]

The legal framework of the European Union also promotes some types of expanding organised crime. The Schengen Area, for example, has made some things easier for smugglers.[53] It is also uncontroversial that there is a connection between

[47] Europol, *Exploring Tomorrow's Organised Crime*, cited in note 20 above, p. 12.

[48] Cf. Arndt Sinn, 'Jurisdictional law as the key to resolving conflicts: comparative-law observations', in Arndt Sinn (ed.), *Conflicts of Jurisdiction in Cross-border Crime Situations*, Osnabrück, V&R Unipress, 2012, p. 531.

[49] Thomas Jäger, 'Transnationale Organisierte Kriminalität', (2013) *Aus Politik und Zeitgeschichte* (38–9), 16 September 2013, p. 3, available at: http://www.bpb.de/apuz/168912/transnatinale-organisierte-kriminalitaet, accessed 7 September 2015.

[50] Europol, *Exploring Tomorrow's Organised Crime*, cited in note 20 above, p. 9, and section 2.4 of this chapter.

[51] Cf. Cyrille Fijnaut, 'The UN Convention and the global problem of organized crime', in Albrecht and Fijnaut, *The Containment of Transnational Organized Crime*, cited in note 27 above, p. 59.

[52] Europol, *Exploring Tomorrow's Organised Crime*, cited in note 20 above, p. 25.

[53] Cf. Christian Steinbrenner, *Zur Verurteilungspraxis deutscher Gerichte auf dem Gebiet der Schleuserkriminalität*, Wiesbaden, Kriminologische Zentralstelle, 2005, p. 23.

VAT carousel fraud and the structure of the EU, where organised crime profits from differences among the member states over the introduction of a unified revenue system, as well as disagreements about risk sharing, division of costs, and audit systems.

2.3.2 Legal aspects of transnational and international crime

As with the term 'organised crime' at its core, there is no single definition of 'transnational organised crime' at the international level, even if many definitions contain identical criteria.

In its strategic analysis of organised crime, the EU assumes that transnational organised crime is a poly-criminal phenomenon, difficult to detect and increasingly more various in its methods, structures, and effects on society.[54] The US Department of Justice characterizes transnational organised crime as having a set of goals: the acquisition of power, expansion of existing influence, attainment of certain financial and economic goals, and the use of illegal, non-transparent methods such as corruption or violence.[55]

At the UN level, the UN Convention Against Transnational Organized Crime defines the phenomenon as present when:

1. the offence is committed in more than one state;
2. it is committed in one state but a substantial part of its preparation, planning, direction or control takes place in another state;
3. it is committed in one state but involves an organised criminal group that engages in criminal activities in more than one state; or
4. it is committed in one state but has substantial effects in another state.[56]

2.3.3 Significant elements, areas of activity, and manifestations

Given the wide variety of factors that influence it, the complexity of developed societies, and the still greater complexity of the relationships that exist among them, there is no fixed scale of activity for transnational organised crime groups. Their activities are not only interrelated, as can be observed by the relationship between money laundering and human trafficking, they are also connected to political developments, such as weak states, economic conditions, the open or closed nature of markets and sanctions, socio-cultural developments such as the significance of clans, families, or other groups, and ecological conditions.[57]

[54] Cf. Europol, EU *Organized Crime Threat Assessment*, The Hague, Europol Police Office, 2011, p. 6, available at: http://www.europol.europa.eu/content/press/europol-organised-crime-threat-assessment-2011-429, accessed 7 September 2015.

[55] Cf. US Department of Justice, 'Overview of the Law Enforcement Strategy to Combat International Organised Crime', Washington DC, 2008, available at: http://www.justice.gov/criminal/icitap/pr/2008/04-23-08combat-intl-crime-overview.pdf, accessed 7 September 2015.

[56] Cf. United Nations, *Legislative Guides*, cited in note 9 above, p. 15.

[57] Jäger, 'Transnationale Organisierte Kriminalität', cited in note 49 above pp. 3–4.

2.3.4 SOCTA 2013 and the current situation in Europe

The SOCTA Report (for Serious and Organized Crime Threat Assessment) is the product of a systematic analysis by Europol of information relevant to law enforcement regarding criminal activities and groupings within the EU.[58] A decision of the Council of the European Union of 6 April 2009 replaced the Europol Convention as the legal basis for the European Police Office.[59] The Lisbon Treaty anchored Europol in statute through Article 88 Treaty on the Function of the European Union (TFEU). Europol in turn developed the SOCTA Report as a way of supporting decision makers in prioritizing the dangers originating in organised crime. SOCTA is the cornerstone of a multi-year political working group begun in 2010 by the EU. The working group is an example of effective cooperation between national law enforcement authorities, EU organs and agencies, and other key partners in combatting serious and organised crime. SOCTA builds on the OCTA (Organized Crime Threat Assessments)[60] and paints the following picture of the situation in Europe.

2.3.4.1 Definitions and factors relevant to crime

Factors relevant to crime include the financial crisis, corruption, legal corporate structures, the increasing importance of internet and online commerce, and markets with high profit potential and low risk. The SOCTA Report assumes the definition of the Framework Decision of 24 October 2008,[61] referring to a 'criminal organisation' as a structured association, established over a period of time, of more than two persons acting in concert with a view to committing offences that are punishable by deprivation of liberty or a detention order of at least four years (or a more serious penalty), to obtain, directly or indirectly, a financial or other material benefit. In keeping with this definition, SOCTA has set out the following list of elements defining an organised crime group:

1. cooperation among more than two people …
2. established over a period of time …
3. acting in concert with a view to committing offences that are punishable by deprivation of liberty or a detention order of a maximum of at least four years or a more serious penalty …
4. to obtain, directly or indirectly, a financial or other material benefit, and
5. active on the international level and/or in third countries.

[58] The following subsection is essentially a summary of the Europol SOCTA report, SOCTA 2013, cited in note 1 above.

[59] Council Decision of 6 April 2009 establishing the European Police Office (Europol) (2009/371/JHA), available at: http:// www.europol.europa.eu/content/page/legal-texts-125, accessed 29 February 2016.

[60] SOCTA 2013, cited in note 1 above, p. 6.

[61] Calderoni, *EU Organized Crime Legislation*, cited in note 8 above, p. 36.

The SOCTA results are based on data collected by the law enforcement agencies of the member states and on publicly available data, though the latter are thoroughly checked to ensure reliability and validity.

2.3.4.2 Structures of offending

The following forms of offending are worthy of note.

2.3.4.2.1 Illegal drugs

The illegal drugs trade continues to be a major feature of the situation in Europe, though it also extends farther. Notable are the logistical routes to Asia (Afghanistan) and Latin America (Colombia). The EU has been determined to rein in the illegal drug trade for a number of years.[62] Its strategy encompasses improvement of law enforcement cooperation in anti-drug operations (on one hand) and prevention and health-care for potential users (on the other).[63] The overall number of offences recorded in connection with the trade in drugs (heroin, cannabis, cocaine) has fallen slightly, though not if one includes prescription drug crime. The illegal trade in synthetic drugs and new psychoactive substances is on the rise, according to SOCTA, primarily because of low prices and increased availability and quality.

2.3.4.2.2 Trade in counterfeit goods

A further profitable field of criminal activity is the trade in all sorts of counterfeit goods, which results not just in theft of intellectual property but also in serious risks to health: the increased trade in counterfeit pharmaceuticals and medical products is potentially devastating.[64] Counterfeit Euro notes made in digital 'print shops' are also an increasing problem. This sector is characterized by low risks and high profits that make it especially attractive.

2.3.4.2.3 Human trafficking

Human trafficking and irregular migration are a significant problem associated with increasing transnationalization. These phenomena include the trade in humans as property for exploitation as prostitutes or cheap labour, as well as the commercial smuggling of asylum-seekers into Europe.[65] Article 4 of the European Convention on Human Rights and Article 5 of the Charter of Fundamental Rights and Freedoms of the EU forbid slavery and forced labour; both recognize that 'slavery' includes modern forms of human trafficking.[66]

[62] SOCTA 2013, cited in note 1 above.

[63] Cf. Bettina Weißer, 'Angleichung von Strafvorschriften zur grenzüberschreitenden (organisierten) Kriminalität', in Martin Böse (ed.), *Europäisches Strafrecht mit polizeilicher Zusammenarbeit*, 1st edn, Baden-Baden, Nomos, 2013, p. 352, para. 23.

[64] Cf. Projekt ALPhA, available at: http:// www.alpha.uni-osnabrueck.de/.

[65] Cf. Jäger, 'Transnationale Organisierte Kriminalität', cited in note 49 above, p. 4.

[66] Cf. EGMR *NJW* 2007, 41, 45.

2.3.4.2.4 Money laundering

Money laundering is a worldwide phenomenon. The UN Office on Drugs and Crime (UNODC) estimates that laundered money makes up between 2 per cent and 5 per cent of the world GDP, meaning that between €651 billion and €1.54 trillion is laundered each year.[67] Anti-money-laundering activities have been expanded each year, but success is still limited, not least because the law in this area lags behind reality.[68] Germany, for example, has been encouraged by the OECD Money Laundering Task Force to improve its money-laundering statutes, especially to assist in the fight against international terrorism.[69] Here, freezing and forfeiture powers are of central importance.

2.3.4.2.5 Environmental crimes

Transnational organised criminal groups commit environmental crimes primarily in the areas of illegal waste trading and trading in endangered species and their products.

2.3.4.2.6 Cybercrime

Internet crime is generally concentrated around financial fraud. A study by the European Commission indicated that, in the EU, about 8 per cent of internet users have been the victim of identity theft, with another 12 per cent suffering from some form of online fraud. Incidences of bank fraud and bank-card cloning increase from year to year; it is thus not surprising that consumer confidence in online banking and online retail is in continual decline.[70]

2.3.4.3 Offender structures

The report speaks of about 3,600 organised crime groups active in the EU. Over 30 per cent of them are so-called 'poly-criminal groups', i.e. active in more than one area of offending. Often, drug trade is one of the areas, combined with smuggling activities or arms trading. In general, illegal trading and smuggling are closely connected with one another. Europol distinguishes between groups with vertical structures and hierarchical leadership on one hand and those with horizontal structures that act as networks on the other. Between these categories are groups whose organisational form contains aspects of both. But, in general, the network model is in the ascendancy, which is itself a sign of high levels of criminal intent, competence, experience, and canniness in groups that have adapted to the state of the world around them, with all its dynamism, mobility, and ease of communication. The size of the group differs across the types of crime: smaller groups tend towards financial crimes, while larger ones tend to be involved in the drug trade and human trafficking.

[67] SOCTA 2013, cited in note 1 above, p. 27.

[68] Michael Kilchling, '§16 Geldwäsche', in Ulrich Sieber, Helmut Satzger, and Bernd von Heintschel-Heinegg (eds), *Europäisches Strafrecht*, 2nd edn, Baden-Baden, Nomos, 2014, p. 332.

[69] Cf. Christian Ramthun, 'OECD: Deutschland versagt im Kampf gegen Geldwäsche', *Wirtschaftswoche*, 26 April 2014, available at: http://www.wiwo.de/politik/deutschland/geldwaesche-oecd-deutschland-versagt-im-kampf-gegen-geldwäsche/9804692.html, accessed 7 September 2015.

[70] SOCTA 2013, cited in note 1 above, p. 28.

2.3.4.4 *Transnational factors*

As mentioned above, international trade, expanding logistics and transport networks, and the extension of the internet and global communications have had a tremendous influence on the development of international network structures in organised crime. The trend is clearly towards groups with a variety of nationalities, and the result is heterogeneous groups unconnected by nationality and ethnicity. Criminals are no longer limited by geographic boundaries and cannot be clearly identified with a given region or centre of action. Nevertheless, there are ethnic, linguistic, and historical connections that continue to be important factors for building trust and for the composition of core groups that steer much larger and more diverse criminal networks.

2.4 Looking to the Future

2.4.1 Introduction

The most recent Europol report ventures into the future of serious and organised crime.[71] It is more than a mere attempt to divine the future in a crystal ball. Instead, predictions come from facts set out by experts in the public and private sectors as well as in academia and European law enforcement. The projections are an attempt to identify the factors that will shape the development of crime and make prognoses based on the likely development of these factors. This is part of a proactive approach meant to counter the criticism that anti-crime policy is too reactive and fails to leverage current developments to predict future scenarios. One of these developments, for example, is that, more and more, serious corporate crime resembles organised crime. Risk factors included in the study include new technology and changes to the economy and society. The report does not claim to make concrete forecasts, nor to paint a comprehensive picture of the future of crime patterns, but it does try to outline plausible developments in the fields of serious and organised crime and to draw attention to these. Law enforcement authorities must constantly balance the competing demands of freedom and security in their work, and must react as flexibly and dynamically as criminal organisations are able to.

2.4.2 Key factors

The report mentions a number of key factors that are likely to influence the future direction of organised crime.

The newest innovations in the transport and logistics sectors enable organised crime groups to commit offences anonymously around the clock and nearly anywhere, without having to be physically present themselves. Navigation apps and real-time user data allow groups to select the most efficient routes and avoid law enforcement. Violence will decline as the focus shifts to infiltration of control systems with new information technologies. Nanotechnology and robotics will open new markets

[71] Cf. Europol, *Exploring Tomorrow's Organised Crime*, cited in note 20 above, p. 9.

to organised crime as well, giving it new tools with which to operate. Nanotechnology can be used to develop and modify psychoactive substances, as well as to counterfeit equipment or drugs. Robotics plays a role primarily in final assembly and health systems, which use computers that will be vulnerable to cyber-attacks on their control systems and extortion attempts. The increasing reliance on 'big data' and personal data will put criminal groups in a position to take the complex forms of identity theft to an entirely new level, beyond even fraud with contactless payment cards and other payment systems. Personal and biometric data can be extremely useful for enterprises, making the illegal trade in such data a lucrative business itself. The use of virtual currencies will allow individuals to offer money laundering as a service without having to resort to criminal infrastructure. In the traditional criminal realms of the trades in arms and drugs, virtual currency will replace all other forms of payment. The illegal trade in electronic garbage will intensify. Increasing reliance on technology and increasing demand for electronic devices of all kinds will greatly increase the amount of electronic scrap in circulation in the coming decade. Integrated precious metals such as gold, silver, nickel, and palladium make electronic scrap very valuable, and lead to its being traded on the global market alongside drugs, weapons, or endangered species. The struggle over natural resources—oil, gas, water, and food—and the trade in these resources cannot be underestimated as a driving force. Increasing population and increasing per capita consumption of energy, food, and other resources will put pressure on supplies in one way or another in every country in the world. Organised crime will take advantage of this situation. Global companies with monopolistic or oligopolistic market positions will be particularly vulnerable; they are highly likely to be infiltrated by organised crime groups. Economic inequality in Europe is making organised crime socially acceptable: criminal groups infiltrate economically weaker communities and offer jobs and services. Poverty and decreasing standards of living will increase illegal immigration and human trafficking, almost certainly leading to increased exploitation of workers.

Ultimately, as mentioned above, demographic change will bring about new markets and opportunities for the sale of illegal goods and services by organised crime. Right now, humans have much higher life expectancies than decades ago: the world average has gone from 48 years in 1950–55 to 68 years in 2005–10. The UN estimates that it will reach 76 years by 2050. Such radical changes in demography change the economy, politics, and society, and will have effects on the nature of crime as well. As the pool of potential victims swells, fraud upon older people will increase, as will fraud in the pension and social security systems. All the while, the potential consumer base for illegal medications and medical products and related services (nursing care, etc.) will be increasing as well.

2.4.3 Changes to types of offending

The organised crime landscape of Europe will be increasingly dominated by loose, undefined, flexible networks created by individual criminal entrepreneurs. These criminals are often engaged on a freelance basis without being a member of a larger network or group. The developments in individual categories of crime are very different, but

Europol monitors and reports on them (e.g. through SOCTA). There are three types of criminal market at the moment:

1. dynamic or growing criminal markets;
2. stable criminal markets; and
3. shrinking criminal markets.

2.4.3.1 Dynamic markets

Growing, dynamic markets need not necessarily be the largest ones. The use of new technologies and the development of new substances requires new methods on the part of law enforcement authorities, especially regarding the development of synthetic drugs and new psychoactive substances. As specific substances are banned, criminal organisations resort to new ones, resulting in a perpetual cycle between law enforcement and criminal organisations. Novel psychoactive substances (NPS), especially, exist in a legal grey area, their position complicated further by widespread societal acceptance and the low hurdles to obtaining them—they are generally available via anonymous transactions in online shops. Also prominent are the role played by 3D printers in the manufacture, supply, and transport of counterfeit goods, as well as the ever-increasing demand for pharmaceuticals.

2.4.3.2 Stable markets

The 'classic' stable markets such as the cannabis trade, organised property crimes, and illegal migration and human trafficking will continue to coexist with the new, dynamic markets. These threats continue and comprise the largest share of serious and organised crime in the EU, as they will in the future.

2.4.3.3 Shrinking criminal markets?

At the same time, the question arises whether certain areas of offending will recede into the background because of developments of technology. One could presume, for instance, that counterfeiting banknotes would be an obsolete criminal undertaking in the era of digital currencies. Yet cash is a stable and anonymous payment method that remains irreplaceable in areas affected by crises, after natural disasters, or in situations where infrastructure does not support digital transactions. Criminals will continue to counterfeit banknotes, and the 'darknet' will serve as an exchange platform for raw materials.

New psychoactive substances that mimic the effects of heroin and cocaine will reduce the market share of the conventional drugs on the European market. But the cocaine trade is extremely profitable for the criminal groups involved, and will remain so in the future. Genetic modification will increase the yield of plants, and the expansion of the Panama Canal means another transport channel for drugs from Central and South America.

2.5 Conclusion

For the international community, there is no such thing as the phenomenon of organised crime—there are criminal organisations, criminal groups, criminal associations, and even gangs, just to name a few examples. The terms only cover the same semantic territory in rare cases. Looking towards the future shows that the definitions currently in use, whether by Europol or the UN, do not adequately account for the phenomena and developments in this area. They are in need of reform. The conception of a new definition requires a national, European, and international perspective.[72] Law enforcement agencies are still too focused on traditional forms of organised crime like mafia organisations, drug cartels, and motorcycle gangs. They should turn their attention towards new forms of offending like cybercrime, financial crimes, and mass fraud and property crimes, because wherever there is a profit to be made, organised crime will try to gain a foothold. The image of the mafia godfather is enduring, but it is only one of many manifestations of organised crime. It must not be forgotten that history, regional differences, and culture lead to organised crime with many different faces, and that understanding one of them does not lead to an understanding of the many others.

It is impossible to guarantee future success, of course. We can, however, point to factors that will increase the success of law enforcement and prosecutors going forward, both in terms of international cooperation among law enforcement authorities as well as cooperation between law enforcement, the private sector, and academia. Information exchange and analysis, mutual trust, and common understanding of law enforcement standards will strengthen the successes of law enforcement.

[72] Cf. Europol, *Exploring Tomorrow's Organised Crime*, cited in note 20 above, p. 60.

3

Transnational Organised Crime and its Impacts on States and Societies

Thomas Feltes and Robin Hofmann

3.1 Introduction

The impacts of transnational organised crime (TOC) on societies are complex and not easy to describe. There is no simple explanation or concept that grasps all the impacts TOC imposes on, and their consequences for, societies, states, and the rule of law. This chapter, therefore, will only try to provide an approximation to the different problems and challenges with which societies are confronted by the emergence of TOC. The fact that TOC is, by definition,[1] a cross-border phenomenon strongly related to the 'darker side'[2] of globalization makes it even more difficult to give a brief, problem-based account. There is no single or single set of impacts that TOC has on societies around the globe. Indeed, the impacts may be similar in different countries but, nevertheless, the consequences for societies differ from country to country and even from region to region. For example, the current war against drugs in Mexico imposes consequences on the Mexican state and on civil society that are devastating and quite different from those of the war on drugs in the USA or The Netherlands. Organised environmental crimes in the south Italian region of Calabria are perceived and dealt with by the Italian state and society in a different manner than in Bangladesh or India.

Another difficulty criminological research is facing when dealing with 'organised crime' is the question of definition, which has not been simplified by adding the term 'transnational' to it. Quite a few criminologists have worked on a definition, but the concept of organised crime remains one of the most contested terms in criminological research.[3] This is due to the fact that the organisational and structural variations of the phenomenon are vast. The problem with the debate about definitions is that it threatens to kill off the substantial debate about the phenomenon itself.[4] This chapter, therefore, will not join this debate. The same counts for the question concerning the difference between organised and transnational organised crime. Organised crime

[1] See—for the matter of definition—Ch. 2, sections 2.1.1, 2.3.2 and Ch. 21 of this book.

[2] Susanne Karstedt, 'Organised crime, democracy, and democratization: how vulnerable are democracies?', in Caroline Robertson-von Trotha (ed.), *Organised Crime: Dark Sides of Globalisation*, Interdisciplinary Studies on Culture and Society 8, Baden-Baden, Nomos, 2013, pp. 95–112.

[3] For a good overview see James Sheptycki *et al.*, 'International organised crime in the European Union', in *Directorate General for Internal Policies. Policy Department C: Citizens' Rights and Constitutional Affairs*. Civil Liberties, Justice and Home Affairs, 2011, pp. 11–12.

[4] James Sheptycki, 'The governance of organised crime in Canada', (2003) 28 *Canadian Journal of Sociology* (4), 489–90.

increasingly operates on a transnational level; even more so as the distinguishing of virtual and geographical borders becomes more and more obsolete, and likewise the distinction between TOC and organised crime.[5] However, a key aspect of the research into TOC is to identify this tipping point at which (domestic) organised crime becomes transnational and to which extent this is the case.[6]

TOC is a complex social phenomenon in an even more complex globalized world and it is constantly adapting itself to challenges imposed by modern conditions. Nevertheless, the world of TOC and the world of civil society are two sides of the same coin. Criminal organisations only exist where a society demands their goods and services, and where an accessible marketplace is provided in which goods and services are offered.[7] In the following pages, an attempt will be made to shed some light on selected aspects of TOC by focussing on areas deemed crucial for getting a grasp on how TOC impacts on societies.

Why are impact assessments important and of what practical use can they be? Understanding the harm done by TOC and developing analytical models tracing those harms back to their roots can be of assistance for policy makers implementing law enforcement policies, allocating financial resources, and evaluating those measures that were taken.[8] In particular, the measurement of the costs of organised crime can play a crucial role when evaluating the impact on crime of the money spent as well as the effectiveness of crime reduction policies. It can help to prioritize and to focus scarce resources on policies that have the potential to actually reduce the harm caused by crime, rather than simply reducing the number of crimes.[9]

3.2 Assessment of Difficulties

Criminological research on organised crime has been quite extensive in recent years.[10] Nevertheless, it seems that this research mainly focused on criminal organisations themselves, the way they are organised, and how they operate. Much less research has been conducted on how societies are affected by TOC, what consequences states and societies face when infiltrated by TOC, and how they perceive and cope with those impacts.[11] A reason for the under-representation of impact research on TOC

[5] Michael P. Roth, 'Historical overview over transnational crime', in Philip Reichel and Jay Albanese (eds), *The Handbook of Transnational Crime and Justice*, 2nd edn, London, SAGE Publications, 2014, p. 7.

[6] Rosemary Barberet, 'Measuring and researching transnational crime', in Reichel and Albanese, *Transnational Crime and Justice*, ibid, p. 50. For a critical view of the concept of TOC see Paolo Campana, 'Governing vs. trading: the functional diversification of Mafia activities across territories', in Ursula Töttel, Gergana Bulanova-Hristova, and Heinz Büchler (eds), *Research Conference on Organised Crime at the Bundeskriminalamt in Germany (Vol. II): Organised Crime—Research and Practice in Western and Northern Europe (2011–12)*, Polizei + Forschung 45, Wiesbaden, Luchterhand Verlag, 2013, p. 51.

[7] Roberto Scarpinato, 'Organised crime in the third millenium', in Robertson-von Trotha, *Organised Crime*, cited in note 2 above, p. 81.

[8] Ernesto U. Savona and Barbara Vettori, 'Evaluating the cost of organised crime from a comparative perspective', (2009) 15 *European Journal on Criminal Policy and Research* (4), 379–93, p. 380.

[9] Sam Brand and Richard Price, *The Economic and Social Costs of Crime*, London, Home Office Research Study 217, 2000, p. 5.

[10] Klaus von Lampe, 'Transnational organized crime challenges for future research', (2009) 58 *Crime, Law and Social Change* (2), 179–94, p. 180.

[11] Barberet, 'Measuring and researching transnational crime', cited in note 6 above, p. 47.

in criminology is certainly due to the methodological difficulties of measuring impacts of crime on societies. However, these problems of criminological harm-research are not particularly related to TOC, but rather occur whenever the harm caused by crime is measured using either official data, victimization data, or self-report data. But the methodological difficulties of measurement are particularly grave when organised forms of crime are in focus. The problems evolve around the question which indicators are best suited to give a precise estimation of the harm caused. A feasible way would be to estimate the financial costs either in absolute numbers, in proportion to income, wealth, or national GDP.[12] In fact, the research into the economic costs of crime has been quite rewarding over the past years.[13] But how does one measure the non-financial or indirect costs, such as the costs of policing and prosecution, environmental degradation, the trauma and suffering of victims, their medical treatment and insurance costs, and the loss of confidence and trust in state institutions either among their own citizens or among other states or business partners? And how does one take into account possible positive monetary side effects of TOC? To an extent some mafia organisations fulfil social functions in their regions of operation, by keeping people employed, running social facilities, and reinvesting profits from illicit commodities in the formal and informal economies.[14] All these impacts of TOC are highly relevant when assessing the impacts on societies but can never be truly captured by applying monetary values.[15]

The same difficulties of measurement apply for victimization surveys, a powerful criminological tool for measuring the dark figure as well as the impact of crime. Ordinary households are seldom directly victimized by organised crime and victimization surveys and, therefore, can hardly be used as a vehicle to measure organised crime.[16] Even when individuals are directly victimized, they may not be aware that organised crime played a role, or might not even become aware that they have been victimized at all. The latter is a phenomenon that often occurs with various forms of cybercrime. Moreover, traditional forms of crime like burglary are almost impossible to classify as domestic or transnational (e.g. when conducted by a transnational burglar ring) by the victims themselves. Despite this missing awareness, a wide range of crimes typically related to organised crime is sometimes called 'victimless', since no individuals are directly affected by the criminal conduct but rather a collective entity, such as companies or states, or simply no one at all. Finally, conventional victim surveys hardly detect typical TOC offences that occur relatively rarely among the civil

[12] Michael Levi, 'States, frauds, and the threat of transnational organized crime', (2012) 66 *Journal of International Affairs* (1), 46.

[13] Claudio Detotto and Edoardo Otranto, 'Does crime affect economic growth?', (2010) 63 *Kyklos* (3), 330–45, p. 330; Brand and Price, *Economic and Social Costs*, cited in note 9 above, p. 5. For a historical overview see Jacek Czabanski, *Estimates of Cost of Crime: History, Methodologies, and Implications*, Berlin, Springer, 2008.

[14] Mark James, 'The other civil society: organised crime in fragile and failing states', (2012) 12 *Defence Studies* (2), 218–56, pp. 218ff.; Jan van Dijk, 'Mafia markers: assessing organized crime and its impact upon societies', (2007) 10 *Trends in Organized Crime*, 39–56, p. 50.

[15] Peter Johnston, Stephen Schneider, *et al. Organized Crime Harm Index: A Scoping and Feasibility Study*, Department of Public Safety Canada, 2010, p. 30.

[16] van Dijk, 'Mafia markers', cited in note 14 above, p. 40.

population, such as human trafficking for sexual exploitation, and are, therefore, only limited in their usefulness in our area. It lies within the very nature of sexual exploitation that the victims are systematically isolated from civil society, so the likelihood of their taking part in a victim survey is very low.[17]

Researching TOC is complicated by the fact that the research is typically conducted on a cross-border level because of the very nature of its study subject. As already mentioned, reliable data on TOC are rare, as the methodological difficulties are hard to overcome. But even where data collections exist, a comparison between different countries is challenging. Different legal systems, cultural differences in the definition of offences, and different crime-data collection systems make the results rarely comparable.[18] This is the case not just across continents or among distant countries but even between EU member states, since a large number of asymmetries exist in standards for measuring organised crime.[19] In addition, TOC is highly flexible and able to adopt to new developments. Hence, state authorities are constantly confronted with new, or variations of old, offences that make reliable recording problematic.[20]

This complexity of TOC has the effect that official statistics of police-recorded or court-recorded crimes may be a source of disinformation rather than illuminating the actual extent of the crimes. Official data provided by states measuring the performance of law enforcement agencies, such as numbers of arrests or convictions for involvement in organised crime, are likely to merely reflect police performance rather than the true extent of criminal activity.[21] Van Dijk assumes

> that in countries where organized crime is most prevalent, investigations into such crimes will be hampered by police corruption and political interference in prosecution and sentencing. Fewer investigations or prosecutions of organized crime will be initiated or successfully completed. Low rates of court cases on corruption or organized crime in a country may point to high rather than low prevalence of such types of crime.[22]

Then again, high numbers of arrests and convictions are likely to indicate a strong police performance, which may lead to a decline in crime rates in the long run rather than indicating a high rate of TOC activities. Unfortunately police-based information tends to be misleading and should therefore be interpreted with caution.

When assessing the impacts of TOC on societies, one has to keep in mind all these inconsistencies and difficulties of measurement and statistics. The results of any research into the impact of organised crime are unlikely to be exact or even remotely accurate but rather have to be treated as broad estimates and more or less reliable

[17] Barberet, 'Measuring and researching transnational crime', cited in note 6 above, pp. 51–2.

[18] Savona and Vettori, 'Evaluating the cost of organised crime', cited in note 8 above, p. 380.

[19] Barbara Vettori, 'Comparing data sources on organised crime across the EU: a first step towards an EU statistical apparatus', in Petrus van Duyne, Almir Maljevic, Marten van Dijk, Klaus von Lampe, and James Newell (eds), *The Organisation of Crime for Profit: Conduct, Law and Measurement*, Nijmwegen, Wolf Legal Publishers, 2006, pp. 43–67, p. 61. For a good overview of the difficulties deriving from the official German BKA statistics on organised crime see Klaus von Lampe, 'Making the second step before the first: assessing organized crime', (2005) 42 *Crime, Law and Social Change* (4–5), 227–59.

[20] Barberet, 'Measuring and researching transnational crime', cited in note 6 above, p. 50.

[21] van Dijk, 'Mafia markers', cited in note 14 above, p. 40.

[22] Ibid, p. 40.

approaches.[23] This is particularly important as crime control strategies are powerful political instruments. As an integral part of the internal security strategies of states crime policies are strongly receptive to subjective needs for security of citizens and may develop a tendency to exploit these needs for political reasons. This counts especially for TOC with its alleged proximity to international terrorism, a phenomenon that has knowingly triggered far-reaching measures and political consequences in all fields of law enforcement in most countries of this world.[24]

3.3 Conditions for the Flourishing of TOC

The conditions for the flourishing of TOC are manifold and cannot be reduced to a single (or a set of the most important) factor(s) promoting the growth of TOC structures. An easy explanation offered would be that the best conditions for the flourishing of TOC are provided by weak state institutions, resulting in a power vacuum where law enforcement is weak or does not exist at all.[25] This view, although intriguing and statistically corroborated, is too simplistic and poses more questions than it is able to answer.[26] There are examples of strong states with functioning institutions being infiltrated by TOC. A number of scholars argue that globalization played a major role in the growth of TOC networks in recent years.[27] Increasing migration, mobility, and transportation, the revolution in information and communication technology, but also social and ethnic distance and major political and economic changes have to be put in that framework. The reduction and disappearance of barriers and frontiers have created new opportunities for the expansion and diversification of organised crime.[28]

Nevertheless, as a precondition for the flourishing of TOC globalization should not be overrated and it should not be indiscriminately applied to all forms of TOC. In some cases it seems that, depending on the local setting and historic conditions, TOC often has strong local and social roots. An example would include the mafia (or mafia-like) organisations in south-eastern Europe and the Middle East, including Albania, former Yugoslavia (especially Kosovo)[29], Turkey, and Lebanon where strong

[23] Johnston,Schneider, *et al.*, *Organized Crime Harm Index* , cited in note 15 above, p. 5.

[24] Louise Shelley *et al.*, 'Methods and motives: exploring links between transnational organized crime and international terrorism', (2005) 9 *Trends in Organized Crime*, 52–67, pp. 4ff.; Augustus Martin, 'Terrorism and transnational organized crime', in Reichel and Albanese, *Transnational Crime and Justice*, cited in note 5 above, pp. 243–61, pp. 243ff.; Tamara Makarenko, 'Foundations and evolution of the crime–terror nexus', in Felia Allum and Stan Gilmour (eds), *Routledge Handbook of Transnational Organized Crime*, Abingdon, Routledge, 2012, pp. 234–49.

[25] Stergios Skaperdas, 'The political economy of organized crime: providing protection when the state does not', (2001) *Economics of Governance*, 180.

[26] Jan van Dijk and Toine Spapens, 'Transnational organized crime networks', in Reichel and Albanese, *Transnational Crime and Justice*, cited in note 5 above, pp. 213–26, p. 217.

[27] Ibid, p. 223; Skaperdas, 'The political economy of organized crime', cited in note 25 above, p. 184; Kelly Hignett, 'Transnational organized crime and the global village', in Allum and Gilmour, *Routledge Handbook of Transnational Organized Crime*, cited in note 24 above, pp. 281–93.

[28] Don Loree, 'Organized crime: changing concepts and realities for the police', (2012) *Trends in Organized Crime*, 75.

[29] Thomas Feltes, 'Peacebuilding and police reform in the New Europe: lessons from Kosovo', in Martin H. W. Möllers and Robert van Ooyen (eds), *Jahrbuch öffentliche Sicherheit 2008/09*, Frankfurt, Verlag für Polizeiwissenschaft, 2008, pp. 439–66.

social support structures are constituted by family units that provide status, protection, and communication and where membership is predominantly defined by blood ties and marriage.[30]

The argument that unstable social economic conditions are significantly related to the growth of TOC networks is also too simplistic. TOC is not confined to a particular social milieu or deeply rooted in the 'underclass', but in a number of instances linked to political elites and business leaders in what von Lampe (in his typology of organised crime) calls a 'mafia-like alliance of upper world and under world'.[31]

Identifying and analysing the conditions for the flourishing of TOC is important for various reasons. The biggest threat from TOC is not that it simply exists, but rather that it keeps on spreading around the globe. To expand, it is dependent on 'safe havens' in which the conditions for prospering are ideal and controls weak.[32] Identifying the safe havens might be the key to preventing criminal conglomerates from expanding and becoming destabilizing factors for states and a threat to global security.

3.3.1 Legal conditions

The legal conditions that promote TOC structures are hard to identify. The simple equation stating that the tougher the legislation criminalizing particular conduct, the better will be the deterrence and prevention of the conduct in question, seldom adds up. Among criminologists, it is common sense that tougher laws are not useful instruments to prevent and deter illegal conduct. On the contrary, the end of drug prohibition policies is discussed as it is believed likely to drive criminal organisations out of the drug market.[33] For this legalization to work, it would require universal laws and world-wide cooperation, which seems to be unrealistic at the moment owing simply to the unwillingness of legislators as well as widely unknown possible side effects such as the estimated increase in demand and the aggravation of drug abuse.[34]

However, it is only half the truth that legalization is the weapon of choice, as coercive strategies have proved inefficient against TOC in the past. A good example of the likelihood that legalization might have no positive effect or, on the contrary, might even trigger off an increase in criminal conduct is human trafficking for sexual exploitation, an area in which TOC groups are typically active. A number of countries like The Netherlands, Australia, and Germany have liberalized their anti-prostitution laws and declared prostitution legal so as, among other reasons, to prevent human trafficking for sexual exploitation, a booming market since the early 1990s.[35] In Germany, since

[30] Klaus von Lampe, 'Organized crime in Europe: conceptions and realities', (2008) 2 *Policing* (1), 7–17, p. 12.

[31] Ibid, p. 15.

[32] van Dijk and Spapens, 'Transnational organized crime networks', cited in note 26 above, p. 222.

[33] Matthew S. Jenner, 'International drug trafficking: a global problem with a domestic solution', (2011) 18 *Indiana Journal of Global Legal Studies* (2), 901–27; Brian Ford, 'From mountains to molehills: a comparative analysis of drug policy', (2013) 19 *Annual Survey of International & Comparative Law*, 197–231.

[34] Matthew S. Jenner, 'Drug trafficking as a transnational crime', in Reichel and Albanese, *Transnational Crime and Justice*, cited in note 5 above, pp. 65–84, pp. 81–2.

[35] Cornelius Friesendorf, 'Pathologies of security governance: efforts against human trafficking in Europe', (2007) 39 *Security Dialogue* (3), 379–402, p. 379.

the new prostitution law came into effect in 2002, prostitutes can take out health insurance and make retirement provision, and can officially register their businesses. The political goals of these legal measures were to stop discrimination against prostitutes, to strengthen their legal position, and to fight crimes typically related to prostitution, such as sexual exploitation or human trafficking, classic fields of organised criminal activity.[36] Soon it became clear that the new prostitution law was causing a fairly small (or even no) reduction in human trafficking for sexual exploitation.[37] For example, after the introduction of a law in Germany to legalize prostitution in 2002 only a very small number of prostitutes registered themselves, not least because they wished to avoid relatively high social security contributions and taxes. Among foreign prostitutes, who still form the majority of workers in the sex industry, the willingness and ability to register was even lower owing to the fact that in many cases the prostitutes do not possess residency and working permits. As far as legalization of prostitution might lead to better working conditions for prostitutes, legal prostitutes might stay longer in the business, which might have the effect of increasing the demand for younger women and girls, a safe source of income for traffickers.[38] Scholars therefore fear that legalizing prostitution might not break the link between organised crime and the sex industry but strengthen it, encourage the growth of the industry, and increase trafficking.[39]

In Sweden, therefore, a different legal approach was adopted to combat human trafficking: while the selling of sexual services was legalized, the purchase of such services was criminalized, punishing clients with the aim of reducing demand and creating an anti-prostitution climate. A similar legislative approach is being discussed in France.

Those examples illustrate the complexity of a legalistic approach to preventing or fighting TOC. It lies within the very nature of TOC to move activities very flexibly and rapidly from one state to another as soon as new legislation is passed against it. That is why loopholes in state legislation are apt to provide safe havens for TOC and only strong cooperation and harmonizing measures provide an effective instrument in the fight.

As regards legal harmonization strategies that are popular in the EU, one should keep in mind that particular legislation developed in a unique legal system is not simply applicable in other states.[40] For example, the Italian anti-mafia legislation has been proven highly effective in recent years. A resultant negative knock-on effect is that Italian mafia organisations seek new, safe havens where legislation and law enforcement is less effective.[41] But to conclude that the implementation of Italian-style

[36] Barbara Kavemann, 'Die praktischen Auswirkungen des deutschen Prostitutionsgesetz', in Thorsten Benkel (ed.), *Das Frankfurter Bahnhofsviertel: Devianz im öffentlichen Raum*, Wiesbaden: V. S. Verlag für Sozialwissenschaften/GWV Fachverlage, 2010, pp. 211–28, p. 214.

[37] Günther Maihold, 'Der Mensch als Ware. Konzepte und Handlungsansätze zur Bekämpfung des globalen Menschenhandels', Stiftung Wissenschaft und Politik Research Paper S24, Berlin, 2011, p. 17.

[38] Friesendorf, 'Pathologies of security governance', cited in note 35 above, pp. 396–7.

[39] Ibid, p. 397 with further references.

[40] For a good overview of the European External Security Strategy against TOC see Daniela Irrera, 'The EU strategy in tackling organized crime in the framework of multilateralism', (2011) 12 *Perspectives on European Politics and Society* (4), 407–19.

[41] Felia Allum, 'Italian organised crime in the UK', (2012) 6 *Policing* (4), 354–9, p. 358.

anti-mafia legislation in other countries might be the best way of dealing with the expansion of the mafia to other territories could be a mistake. Legal systems, even inside the European Union, are too different to allow the simple copying of legal strategies rather than taking a jurisdiction-specific and more pragmatic approach.[42] A good example of such a pragmatic approach to harmonizing different legislation is the European Arrest Warrant (EAW), which has simplified extradition procedures in the EU significantly. On the downside, the criticism has been offered that the EAW and its pragmatic and informal approach have had a negative effect on the rights of people who are extradited.[43] In sum, differences in legislation and policies across states might prove beneficial for highly mobile TOC actors and result in uneven progress in the fight against TOC groups, since they might simply move their operations to a less risky jurisdiction.[44]

3.3.2 Institutional conditions

A simple model of stable states suggests three elements as a precondition for stability: governance/the rule of law, economic/infrastructure development, and security.[45] All three elements are interdependent and all three are vulnerable to influence in one way or another by TOC. When determining the extent of TOC activities in states, the quality of the institutions responsible for the rule of law, such as competent police services and independent courts complying with the standards of professional integrity, is a crucial factor. The effectiveness of the criminal justice system relates negatively to the performance of organised crime groups at the country level. According to van Dijk's study on mafia markers, high levels of organised crime rarely go together with effective policing and strong maintenance of the rule of law.[46] Interestingly, the collected data suggest that this effect is lower for the fight against conventional crime than it is for organised crime. Van Dijk concludes that the impact of police services and independent professional judiciaries on fighting conventional crimes may have been somewhat overrated while the importance of the criminal justice system fighting complex crimes such as TOC seems to be underrated.[47]

Among the most important prerogatives of states and their institutions are the provision of protection, legal services, and services to facilitate exchange and contracts. But when state institutions are weak, illicit organisations may act as illegal suppliers of governance and protection and become credible alternatives to state institutions, as is

[42] Paolo Campana, 'Understanding then responding to Italian organized crime operations across territories', (2013) 7 *Policing* (3), 316–25, p. 324.

[43] Michael Böhm, 'Das neue europäische Haftbefehlsgesetz', (2006) 36 *Neue Juristische Wochenschrift*, 2592–6; Stefan Braum, 'Europäisches Strafrecht im Fokus konfligierender Verfassungsmodelle. Stoppt das Bundesverfassungsgericht die europäische Strafrechtsentwicklung?', (2009) 4 *Zeitschrift für Internationale Strafrechtsdogmatik* (8–9), 418–26, available at: http://www.zis-online.com/dat/artikel/2009_8-9_348.pdf, accessed 29 January 2016.

[44] Joseph Wheatley, 'Transnational organized crime: a survey of laws, policies and international conventions', in Allum and Gilmour, *Routledge Handbook of Transnational Organized Crime*, cited in note 24 above, pp. 65–79, p. 77.

[45] James, 'The other civil society', cited in note 14 above, p. 227.

[46] van Dijk, 'Mafia markers', cited in note 14 above, p. 47.

[47] Ibid, p. 47.

the case with some mafia organisations in Italy or in a number of post-conflict countries.[48] Weak states are defined by weak institutions and organised crime actors may prey on that. As self-evident as this may seem, the same is not true for economically weak states as there is no significant relation between poverty and the quality of the rule of law, as will be explained in chapter 4 of this book.

A complicating factor for the simple scheme that seeks to link TOC to the weak state institutions that are particularly found in developing countries is the fact that, particularly in fragile and failed states, state institutions are not the only source of authority. In a number of poor and developing countries, the boundaries between state and society are widely unclear.[49] Very often stability is more of a constant bargaining process of distribution and limitation of power between government and its institutions, competing elites, and civil society.[50] In these constellations, TOC may act more or less independently of weak or strong state institutions, serving only its own political agendas and functions. The latter do not necessarily have a negative impact on societies, but rather develop a number of positive and stabilizing potentials.[51]

There is not much doubt that one of the most important institutional conditions for the flourishing of organised crime is the receptiveness of state institutions to corruption. This receptiveness occurs in various forms, such as direct bribery of law enforcement agencies and state institutions, of political institutions by paying off politicians, or through the funding of political parties. Corruption functions by opening doors for organised crime actors into state institutions. Van Dijk, therefore, refers to organised crime and corruption as two sides of the same coin.[52] Most directly affected by corruption are law enforcement institutions, particularly the police, that seem to have a high level of vulnerability to corruptive practices. The reasons for this are various and range from the systematic recruitment of relatively poorly educated officers (arising from low prestige attached to joining the police force), to a predominant lack of meritocracy in the police force (preventing exposure of unprofessional or even illicit behaviour).[53]

In and of itself, corruption does not generate negative effects, and may even contribute to stability, especially in fragile states.[54] But the example of Mexico shows how illusory this stability may be in the long run. Here, corruption in the past contributed to a

[48] Campana, 'Understanding then responding to Italian organized crime', cited in note 42 above, p. 322. Also see Center for the Study of Democracy, *Examining the Links Between Organised Crime and Corruption*, Irvine, California, 2010, p. 150.

[49] James, 'The other civil society', cited in note 14 above, p. 228.

[50] Tilman Feltes, 'Jugend und Demokratie. Die Förderung der Partizipation Jugendlicher durch die internationale Gemeinschaft im Kosovo', (2013) 1 *Südosteuropäische Hefte* (2), 45–57, available at: http://suedosteuropaeischehefte.files.wordpress.com/2012/12/sh_1_2_feltes.pdf.

[51] See James, 'The other civil society', cited in note 14 above; William Reno, 'Understanding criminality in West African conflicts', in James Cockayne and Ada Lupel (eds), *Peace Operations and Organised Crime: Enemies or Allies?*, London, Routledge, 2011; van Dijk, 'Mafia markers', cited in note 14 above, pp. 50ff.

[52] van Dijk, 'Mafia markers', cited in note 14 above, p. 49; also see Stephen D. Morris, 'Corruption, drug trafficking, and violence in Mexico', (2012) *Brown Journal of World Affairs* (11), 29–43, p. 30.

[53] For the European Police see CSD, *Examining the Links*, cited in note 47 above, p. 150.

[54] Philippe Le Billon, 'Buying peace or fuelling war: the role of corruption in armed conflicts', (2003) 15 *Journal of International Development* (4), 413–26.

low level of violence and relative stability, but began to fuel an unprecedented amount of violence in recent years. This paradox can be explained by a number of changes that together have altered the patterns and impact of corruption as it relates to drug trafficking and organised crime. In the past, corruption provided the cartels with a relatively secure state-sponsored protection and linked the state and narco-trafficking discreetly together, to the degree that centralized political authorities essentially managed the drug business.[55] But since 2006 and the launch of president Calderón's war on drugs the level of corruption skyrocketed owing to the weakening of the large cartels and the growing number of rival and splinter organisations that increasingly infiltrated the state via corruption to maintain the operation of their drug-related businesses.[56] Today an essential part of the war on drugs in Mexico is against the state's own officials. In the long run, corruption is likely to become a Trojan horse within the walls of governments.[57]

Nevertheless, one should not overestimate the corruptive practices of organised crime actors as means to gain power in governments and infiltrate societies. In most cases money is only invested when it seems beneficial for the conducted crime trades. Long-term investment strategies for building power sustainably in different branches of the government and the economy are not very common.[58]

3.3.3 Socio-economic conditions

To assume that the weakness of state institutions correlates with the economic performance of the state is too simplistic. The strong relationships that exist between the measures of governance and economic growth or performance do not necessarily imply that a strong economy is followed by a high quality of institutions. In fact, it seems more plausible that good governance with highly independent law enforcement agencies does not require expenditures only affordable by rich countries with vast resources, but is rather dependent on sound legislation and political will.[59] On theoretical grounds, the relationship between favourable socio-economic conditions for TOC is a more indirect one, following the logic that weak institutions lead to less wealth and poorer societies that provide good breeding grounds for TOC activities. Those activities may reach an extent where they re-impact the legal economy and state institutions resulting in a vicious circle the dynamics of which are further explained below in section 3.5.1 of this chapter, 'Economic impacts'.

However, poverty often goes hand-in-hand with political instability and both constitute an important force driving the flourishing of TOC. In fragile states, such as some parts of northern Africa, power and investment vacuums in the public and private sector are likely to be filled by TOC, particularly through providing essential

[55] Morris, 'Corruption, drug trafficking, and violence in Mexico', cited in note 52 above, pp. 34–6 with further references.

[56] Ibid, p. 38.

[57] van Dijk, 'Mafia markers', cited in note 14 above, p. 54.

[58] Petrus van Duyne, 'Organized crime, corruption and power', (1997) *Crime, Law & Social Change* (26), 201–38, pp. 218ff.

[59] van Dijk, 'Mafia markers', cited in note 14 above, p. 48.

goods and services such as transport infrastructure, food, and fuel.[60] Thanks to the global economic crisis, however, not only African states are suffering from a high rate of unemployment, especially among young people. In nearly all parts of the world, poverty and unemployment provide a nearly unlimited recruiting pool of foot soldiers for illicit organisations.[61] The absence of opportunities and participation in the labour market has a strong effect on human trafficking of labourers and on sexual exploitation, as unemployment is a significant push-factor. Victimization of both kinds becomes more likely for (young) people living in insecure economic circumstances.[62]

We have already mentioned how TOC may generate benefits and positive impacts for society by employing people or reinvesting money derived from their illicit activities. However, the real problem with the profits of TOC is that they are mainly funnelled to transnational crime syndicates where they are used to maintain or establish new trade networks, while the labour force at the base of such syndicates only receives a minor part of the profits made from the trade. The coca farmer from Peru, the organ donor from Pakistan, or the prostitute from Bulgaria only receive a tiny fraction of the retail earnings of their contribution.[63]

Among scholars of TOC there is broad consensus that the economic liberalization that goes hand-in-hand with globalization has been a factor facilitating the evolution and expansion of criminal organisations.[64] As a consequence, the absence of effective regulatory oversight and the establishment of offshore financial centres made money laundering easier.[65] The increasing desire for mobility paralleled by the hardening of border protection and tightening of immigration laws created a new variety of opportunities for human traffickers. More generally expressed: the global economy has created socio-economic inequalities around the world as well as an extensive mobility of goods and people that, in turn, has created circumstances described as 'criminogenic asymmetries', offering a variety of opportunities to criminal organisations while complicating regulation by states.[66]

3.4 TOC and its Impact on Societies

When analysing the impacts of TOC on society, it would be one-dimensional to focus solely on the negative and devastating consequences associated with organised crime. Contrary to popular belief, to a certain extent TOC may actually contribute to regional development, particularly in some regions of the southern part of the globe.

[60] Europol, *EU Organised Crime Threat Assessment, OCTA 2011*, The Hague, Europol Police Office, 2011, p. 49.

[61] Antonio Maria Costa, 'The economics of crime: a discipline to be invented and a Nobel Prize to be awarded', (2010) *Journal of Policy Modeling*, 660.

[62] Maihold, 'Der Mensch als Ware', cited in note 37 above, p. 9.

[63] Jeremy Haken, *Transnational Crime in the Developing World*, Washington DC, Center for International Policy, 2011.

[64] See Tim Hall, 'Economic geography and organized crime: a critical review', (2010) *Geoforum* (41), 841–5, p. 842.

[65] Tim Hall, 'Geographies of the illicit: globalization and organized crime', (2013) 37 *Progress in Human Geography* (3), 366–85, p. 371.

[66] Hall, 'Economic geography and organized crime', cited in note 64 above, p. 842.

These positive effects should be recognized but not overestimated. It is argued that through violent and corruptive practices, particularly through the diversion of resources from the legitimate economy and the tendency to destabilize state institutions, the net developmental impacts of TOC are inevitably negative.[67] However, the terms 'negative' or 'positive' impact may oversimplify the complexity of the effects of TOC. The benefits in one community may result in a downside for a community somewhere else, though probably not in the short term but rather in the long run.[68] TOC can best be understood by its mutual interdependencies and strong ties with civil societies. As much as TOC's impacts and threats have shaped civil societies, these societies in turn leave their mark on the underworld and shape it by their own transformative processes from a once merely domestic phenomenon to a plural and highly internationalized terrain.[69]

3.4.1 Direct vs indirect impacts

Criminological research in recent years has increasingly focused on the indirect impacts of crime, particularly by assessing its economic costs. This perspective allows for the analysis of data that were not directly connected to crime data collected by the law enforcement agencies and the measurement of economic impact. Simply put, direct impacts are the more or less intentional result of a given activity conducted by organised crime actors; indirect impacts are non-intentional, or at least not known to be a goal of TOC actors, but still are a specific result or outcome of the activity.[70]

The difference between direct and indirect impacts, as well as the need for drawing a distinction between them, is best illustrated by the example of drug trafficking and drug abuse. Here, the indirect costs of use and abuse sometimes far outweigh the direct costs. Sometimes the estimated indirect costs seem to be far-fetched. For example, it is argued that the increased transnational smuggling of tobacco tends to result in lower prices for cigarettes on the black market, which makes tobacco more attractive and affordable for everyone, especially younger consumers. But the younger the consumers, the more vulnerable they are to the addictive and health-damaging effects of tobacco. The probable lower quality of smuggled tobacco may aggravate those devastating effects. The impact of these dynamics on state health systems are immense, though quite difficult to measure.

Another indirect effect is that different licit and illicit drugs may interrelate with each other and the consumption of one drug can influence the consumption of another.[71] For example, reducing the supply of marijuana through increased law enforcement activities, including seizure, may lead to a rise in prices. This scarcity may drive drug users to alternative drugs such as alcohol, or even worse, synthetic

[67] Ibid, p. 371. [68] James, 'The other civil society', cited in note 14 above, p. 247.

[69] Hall, 'Economic geography and organized crime', cited in note 64 above, p. 371.

[70] For direct and indirect impacts of organised drug crimes on young people see Holly Richter-White, 'The direct and indirect impacts of organized crime on youth, as offenders and victims', (2002) *Trends in Organized Crime*, 83.

[71] Ibid, 85.

drugs or opiates.[72] Getting tough on one drug may aggravate the drug problem instead of actually solving it.

The gateway drug problem is another indirect dilemma societies are confronted with and for which no easy answers can be found. Closely related to this question of impacts on health systems is the controversy about legalizing weaker drugs such as marijuana. A different, but still widely related, indirect impact of drugs would be the harm and damage caused by traffic accidents from people under the influence of drugs. Quite apart from the cost for law enforcement this list of indirect impacts could be easily extended. For example, productivity losses in the workforce attributable to drug abuse by employers and employees are nearly impossible to measure. Furthermore, it is worth noting the link between drug trafficking and terrorism: drug consumption may directly or indirectly finance terrorism which, again, leads to enormous cost in the field of internal security.

In conclusion, the direct impacts of TOC may be easier to measure than the indirect impacts. But the collected data give an incomplete picture that only allows limited conclusions. The informative value of data measuring indirect impacts is much higher and the derived picture may be broader, but collecting reliable data is difficult and costly.

3.4.2 Moral panics and TOC

According to Goode and Ben-Yehuda,[73] a moral panic can be identified by five crucial elements or criteria. First, there must be a heightened level of concern over a particular behaviour, which can be measured, as through media attention for example. Second, an increased amount of hostility is required towards the people seemingly engaging in the behaviour, which is allegedly harmful to the society. Third, a consensus has to be reached in the form of a minimal agreement fairly widespread among the population that the behaviour in question is real and serious. Fourth, a certain disproportion has to be reached, meaning that the moral panic is in fact considerably greater than empirical evidence would support. The fifth element is described as a certain volatility of moral panics, meaning that they subside as suddenly as they have erupted, although they might have been latent for relatively long periods. Garland adds two further elements to this conceptualization, namely '(i) the moral dimension of the social reaction, particularly the introspective soul-searching that accompanies these episodes; and (ii) the idea that the deviant conduct in question is somehow symptomatic'.[74]

When applied to TOC, the concept of moral panics offers some enlightening insights into the peculiar dynamics of crime policies.

[72] For an interesting overview of possible impacts of drug seizures see Joseph McGallagly and Neil McKeganey, 'The impact of drug seizure on local communities', in Töttel, Bulanova-Hristova, and Büchler, *Research Conference on Organised Crime, Vol. II*, cited in note 6 above, pp. 81–105.

[73] Erich Goode and Nachman Ben-Yehuda, 'Moral panics: culture, politics, and social construction', (1994) *Annual Review of Sociology* (20), 149–71, pp. 156–8. The 'classic' work about moral panics is that by Stuart Hall, Chas Critcher, Tony Jefferson, John Clarke, and Brian Roberts, *Policing the Crisis: Mugging, the State and Law and Order*, 2nd edn, Basingstoke, Palgrave Macmillan, 2013.

[74] David Garland, 'On the concept of moral panic', (2008) 4 *Crime, Media, Culture* (1), 9–30, p. 11.

First of all, organised crime seems to be a taboo topic in a number of countries. The reasons for that may be that the existence of organised crime is associated with failed governance and public distrust, political corruption, and economic leeway, as well as human rights violations. Political discourses about TOC may have a negative impact on the reputation of governments and state institutions, as viewed either by external states or companies, or by its own citizens.[75] This tendency to disguise organised crime discussions in a shroud of secrecy is not restricted to the politics level, but also practised on the law enforcement and police level, as these institutions are under nearly the same pressure of public opinion as politicians.[76]

Second, the media plays a crucial role in influencing and shaping public perceptions about TOC through entertainment programming as well as information and news, and is only to a limited extent controllable by political agendas. Media discourses about TOC seems somehow to suffer from a certain hypocrisy: on one side, the entertainment branch glorifies organised criminals in movies and TV shows (*The Godfather, The Sopranos, Scarface, Breaking Bad*, etc.), and on the other side it engages shamelessly in moral panicking by overestimating the violent side of organised crime by, for example, strongly concentrating on crimes by violent motorcycle gangs ('biker wars').[77] Depending on their own agenda, some of those motorcycle gangs in their turn try to influence public perception either by creating a positive image through charity activities, or by keeping up with the 'bad boy' image.[78] Public relations strategies of organised crime actors may reach a point at which the organisation itself is only living by its reputation, which is fuelled by journalistic and law enforcement speculation, as was suspected of 'La Cosa Nostra' in New York City or the Russian 'thieves in law'.[79]

Third, for various reasons, some forms of organised crime go entirely unnoticed by the media and the public. In the past, this was the case for a variety of environmental crimes, corporate crimes, and contraband activities. This is particularly noteworthy for white-collar crimes, where it seems that the usual moral panic dynamics and the demonizing of the criminals at least in the long run seem to be rendered ineffective by economic power, respectability, and prestige.[80]

A similar disinterest has been the case for TOC as well which, according to Irrera, has positioned itself silently and has widely gone unnoticed by the media as a dangerous global threat.[81] One reason might be that, as with white-collar criminals,

[75] Cyrille Fijnaut, 'Organised crime in Europe and beyond: some general considerations', in Robertson-von Trotha, *Organised Crime*, cited in note 2 above, p. 13.

[76] Richter-White, 'Direct and indirect impacts', cited in note 70 above, p. 100.

[77] Judith Dubois, 'Media coverage of organized crime—police managers survey', (2002) *Trends in Organized Crime*, pp. 52ff.; Loree, 'Changing concepts and realities', cited in note 28 above, pp. 74–5; Sheptycki, 'Organised crime in Canada', cited in note 4 above, p. 501. For a good overview of the role of TOC in the modern media see Paddy Rawlinson, 'Transnational organized crime: media, myths and moralities', in Allum and Gilmour, *Routledge Handbook of Transnational Organized Crime*, cited in note 24 above, pp. 294–306.

[78] For a good overview of motorcycle gangs and moral panic, see Karen Katz, 'The enemy within: the outlaw motorcycle gang moral panic', (2011) 36 *American Journal of Criminal Justice* (3), 231–49.

[79] Richter-White, 'Direct and indirect impacts', cited in note 70 above, p. 99.

[80] Michael Levi, 'Suite revenge?: The shaping of folk devils and moral panics about white-collar crimes', (2009) 49 *British Journal of Criminology* (1), 248–67, p. 251.

[81] Irrera, 'The EU strategy in tackling organized crime', cited in note 40 above, p. 411.

transnational organised criminals may today have more in common with respectable and distinguished businessmen than with the violent thug of ancient mafia organisations. Another reason might be found in the transnational aspect of organised crime itself. This, on one hand, offers the possibility for politicians and law enforcement institutions to constitute a 'particular form of othering' where the organised criminal is presented as an external threat and not a product of poor security governance, and through that, reinforce those politicians' and institutions' own political agenda.[82] On the other hand, this outsourcing of societal problems connected to TOC, as well as its blurred and ghostlike appearance, may have the effect that the critical mass of interest to set off the discourse dynamics of moral panics based on the identification of folk-devils may not be reached.

3.4.3 Organised exploitation

When it comes to organised exploitation, one might primarily think of the most prominent branches such as sexual exploitation of women and children or the exploitation for labour, both classic fields in which TOC has been widely active for years. Accordingly, it has played an important role in crime policies, and the research activities in that field have been extensive over recent years.[83] But the exploitation of human beings is not limited to sexual or labour services. It rather has a number of different faces: it encompasses sexual exploitation of men and boys, the mail-order bride business, the trade in children offered for adoption, and the illicit trade in human organs.[84] All these phenomena of exploitation have at least one characteristic in common: most of the victims come from socially and economically precarious backgrounds where unemployment rates, poverty, or inequalities are high, and where educational perspectives and prospects for social and economic advancement are low.[85] Compared with the sexual exploitation of women and exploitation for labour, the other named fields of exploitation have gained less attention in the past and are not well researched. These fields are constantly growing and are likely to become more and more important in the future. For example, inter-country adoptions of children, particularly from very poor sending nations, has dramatically increased over the past years. A whole industry of adoption agencies has been developed, sometimes perverting the humanitarian aid system to meet the growing demand. To grasp that phenomenon, Smolin coined the term 'child laundering',

[82] See, for the concept of 'othering', Michael Woodiwiss and Dick Hobbs, 'Organized evil and the Atlantic Alliance: moral panics and the rhetoric of organized crime policing in America and Britain', (2009) 49 *British Journal of Criminology* (1), 106–28, p. 124.

[83] Maria O'Neill, 'Trafficking in human beings and the European Neighbourhood Policy: new challenges for the EU Justice and Law Enforcement Framework', in Maria O'Neill, Ken Swinton, and Aaron Winter (eds), *New Challenges for the EU Internal Security Strategy*, Cambridge, Cambridge Scholars Publishing, 2013, pp. 188–216; Brenda Breuil, Diana Siegel, Piet van Reenen, Annemaricke Beljer, and Linda Roos, 'Human trafficking revisited: legal, enforcement and ethnographic narratives on sex trafficking to Western Europe', (2011) *Trends in Organized Crime*; Manfred Paulus, 'Sexual slavery and trafficking in women—a summary of current developments in Europe', in Robertson-von Trotha, *Organised Crime*, cited in note 2 above, pp. 127–36.

[84] Friesendorf, 'Pathologies of security governance', cited in note 35 above, pp. 379–80.

[85] Maihold, 'Der Mensch als Ware', cited in note 37 above, p. 9.

which describes the obtaining of children illicitly through force, fraud, or financial inducement, providing false paperwork that identifies such illicitly obtained children as legally abandoned or relinquished 'orphans', and offering or putting them up for adoption.[86] Child laundering is conducted by a highly organised, commercialized, and corrupt system of adoption agencies that operate behind a perfidious humanitarian facade and are driven by the demand of rich Western adults for children.[87] However, the questions how this system qualifies as, and is linked to, TOC and human trafficking remain controversial. A quite similar field is the 'mail-order bride' system, where a whole industry of agencies pair Western men with women mostly from Eastern Europe for marriage. Statistical data and research on that topic are rare, but available information suggests that mail-order brides are likely to become victims of human trafficking and sexual exploitation by a system of agencies operating with the same patterns as TOC.[88]

The trade in organs has become a multibillion-dollar industry ranked among the ten most profitable illegal trading activities, such as the illicit trade in arms, diamonds, and humans. Both the mere commercialism, such as organ tourism, and the actual trafficking in organs, the latter encompassing coercion or fraud, are prohibited in nearly every country of the world.[89] The global shortage of organs has fuelled the controversial debate over how this prohibition of the commercial trade contributes to trafficking and exploitation of human beings for the purpose of organ transplantation. Organ trafficking is strongly linked to TOC activities, especially in the developing world.[90]

3.5 TOC and its Impact on States

TOC impacts states mainly on three levels: the economic, the political, and the rule of law levels. However, these different levels of impact cannot be strictly separated. Van Dijk describes the complex interplay by stating that organised crime activities tend to erode public trust in state institutions by targeting the integrity of those holding public offices, including those responsible for upholding the rule of law.[91] The greater

[86] David M. Smolin, 'Child laundering and the Hague Convention on Intercountry Adoption: the future and past of intercountry adoption', (2010) 48 *University of Louisville Law Review [Online]* (3), 441–98, available at: http://works.bepress.com/david_smolin/8, accessed 24 April 2014, pp. 443–4.

[87] David M. Smolin, 'Child laundering: how the intercountry adoption system legitimizes and incentivizes the practices of buying, trafficking, kidnapping, and stealing children', (2006) 52 *Wayne Law Review [Online]* (1), 113–200, available at: http://works.bepress.com/david_smolin/1/, accessed 24 April 2014, p. 116.

[88] Kirstin M. Lindee, 'Love, honor, or control: domestic violence, trafficking, and the question of how to regulate the mail-order bride industry', (2007) 16 *Columbia Journal of Gender and Law* (2), 551–601, p. 554.

[89] Haken, *Transnational Crime In The Developing World*, cited in note 63 above, p. 22.

[90] For the discussion see Frederike Ambagtsheer and Willem Weimar, 'A criminological perspective: why prohibition of organ trade is not effective and how the Declaration of Istanbul can move forward', (2012) 12 *American Journal of Transplantation* (3), 571–75; for a good overview of the global organ trade see Debra A. Budiani-Saberi and Francis L. Delmonico, 'Organ trafficking and transplant tourism: a commentary on the global realities', (2008) 8 *American Journal of Transplantation* (5), 925–9.

[91] van Dijk, 'Mafia markers', cited in note 14 above, p. 54.

the power of organised crime groups, the more biased are legislation, policy-making, and legal rulings serving the interest of a few rather than the majority. This pervasive bias undermines market efficiencies, impedes on investments and sustainable development, and results in economic decline. These impacts are considered to have the potential and capacity to destabilize states economically, socially, and politically to an extent at which TOC is perceived as a threat not just to security, but also to the existence of countries themselves.[92] Particularly in those countries where TOC refrains from merely evading or infiltrating law enforcement agencies, but rather chooses the open confrontation, the state is in significant danger. But there are also positive examples of countries, such as Botswana, Jordan, or Chile, that illustrate how proper legal infrastructures and zero tolerance for organised crime and corruption may promote economic growth and societal wealth.

3.5.1 Economic impacts

The global economic impact of TOC is impossible to estimate precisely. Although strenuous efforts are made by international organisations, such as the UNODC, to harmonize official data from around the world, reliable numbers are scarce. The same goes for empirical studies and the weaknesses and relative merits of every new study are contested by experts.[93]

Despite those concerns, it seems clear that the profits made by TOC are enormous. Haken, for example, estimates the global illicit flow of goods, weapons, people, and natural resources at approximately $650 billion, whereas the illicit drug trade accounts for $320 billion and counterfeiting for $250 billion.[94] Transit crimes, such as international smuggling, seem to be among the most profitable branches and are, therefore, among the main activities of TOC.[95]

Apart from the estimation of profits, the economic impacts on states are even harder to quantify. For example, the German Federal Police Office (BKA) publishes annual reports in which the monetary damage of organised crime in Germany is measured. The overall figure for the year 2012 reached €1.1 billion, while one organised crime group alone was responsible for damage worth €320 million.[96] However, this report gives just a very rough estimate of the actual economic impact, since it specifically does not account for the dark figure, nor for the indirect economic impacts.

One of the crucial, devastating, economic effects of TOC networks, according to Haken, is the fact that, particularly in under-developed countries, organised crime networks have very little incentive to bolster the legitimate economy.

[92] Helena Carrapiço, 'Transnational organized crime as a security concept', in Allum and Gilmour, *Routledge Handbook of Transnational Organized Crime*, cited in note 24 above, pp. 19–35, p. 19.

[93] Edward R. Kleemans, 'Organized crime and the visible hand: a theoretical critique on the economic analysis of organized crime', (2013) 13 *Criminology and Criminal Justice* (5), 615–29, pp. 616–17.

[94] Haken, *Transnational Crime In The Developing World*, cited in note 63 above, p. 5; for a good overview of the economic impacts of TOC see UNODC, *The Globalization of Crime. A Transnational Organized Crime Threat Assessment*, Vienna, 2010.

[95] Kleemans, 'Organized crime and the visible hand', cited in note 93 above, p. 620.

[96] Bundeskriminalamt, *Bundeslagebild Organisierte Kriminalität*, Hamburg, 2012, p. 7.

> Unregulated, they minimize overheads in developing source countries by exploiting local labour forces, often resorting to forced or child labour, dodging environmental and safety regulations, and evading trade tariffs.[97]

It is, therefore, in the best interest of TOC to not just search for weak states as 'safe havens' for their activities, but to actively contribute to the weakening of states by impairing the capacity of governments to promote sustainable economic growth.[98] This, in turn, will deter local as well as foreign investors, leaving a vacuum preferably filled by illicit actors perpetuating the parasitic dependence of economically underdeveloped states on TOC.

3.5.2 Political impacts

From a political perspective, the occurrence of growing TOC networks alongside globalization have led to a number of impacts. First of all, TOC is included in the political agenda on a global scale owing to its similarities and actual links to global terrorism. The fight against TOC has turned into an approach like warfare, with similar political implications to the 'war on terror'.[99]

Nevertheless, this warfare cannot be considered to have the same exclusive policy priority as the 'war on terror'. This may derive from the fact that the political differences in position among the main actors in the fight against TOC, such as the USA, the EU, and the UN, are significant.[100] This is reflected in national legislations and statutes that focus on domestic organised crime and seldom refer to the transnational or international aspect of an offence. As a consequence, the combat against TOC differs in each country, even if it is a signatory of the Palermo Convention. In addition to this statutory variety, domestic policy initiatives and law enforcement strategies to fight TOC differ from each other significantly.[101] But with a view to the aforementioned tendency of TOC to develop strong local roots, domestic law enforcement and policy approaches specifically tailored to the local TOC activities may be successful in the long run. Nevertheless, stronger international cooperation and coordination seems inevitable, taking into account how easily TOC groups move across borders and how difficult the same might be in turn for national law enforcement authorities.[102]

Political impacts on developing countries may differ from this discussion about stronger legal cooperation and law enforcement measures to erase TOC. Here, the question of fighting TOC effectively boils down to approaches encouraging organised crime actors to become less predatory, but rather parasitic and symbiotic (and thereby less violent), or even to transform to licit actors.[103] When state institutions are

[97] Haken, *Transnational Crime In The Developing World*, cited in note 63 above, p. 5.

[98] van Dijk, 'Mafia markers', cited in note 14 above, p. 51.

[99] van Dijk and Spapens, 'Transnational organized crime networks', cited in note 26 above, p. 222.

[100] Irrera, 'The EU strategy in tackling organized crime', cited in note 40 above, p. 407.

[101] Wheatley, 'Transnational organized crime', cited in note 44 above, p. 77.

[102] van Dijk and Spapens, 'Transnational organized crime networks', cited in note 26 above, p. 224; Wheatley, ibid, p. 77.

[103] James Cockayne and Ada Lupel, 'From iron fist to invisible hand: peace operations, organized crime and intelligent international law enforcement', in James Cockayne and Ada Lupel (eds), *Peace Operations and Organised Crime: Enemies or Allies?* London, Routledge, 2011, pp. 190–208.

weak and political branches are infiltrated by TOC, pragmatic approaches to accept it as a political player are considered to be an alternative, at least in the short term. The reasoning behind this is the assumption that a hypothetical successful removal of all TOC structures in developing societies would lead to destabilization, as it is unclear what would emerge to replace these structures. Moreover, the primary drivers for TOC, such as poverty, social inequality, unemployment, weak borders, and government structures, as well as the demand for the illicit goods in question, would remain present.[104]

Despite these legitimate concerns, it was argued before that considering TOC as a stabilizing factor in societies is a dangerous approach that is apt to misjudge the highly subversive and destabilizing risks TOC unfolds in all societal spheres. Political strategies in the developing world face this dilemma of finding a balance between fighting and taming TOC by including it in the political process.[105] The international community may play a crucial role in these transformation processes, not only by stressing the law enforcement aspect, but also by supporting political and economic reforms.[106]

3.5.3 Impacts on the rule of law

It has been established that in countries where the rule of law is weak and the perceived independence of the judiciary is low, organised crime structures are more prevalent.[107] When assessing the impact of TOC on the rule of law, distinguishing between conditions for the flourishing of TOC and its impacts is not a simple task. This is particularly the case for developing and post-conflict countries in which the relationship between corruption in the public sector and TOC is strong.[108] Corruption tends to unfold a dynamic, in German called '*anfüttern*' (feeding). This term describes the deliberate development of a relationship based on the dependency of the bribed. The bribed become dependent on more bribes to finance their improved lifestyle, which was made possible by accepting bribes in the first place. Simply put, corruption tends to create its own demand. On the state level, this dynamic is reflected in the devastating impact corruption has on economic performance. The damage to national budgets is enormous, contributing to the inability to pay public servants adequately. This, in turn, makes public servants more susceptible to bribes paid by criminals to foster their illicit goals.

This threat posed by TOC undermining the rule of law through corruption and violence is widespread around the globe. Even relatively strong states are not immune to this dynamic. But the most devastating effects unfold where organised criminals are seeking to directly confront governments rather than simply to undermine them. This has recently been the case in some parts of Mexico and in West Africa. The

[104] For the discussion see James, 'The other civil society', cited in note 14 above, pp. 248ff.

[105] Reno, 'Understanding criminality in West African conflicts', cited in note 51 above, p. 49.

[106] James, 'The other civil society', cited in note 14 above, pp. 248ff.

[107] van Dijk, 'Mafia markers', cited in note 14 above, pp. 46–7.

[108] Edgardo Buscaglia and Jan van Dijk, 'Controlling organized crime and corruption in the public sector', in *Forum on Crime and Society* 3, Nos 1 and 2, Geneva, United Nations Publication, 2003, p. 32.

symptoms remain the same in these regions: investigators, prosecutors, judges, and even journalists and activists who pursue organised crime, are threatened and killed. Corruption has taken over large parts of government and law enforcement agencies are paralysed by mistrust.[109] Military forces are deployed to get the situation back under control and enforce public authority, which may have short-term successes, but is itself a threat to civil liberties and the rule of law in the long run. Civil society may react by forming militia and civilian vigilante groups to take security into their own hands, operating widely uncontrolled. These groups may become a security threat to the rule of law over time similar to the criminals they were formed to combat.[110] These might be extreme examples, but they illustrate very clearly the consequences that may arise from organised crime networks taking advantage of weak rule-of-law structures.

This dynamic is drastically illustrated in the case of Kosovo and the failure of the international organisations. Just one of many examples is the story of an African citizen who was hired to rebuild the Kosovo railway system, although he personally had no experience with railways.

> Mr Bangura teaches the Kosovans how to run a railway and is paid some €8,000 a month. Local railwaymen who are supposed to live on €150 feel a bit humiliated by the project, especially since Mr Bangura knows nothing about railways. How could he? He is from Sierra Leone where the last train stopped in 1975. He is an expert in harbours.[111]

As if that wasn't enough, in 2007 a high-ranking US police officer, working for the UN Interim Administration Mission in Kosovo (UNMIK), was prosecuted for sexual exploitation of women and cooperation with organised criminals. Corruption scandals, some of them at the highest level, have damaged the reputation of the international administration. The former director of the Kosovo Electricity Corporation, KEK (from 2001–3), a 36-year-old German, was only one example. US$4.5 million from international donors disappeared from his books at KEK. He sold electricity to other countries, and the money was transferred to his private account in Gibraltar. He was sentenced to probation in 2007 in Bochum—not for fraud or corruption in Kosovo, but for using false doctorate titles while applying for jobs in Germany.

The rise in organised crime marked a serious failure by the UN administration. More than ever, Kosovo is at the heart of the European trafficking in drugs and human beings. The 'Balkans … already distribute most of Europe's heroin, facilitate illegal migration and are responsible for nearly 30 per cent of women victims of the sex trade

[109] UNODC, *Crime and Instability: Case Studies of Transnational Threats* Vienna, 2010, pp. 1–2.

[110] Ibid, p. 2.

[111] Maciej Zaremba, 'Koloni Kosovo. Part 1: Report from Unmikistan, land of the future', available at: http://www.dn.se/kultur-noje/kulturdebatt/part-1-report-from-unmikistan-land-of-the-future/; 'Koloni Kosovo. Part 2: The UN state and the seven robbers', available at: http://www.dn.se/kultur-noje/kulturdebatt/part-2-the-un-state-and-the-seven-robbers/; 'Koloni Kosovo. Part 3: Complain in Azerbaijan', available at: http://www.dn.se/kultur-noje/kulturdebatt/part-3-complain-in-azerbaijan/; 'Koloni Kosovo: Part 4: Prowess, courage and plastic socks', available at: http://www.dn.se/kultur-noje/kulturdebatt/part-4-prowess-courage-and-plastic-socks/, all in *Dagens Nyheter*, 25 June 2007, all accessed 29 October 2015.

worldwide'.[112] Illicit trade is developing on its borders. Albanian groups organize 80 per cent of the smuggling of heroin in Northern Europe and 40 per cent of that in Western Europe, and four to five tons of heroin cross the borders of Kosovo every month.[113] The UN police works closely with the Kosovo Police, but some members of the service are known for their good contacts with local and international criminals, and the same is true for the always necessary language assistants, some of whom have made tremendous careers in recent years, because the internationals needed them and good and reliable interpreters are rare for a language that was used rarely on an international level before. A monthly list, issued by UNMIK, lists some 140 brothels, officially 'off limits' to UN employees—for a country of some 2 million people.

> Mr Bhattacharya from Bangladesh ... is an expert in nothing. He is a parking guard, without a driver's licence and speaks only Bengali, but he must have paid handsomely in Dhaka, because now he is a UN policeman. There are hundreds of them, incompetent people, within the UN police, within finance, and even within the justice system.[114]

They are called 'domestic internationals', 'project addicts', or, when working for one of the estimated 4,000 NGOs in Kosovo, 'MANGOs' (short for MAfia-Non-Governmental Organization).

3.6 Final Observations

To analyse the 'impact' of TOC on societies is to some extent misleading. The notion 'impact' might suggest that TOC is taking a position somewhere outside societies from where it unfolds its activities and invades the society. This view is only partly true. TOC has its roots within societies around the world. Within these societies, it follows the same social patterns, adopts the same societal developments and changes, takes advantage of weaknesses, preys on state failures, and operates its business in an economic system provided by the international community, obeying some of its rules while violating others. As much as TOC is a measurable and observable phenomenon, it is more of a social construction defined and influenced by societal perceptions and projections. With disregard to the positive or stabilizing role TOC might play in some regions of the world, one might still consider TOC as a tumour or parasite feeding on the blood of its host. But this metaphor, although popular, is somehow crooked as it describes TOC as an outsider; which it simply is not. If a metaphor is needed at all, one might compare TOC more to a limping leg on the body of society: it slows us down and might hurt from time to time, but it is still a functional leg and sometimes we might not even realize that it is limping. And whether we like it or not, the leg remains a part of our body.

[112] International Crisis Group, 'Breaking the Kosovo stalemate: Europe's responsibility', (2007) Europe Report 185, available at: http://www.crisisgroup.org/~/media/Files/europe/185_breaking_the_kosovo_stalemate___europe_s_responsibility.ashx.

[113] Walter Mayr, 'Elefanten vor dem Wasserloch', (2008) 17 *Der Spiegel*, 128–30.

[114] Zaremba, 'Koloni Kosovo', cited in note 111 above.

4

The EU and the Fight against Organised Crime

Bernd Hecker

4.1 Origins

4.1.1 Transnational organised crime—appearances and dangers

Transnational organised crime (TOC) generates billions in profits annually for criminal organisations. These earnings are typically introduced into the legal, financial, and economic cycles.[1] In addition to illegal drug trafficking and racketeering, money laundering, smuggling of illegal migrants, trafficking in human beings (such as labour exploitation and sexual exploitation of women and children), the arms trade, vehicle trafficking, and trafficking of high-quality goods are especially lucrative fields of activity for TOC. Rapidly progressive developments in communication and transportation technologies present criminal networks operating across borders with new technical possibilities of criminal offence. The manifold appearances and dangers of TOC are partly cited as the reasons for the creation of the European Parliament resolution of 23 October 2013 on organised crime, corruption, and money laundering,[2] which greatly illuminates the vastness of these enterprises in stating that:

- criminal organisations have gradually extended their operating range on an international scale, exploiting economic globalization and new technologies, and entering into alliances with criminal groups in other countries in order to carve up markets and spheres of influence;
- increasingly, criminal groups are diversifying in their operations, with links growing between drug trafficking, the trafficking of human beings, the facilitation of illegal immigration, weapons trafficking, and money laundering;
- corruption and organised crime are serious threats in terms of costs to the EU economy;
- organised crime is increasingly resembling an economic global player with a strong business orientation, enabling it to supply different kinds of illegal—but also, to an increasing extent, legal—goods and services at the same time, and is

[1] Pierre Hauck and Sven Peterke, 'Organized crime and gang violence in national and international law', 92 *International Review of the Red Cross* (100), 407; Claus Kreß and Nicolaos Gazeas, 'Organisierte Kriminalität', in Ulrich Sieber, Helmut Satzger, and Bernd von Heintschel-Heinegg (eds), *Europäisches Strafrecht*, 2nd edn, Baden-Baden, Nomos, 2014, para. 18: see recital 1; Bettina Weißer, 'Angleichung von Strafvorschriften zur grenzüberschreitenden (organisierten) Kriminalität', in Martin Böse (ed.), *Europäisches Strafrecht*, Baden-Baden, Nomos, 2013, para. 9: see recital 1.

[2] P7_TA(2013)0444.

having an increasing impact on the European and global economy, significantly affecting tax revenues of the member states and the EU as a whole, and at a cost to business estimated at more than €670 billion annually;

- organised crime is a major, cross-border, internal security threat in the EU in terms of the number of victims;
- organised crime makes huge profits from trafficking in human beings, illegal trafficking in and smuggling of organs, arms, drugs and their precursors, nuclear, radiological, biological and chemical substances, prescription drugs, counterfeiting of everyday consumer goods such as foodstuffs, protected animal and plant species and parts of them, tobacco in all its forms, works of art, and various other—often counterfeit—products;
- mafia-type organised crime relating to the environment—involving various forms of illegal waste trafficking and disposal and the destruction of environmental, landscape, artistic, and cultural heritage—has now assumed an international dimension;
- numerous criminal organisations have a network structure characterized by high levels of flexibility, mobility, connectivity, and inter-ethnicity, as well as a heightened capacity for infiltration and camouflage;
- the 2013 Europol SOCTA report estimates that 3,600 international criminal organisations are operating in the EU and that, of those, 70 per cent have a geographically heterogeneous composition and range of action and more than 30 per cent are poly-crime groups;
- criminal organisations can take advantage of a grey area of collusion with other parties, merging for the purpose of carrying out certain activities with white-collar perpetrators (entrepreneurs, public officials at all levels of decision making, politicians, banks, professionals, etc.), who, while not actually belonging to criminal organisations, have mutually lucrative business relations with them;
- the financial flows generated by the international drug traffic operated by mafia-type organisations, in a good many cases, have been handled by banks in several parts of the world;
- the transnational dimension of organised crime has been heightened by the ease with which criminal groups use every means of transport, tried and tested routes, and existing infrastructure, extending outside the EU;
- the victims of the trafficking in human beings are recruited, transported, or harboured by force, coercion, or fraud with the purpose of sexual exploitation, forced labour or services, including begging, slavery, servitude, criminal activities, domestic service, adoption or forced marriage, or the removal of organs;
- operations involving trafficking in human beings and human organs, forced prostitution or enslavement, and the establishment of labour camps are often run by transnational criminal organisations;
- while, in particular, trafficking in human beings generates an estimated profit of €25 billion each year and this crime concerns all EU countries;

- the revenues generated by trafficking in wildlife species and body parts are estimated at €18 to 26 billion per year, with the EU being the foremost destination market in the world;
- cybercrime is creating increasingly significant economic and social damage affecting millions of consumers and is causing annual losses estimated at €290 billion;
- in many cases, for organised crime, the bribery of public officials aids illegal trafficking in that, amongst other things, it provides access to confidential information, enables false documents to be obtained, public procurement procedures to be guided, proceeds to be recycled, and law enforcement actions by the police and courts to be evaded;
- systemic corruption in the public sector, which is one of the main impediments to efficiency, foreign direct investment, and innovation, is thus preventing the proper functioning of the monetary union;
- flows of dirty money through transfers of funds can damage the stability and reputation of the financial sector and threaten the internal market of the Union;
- the activities of organised crime increasingly include the counterfeiting of all kinds of products, from luxury goods to everyday items; and
- the increasing number of crimes being perpetrated against the agri-food sector are not only seriously endangering the health of European citizens but also causing considerable damage to those countries that have made food excellence their major asset.

4.1.2 European criminal policy

Since the mid-1990s the European criminal policy has been concerned with increasing the intensity of the control of TOC. Previously the fight against crime played a relatively minor role compared with other policies of the European Community. European integration should be promoted above all in economic sectors, so in an area in which the member states seem to be ready earliest to renounce sovereignty reservations. The fact that the police of and judicial cooperation among the member states came more into the focus of EU politics is associated above all with the serious increase of TOC. Not only respectable citizens profit from the discontinuation of controls in the internal frontiers and the freedom of passenger traffic, service traffic, and movement of goods. The centres of the affluent societies of the EU member states represent popular outlet markets for illegal products and services of all kinds. They form a target for criminal attacks on regular finance, economy, and competitive processes. It must be kept in mind that the European house is infected by the virus of corruption and mafia-like structures. There is also the ever-present menace of international terrorism to contend with. The discovery that national criminal proceeding systems in themselves were helpless against the globalization of crime and its manifold potential of menaces generated massive political pressure for action to counter this criminal activity. This forced back national sovereignty reservations and prompted a revaluation of the police and judicial cooperation in criminal cases, emphasizing these as an important pillar of European integration politics. The EU strategies for the creation of a union of freedom, security, and justice, which are laid down in the programmes the European Council adopted at Tampere (1999–2004), The Hague (2005–9), Stockholm (2009–14), and Ypres/Brussels (2015–20), testify to the fact that fighting TOC, with the aim of actual prevention of it, which appears in varied manifestations, belongs to the central aims of European criminal politics.[3]

4.1.2.1 Towards a union of freedom, security, and justice: the Tampere milestones (1999–2004)

Following the declaration of the European Council from 15/16 October 1999 in Tampere,[4] people have the right to expect the Union to address the threat to their freedom and legal rights posed by serious crime. To counter these threats a common effort is needed to fight and prevent crime and criminal organisations throughout the Union. The joint mobilization of police and judicial resources is needed to guarantee that there is no hiding place for criminals or the proceeds of crime within the Union. Efforts by national criminal law to agree on common definitions, incriminations, and sanctions should focus in the first instance on a limited number of sectors of particular relevance, such as financial crime (money laundering, corruption, Euro counterfeiting), drugs trafficking, trafficking in human beings, particularly exploitation of women and sexual exploitation of children, high-tech crime, and environmental crime. As well as demanding better access to justice and improvement of the exchange of information for the fight against criminal activity, a *principle of mutual recognition* inspired by the internal market was stated. This principle should cause the two-stage procedure model of mutual legal aid, request and approval, to change to a single-step construction under which judicial decisions should find immediate recognition in and obedience by all other member states. The conclusions also illustrated a narrow *similarity of criminal law alignment and cooperation in criminal cases* and laid the foundations for the criminal-political concept of the member states that has dominated up to the present.

4.1.2.2 The Hague programme: strengthening freedom, security, and justice in the European Union (2005–9)

In the Hague programme accepted on 4/5 November 2004 the European Council reaffirmed the priority it attaches to the development of an area of freedom, security,

[3] Hauck and Peterke, 'Organized crime and gang violence', cited in note 1 above, p. 426; C. Kreß and N. Gazeas, 'Organisierte Kriminalität', cited in note 1 above, para. 18: see recital 5; B. Weißer, 'Angleichung', cited in note 1 above, para. 9: see recital 2; Fritz Zeder, 'Europastrafrecht, Vertrag von Lissabon und Stockholmer Programm "Mehr Grundrechtsschutz?"', (2012) *Europarecht*, 34.

[4] See Tampere European Council, Presidency Conclusions (SN 200/99) as well as Frank Meyer, 'Titel V: Der Raum der Freiheit, der Sicherheit und des Rechts', in Hans von der Groeben, Jürgen Schwarze, and Armin Hatje (eds), *Europäisches Unionsrecht*, 7th edn, Baden-Baden, Nomos, 2015, before Art. 82ff. AEUV: see recital 15.

and justice.[5] Implementing the principle of mutual recognition of penal-judicial decisions should be made easier by the *application of criminal regulations* and especially so in serious offence areas with an international dimension. Moreover, the European Council considered that it requires the international exchange of information about criminal prosecutions to improve. As an innovative concept the *principle of availability* was introduced, under which the criminal prosecuting authorities of a member state should be able to perform their duties widely unhindered, since all useful information available to criminal prosecuting authorities in other member states would be made universally accessible.[6]

4.1.2.3 The Stockholm Programme—an open and secure Europe serving and protecting citizens (2009–14)

On 10/11 December 2009 the Stockholm Programme was adopted by the European Council,[7] to express the Council's conviction that the strengthening of measures at the European level in connection with better coordination at regional and national levels are of central necessity for the protection from transnational menaces, in particular terrorism and organised crime (OC), drug trafficking, corruption, trafficking in human beings, smuggling, and the unlawful arms trade. The European Council and Commission were asked to develop a comprehensive internal security strategy for the EU. They adopted, on 22 November 2010, an EU strategy for internal security in which serious and organised crime formed one of the five main issues for the Union to address. The fight against trafficking in human beings, sexual exploitation of children and child pornography, cybercrime, economic criminal activity and corruption, criminal drug activity, and terrorism became priorities.[8] The chief aim was seen as the *weakening of international criminal networks.*[9]

4.1.2.4 'Post-Stockholm-Programme' (2015–20)

The strategic guidelines for legislative and operational planning for 2015–20 were defined at the conference of the European Council on 26/27 June 2014 in Ypres/Brussels.[10] The 'Post-Stockholm Programme' focuses on consolidation and the actual implementation of the already created *acquis communautaire*. Recital 10 confirms the aim of guaranteeing a genuine area of security for European citizens through operational

[5] OJ (2005/C 53/01). See also Meyer, ibid.

[6] See also M. Böse, *Der Grundsatz der Verfügbarkeit von Informationen in der strafrechtlichen Zusammenarbeit der EU*, Bonn, V&R Unipress, 2007, p. 46.

[7] OJ (2010/C 115/01), p. 21. See also Meyer, 'Titel V', cited in note 4 above, recital 23; Zeder, 'Vertrag von Lissabon und Stockholmer Programm', cited in note 3 above, pp. 34, 51.

[8] COM (2010) 673 final, p. 5; see also the European Parliament resolution of 25 October 2011 on organised crime in the European Union, P7_TA(2011)0459.

[9] See also COM (2014) 154 final, p. 10.

[10] OJ (2014/C 240/13); see also Dominik Brodowski, 'Strafrechtsrelevante Entwicklungen in der Europäischen Union—ein Überblick', (2015) *Zeitschrift für Internationale Strafrechtsdogmatik*, 79.

police cooperation and preventing and combating serious and organised crime, including human trafficking and smuggling, as well as corruption. The European Council calls on the EU institutions and the member states to ensure the appropriate legislative and operational follow-up to these guidelines and will hold a mid-term review in 2017 (Article 13).

4.2 Legal Bases

4.2.1 The Maastricht Treaty

Long before the introduction of the Lisbon (reform) Treaty (see section 4.2.3 of this chapter) the collective actions of the EU member states within the sphere of internal security and justice crystallized as central and prominent factors in the areas of the international, work-sharing fight against crime. The Maastricht Treaty (Treaty on European Union; TEU) , which came into force on 1 November 1993, created for the first time *common structures* for intergovernmental cooperation on matters of common interest. Part of this entailed *cooperation in the fields of justice and home affairs (JHA)*.[11] The procedures for cooperation of all EU member states were finally fixed by the implementation of the JHA in the TEU framework.[12] The integration of JHA in that framework was justified by the growing international dimension of many domestic political and judicial-political problem areas. Nine policy areas that the member states regarded as *'affairs of common interest'* were listed in Article K.1 TEU (in the Maastricht Treaty version), including judicial cooperation in criminal and civil cases, and customs cooperation (*Zollwesen*) such as police cooperation to prevent and abate serious forms of international crime like terrorism and drug trafficking. The Maastricht Treaty's chief merit is to have transferred an—until then—informal cooperation practised by various working groups into a form of contract based on international law,[13] and thereby into an institutionalized form of cooperation.[14] Since then the justice policy and internal policy has been part of the most dynamic policy field in the EU.[15]

The JHA brought forth on 16/17 June 1997 the adoption by the European Council in Amsterdam of the *Action Plan to combat organised crime*. This high-level group on OC was devised and implemented by the European Council in Dublin (13/14 December

[11] Bernd Hecker, *Europäisches Strafrecht*, 5th edn, Heidelberg, Springer, 2015, para. 5: see recital 54ff.; Arndt Sinn, 'Europäische Gemeinschaften', in Walter Gropp and Barbara Huber (eds), *Rechtliche Initiativen gegen organisierte Kriminalität*, Freiburg im Breisgau, Iuscrim MPI, 2001, p. 296.

[12] Compare with Meyer, 'Titel V', cited in note 4 above: recital 8; Peter-Christian Müller-Graff (ed.), *Europäische Zusammenarbeit in den Bereichen Justiz und Inneres*, Baden-Baden, Nomos, 1996, *passim*.

[13] Compare with the TREVI working group: Hecker, *Europäisches Strafrecht*, cited in note 11 above, para. 5: see recital 26ff.

[14] Sabine Gleß, 'Kontrolle über Europol und seine Bedienstete', (1998) *Europarecht*, pp. 748, 749; Ursula Nelles, 'Europäisierung des Strafverfahrens—Strafprozessrecht für Europa?', (1997) 109 *Zeitschrift für die gesamte Strafrechtswissenschaft*, pp. 727, 734.

[15] Jens Jokisch and Moritz Jahnke, 'Der Raum der Freiheit, der Sicherheit und des Rechts', in Sieber, Satzger, and von Heintschel-Heinegg, *Europäisches Strafrecht*, cited in note 1 above, para. 2: see recital 1.

1996).[16] This first Action Plan followed the Joint Action 98/733/JI concerning the punishability of the participation in a criminal organisation in the Member States of the European Union of 21 December 1998,[17] though which for the first time at EU level a legislative act was created to fight OC.

4.2.2 Treaty of Amsterdam

The next significant development came in the Treaty of Amsterdam that came into force on 1 May 1999, and created the base for the new Union objectives (*Unionsziel*) for the development of an 'area of freedom, security and justice' (ex-Article 29 TEU). The former JHA was restructured into *police and judicial cooperation in criminal matters (PJCC)* in the insertion to Article 29–42 TEU. PJCC specified and extended the police and judicial cooperation previously practised and furthered integration. It was conceived as a cooperation of sovereign states in which the instruments of Community law do not apply. Rather, cooperation took place in accordance with the closing list of actions in ex-Article 34(2)[(a)–(d)] TEU, to which especially the unanimous adoption of framework decisions belonged. Urgent areas for the PJCC to address, areas in which according to ex-Article 29 TEU a 'common action of the Member States' was to be developed, were on one hand protection of EC finance interests under criminal law and on the other the fight to prevent transnational crime, including but not limited to terrorism, trafficking in human beings, criminal offences against children, illegal trafficking in drugs and arms, corruption, money laundering, and other manifestations of serious organised and non-organised crime.[18] The Union aim to create an 'area of freedom, security and justice' should be achieved by closer cooperation of police, customs, and the justiciary as well as the *alignment and harmonization of criminal law in the member states*. On this basis the Council created a 'third pillar of the EU', an intergovernmentally structured multiplicity of framework decisions with minimum rules relevant for criminal law that applied across the whole range of serious international crime, notably terrorism, OC, counterfeiting of money, drug-related crime, money laundering, trafficking in human beings, smuggling, child pornography, and cybercrime.[19] Thereto belonged Framework Decision 2008/841/JHA of 24 October 2008 on the fight against organised crime (FD OC 2008) which came into effect on 11 November 2008.[20] This Framework Decision replaced the 1998 Joint Action (see section 4.2.1 of this chapter) and defines the minimum standard for the levying of penal provisions by the member states (considered further in section 4.2.5.1).

[16] OJ (1997/C 251/01); see for detail Sinn, 'Europäische Gemeinschaften', cited in note 11 above, p. 311. Numerous other resolutions and action plans followed; compare the listing in Article 1.2 of the Communication from the Commission about 'Developing a strategic concept on tackling organised crime' from 2 June 2005, COM (2005) 232 final.

[17] GM 98/733/JI: OJ (1998/L 351/01); compare Claus Kreß, 'Das Strafrecht in der Europäischen Union vor der Herausforderung durch organisierte Kriminalität und Terrorismus', (2005) *Juristische Arbeitsblätter*, 220; Sinn, 'Europäische Gemeinschaften', cited in note 11 above, p. 359.

[18] Meyer, 'Titel V', cited in note 4 above: see recital 13.

[19] For the current valid framework decisions, see Hecker, *Europäisches Strafrecht*, cited in note 11 above, para. 11: see recital 10.

[20] OJ (2008/L 300/42). Compare Art. 9 of the Protocol on Transitional Provisions, No. 36, OJ (2008/C 115/322).

4.2.3 Treaty of Lisbon

With the entry into force of the Lisbon Treaty on 1 December 2009 a new era for PJCC began.[21] Through it the contracting parties founded a European Union ('Union') to which the member states transfer competences in order to realize their common objectives. The Union replaced the European Community, as a legal successor. The European Nuclear Society was separated from the former EU umbrella organisation and set up as an independent international organisation. The primary legal basis of the Union is now the TEU and the Treaty on the Functioning of the European Union (TFEU), in place of the Treaty of the European Community. The guarantee of an 'area of freedom, security and justice' is set out in Article 3(2) TEU. This objective also appears in Article 67(1) TFEU, which requires respect for the fundamental rights and the different legal systems and legal traditions of the member states. Moreover, internal security politics are set down in Article 67(3) TFEU and the programme laid down there:[22] to achieve a high level of safety the Union contributes through measures for preventing and fighting crime, coordination and cooperation of institutions for criminal justice (*Strafrechtspflege*), mutual recognition of penal decisions (*strafrechtliche Entscheidungen*), and if necessary by the approximation of criminal legal regulations. In particular, the strategic guidelines for European criminal policy are fixed by the European Council (cf. Article 68 TFEU). Every legal area relating to the defined areas of freedom, security, and justice is harmonized under Articles 67–89 TFEU and thus is created a supranational legal area.

4.2.4 Primary EU law

The Treaty of Lisbon (see section 4.2.3 of this chapter) introduced, with Article 83 TFEU, a general competence for the approximation of substantive criminal law by means of directives. The article distinguishes between approximation of *particularly serious crimes with a cross-border dimension* (para. 1) and approximation to ensure the effective implementation of a Union policy in an area that has been subject to harmonization measures, the 'annex competence' (para. 2).[23] As subject to a possible unification of domestic criminal law, Article 83(I)(2) TFEU appoints—as already stated in Article 31(e) TEU—an explicit scope for OC although no legal definition of the term is found in European Union law.[24] It receives certain contours from the fact that crimes that should be attributed to

[21] Hecker, *Europäisches Strafrecht*, cited in note 11 above, para. 1: see recital 3; Meyer, 'Titel V', cited in note 4 above: see recital 21; U. Sieber, 'Die Zukunft des europäischen Strafrechts', (2009) 121 *Zeitschrift für die gesamte Strafrechtswissenschaft* (1), 57.

[22] Compare Jokisch and Jahnke, 'Freiheit, Sicherheit und Rechts', cited in note 15 above, para. 2: see recital 1ff.; Meyer, 'Titel V', cited in note 4 above, recital 25ff.

[23] See H. Satzger, *International and European Criminal Law*, Munich, C. H. Beck, 2012, para. 7: see recital 31ff.

[24] Hauck and Peterke, 'Organized crime and gang violence', cited in note 1 above, p. 407; Kreß and Gazeas, 'Organisierte Kriminalität', cited in note 1 above, para. 18: see recital 2; Weißer, 'Angleichung', cited in note 1 above, para. 9: see recital 5.

OC must be committed in a typically systematic and collaborative manner by a minimum of three organisationally connected persons for a long period and with the intention of making profits.[25] Article 83(I) TFEU lists approximated offences that should be considered as affiliated to organised crime, such as organised and gang offences in the stricter sense of the term, but criminal offences that do not demonstrate the organised cooperation of several perpetrators may form an element of the offence since they are typically committed using technical, logistical, financial, and personal instruments within the framework of an organisation acting collaboratively in the pursuit of profit. Measures aiming at harmonization of the substantive criminal law of the member states for particular areas of crime are covered by Article 83(I) TFEU, such as the enactment of minimum rules to evaluate the relevant facts for the special purposes of criminal law. For example, they can be included in a common definition that describes the essential objective and subjective characteristics of the action(s) forming the offence, which need not exclude the detailed or progressing definition in domestic law. Member states are not allowed to pass sentences below the minimum tariffs for criminal offences in a legislative act by establishing additional (criminal) conditions. The responsibility for harmonization in Article 83(I) TFEU also requires that aid be offered to implement regulations governing the general part of criminal law as needed to arrack offences effectively, and that intervention in the basic structure of domestic criminal justice systems be systematic.[26] Some areas are not problematic, for example the area specific to standards for criminal offences, which makes sure that criminal sanctions are imposed for attempting a specified criminal offence and participation in it (incitement, allowance). Member states may provide for the responsibility (although not the competence) of juristic entities so long as they leave wide room for manoeuvre in implementation, such as limiting non-criminal sanctions. Furthermore, sanctions in the criminal areas covered by the Treaty are subject to a minimum of harmonization, which can take the form of minimum–maximum penalty specification: determining the minimum and maximum levels of a planned penalty in domestic criminal law. Hereby, legal provisions in member states approximate only the penalties applicable, not the sentence to be imposed in fact. In this respect the principle of adequate punishment for the act applies, and from the outset the liability and independence of courts set limits to the approximation of laws. Likewise, offence-specific guidelines relating to jurisdiction and aggravating or mitigating circumstances can be based on Article 83(I) TFEU.[27]

[25] See Hauck and Peterke, 'Organized crime and gang violence', cited in note 1 above, p. 407, 426; Kreß and Gazeas, 'Organisierte Kriminalität', cited in note 1 above, para. 18: see recital 2.

[26] Martin Böse, 'Kompetenzen der Union auf dem Gebiet des Straf- und Strafverfahrens', in Böse, *Europäisches Strafrecht*, cited in note 1 above, para. 4: see recital 14; Hecker, *Europäisches Strafrecht*, cited in note 11 above, para. 11: see recital 6; Meyer, 'Titel V', cited in note 4 above: see recital 21.

[27] Jörg Eisele, 'Jurisdiktionskonflikte in der Europäischen Union—Vom nationalen Strafanwendungsrecht zum Europäischen Kollisionsrecht?', (2013) 125 *Zeitschrift für die gesamte Strafrechtswissenschaft*, 12; Bernd Hecker, 'Harmonisierung', in Sieber, Satzger, and von Heintschel-Heinegg, *Europäisches Strafrecht*, cited in note 1 above, para. 10: see recital 35.

4.2.5 Secondary EU law

4.2.5.1 Council Framework Decision 2008/841/JHA on the fight against organised crime

4.2.5.1.1 Object of regulation

The Framework Decision on Organised Crime (FD OC) was issued within the scope of the third pillar of the EU (PJCC; see section 4.2.2 of this chapter), came into force on 11 November 2008, and is valid until further notice.[28] It is based on the guidelines in the United Nations Convention against Transnational Organized Crime ('the Palermo Convention') of 15 November 2000, which the Community joined by resolution of the Council on 29 April 2004.[29] The Framework Decision aims to approximate the definitions of criminal offences that are committed in connection with participation in a criminal organisation. The object is to facilitate mutual recognition of decisions and judgments, and police and judicial cooperation.

4.2.5.1.2 Definition of criminal organisations

Article 1(1) FD OC defines a 'criminal organisation' as

> a structured association, established over a period of time, of more than two persons acting in concert with a view to committing offences which are punishable by deprivation of liberty or a detention order of a maximum of at least four years or a more serious penalty, to obtain, directly or indirectly, a financial or other material benefit.

The conceptual characteristic of 'structured association' in the Article is defined in Article 1(2) as 'an association that is not randomly formed for the immediate commission of an offence, nor does it need to have formally defined roles for its members, continuity of its membership, or a developed structure'.

Thus the Union's term 'criminal organisation' contains *personal* (minimum three persons), *temporal* (longer period), *organisational* (not just a random fusion), and *voluntary* elements (intention to commit criminal offences collaboratively).[30] Furthermore, only offences against property in the broadest sense (financial or other material advantage) are taken into account.

4.2.5.1.3 Culpable behaviour

Article 2 of the Framework Decision of Organised Crime 2008 obliges member states to define one or both of the following behaviours, in the context of a criminal organisation, as criminal:

> [a] the behaviour of a person, who intentionally and in the knowledge of the aim and the general activity of the criminal organisation or the intention of the organisation, contributes actively to the criminal activities of the organisation, including the provision of information or material resources, the recruitment of

[28] OJ (2008/L 300/42). [29] OJ (2004/L 261/69).

[30] Kreß and Gazeas, 'Organisierte Kriminalität', cited in note 1 above, para. 18: see recital 14; Weißer, 'Angleichung', cited in note 1 above, para. 9: see recital 6.

new members or any kind of financing the activities of the organisation and who appreciates, that the participation supports the provision in criminal activities of the organisation (this is called the 'organisational model');[31] and/or

[b] the behaviour of a person, that insists on making an agreement with one or more persons about the exercise of the activity, that—in case of implementation—matches with the perpetration of a criminal offence named in Article 1; even if the person is not involved into the actual implementation of the activity (this is called the 'conspiracy model').[32]

The organisational model (Article 2(a)) implies an expansion of the sphere of criminality by criminalizing acts carried out separately from punishable offences of the criminal organisation. Beside classic 'aiding', such as providing information or recruiting members, liability is extended to the contribution of a perpetrator. In contrast a criminal offence that is based on the conspiracy model (Article 2(b)) does not require a unified structure: it is sufficient that at least two persons arrange to perpetrate a specific offence with the aim of making profits. It is not necessary that the involved person actually contributes to the implementation of the offence arranged between them.[33]

4.2.5.1.4 Sanctions

Article 3(I) applies to those criminal offences named in Article 2(a) and (b) that attract a minimum sentence of two, and a maximum sentence of five, years. If a member state follows the conspiracy model of Article 2(b), it has the option to set the same range of sentences for the offence and for the criminal offence that depends on the agreement forming the 'conspiracy' (Article 3(I)(b)). Hence Article 3(II) demands the guarantee that committing a criminal offence listed in Article 2 within the scope of a criminal organisation can be seen as an aggravation of the offence. Implementation need not mandate a qualifying fact to be proved in the case. In fact, an additional penalty for aggravation can be imposed within the general sentencing framework.[34] Article 4 allows member states to commute sentences to the full extent of the penalty in cases of serious repentance and for Crown witnesses.

4.2.5.1.5 Responsibility of legal persons

Article 5(I) requires member states to make sure that a legal person can be prosecuted for criminal activity contrary to Article 2: a crime that has been committed by a person for his/her benefit, whether acting alone or as part of a group constituting the legal person, and in the latter case holding a leading position within the legal person. Under Article 6(I) it must be possible to impose proportional and deterrent sanctions against responsible legal persons under Article 5(I) that include criminal or

[31] Kreß and Gazeas, 'Organisierte Kriminalität', cited in note 1 above, para. 18: see recital 10; Weißer, 'Angleichung', cited in note 1 above, para. 9: see recitals 5 and 7.

[32] Kreß and Gazeas, 'Organisierte Kriminalität', cited in note 1 above, para. 18: see recital 16; Weißer, 'Angleichung', cited in note 1 above, para. 9: see recitals 5 and 9.

[33] Weißer, 'Angleichung', cited in note 1 above, para. 9: see recital 9.

[34] Kreß and Gazeas, 'Organisierte Kriminalität', cited in note 1 above, para. 18: see recital 18.

non-criminal fines and other sanctions, for example exclusion from public funds or aid, a temporary or constant prohibition from exercising a commercial activity, judicial supervision, judicially ordered resolution, or the temporary or final closing of facilities that were used for the commitment of the criminal offence.

4.2.5.1.6 Jurisdiction

Article 7(I) obliges member states to ensure that their jurisdiction extends to at least three situations in which the criminal offence contrary to Article 2 has been

(a) totally or partly committed in the national territory, regardless of the place where the criminal organisation has its base of operations or commits its criminal activities;

(b) committed by one of its national subjects/citizens; and/or

(c) committed in favour of a legal person who is settled in the sovereign territory of the member state.

It is worthy of note that member states must extend *outside the EU* their competence to prosecute crimes under Article 2 that were totally or partly committed on their territory with the participation of a foreign criminal organisation.[35]

As long as a member state does not undermine the rights of its citizens, it must lay the foundations in accordance with Article 7(III) for offences committed abroad to be pursued via domestic criminal justice.

4.2.5.2 Absorption of unlawfully acquired assets (Directive 2014/42/EU)

The Stockholm Programme (see section 4.1.2.3 of this chapter) stated that identification of unlawfully acquired assets must improve to remove the financial incentives for criminal networks to commit the related acts. In implementing this part of the Programme European law against skimming off excess profits experienced a significant transformation through Directive 2014/42/EU of the European Parliament and of the Council of 3 April 2014 on the freezing and confiscation of instrumentalities and proceeds of crime in the European Union, which came into force on 19 May 2014.[36] In the view of the EU legislator the hope for profit is the most important force driving TOC. That is why efficient tracing and the freezing and confiscation of instruments and the proceeds of crimes require the most effective measures. The existing regulations for expanded confiscation and the mutual recognition of decisions about securing and confiscation have only limited effect; member state regulations covering securing and confiscation should approximate through accepting minimum rules (Article 1(I)). The responsible authorities should obtain instruments to enable them to determine, secure, manage, and confiscate the profits acquired by the criminal offence.

[35] Ibid, para. 18: see recital 22.

[36] OJ (2014/L 127/39). The directive does not bind Denmark or the UK. See Hecker, *Europäisches Strafrecht*, cited in note 11 above, para. 11: see recital 57ff.; Michael Kilchling, 'Geldwäsche', in Sieber, Satzger, and von Heintschel-Heinegg, *Europäisches Strafrecht*, cited in note 1 above, para. 16: see recital 21.

The concept of absorption of illegal profits from criminal offences should be specified in a way that does not include merely the profits acquired directly from the criminal act but also the indirect advantages that result from a later reinvestment or transformation of direct profits (Articles 2(1) and 3(a)–(k)). 'Profits' must include all items of property including any transformed partly or wholly into other items of property, or any mixed with items of property from licit sources, up to the amount of the total estimated value of the mixed profits. They can also include revenues or other gains that stem from profits of the criminal offences, or items of property in or by which such profits have been transformed, changed, or mixed.

Article 2(2) contains an elongated definition of the term 'items of property' that can be secured and confiscated. This definition extends to legally relevant writs and documents that verify rights to or over items of property. These writs or documents can be financial instruments or instruments that can justify creditor claims and that are normally held by persons involved in the procedure concerned.

In order to fight TOC effectively, on a criminal conviction not just items of property having any connection to a specific criminal offence, but also other items of property that the court views as profits of other criminal offences, should be confiscated ('extended withdrawal'; cf. Article 5(I)). The earlier Council Framework Decision 2005/212/JHA of 24 February 2005 on Confiscation of Crime-Related Proceeds, Instrumentalities and Property provided three instances in which member states could decide on extended confiscation.[37] When implementating the Framework Decision member states have chosen different options that lead to non-uniform concepts of extended confiscation in domestic law. In the view of the European legislator these differences interfere with cross-border cooperation in cases of confiscation. Accordingly, the regulations for extended confiscation should be harmonized in line with a uniform minimum rule set out as a guideline (Article 5(II) Directive 2014/42/EU).

4.2.5.3 Fighting specific outward forms of TOC

4.2.5.3.1 Illegal drug trafficking

Illegal drug trafficking constitutes a main activity of TOC. For this reason the drug policy of the EU includes health-related drug prevention policy programmes and measures for monitoring the trade in raw materials for drugs as well specific instruments against crime involving narcotic drugs.[38] With the cooperation of the justice and home affairs sectors (cf. section 4.2.1 of this chapter) the Council agreed on Joint Action 96/750/JHA concerning the approximation of the laws and practices of the Member States of the European Union to combat drug addiction and to prevent and combat illegal drug trafficking on 17 December 1996.[39] Ex-Article 29 TEU emphasized that prevention and combating illegal drug trafficking are a central aim of the

[37] OJ (2005/L 68/49).

[38] Martin Böse, 'Drogenhandel', in Sieber, Satzger, and von Heintschel-Heinegg, *Europäisches Strafrecht*, cited in note 1 above, para. 20: see recital 3ff.

[39] OJ (1996/L 342/6).

Union. After Article 31(e) TEU the mutual approach of the member states in the fields of police and judicial cooperation in criminal matters (PJCCM; cf. section 2.2 of this chapter) included a step-by-step acceptance of measures to establish minimum rules about characteristic facts of criminal offences and penalties across the range of illegal drug trafficking. Based on this the Council agreed Framework Decision 2004/757/JHA of 25 October 2004, laying down minimum provisions on the constituent elements of criminal acts and penalties in the field of illicit drug trafficking, as regards the definition of drug,[40] in force until further notice. The Framework Decision sets a minimum standard to be met by domestic criminal laws on narcotics.[41] In an October 2011 notification to the Council and Parliament the Commission demanded a more purposeful approach, progressive measures to combat the networks of TOC groups and cross-border drug trafficking more effectively.[42]

4.2.5.3.2 Human trafficking

Human trafficking—a form of modern slavery—is one of the most lucrative and perverse fields of activity of TOC.[43] In a narrow sense human trafficking, which needs to be distinguished from people smuggling ('smuggler and tugboat crime'; see section 4.2.5.3.3 of this chapter), can be described as the transfer of a person against their will by employing violence or menace, making use of a dependence relationship, or trickery. The particular characteristics of human trafficking lie in the outward forms of sex tourism, 'mail-order' marriage, organ trafficking, and the trade in adopted children.

Directive 2011/36/EU of the European Parliament and the Council of 5 April 2011 on preventing and combating trafficking in human beings and protecting its victims came into being on 15 April 2011,[44] and replaced Council Framework Decision 2002/629/JHA of 19 July 2002 on combating trafficking in human beings. The Directive aims to counter human trafficking with a comprehensive criminal definition, which is of integral importance for protecting victims. Under Article 2(I) every member state must take the necessary measures to make sure that the following deliberate acts, including incitement, aiding and attempt (Article 3), are made punishable:

> The recruitment, transportation, shipment, lodging or inclusion of persons, including the delivery or takeover of the control of the persons, through the threat or use of violence or other forms of compulsion, through kidnapping, fraud, illusion, misuse of power or utilization of need for protection or through granting or receipt of

[40] OJ (2004/L 335/8). See M. Böse, 'Drogenhandel', cited in note 38 above, para. 20: see recital 6ff.; Hecker, *Europäisches Strafrecht*, cited in note 11 above, para. 11: see recital 45; Weißer, 'Angleichung', cited in note 1 above, para. 9: see recital 27ff.

[41] See report from the Commission on the implementation of Framework Decision in COM (2009) 669 final.

[42] COM (2011) 689 final.

[43] Barbara Huber, 'Menschenhandel', in Sieber, Satzger, and von Heintschel-Heinegg, *Europäisches Strafrecht*, cited in note 1 above, para. 21: see recital 1; Weißer, 'Angleichung', cited in note 1 above, para. 9: see recital 41.

[44] OJ (2011/L 101/1). See Hecker, *Europäisches Strafrecht*, cited in note 11 above, para. 11: see recital 25ff.; Huber, 'Menschenhandel', cited in note 43 above, para. 21: see recital 19ff.; Weißer, 'Angleichung', cited in note 1 above, para. 9: see recital 47ff.

payments or advantages for obtaining the consent of a person, which has the control over another person, for the purpose of exploitation.

A *special need for protection* occurs if the trafficked person does not have a real or acceptable alternative to submitting to the abuse (Article 2(II)). *Exploitation* includes at minimum prostitution or other forms of sexual exploitation, forced labour or forced services including begging, slavery, or slavery-like practices, serfdom, or the utilization of criminal action, or organ removal (Article 2(III)). The victims' acquiescence in the intended or actual exploitation is *insignificant*, if one of the methods listed in Article 2(I) has been used (Article 2(IV)). Where an act under Article 2(I) affects a child (aged less than 18 years), it must be punishable as human trafficking even if none of the criteria listed in Article 2(I) apply (Article 2(V)). Criminal offences under Article 2 must be punishable with a custodial sentence of up to five years (Article 4(I)). A maximum penalty of ten years must be laid down for particular criminal offences, especially ones directed against children (Article 4(II)(a)) or that were committed within a criminal organisation (Article 4(II)(b)).

The criminal protection of children against sexual exploitation is complemented by Directive 2011/93/EU of the European Parliament and the Council of 13 December 2011 on combating the sexual abuse and sexual exploitation of children and child pornography, and replacing Council Framework Decision 2004/68/JHA, which came into being on 17 December 2011.[45]

4.2.5.3.3 People smuggling

In view of the pressure on the external borders of the EU exerted by high immigration levels, the development of a coordinated asylum, immigration, and border security policy became a core area of European domestic and justice policy. Since the diverging regulations of different member states lead to different loads and inefficiency, only by an agreed procedure can people smuggling be prevented. In addition, the use of penal provisions to fight illegal migration is rightly conceived as a significant control element in European migration policy.[46] The reason is that people smuggling—by which I mean participation in illegal migration—confronts law enforcement agencies with transboundary, organised, perpetrator structures.[47]

At Union level the central legal instrument in the fight against people smuggling is still Framework Decision 2002/946/JI v. 28. 11. 2002 concerning the reinforcement of the criminal framework for the fight against facilitation of unauthorized entry, transit, and residence, which came into force on 6 December 2012.[48] This Framework Decision requires member states to combat actions contrary to

[45] OJ (2011/L 235/1), corrected OJ (2012/L 18/7). See Hecker, *Europäisches Strafrecht*, cited in note 11 above, para. 11: see recital 34ff.; Huber, 'Menschenhandel', cited in note 43 above, para. 23: see recital 39; Weißer, 'Angleichung', cited in note 1 above, para. 9: see recital 63ff.

[46] COM (2000) 757 final, pp. 11.

[47] M. Kilchling and Annette Herz, 'Schleuserkriminalität', in Sieber, Satzger, and von Heintschel-Heinegg, *Europäisches Strafrecht*, cited in note 1 above, para. 22: see recital 2; Wolfgang Oegel, 'Die Internationalität der Schleusenkriminalität', in Günter Gehl (ed.), *Europa im Griff der organisierten Kriminalität*, Weimar, Bertuch, 2006, p. 39ff.

[48] OJ (2002/L 328/01).

Article 1 of Council Directive 2002/90/EC of 28 November 2002 defining the facilitation of unauthorized entry, transit, and residence,[49] defined as the facilitation of the three named forms of smuggling (acts to facilitate illegal immigration) with criminality occurring on the unauthorised crossing of a border in the strict sense or when a network is maintained that exploits human beings. Article 1(III) requires that in all cases all actions that any person committed for financial gain within the context of a criminal organisation should attract imprisonment for a minimum of eight years.

4.2.5.3.4 Forgery of means of payment

The main field of this type of TOC is the production and use of counterfeit money. Counterfeiting of currencies has always been criminal. The EU considers halting the use of counterfeit currency indispensable to maintaining the trust of all citizens and companies in the currency. This applies in particular to the euro, which is the single currency for more than 330 million people and is the second-largest international currency. On 22 May 2014, Directive 2014/62/EU of the European Parliament and the Council of 15.05.2014 on the criminal law protection of the euro and other currencies against counterfeiting, replacing Council Framework Decision 200/383/JI, came into force.[50] Approximation within member states' criminal offences should ensured that the euro and other currencies are effectively protected in the EU regions. The Directive also includes provisions to strengthen the fight against, and better define, such offences, as well as better cooperation strategies for the different law enforcement agencies.

In the field of non-cash financial transactions Framework Decision 2001/413/JI v. 28.5.2001, which came into force on 3 June 2001, lists obligations designed to ensure an equivalent level of safety while strengthening criminal protection against fraud and the counterfeiting of non-cash means of payment.[51]

4.2.5.3.5 Corruption

In view of the global economic interdependence, the fight against corruption has moved from the national level to the European and international levels and expanded to the private sector.[52] This is reflected in EU guidelines in which the Council of Europe, the UN, and OECD provisions against private and public corruption were set out. To combat attacks on the institutions of the Community, with relevance to officer corruption, the Council accepted a protocol to combat active and passive bribery from

[49] OJ (2002/L 328/17). For Directive, see note 44.

[50] OJ (2014/L 151/1). See Lothar Kuhl, 'Geldfälschung', in Sieber, Satzger, and von Heintschel Heinegg, *Europäisches Strafrecht*, cited in note 1 above, para. 14: see recital 3ff.

[51] OJ (2001/L 149/01). See Gerhard Dannecker, 'Einführung von Tatbeständen mit supranationaler Schutzrichtung (Europadelikte)', in Böse, *Europäisches Strafrecht*, cited in note 1 above, para. 8: see recital 16ff.; Bernd-Roland Killmann, 'Unbare Zahlungsmittel', in Sieber, Satzger, and von Heintschel-Heinegg, *Europäisches Strafrecht*, cited in note 1 above, para. 15: see recital 1ff.

[52] Dannecker, 'Europadelikte', cited in note 51 above, para. 8: see recital 79ff.; Barbara Huber, *Combatting Corruption in the European Union*, Cologne, Bundesanzeiger, 2002, p. 95; Killmann, 'Unbare Zahlungsmittel', cited in note 51 above, para. 13: see recital 1ff.

27 January 1996,[53] which came into force on 17 October 2002 together with an agreement on the protection of the financial interests of the EC (the PIF Convention).[54] On 26 May 1997 was adopted a Convention on corruption and with which officials of the European Community or member states of the European Union are involved (EU Convention on corruption),[55] which came into force on 28 September 2005. This Convention led to criminal law sanctions being extended to bribery, to prevent damage to Community financial interests and to ensure that domestic criminal law would extend to bribery of Community officials and officials of other member states. According to the Council corruption in the private sector poses a threat to law-abiding society,[56] as well as distorting competition in relation to the procurement of goods or commercial services, and impeding sound economic development. Framework Decision 2003/568/JI from 22.7.2003 to fight against corruption in the private sector aims to guarantee that in all member states corruption in the private sector is made punishable, that legal persons can be held liable for this offence, and that penalties should be effective and deterrent.

In a Notification on the fight against corruption in the EU from 6 June 2011, the Commission announced that, starting from 2013 at two-year intervals, they will publish an EU anti-corruption report in which the actions of the member states against corruption will be evaluated.[57]

4.2.5.3.6 Attacks on information systems

Electronic information systems are very important for the modern information society. Financial systems, production management functions in companies, air and rail infrastructure, power supply, control of power stations, public administration, military systems, and—in general—the communication infrastructure depend on their functioning. Existing technical security holes provide great scope for manipulation and all sorts of damaging effects, which can be instigated from all over the world over the internet.[58] Offences such as computer espionage (unauthorized intrusion to external computers to investigate foreign data—'hacking'), computer sabotage (damage or destruction of data), computer manipulation (changing data with the aim of influencing the result of a data processing program), and copyright infringement (unauthorized use and exploitation of computer programs and data) are of particular concern. The tools developed for such actions are often the *modus operandi* for the computer-aided committing of fraud, economic crimes, and illegal gambling as well as the spread of illegal material on the internet (e.g. child pornography).

[53] OJ (1996/C 313/02). See Gerhard Dannecker and Roman Leitner (eds), *Handbuch Korruption*, Vienna, Finanzstrafrecht, 2012, pp. 159, 167; Killmann, 'Unbare Zahlungsmittel', cited in note 51 above, para. 13: see recital 3ff.

[54] OJ (1995/C 316/48). See Dannecker, 'Europadelikte', cited in note 51 above, para. 8: see recital 33ff.

[55] OJ (1997/C 195/01). See Dannecker, 'Europadelikte', cited in note 51 above, para. 8: see recital 93ff.

[56] OJ (2003/L 192/54). See Dannecker, 'Europadelikte', cited in note 51 above, para. 8: see recital 97; Killmann, 'Unbare Zahlungsmittel', cited in note 51 above, para. 13: see recital 8ff.

[57] COM (2011) 308 final.

[58] Ulrich Sieber, 'Computerkriminalität', in Sieber, Satzger, and von Heintschel-Heinegg, *Europäisches Strafrecht*, cited in note 1 above, para. 24: see recital 1ff.

The Union considers that attacks on information systems threaten the building of a safe information society. Such attacks are growing, launched by TOC and by terrorists against information systems integral to the critical infrastructure of the member states. Given this assessment of the situation, on 24 February 2005 the Council accepted Framework Decision 2005/222/JI about attacks on information systems,[59] which came into force on 16 March 2005 and, in large parts, went beyond the Council of Europe's Cybercrime Convention of 23 November 2001.[60] On 12 August 2013 the European legislator finally passed Council Directive 2013/40/EU of the European Parliament and the Council relating to attacks against information systems, which came into force on 10 September 2013.[61] This replaced Framework Decision 2005/222/JI of the Council.

A common minimum level of approximation of criminal law should ensure that all attacks on information systems are uncovered, pursued, and avenged with the techniques and methods available. It should achieve a sufficient deterrent effect and mutual prosecution and traceability, which are necessary for international legal assistance.[62]

4.2.5.3.7 Money laundering

Money laundering is the process of hiding the illegal existence, source, or use of money or monetary goods and changes them in such a manner that they seem to be legal.[63] It is clear that the liberalized economic and financial structures of an ever closer Europe have opened up new possibilities for TOC to integrate dirty money in the legal economic circle of the internal market, exploit it, and use it again for illegal activities.[64] Since the beginning of the 1990s, the EU has taken criminal law and other measures to fight money laundering.[65] To their satisfaction these actions can now be brought on a European level. However, it was feared that the aim of completing the internal market had suffered setbacks when member states took different measures to defend their respective national financial sectors.[66]

The minimum definition for money laundering offence laid down by Union law is currently set out in Directive (EU) 2015/849 of the European Parliament and the Council of 20 May 2015 on the prevention of the use of the financial system for the purposes of money laundering or terrorist financing, amending Regulation (EU) No. 648/2012 of the European Parliament and of the Council, and repealing Directive 2005/60/EC of the European Parliament and of the Council and Commission Directive 2006/

[59] OJ (2005/L 69/67). [60] ETS no. 185.

[61] OJ (2013/L 218/08). See Sieber, 'Computerkriminalität', cited in note 58 above, para. 24: see recital 70ff.

[62] See Eric Hilgendorf, 'Tendenzen und Probleme einer Harmonisierung des Internetstrafrechts auf Europäischer Ebene', in Christian Schwarzenegger, Oliver Arter, and Florian Jörg (eds), *Internet-Recht und Strafrecht*, Bern, Stämpfli, 2005, pp. 257 and 271ff.

[63] Dannecker, 'Europadelikte', cited in note 51 above, para. 8: see recital 120.

[64] Arndt Sinn, 'Das Lagebild der OK in der EU-Tendenzen, rechtliche Initiativen und Perspektive einer wirksamen OK-Bekämpfung', in Walter Gropp and Arndt Sinn (eds), *Organisierte Kriminalität und kriminelle Organisationen*, Baden-Baden, Nomos, 2006, pp. 503 and 509ff.

[65] Dannecker, 'Europadelikte', cited in note 51 above, para. 8: see recital 128ff.; Hecker, *Europäisches Strafrecht*, cited in note 11 above, para. 8: see recital 11ff.; Kilchling, 'Geldwäsche', cited in note 36 above, para. 16: see recital 1ff.

[66] Dannecker, 'Europadelikte', cited in note 51 above, para. 8: see recital 129.

70/EC (fourth Money Laundering Directive);[67] the directive takes over regulation of criminal law from the third Money Laundering Directive.[68]

The specific risk potential of money laundering arises from criminal proceeds infiltrating the legal economic circuit though an illusion. Article 1(II)(a)–(c) adopted partially overlapping criteria (elements of concealment, intentional offence, and the offence of receiving stolen goods with other assets) but made the illusion element of money laundering (whether objective or subjective) the normative element.[69] Under Article 3(5)(a)–(f) such actions are classified by the member states as offences predicate of money laundering. In addition to criminal penalties, ensuring identification and confiscation of the proceeds (skimming of excess profits) are other instruments in the fight against money laundering (see section 4.2.5.2 of this chapter).

4.3 Institutionalizing Cooperation against TOC

In view of the fact that criminal networks operate across borders the EU agencies Europol and Eurojust play a central role in international cooperation to enforce the law.[70]

4.3.1 Europol

Europol supports and reinforces actions by the responsible authority in the member states and facilitates their cooperation in the prevention and the fight against TOC, terrorism, and other forms of serious crime, when two or more member states are affected. The focus of its work is to collect, store, process, analyse, and exchange information and findings ('intelligence work') as well as to inform and support the responsible authority in the member states. With the help of Europol, the national investing authorities should gain specialized knowledge, be offered consultations and strategic insights, and receive general reports on the state of work submitted. Europol fulfils this task with the help of an automated collection of information, the Europol information and analysis system.[71] Europol has no independent executive or investigatory power. Article 88(III) TFEU allows Europol to take operational measures only in connection and consultation with the authority of the affected member state. *De facto*,

[67] OJ (2015/L 141/73).

[68] See COM (2013) 45 final. On 20 April 2015, the Council accepted a previously negotiated compromise on the fourth Money Laundering Directive.

[69] Bernd Hecker, 'Die gemeinschaftlichen Strukturen der Geldwäschestrafbarkeit', in Thomas Görgen *et al.* (eds), *Festschrift für Arthur Kreuzer*, Frankfurt am Main, Verlag für Polizeiwissenschaft, 2008, p. 216; Joachim Vogel, 'Geldwäsche—ein europaweit harmonisierter Straftatbestand?', (1997) 109 *Zeitschrift für die gesamte Strafrechtswissenschaft*, 335, p. 339.

[70] COM (2012) 673 final, p. 6. See Satzger, *International and European Criminal Law*, cited in note 23 above, para. 8: see recital 3ff. and for more detail, Robert Esser, 'Die Rolle von Europol und Eurojust bei der Bekämpfung von Terrorismus und OK', in Arndt Sinn and Mark A. Zöller (eds), *Neujustierung des Strafrechts durch Terrorismus und Organisierte Kriminalität*, Heidelberg, C.F. Müller, 2012, p. 61.

[71] Esser, ibid, pp. 61, 70; Dietrich Neumann, 'Europol', in Sieber, Satzger, and von Heintschel-Heinegg, *Europäisches Strafrecht*, cited in note 1 above, para. 44: see recitals 25ff. and 29ff.; Satzger, *International and European Criminal Law*, cited in note 23 above, para. 8: see recital 7ff.

Europol is often part of 'Joint Investigation Teams' and for that reason part of the operative missions of the national police and customs office.

Real-life examples include the coordination of controlled deliveries (drug deals monitored by the police) across Europe, support in task forces of the EU Baltic States against traffic in vehicles, and targeted combat of serious and organised crime and their infrastructure in the course of 'Operation Archimedes', which was coordinated by Europol in September 2014 and in which more han 20,000 police and security officers in 34 countries were involved.[72]

4.3.2 Eurojust

The task of Eurojust—based on Europol analyses and in close collaboration with the European Judicial Network—is to facilitate the optimal coordination of action for investigations and prosecutions, to simplify criminal investigations in transnational criminality, and to simplify the execution of letters rogatory.[73] The responsibility of Eurojust ranges across all forms of crime that fall within their competence. Eurojust can, for example, encourage the competent authority to carry out investigations to establish criminal facts, to start a prosecution, or to agree on the acquisition of the necessary investigation or prosecution by another member state. The agency supports the coordination of investigations by member states, assists in the formation of joint investigation teams, receives requests for assistance, and provides for the exchange of all information that is deemed useful for the optimum performance of tasks. The national members provide for reciprocal notification of member state competent authorities about investigations and prosecutions of which Eurojust has knowledge and which concern the member states.

Currently Eurojust is a pure service and coordination centre. The agency could also evolve towards a European prosecution, as envisaged in Article 86 TFEU.[74]

4.4 Final Observations

Since the middle of the 1990s common tools have been created in the EU to protect society and the European economy against serious and organised crime. The task now is to consolidate the *acquis communautaire* thus created under the umbrella of the PJCC, to implement, and continuously to evaluate.

[72] For this and more activities see the annual reports of Europol, available at: http://www.europol.europa.eu.

[73] Esser, 'Die Rolle von Europol und Eurojust', cited in note 70 above, pp. 61 and 78ff.; Michael Grotz, 'Eurojust', in Sieber, Satzger, and von Heintschel-Heinegg, *Europäisches Strafrecht*, cited in note 1 above, para. 45: see recital 8ff.; Satzger, *International and European Criminal Law*, cited in note 23 above, para. 8: see recital 12ff.

[74] On the proposal for a Council regulation on the establishment of the European Public Prosecutor, see COM (2013)534 final and Robert Esser, 'Die Europäische Staatsanwaltschaft: Eine Herausforderung für die Strafverteidigung', (2014) *Strafverteidiger*, 494, 496ff.; Hecker, *Europäisches Strafrecht*, cited in note 11 above, para. 14: see recital 40ff.; Edward Schramm, 'Auf dem Weg zur Europäischen Staatsanwaltschaft', (2014) *Juristenzeitung*, 749ff.

TOC continues to pose a significant threat to the internal security of the EU and can have a destabilizing effect on third countries.[75] The EU is therefore called upon to continuously adapt its response to this threat and to coordinate measures within and outside its borders. In this effort operational cooperation between the authorities of the member states plays a central role. The trust between these authorities should be strengthened to improve the use of joint investigation teams when they are required. The exchange of information between the law enforcement authorities of the member states and EU agencies should be intensified and made more effective.

Criminal organisations are guided by big profits, which they achieve through smuggling, corruption, financial crime, and other criminal activities. Combating these incentives and protecting the licit economy against smuggling of illegal income needs greater effort. Directive 2014/42/EU on the freezing and confiscation of the proceeds of crime in the EU (see section 4.2.5.2 of this chapter) must be implemented immediately.

Asset recovery offices, prosecution authorities, courts, and public authorities should extend their cooperation to improve the tracing of assets.

Given the likely increase in cyber-attacks over the next few years, the operational capacity to combat cybercrime should be strengthened. On 11 January 2013, the EU set up a European centre for fighting cybercrime at Europol ('European cybercrime centre'). In its first year alone the centre proved its worth by supporting criminal investigations conducted by member states in matters ranging from fraud to sexual abuse of children on the internet. The future role of the EU is to encourage member states to develop their ability to combat crime. Ideally, all member states should have a centre to combat cybercrime. The Union has already agreed to a tightening of laws against cybercrime (see section 4.2.5.3.7 of this chapter), which must be implemented with haste. For an effective approach in this area, it is also necessary to intensify cooperation with the private sector. The effective fight against all types of TOC remains, in the future, a central task of the international collaborative criminal justice of the Union. European criminal policy is facing the challenge of striking an equitable balance between the interests of ensuring an effective criminal justice system on one hand, and the protection of civil rights through the rule of law on the other.[76]

[75] See for this and the following COM (2014) 154 final, 'An open and secure Europe making it happen'.

[76] See 'Manifest for the European Criminal Law', which was published by the European Criminal Policy Initiative, (2013) *Zeitschrift für Internationale Strafrechtsdogmatik*, 412 (English version in (2011) *European Criminal Law Review*, 86ff.). See also Satzger, *International and European Criminal Law*, cited in note 23 above, para. 7: see recital 53ff.

5

Transnational Organised Crime and Terrorism

Bettina Weißer

5.1 Historical Evolution of Terrorism

5.1.1 Eighteenth- and nineteenth-century precedents

The roots of the term 'terrorism' can be traced back to the aftermath of the French Revolution when the general prosecutor of Paris, Maximilian de Robespierre, installed a regime of terror (*régime de la terreur*, 1792–94)[1] in order to regain rule and order in the revolutionized French society. Whilst this first occurrence of the term terrorism is linked to a state-governed regime terrorizing civil society in order to regain political order, the following historical cornerstones of terrorism are linked to movements that were aimed at the disturbance or destruction of existing state orders.

In the nineteenth century, anarchist movements evolved as a first wave of transnational terrorism.[2] The anarchist movement was driven by political objectives: the prevailing political order was to be destroyed. Official governments maintaining an unfair distribution of goods and power were to be eliminated and replaced by social groups and their individual members agreeing on the rules they wanted to govern their lives. The protagonists of the anarchist theory were active in numerous countries and inspired themselves mutually: Nechayev (1847–82), Kropotkin (1842–1921), and Bakunin (1814–76) in Russia, Proudhon (1809–65) in France,[3] and other theorists in Spain, Italy, the Balkans, the Americas (United States and other), and Asia.[4] After the invention of dynamite by Alfred Nobel (1866), the protagonists of the anarchist movement directed bomb attacks on heads of states (for example the assassination of Tsar Alexander II in 1881; attempts on the German Kaiser, the Italian King, and the Spanish King in 1878; assassination of the Spanish Prime Minister and the Italian King in 1897, of Empress Elisabeth of Austria in 1898, and of US President William McKinley in 1901)[5] and other important officials (the police chief of Frankfurt, 1885). These terrorist attacks were part of a 'propaganda by the deed' that was meant not only to spread fear and terror amongst political leaders but also to inform and teach

[1] Bruce Hoffman, *Inside Terrorism*, New York, Columbia University Press, 2006, p. 3.

[2] David C. Rapoport, 'The four waves of modern terrorism', in Steven M. Chermak and Joshua D. Freilich (eds), *Transnational Terrorism*, Farnham, Ashgate 2013, pp. 46–73 at pp. 47 and 50.

[3] Proudhon coined the anarchists' popular maxim 'property is theft'.

[4] For details see Richard Jensen, 'Daggers, rifles and dynamite: anarchist terrorism in nineteenth century Europe', (2004) 16 *Terrorism and Political Violence* 116–53, p. 120; Gus Martin, *Understanding Terrorism*, 3rd edn, SAGE Publications 2010, pp. 216ff.; Rapoport, 'The four waves', cited in note 2 above, p. 7.

[5] For details see Jensen, 'Daggers, rifles and dynamite', cited in note 4 above, p. 134.

the society about the movement's goals.[6] The selection of victims was based on their symbolic value—the more prominent and important in society, the more attractive a person became as a possible target.

One of the main features of anarchist terrorism is this restricted use of violence against political leaders[7]—illustrated by the fact that an attempt to kill Tsar Alexander II was abandoned when the perpetrators realized that the bomb would also injure his children.

5.1.2 Nationalist-separatist terrorism

After the Second World War the distinction between terrorism and liberation movements emerged in international debate. In many countries, opposition against colonial powers sprang up. The anti-colonial groups resorted more and more to the use of violence in the struggle for liberation of their countries from colonial powers. Yet in spite of the use of violence, the actors held that they pursued the legitimate ends of liberation movements and thus were not terrorists but freedom fighters.[8] It is this anti-colonial movement that generated the conundrum of a distinction between good and bad violence—between criminal terrorism and legitimate liberation movements.[9]

Some of the nationalist-separatist movements succeeded in freeing their countries from colonial authority and former terrorists/freedom fighters assumed leading roles in the newly established domestic legal orders. For example, the Irgun in Palestine committed terrorist acts in a fight against the British colonial power in order to gain legal authority over that territory.[10] Finally the British gave in and declared their withdrawal from Palestine. When the state of Israel was founded on 15 May 1948, Menachem Begin, the leader of the Irgun, became a member of the Israeli parliament (Knesset). Later on, he even became Prime Minister of Israel.

This is only one example of a national-separatist terrorist movement that achieved its goals. Other national-separatist powers succeeded in Kenya, Cyprus, Algeria, etc.[11] The same is true—although only partially—for the IRA (Irish Republican Army), the ETA (Euskadi Ta Askatasuna, the Basque separatist movement), and the PLO (Palestine Liberation Organization),[12] which—to different degrees—at least achieved

[6] The term was coined by the Italian anarchist Carlo Pisacane (1818–57). It became a famous legitimizing label for violent attacks against political leaders. See also Alex P. Schmid, 'The links between transnational organized crime and terrorist crimes', (1996) 2 *Transnational Organized Crime*, 40–82, p. 56.

[7] Speaking of 'traditional terrorism', Walter Laqueur, 'Terrorism: a brief history', (2007) *eJournal USA*, 20–23, p. 22.

[8] Compare Rapoport, 'The four waves', cited in note 2 above, p. 11.

[9] See section 2.2.2 of this chapter.

[10] The terrorist acts targeted infrastructure representing the British authorities, such as immigration and land registry offices. Well known is the bombing of the King David Hotel in Jerusalem (1946) that cost the lives of ninety-one people. The hotel was chosen because British government authorities resided there.

[11] Further examples are the Front de Libération National Corse and the Front de Libération de Quebec. For details see Hoffman, *Inside Terrorism*, cited in note 1 above, p. 53.

[12] The PLO is an umbrella organisation of numerous bodies fighting for the Palestinian population, e.g. Fatah, Hamas, Al Aqsa Brigades. For details see Hoffman, *Inside Terrorism*, cited in note 1 above, p. 71; James M. Lutz and Brenda J. Lutz, *Global Terrorism*, 3rd edn, Abingdon, Routledge, 2013, p. 125.

some level of recognition and protection of their rights as separate national/ethnic groups.[13] An explanation of the success of such nationalist-separatist movements might be that they can sometimes rely on the tacit agreement of parts of the population. In their violent acts, they communicate a sense of self-assertion by certain parts of the citizenry who (in some cases only surreptitiously, in others openly) favour their goals. Terrorist attacks are seen as unwanted but necessary acts of wrongdoing in order to gain enough public consideration for a population that it represents and that suffers under an illegitimate government. Once the group's political influence is manifest, terrorist acts are no longer needed.[14]

5.1.3 Social revolutionary terrorism

The first terror wave of the anarchist movement was at the same time a first manifestation of social revolutionary terrorism, which was followed by many social-revolutionary terrorist movements. Triggered by the opposition against the Vietnam war, social-revolutionary movements emerged in the 1960s and 1970s: the Montoneros in Argentina, the Weathermen in the United States, GRAPO (Grupos de Resistencia Antifascista Primero de Octubre) and FRAP (Frente Revolucionario Antifascista y Patriota) in Spain, Action Directe in France, the RAF (Rote Armee Fraktion) and the Bewegung 2. Juni in Germany, the Brigate Rosse in Italy.[15] They shared a rejection of the imperialistic Western world, mostly represented by the United States as the dominant international player. Also, they connected with the PLO, since they understood the PLO's fight for land for the Palestinians as a parallel to the left-wing fight against capitalistic domestic establishments. Apart from this, the PLO had already gained some 'expertise' in the commission of terrorist acts. Terrorists from all over the world obtained training in PLO training camps in the Middle East—the money paid for the training funded the activities of the PLO. In contrast to the partial success of the PLO, social-revolutionary terrorist movements in Europe were not able to gain political power and finally ceased to exist. The leaders of the German RAF, for example, committed suicide in a concerted action in prison in the year 1977. Yet by that time European societies had already reacted to the terrorist threat with numerous legislative acts (e.g. granting law enforcement authorities far-reaching means of investigation) that are still in force.[16] This was only the starting point of a continuing development: as terrorist activities evolve, so do anti-terrorist laws on the domestic and the international law level (see section 5.2.1 of this chapter).

[13] In the aftermath of the Six-Day War in 1967 that ended in the occupation of the West Bank, the Gaza Strip, the Golan Heights, and the Sinai Peninsula by Israel, the PLO resorted to terrorist attacks for a longer period of time. More recently, the PLO began to take part in negotiations with the Israeli government and finally gained autonomy over Palestinian territory: for details see Lutz and Lutz, ibid, p. 125. On 22 November 1974 the PLO was afforded 'non-state observer' status by the United Nations (A/RES/3237 (XXIX)). On 29 November 2012 the PLO gained the status 'observer state' (A/RES/67/19).

[14] See the case study on the PLO in Lutz and Lutz, *Global Terrorism*, cited in note 12 above, p. 125.

[15] Ibid, Ch. 7; Martin, *Understanding Terrorism*, cited in note 4 above, p. 235.

[16] For details see Anna Oehmichen, *Terrorism and Anti-Terrorism Legislation: The Terrorised Legislator?*, Mortsel, Belgium, Intersentia, 2009, Chs 4–9.

5.1.4 Religious terrorism

Fundamentalist terrorists exist in various religious groups, from Aum Shinrikyo in Japan, to Islamic and Jewish religious fanatics, to the Christian Patriots in the United States of America. All of them—and many more—have committed serious terrorist attacks on those they perceive to be non-believers. Contemporary examination of terrorist phenomena mostly centres on terrorist groups that claim to act in the name of Islam. The Al-Qaeda attacks on the World Trade Center on 11 September 2001 are still the hallmark of a new dimension of religiously motivated terrorism. They were followed by numerous attacks committed by Islamic fundamentalists: in Madrid (2004), Bali (2005), London (2005), Mumbai (2008), Paris (January and November 2015), Tunisia (2015) and Brussels (2016).

Nowadays, the most prominent religiously motivated terror group is the 'Islamic State of Iraq and the Levant' (ISIL). The group aims to conquer territory in order to establish a 'Caliphate', a religious state that obeys the rules of *shari'a* and is dominated by its religious leaders. ISIL already controls certain territories in Iraq, Syria, and smaller parts of other neighbouring countries. The group claims that its final goal is to establish a world-wide Caliphate that would be ruled exclusively by ISIL's religious leaders (the most prominent being Abu Bakr al-Baghdadi). The group renamed itself 'Islamic State' in 2014—expressing that it no longer limits itself to the territory of Iraq and Syria but extends its claims of power to further countries (for example Lebanon, Libya, Nigeria, and the Yemen, where the group has already gained control over certain territories)—and underlining that in the end it strives for a world-wide Caliphate obeying the Islamic State's orders.

The prevailing feature of this form of terrorism is that it aims explicitly at the indiscriminate killing of as many 'infidel' as possible whilst the perpetrators themselves are willing to sacrifice their own lives in the attack. It is one of the major problems in countering religious terrorism that the alleged metaphysical justification for terrorist acts makes worldly estimations of good and evil, of crime and terror, inapplicable. Religious terrorists play by different rules. Ordinary categories of wrongdoing and guilt cannot prevent them from planning and committing terrorist acts. A person who believes in a reward after the end of life on Earth cannot be deterred from committing terrorist acts by the threat of any 'worldly' punishment.[17] What is more, even the knowledge of certain death cannot influence convinced religious terrorists—they believe that martyrdom will bring them to Paradise even sooner.

5.1.5 Concluding considerations

Three conclusions can be drawn from this brief introduction to the historical evolution of terrorism: first, terrorist groups cannot always be classified into one of the mentioned categories. Some of them have characteristics of different 'types' of terrorism. Not only is the Islamic State religiously motivated, for example, but it also aims

[17] Javaid Rehman, 'Islam, terrorism and international law', in Ben Saul (ed.), *Research Handbook on International Law and Terrorism*, Cheltenham, Edward Elgar Publishing, 2014, pp. 177–91, at p. 180.

at a completely new society that will be dominated by religious leaders only—in a way, the Islamic State can be seen as a revolutionary group. The terrorist attack by Anders Breivik that cost the lives of seventy-seven people in Norway in 2011, on the other hand, was motivated by religious hatred of Muslims and at the same time represented a very strong nationalist and xenophobic attitude. Religious motivations as well as an ultra-right-wing political conviction characterize this perpetrator.

Also, the Irgun (see section 5.1.2 of this chapter) can be seen as a nationalist–separatist movement fighting for independence from the British authorities, and at the same time the new state was dedicated to the Jewish people—making the Jewish faith the most distinctive feature of the Irgun movement.

The second conclusion can be drawn by considering the outcome of the different terrorist movements: it can be observed that social-revolutionary terrorism seems to have a tendency to fail, whilst national-separatist movements sometimes succeed in gaining control of certain territories (for details see sections 5.1.2 and 3 of this chapter).

The third conclusion shows a drastic paradigm change in the use of violence. Whilst early terrorist movements selected their victims carefully and tended to restrain the use of violence, nowadays terrorist acts deploy violence indiscriminately and seek to hit as many victims as possible and to cause as impressive damage as possible. The victims are no longer targeted because of any personal features, but as means to convey a particular message to society as a whole.

5.2 Concept of Terrorism

The historical introduction has shown that terrorism appears in various forms. This section of the chapter seeks to elaborate on definitions of terrorism: international law instruments on terrorism created by the United Nations (in section 5.2.1.1), by the Council of Europe (in 5.2.1.2), and by the European Union (in 5.2.1.3) are analysed in order to find the common characteristics of terrorist crimes. Section 5.2.2 is dedicated to the remaining definitional problems concerning terrorism.

5.2.1 The international law on terrorism

5.2.1.1 United Nations anti-terrorism law

The United Nations concluded a number of conventions on specific aspects of terrorism in a 'sectoral' approach.[18] The earliest conventions deal with crimes committed on board aircraft: the Tokyo Convention (1963) on Offences and Certain Other Acts Committed on Board Aircraft and the Hague Convention (1970) for the Suppression of Unlawful Seizure of Aircrafts do not explicitly address terrorism but lay a duty on the member states to establish jurisdiction for crimes committed on board aircraft.[19] The

[18] See Samuel Witten, 'The International Convention for the Suppression of Terrorist Bombings', in Saul, *Research Handbook*, cited in note 17 above, pp. 136–62, at p. 154.

[19] Tokyo Convention: UNTS Vol. 704, 220ff. Hague Convention: UNTS Vol. 860, 106ff. This also holds true for the most recent (2010) Convention on the Suppression of Unlawful Acts Relating to International Civil Aviation, ICAO Doc. 9960. However, the convention is not yet in force.

1979 Convention against the Taking of Hostages is the first convention that mentions the phenomenon 'terrorism'.[20] The preamble states a necessity to prosecute the taking of hostages as 'manifestations of international terrorism', although the description of the offence contains no explicit reference to terrorism. Nevertheless, the characteristic feature of terrorist crimes, namely the perpetrator's aim 'to compel ... a State, an international intergovernmental organization, a natural or juridical person, or a group of persons, to do or abstain from doing any act' forms part of the description of the offence in Article 1 of the Convention.

The 1997 Terrorist Bombing Convention explicitly addresses terrorism,[21] though a specific 'terrorist' feature is not included in the description of the offence in Article 2 of the Convention. An offence under Article 2 is committed if the perpetrator delivers, places, discharges, or detonates an explosive with the intent to cause death, serious bodily injury, or extensive destruction. Article 5 stipulates that member states are obliged to penalize such crimes in their domestic laws,

> ... in particular where [the crime] is intended or calculated to provoke a state of terror in the general public or in a group of persons or particular persons.

The 1999 Convention for the Suppression of the Financing of Terrorism requires member states to punish the financing of crimes that are listed in existing international treaties (amongst them the UN Conventions on Terrorist Bombings and Aircraft Hijacking).[22] Moreover, the Convention contains a first notion of terrorist crimes in general: according to Article 2(1)(b), the Convention also encompasses the financing of

> any other act intended to cause death or serious bodily injury to a civilian, or to any other person not taking an active part in the hostilities in a situation of armed conflict, when the purpose of such act, by its nature or context, is to intimidate a population, or to compel a government or an international organization to do or to abstain from doing any act.

This attempt at definition already addresses the characteristic elements of terrorism: terrorist crimes are understood as acts that are intended to bring about a given immediate result—the death or serious bodily injury of another person. In stating that the intended victim should be a civilian, the Convention excludes attacks against combatants in armed conflict from the ambit of terrorist crimes.[23] Furthermore, a specific *mens rea* is required for terrorist crimes: terrorist acts must be aimed at the intimidation of a population or the putting of pressure on a government or an international organisation.

The 2005 Convention for the Suppression of Acts of Nuclear Terrorism follows the same path:[24] it requires member states to penalize the possession or use of radioactive material with intent to cause serious bodily injury or death, or substantial damage to

[20] UNTS Vol. 1316, 206ff.
[21] International Convention for the Suppression of Terrorist Bombings, UNTS Vol. 2149, 256ff.
[22] UNTS Vol. 2178, 197ff.
[23] See section 5.2.1.4 of this chapter.
[24] UNTS Vol. 2445, 89ff.

property or to the environment. Article 2(1)(b)(iii) extends the Convention's ambit to the use of radioactive material with the intent to compel a natural or legal person, an international organisation or a state to do or refrain from doing any act—thereby adopting the approach of the 1999 Convention for the Suppression of the Financing of Terrorism.[25]

Apart from these UN conventions, the UN Security Council adopted a number of resolutions in respect of terrorist crimes. In the wake of the shocking terrorist attacks on the World Trade Center and the Pentagon on 11 September 2001, UN Security Council Resolution No. 1368 (2001) of 12 September 2001 was the first international reaction and contained a general commitment to bring terrorists to justice. The subsequent UN Security Council Resolution No. 1373 (2001) of 28 September 2001 was aimed in particular at combating the financing of terrorist activities and obliged member states to prevent and suppress the preparation and financing of terrorist acts by the freezing of assets and other measures.[26] The same is true of the more recent Security Council Resolutions No. 2161 (2014) of 17 June 2014 and No. 2178 (2014) of 24 September 2014: Resolution No. 2161 imposes manifold obligations on UN member states concerning members and supporters of Al-Qaeda (e.g. asset-freezing or travel bans). Resolution No. 2178 (2014) relates to terrorism in general and requires member states to criminalize the (attempt to) travel abroad for the purpose of the perpetration, planning, preparation of, or participation in, terrorist acts, or the providing or receiving of terrorist training. The support of another's travel as well as the funding of such acts must also be penalized, under paragraph 6(a)–(c). Although these Security Council Resolutions impose immediate legislative duties on the member states,[27] they do not contain an explicit definition of the terrorist acts that must be prevented by the required measures.[28]

In concentrating on certain manifestations of terrorist activity, the UN managed to agree on numerous conventions that require the member states to criminalize certain kinds of terrorist crime. This sectoral approach allowed the UN to work their way around a comprehensive definition of terrorism. Still, efforts have been undertaken in order to reach a general definition of terrorism on the UN level: in 1996, the UN General Assembly established an Ad Hoc Committee to elaborate an international

[25] Another interesting feature of this Convention is the regulation in Art. 4(2), excluding actions in an armed conflict from the ambit of the convention. The law of armed conflict shall be governed exclusively by international humanitarian law (see section 5.2.2.1 of this chapter and note 60 below). Furthermore, the Convention does not apply to the use or threat to use nuclear weapons by states: Art 4(4).

[26] For details see Ben Saul, 'Criminality and terrorism', in Ana María Salinas de Frías, Katja L. H. Samuel, and Nigel D. White (eds), *Counter Terrorism*, Oxford, OUP, 2012, pp. 133–70, at pp. 144–7.

[27] The resolutions were enacted as measures under Chapter VII of the Charter of the United Nations, since stipulating immediate legislative duties for the member states. Their consequently binding character led to criticism in the international debate, as some scholars took the view that the Security Council did not have a right to impose such duties on the member states. For details about this debate see Matthew Happold, 'Security Council Resolution 1373 and the Constitution of the United Nations', (2003) 16 *Leiden Journal of International Law*, 593–610; Stefan Talmon, 'The Security Council as world legislature', (2005) 99 *American Journal of International Law*, 175–93.

[28] This also holds true of numerous further UN documents that address terrorism: compare UN SC Res. No. 1540 (2004) of 28 April 2004; UN SC Res. No. 1624 (2005) of 14 September 2005; UN SC Res. No. 2133 (2014) of 27 January 2014; UN GA Res. No. 60/288 of 8 September 2006; UN GA Res. No. 66/105 of 9 December 2011; UN GA Res. No. 66/282 of 29 June 2012; UN GA Res. No. 68/178 of 18 December 2013.

convention concerning international terrorism.[29] In the year 2010, the Committee arrived at a Draft Comprehensive Terrorism Convention containing the following definition of terrorism:

> 1. Any person commits an offence within the meaning of the present Convention if that person, by any means, unlawfully and intentionally, causes:
>   (a) death or serious bodily injury to any person; or
>   (b) serious damage to public or private property, including a place of public use, a State or government facility, a public transportation system, an infrastructure facility or to the environment; or
>   (c) damage to property, places, facilities or systems referred to in paragraph 1(b) of the present article resulting or likely to result in major economic loss,
>
> when the purpose of the conduct, by its nature or context, *is to intimidate a population, or to compel a Government or an international organization to do or to abstain from doing any act. …*[30]

The threatening of as well as attempts and participation in such acts are also covered. In brief: the *actus reus* required is an act of violence with serious consequences to the physical integrity of (a) person(s) or to important private or public property. The *mens rea* required is twofold: apart from the ordinary intent to commit the criminal act, a *dolus specialis* requirement entails the specific terrorist impetus of the crime: the act must aim at intimidating a population or at compelling a government or an international organisation to do or to abstain from doing any act.

The elements of this definition reflect some of the regulations in the UN Conventions mentioned earlier in this section. It has to be borne in mind, though, that complete congruence between the existing conventions and a future umbrella convention on terrorism in general need not be achieved. The goal of a comprehensive terrorism convention consists of the creation of a generally acceptable description of terrorism as such. This does not preclude that certain manifestations of terrorist crimes are specified in sectoral conventions. But a comprehensive terrorism convention would finally establish the so-far-missing foundation for the manifold conventions on single aspects of terrorist crimes.

Although it can be assumed that the elements of the Ad Hoc Committee's definition are agreeable, the work on a comprehensive convention seems to be stuck in a gridlock—the last meeting of the UN Ad Hoc Committee took place in 2013—and it has already been announced that the Committee will not meet in 2016 either.[31] It seems that the delicate matter of defining terrorism on the UN level has been put on the farthest-back burner. The main reason for this standoff lies in the unresolved question whether excessive use of force exerted by a state can amount to terrorism.[32] This controversy on the definition of state terror is complemented by a second unresolved question, regarding the demand for an explicit exclusion of liberation movements

[29] UN GA Res. No. 51/210 of 17 December 1996.

[30] UN GA, A/C.6/65/L.10 of 3 November 2010, p. 6.

[31] See http://legal.un.org/committees/terrorism/, accessed 29 February 2016.

[32] See the comments of delegations to the draft Comprehensive Terrorism Convention, UN GA, A/C.6/65/L.10 of 3 November 2010, No. 8, p. 22.

from any definition of terrorism.[33] The debate on these questions is still going on. Still, a solution is not likely to be forthcoming any time soon. In line with this presumption is the fact that the most recent UN Security Council Resolution mentioned above, No. 2178 (2014) regarding terrorist 'travellers' does not contain a single word about what exactly is meant by the term terrorism.[34]

5.2.1.2 *Council of Europe*

On the regional level, the 2005 Council of Europe Convention on the Prevention of Terrorism follows the same approach as the UN instruments:[35] Article 1 of the Convention defines a terrorist crime as an offence described in earlier international treaties that are listed in the Convention's appendix (for example the UN Hague Convention of 16 December 1970, and the UN Terrorist Financing Convention of 9 December 1999). The Council of Europe Convention requires the criminalization of public provocation to commit terrorist offences (Article 5), of recruitment and training for terrorism (Articles 6, 7) , and of several ancillary offences. Again, the Convention itself does not provide a general definition of terrorism.

5.2.1.3 *European Union*

The main instrument concerning terrorism on the European Union level is the Framework Decision 2002/475/JHA on combating terrorism.[36] It lists specific crimes (e.g. attacks upon a person's life or physical integrity, taking of hostages, seizure of aircraft, interfering with or disrupting the supply of water, power, or any other fundamental resource) that 'given their nature or context, may seriously damage a country or an international organisation'. These crimes shall be deemed terrorist offences if they are

> committed with the aim of:
> — seriously intimidating a population, or
> — unduly compelling a Government or international organisation to perform or abstain from performing any act, or
> — seriously destabilising or destroying the fundamental political, constitutional, economic or social structures of a country or an international organisation.

[33] Ibid, No. 11, p. 22. Compare also Kai Ambos and Anina Timmermann, 'Terrorism and customary international law', in Saul, *Research Handbook*, cited in note 17 above, pp. 20–38, at p. 33.

[34] UN Resolution 2178, adopted on 24 September 2014. The Resolution requires the member states to penalize the facilitation of another person's travel to a foreign country for terrorist purposes. Such purpose can be confined to merely preparation of terrorist acts or even receiving terrorist training: S/RES/2178 (2014), p. 5, para. 6(c).

[35] ETS No. 196, of 16 May 2005.

[36] Council Framework Decision 2002/475/JHA of 13 June 2002 on combating terrorism, OJ, 22/6/2002, L 164/3. The Framework Decision was amended by Council Framework Decision 2008/919/JHA of 28 November 2008, OJ, 9/12/2008, L 330/21. The amendments require the member states to criminalize public provocation to commit a terrorist offence, recruitment for terrorism, training for terrorism, and several modes of participation (aiding, abetting, inciting, attempting). The amendments do not influence the overall definition of terrorism as provided by the Framework Decision of 2002. For a recent report on the implementation of the 2008 requirements in the member states see Com. (2014) 554 final of 5/9/2014.

Like the instruments on the European Council and UN levels, the European Union Framework Decision relates to certain listed offences. They assume terrorist character by the familiar *mens rea* component: an intention to spread fear and/or put pressure on a government or the social fabric as a whole. The third aim mentioned, however, envisages an additional form of terrorist goal: the will to destroy or seriously damage fundamental political, constitutional, economic, or social structures of a state or an international organisation.

5.2.1.4 Conclusion

Despite the complex framework of international legislation on terrorism, to date no detailed, internationally acknowledged definition of terrorism exists.[37] However, the paramount question of how to define terrorism does not remain entirely unresolved. The international instruments are converging over at least some of the main features of terrorist acts. Common denominators of terrorist acts are the unlawful use of violence that results in serious physical harm or death. Only some of the conventions addressing terrorist offences (Terrorist Bombing Convention, Maritime and Aviation Convention)[38] also define damage to (public) property as a possible target of terrorist crimes.

The most characteristic feature of a terrorist attack is that the perpetrators aim at affecting another (or a greater) group of people than the immediate victims that are actually targeted.[39] The terrorist's specific intent is to intimidate, to spread terror and fear amongst a population, and/or to put a state, an international organisation or even the whole social fabric under pressure.[40]

This terrorist intent must be distinguished from the traditional approach that terrorism is characterized by the pursuance of a specific (political, ethnic, moral, religious, or other) motive.[41] Such motivation does not form part of the characteristics of terrorist crimes that international legislators so far consent to. This is not

[37] For a different view see Antonio Cassese arguing that a crime of international terrorism in fact does exist: 'The multifaceted criminal notion of terrorism in international law', (2006) 4 *Journal of International Criminal Justice*, 933–58.

[38] See Art. 2(1)(a) of the 1997 Convention for the Suppression of Terrorist Bombings, UNTS Vol. 2149, 285; Art. 3(1)(c), (d), (e) of the 1988 Convention for the Suppression of Unlawful Acts against the Safety of Maritime Navigation, UNTS Vol. 1678, 225; Art. 1 of the 2010 Convention on the Suppression of Unlawful Acts Relating to International Civil Aviation, ICAO Doc. 9960, not yet in force.

[39] See Art. 2(1)(b) of the 1999 Convention for the Suppression of the Financing of Terrorism, UNTS Vol. 2178, 230; Art. 2 of the Ad Hoc Committee's Draft Comprehensive Terrorism Convention, UN GA, A/C.6/65/L.10 of 3 November 2010, p. 6. See also Cyrille Begorre-Bret, 'The definition of terrorism and the challenge of relativism', (2005/6) 27 *Cardozo Law Review*, 1987–2004, p. 1996; Schmid, 'The links between TOC and terrorist crimes', cited in note 6 above, pp. 58ff.

[40] Marcello Di Filippo, 'The definition(s) of terrorism in international law', in Saul, *Research Handbook*, cited in note 17 above, pp. 3–19, at p. 11; Oehmichen, *Terrorism and Anti-Terrorism Legislation*, cited in note 16 above, p. 127; Reuven Young, 'Defining terrorism: the evolution of terrorism as a legal concept in international law and its influence on definitions in domestic legislation', (2006) 29 *Boston College International and Comparative Law Review*, 23–105, p. 57. The emphasis on this subjective component is criticized by George Fletcher, 'The indefinable concept of terrorism', (2006) 4 *Journal of International Criminal Justice*, 894–911, p. 903, who points out that the alleged intention will in most cases be inferred from the objective context of the terrorist attack. See also Jacqueline Hodgson and Victor Tadros, 'The impossibility of defining terrorism', (2013) 16 *New Criminal Law Review*, 494–526, p. 522.

[41] See Cassese, 'The multifaceted criminal notion', cited in note 37 above, p. 940; Hodgson and Tadros, 'The impossibility of defining terrorism', cited in note 40 above, p. 500.

undisputed: while some commentators reject the notion of a specific (religious, political, ethnic, etc.) motivation as a definitional part of terrorism,[42] others propose that a specific, non-personal motivation should be acknowledged as a distinctive component, setting terrorism apart from ordinary crimes.[43] The reason for the rejection of such a component from the international anti-terrorism instruments is that an assessment of the perpetrator's motive would cause intricate problems for law enforcement authorities.[44] In contrast to this, confining terrorist intent to the aim of spreading fear and intimidation connects it closely to the terrorist's conduct. The offence must at least have the potential to achieve the wanted terrorizing effect. Therefore, the subjective terrorist element has a strong foundation in the way the crime is committed and thereby avoids the vagueness of a motivational element.[45]

Furthermore, some commentators suggest an organisational element of terrorist crimes[46]—stating that terrorist crimes can only be committed with a certain organisational background and sufficient 'manpower'. But it has to be borne in mind that nowadays the phenomenon of the 'lone terrorist fighter' or 'sleeper' occurs frequently and that religious terrorism in particular is performed in very loosely connected cells.[47] Moreover, even individuals can become radicalized by simply sitting in front of their computers and surfing the internet. As a result, the requirement of an organisational element for terrorist crimes seems outdated and should not be adopted as a prerequisite for defining such crimes.

5.2.2 Remaining definitional problems

The reason for the lack of a comprehensive international definition of terrorism is that some definitional problems remain unresolved: contentious issues are the delimitation of terrorism from state terror (see section 5.2.2.1 of this chapter) on one hand and from liberation movements (see section 5.2.2.2) on the other hand.

5.2.2.1 Delimitation from state terror

Some commentators suggest that an internationally accepted definition of terrorism should include state terror.[48] Traditionally, a fine line is drawn—not just

[42] Di Filippo, 'The definition(s) of terrorism', cited in note 40 above, p. 11; Oehmichen, *Terrorism and Anti-Terrorism Legislation*, cited in note 16 above, p. 126; Young, 'Defining terrorism', cited in note 40 above, pp. 58 and 64.

[43] Cassese, 'The multifaceted criminal notion', cited in note 37 above, p. 941; Ben Saul, *Defining Terrorism in International Law*, Oxford, OUP, 2006, p. 61; Thomas Weigend, 'The universal terrorist', (2006) 4 *Journal of International Criminal Justice*, 912–32, p. 924.

[44] Cassese, 'The multifaceted criminal notion', cited in note 37 above, p. 941; Hodgson and Tadros, 'The impossibility of defining terrorism', cited in note 40 above, p. 525.

[45] Compare Di Filippo, 'The definition(s) of terrorism', cited in note 40 above, p. 16.

[46] Compare ibid, pp. 3–19; Lutz and Lutz, *Global Terrorism*, cited in note 12 above, p. 10.

[47] Compare Steven Hutchinson and Pat O'Malley, 'A crime–terror nexus? Thinking on some of the links between terrorism and criminality', (2007) 30 *Studies in Conflict & Terrorism*, 1095–1107, pp. 1098ff.

[48] Upendra D. Acharya, 'War on terror or terror on wars: the problem in defining terrorism', (2008/9) 37 *Denver Journal of International Law and Policy*, 653–79, pp. 660 and 669; Adam Roberts, 'Countering terrorism: a historical perspective', in de Frías, Samuel and White, *Counter-Terrorism*, cited in note 26 above, pp. 3–41, at p. 10; Weigend, 'The universal terrorist', cited in note 43 above, p. 923.

terminologically—between state terror and 'ordinary' terrorism. State terror is characterized by state authorities establishing their power by using violence against opponents. This has to be strictly distinguished from a state's (tacit) support of terrorist groups—for example, by lending funding or logistic support to terrorist organisations (either for domestic terror groups that favour the state order or for terror organisations abroad).[49]

Numerous examples of devastating state terror can be found in the history of the twentieth century: the murderous regimes installed by Hitler and Stalin or the Khmer Rouge regime in Cambodia are undisputed cases.[50]

Extending an international definition of terrorism to state terror would bring along numerous most difficult implications:[51] apart from the fact that a concise definition of state terror is hard to achieve, the question who should assess whether a state actually commits terrorist acts is a most delicate matter. Moreover, no international institution vested with the power to prosecute state terror exists.[52]

In fact, it is questionable whether the furtherance of a definition that explicitly includes state terror is even worth pursuing.[53] The chance of attaining universal agreement is close to none.[54] Moreover, state terror is already addressed by international humanitarian law:[55] if a state deprives a civilian population of fundamental human rights, this is punishable as crime against humanity under international law. Terrorist acts against other states amount to the crime of aggression under international criminal law. Although the International Criminal Court (ICC) cannot yet exert jurisdiction over this crime, it is at least conceivable that in the future this might be achieved. Finally, the international law on war crimes might be applied to state terror. If the precondition of an (international or otherwise) armed conflict is met, excessive acts of violence performed by a state can amount to war crimes under international criminal law.[56] This has led the majority of commentators to the view that state terror should not be addressed by a future international law definition of terrorism.[57] In the same vein is the position presented by the UN High-level Panel on Threats, Challenges, and Change in its 2004 report 'A More Secure World: Our Shared Responsibility'.[58] The

[49] For details on terror supported by the state see Hoffman, *Inside Terrorism*, cited in note 1 above, p. 257; and Martin, *Understanding Terrorism*, cited in note 4 above, p. 102.

[50] Hodgson and Tadros, 'The impossibility of defining terrorism', cited in note 40 above, p. 512, also mention the nuclear bombings of Hiroshima and Nagasaki during the Second World War, as well the air raids on Coventry, England, and Dresden, Germany.

[51] Compare ibid, p. 522.

[52] The ICC does not have jurisdiction over crimes of terrorism in general.

[53] Claudia Martin, 'Terrorism as a crime in international and domestic law: open issues', in Larissa van den Herik and Nico Schrijver (eds), *Counter-Terrorism Strategies in a Fragmented International Legal Order*, Cambridge, CUP, 2013, pp. 639–66; Young, 'Defining terrorism', cited in note 40 above, p. 63.

[54] Fiona de Londras, 'Terrorism as an international crime', in William Schabas and Nadia Bernaz (eds), *Routledge Handbook of International Criminal Law*, Abingdon, Routledge, 2013, pp. 169–80, at p. 170.

[55] Compare Helen Duffy, *The 'War on Terror' and the Framework of International Law*, 2nd edn, Cambridge, CUP, 2005, pp. 125ff.

[56] See on this de Londras, 'Terrorism as an international crime', cited in note 54 above, pp. 173–5.

[57] For further reasons see Martin, 'Terrorism as a crime', cited in note 53 above. A different view is presented by Weigend, 'The universal terrorist', cited in note 43 above, p. 923. Compare also Duffy, *The 'War on Terror'*, cited in note 55 above, pp. 53–7.

[58] The former UN Secretary-General Kofi Annan founded this panel of independent experts.

report states that the use of force by states is already sufficiently regulated by the international law (the Charter of the United Nations, the Geneva Conventions, the Statute of the ICC) and therefore need not be addressed additionally by an internationally accepted definition of terrorism.[59] So far as the use of force occurs in the context of an armed conflict, this is also reflected in several UN conventions that explicitly confine descriptions of the offence of terrorist activities to attacks against civilians.[60] This clarifies that the use of force by and against military personnel in armed conflicts is exclusively subjected to international humanitarian law.

5.2.2.2 Delimitation from liberation movements

Another field of contention is the quest for an explicit exclusion of liberation movements from an international definition of terrorism.[61] The call for a distinction between unlawful terrorism and legitimate claims of peoples' rights to self-determination is rooted in the anti-colonial movements mentioned in section 5.1.2 of this chapter. It was one of the remaining problems unresolved during the negotiations of the UN Ad Hoc Committee on a comprehensive definition of terrorism.[62] An agreement on this issue could not be reached. The reason for this lies in the fact that a precise distinction between offences that are motivated by a legitimate claim for self-determination and terrorist crimes presupposes a close scrutiny of the perpetrator's motives for the elements that can undergird an assumption of a comprehensible political 'liberation motivation'.[63] But to distinguish 'good' from 'bad' political reasons is not easy—and in most cases the result of such an assessment will depend on the decision maker's own political views. Consequently, an attempt to introduce clear-cut criteria for legitimate liberation movements in the framework of international anti-terrorism instruments would most likely lead to failure. Accordingly, the prevailing view at the international level is not to explicitly exclude liberation movements from the definition of terrorism. This is reflected by more recent UN conventions that explicitly preclude the claim of allegedly legitimate motives as grounds for an exemption from their scope.[64]

[59] UN High-level Panel on Threats, Challenges and Change, 'A more secure world: our shared responsibility', New York, UN, 2004, nos 158, 160, p. 48.

[60] Art. 2(1)(b) of the 1999 Convention for the Suppression of the Financing of Terrorism; Art. 4(2) of the 2005 Convention for the Suppression of Acts of Nuclear Terrorism excludes actions in armed conflict from its scope.

[61] Hodgson and Tadros, 'The impossibility of defining terrorism', cited in note 40 above, p. 525. An outline of the discussion is provided by Cassese, 'The multifaceted criminal notion', cited in note 37 above, p. 951 and Weigend, 'The universal terrorist', cited in note 43 above, p. 921.

[62] See UN GA, A/C.6/65/L.10 of 3 November 2010, 'Measures to eliminate international terrorism. Report of the Working Group', p. 22.

[63] See also Hodgson and Tadros, 'The impossibility of defining terrorism', cited in note 40 above, p. 525: general distinctions cannot be made without making political judgements.

[64] Compare Art. 6 of the 2005 International Convention for the Suppression of Acts of Nuclear Terrorism, UNTS Vol. 2445, 140:

> Each State Party shall adopt such measures as may be necessary, including, where appropriate, domestic legislation, to ensure that criminal acts within the scope of this Convention, in particular where they are intended or calculated to provoke a state of terror in the general public or in a group of persons or particular persons, are under no circumstances justifiable by considerations of a political, philosophical, ideological, racial, ethnic, religious or other similar nature and are punished by penalties consistent with their grave nature,

As a result, the classification of a violent attack as a terrorist crime depends on the general criterion of an *actus reus* consisting of a serious use of violence that is driven by the aim to intimidate a population, public authorities, or organisations in order to make them do or abstain from doing certain acts. If this requirement is met, a perpetrator's political motivation to 'liberate' a population from illegitimate authorities does not provide an exclusion from the scope of the terrorism definition.

From a doctrinal perspective it might be more convincing to strive for a definition that includes state terror and at the same time defines criteria for excluding legitimate freedom fighters from its ambit. However, the development of international law is driven by the need to compromise: a solution for the most intricate political problems that are almost naturally evaluated differently from country to country is very unlikely to emerge in the process of designing an internationally agreeable definition of terrorism. For this reason, it might be wiser to push the questions of state terror and freedom fighters down the international law agenda and to content oneself with the basic consensus that has been reached so far.[65]

5.3 The Distinction between TOC and Terrorism

The distinction between TOC and terrorism would be easy if an authoritative international definition of TOC existed.[66] Yet this is not the case (see for details Chapter 1 of this book): as with terrorism, transnational organised crime is tackled in various international treaties that address certain aspects of TOC.[67] But these aspects are not gathered under the umbrella of any general international definition of TOC.

with Art. 6 of the 1999 Convention for the Suppression of the Financing of Terrorism, UNTS Vol. 2178, 232, and Art. 5 of the 1997 International Convention for the Suppression of Terrorist Bombings, UNTS Vol. 2149, 286. Compare also UN SC Res. No. 1566 (2004) of 8 October 2004: '… criminal acts … are under no circumstances justifiable by considerations of a political, philosophical, ideological, racial, ethnic, religious or other similar nature' and the report of the UN High-level Panel on Threats, Challenges and Change (cited in note 59 above) No. 160, p. 48: '… there is nothing in the fact of occupation that justifies the targeting and killing of civilians'.

[65] The debate on the question whether terrorism can be considered one of the core crimes under customary international criminal law (advocated by Cassese, 'The multifaceted criminal notion', cited in note 37 above; Antonio Cassese *et al.*, *International Criminal Law*, 3rd edn, Oxford, OUP, 2013, Ch. 8; and in the Special Tribunal for Lebanon's Interlocutory Decision on the Applicable Law, STL Case No. 11-1 of 16 February 2011, paras 83ff.) is not further addressed in this chapter. Commentators almost unanimously state that there is no such agreed definition of terrorism as a discrete crime under customary international law; compare Ambos and Timmermann, 'Terrorism and customary international law', cited in note 33 above, p. 27; Kai Ambos, 'Judicial creativity at the Special Tribunal for Lebanon: is there a crime of terrorism under international law?', (2011) 24 *Leiden Journal of International Law*, 655–75, pp. 667ff.; Matthew Gillett and Matthias Schuster, 'Fast-track justice', (2011) 9 *Journal of International Criminal Justice*, 989–1020, pp. 1008–14; Guénael Mettraux, 'The United Nations Special Tribunal for Lebanon: prosecuting terrorism', in Saul, *Research Handbook*, cited in note 17 above, pp. 651–65; Ben Saul, 'Legislating from a radical Hague: the United Nations Special Tribunal for Lebanon invents an international crime of transnational terrorism', (2011) 24 *Leiden Journal of International Law*, 677–700, p. 699; Saul, *Defining Terrorism*, cited in note 43 above, pp. 191ff., 270; Weigend, 'The universal terrorist', cited in note 43 above, p. 926.

[66] See also Sinn, Chapter 2 of this book and Thielbörger, Chapter 17 of this book, section 17.3.2.

[67] For example the 1988 Convention against Illicit Traffic in Narcotic Drugs and Psychotropic Substances, UNTS Vol. 1582, 95ff. (and see Ch. 6 of this book); the 2003 Convention against Corruption, UNTS Vol. 2349, 41ff. (and see Ch. 11 of this book).

Traditionally, organised crime and terrorism were understood as offences that excluded one another mutually. While the use of violence is the core element of terrorism, organised crime does not necessarily involve the use of physical violence. And even when organised crime is violent, the violence is not used as a means to achieve certain psychological effects (intimidation of a population, put pressure on the authorities), but merely to secure the best financial outcome for the organised activity. Furthermore, the terrorist's aim to intimidate or pressure a population or government can only be achieved if the terrorist crime actually succeeds in attracting its target's attention. This presupposes a certain degree of publicity. Moreover, it is vital that the actual terrorist/organisation behind the crime is identified. Thus, while both 'ordinary' organised and terrorist crimes are planned clandestinely, the 'successful' commission of organised crime depends upon the organisation's ability to maintain its cover. Consequently, perpetrators of organised criminal offences will do their very best to avoid being detected and identified. Terrorist crimes, on the other hand, can only advance their messages if the public as a whole or at least the target of the terrorist threat realizes not only the terrorist character of the crime but also identifies its *spiritus rector* in order to link it to the organisation's specific agenda. Therefore, terrorist organisations tend to publicly spell out their involvement in committed crimes.[68] Linked to this is the fact that, although a certain political, ideological, or religious motivation is no legal prerequisite for terrorism, terrorists act within an ideological framework. It defines the goals of their crimes and at the same time provides a 'justification' for committing them. Organised crime syndicates, on the other hand, do not have an ideological background, but aim simply at gaining illicit profits.[69]

5.3.1 Links between TOC and terrorism—the debate on the crime-terror continuum

In spite of these differences between terrorism and TOC, the view is emerging that terrorism and organised criminal offences are sometimes converging and that this development will last.[70] Since the end of the Cold War, state sponsorship has no longer been available for terrorist groups to the same extent,[71] so terrorist organisations have increasingly engaged in organised crime to gain financial resources in order to fund their

[68] Hutchinson and O'Malley, 'A crime–terror nexus?', cited in note 47 above, p. 1100; Schmid, 'The links between TOC and terrorist crimes', cited in note 6 above, p. 66.

[69] James H. Andersen and Stephen R. Bowers, 'Terrorism and crime: critical linkages', (2009) *Liberty University, Faculty Publications and Presentations*, Paper 19, p. 5.

[70] Tamara Makarenko, 'The crime–terror continuum: tracing the interplay between transnational organised crime and terrorism', (2004) 6 *Global Crime*, 129–45; Louise I. Shelley and John T. Picarelli, 'Methods and motives: exploring links between transnational organized crime and international terrorism', (2005) 9 *Trends in Organized Crime*, 52–67.

[71] Andersen and Bowers, 'Terrorism and crime', cited in note 69 above, p. 16 (providing several examples); Frank Bovenkerk and Bashir Abou Chakra, 'Terrorism and organized crime', (2004) 4 *Forum on Crime and Society*, 3–15, p. 7; Hutchinson and O'Malley, 'A crime–terror nexus?', cited in note 47 above, p. 1095. For a different view see Schmid, 'The links between TOC and terrorist crimes', cited in note 6 above, p. 62, stressing also that state sponsoring of terrorism was not confined to communist states. See also Walter Laqueur, 'Postmodern terrorism', (1996) 75 *Foreign Affairs*, pp. 24ff., 26ff., and 34, who exemplifies some cases of today's state-sponsored terrorism.

activities.[72] A study carried out by the Financial Action Task Force states that the funding requirements of terrorist organisations pertain not only to financing terrorist attacks,[73] but also to the establishment and maintenance of an organisational structure.[74] Also, an ideology can only be advanced and implemented if its public dissemination is ensured. This requires significant expense. Besides state sponsoring and donations by supporters or charity organisations, common funding sources lie in terrorist organisations' engagement in the drug trade,[75] kidnapping, trafficking in weapons, smuggling, and money laundering.[76]

This very widely known connection between TOC as a funding source and terrorism can also be established in the opposite direction: terrorist acts are sometimes committed by organised crime syndicates as a means to destabilize the legal order and/or to hamper the enforcement of the law on criminal organisations and thus assist the organisation's activities. This has been observed for mafia organisations that used terrorist attacks to deter politicians from enacting valid anti-mafia legislation,[77] or to stop law enforcement agencies from effective prosecutions.

[72] Makarenko, 'The crime–terror continuum', cited in note 70 above, p. 133; Louise Shelley, *Dirty Entanglements*, Cambridge, CUP, 2014, p. 111 *passim*; Phil Williams, 'Terrorist financing and organized crime. nexus, appropriation, or transformation?', in Thomas J. Biersteker and Sue E. Eckert (eds), *Countering the Financing of Terrorism*, Abingdon, Routledge, 2008, pp. 126–49, at p. 130. For example, the funding of Al-Qaeda is suspected to be based to a certain degree on the systematic commission of credit card fraud—compare Rohan Gunaratna, *Inside Al Qaeda: Global Network of Terror*, New York, Columbia University Press, 2002, p. 65.

[73] The Financial Action Task Force (FATF) is an intergovernmental body established in 1989 by the ministers of its thirty-four member jurisdictions (amongst them the United Kingdom, the USA, China, Germany, and France).

[74] FATF, 'Terrorist Financing' (29 February 2008), available at: http://www.fatf-gafi.org/media/fatf/documents/reports/FATF%20Terrorist%20Financing%20Typologies%20Report.pdf, accessed 26 July 2015, pp. 7f. Compare also Shelley, *Dirty Entanglements*, cited in note 72 above, pp. 177f.

[75] Often mentioned examples for terrorist organisations funded by their engagement in the drug trade are FARC in Colombia, Hamas and Hezbollah in the Tri-Border area of Central America, PKK (Kurdish workers party) in Turkey; and the Taliban in Afghanistan fund Al Qaeda through drug crimes. Compare Hutchinson and O'Malley, 'A crime–terror nexus?', cited in note 47 above, p. 1096. A recent assessment of today's drug trade and drug consumers is provided by the UN 'World Drug Report 2015', available at: http://www.unodc.org/documents/wdr2015/World_Drug_Report_2015.pdf, accessed 26 July 2015. Compare also the case studies provided by the European Parliament, Directorate-General for Internal Policies, 'Europe's crime–terror nexus: links between terrorist and organised crime groups in the European Union' (2012), available at http://www.europarl.europa.eu/document/activities/cont/201211/20121127ATT56707/20121127ATT56707EN.pdf, accessed 26 July 2015, pp. 20ff., and by John Rollins, Liana Sun Wyler, and Seth Rosen, 'International terrorism and transnational crime', Congressional Research Service, Report for Congress (5 January 2010), available at http://fas.org/sgp/crs/terror/R41004-2010.pdf, accessed 26 July 2015, p. 16. and by Louise Shelley and Sharon Melzer, 'The nexus of organised crime and terrorism: two case studies in cigarette smuggling', (2008) 32 *International Journal of Comparative and Applied Criminal Justice*, 1.

[76] Hutchinson and O'Malley, 'A crime–terror nexus?', cited in note 47 above, p. 1097; Loretta Napoleoni, 'The new economy of terror', (2004) 4 *Forum on Crime and Society*, 31–48; Shelley, *Dirty Entanglements*, cited in note 72 above, p. 179. The UN FATF report on 'Financing of the terrorist organisation Islamic State in Iraq and the Levant (ISIL)' (February 2015), available at: http://www.fatf-gafi.org/publications/methodsandtrends/documents/financing-of-terrorist-organisation-isil.html, accessed 2 March 2016, p. 5, states that ISIL engages in bank looting and extortion, kidnapping for ransom, theft, and other criminal activities. ISIL also exploit oil and gas fields on conquered territory: p. 13. Besides, donations are given to ISIL by persons hiding behind non-profit organisations.

[77] See Peter Grabosky and Michael Stohl, *Crime and Terrorism*, Thousand Oaks, California, SAGE Publications, 2010, pp. 6ff.; Makarenko, 'The crime–terror continuum', cited in note 70 above, pp. 131ff. and 134; Williams, 'Terrorist financing and organized crime', cited in note 72 above, p. 131.

The forging of links between terrorism and organised crime has been described as a linear evolution passing through different stages ('terror-crime interaction spectrum'):[78] first, terrorists merely imitate organised crime activities to garner financial benefits. This first step, 'activity appropriation' does not necessarily entail any actual contact between terrorist and organised crime groups but can be confined to a transfer of techniques (like credit card fraud, etc.).[79] The next step consists of an 'outsourcing' of certain services that can be provided properly by 'organised crime experts'—e.g. passport forgery is best performed by the members of organised crime syndicates who have greater know-how and 'infrastructure' at their disposal.[80] If the provision of certain services by one group to the other continues, it might be elevated to the next level of a closer cooperation—group members might start to actually work together. A natural consequence of this convergence would be that the group members start to share their respective goals. For this reason, this stage is characterized as a 'symbiotic relationship'.[81] Some commentators claim that there is not enough empirical evidence to assert that such effects occur often.[82] Yet the majority in this debate adhere to the notion of a growing importance for this crime–terror nexus. The longer the cooperation between terrorist and organised crime groups lasts, the closer the relationship becomes, the more the differences between the groups dissipate—and in the end, a hybrid group containing both former terrorists and former 'pure' criminals evolves. Such a development has been described for several geographic regions (Paraguay, Brazil, Argentina, and Chechnya).[83] It is also possible that a former terrorist group will abandon its idealistic goals and concentrate its future activities on the pursuit of profits.[84] This would amount to a transformation of a terrorist group into an organised crime syndicate.[85] Naturally, the same evolution can occur in the opposite direction: a former organised crime group can assume a political agenda, become radicalized, and thus transform into a terrorist organisation.[86]

It has been observed that hybrid groups thrive in states with a weak legal order and poor law enforcement strategies—or even failed states.[87] In some regions, the unholy alliance of terrorism and organised crime has led to a piecemeal assumption of state-like

[78] Shelley and Picarelli, 'Methods and motives', cited in note 70 above, p. 53.

[79] Ibid, p. 53; Williams, 'Terrorist financing and organized crime', cited in note 72 above, p. 130.

[80] Makarenko, 'The crime–terror continuum', cited in note 70 above, p. 131; Shelley and Picarelli, 'Methods and motives', cited in note 70 above, p. 53, describe this stage as 'nexus'; compare also Williams, 'Terrorist financing and organized crime', cited in note 72 above, p. 128.

[81] Shelley and Picarelli, 'Methods and motives', cited in note 70 above, p. 53. For a different view see Hutchinson and O'Malley, 'A crime–terror nexus?', cited in note 47 above, p. 1104.

[82] Hutchinson and O'Malley, 'A crime–terror nexus?', cited in note 47 above, p. 1105; Williams, 'Terrorist financing and organized crime', cited in note 72 above, pp. 136 and 145.

[83] Andersen and Bowers, 'Terrorism and crime', cited in note 69 above, p. 8; Shelley, *Dirty Entanglements*, cited in note 72 above, p. 116; Shelley and Picarelli, 'Methods and motives', cited in note 70 above, p. 60.

[84] Makarenko, 'The crime–terror continuum', cited in note 70 above, p. 136. This has been described for the IRA: see Shelley, *Dirty Entanglements*, cited in note 72 above, p. 116.

[85] Compare European Parliament, 'Crime–terror nexus', cited in note 75 above, p. 17. Shelley and Picarelli, 'Methods and motives', cited in note 70 above, p. 54.

[86] See Williams, 'Terrorist financing and organized crime', cited in note 72 above, pp. 133ff. and 143ff., who claims that such development poses the most dangerous threat to society.

[87] Andersen and Bowers, 'Terrorism and crime', cited in note 69 above, p. 19; Makarenko, 'The crime–terror continuum', cited in note 70 above, p. 138; T. Makarenko, 'Criminal and terrorist networks: gauging interaction and the resultant impact on counter-terrorism', in Esther Brimmer (ed.), *Five Dimensions*

powers by terrorist groups. An example is the Fuerzas Armadas Revolucionarias de Colombia (FARC)—a terror organisation that began to use the drug trade to fund its activities in the 1980s. The FARC even attained governing power over certain territories of Colombia.[88] This growing influence of drug-funded terror has led to the coining of the term 'narco-terrorism'.[89] More and more state orders are threatened by powerful terror–organised crime syndicates: Afghanistan, Mexico, Peru, Pakistan, and other countries seem in some parts of their territories to have already lost the fight against terror–crime syndicates.

An obvious conclusion from this growing nexus should be a broadening of the view on terrorist crime—it should take organised crime into account, too. Even more: the detection of organised crime will most likely lead to a discovery of terrorist networks as well. Consequently, law enforcement should not detach the fight against terrorism from that against organised crime—their connection is in fact very close because of the need to obtain financial resources.

5.3.2 Applicability of the international law on terrorism to TOC

Usually, the fight against TOC is understood as a means to also fight terrorist crimes because organised crime can serve as a means to provide the needed funding for terrorist acts. Therefore, the fight against TOC and the international treaties on TOC are perceived as an ever-more-important instrument to prevent terrorist acts, too. However, a different question has not been examined very closely so far: the question whether international law on terrorism might also have effects on TOC. For this reason the following part of this chapter focuses on the question whether the instruments of international law on terrorism allow of application to TOC as well.

The early UN conventions on aircraft terrorism do not contain any provisions that could be applied to TOC offences.[90] However, if TOC offences are used as a means to finance terrorist crimes, they can at the same time amount to an offence consisting of the aiding/assisting or other support of terrorist crimes. If the profit from TOC offences is applied to the commission of terrorist crimes, this may constitute assistance of terrorist crimes. The connection is obvious and addressed as a discrete area in the 1999 Terrorist Financing Convention,[91] which targets funding activities directly.[92] The Convention stipulates it as a crime under international law if a person

of Homeland and International Security, Washington DC, Center for Transatlantic Relations, 2008, pp. 57–72, p. 59; Shelley, *Dirty Entanglements*, cited in note 72 above, p. 118; Shelley and Picarelli, 'Methods and motives', cited in note 70 above, p. 53.

[88] Compare Makarenko, 'The crime–terror continuum', cited in note 70 above, p. 137 (estimated 40 per cent of Colombian territory in the year 2000); Williams, 'Terrorist financing and organized crime', cited in note 72 above, p. 132; Shelley, *Dirty Entanglements*, cited in note 72 above, p. 228. Shelley also suggests that Colombia is in a state of recovery, while the drug crime threat seems to have been moved to Central America and Mexico, p. 230. Compare also the case study by Rollins, Wyler and Rosen, in 'International terrorism and transnational crime', cited in note 75 above, p. 16.

[89] Compare Schmid, 'The links between TOC and terrorist crimes', cited in note 6 above, p. 66; Shelley, *Dirty Entanglements*, cited in note 72 above, p. 112.

[90] See section 5.2.1.1 of this chapter.

[91] UNTS Vol. 2178, 197ff. (and UN SC Res. No. 1373 (2001) of 28 September 2001).

[92] See Art. 2(1), UNTS Vol. 2178, 230.

by any means, directly or indirectly, unlawfully and wilfully, provides or collects funds with the intention that they should be used or in the knowledge that they are to be used, in full or in part, in order to carry out … [a terrorist crime].[93]

The Terrorist Financing Convention aims at exterminating terrorist organisations' roots in preventing their funding. To this end, it requires the UN member states to criminalize fundraising for terrorist(s) (organisations) and to cooperate effectively in the prosecution of acts financing terrorism. If terrorist acts or terrorist organisations in general are financed by profits garnered through the commission of organised crimes, the collecting of illegal benefits can at the same time amount to an act of organised crime and an act falling within the purview of the Terrorist Financing Convention. Yet this presupposes that the organised crime offences were meant to fund terrorist acts or for the support of a terrorist organisation in general. It would not suffice if the dedication of illegally gained profits to a terrorist organisation is detached from the actual criminal offence that was committed to gain the financial benefits at the outset—for example, if the members of an organised crime syndicate decide to 'donate' a certain amount to a terrorist organisation after the commission of the initial crime. If the commission of the organised crime offence was not meant to also gain benefits for future funding of terrorist crimes, the link between TOC and terrorism is not established. The subsequent donation of the illegally obtained profit to a terrorist organisation, however, would amount to terrorist financing.

In contrast to this restriction it has to be pointed out that under the Terrorist Financing Convention a crime under the convention is committed even by participation in the financing of terrorist crimes.[94] From the perspective of the ultimate terrorist act this amounts to mere assistance (provided to the person who finances terrorism) in the commission of terrorism (by financing). Hence, as described, the offence somehow predates the punishable act twice.

In addition to the far-fetched ambit of the Terrorist Financing Convention, modern conventions on terrorist crimes contain provisions that extend the ambit of criminalized behaviour far into even remote acts of support. Acts of assisting/supporting terrorist activities are encompassed by the modern conventions. This holds true for the Terrorist Bombing Convention (1997),[95] the Nuclear Terrorism Convention (2005),[96] and the Convention on the Suppression of Unlawful Acts Relating to International Civil Aviation (2010, the 'Beijing Convention').[97] As long as TOC is used as a means to generate funds for the commission of terrorist crimes, this activity might also fall within the purview of these conventions. Yet since the Terrorist Financing Convention already defines the act of financing very broadly, a separate application of other terrorist conventions on the acts of financing is not needed to cover the funding activity.

[93] See for details section 5.2.1.1 of this chapter.

[94] See Art. 2(5): 'Any person also commits an offence if that person: (a) participates as an accomplice …; (b) organizes or directs others to commit an offence …; (c) contributes to the commission of one or more offences …'.

[95] Art. 2(3)(a), (b), (c), UNTS Vol. 2149, 286.

[96] Art. 2(4)(a), (b), (c), UNTS Vol. 2445, 139.

[97] Art. 1(5)(b), ICAO Doc. 9960. This convention is not yet in force.

A different question is whether TOC instruments already encompass the financing of terrorism. This is not the case whenever the act generating financial benefits is itself lawful—for example if an organised crime syndicate also engages in lawful business like real estate trading, etc. Such cases are only addressed by the Terrorist Financing Convention—for TOC Conventions clearly presuppose that the organised crime is a crime in itself.

5.3.3 Conclusions

It has become obvious that the growing nexus between terrorism and TOC should not be underestimated. Efforts to prosecute and prevent international crime should take this link into account. The international community should strengthen its efforts to fight the modern threats of TOC, terrorism, and the combination of the two phenomena with a broadened agenda considering cooperation, convergences, the growth of powerful organisational structures, and even the partial gain of control over territory by criminal networks. The UN Security Council has already acknowledged the threat posed by the convergence of terrorism and organised crime; it stated in the year 2001 that it:

> [n]otes with concern the close connection between international terrorism and transnational organized crime, illicit drugs, money-laundering, illegal arms-trafficking, and illegal movement of nuclear, chemical, biological and other potentially deadly materials, and in this regard emphasizes the need to enhance coordination of efforts on national, subregional, regional and international levels in order to strengthen a global response to this serious challenge and threat to international security.[98]

It is vital that the international community follow this path in the future.

[98] UN SC Res. No. 1373 (2001) of 28 September 2001, no. 4. See also the recommendations of the European Parliament, 'Europe's crime–terror nexus', cited in note 75 above.

PART II

UN CORE CONVENTIONS ON TRANSNATIONAL ORGANISED CRIME

6

The Convention against Illicit Traffic in Narcotic Drugs and Psychotropic Substances 1988 and the Global War on Drugs

Richard Vogler and Shahrzad Fouladvand

6.1 Introduction

The problem of drug control in the contemporary world is a deeply paradoxical one. Although the three Drug Conventions that were agreed between 1961 and 1988 are amongst the most successful international instruments ever created in terms of state participation, it is fair to say that their operation has been an almost unmitigated failure, producing consequences directly opposite to those envisaged. Drugs themselves represent what Herschinger has described as 'ambivalent materiality', having both therapeutic and addiction-forming characteristics, which can both cure and destroy.[1] They represent pleasure and pain in equal measure and while the great majority of the global population are in desperate need of basic painkillers, the world's attention and its resources have been engrossed by the abuse of drugs by a small minority. The purpose of this chapter is to explore these ambiguities insofar as they concern the origin, nature, and the field of operation of the 1988 Convention Against Illicit Traffic in Narcotic Drugs and Psychotropic Substances (the Trafficking Convention), which represents one of the cornerstones of the global drug prohibition regime.

This exploration charts the way in which a humanistic and philanthropic enterprise, represented by the Trafficking Convention and supported by overwhelming international sentiment, has become distorted by state policy and international criminality to become the source of wars, offending, disease, and loss of life on an unprecedented scale. There is no doubt that the period since the Single Convention on Narcotic Drugs (Single Convention) was opened for signature in 1961 has witnessed the largest increase in drug production, trafficking, and abuse in human history, promoted by organised crime networks that have grown exponentially and acquired fabulous wealth on the proceeds. Whether this would have happened without the creation of a global prohibition regime is a matter for debate. But it is certainly true that the regime itself provided ideal conditions for these organisations to flourish. This chapter will begin by examining briefly the relationship between organised crime and drug trafficking, before moving on to consider the origins of prohibition

[1] Eva Herschinger, 'The drug *dispositif*: ambivalent materiality and the addiction of the global drug prohibition regime', (2015) 46 *Security Dialogue* (2), 183–201.

and the creation of the International Narcotics Convention System between 1961 and 1988. It will then focus on the Trafficking Convention itself as the central achievement of this process, before considering ways in which states have sought to escape from its restrictions and the strong contemporary drive for the reform of its provisions.

6.2 Organised Crime and International Drug Trafficking

The link between organised crime and the rise of the drug trafficking phenomena in the last half-century is well established and extensively documented.[2] It is difficult nevertheless to estimate the actual value of business involved in these illegal operations, but it is probably in the region of $500 billion annually,[3] while the number of consumers of illicit drugs is believed to be in excess of 246 million people in 2013, or 5 per cent of the global adult population.[4] The annual number of drug-related deaths in the same year was estimated at 187,100.[5] The extent of drug consumption is notoriously difficult to quantify. For example, data based on seizures suggest that over 500 kg of cocaine enters the United States every day.[6] With probably greater accuracy, extrapolated analysis of urinary biomarkers of cocaine in the sewerage of nineteen European cities indicates a daily use of 365 kg of cocaine for the entire continent.[7] Despite this widespread use, production of illicit drugs is relatively localized around the globe. Cannabis resin production is centred on a few countries in North Africa, the Middle East, and South-West Asia, while the cultivation of coca bush is largely confined to South America. The 'Golden Crescent' (Afghanistan, Iran, and Pakistan) and the 'Golden Triangle' (Thailand, Myanmar, and Laos) account for most of the world's production of illicit opium poppy while cannabis herb and amphetamine-type stimulants are the exceptions that can be produced anywhere.[8] The lengthy distribution and supply chains necessitated by this pattern of production require organisation on a global scale and have facilitated the growth of criminal enterprises that mirror the structures of legitimate multinational corporations.[9]

The role of organised crime in the illicit drug industry has developed rapidly since the 1960s and a few instances will suffice to demonstrate how the era of international drug prohibition over the last half-century offered extraordinary opportunities for this type of criminal undertaking and actually promoted its growth. Colombia, for

[2] See e.g. Matthew S. Jenner, 'Drug trafficking as a transnational crime', in Philip Reichel and Jay Albanese (eds), *Handbook of Transnational Crime and Justice*, Thousand Oaks, California,SAGE, 2014, pp. 65–85; Bruce M. Bagley and Jonathan D. Rosen, *Drug Trafficking, Organized Crime, and Violence in the Americas Today*, Gainesville, University Press of Florida, 2015.

[3] Jenner, 'Drug trafficking as a transnational crime', cited in note 2 above, p. 65.

[4] United Nations, *World Drug Report 2014*, Vienna, United Nations Office on Drugs and Crime (UNODC), 2014.

[5] Ibid. [6] Jenner, 'Drug trafficking as a transnational crime', cited in note 2 above, p. 82.

[7] Kevin V. Thomas, *et al.* 'Comparing illicit drug use in 19 European cities through sewage analysis', (2012) *Science of the Total Environment*, 432, 432–9.

[8] United Nations, *World Drug Report 2014*, cited in note 4 above, p. 14.

[9] Chantal Thomas, 'Disciplining globalization: international law, illegal trade, and the case of narcotics', (2002) *Michigan Journal of International Law*, 24, 549–75.

example, from its independence, had always suffered high levels of violence associated with paramilitary organisations and small-scale criminal organisations.[10] However, as Thoumi has argued, the development of a major illegal drug industry from the 1970s enabled many of these local organisations to become 'globalized' by establishing links with overseas crime groups,[11] a process that could only have occurred because of the global drug prohibition regime. Once the regional power and wealth of the Medellin and Cali cartels had reached a point at which they were considered by the United States government as threats to its regional hegemony, concerted military operations ('Plan Colombia') were launched against them in the 1990s that resulted in their almost complete eradication.[12] Whilst this might be considered an excellent example of the cooperative, multinational interdiction strategy envisaged by the Trafficking Convention, the long-term outcome clearly demonstrates the inadequacies of this approach. Not only did the larger organisations simply diversify into smaller *cartelitos*, with a broader range of criminal activities and more extensive state penetration,[13] but much of the transit business to the United States was simply appropriated by the Mexican cartels that subsequently plunged their own country into a period of internecine warfare, just as brutal and protracted as that which had affected Colombia in the previous decades.[14] In short, the interdiction strategy envisaged by the international drug Conventions, when carried out with the rigour and commitment that characterized 'Plan Colombia', simply displaced the criminal activity and encouraged the formation of less hierarchical and more resilient criminal organisations.[15]

The counter-narcotics policies adopted by the Western allies in Afghanistan have met with equally little success. Extensive eradication campaigns backed by military force, as envisaged by Article 14 of the Trafficking Convention, have failed dismally to discourage opium production, which has actually increased since the 2001 intervention.[16] In short, the illicit drugs market is simply too lucrative to be restrained in this way and interdiction and eradication campaigns simply increase unit value and encourage competition and positive restructuring amongst organised crime groups. In order to understand how the world community has first developed and then clung so tenaciously to these manifestly counter-productive policies, it is worthwhile to look at the origins of prohibition.

[10] Francisco E. Thoumi, 'Colombian organized crime: from drug trafficking to parastatal bands and widespread corruption', in Dina Siegel and Henk van de Bunt (eds), *Traditional Organized Crime in the Modern World: Responses to Socioeconomic Change*, New York, Springer, 2012, pp. 131–48, pp. 131–2.

[11] Ibid, pp. 134–41.

[12] Jenner, 'Drug trafficking as a transnational crime', cited in note 2 above, pp. 78–9.

[13] Thoumi, 'Colombian organized crime', cited in note 10 above, p. 141; Bruce M. Bagley, *Drug Trafficking and Organized Crime in the Americas*, Washington DC, Woodrow Wilson Center, 2012, p. 17.

[14] Viridiana Ríos, 'Why did Mexico become so violent? A self-reinforcing violent equilibrium caused by competition and enforcement', (2013) 16 *Trends in Organized Crime* (2), 138–55.

[15] Thoumi, 'Colombian organized crime', cited in note 10 above, p. 141.

[16] David M. Catarious Jr and Alison Russell, *Counternarcotics Efforts and Afghan Poppy Farmers: Finding the Right Approach*, Washington DC, Environmental Law Institute and United Nations Environment Programme, 2012.

6.3 Prohibition and the Global Drug Control Regime

The origins of the prohibitionist global drug control regime, which reached its culminating achievement with the Trafficking Convention, are complex. Its ideological roots lie in the British and North American temperance movements of the nineteenth century, which campaigned against all intoxicants. The association of alcohol and drugs with unruly immigrant communities and the global south also contributed to the anxieties of these groups.[17] However, when it became apparent that alcohol prohibition in the United States during the 1920s had done little more than exacerbate already high levels of offending and deliver many cities and communities directly into the hands of organised crime,[18] narcotic drug prohibition was strategically separated by its prominent supporters such as Harry Anslinger, from its discredited counterpart. The lessons were not learned, however. Drug prohibition on a global scale has sadly produced identical outcomes to domestic alcohol prohibition but on a vastly greater and more catastrophic scale.

It is hard to see why, in view of the obvious failure of alcohol prohibition in the USA, narcotic drug prohibition should have been embraced so enthusiastically around the world for over half a century. No international treaty system has been so widely supported. As Levine put it:

> Capitalist democracies took up drug prohibition, and so did authoritarian governments. German Nazis and Italian Fascists embraced drug prohibition, just as American politicians had. Various Soviet regimes enforced drug prohibition, as have their successors. In China, mandarins, militarists, capitalists, and communists all enforced drug prohibition regimes. Populist generals in Latin American and anti-colonialist intellectuals in Africa backed drug prohibition.[19]

The answer is that prohibition was functional for a wide variety of state and non-state organisations. Prohibition brought political opponents into agreement and provided important legitimization for police, military, and a wide range of government and non-government agencies.[20] As a result, the need to eradicate the international traffic in drugs became a 'taken for granted' universal knowledge that could never be questioned. It was a founding principle for the nascent regime of global governance, explicitly referenced in the early documents of both the League of Nations in 1920 and the United Nations in 1945.[21] It also served the hegemonic interests of the USA throughout the twentieth century and beyond, playing a crucial role in policy from Vietnam and Laos to Central America and Afghanistan.[22] Animated by an 'implacable and

[17] Ethan A. Nadelmann, 'Global prohibition regimes: the evolution of norms in international society', (1990) 44 *International Organization* (4), 479–526, pp. 504–5.

[18] Nora V. Demleitner, 'Organized crime and prohibition: what difference does legalization make?', (1994) 15 *Whittier Law Review*, 613–46.

[19] Harry G. Levine, 'Global drug prohibition: its uses and crises', (2003) 14 *International Journal of Drug Policy* (2), 145–53, p. 147.

[20] Ibid. [21] Ibid, p. 146.

[22] Alfred W. McCoy, *The Politics of Heroin: CIA Complicity in the Global Drug Trade, Afghanistan, Southeast Asia, Central America*, Chicago, Lawrence Hill, 2003.

almost religious commitment to prohibition'[23] the United States drove forward relentlessly the creation and enforcement of the global legal regime, notwithstanding that its secret services continued to establish mutually beneficial contacts with organised criminals engaged in drug trafficking, when the situation appeared to demand it.[24]

In many ways, commitment to the drug Conventions was viewed by the United States and its allies as evidence of commitment to international governance, peace, and security itself. In the discourse underpinning the Conventions, the lawfulness and order of the global 'self', represented by drug prohibition, is contrasted sharply with the evil 'otherness' of those who opposed it. As Crick puts it, '(a)t each stage of the development of the "drugs as an existential threat" discourse, there was an individualization of the "antagonistic drug Other"'.[25]

The long development of the global prohibition regime that reached its climax with the Trafficking Convention can be seen in two stages. The first was characterized by an uncompromising focus on the supply of narcotic drugs, to the exclusion of any concern with demand in the Western nations:

> rather than address both demand—the socio-medical nature of such problems—and supply, they focused uniquely on the latter and attempted to stem the flow of drugs into their territories. In doing so, they earned political capital back home and shifted the cost and burden of drug control to predominantly Asian and Latin American developing countries with no cultural inclination or resources to take on such an intrusive task—and no economic or military power to refuse what was imposed on them.[26]

The creation of the Trafficking Convention in 1988 marked a new stage in international drug prohibition, with the mandating, for the first time, of a network of specific domestic penal controls on demand-side consumption alongside more effective controls on production and trafficking. It can therefore be seen as a critical moment in the development of international drug prohibition and a significant escalation in penal control. Its roots lie deep in the United States' approach to the colonial project and its own global role.

6.4 Early Attempts to Establish a Global Drug Control Regime

The historic importance of opium as a major international trading commodity cannot be overstated. It fuelled the rise of European Asiatic empires and, so it has been claimed, the whole development of global capitalism.[27] Its role was certainly crucial

[23] Alex Wodak, 'The international drug treaties: "paper tigers" or dangerous behemoths?', (2003) 14 *International Journal of Drug Policy* (2), 221–3, p. 221.

[24] McCoy, *The Politics of Heroin*, cited in note 22 above.

[25] Emily Crick, 'Drugs as an existential threat: an analysis of the international securitization of drugs', (2012) 23 *International Journal of Drug Policy* (5), 407–14, p. 408.

[26] Jay Sinha, *The History and Development of the Leading International Drug Control Conventions*, Ottawa, Parliamentary Research Branch, 2001, p. 1.

[27] Carl A. Trocki, *Opium, Empire and the Global Political Economy. A Study of the Asian Opium Trade 1750–1950*, London, Routledge, 1999, p. 7.

in the establishment of British imperial rule in Asia. Not only did the opium trade for the first time reverse the flows of capital in favour of the European colonialists but it also played a major role in destabilizing existing political economies and enabling them to be replaced by colonial ones.[28] Almost all the great European overseas merchant houses, banks, and insurance companies had their origins in the opium trade.[29] According to Trocki:

> [o]pium came to be an essential element, indeed the cash cow, in the finances of every Asian state structure during the nineteenth and even during the first part of the twentieth century.[30]

It is not surprising, therefore, that the British were prepared to fight continental wars with the Chinese to preserve their trading monopoly in opium.[31] The addictive epidemic that resulted from the opium trade across Asia during this period has been compared to the similar 'drug plague' that has engulfed Europe and the United States since the enactment of the Single Convention in 1961.[32] However, whereas the nineteenth century opium trade was financed and organised by European venture capital with extensive support from imperial governments, the contemporary traffic, which it resembles in many other ways, is monopolized by organised crime. By 1906 Britain, France, Portugal, and the Netherlands were enjoying highly lucrative drug monopolies in Asia and also controlled the supply of pharmaceuticals to Europe and the United States.[33]

Opposition to Britain's involvement in opium trafficking was organised largely by Nonconformist religious groups which, in 1874, founded the Anglo-Oriental Society for the Suppression of the Opium Trade.[34] As a result of this increasing pressure, the reforming Liberal government that gained power in Britain in 1906 negotiated a 'ten year agreement' with China and India—regarded as the first international drug treaty—for a mutual reduction of production. This proved surprisingly effective until the fall of the Manchu dynasty in 1911 when drug production was again revived by competing warlords.[35] Japanese imperial ambitions in China and South-East Asia from 1895 to 1945 were also underpinned by the opium trade just as those of the Europeans had been earlier.[36] However, the policy of another new colonial power, the United States, which acquired the Philippines in 1898 at the conclusion of the Spanish-American War, was radically different and aimed at disrupting the existing trade monopolies of the European powers. Charles Henry Brent, the newly appointed American Episcopal

[28] Frank Dikötter, *et al.* 'Narcotic culture. A social history of drug consumption in China', (2002) 42 *British Journal of Criminology* (2), 317–36, p. 321.

[29] Trocki, *Opium, Empire,* cited in note 27 above, p. 10.

[30] Ibid, p. 10.

[31] Julia Lovell, *The Opium War,* London, Picador, 2011.

[32] Dikötter, Laamann, *et al.* suggest that there were more than 30 million opium users in China alone by the 1880s: 'Narcotic culture', cited in note 28 above, p. 321.

[33] Martin Jelsma, *The Development of International Drug Control: Lessons Learned and Strategic Challenges for the Future*, Amsterdam, Transnational Institute, 2011, p. 2.

[34] Nadelmann, 'Global prohibition regimes', cited in note 17 above, pp. 503–4.

[35] Sinha, *The Leading International Drug Control Conventions*, cited in note 26 above, p. 6.

[36] John M. Jennings, *The Opium Empire: Japanese Imperialism and Drug Trafficking in Asia, 1895–1945*, Westport, Connecticut, Praeger, 1997.

Bishop of the Philippines, had strong links with the British and American temperance movements and enjoyed considerable influence with US President Theodore Roosevelt. The latter was anxious to gain access to Chinese markets for American exports and the expression of vocal opposition to the European opium monopolies was an important element in that policy. With Roosevelt's support, Brent chaired the first meetings of the International Opium Commission in Shanghai in 1909.[37] The organisation was dominated by the founding fathers of the international drug prohibition regime, who Webster has described as 'a remarkably small coterie of messianic do-gooders, the remnants of 19th century radical temperance movements'.[38] However, despite the efforts of Brent and his colleague Dr Hamilton Wright, there was no international agreement other than an expression of intent to suppress opium smoking, signed by only twelve countries.[39]

Greater success was achieved three years later in 1912 when the Hague International Opium Convention became the first legally binding multilateral drug control treaty.[40] However, the Convention merely mandated domestic import and export controls on opium and made no attempt to prohibit or criminalize production or trade.[41] What is significant about the Convention, however, was its use by Wright to persuade the US government to enact the first domestic drug control instrument, the 1914 Harrison Narcotics Act.[42] Further activity was curtailed by the First World War and it was not until 1924–5 that a new series of international conferences was convened at the Hague. By this time the temperance movement in the United States had succeeded in establishing domestic alcohol prohibition (1920–33),[43] a policy that the Federal government attempted to replicate at the international level in relation to drugs. This approach proved so unpopular with other countries that, together with the Chinese, the United States delegates felt obliged to walk out of the Hague negotiations in protest at the lack of enthusiasm for extreme prohibitionist measures.[44] Nevertheless, under the first Geneva Convention it was agreed that signatories would allow the sale of opium only through government agencies, before ending the trade entirely within fifteen years. The 1925 International Opium Convention (which for the first time included other drugs such as cannabis) established reporting requirements and created the Permanent Central Opium Board under the auspices of the League of Nations,[45] with

[37] Sinha, *The Leading International Drug Control Conventions*, cited in note 26 above, p. 7.

[38] Peter Webster, 'Learning from history: a review of David Bewley-Taylor's *The United States and International Drug Control, 1909–1997*', (2003) 14 *International Journal of Drug Policy* (4), 343–6, p. 343; Nadelmann, 'Global prohibition regimes', cited in note 17 above, p. 504.

[39] David Bewley-Taylor and Martin Jelsma, 'Regime change: re-visiting the 1961 Single Convention on Narcotic Drugs', (2012) 23 *International Journal of Drug Policy* (1), 72–81, p. 73.

[40] Convention Relating to the Suppression of the Abuse of Opium and Other Drugs. Signed at The Hague on 23 January 1912, 38 Stat 1912, TS No. 612, 1 Bevans 855, 8 LNTS 187.

[41] At the insistence of the British and Americans, its provisions were incorporated directly into the Versailles Peace Treaty of 1919. Crick, 'Drugs as an existential threat', cited in note 25 above, p. 409.

[42] Sinha, *The Leading International Drug Control Conventions*, cited in note 26 above, p. 11.

[43] Demleitner, 'Organized crime and prohibition', cited in note 18 above.

[44] Jelsma, *The Development of International Drug Control*, cited in note 33 above.

[45] Later to be transformed into the International Narcotics Control Board. International Opium Convention, signed in Geneva on 19 February 1925, entered into force 25 September 1928, 81 LNTS 317, reprinted in 23 *American Journal of International Law* 135 (1929).

the power to set limits on production and importation.[46] This represented the first international and collective attempt to reduce the trade in drugs, although restrictions were largely ineffective as consignments could be shipped via non-signatory nations.

In the 1930s, however, the involvement of the nascent International Criminal Police Organization (later, Interpol) encouraged a significant shift in international attention, which for the first time began to view the issue of drug trafficking as an international crime rather than simply as a trading matter. As a result, the signatory states to the 1936 Geneva Trafficking Convention agreed to make the necessary legislative provisions for 'severely punishing, particularly by imprisonment'[47] a number of acts connected with the transit, importation, and exportation of a wide range of narcotic drugs.[48] Although this Convention can be seen as the direct precursor of the 1988 Trafficking Convention, the United States considered it to be insufficiently robust and declined to sign, ensuring that the provisions were little used.[49] Similarly ineffective was the 1953 New York Opium Protocol which, although containing articles limiting the use of opium exclusively to medical and scientific needs,[50] did not come into force until 1963 when it had been effectively overtaken by the 1961 Single Convention. From the point of view of the prohibitionists, the outcome of a half-century of struggle to establish international agreement on drug control was less than impressive. Many countries had not participated. There were no agreed definitions of the subject-matter drugs, no effective international regime for the suppression of the drug trade, and no obligations to enact domestic legislation criminalizing manufacture, use, or dealing. This was to change dramatically during the period 1961 to 1988.

6.5 The Creation of the International Drug Convention System, 1961–88

The drug control conventions that were opened for signature between 1961 and 1988 were unprecedented in their scope and represented extraordinary international interventions in the domestic affairs of states.[51] Collectively they form the statutory basis of what has been described as the 'global drug prohibition regime',[52] largely crafted by the United States with the collusion of a number of other powerful consumer nations. The regime is one of the earliest and most effective examples of what Bassiouni has described as the indirect control system, by which states undertake certain international

[46] Sinha, *The Leading International Drug Control Conventions*, cited in note 26 above, p. 12.

[47] The Convention of 1936 for the Suppression of the Illicit Traffic in Dangerous Drugs. Signed in Geneva on 26 June 1936, entered into force 26 October 1939, 31 *American Journal of International Law* 31 (1937).

[48] The Convention of 1936 for the Suppression of the Illicit Traffic in Dangerous Drugs, 26 June 1936, Art. 2.

[49] Sinha, *The Leading International Drug Control Conventions*, cited in note 26 above, p. 15.

[50] Protocol for Limiting and Regulating the Cultivation of the Poppy Plant, the Production of, International and Wholesale Trade in, and use of Opium. New York, 23 June 1953, Art. 2, available at: https://www.unodc.org/unodc/en/data-and-analysis/bulletin/bulletin_1953-01-01_3_page015.html.

[51] Robin Room, 'Reform by subtraction: the path of denunciation of international drug treaties and reaccession with reservations', (2012) 23 *International Journal of Drug Policy* (5), 401–6, p. 401.

[52] Sophie O'Manique, 'From prohibition to decriminalization: interrogating the emerging international paradigm shift in the war on drugs discourse', MA thesis, Carleton University Ottawa, 2014, p. 35.

obligations based on their treaty obligations and accept the responsibility for carrying them out through their national legal system.[53]

Work began in 1948 on what has been described as the 'foundational document of the international drug control system':[54] the 1961 Single Convention on Narcotic Drugs (Single Convention). The initiative came from a US-drafted resolution requesting the UN Secretary-General to prepare a new single convention to replace the numerous existing treaties that had been created since 1912. What was intended was above all a simplification and codification exercise although, in the three drafts that the Convention underwent between 1950 and 1958,[55] the text began to develop a more radical framework. In the immediate post-war world, drug production, trafficking, and consumption were not seen as serious social problems and the usage of drugs was largely confined to very marginal groups, widely regarded as deviant.[56] The driving forces behind the new Convention were therefore very much religious, moralist, and medical interest groups, predominately in the United States. The preamble expresses its drafters' concerns for the health and welfare of mankind and announces, in almost religious terms, a collective duty to prevent and combat the 'evil' of drug use.

Agreement on a final draft was delayed largely because of concerns expressed by nations such as the UK, West Germany, The Netherlands, and Canada which felt that their commercial and pharmaceutical interests might be affected, and some producer nations such as Iran and Turkey.[57] The concerns of the negotiators were very much centred on supplier countries and very little effort was made to reduce demand. Amongst the three main objectives of the Single Convention, which was adopted on 30 March 1961, were the consolidation of existing international treaties, the extension of the control system to include plant-based substances such as coca, cocaine, and cannabis,[58] and the reorganisation of the United Nations drug enforcement mechanisms. Consolidation was achieved with a marked preference for the penal aspects of previous agreements, emphasizing the sharp distinction between lawful trade and unlawful trafficking, and requiring states to establish control measures.[59] Under Article 4, the parties were required to put in place legislative and administrative measures to give effect to and carry out the provisions of the Convention within their own territories, and to cooperate with each other in furthering its aims. Under Article 33 the parties agreed not to permit the possession of drugs except under legal authority, although no specific penal provisions were recommended. However, subject to constitutional limitations, each party was obliged to adopt such penal measures as would

[53] Mahmoud Cherif Bassiouni, 'Critical reflections on international and national control of drugs', (1989) 18 *Denver Journal of International Law and Policy* (3), 311–37, p. 317.

[54] Single Convention on Narcotic Drugs, New York, adopted 30 March 1961, entered into force 13 December 1964, 520 UNTS 151. See also Joseph Spillane and William B. McAllister, 'Keeping the lid on: a century of drug regulation and control', (2003) 70 *Drug and Alcohol Dependence* (3, Supplement), S5–S12, S7.

[55] Bewley-Taylor and Jelsma, 'Regime change', cited in note 39 above, p. 74.

[56] F. E. Thoumi, 'The international drug control regime's straight jacket: are there any policy options?', (2010) 13 *Trends in Organized Crime* (1), 75–86, p. 78.

[57] Crick, 'Drugs as an existential threat', cited in note 25 above, p. 410.

[58] Sinha, *The Leading International Drug Control Conventions*, cited in note 26 above, p. 2.

[59] Spillane and McAllister, 'Keeping the lid on', cited in note 54 above, S7.

ensure that cultivation, production, manufacture, extraction, preparation, possession, offering, offering for sale, distribution, purchase, sale, etc. were prohibited, except for medical and scientific purposes. Some one hundred narcotic substances were allocated to four schedules, each with a different level of control. Any transitional arrangements based on the cultural traditions of states parties were to be subject to the overriding ambition to abolish the 'quasi-medical' use of opium within fifteen years, and the chewing of coca leaf and use of cannabis for other than medical and scientific purposes within twenty-five years.[60] Almost no attempt was made to address drug consumption problems apart from a very general requirement in Article 38 for states parties to 'take all practicable measures for the prevention of abuse of drugs and for the early identification, treatment, education, after-care, rehabilitation and social reintegration of the persons involved'. In view of the drug epidemic that was about to engulf the world, this was wholly inadequate and placed the moralistic tone of the Preamble in a somewhat questionable light. The Convention also established a secretariat that eventually became the highly influential United Nations Office of Drugs and Crime (UNODC), which was given the responsibility of monitoring the implementation of all United Nations drug Conventions.

Despite the initial disappointment of the United States that it was not more stringent,[61] there is no doubting the historic importance of the Single Convention. It was to become the most important international weapon in the armoury of the first stage of the 'War on Drugs' that was launched by the American President, Richard Nixon, in the following decade, and it has been widely hailed as one of the most successful international agreements.[62] After the UN Charter and the four Geneva Conventions of 1949, it has attracted the largest number of states party.[63] It can be seen as the turning point in the use of drugs in contemporary society and, for better or worse, it transformed the global drug market.

While the Single Convention was aimed predominantly at plant-based substances, by the 1970s a considerable industry had developed in synthesizing drugs that were widely marketed in North America and Europe. The 1971 Convention on Psychotropic Substances (the Psychotropic Convention) appears, on the face of it, to be an attempt merely to extend the provisions of the Single Convention into the area of synthetic drugs. It reproduces the structure and approach of the Single Convention, addressing the problem as one of supply, dividing synthetic drugs into four schedules, and applying controls through a similar infrastructure. However, similarities end at this point. While the terms of the Single Convention were imposed on the relatively weak supplier nations of organic drugs, the drafters of the Psychotropic Convention were confronted with the collective opposition of the international pharmaceutical industry, anxious to protect itself from regulation.[64] There is no mention of 'evil' in the preamble and

[60] Art. 49(2). [61] Bewley-Taylor and Jelsma, 'Regime change', cited in note 39 above, p. 78.

[62] Spillane and McAllister, 'Keeping the lid on', cited in note 54 above.

[63] Bassiouni, 'Critical reflections', cited in note 53 above, p. 313.

[64] Convention on Psychotropic Substances, Vienna, adopted 21 February 1972, entered into force 16 August 1976, 1019 UNTS 175. Sinha, *The Leading International Drug Control Conventions*, cited in note 26 above, p. 25.

the Convention reverses the presumption of illegality. Under the Single Convention organic drugs are deemed to be unlawful unless it is proved otherwise while under the Psychotropic Convention synthetic drugs are to be considered lawful until and unless it is proved otherwise. No clearer illustration could be provided of the relative power of the states producing organic, plant-based drugs and the states with developed pharmaceutical industries to influence the text of international conventions.

Article 2 created a process whereby the World Health Organization (WHO) was made responsible for evaluating the capacity of a substance to produce 'a state of dependence' and central nervous system stimulation or depression, resulting in 'hallucinations or disturbances in motor function or thinking or behaviour or perception or mood'. Only then and where there was sufficient evidence that the substance is being or is likely to be abused so as to constitute a public health and social problem, can it be scheduled as unlawful. The Convention included a range of drug classes, including stimulants, depressants, and hallucinogens in its schedules. However, the controls adopted were considerably weaker than those under the Single Convention,[65] and a more significant attempt was made in Article 20 to address the prevention of drug abuse in consumer countries. In particular, Article 36 asserted that 'measures of treatment, education, after-care, rehabilitation and social reintegration' could be used as an alternative to conviction or punishment, or in addition to conviction or punishment. Shortly afterwards, the Single Convention itself was amended by Protocol to reflect the rather more rehabilitative approach taken in Articles 20 and 36 of the Psychotropic Convention.[66] Nevertheless, enthusiasm for the Psychotropic Convention amongst most members of the international community, mindful of the importance of their own pharmaceutical industries, was considerably weaker than that for the Single Convention.[67]

6.6 The Convention against Illicit Traffic in Narcotic Drugs and Psychotropic Substances 1988

By the late 1980s the level of illicit drug traffic that had developed since the entry into force of the two previous Conventions was causing serious global concern. In the declining years of the Cold War, the United States was beginning to regard defence against the drug threat as less of a moralistic crusade and more of a challenge to its national security, requiring a disciplinary, militarized response. This 'securitization' of the drug problem led to the transfer of military resources from confrontation with the Soviet Union to containment of the drug threat, particularly in Latin America. According to Hesselroth:

> Such a securitization emphasises the application of state-centred policies and military means to face drug trafficking and the complex problems related to it.[68]

[65] Ibid, p. 24.

[66] Protocol Amending the Single Convention on Narcotic Drugs, 1961, Geneva, adopted 25 March 1972, entered into force 8 August 1975, 976 UNTS 3.

[67] Spillane and McAllister, 'Keeping the lid on', cited in note 54 above, S10.

[68] Alba Hesselroth, 'Struggles of security in US foreign drug policy towards Andean countries', (2004) 5 *Journal of Peace, Conflict and Development*, 1–29, p. 1.

From 1986 the United States was also increasingly willing to use its 'Certification Scheme' to link its aid programmes directly to the compliance of the recipient state with the two Conventions. States that refused to cooperate in enforcing their obligations were simply excluded from US trade and aid deals,[69] and could be subject to sanctions.[70] The idea that drugs represented a vital national security threat to the United States, connected directly to terrorism and anti-democratic insurgent activity, was very evident in the wording of the National Security Decision Directive 221 that was signed by President Ronald Reagan in 1986.[71] The general tone and in some cases the wording of this Directive are also very close to those of the Trafficking Convention.

A draft of the Trafficking Convention was prepared during the 1987 UN Conference on Drug Abuse and Illiciit Trafficking, which resolved to take 'vigorous international actions against drug abuse and international trafficking as an important goal of our policies'. In pursuit of this aim and in addition to calling for wider participation in the regimes of the existing Conventions, the Conference demanded the 'urgent yet careful finalization' of the Trafficking Convention and its entry into force at the earliest possible date.[72] The representatives of 106 states and other interest groups met in Vienna in November 1988, accepting the text of the Trafficking Convention on 20 December. The Trafficking Convention signalled a very significant escalation of the war against drugs. For the first time, the preamble explicitly identified illicit traffic in drugs as an international criminal activity and noted the links between 'illicit traffic and other related organised criminal activities that undermine the legitimate economies and threaten the stability, security and sovereignty of States'.[73] Under Article 3 of the Convention, states parties were directly required to establish criminal offences under their domestic law, covering a range of activities that included the production, manufacture, extraction, preparation, offering, offering for sale, or involvement in trafficking of any narcotic drug or any psychotropic substance identified by the provisions of the two previous Conventions. Organising or financing such activities should also be penalized. Article 14 dealt with eradication, requiring 'all parties to take appropriate measures to prevent illicit cultivation of and to eradicate plants containing narcotic or psychotropic substances, such as opium poppy, coca bush and cannabis plants, cultivated illicitly

[69] Ibid.

[70] Jelsma, *The Development of International Drug Control*, cited in note 33 above, p. 5.

[71] Ronald Reagan, National Security Decision Directive 221 (NSDD-221), 'Narcotics and National Security', 8 April 1986, partially declassified on 7 November 1995, redacted version available at www.fas.org/irp/offdocs/nsdd/nsdd-221.htm. O'Manique, 'From prohibition to decriminalization', cited in note 52 above, p. 42.

[72] 'Declaration of the International Conference on Drug Abuse and Illicit Trafficking' 1987, para. 3. Adopted by the International Conference on Drug Abuse and Illicit Trafficking held in Vienna, 17–26 June 1987, and affirmed by the General Assembly of the United Nations by its resolution 42/112 of 7 December 1987, in Resolution and Decisions adopted by the General Assembly during its 42nd session, Vol. I, Supplement No. 49, UN Document A/42/49, p. 211. Available at www.unodc.org/documents/commissions/CND/Political_Declaration/Political_Declaration_1987/1987_DECLARATION_OF_THE_INTERNATIONAL_CONFERENCE_ON_DRUG_ABUSE_AND_ILLICIT_TRAFFICKING.pdf.

[73] Convention against Illicit Traffic in Narcotic Drugs and Psychotropic Substances, Vienna, adopted 20 December 1988, 1582 UNTS 95; entered into force 11 November 1990.

in its territory'. On a more individual level, the Trafficking Convention even required states to prohibit the possession, purchase, or cultivation of narcotic drugs or psychotropic substances for personal consumption;[74] activities that suggest an extremely elastic definition of 'trafficking'.

Jelsma has described these provisions as 'the radicalization of the system towards more repressive implementation',[75] while Aoyagi has characterized them as 'the most stringent punitive measures to date'.[76] They also represent a very significant reorientation of the drug control system towards the policing of domestic consumption in a way that is very different to the approach adopted by the other two Conventions. The language of the central penal section, Article 3, is unrelentingly admonitory, emphasizing on at least three occasions the 'grave nature' of many of these offences and that they are 'particularly serious'.[77] In two respects, however, the Trafficking Convention appears initially to offer concessions to a liberal approach. First, it reproduces the more humane alternatives of 'treatment, education, aftercare, rehabilitation or social reintegration' that had been introduced into the other two Conventions in 1961–2. However, whereas previously these measures had been seen as 'alternatives to conviction',[78] in the Trafficking Convention they were expressed to be 'in addition to conviction or punishment' or only for 'appropriate cases of a minor nature'.[79] Where the Trafficking Convention broke new ground is in its reference, for the first time in any drug convention, to 'human rights'. Article 14(2) specifically required states parties undertaking drug cultivation eradication programmes to adopt measures that respect fundamental human rights and to take due account of traditional licit uses as well as the protection of the environment.

No such concerns needed to arise, however, in respect of the draconian measures contained in Article 3 and the only rights that were envisaged by the Convention in this respect were those of presence at trial and respect for the domestic law (whatever that happens to be).[80] Curiously, the offences scheduled in Article 3(1) are limited to those committed intentionally, while by contrast those in Article 3(1)(c) were to be enacted subject to constitutional principles and the basic concepts of the local legal system! Possession, purchase, or cultivation for personal consumption under Article 3(2) must be subject to both. This rather complex wording clearly offers the potential for loophole defection from the Convention by countries with constitutional courts that are prepared to assert that the enforcement of these offences would be contrary to their constitutional principles and to the basic concepts of their legal system.[81] This is particularly important, given that Article 3 imposes the only explicit, direct, and binding international obligation to penalize domestic consumption in any of the three Conventions. The Trafficking Convention launched a 'new era in UN drug control

[74] Art. 3(2).

[75] Jelsma, *The Development of International Drug Control*, cited in note 33 above, p. 1.

[76] Melissa T. Aoyagi, 'Beyond punitive prohibition: liberalizing the dialogue on international drug policy', (2004) 37 *New York University Journal of International Law and Politics* (3), 555–610, p. 579.

[77] Art. 3(4)(a), (5), and (7).

[78] Psychotropic Convention, Art. 22.

[79] Art. 3(4)(b) and (c).

[80] Arts 3(9) and (11).

[81] Bewley-Taylor and Jelsma, 'Regime change', cited in note 39 above, p. 177.

efforts'[82] and the UK representative Richardson announced that '(t)his is an instrument with teeth, and we need to make it bite'.[83]

Since 1988, the Trafficking Convention has indeed bitten hard. In the absence of any effective human rights protections written into any of the three Conventions,[84] policies of interdiction, eradication, and criminalization have been pursued relentlessly by many states. Many of those arrested, even for low-level involvement, have faced the death penalty, particularly in countries, such as Iran, Vietnam, and China, with poor due process protections. Notwithstanding the professed opposition of the international community to the death penalty, it has colluded actively in this sanguinary process by providing funds and even celebrating the process's success, for example in helping catch 61 traffickers in Iran and in extraditing 128 to China, all of whom were probably executed.[85] Drug arrestees, usually drawn from the most marginalized and impoverished populations, have filled the world's prisons, particularly in the United States and in Latin America.[86]

6.7 Undermining the Conventions

Nevertheless, some signatory states, recognizing these and other 'unintended consequences' of the international drugs control regime, have adopted a variety of methods of defection or resistance. It is fair to say that no international convention regime has been interpreted in such widely different ways by states parties, from the aggressive policing of 'narco-terrorism' in 'Plan Colombia', to the liberalism of the Californian and Dutch models, and the abstentionism of states such as Portugal and Bolivia. The different pragmatic strategies adopted to undermine or evade the stricter terms of the Conventions can be grouped under three headings.

The first can be characterized as the active use of 'loopholes', such as the unusual wording of Article 3 of the Trafficking Convention, referred to in section 6.6 of this chapter. An increasing number of states have entered reservations to the Treaties, particularly the Trafficking Convention.[87] Moreover, Article 32(4) of this instrument explicitly permitted states parties to enter a reservation rejecting the compulsory jurisdiction of the International Court of Justice over disputes. Bolivia has attempted to renounce and then re-accede to the Single Convention with further reservations,[88] a manoeuvre that was met with implacable opposition by the United States and its supporters.[89]

[82] Jelsma, *The Development of International Drug Control*, cited in note 33 above, p. 183.

[83] Ibid, p. 183.

[84] With the exception of Art. 14(2) of the Trafficking Convention, referred to above.

[85] Damon Barrett, *Reflections on Human Rights and International Drug Control*, London, London School of Economics, 2010, p. 61.

[86] Pien Metaal and Coletta Youngers, *Systems Overload. Drug Laws and Prisons in Latin America*, Washington DC, Washington Office on Latin America, 2011.

[87] Room, 'Reform by subtraction', cited in note 51 above, pp. 403–4.

[88] Thoumi, 'Straight jacket', cited in note 56 above, p. 78; Room, ibid, p. 405.

[89] Bewley-Taylor and Jelsma, 'Regime change', cited in note 39 above, p. 62.

The second approach has been described as 'soft defection', whereby states attempt to circumvent the accepted provisions of the Conventions through creative interpretation. According to Bewley-Taylor and Jelsma, 'detailed and robust legal justifications put forward by many states demonstrate that the policy choices are defensible within the boundaries of the existing treaty framework'.[90] Many countries have simply relaxed the intensity with which the users of, or dealers in, certain drugs are pursued by the authorities. Switzerland, Luxembourg, Belgium, Spain, Portugal, Ireland, the Czech Republic, and thirteen US states have introduced legislation to decriminalize the possession of minor quantities of cannabis and others have achieved the same result through policing policy.[91]

The European Union has not sought to impose any collective approach to the international treaties on member states.[92] The Netherlands, for example, has adopted a relatively permissive approach to consumption under a 'separation of the markets' policy, whereby cannabis use is decriminalized and the possession and small-scale sale of cannabis in coffee shops is an accepted part of life. Cultivation and supply of cannabis nevertheless remain illegal.[93] This contrasts sharply with the approach adopted by the UK and Sweden. In the latter case, a strictly prohibitionist regime has focused on 'abstention-based and coercive treatment programs'.[94] As a result, Sweden has somewhat lower rates of drug use than The Netherlands but a higher drug-related death rate, although such differences are negligible in global terms.[95] The decriminalization of certain classes of drugs by Portugal in 2001 resulted in significant reductions in the prison population but little indication of any increase in the harmful use of drugs.[96]

The third approach can be broadly characterized as 'harm reduction'[97] and has been actively championed, sometimes in direct opposition to the Conventions and their supporters, by international agencies such as the International Red Cross[98] and the WHO.[99] Much of the debate over the 'medicalization' of approaches to addiction has centred around the use of 'drug injection rooms' that have been shown to have largely achieved their initial, health-related objectives without increasing levels of drug use or drug trafficking.[100]

[90] Ibid, p. 61.

[91] Jelsma, *The Development of International Drug Control*, cited in note 33 above, p. 9.

[92] Caroline Chatwin, *Mixed Messages from Europe on Drug Policy Reform: The Cases of Sweden and the Netherlands*, Washington DC, Brookings Institution, 2015, p. 2.

[93] Ibid, pp. 5–7. [94] Ibid, pp. 4–5.

[95] Jean-Paul Grund and Joost Breeksema, *Coffee Shops and Compromise. Separated Illicit Drug Markets in the Netherlands*, New York, Open Society, 2013. Chatwin, ibid, p. 9.

[96] Jelsma, *The Development of International Drug Control*, cited in note 33 above, p. 8; Hannah Laqueur, 'Uses and abuses of drug decriminalization in Portugal', (2015) 40 *Law & Social Inquiry* (3), 746–81.

[97] Patricia G. Erickson *et al.*, *Harm Reduction: A New Direction for Drug Policies and Programs*, Toronto, University of Toronto Press, 2015.

[98] International Federation of Red Cross and Red Crescent Societies, *Out of Harm's Way. Injecting Drug Users and Harm Reduction*, Geneva, IFRC, 2010.

[99] Robin Room, 'Harm reduction, human rights and the WHO Expert Committee on Drug Dependence', in Patricia G. Erickson, Diane M. Riley, Yuet W. Cheung, and Pat A. O'Hare (eds), *Harm Reduction: A New Direction for Drug Policies and Programs*, Toronto, University of Toronto Press, 1997, pp. 119–30; Robin Room and Peter Reuter, 'How well do international drug conventions protect public health?', (2012) 379 *The Lancet* (9810), 84–91.

[100] Chloé Potier *et al.*, 'Supervised injection services: what has been demonstrated? A systematic literature review', (2014) *Drug and Alcohol Dependence*, 145, 48–68.

6.8 The Road to Reform of the Conventions

At the turn of the millennium, the prospects for reform of the 1961, 1972, and 1988 Conventions looked bleak. In 1995, the findings of the extensive 'WHO/UNICRI Cocaine Project' were allegedly suppressed and,[101] after repeated requests from Mexico and other producer nations, a United Nations General Assembly Special Session (UNGASS) on Drugs was held in 1998, which (disappointingly) merely endorsed existing policies. Jelsma has recorded the 'unwritten history' of this event, noting the 'extent to which the hardliners have gone to maintain the status quo through rhetoric, denial, manipulation, selective presentation, misrepresentation and suppression of evidence, selective use of experts, threats to funding, and purging "defeatists" from the UN system'.[102]

Despite the pessimism of many commentators, there appears to be an increasing volume of international demand for a 'recalibration' of the Conventions.[103] Part of this developing confidence arises from the obvious and sometimes very public institutional disagreements that have taken place between international agencies such as the WHO, the UNODC, and the International Narcotics Control Board.[104] UNODC, for example, in a trenchant 2008 intervention that implied strongly that the drug control system was 'not fit for purpose', identified a number of 'unintended negative consequences' of the current system. Amongst these were the creation of the criminal market for drugs as a by-product of a supply-focused international system that inflated criminal market prices, policy displacement from health to law enforcement, geographic displacement (the balloon effect) as an inevitable consequence of supply reduction efforts and the stigmatization and marginalization of target populations.[105] More importantly, the bloody conflicts over drugs in Mexico and Afghanistan show no sign of abatement and the evidence for the futility of these policies and their environmental and social costs continued to accumulate.

In 2011, the Global Commission on Drug Policy (GCDP), an organisation funded by the Open Society Foundation and comprising twenty-two international 'Ambassadors', including the former Secretary-General of the United Nations, Kofi Annan, Richard Branson the entrepreneur, and the former Presidents of Brazil, Chile, Colombia, Mexico, Portugal, and Switzerland, amongst other luminaries, issued a Report that began:

> The global war on drugs has failed, with devastating consequences for individuals and societies around the world. Fifty years after the initiation of the UN Single Convention on Narcotic Drugs, and 40 years after President Nixon launched the US

[101] Jelsma, *The Development of International Drug Control*, cited in note 33 above, pp. 188–9.

[102] Martin Jelsma, 'Drugs in the UN system: the unwritten history of the 1998 United Nations General Assembly Special Session on Drugs', (2003) 14 *International Journal of Drug Policy* (2), 181–95, p. 181.

[103] Bewley-Taylor and Jelsma, 'Regime change', cited in note 39 above, p. 67.

[104] Ibid, p. 60.

[105] UNODC, *Making Drug Control 'Fit for Purpose': Building on the UNGASS Decade*, Vienna, UNODC, 2008.

government's war on drugs, fundamental reforms in national and global drug control policies are urgently needed.[106]

In the following year, the organisation Count the Costs of the War on Drugs published its *Alternative World Drug Report* setting out the 'seven costs' of the international drug prohibition regime. These included 'undermining development and security, fuelling conflict, threatening public health, spreading disease and death, undermining human rights, promoting stigma and discrimination, creating crime, enriching criminals, deforestation and pollution and wasting billions on drug law enforcement'.[107] Two former US Presidents, Jimmy Carter and Bill Clinton,[108] have joined the growing campaign. Latin America has also taken a prominent role in opposition. The 2012 Cartagena Summit of the Americas, for example, gave the Organization of American States a mandate to explore possible alternative drug policy scenarios for the hemisphere.[109]

The GCDP published further powerful reports, including, in 2014 *Taking Control. Pathways to Drug Policy Reform Around the World*, which called for the international community to abandon the criminalization of drug use and possession and to focus on reducing the power of criminal organisations and the violence and insecurity that result from their competition with both one another and the state. In 2015 GCDP published *The Negative Impact of Drug Control on Public Health: The Global Crisis of Avoidable Pain*, which called for a renewed emphasis on harm reduction, a revision of the 1961 and 1971 Conventions' schedules in light of scientific evidence and an emphasis on providing therapeutic drugs and pain relief for the estimated 75 per cent of the global population with no access to these.[110] According to the GCDP, 'change was in the air'.

One of the main sources for optimism amongst the 'moral entrepreneurs' working with and within these organisations was the imminence of the next UNGASS, which has been brought forward to 2016 from 2019 on a motion co-sponsored by Mexico and ninety-five other countries.[111] Nevertheless, resistance to Convention change amongst the more powerful nations appears to be as firm as ever. In September 2014 United States President Barack Obama issued a Presidential Determination ... for Fiscal Year 2015, which asserted that '(t)he essential underpinnings of our unified stance against criminal enterprise are embodied in longstanding international agreements, including the 1961, 1971, and 1988 UN Conventions...'[112] Russia has been actively promoting

[106] Global Commission on Drugs Policy, *Report on the Global Commission on Drugs Policy*, Rio de Janeiro, GCDP, 2011, p. 2.

[107] Count the Costs of the War on Drugs. Alternative World Drug Report, 2012, available at: http://www.countthecosts.org/alternative-world-drug-report.

[108] Carter, 'Call off the drug war', *New York Times*, 16 June 2011. 'Bill Clinton apologizes to Mexico for war on drugs', *Huffington Post*, 13 February 2015.

[109] Martin Jelsma, *UNGASS 2016: Prospects for Treaty Reform and UN System-Wide Coherence on Drug Policy*. Washington DC, Brookings Institution, 2015, p. 15.

[110] Global Commission on Drugs Policy, *Taking Control. Pathways to Drug Policy Reform Around the World*, Rio de Janeiro, GCDP, 2014 and *The Negative Impact of Drug Control on Public Health: The Global Crisis of Avoidable Pain*, Rio de Janeiro, GCDP, 2015, p. 6.

[111] Jelsma, *UNGASS 2016*, cited in note 109 above.

[112] Available at: https://www.whitehouse.gov/the-press-office/2015/09/14/presidential-determination-major-drug-transit-or-major-illicit-drug.

its 'Rainbow-2' drug eradication programme in Afghanistan, positioning itself as 'a major advocate for the continuation of prohibitionist policy',[113] while China has continued to pursue a brutal policy of domestic repression of drug trafficking, justifying its actions by reference to the international Conventions.[114] Europe, on the other hand, is increasingly likely to advocate a 'balanced approach' combining the fight against trafficking with demand and harm reduction strategies.[115] A further round of confrontation in the international community can certainly be anticipated, in which the three Conventions, and especially the Trafficking Convention, will provide the major battleground.

6.9 Conclusion

Much of the debate at UNGASS 2016 will no doubt turn on the supposed 'unintended consequences' of the global campaign against drug trafficking and use. It has been argued here that the uncompromising character of the Trafficking Convention is the outcome of a long historical process, involving the negotiated geopolitical and economic interests of a number of extremely powerful states. So far from being unintended, many of the consequences of the Trafficking Convention, notably the securitization and militarization of the global response that it effectively authorized, are highly functional for many countries. They permit intervention in neighbouring states, the maintenance of extensive military, police, and security agencies and networks of surveillance that, with the colonization of the darkweb by drug dealers, now penetrate deep into cyberspace.[116] The characterization of drug trafficking as an international crime by the Trafficking Convention, and the acknowledgement of an explicit linkage with organised crime networks, allow these same states to portray themselves as guardians of global order, when it is the policies that they have adopted in response that have magnified the criminality of the drug economy.

The victims of this confluence of interest around the Trafficking Convention and its antecedent treaties are increasingly numerous. They do not just consist of the growing number of drug users denied therapeutic treatment by an exclusively penal response to their addiction, nor the huge numbers of impoverished and desperate individuals drawn into menial roles in the trafficking networks and then abandoned to lengthy imprisonment or execution, justified by the severity demanded by Article 3. They also include the victims of drug wars in Mexico, Afghanistan, and elsewhere, the farmers displaced by eradication campaigns mandated by Article

[113] Crick, 'Drugs as an existential threat', cited in note 25 above, pp. 411–12.

[114] Bin Liang, 'Drugs and drug control in the People's Republic of China (1949–present)', in Liqun Cao, Yvan Sun, and Bill Hebenton (eds), *The Routledge Handbook of Chinese Criminology*, Abingdon, Routledge, pp. 183–96.

[115] Jorg Friedrichs, *Fighting Terrorism and Drugs: Europe and International Police Cooperation*, Abingdon, Routledge, 2008, p. 114.

[116] Alexia Maddox *et al.*, 'Constructive activism in the dark web: cryptomarkets and illicit drugs in the digital "demimonde"', (2015) *Information, Communication & Society*, 1–16.

14, and the many millions denied health-care, education, or access to basic necessities by the large sums of tax money wasted by their governments in attempted compliance with the penal provisions of the Convention. These unbearable costs must be in the forefront of discussion both at UNGASS 2016 and thereafter, when as Secretary-General of the United Nations Ban Ki-moon has urged, all options must be considered.[117]

[117] Jelsma, *UNGASS 2016*, cited in note 109 above, p. 24.

7

The UN Convention against Transnational Organised Crime 2000

*Neil Boister**

7.1 Introduction

The UN Convention against Transnational Organised Crime (Palermo Convention, UNTOC or UNCTOC) adopted in Palermo in 2000[1] is designed to be the premier global crime suppression convention in the fight against organised crime. With 185 states parties as at May 2015, this comprehensive legal armoury has enjoined considerable formal support.[2] Three Protocols—the Human Trafficking Protocol,[3] the Migrant

* Professor, Te Piringa Faculty of Law, University of Waikato, New Zealand. Research was completed while the author was a visiting scholar at the University of Hamburg, funded by the receipt of a Friedrich Wilhelm Bessel Prize from the Alexander von Humboldt Foundation. My thanks to Professor Florian Jessberger (University of Hamburg), and to the Humboldt Foundation, for their generosity.

[1] The United Nations Convention against Transnational Organized Crime, opened for signature 15 November 2000, 2225 UNTS 209, in force 29 September 2003. See generally the contributions to Hans-Jörg Albrecht and Cyrille Fijnaut (eds), *The Containment of Transnational Organised Crime: Comments on the UN Convention of December 2000*, Freiburg im Breisgau, Edition Iuscrim, 2002; the contributions to Stefano Betti (ed.), *Symposium: The United Nations Convention against Transnational Organised Crime: requirements for effective implementation*, Turin: UNICRI *et al.*, 2002; Roger S. Clark, 'The United Nations Convention against Transnational Organized Crime', (2004) 50 *Wayne Law Review* 161; Carrie-Lyn Donigan Guymon, 'International legal mechanisms for combating transnational organised crime', (2000) 18 *Berkeley Journal of International Law*, 53; Matti Joutsen, 'International cooperation against transnational organized crime: criminalizing participation in and organized criminal group', (2002) 59 *UNAFEI Resource Materials* 417; Gerhard Kemp, 'The United Nations Convention against Transnational Organized Crime: a milestone in international criminal law', (2001) 14 *South African Journal of Criminal Justice* 152; David McClean, *Transnational Organized Crime: A Commentary on the UN Convention and its Protocols*, Oxford, OUP, 2007; Tom Obokata, *Transnational Organised Crime in International Law*, Oxford, Hart, 2010, pp 25–80; Alexandra V. Orlova and James W. Moore, '"Umbrellas" or "building blocks"?: Defining international terrorism and transnational organised crime in international law', (2005) 27 *Houston Journal of International Law* (2), 267; Andreas Schloenhardt, 'Transnational organised crime', in Neil Boister and Robert J. Currie (eds), *The Routledge Handbook of Transnational Criminal Law*, London, Routledge, 2014, p. 409; Dimitri Vlassis, 'The United Nations Convention against Transnational Organized Crime and its Protocols: a new era in international cooperation', in International Centre for Criminal Law Reform and Criminal Justice Policy (eds), *The Changing Face of International Criminal Law*, Vancouver, BC, International Centre for Criminal Law Reform and Criminal Justice, 2002, p. 75.

[2] United Nations Treaty Collection, Status, as at 28 May 2015 available at https://treaties.un.org/pages/viewdetails.aspx?src=ind&mtdsg_no=xviii-12&chapter=18&lang=en.

[3] Protocol to Prevent, Suppress, Punish Trafficking in Persons, Especially Women and Children, supplementing the United Nations Convention Against Transnational Organized Crime, New York, 15 November 2000, 2237 UNTS 319, in force 25 December 2003.

Smuggling Protocol,[4] and the Firearms Protocol[5]—deal with specific crimes stipulated as sufficiently serious to justify application of the UNTOC's regime for international cooperation, and many of the provisions of the UNTOC were specifically designed to be used to implement the Protocols.[6] As spelled out in Article 1, the UNTOC's purpose is to 'promote co-operation to prevent and combat transnational organised crime more effectively'. This is to be achieved through legislative harmonization and more effective suppression while remaining within the bounds of human rights safeguards.[7]

The authors of the UNTOC had to clear a difficult conceptual hurdle to realize this programme: the controversial nature of its foundational concept, 'organized crime', and by extension its transnational extrapolation, 'transnational organized crime'.[8] Critics deny that 'organized crime' reflects social reality and point to its malleability and use as a political tool.[9] Levi, for example, argues that the causes of, form of, and policy responses to illicit markets cannot be adequately described by 'organized crime', 'which provides little more than a floating signifier of social danger, allowing interpreters to read what they like into it'.[10] Even amongst those more accepting of the validity of the terms 'organized crime' and 'transnational organized crime' there are differences over precisely what 'organised' means (from monolithic shadow governments to diversified logistical networks) and how a cross-border context changes the nature of the activity or the threat it offers.[11] This chapter illustrates how the authors of the UNTOC overcame the difficulty of getting agreement on a concept of organised crime for the purposes of substantive criminal law by criminalizing participation in organised criminal groups in serious crimes.

The UNTOC's elaborate framework for international cooperation, which ranges from more informal police cooperation to more formal legal assistance, is so extensive that it suggests that cooperation rather than criminalization is the main subject matter of the UNTOC. There is a sense, however, that fifteen years after its adoption the UNTOC's aims of promoting cooperation to prevent and combat transnational

[4] Protocol Against the Smuggling of Migrants by Land, Sea and Air, supplementing the United Nations Convention Against Transnational Organized Crime, New York, 15 November 2000, 2241 UNTS 507, in force 28 January 2004.

[5] Protocol against the Illicit Manufacturing of and Trafficking in Firearms, Their Parts and Components and Ammunition, supplementing the United Nations Convention against Transnational Organized Crime, New York, 31 May 2001, 2326 UNTS 208, in force 3 June 2005.

[6] Legislative Guide 329. In terms of Art. 37 a state can become party to UNTOC alone but not to a protocol without becoming party to UNTOC.

[7] Vincenzo Militello, 'Participation in an organised criminal group as international offence', in Albrecht and Fijnaut, *Containment of TOC*, cited in note 1 above, p. 97, p. 106.

[8] See—for the matter of definition—Chapter 2 of this book, sections 2.1.1 and 2.3.2 and Chapter 21 of this book.

[9] See, for example, James W. E. Sheptycki, 'Transnational crime: an interdisciplinary perspective', in Boister and Currie, *Routledge Handbook of Transnational Criminal Law*, cited in note 1 above, p. 41, pp. 42–6.

[10] Michael Levi, 'The organization of serious crime for gain', in Mike Maguire, Rod Morgan, and Robert Reiner (eds), *The Oxford Handbook of Criminology*, Oxford, OUP, 2012, p. 595.

[11] See, for example, Phil Williams and Ernesto U. Savona, 'Problems and dangers posed by organized transnational crime in the various regions of the world', in Phil Williams and Ernesto Savona (eds), *The United Nations and Transnational Organized Crime*, London: Frank Cass, 1996, p. 1, p. 6.

organised crime more effectively have not been fully realized. The 2015 Doha Declaration, for example, calls on states parties 'to implement and make more effective use of' the UNTOC.[12] The aim of this chapter is to examine the criminalization provisions in the UNTOC to try to draw some conclusions about whether and if so how they have impacted on its implementation and thus on the suppression of organised crime.

7.2 Development of the UNTOC

The UNTOC's development is well documented.[13] An influential step was taken domestically by the USA in the 1970 Racketeer Influenced and Corrupt Organizations Act (RICO).[14] Built around the notion of a legal enterprise such as a trade union being used to run a racket, RICO criminalized direct and indirect participation in patterns of criminal activity used as a means to extort, infiltrate, or control either licit or illicit enterprises. A different approach was taken by Italy in 1982 when in Article 416*bis* of the Italian Penal Code it adopted an organisational model of criminality by criminalizing the act of being part of a mafia-type organisation made up of three or more persons. The term 'transnational crime' had already been coined in 1974 by the UN Crime Prevention and Criminal Justice Branch to mean 'certain criminal phenomena transcending international borders, transgressing the laws of several states or having an impact on another country'.[15] The 1980s also saw growth in bilateral and regional mutual legal assistance treaties and an increase in broader multilateral cooperation against drugs and money laundering through the 1988 United Nations Convention against Illicit Traffic in Narcotic Drugs and Psychotropic Substances and the foundation of the Financial Action Task Force in 1989.[16]

Driven from within the UN crime prevention and criminal justice programme, progress towards a new convention dealing with transnational organised crime drawing on these instruments was fairly rapid. In 1990, the UN General Assembly signalled its

[12] The Declaration on Integrating Crime Prevention and Criminal Justice into the wider United Nations Agenda to address social and economic challenges and to promote the rule of law at the national and international levels, and public participation, adopted at the 13th UN Congress on Crime Prevention and Criminal Justice, 12–19 April 2015, Doha: UN Doc A/CONF.222/L.6, 31 March 2015.

[13] See M. Cherif Bassiouni and Eduardo Vetere (eds), *Organized Crime: a Compilation of UN Documents, 1975–1998*, Ardsley, New York, Transnational, 1998; 'Introduction', *Travaux Préparatoires of the Negotiations for the Elaboration of the United Nations Convention against Transnational Organized Crime and the Protocols thereto*, New York, United Nations, 2006, UN Pub. Sales No. E.06.V.5, p. ixff. See also Roberta Barberini, 'Italy and the international community in the fight against organized crime', in Betti, *Symposium: UNTOC*, cited in note 1 above, pp. 25–7; Peter Gastrow, 'The origin of the Convention', in Albrecht and Fijnaut, *Containment of TOC*, cited in note 1 above, p. 19ff.; Guymon, 'International legal mechanisms', cited in note 1 above, p. 90ff.; Almir Maljević, *Participation in a Criminal Organisation and Conspiracy; Different Legal Models and Criminal Collectives*, Berlin: Duncker and Humblot, 2011, p. 123ff.

[14] Title 18 of the USC, para. 1961.

[15] Gerhard Mueller, 'Transnational crime: definitions and concepts', in Phil Williams and Dimitri Vlassis (eds), *Combating Transnational Crime*, Milan/London, ISPAC/Frank Cass, 2001, p. 13.

[16] Trafficking Convention: Vienna, 20 December 1988, 1582 UNTS 95; in force 11 November 1990. The FATF's Forty Recommendations were originally published in April 1990; the latest iteration was adopted 16 February 2012, and is available at: http://www.fatf-gafi.org/topics/fatfrecommendations/documents/fatf-recommendations.html.

concern about the growth of cross-border crime in the post-Cold War world and the necessity for the development of preventive and control strategies.[17] In July 1992 the UN Economic and Social Council (ECOSOC) put 'action against national and transnational organized and environmental crime' on the agenda of the UN Congress on the Prevention of Crime and Treatment of Offenders.[18] In December 1992 the General Assembly called for 'global efforts' against 'national and transnational crime'.[19] Prompted by recommendations from the UN Commission on Crime Prevention and the General Assembly,[20] a World Ministerial Conference on Organised Transnational Crime was held in Naples in 1994. It adopted the Naples Political Declaration and Global Action Plan against Organized Transnational Crime,[21] which called in general terms for action against transnational organised crime including the elaboration of an international instrument on organised crime that defined the term.

Yet in spite of broad support for international action at Naples there was resistance to the idea of a convention, especially from the 'Western Europe and other' group (WEOG). Gastrow summarizes their objections:

> Those who were sceptical of the need for a new convention argued that the concept of organised transnational crime was too vague, that it appeared in too many forms to be dealt with except on a high level of generality, and that existing instruments on extradition and mutual legal assistance—if promoted and properly implemented—could already provide an adequate basis for international cooperation.[22]

The WEOG were raising two important questions: first, could a treaty be agreed that articulated a concept of organised crime that was of sufficient generality that it would include within its scope all forms of organised criminality, yet be sufficiently specific that it actually addressed the problem of organised crime? Second, could a treaty based on such a concept provide a practical basis for effective international cooperation? Developing states in contrast were generally in favour of the treaty. They felt it would help them tackle a phenomenon that was beginning to penetrate their territories and impede their development and for which they were totally unprepared. Moreover, development within the UN meant the treaty would be built using a process of consensus under which they would enjoy relative parity with the developed states. Finally, the convention would make provision for mechanisms of international cooperation that they had not been able to develop because they had neither the resources nor the negotiating power to address this need through bilateral or regional arrangements.[23]

Calls for action against organised crime were lent political impetus when US President Bill Clinton classified it as a threat to national security in Presidential

[17] UN GA Res. 45/108 of 14 December 1990 (UN Doc. A7RES746/152).

[18] ECOSOC Res. 1992/24 of 30 July 1992.

[19] UN GA Res. 47/87 of 16 December 1992 (UN Doc. A/RES/47/87).

[20] UN GA Res. 48/103 of 20 December 1993 (UN Doc. A/RES/48/103).

[21] Report of the World Ministerial Conference on Organised Crime: Report of the Secretary-General, UN GAOR, 49th Sess., Agenda Item 96, 1994. It was approved in UN GA Res. 49/159 of 23 December 1994.

[22] Gastrow, 'The origin of the Convention', cited in note 13 above, p. 29; see also Vlassis, 'The UNTOC and its Protocols', cited in note 1 above, pp. 78–9.

[23] Vlassis, 'The UNTOC and its Protocols', cited in note 1 above, pp. 79–80.

Directive 42 of 1995. A group of senior experts on transnational organised crime was set up by the G7 plus Russia and made a set of recommendations that set the stage for further developments.[24] In July 1996 ECOSOC called for a thorough analysis of the attitude of states to the possible elaboration of a convention or conventions against transnational organised crime.[25] Pre-empting further debate, in October 1996 the Polish government submitted a draft convention to the UN General Assembly.[26] In 1998 the UN General Assembly endorsed the development of a convention and set up an intergovernmental meeting of experts that met in Warsaw and drafted a list of options.[27] Ten sessions of a UN ad hoc Committee open to all states were held between 1999 and 2000,[28] producing a draft convention and three supplementary protocols. These instruments were formally adopted and opened for signature symbolically in Palermo in 2000.

What emerged was an uneven mixture of complex technical provisions drawn from the law and practice of Western states, with lowest-common-denominator provisions distilled in treaty negotiations filling the gaps. During the negotiations the initial enthusiasm of developing states had been dampened by the complexity of the obligations being developed and the sense that the now enthusiastic Western states were beginning to impose approaches that would expand extra-territorial jurisdiction and require considerable resources to meet.[29] The policy models used can give the impression that the UNTOC was intended mainly as a measure to protect the West, something that would inevitably impact negatively on its global implementation.[30] Samuel Witten, a legal advisor to the State Department, argued before the Senate for US ratification of the UNTOC as follows: 'The value of these Convention provisions to the United States is that they oblige other countries that have been slower to adapt to the threat of transnational organized crime to adopt new laws in harmony with ours.'[31]

7.3 Criminalizing the Organisation of Serious Crime for Benefit

7.3.1 From organised crime to organised criminal group

The authors of the UNTOC may have agreed to the political concept of organised crime but they struggled to clothe it in acceptable legal flesh. While concepts of

[24] Ibid, p. 80.

[25] ECOSOC Res. 1996/27 on the implementation of the Naples Political Declaration and Global Action against organised transnational crime, 24 July 1996.

[26] *Question of the Elaboration of an International Convention against Organized Transnational Crime*, UN Doc. A/C.3/51/7, 1 October 1996; see also Vlassis, 'The UNTOC and its Protocols', cited in note 1 above, p. 81.

[27] Established by UN GA Res. 52/85, 30 January 1998.

[28] See Reports of the Ad Hoc Committee on the Elaboration of a Convention against Transnational Organized Crime on the work of its first to eleventh sessions, UN Doc. GA A/55/383, 2 November 2000, 40 *ILM* 335 (2001).

[29] Vlassis, 'The UNTOC and its Protocols', cited in note 1 above, pp. 90–91.

[30] See also C. Fijnaut, 'The UN Convention and the global problem of organized crime', in Albrecht and Fijnaut, *Containment of TOC*, cited in note 1 above, p. 55, p. 59.

[31] Peter Andreas and Ethan Nadelmann, *Policing the Globe: Criminalization and Crime Control in International Relations*, Oxford, OUP, 2006, p. 173.

organisational hierarchy and use of violence, intimidation and corruption permeated the Naples Declaration's characterization of organised crime,[32] by the Polish draft definition the focus was shifting to the structural features of criminal organisations, such as membership. The Intergovernmental Group of Experts commented in 1998:

> While the contours of organized crime were generally understood, there continued to be divergences of a legal nature that made it difficult to reach a comprehensive definition. Engaging in such an endeavour might require considerable time, whereas there was a general feeling of the urgency of action in the direction of elaborating the new convention. Organized crime continued to evolve and manifest itself in different ways. As there was a general understanding of criminal organizations, efforts to determine the scope of the convention should build on that understanding, focusing action under the new convention against those groups; …[33]

This shift in focus led to the development of a definition of 'organised criminal group (OCG)', membership of which would lead to criminal liability, thus overcoming the difficulty of attributing criminal liability to individuals in a controlling position but who as a matter of evidence could only be established to have little or limited involvement in the actual offences committed. Article 2(a) of the Convention defines 'organized criminal group' as:

> a structured group of three or more persons, existing for a period of time and acting in concert with the aim of committing one or more serious crimes or offences established in accordance with this Convention, in order to obtain, directly or indirectly, a financial or other material benefit.

The definition in Article 2(a) incorporates the notion that what distinguishes organised crime is not the type of crime committed, nor the type of criminal, but the process by which it is carried out, which is claimed to increase social threat.[34] Many of the elements in Article 2(a) that establish the existence of an OCG were analytical concepts developed by the EU;[35] in 1998 the EU adopted a definition of a criminal organisation in very similar terms.[36]

7.3.2 Defining the organised criminal group (OCG)

Article 2(a) requires the participation of at least three persons which sets a very low size-threshold for what the states parties consider to be offering an increase in social danger.

The group must be 'structured', but only very loosely, with no requirements of membership formality, stability, or hierarchy. Under Article 2(c) this means a group 'that is not randomly formed for the immediate commission of an offence and that does

[32] See also McClean, *Transnational Organized Crime*, cited in note 1 above, pp. 3–4.
[33] See also UNODC, *Travaux Préparatoires,* cited in note 13 above, p. xxii.
[34] Willy Bruggeman, 'The Fight against organised crime: possibilities, problems and opportunities, with a special focus on the EU', in Albrecht and Fijnaut, *Containment of TOC*, cited in note 1 above, p. 67, p. 68.
[35] Ibid, p. 68.
[36] Joint Action 98/733/JHA of 21 December 1998.

not need to have formally defined roles for its members, continuity of its membership or a developed structure'. In an interpretative note about 'structured group' the Ad Hoc Committee for the Elaboration of the Convention states that the term 'is to be used in a broad sense so as to include both groups with hierarchical or other elaborate structure and non-hierarchical groups where the roles of the members need not be formally defined'; commentators suggest this renders the concept practically meaningless.[37] Although it appears to exclude mere complicity based on assistance by one to others,[38] it does have a very broad scope that can include a range of organizational forms from the highly structured to the relatively unstructured.

The requirement that the persons act in concert has been suggested to mean, not that they act simultaneously together, but that they act to achieve the same goal pursuing the same plan, so that their actions supplement each other.[39]

The group must exist for a period of time, but this period is undefined. Article 2(c) makes it clear that it must last longer than for the immediate commission of an offence. It has been argued that such groups usually commit more than one offence so it would have to exist for a period sufficient to commit at least two.[40] However, Article 2(c) excludes random formation for the immediate commission of an offence. A more deliberate formation for a period of time even prior to the commission of an offence should be sufficient, because it will allow authorities to take preventive action in pursuit of the general aims of the UNTOC.

The aim of the group must be to commit one or more serious crimes or offences established in accordance with the UNTOC for the purpose of obtaining a material benefit. This excludes groups whose aims are purely political, religious, philosophical, humanitarian, etc., but should be interpreted broadly to include those groups that might seek sexual gratification through, for example, trading child pornography.[41]

The model adopted permits the UNTOC to be used against a diverse range of networks from the ephemeral ranging all the way to the essentialist mafia-like stereotype that dominate the discourse.[42] In theory it is flexible enough to be used against new manifestations of organised crime as they appear, ensuring its continued relevance.[43] What it does not do is specifically label and denounce high-end, large-scale organisations, while it does create the potential for over-condemning low-end, small-scale organisations (even three youths engaged in a serious crime would qualify as an OCG).[44]

[37] *Travaux Préparatoires,* cited in note 13 above, [4]; Orlova and Moore, '"Umbrellas" or "building blocks"?', cited in note 1 above, p. 283.

[38] Maljević, *Participation in a Criminal Organisation*, cited in note 13 above, p. 150.

[39] Ibid, p. 151.

[40] Maljević, *Participation in a Criminal Organisation*, cited in note 13 above, p. 150.

[41] Ibid, p. 154; Obokata, *Transnational Organised Crime in International Law*, cited in note 1 above, p. 28.

[42] Letizia Paoli and Tom Vander Beken, 'Organized crime: a contested concept' in Letizia Paoli (ed.), *The Oxford Handbook of Organized Crime*, Oxford, OUP, 2014, p. 13, p. 24.

[43] Pino Arlacchi, 'After the Palermo Convention: new international prospects in the fight against organised crime', in Betti, *Symposium: UNTOC*, cited in note 1 above, 15, p. 17.

[44] Michael Tonry, 'Transnational organised crime—prospects for success of the UN Convention', in Albrecht and Fijnaut, *Containment of TOC*, cited in note 1 above, p. 253, p. 261.

Militello criticizes the breadth of the definition in Article 2(a) because it 'eclipses the distinction between the simple complicity of two persons in a single crime and the specific danger represented by an organisation whose programme covers an indeterminate number of crimes'.[45] Beare complains that, as a whole, these elements do not set up a set of conditions 'that address the "extra" risk that such an organisation ought to pose in order to rank among the truly "organized crime operations"', which she considers to be the capacity to extort and intimidate.[46] To be fair, though, when the UNTOC was developed the UN's own research indicated a startling diversity of criminal organisations, many small (three or four people) and loosely structured.[47] A further criticism is that the elementary way in which the OCG is described removes it from the social and political context in which it is formed and will not help us to understand why it exists and what needs to be done to prevent the formation of similar groups.

Legislative activity to implement this concept has occurred but is patchy. Even in Europe a common understanding of a concept of criminal organisation 'is far from being realized and legal approaches vary significantly among national legal systems'.[48] Criticisms of the very similarly worded EU Framework Definition, for being so vague that most EU member states did not need to change their legislation to comply with it,[49] are also apposite to the UNTOC definition. A study of implementation in the Asia-Pacific region suggests little legislative change and, where it has occurred, a lot of tailoring to local contexts.[50] Article 1 of Brazil's Organized Crime Act defines organised crime group as 'a group or association of four or more persons, hierarchically organized, acting in concert to obtain, directly or indirectly, a financial or other material benefit by committing any criminal offences punishable by at least four years incarceration or international criminal offences'.[51] The differences were apparently introduced so as not to confuse this crime with Article 282, which covers conspiracy.[52] Domestic tailoring of this kind is present in many other states including China, which reformed its law to respond not only to transnational organised crime but to other perceived threats to its internal security, revenue protection, and territorial integrity.[53]

[45] Militello, 'Participation in an OCG', cited in note 7 above, p. 103.

[46] Margaret E. Beare, 'Shifting boundaries—between states, enforcement agencies, and priorities', in Albrecht and Fijnaut, *Containment of TOC*, cited in note 1 above, p. 171, p. 183.

[47] Jan van Dijk and Toine Spapens, 'Transnational organized crime networks across the world', in Jay Albanese and Philip Reichel (eds), *Transnational Organized Crime, A View from Six Continents*, 2nd edn, Thousand Oaks, California, SAGE, 2014, p. 7.

[48] Francesco Calderoni, '"A definition that does not work": the impact of the EU Framework Decision on the Fight against Organized Crime', (2012) 49 *Common Market Law Review*, 1365, 1384.

[49] Ibid, p. 1366.

[50] For a study of implementation see also Andreas Schloenhardt, *Palermo in the Pacific: Organised Crime Offences in the Asia Pacific Region*, Leiden/Boston, Martinus Nijhoff Publishers, 2009.

[51] Law 12.850 of 2 August 2013.

[52] See also Fabio H. C. Gandara, 'New legislation defines "organized criminal group" and related criminal procedures', (2013) 29 *International Law Enforcement Reporter* (11), 429–30.

[53] See also Roderic Broadhurst and Nicholas Farrelly, 'Organized crime "control" in Asia: experiences from India, China and the Golden Triangle', in Paoli, *Oxford Handbook of Organized Crime*, cited in note 42 above, p. 634, p. 642.

7.3.3 Defining 'transnational'

The UNTOC does not cover the entire field of organised crime. The authors of the UNTOC have separated out transnational organised crime from both transnational crime—which is all cross-border crime whether organised or not—and organised crime—which may include purely intra-state crime.[54] Article 3(2) defines an offence as 'transnational' for the purposes of the UNTOC if:

(a) It is committed in more than one State;
(b) It is committed in one State but a substantial part of its preparation, planning, direction or control takes place in another State;
(c) It is committed in one State but involves an organised criminal group that engages in criminal activities in more than one State; or
(d) It is committed in one State but has substantial effects in another State.

Critics point out that much organised criminal activity is actually local or 'glocal' (global and local),[55] and even when transnational the actual crossing of the border (whether by contraband, criminal, or proceeds) is relatively limited in scope, and much of the productive and supply activity is local.[56] But Article 3(2) is primarily of jurisdictional, not phenomenological, importance and better understood as a trigger providing a legal justification for other states' interest in domestic organised crime activities. This point is reinforced by the fact that Article 34(2) requires that national laws criminalizing participation in an OCG (Article 5), the laundering of criminal proceeds (Article 6), corruption (Article 8), or obstruction of justice (Article 23), and the various Protocol offences must be established independently of any transnationality requirement.

7.3.4 From every crime to serious crime

The deliberations of the Expert Group led to a move away from organised crime defined in terms of 'all crimes', to focusing only on groups that participate in serious crimes.[57] While some delegates preferred to articulate criteria of gravity such as the use of violence, others preferred to list crimes associated with organised crime such as *inter alia* drug trafficking, money laundering, human trafficking, and the like. An enumeration, however, was considered too restrictive because it excluded emerging forms of organised criminal activity. An approach based on the seriousness of the offence was opted for, but recognizing that the concept of seriousness is not as meaningful in all national systems, it was agreed it should be derived from the penalty applied in national legislation. Article 2(b) defining 'serious crime' as 'conduct constituting

[54] Michael Kilchling, 'Substantive aspects of the UN Convention against Transnational Organised Crime', in Albrecht and Fijnaut, *Containment of TOC*, cited in note 1 above, p. 84, fn. 3.

[55] Richard Hobbs, 'Going down the glocal: the local context of organised crime', (1998) 37 *The Howard Journal of Criminal Justice* (4), 407, p. 419.

[56] Fijnaut, 'The UN Convention and the global problem', cited in note 30 above, pp. 57–8.

[57] *Travaux Préparatoires*, cited in note 13 above, pp. xxii–iii; 'The notion of serious crime in the United Nations Convention against Transnational Organized Crime, note by the Secretariat', UN Doc. CTOC/COP/2012/CRP.4, 20 September 2012, paras 21–2.

an offence punishable by a maximum deprivation of liberty of at least four years or a more serious penalty', became a linchpin for the UNTOC. The four-year minimum was settled after an analytical study by the UN Secretariat for the Ad Hoc Committee revealed that a typical minimum sentence for serious offences ranged from one to five years with the average at three years.[58] Four rather than three years may have been chosen because the three-year threshold left out a range of serious offences.[59]

The definition of 'serious crime' in Article 2(b) was the first time a suppression convention took the discretion to decide what is a serious crime away from states parties, and set an objective normative benchmark for seriousness. Although it escapes the inherent redundancy of an enumeration, it has been subject to criticism. Fijnaut complains that 'the concept of organised crime actually no longer has any specific meaning' because 'all types of more or less serious crime fall within the scope of the Convention'.[60] Militello points out: 'a fixed level of sanctions as reference of "serious crime" disregards the considerable differences that exist among the criminal law systems of the more than 190 UN Member States in the matter of establishing sanctions for crimes'.[61] Moreover, basing on a maximum penalty threshold takes no account of the fact that in some states parties a minimum threshold is used to denote serious crime.[62] There was also no agreement on a maximum length of imprisonment, because of differences about the seriousness of each crime and how to punish it.[63] The more conceptual criticism is whether a punishment threshold is a suitable criterion at all. While Article 2(b) accepts that what may be considered serious in one state party might not be serious in another, setting a four-year threshold suggests a harmonization of the measure of just desert across the globe which did not exist in 2000 (although it may be created as a result of the operation of this provision). A more political criticism might be that this threshold turns the UNTOC into a serious crime convention, and makes it at least in part an expression of the US policy objective of establishing instruments for international cooperation that are of general application.[64]

What the UNTOC lacks is a provision to enable its Conference of the Parties (CoP) to take decisions that oblige states parties to amend their penalties, pushing them over the four-year-or-more threshold in regard to certain offences as they become more of a threat. A conference-room paper on the notion of serious crime prepared for the 2012 UNTOC CoP (CoPU) notes that states parties are not required to introduce a definition of serious crime into their national law but points out that the (UN) Commission on Crime Prevention and Criminal Justice (CCPCJ) and CoPU had identified certain kinds of crime as associated with organised crime and urged states

[58] See also 'Analytical study on serious crime: report by the Secretariat', UN Doc. A/AC.254/22.

[59] Maljević, *Participation in a Criminal Organisation*, cited in note 13 above, p. 153.

[60] Fijnaut, 'The UN Convention and the global problem', cited in note 30 above, p. 56. See also Clark, 'The UNTOC', cited in note 1 above, p. 169, who notes that it is 'specific content free'.

[61] Militello, 'Participation in an OCG', cited in note 7 above, p. 102.

[62] Kilchling, 'Substantive aspects of the UNTOC', cited in note 54 above, p. 90, referring to Germany (para. 12 of the *Strafgesetzbuch*) as the example.

[63] Obokata, *Transnational Organised Crime in International Law*, cited in note 1 above, p. 27.

[64] See also Witten quoted in Andreas and Nadelmann, *Policing the Globe*, cited in note 31 above, p. 174.

parties to consider adopting them as serious crimes by application of the four-year penalty threshold.[65] For example, in Resolution 66/180 of 19 December 2011 the UN General Assembly invited states 'to make trafficking in cultural property, including stealing and looting at archæological and other cultural sites, a serious crime, as defined in article 2 of the United Nations Convention against Transnational Organised Crime, with a view to fully utilising that Convention for the purpose of extensive international cooperation in fighting all forms and aspects of trafficking in cultural property and related offences'. Similar recommendations have been made in regard to trafficking in fraudulent products, trafficking in endangered species, identity crimes, kidnapping, piracy, and trafficking in fraudulent medicines.[66] It appears that some states parties have been increasing penalties to make the use of the UNTOC possible, but either because of pressure from partners or to suit themselves. In 2002 New Zealand, for example, became a party to the UNTOC and in 2003 it imposed a maximum five-year penalty for making or dealing with objects that infringe copyright in section 131(1) of the Copyright Act 1962.[67] It is not certain to what extent the threshold influences choices like that made by Canada, which in 2015 introduced a new indictable offence of tobacco smuggling in section 121(1)(a) of its Criminal Code, which carries a maximum penalty of five years,[68] but given how heavily involved organised crime is in tobacco smuggling, imposing a punishment over the threshold is likely to have been a conscious decision.

7.3.5 The scope of application

The various elements of the concept of OCGs engaging in serious transnational crimes come together in Article 3(1), entitled 'Scope of Application':

> 1. This Convention shall apply, except as otherwise stated herein, to the prevention, investigation and prosecution of:
>   (a) the offences established in accordance with articles 5, 6, 8 and 23 of this Convention; and
>   (b) serious crime as defined in article 2 of this Convention;
>
>   where the offence is transnational in nature and involves an organised criminal group.

The key provision is Article 3(1)(b)'s residual application of the UNTOC to all serious crime in which OCGs participate, where the crime is transnational in nature. It makes for a Convention with a very broad scope. Moreover, the specific offences in the UNTOC to which it applies in terms of Article 3(1)(a) (discussed in section 7.4 of this chapter) also contain within their elements the OCG, serious crime, and transnationality concepts, showing how all-pervading these concepts are as triggers to enable international cooperation within the UNTOC.

[65] 'Notion of serious crime in the UNTOC', cited in note 57 above, para. 4.
[66] Ibid, paras 28–33.
[67] S. 131(5). It was amended by s. 201 of the Trade Marks Act 2002 (2002 No. 49).
[68] S. 121(1)(4)(a).

7.4 Offences in the UNTOC

7.4.1 The double strategy—basic crimes and organisational/infrastructural crimes

The UNTOC obliges states parties to enact certain offences targeting different aspects of the activities of OCGs, to enable both national suppression of this conduct and international cooperation in the prosecution of these offences. But its role is not merely to ensure double criminality in order to enable cooperation. These offences are designed to attack organised crime; they are aimed at the organisational aspects of organised crime, the aspects that constitute the specific dimensions of organised crime and give it a specific danger.[69] These organisational/logistical aspects make possible the implementation of the basic profit-making crimes, and are considered the key to organised crime, especially when the basic activities are diverse.[70] These basic crimes could not be carried out without these entrepreneurial structures. Mobilizing criminal labour, both skilled and unskilled, is just one common feature of the basic crimes that make this organisation necessary.[71] In response the authors of the UNTOC have pursued a double strategy of prevention[72]—one strategy against the basic crimes (those proscribed in the Protocols and as serious crimes by the parties) and one against the logistical/organisational crimes (those proscribed in the UNTOC itself—participation in an organised criminal group, corruption, money laundering, and obstruction).

The list of basic crimes is at least potentially open-ended—through the discretion given to states parties using the four-year punishment threshold for serious crimes and the built-in capacity for the UNTOC to be supplemented by new protocols in the future as organised criminals participate in new types of basic offences.[73] While the former has occurred, the latter has not because of organisational fracturing within the UN,[74] or perhaps out of wariness at the political impact of the UNTOC itself. The list of organisational crimes is closed, yet it is not comprehensive because it does not include violent crimes directed for instrumental purposes by the OCGs.[75]

Participation in the organisational offences can be seen as an aggravated form of participation in the basic offences, deserving both of punishment in itself (which may in turn lead to aggravated sentences) and of justifying international cooperation to deal with these offences. The authors of the UNTOC understood that, just because the basic offences are not the subject of international cooperation in the UNTOC, this

[69] Kilchling, 'Substantive aspects of the UNTOC', cited in note 54 above, pp. 84–6.

[70] Ibid. Verbruggen uses the terms 'core' and 'functional'—see also Frank Verbruggen, 'On containing organized crime using "container offences": some reflections on substantive criminal law issues, in, Albrecht and Fijnaut, *Containment of TOC*, cited in note 1 above, pp. 113–34, pp. 113–14.

[71] Vincenzo Ruggiero, 'Legal pre-requisites and socio-economic structures for a successful implementation of the Palermo Convention', in Betti, *Symposium: UNTOC*, cited in note 1 above, p. 149, p. 150.

[72] Kilchling, 'Substantive aspects of the UNTOC', cited in note 54 above, p. 86, citing *inter alia*, Ulrich Sieber (ed.), *International Organisierte Kriminalität*, Cologne, 1997.

[73] Kilchling, 'Substantive aspects of the UNTOC', cited in note 54 above, p. 87.

[74] See also Neil Boister, 'The (un-) systematic nature of the UN criminal justice system: the (non) relationship between the draft Illicit Tobacco Trade Protocol and the UN Convention against Transnational Organised Crime', (2010) 21 *Criminal Law Forum*, 361–97.

[75] Kilchling, 'Substantive aspects of the UNTOC', cited in note 54 above, pp. 87–8.

does not preclude cooperation in regard to the logistical/organisational offences; the organisational offences are not simply forms of complicity in the basic offences but stand-alone offences.

7.4.2 Participation in an OCG

The offence that states parties are obliged to enact under Article 5, entitled 'criminalization of participation in an organized criminal group', most deserves the criticism of the UNTOC that the Convention instantiates a mafia-type concept of organised crime bred in the West rather than more fluid networks.[76] An echo of Articles 9 and 10 of the Nuremberg Charter that entitled the Nuremberg International Military Tribunal to classify an organisation as criminal,[77] which were interpreted as entitling convictions to be based solely on membership of that group,[78] it too is vulnerable to criticism that it relies on collective rather than personal criminality, criticism only somewhat ameliorated by the requirement that participation in the OCG occur with some subscription to or knowledge of the group's criminal purposes.[79]

The authors of Article 5 had a number of national models that they could draw on: conspiracy (the common law concept of both an inchoate offence and a form of participation in crime), criminal associations (recognized in many civilian criminal legal codes), the racketeering offences (United States), and mafia-type associations (Italian Penal Code).[80] A difficulty with the specific measures was that they had been pioneered against the organised mafias operating in the United States and Italy, which were not present in most states, and had not proved successful in the USA or Italy themselves.[81] In the cause of coverage and compromise the authors of the UNTOC settled for two options,[82] although parties can opt for both if they choose.[83] The *chapeau* in Article 5(1)(a) also clarifies that whichever option is chosen, the new offence must be 'distinct from those involving the attempt or completion of the criminal activity', clarifying their stand-alone character.

The first option, the conspiracy model,[84] reflects the common law offence of conspiracy, with all of its attendant difficulties. Article 5(1)(a) requires criminalization of:

(i) Agreeing with one or more other persons to commit a serious crime for a purpose relating directly or indirectly to the obtaining of a financial or other material

[76] See also Margaret E. Beare and Michael Woodiwiss, 'US organized crime control policies exported abroad', in Paoli, *Oxford Handbook of Organized Crime*, cited in note 42 above, p. 545, p. 563.

[77] Annexed to the Agreement for the Prosecution and Punishment of the Major War Criminals of the European Axis, 8 August 1945.

[78] Allied Control Council Law No. 10.

[79] Stanislaw Pomorski, 'Conspiracy and criminal organization', in George Ginsburg and Vladimir Kudriavtsev (eds), *The Nuremberg Trial and International Law*, Dordrecht, Martinus Nijhoff Publishers, 1990, p. 213, p. 243.

[80] Barberini, 'Italy and the international community', cited in note 13 above, p. 28.

[81] Paoli and Vander Beken, 'A contested concept', cited in note 42 above, p. 24.

[82] Calderoni, 'A definition that does not work', cited in note 48 above, p. 1374.

[83] See also Maljević, *Participation in a Criminal Organisation*, cited in note 13 above, p. 128.

[84] Verbruggen, 'Using "container offences"', cited in note 70 above, p. 118; Clark, 'The UNTOC', cited in note 1 above, p. 171.

> benefit and, where required by domestic law, involving an act undertaken by one of the participants in furtherance of the agreement or involving an organized criminal group[.]

Common law states do not usually require the agreement to take a particular form or even be express, so long as two or more people agree to commit a crime.[85] If the agreement only involves two persons it will not meet the requirements for an OCG in Article 2(a), which means the UNTOC is internally inconsistent. Criminality arises upon agreement; once the accused has agreed it does not matter if they later withdraw.[86] As described, this form of conspiracy is much narrower than that which applies in many common law systems where any agreement to commit an indictable offence is itself criminal.[87] Article 5(1)(a)(i) imposes restrictions. The agreement must be for the purpose of obtaining a financial or other material benefit. It will not require any legislating by states parties that already apply the normal common law offence. For those states that require it, the provision also makes allowance for criminalization only if a material act has been perpetrated pursuant to the unlawful agreement with the novel addition of involvement of an OCG. As for *mens rea*, it appears to require that the parties to the agreement have knowledge of the object of the agreement, i.e. the commission of the crime (but not a serious crime), and of each other's agreement to commit it, and that they should intend to agree to commit it, and intend to carry it out, but additionally have the purpose of material benefit.[88] Under Article 5(2) states parties will have to permit courts to infer this state of mind from objective circumstances. The conspiracy option has been criticized for not reflecting the specific danger presented by a criminal organisation.[89] It also has practical limitations. Apart from the complexity and resource-intensiveness of such trials, it may be difficult to prove that all defendants in an OCG are party to the same agreement if the group is broken up into subgroups, or that senior members have participated in an overt act where this is required, or have agreed in a sufficiently specific fashion to the commission of the particular crimes.[90]

The second option, the 'associative offence' model,[91] is set out in Article 5(1)(a)(ii). It requires criminalization of

> (ii) Conduct by a person who, with knowledge of either the aim and general criminal activity of an organized criminal group or its intention to commit the crimes in question, takes an active part in:
> a. criminal activities of the organized criminal group;
> b. other activities of the organized criminal group in the knowledge
> that his or her participation will contribute to the achievement of the above described criminal aim[.]

[85] See also Maljević, *Participation in a Criminal Organisation*, cited in note 13 above, pp. 140–41.
[86] See also ibid, p. 143. [87] See also ibid, p. 143. [88] See also ibid, pp. 144–5.
[89] Militello, 'Participation in an OCG', cited in note 7 above, p. 104.
[90] See also Schloenhardt, 'Transnational organised crime', cited in note 1 above, p. 425.
[91] Verbruggen, 'Using "container offences"', cited in note 70 above, p. 118; Clark, 'The UNTOC', cited in note 1 above, p. 172.

This provision resembles the *association de malfaiteurs* in Article 450-1 of the French Penal Code more closely than Article 416*bis* of the Italian Penal Code. The objective elements are participation in the activities of an OCG as defined by the UNTOC (and as explored earlier in this section). What is critical is the forms of participation themselves and the associated subjective elements.[92] Participation is the taking of an active part in the criminal activities of the OCG or in other activities, knowing of either the aim and general criminal activity of the OCG or its intention to commit the crimes in question, and knowing that one's participation will contribute to the achievement of the criminal aims of the OCG. The participation must be distinct from the attempt at or completion of the criminal activity itself. Thus a person who joins an OCG and takes active part in drug trafficking will be guilty of two offences, drug trafficking and the participation offence.[93] The scope of the offence is broader than the conspiracy option, because there is no requirement that the object of the agreement be the commission of a serious crime.[94] The scope also covers those within the group (three or more) plus those outside it who contribute to its criminal aims.[95] The provision of apparently innocent services to the group raises difficulties of how close the involvement must be. The question whether accounting services, food, transport, etc., may be regarded as participating in an activity of the OCG is one of degree—some services may be closely related to the group's activities and aims and thus implicate the provider, others more mundane and thus for policy reasons not impeachable. In every case, however, the accused must know that providing the service will contribute to the aims of the group.

Article 5(1)(b) increases the scope of criminality by obliging states parties to criminalize '[o]rganising, directing, abetting, facilitating, or counselling the commission of serious crime involving an organised criminal group'. They promise to criminalize secondary participation in the serious crimes committed by the OCG, beyond the scope of the principal offences discussed above. It does not require criminalization of participation in the OCG per se but some form of furthering of the perpetration of the serious crimes by the OCG.[96] It is not clear whether this includes inchoate forms of serious crime such as attempts or incitement,[97] but it would be redundant to include conspiracy as this is a form of participation in the organised crime group. The scope ranges from leadership to less consequential contributions. While the less consequential forms are familiar, 'organising' and 'directing' are novel, and are intended to reach leaders of the groups who do not personally participate in the commission of the serious crimes.[98] There does appear to be considerable overlap between this provision and participation in an OCG as defined by Article 5(1)(a).[99]

When it comes to implementation of Article 5's offences, the picture is mixed. This is occurring globally on an ad hoc basis and there is no doubt that the term

[92] See also Maljević, *Participation in a Criminal Organisation*, cited in note 13 above, pp. 154–8.
[93] Joutsen, 'International cooperation against TOC', cited in note 1 above, p. 426.
[94] Maljević, *Participation in a Criminal Organisation*, cited in note 13 above, p. 154.
[95] Militello, 'Participation in an OCG', cited in note 7 above, p. 109. [96] Ibid, p. 105.
[97] Schloenhardt, 'Transnational organised crime', cited in note 1 above, p. 430.
[98] McClean, *Transnational Organized Crime*, cited in note 1 above, p. 64.
[99] Maljević, *Participation in a Criminal Organisation*, cited in note 13 above, p. 156.

'participation in an OCG' has entered legal parlance.[100] In Europe, the EU has followed the definition of OCG in its own adaptations.[101] At a national level the pattern of implementation in Europe is not uniform. There has been a marked resistance from Scandinavian states, reliance by common law states on conspiracy with some introduction of new participation in OCG offences, while civil law states have used a wide variety of approaches from reliance in Western Europe on existing association provisions to a more enthusiastic remodelling of law in Eastern Europe to meet EU and UNTOC obligations.[102] Outside Europe the picture is even more uneven. Some states have enacted specific offences of participation in an organised criminal group close to the original idea in Article 5. New Zealand, for example, enacted section 98A of the Crimes Act 1961 (inserted by section 5 of the Crimes Amendment Act 2002), which requires the participation of three or more people who share the purpose of obtaining material benefits, but the accused need not actually share that purpose, only know of its existence.[103] But others, such as Japan, have been content to rely on home-grown legal measures like the Anti-Boryodukan Law 1991 which have nothing to do with punishing participation in an organised criminal group that pursues serious crimes.[104] There is a clear pattern of national law-making based on local concepts of what is a criminal organisation. Some laws are drafted in such a way as to be very broad in scope, so as to include individuals who simply cooperate with each other in the commission of crimes.[105] Divergent approaches among the states parties may not be suitable to establish a unitary approach to punishing participation in an OCG, but to some extent this divergence reflects the flexibility built into the UNTOC. Many states parties did not have to amend or modify their legislation to comply because their law usually catered for either option already. This leaves largely untested and untestable the question whether the concept of an OCG used by the UNTOC is actually suitable for realizing the hope that attacks on organisation/logistics through the 'double strategy' will produce greater crime reduction.[106]

7.4.3 Money laundering

The laundering of the proceeds of its activities is useful to organised crime because it can disguise the illicit origins of those proceeds and render them reusable for further investment in criminal activities. The authors of the UNTOC made the attack on laundering a priority. Article 6 builds on the obligation to criminalize money laundering in Article 3(1)(b) of the 1988 UN Drug Trafficking Convention by following the

[100] Paoli and Vander Beken, 'A contested concept', cited in note 42 above, p. 25.

[101] See Arts 1 and 2, EU, Framework Decision on the Fight against Organized Crime, 2008/841/JHA—Francesco Calderoni, *Organized Crime Legislation in Europe: Harmonization and Approximation of Criminal Law, National Legislations and The EU Framework Decision on the fight against Organized Crime*, Heildelberg, Springer, 2010, p. 37.

[102] See also Calderoni, ibid, p. 115.

[103] See also Julie Ayling and Rod Broadhurst, 'Organized crime control in Australia and New Zealand', in Paoli, *Oxford Handbook of Organized Crime*, cited in note 42 above, p. 612, pp. 620–21.

[104] See also Schloenhardt, *Palermo in the Pacific*, cited in note 50 above, p. 271.

[105] Paoli and Vander Beken, 'A contested concept', cited in note 42 above, pp. 25–6.

[106] See also Schloenhardt, 'Transnational organised crime', cited in note 1 above, p. 431.

trend to criminalize 'all crimes' money laundering, not just drug money laundering, that is found in the FATF's forty recommendations,[107] and the Council of Europe's Convention on The Laundering, Search, Seizure and Confiscation of the Proceeds of Crime.[108] The UNTOC defines the proceeds of crimes broadly, in Article 2(e), as 'any property derived from or obtained, directly or indirectly, through the commission of an offence'—not just drug offences or even 'serious' offences—and defines 'property' broadly, in Article 2(d), as 'assets of every kind, whether corporeal or incorporeal, movable or immovable, tangible or intangible, and legal documents or instruments evidencing title to, or interest in, such assets'.

Article 6 aims to suppress three different kinds of laundering activities with different kinds of *mens rea*. The first two are clear obligations, the third conditional.

Article 6(1)(a)(i) requires states parties to criminalize 'the conversion or transfer of property'. The action of conversion or transfer must have a cognitive component—the accused must have 'knowledge that such property is the proceeds of crime'. It must also have a purposive component—the accused must have 'the purpose of concealing or disguising the illicit origin of the property or of helping any person who is involved in the commission of the predicate offence to evade the legal consequences of his or her action'. The emphasis on a purposive mental state means that the offence cannot be committed by mistake, no matter how negligent.

The offence in Article 6(1)(a)(ii) requires states parties to criminalize the '[t]he concealment or disguise of the true nature, source, location, disposition, movement or ownership of or rights with respect to property'. In this case the *mens rea* required is only cognitive—the accused must do so 'knowing that such property is the proceeds of crime'. No explicit laundering purpose is required although it is implied in the actions of concealment and disguise.[109]

The offence in Article 6(1)(b)(i) is subject to basic concepts in the party's legal system. Attacking simple receipt of proceeds, it is designed in Verbruggen's terms to render the proceeds of crime 'untouchable'[110] because of its ease of use against financial entities that do not have a laundering purpose but only a commercial one. If compatible, it requires states parties to criminalize '[t]he acquisition, possession or use of property'. The *mens rea* required is that the accused do so 'knowing, at the time of receipt, that such property is the proceeds of crime'. Again, no special purpose is required.

Finally, Article 6(1)(b)(ii) criminalizes 'participation in, association with, conspiracy, attempt, aiding, abetting, facilitating and counselling the commission of laundering offences' but this expansion of the scope of the money laundering offence to include secondary participants is also subject to basic concepts in the states parties' legal systems.

The novel step taken in the UNTOC was to expand the range of predicate offences. Under Article 6(2)(a) states parties agree to 'seek to criminalize laundering of proceeds from the widest range of predicate offences' while more specifically they agree to include as predicate offences all 'serious crime' as defined in Article 2 of

[107] Cited in note 16 above.

[108] ETS 141.

[109] Verbruggen, 'Using "container offences"', cited in note 70 above, p. 121.

[110] Ibid, p. 121.

the UNTOC and the offences established in accordance with Articles 5, 8, and 23 of the UNTOC.

Laundering is usually transnational, so Article 6(2)(c) provides that such laundering will be an offence regardless of whether the predicate offences were committed within or outside the jurisdiction of the state claiming jurisdiction over the laundering. But a double criminality requirement is also imposed; the predicate must be a crime both where it occurs and in the state with jurisdiction over laundering.

Under Article 6(2)(e) the states parties must punish the authors of a predicate offence for the separate offence of laundering but can exclude them if such is incompatible with fundamental principles of their domestic law. States parties with such principles agree that they will still render international legal cooperation to states parties that do not have them and are prosecuting self-laundering.

Although Article 6(2)(f) does allow 'knowledge, intent, or purpose' to be inferred, Article 6 does not reach negligent behaviour that is ignorant, but new state practice (such as the Bahamian law that applies 'reasonable grounds to believe') does.[111]

Developed states pushed for adherence to the FATF recommendations and implementation of its periodic monitoring mechanisms as binding treaty obligations but this was resisted by bank-secrecy states and developing states that feared loss of sovereignty.[112] Nonetheless, in something of an innovation for the time Article 7(a) calls upon states parties to institute a comprehensive domestic regulatory and supervisory regime for banks and non-bank financial institutions. State practice with regard to money laundering has been driven and monitored by the FATF in reliance on provisions like Article 6, and is far more developed than that relating to criminalizing participation in organised crime.[113] It is difficult to sum up the impact of this offence. Clearly a great deal of anti-money laundering reform and institutional development has occurred around the world, but critics believe that the impact on criminal justice performance has been modest and on crime suppression negligible.[114]

7.4.4 Corruption

Attempting to address the growing realization that organisational deviance mixes with governmental deviance,[115] the authors of the UNTOC drew heavily on existing anti-corruption instruments to adopt Article 8, which obliges states parties to establish a range of corruption offences. Article 8(1)(a) obliges states parties to criminalize active corruption, 'the promise, offering or giving to a public official, directly or indirectly, of an undue advantage, for the official himself or herself or another person or entity, in order that the official act or refrain from acting in the exercise of his or her official duties'. Article 8(1)(b) obliges states parties to criminalize passive corruption,

[111] Section 43 of the Proceeds of Crime Act 2000.

[112] Barberini, 'Italy and the international community', cited in note 13 above, p. 28.

[113] See also W. Gilmore, 'Money laundering', in Boister and Currie, *Routledge Handbook of Transnational Criminal Law*, cited in note 1 above, p. 342.

[114] Michael Levi, 'Money laundering' in Paoli, *Oxford Handbook of Organized Crime*, cited in note 42 above, p. 419, pp. 434–5.

[115] Ruggiero, 'Legal pre-requisites and socio-economic structures', cited in note 71 above, p. 152.

'the solicitation or acceptance by a public official, directly or indirectly, of an undue advantage, for the official himself or herself or another person or entity, in order that the official act or refrain from acting in the exercise of his or her official duties'. Falling somewhat behind the lead provided by the OECD's 1997 Convention on Combating Bribery of Foreign Public Officials in International Business Transactions,[116] Article 8(2) only requires states parties to consider criminalizing these forms of conduct when they involve a 'foreign public official or international civil servant'. Article 8(4) clarifies that a 'public official' is someone who is such an official or provides such a public service according to domestic law. Article 8(3) provides for criminalization of participation as an accomplice. Article 8(4) also invites the states parties to consider criminalizing other forms of corruption such as private corruption and trading in influence, but the weakness of this provision and that of Article 9 for prevention of corruption, all points to why the much broader UN Convention against Corruption has largely transcended the UNTOC in regard to corruption.[117]

7.4.5 Obstruction of justice

Article 23 is designed to suppress actions that try to neutralize states parties' law enforcement activities against organised crime. It is not comprehensive. It does not, for example, cover intentional destruction of documentary evidence or tampering with evidence.[118] Article 23(a) requires criminalization of 'the use of physical force, threats or intimidation or the promise, offering or giving an undue advantage'. The action must be intentional but must also be accompanied by a special purpose—'to induce false testimony or to interfere in the giving of testimony or the production of evidence in proceedings related to offences covered by this Convention'. In this way the obstruction must be linked to the UNTOC offences including serious crimes. Ironically, the offence could apply to law enforcement officers who pressurize prosecution witnesses in organised crime cases.[119] Article 23(b) requires criminalization of the 'use of physical force, threats or intimidation'. Again, it must be intentional and with a special purpose—'to interfere with the exercise of official duties by a justice or law enforcement official in relation to the commission of offences covered by this Convention'. Article 24 supplements this provision by requiring states to provide for the protection of witnesses.

7.4.6 Corporate liability

In an innovative provision designed to provide for corporate liability, Article 10(1) obliges each state party 'to adopt such measures as may be necessary, consistent with its legal principles, to establish the liability of legal persons for participation in

[116] 18 December 1997, 37 *ILM* 1; in force 15 February 1999.

[117] United Nations Convention against Corruption, New York, 31 October 2003, 2349 UNTS 41, in force 14 December 2005.

[118] Verbruggen, 'Using "container offences"', cited in note 70 above, p. 126.

[119] Ibid, pp. 126–7.

serious crimes involving an organized criminal group', but Article 10(2) recognizes legal diversity by allowing that such liability may be criminal, administrative, or civil. Although it again relies on the serious crimes concept, Article 10 does not lay down any substantive criteria for how corporate liability should be achieved, leaving this to the particular legal system.[120] Using the example of the ENRON Corporation, Beare complained that when the UNTOC was settled there was little recognition that a corporation could itself be an OCG, and not just an entity that assisted or profited from an OCG.[121] Despite prosecution of corporate entities in certain countries for corruption and money laundering, this concept is still an uncomfortable fit.

7.4.7 Penalties

In a provision designed to reform state law that may be too lenient,[122] Article 11 provides that sanctions applied to the UNTOC offences discussed above must take into account the gravity of the offence. The detail is left to the states parties. The EU has introduced a minimum-maximum penalty of between two and five years.[123] Article 11(4) warns about being too generous with parole and Article 11(5) suggests a long statute of limitations.

7.4.8 Confiscation

The promise of confiscation was that it would take the profit out of crime.[124] Article 12(1) requires states parties to adopt measures 'to the broadest extent possible' that enable confiscation of the proceeds of, and property, equipment, and instrumentalities used in or destined for use in, 'offences covered by this convention'. This appears to include the UNTOC and Protocol offences, but it is not clear whether it also covers other 'serious crimes' carrying a four-year or longer sentence.[125] Confiscation means permanent deprivation by lawful procedure and includes forfeiture where applicable.[126] Article 12(2) also requires each state party to adopt preliminary measures to enable the identification, tracing, freezing, and seizing of items for the purpose of eventual confiscation. Although lacking the symbolic impact of confiscation of the actual proceeds, Article 12(3) and (4) permit extension to value confiscation, which means that concealment, displacement, or loss of actual proceeds becomes irrelevant and authorities can confiscate property legally held without the need to rely on the shifting onus of proof of origins.[127] Article 12(7) makes it clear that while states parties can, they do not have to, adopt a reversal of onus of proof in the confiscation process. Although their systems vary from the administrative, to civil, to penal, states have

[120] Kilchling, 'Substantive aspects of the UNTOC', cited in note 54 above, p. 90.
[121] Beare, 'Shifting boundaries', cited in note 46 above, p. 184.
[122] Verbruggen, 'Using "container offences"', cited in note 70 above, p. 127.
[123] Art. 3 of the Framework Decision, 2008/841/JHA.
[124] Kilchling, 'Substantive aspects of the UNTOC', cited in note 54 above, p. 91 and authors cited there.
[125] See also McClean, *Transnational Organized Crime*, cited in note 1 above, p. 141.
[126] Art. 2(g).
[127] Kilchling, 'Substantive aspects of the UNTOC', cited in note 54 above, p. 92

responded positively by amending their laws to make it possible to seize and confiscate the proceeds of crime.[128] The scale of confiscation is increasing. South Korea has indicated, for example, that the amounts confiscated rose from US$121 million in 2008 to US$854 million in 2014.[129] Claims of the effectiveness of confiscation are, however, questioned. Following the money did not lead to the winning of the war on drugs,[130] and it is unlikely to do the same in the war on organised crime.

7.4.9 Legality or over-criminalization?

In a preventive form of crime control international society has chosen to intervene against the organisation of crime itself,[131] by creating a range of organisational/logistical offences. The perception was that the harm being caused by these organisations might become so great that waiting for it to manifest itself was out of the question. But there was little clarity as to the specific legal interest that these provisions protect and that justified the use of criminal law; indeed, the main driver appears to be the difficulty of enforcing existing property, moral, and personal harm crimes against the organisers of these crimes. This has led to flexible offences with a very broad scope. While Article 11(6) reserves the description of offences and applicable defences 'to the domestic law of the State Party', which preserves state autonomy over how to criminalize and prevents, for example, civil law states from having to violate their principles by criminalizing conspiracy,[132] the impact on the principle of legality and *lex certa* is more difficult to assess.

7.5 The Provisions for International Cooperation

The UNTOC contains the 'minimum' procedural framework to be used to enable cooperation in regard to the offences in the Convention and in the Protocols.[133] It provides for obligations to enhance the requirements for effective police cooperation and exchange of information,[134] and to adopt specific policing measures.[135] It sets up a detailed platform for greater formal legal assistance,[136] and provides for a similar platform for extradition.[137] Finally, provision is made for cooperation in confiscation and retrieval of assets.[138] Transnationality and the involvement of an OCG operate as triggers for the application of this procedural regime. In essence the container offences set up by the UNTOC, which are ultimately derived from serious but unidentified

[128] See also M. Kilchling, 'Finance oriented strategies of organized crime control', in Paoli, *Oxford Handbook of Organized Crime*, cited in note 42 above, p. 655, p. 663.

[129] UNCCPCJ, 18 May 2014.

[130] Beare, 'Shifting boundaries', cited in note 46 above, p. 188.

[131] Verbruggen, 'Using "container offences"', cited in note 70 above, p. 130.

[132] M. G. Vietti, 'The Palermo Convention: Italy's ratification and the need to adapt national legislation', in Betti, *Symposium: UNTOC*, cited in note 1 above, p. 39, p. 42.

[133] M. Mackarel, 'Procedural aspects of the Convention against Transnational Organised Crime', in Albrecht and Fijnaut, *Containment of TOC*, cited in note 1 above, p. 145, p. 147; see also Clark, 'The UNTOC', cited in note 1 above, p. 182.

[134] Arts 27 and 28. [135] Arts 19, 20, and 29. [136] Art. 18. [137] Art. 16.

[138] Arts 13 and 14.

domestic offences, make cooperation possible in a container-to-container fashion, as it were, dispensing with any meaningful condition of double criminality for such cooperation.[139] This also dispenses with an implicit criterion of proportionality between the seriousness of the basic offence and the level of cooperation offered by a requested state party. It may be that instead of engendering the mutual trust necessary for cooperation, it engenders suspicion among states parties.[140] Some responsibility for this must lie with the negotiators (some from the WEOG) who pursued the development of a 'tool box' on modes of international cooperation and did not deal adequately or with any enthusiasm with the conceptual issue of defining organised crime.[141] In essence, the conceptual issue became secondary to the pursuit of a global legal assistance convention.

7.6 Implementation

Under Article 34(1) of the UNTOC, its states parties are obliged to take the measures necessary, including legislative and administrative measures, in accordance with the fundamental principles of their domestic law, to ensure implementation. Recognizing the impecunious position of many potential parties, Article 30(2)(b) provides the basis for states parties to enhance financial and material assistance to support developed states to implement, while Article 30(2)(c) provides for technical assistance. The main follow-up mechanism for implementation is provided by Article 32, which establishes a CoPU to periodically review the implementation of the UNTOC, recommend how to improve and implement it, and cooperate with relevant international and regional intergovernmental and non-governmental organisations (IGO and NGO). Under Article 33 the UNODC serves as the secretariat. From the first session of the CoPU held in 2004 the goal of establishing a mechanism to review implementation by states parties has regularly been discussed, but as yet no such mechanism has been agreed. It appears that many states parties fear the system will be too expensive and be a drain on resources.[142] In Resolution 67/189 of 20 December 2012 the UN General Assembly both affirmed the centrality of the UNTOC in the fight against transnational organised crime and urged states parties to actively engage in the endeavour to agree such a mechanism. In the absence of a review mechanism, as we have seen there is only anecdotal evidence as to how the treaty is performing, but there are concerns. At the 2015 UN CCPCJ meeting the US delegate stated 'we do not have a shortage of conventions, what we have is a gap in their implementation'.[143]

[139] Verbruggen, 'Using "container offences"', cited in note 70 above, pp. 129–30.

[140] Calderoni, 'A definition that does not work', cited in note 48 above, p. 1390.

[141] See also Orlova and Moore, '"Umbrellas" or "building blocks"?', cited in note 1 above, p. 285, citing an interview with the Canadian negotiator.

[142] Vienna, UNCCPCJ, Tuesday 21 May (author's personal notes)—statements by Canada, Norway, Austria, USA.

[143] UNCCPCJ, 18 May 2015 (notes on file with author). The French were of much the same opinion: 20 May 2015.

7.7 Final Observation

Obokata notes that as the UNTOC is not subject-specific, unlike other crime suppression conventions, 'its benefit is that it can be used to prosecute and punish a variety of criminal activities, provided they are serious crimes committed by criminal groups as defined in the ... Convention'.[144] However, while the UNTOC may provide a reasonable model for an evolutionary approach to the combating of transnational organised crime, it may be too advanced for many states parties to use to its full potential. Although more states, NGOs, and IGOs are now involved in activity against transnational organised crime, that activity appears to be fragmentary and focused on particular types of organised crime. States parties may be leery of using the UNTOC, not because of what the UNTOC is, but what they take it to be. There is little in the UNTOC concept for states to fix on, to legislate and train around—because the concept is largely content-free. Promoted perhaps by a reluctance to embrace a too-broad concept of organised criminality, even EU members have not adopted legal instruments on criminalization of transnational organised crime, making investigation and asset recovery impossible.[145] This has prompted advocates of the Italian approach to return to the conceptual basis of action against organised crime and call for a standardized definition of organised crime.[146] In a development that suggests implicit criticism of the UNTOC definition, in 2011 the EU Parliament asked the Commission to begin work on a concept of organised crime that better identified the organisational features of the phenomenon,[147] and in 2013 the EU Parliament Special Committee on Organised Crime recommended the adoption of a single EU-wide definition of mafia-related crimes that fully covers the phenomenon because of the different legal definitions of organised crime in different EU countries which make cooperation difficult.[148] However, in 2013 the Council of Europe's Special Group of Experts on Organised Crime felt there was no need for a new convention or new definition.[149] The fact is that a more precise model may not be the answer. Article 416*bis* of the Italian Penal Code, for example, has not proved that useful to reach loosely interconnected groups like the hacktivist group 'Anonymous'. It has been argued that the UNTOC was a measure of a kind dictated by the level of knowledge at the time and by an emotional attachment to models of organisational structure dictated by the mafia legacy.[150] As Levi notes, it is an error to move from the acceptable proposition that there is considerable harm

[144] Obokata, *Transnational Organised Crime in International Law*, cited in note 1 above, p. 40.

[145] See also Parliamentary Committee of Inquiry into Mafia-related and Other Criminal Organisations, 'Report of the Italian Presidency of the EU on the fight against mafia-related crime in Europe and outside Europe' (2014).

[146] Ibid, Conclusions, Recommendation (i).

[147] EU Parliament, Resolution on organized Crime in the European Union, Resolution 25 October 20111, P7_TA(2011)0459.

[148] European Parliament, 'Equipping the EU to tackle the Mafia', 15 October 2012; see also Bruce Zagaris, 'EU committee recommends action to combat transnational organised crime', (2013) 29 *International Law Enforcement Reporter* (1), 501.

[149] Michael Plachta, 'First meeting of Council of Europe's Special Group of Experts on Organized Crime', (2013) 29 *International Law Enforcement Reporter* (10), 387.

[150] Levi, 'The organization of serious crime for gain', cited in note 10 above, p. 599.

being done, to the indefensible proposition that these impacts can be described with certainty 'and that they arise from a common coherent delivery mechanism called "organised crime"'.[151]

Yet the delivery mechanism described in the UNTOC—the definitions of 'organised criminal group', 'transnational', and 'serious crime'—are so unspecific as to undermine this argument. The catchy label 'transnational organised crime' suggests one thing, but the actual treaty is broad in scope: it potentially captures all transnational serious crime. But the strength of the UNTOC—its flexibility, which means it can be adapted for use against emerging criminal activity while meeting relatively simple factual conditions—is also its weakness—it cannot be used to prescribe to states parties what to criminalize and when to use its provisions, because the discretion remains with those parties. In the 'organised criminal group' the authors of the UNTOC created a new general principle not a specific crime, a form of complicity linked to non-specified serious crimes of the state party's own making. Perhaps it would have been more practical to enumerate a list of crimes that OCGs participate in, or add elements that described the production, logistical, and distribution capacities of OCGs (such as finance, human resources, equipment and transportation, conversion of the products of crime into money and other usable assets, storage facilities, neutralization of law enforcement), in order to give the term some substance.[152] A listing of such activities was abandoned during the negotiations because of absence of agreement, leading commentators at the time to note that this would make it easier for states parties to ignore the manifestations of organised crime within their territory.[153] In the absence of a fuller embrace by states parties of the essential flexibility of the UNTOC, there is a very real danger that the Convention could be considered just one more suppression convention.[154]

[151] Ibid, p. 596.
[152] Levi, 'The organization of serious crime for gain', cited in note 10 above, p. 602.
[153] Guymon, 'International legal mechanisms', cited in note 1 above, p. 93.
[154] Krzysztof Krajewski, 'Some legal and criminological aspects of implementation', in Albrecht and Fijnaut, *Containment of TOC*, cited in note 1 above, p. 235, p. 245.

8

The UN Protocol to Prevent, Suppress, and Punish Trafficking in Persons 2000

Hans-Joachim Heintze and Charlotte Lülf

8.1 Introduction

Human trafficking and the exploitation of human beings and their vulnerabilities has evolved as one highly lucrative facet of transnational organised crime.[1] There exist endless varieties of ways to traffic persons; among others, relatives, employment agencies, or kidnappers sending them into traffickers' arms under false pretences. The amount of money involved, an estimated $150.2 billion annually in illegal profits,[2] establishes autonomous economies, which makes comprehensive counter-measures even more challenging. In the age of globalization this is one enormous aspect of international migration and it cannot be seen in isolation from the broader socio-economic developments that drive it. It is doubtless a growing form of transnational organised crime,[3] especially since the criminal perspective is too narrow. Trafficking follows in the tracks of poverty and inequality, the lack of educational opportunity and access to health-care, gender discrimination including gender-based violence, or racial inequality. Accordingly, trafficking occurs worldwide, although most victims are trafficked from poor countries to richer regions. Agriculture and horticulture, construction, garments and textiles, hospitality and catering, mining, logging and forestry, fishing, food processing and packaging, transportation, domestic service, and other care and cleaning work have been identified as sectors that are most exposed to trafficking in persons—with businesses themselves involved in the trafficking. Between 2007 and 2010, victims of 136 nationalities were detected in 118 countries worldwide, and while approximately 58 per cent were trafficked for the purpose of sexual exploitation around 36 per cent were trafficked to forced labour. Several related offences accompany the act of trafficking, such as among others breaches of immigration laws, document forgery, corruption, tax evasion. These parallel the offences directed at the individual, such as unlawful coercion or threat, extortion, aggravated or sexual assault, and even murder.[4] Owing to this multitude of rights violations, their severity and

[1] Louise Shelley, 'The crime of human trafficking', (2008) 4 *Global Studies Review* (2), available at: http://www.globality-gmu.net/archives/622, accessed 24 March 2016.

[2] International Labour Office, *Profits and Poverty: the Economics of Forced Labour*, Geneva, ILO, 2014, p. 13.

[3] Shelley, 'The crime of human trafficking', cited in note 1 above.

[4] UNODC (ed.), *Assistance for the Implementation of the ECOWAS Plan of Action against Trafficking in Persons*, New York, United Nations Press, 2006, pp. 3 and 33.

scale, human trafficking is often considered as a modern form of slavery or slave trade,[5] and 'the very antithesis of the Universal Declaration of Human Rights'.[6] Against this background, trafficking in human beings has become a focus of government policy and NGO activities and provoked the elaboration of international, regional, and national legal acts, 'inspiring states to devote enormous financial and bureaucratic resources to its eradication'.[7] In light of the recent increase in both smuggling and trafficking in the context of the refugee and migration flows in the Mediterranean, former United Nations (UN) Special Rapporteur on Trafficking in Persons, Joy Ezeilo, offered this criticism: 'States are still grappling with integrating a human-rights-based approach; a child-centred approach; and an approach that pays attention to causes and vulnerability factors, including the creation of opportunities for legal, gainful and non-exploitative migration, which is crucial for preventing future trafficking.'[8]

This chapter will turn its attention towards the major international legal instrument on human trafficking at the international level, the Protocol to Prevent, Suppress and Punish Trafficking in Persons, especially Women and Children (hereafter the Trafficking Protocol), adopted by General Assembly Resolution 55/25 and in force since 25 December 2003. Initially, this chapter will address the historical developments and the predecessor instrument leading to the drafting and entry into force of the Protocol. The main focus will then be laid on the core instrument, the Protocol itself. The debate on definitions, scope of application, and delimitation is subsequently portrayed and analysed in detail and delimitations from neighbouring fields such as human trafficking and slavery are highlighted. The implementation of the Protocol by its member states is considered by reference to state practice and the overall assessment of a legal response to trafficking in persons made in the light of recent regional initiatives.

8.2 Through a Gendered Lens—The Development of Trafficking Instruments until 2000

Combating trafficking was addressed at the early stage of the League of Nations within its human rights framework, although exclusively with a focus on women and children; regulations on trafficking in women were incorporated in its 1933 International Convention for the Suppression of the Traffic in Women of Full Age. Addressing the vulnerability of women also shaped the first approaches to transnational crimes of its successor, the UN, which codified provisions on trafficking as one specific form of gender-based violence. The UN regulated the 'white slave trade' in several of their

[5] David Weissbrodt and Anti-Slavery International, *Abolishing Slavery and its Contemporary Forms*, New York/Geneva, OHCHR, 2002, pp. 18, 26ff.

[6] 'The Global Problem of Trafficking in Persons: Breaking the Vicious Circle on Trafficking of Women and Children in the International Sex Trade', Before the House Committee on International Relations, 106th Congress 2 (1999), Testimony of Harold Hoju Koh, Assistant US Secretary of State.

[7] Janie Chuang, 'Exploitation creep and the unmaking of human trafficking law', (2014) 108 *American Journal of International Law*, 609.

[8] Joy Ezeilo, 'Achievements of the Trafficking Protocol: perspectives from the former UN Special Rapporteur on Trafficking in Persons', (2015) 4 *Anti-Trafficking Review*, 144–8.

early treaties, with Radhika Coomaraswamy, Special Rapporteur on Violence against Women, clarifying, 'historically, anti-trafficking movements have been driven by perceived threats to the "purity" or chastity of certain populations of women, notably white women'.[9] In 1949, the Convention for the Suppression of the Traffic in Persons and the Exploitation of the Prostitution of Others was drafted, but it was never widely ratified.[10] One major shortcoming was the lack of any definition on trafficking. The 1967 General Assembly Declaration on the Elimination of Discrimination against Women stated in Article 8 that 'all appropriate measures, including legislation, shall be taken to combat all forms of traffic in women and exploitation of prostitutions of women'. Comparable protection against trafficking was also included in the 1981 Convention on the Elimination of All Forms of Discrimination Against Women in Article 6, which obliged states parties to 'take all appropriate measures, including legislation to supress all forms of traffic in women and exploitation of prostitution of women'. The Committee on the Elimination of Discrimination against Women described trafficking as form of gender-based violence in its General Recommendation No. 19 of 1992 and addressed the interrelatedness of trafficking with women's economic standard and their vulnerability to armed conflicts and violence: 'Poverty and unemployment increase opportunities for trafficking in women. In addition to established forms of trafficking, there are new forms of sexual exploitation … These practices are incompatible with the equal enjoyment of rights by women and with respect for their rights and duties.'[11]

While the historical development of anti-trafficking mechanisms benefited from the increasing awareness and incorporation of women's rights, the narrow focus and application of these legal instruments, addressing the issue solely in relation to women, limited the application of this legal protective mechanism; moreover, the first instruments, such as the 1949 Convention, recognized trafficking exclusively in relation to prostitution. Special Rapporteur Coomaraswamy criticized in these terms: 'The 1949 Convention does very little to protect women from and provide remedies for the human rights violations committed in the course of trafficking, thereby increasing trafficked women's marginalisation and vulnerability to human rights violations. Further, by confining the definition of trafficking to trafficking for prostitution, the 1949 Convention excludes vast numbers of women from its protection.'[12]

In the following decades, with concern for international human rights law on the rise, codification of the general protective rules that articulated rights and duties regarding or implicitly addressing trafficking greatly improved. Thereby, the issue was slowly but steadily detached from the narrow concept of trafficking women for prostitution and incorporated into the larger framework of general human rights law and

[9] Economic and Social Council, Commission on Human Rights, 'Report of the Special Rapporteur on Violence against Women, its Causes and Consequences, submitted in accordance with Commission on Human Rights Resolution 1997/44', UN Doc. E/CN.4/2000/68, 29 February 2000, p. 10.

[10] Eighty-two states currently have ratified the Convention.

[11] Para. 14 of Recommendation 19; available at: http://www.un.org/womenwatch/daw/cedaw/recommendations/recomm.htm#recom19, accessed 24 March 2016.

[12] 'Report of the Special Rapporteur on Violence against Women, its Causes and Consequences', UN Doc. E/CN.4/1997/47/Add.1, 10 December 1996.

instruments protecting vulnerable groups. Among others, the International Covenant on Civil and Political Rights (ICCPR) and its counterpart the International Covenant on Economic, Social and Cultural Rights (ICESCR) established fundamental guarantees with respect to life and living conditions. Labour law instruments provided further protection mechanisms: the International Labour Organization Forced Labour Convention and the Abolition of Forced Labour Convention lay down the obligation to suppress forced or compulsory labour, i.e. 'all work or service which is exacted from any person under the menace of any penalty and for which the said person has not offered himself voluntary[il]y'.[13]

During the 1990s the contemporary instruments that cover trafficking in women were drawn up under the broad umbrella of human rights violation. This new approach became apparent in 1993 at the Second World Conference on Human Rights. The Conference's Vienna Declaration highlighted that

> the human rights of women and of the girl-child are an inalienable, integral and indivisible part of universal human rights ... Gender-based violence and all forms of sexual harassment and exploitation, including those resulting from cultural prejudice and international trafficking, are incompatible with the dignity and worth of the human person, and must be eliminated.[14]

The Declaration lacked the traditional equation of trafficking with prostitution and furthermore called for the establishment of the position of the Special Rapporteur, the drafting of a UN Declaration on the Elimination of Violence against Women, and the Inter-American Convention on the Prevention, Punishment and Eradication of Violence against Women. In Article 2 the UN Declaration (mirrored in Article 1 of the Inter-American Convention) explicitly expanded the notion of violence against women:

> Violence against women shall be understood to encompass, but not be limited to, the following ... Physical, sexual, and psychological violence occurring in the family ... Physical, sexual, and psychological violence occurring within the general community, including rape, sexual abuse, sexual harassment, and intimidation at work, trafficking in women and forced prostitution; physical, sexual and psychological violence perpetrated or condoned by the State, wherever it occurs.

In 1996 and 1997, Special Rapporteur Coomaraswamy submitted prominent reports on trafficking, forced prostitution, and violence against women. She addressed not only the dynamics but also recruitment methods, routes, and problems of prosecuting perpetrators. Especially in the latter report she called attention to the 'slavery-like conditions' to which women were trafficked and emphasized the need for international standards and efforts owing to the massive cross-border implications of trafficking, which current instruments were neither able to prevent nor restrict.[15]

[13] Art. 2 (1) ILO Forced Labour Convention of 1930, No. 29.

[14] Vienna Declaration and Programme of Action, adopted by the World Conference on Human Rights in Vienna on 25 June 1993.

[15] UN Doc E/CN.4/1997/47/Add.1, (above, n. 12) and UN Doc. E/CN.4/1997/47, 12 February 1997.

8.3 The United Nations Protocol to Prevent, Suppress and Punish Trafficking in Persons, especially Women and Children

8.3.1 Development and drafting of a new instrument

Since the early 1990s, the international community has considered the cross-border dimension of contemporary crime to be a threat. Certainly, the concept of organised crime emerged in the 1920s in the USA in connection with mafia-type organisations, but in our day it has become internationalized.[16] In principle it can be understood as entrepreneurial crime, and initially it was linked to the rapid expansion of illegal markets for drugs. Nowadays, transnational organised crime manifests itself in various forms ranging from drug trafficking, the arms trade, and smuggling migrants to human trafficking. This makes a definition of organised crime and the establishment of a specialized legal framework complicated.[17] Thus, most of the definitions one can find in national legislation are quite vague. It is therefore not surprising that the approach of the UN since the 1990s has also been rather broad. In 1998, following a recommendation of the UN Commission on Crime Prevention and Criminal Justice and the Economic and Social Council, the UN General Assembly initiated a new process: calling for the establishment of an ad hoc committee to address trafficking in its Resolution 53/11, these developments finally led to the establishment of the contemporary legal framework.[18] Based on evidence from a study on trafficking published by the International Organization of Migration in 1999 indicating that the majority of the more than 700,000 trafficked persons came from Eastern and Central Europe, not the expected Africa or Asia, the need to adapt perceptions on trafficking was articulated. The General Assembly therefore recommended drafting a protocol without any limitation as a comprehensive, universal new mechanism:[19] the UN Convention against Transnational Organized Crime of 15 December 2000 (often called the Palermo Convention).[20] The Convention is supplemented by three Protocols, which target specific areas and manifestations of organised crime: the Protocol to Prevent, Suppress and Punish Trafficking in Persons, Especially Women and Children; the Protocol against the Smuggling of Migrants by Land, Sea, and Air; and the Protocol against the Illicit Manufacturing of and Trafficking in Firearms, their Parts and Components and Ammunition. The Palermo Convention represents recognition by member states of the seriousness of the problems posed by transnational crimes. States that ratify this instrument commit themselves to taking a series

[16] Ulrich Sieber, 'Legal order in a global world', in Armin von Bogdandy and Rüdiger Wolfrum (eds), *Max Planck Yearbook of United Nations Law*, Vol. 14, Leiden/Boston, Martinus Nijhoff Publishers, 2010, p. 2.

[17] See—for the matter of definition—Chapter 2 of this book, sections 2.1.1 and 2.3.2 and Chapter 21.

[18] UN Doc. A/Res/53/111, 20 January 1999, para. 10.

[19] UN Doc. A/Res/55/25, 8 January 2001; Hans-Joachim Heintze and Sven Peterke, 'Inhalt und Bedeutung des VN-Protokolls zur Verhütung, Unterdrückung und Bestrafung des Menschenhandels (2000)', (2008) 1 *Journal for International Law of Peace and Armed Conflict*, 10.

[20] Adopted by General Assembly Resolution 55/25 of 15 November 2000.

of measures against these crimes including the creation of domestic criminal offences. The Convention underlines the necessity of mutual legal assistance and cooperation in law enforcement, and is the first global, legally binding instrument with an agreed definition on trafficking in persons.

The Trafficking Protocol is the major international legal instrument to address the crime of trafficking. Prior to the adoption of the UN Protocol, a number of countries had no specific provision addressing trafficking in their criminal legislations, or, owing to the origin of the trafficking framework, these were solely focused on women and children. Furthermore, various definitions existed in different instruments of international law, stemming from its various fields, most often international human rights law and criminal law. This has changed. In its Article 2, the Protocol established the overall goal to 'prevent and combat trafficking in person, paying particular attention to women and children; to protect and assist the victims of such trafficking, with full respect for their human rights; to promote cooperation among States Parties in order to meet those objectives'. Following the entry into force of the Protocol, legislation criminalizing trafficking has been adopted increasingly. In 2012, only nine countries out of the 162 a UNODC report included had no specific legislation; all the other states had drafted or amended their laws.[21]

Although trafficking is more often addressed through the human rights lens, the UN Trafficking Protocol itself is not a human rights instrument but was established through the UN Crime Commission with the incentive to fight the growing threat and consequences deriving from transnational organised crime. Thus, the Protocol is considered a law enforcement instrument, addressing aspects of prevention, prosecution, and protection.[22] The Trafficking Protocol can only be signed and ratified by parties to the UN Convention, currently 167 states.[23] The special focus on women and children within the Protocol was adopted following the tradition of predecessor legal mechanisms and mirroring experiences that remain valid: current numbers indicate that women amount to 55 to 60 per cent of all victims; women and girls together 75 per cent.[24] Unlike its predecessors it does not contain gender limitations, and it assigned rights to all trafficked persons. With the Protocol a focus on trafficking was introduced that stems from the field of international criminal law and 'despite the weakness in human rights protection offered by the Protocol, it represents a strategically important re-conceptualisation of trafficking in women'.[25]

[21] UNODC (ed.), *Global Report on Trafficking in Persons 2012*, New York, United Nations Publications, 2012, p. 82.

[22] LeRoy G. Potts, 'Global trafficking in human beings: assessing the success of the United Nations Protocol to Prevent Trafficking in Persons', (2003) 35 *George Washington International Law Review*, 239.

[23] For a list of states party to the Protocol, see UNODC at:, https://www.unodc.org/unodc/en/treaties/CTOC/countrylist-traffickingprotocol.html, accessed 25 May 2014.

[24] UNODC, *Global Report on Trafficking*, cited in note 21 above, p. 11.

[25] Minnesota Advocates for Human Rights, Stop Violence against Women, 'Trafficking in women—law and policy', available at: http://www1.umn.edu/humanrts/svaw/trafficking/law/, accessed 3 February 2016.

8.3.2 Trafficking in persons as a transnational crime

The Trafficking Protocol and its siblings were drafted to supplement the Palermo Convention. While the Convention enshrines the more general provisions of transnational organised crime, among others on matters of legal assistance and extradition, the specific subject matter on trafficking or smuggling is contained in its supplementary Protocols. The Protocols cannot be signed and ratified as independent international treaties; states are required to ratify the parent Convention to also become party to its Protocols. This relationship is defined in Articles 1 and 37 of the Protocol: 'No country can be a party to the Protocol unless it is also a Party to the Convention … The Convention and the Protocol must be interpreted together.'

As a specialized part of the Convention against transnational crime, trafficking is framed in a specific way and the commitment of the international community to address a transnational threat is mirrored in a multinational response.[26] The involvement of an organised criminal group and the transnational character of the crime are enshrined as conditions for the application of the Protocol. The transnational dimension of the crime is defined in Article 3 paragraph 2 of the Convention as an offence committed by more than one state; in one state but a substantial part taking place across borders; under the involvement of an organised criminal group that is engaged in more than one state; or as offence committed in one state that has substantial effects in another. An organised criminal group is, as defined by Article 2(a), 'a structured group of three or more persons existing for a period of time and having the aim of committing a serious crime in order to, directly or indirectly, obtain a financial or other material benefit'. Following these Articles, the scope of the Protocol does not explicitly cover internal trafficking of domestic workers or trafficking only by single individuals. These layers of trafficking should be covered by domestic legislation but, since they lack a transnational dimension, are excluded from the scope of application of this Protocol and the Convention.

8.3.2.1 Defining the terms—a controversial effort

The definition of trafficking in persons as detailed by the Trafficking Protocol is tailored to include forms of sexual exploitation but also covers a broader range of conduct: situations of servitude and forced labour, or exploitation by removal of organs.

The major progress of the Protocol in comparison to its predecessors was the definition of trafficking contained in Article 3 (a):

> 'Trafficking in persons' shall mean the recruitment, transportation, transfer, harbouring or receipt of persons, by means of the threat or use of force or other forms of coercion, of abduction, of fraud, of deception, of the abuse of power or of a position of vulnerability or of the giving or receiving of payments or benefits to achieve the consent of a person having control over another person, for the purpose of exploitation. Exploitation shall include, at a minimum, the exploitation of the prostitution

[26] Frank Laczko, 'Data and research on human trafficking', (2005) 43 *International Migration* (1–2), 6.

of others or other forms of sexual exploitation, forced labour or services, slavery or practices similar to slavery, servitude or the removal of organs.

The definition in Article 3 is based on three constitutive and cumulative elements: the act, the means, and the purpose. Through the lens of criminal law, two elements can be considered material while the third constitutes the necessary mental element. The *actus reus* requirement is split into two parts, encompassing the necessary conduct and the respective means: the Protocol lists as acts within its definition recruitment, transportation, transfer, harbouring or receipt of persons; the means potentially used encompass threat or use of force, coercion, abduction, fraud, deception, abuse of power or vulnerability, and giving payments or benefits to a person in control of the victim.

The *mens rea* element of trafficking, reflecting the perpetrator's state of mind, is given in a non-exhaustive list: 'the purpose refers to exploitation, which includes exploiting the prostitution of others, sexual exploitation, forced labour, slavery or similar practices and the removal of organs'.[27]

The previously dominant view of trafficking as an instrument of sexual exploitation is still included in the definition; however, in renouncing the narrow interpretation, the definition and with it the Protocol's scope of protection codifies a much broader approach to trafficking, by referring to forced labour, slavery, and servitude. Deliberately, the term 'trafficking' itself was not further defined by the Protocol. During preparatory meetings and drafting procedures, the delegates were unable to agree on an exact definition, arguing about a potential inclusion of any form of prostitution as trafficking. Finally, they left the term itself only so circumscribed as to allow for domestic interpretations and solutions—an aspect that was subsequently criticized for leaving too large a scope for interpretation and thereby a margin of appreciation for national stakeholders and domestic courts.[28]

The interpretation of the single elements of prohibited conduct as contained in Article 3(a) is given by reference to other instruments of international law. The International Labour Organization (ILO) Convention Concerning Forced Labour No. 29 defines 'forced labour' in its Article 2(1),[29] the UN Slavery Convention includes 'slavery' in Article 1(1),[30] and the UN Supplementary Convention on the Abolition of Slavery, the Slave Trade, and Institutions and Practices Similar to Slavery does likewise in Article 1(a)–(d). It also lists examples of conduct considered as 'servitude'.

Paragraph (b) of Trafficking Protocol Article 3 stipulates further 'the consent of a victim of trafficking in person to the intended exploitation ... shall be irrelevant where any of the means set forth have been used', enshrining the common understanding in international law that consent given under distress cannot be legally valid. This

[27] Art. 3.

[28] As stated by the Interpretative Notes: 'the terms "exploitation of the prostitution of others" or "other forms of sexual exploitation" are not defined in the Protocol, which is therefore without prejudice to how States Parties address prostitution in their respective domestic laws', p. 8.

[29] 'For the purposes of this Convention the term forced or compulsory labour shall mean all work or service which is exacted from any person under the menace of any penalty and for which the said person has not offered himself voluntarily.'

[30] 'Slavery is the status or condition of a person over whom any or all of the powers attaching to the right of ownership are exercised.'

reflects the general understanding that an individual cannot consent to being tortured or abused. No one can give consent to being exploited.[31] In a number of trafficking cases initial consent is given by the victims to be transported to another country, for instance, being promised a working or residence permit. As Article 3 paragraph (b) indicates, consent becomes irrelevant if the means listed above are used. Even in cases of trafficking to prostitution, knowing about the nature of the work would not change its trafficking character if the element of exploitation remained.[32] The UN Interpretative Note to the first requirement of the definition underlines that use of force on trafficked persons is not a necessary precondition, since the wording 'abuse of a position of vulnerability' already encompasses the possibility that victims have no option to refuse even where they seem to voluntarily submit.

Even in cases in which none of the means listed in Article 3(a) are employed, children cannot give their consent to the act of trafficking for the purpose of being exploited. The reference to children's rights set forth in paragraph (c), a child being a person under 18 years of age, is in addition to section 6(4) on assistance and protection of victims, the only explicit mention of children and special needs. The lack of explicit provisions was criticized during and after drafting by the United Nations Children's Fund (UNICEF), the Human Rights High Commissioner, the Human Rights Caucus, and the International Organization for Migration. The Annotated Guide to the Complete UN Trafficking Protocol strongly advises governments to fill the gap by incorporating the respective provisions from the Convention on the Rights of the Child, found within its Optional Protocol, the ILO Convention Concerning the Prohibition and Immediate Action for the Elimination of the Worst Forms of Child Labour No. C182 (1999).[33]

8.3.2.2 Considering delimitations—trafficking, slavery, smuggling

The complex field of voluntary and involuntary migration, the multi-causality of movement and displacement, makes it problematic to allocate individuals to the distinct legal categories that were established to differentiate between refugees, migrants, trafficked, and smuggled persons. Man-made and natural disasters are often considered as common root causes of smuggling and trafficking and distinction between the two is difficult, as they are often strongly interrelated, 'a continuum from tolerable forms of labour migration to trafficking, perhaps particularly in the context of humanitarian crisis'.[34]

Forced marriages, forced servants, abduction, and conscription of children to the armed forced might constitute trafficking; child adoption markets can constitute another form of human trafficking if the three requirements defined in the UN Protocol

[31] UNODC (ed.), *Anti-Human Trafficking Manual for Criminal Justice Practitioners*, New York, United Nations Publications, 2009, p. 8.

[32] UNODC, *Assistance for the Implementation of the ECOWAS Plan of Action*, cited in note 4 above, p. 6.

[33] Ann D. Jordan, 'Annotated guide to the complete UN Trafficking Protocol', May 2012, Washington DC, International Human Rights Law Group, p. 11.

[34] Elzbieta Gozdiak and Alissa Walter, 'Misconceptions about human trafficking in a time of crisis', (2014) 45 *Forced Migration Review*, 58.

are met. There are strong overlaps between the crime of slavery and trafficking, especially as 'trafficking in human beings will almost always involve slavery or slavery-like practices …',[35] in particular as a consequence of the primary act of moving a person. While national laws often treat trafficking as enslavement, the UN Protocol solely applies to transnational movements of persons. An elaboration of the predominant definition of slavery was provided by the International Criminal Tribunal for the Former Yugoslavia in *Kunarac et al.*[36] Furthermore, the Rome Statute of the International Criminal Court established the relationship in its Article 7 paragraph 2(c), defining the crime of slavery: '"Enslavement" means exercise of any or all of the powers attaching to the right of ownership over a person and includes the exercise of any or all persons, in particular women and children'.

Distinguishing between trafficking and smuggling as further discussed in Chapter 9 of this book is equally difficult, as they do overlap to some extent. Trafficking, however, mostly goes beyond the illegal entry of individuals to the territory of foreign states. In this regard, the question of consent (as discussed in section 8.3.2.1 of this chapter) again becomes relevant, since consent to being smuggled is the main difference between smuggling and trafficking, as smuggling victims often consent to being smuggled as one and often the only way to circumvent national immigration laws. This, however, should not be considered a 'victimless crime', although it mostly starts with some form of complicity.[37] In comparison, trafficking is often defined by long-term exploitation to the benefit of the traffickers that goes far beyond the irregular crossing of state borders.

8.3.3 Effective remedy for and protection of victims of trafficking

Although the UN Trafficking Protocol is not by design a human rights instrument and does not focus on victims' rights, the Protocol contains a specific second section on the 'assistance to and protection of victims of trafficking in persons'.

A basis for the following Articles is given by Article 24 of the Palermo Convention that obliges its member states to employ effective domestic measures to protect victims from intimidation and retaliation, in particular if testifying as witnesses.[38] Article 6 of the UN Trafficking Protocol additionally addresses the necessity to implement effective protection of the identity and personal privacy of victims from the long arm of transnationally operating criminal groups. In paragraph 2, special emphasis is laid on providing the information required for court proceedings, such as (for instance, and herewith mirroring traditional human rights law) by providing translators for trial proceedings. Paragraph 3 upholds the importance of various aspects of recovery and the basic needs of trafficked persons: 'each State Party shall consider implementing

[35] Ryszard Piotrowicz, 'The legal nature of trafficking in human beings', (2009) 4 *Intercultural Human Rights Law Review*, 179.

[36] *Prosecutor v Dragoljub Kunarac Radomir Kovac and Zoran Vukovic* Cases IT-96-23 and IT-96-23/1-A (2002), para. 543.

[37] Jacqueline Bhaba and Monette Zard, 'Smuggled or trafficked?', (2005) 25 *Forced Migration Review*, 6.

[38] Heintze and Peterke, 'Inhalt und Bedeutung', cited in note 19 above, p. 13.

measures to provide for the physical, psychological, and social recovery of victims of trafficking in person', and provides a list of examples of appropriate housing, counselling, medical, psychological, and material assistance, or employment, educational, and training opportunities.[39]

During the drafting sessions, how to handle victims that had been rescued from traffickers was debated. Representatives feared turning the UN Protocol into a migration convention if measures were adopted to facilitate their remaining in the destination country. On the other hand, return to their country of origin would put them in potential danger of being returned to the traffickers.[40] With the obligation to provide adequate housing, in conjunction with the requirement of Article 14 to respect international obligations under human rights law, international humanitarian law, the 1951 Refugee Convention, and first and foremost the fundamental principle of non-*refoulement*, the potentially devastating effects of returning victims to their country of origin is considered and inscribed in the UN Protocol. Furthermore, with reference to adequate housing, the practice of keeping victims in detention centres, often employed in reality, is in focus and here again appears the goal of the Protocol to not punish victims of the trafficking for aspects of the crime itself, such as for instance illegal entry to a state's territory without valid permits.[41] Article 7 reaffirms the potential harm that might follow return of trafficked persons that illegally entered or worked in a foreign country, by recommending a state to '*consider* adopting legislative or other appropriate measures that permit victims of trafficking in persons to remain in its territory, temporarily or permanently, in appropriate cases'.[42] The reference to paragraph 2, 'each State party shall give appropriate consideration to humanitarian and compassionate factors', is evaluated as primarily showing political commitment.[43]

The actual return of trafficked persons is further regulated by Article 8. Finding its basis in protection of victims having the nationality of a particular state or a permanent residence permit, the obligation is in practice rendered quite ineffective. Trafficked persons often are not protected by their state of nationality as valid documentation is missing and the countries of origin repeatedly hinder return to their territory.

The obligation of paragraph 5 specifically addresses domestic legislation and domestic practices and enshrines the duty to transpose or implement domestic laws to guarantee the fundamental physical safety of victims. The prosecutorial nature of the Protocol is mirrored, requesting states to criminalize and penalize trafficking in human beings: 'each State Party shall adopt such legislative and other measures as may be necessary to establish as criminal offences the conduct set forth in article 3 of this Protocol, if committed intentionally'. Through the relationship between the Palermo Convention and its Supplementary Protocol discussed earlier, Article

[39] See Art. 6 para. 3(a)–(d) UN Trafficking Protocol.

[40] UN Doc./A.AC.254/4/Add.1/Rev.6, (2000), p. 7.

[41] Christopher Ram, 'The United Nations Convention Against Transnational Organized Crime and its Protocols', (2001) 1 *Forum on Crime and Society* (2), 135, p. 143.

[42] Art. 7, para. 2.

[43] Heintze and Peterke, 'Inhalt und Bedeutung', cited in note 19 above, p. 14.

10 of the Convention becomes equally applicable, entailing the liability of legal entities. This should be read in conjunction with Article 8 of the Convention concerning corruption of public officials, which supplements the provisions of the Protocol and mirrors the complementary and sometimes even overlapping scope of application of both the Convention and its Protocol. The United Nations Office on Drugs and Crime (UNODC) indicates that around 134 countries have currently incorporated in their legislation specific trafficking offences that are in line with the UN Trafficking Protocol's provision. However, the actual conviction rate stays low. Of the 132 countries the *Global Report 2012* cites, 21 did not have one conviction in the years between 2007 and 2010 with Africa and the Middle East as regions where the fewest convictions were observed.[44]

Finally, in paragraph 6 compensation for damages is enshrined as 'the possibility [of] obtaining compensation for damages suffered'. As the Annotation guide discusses, the UN Protocol establishes just the possibility, not the right, to seek compensation and it thus has little priority.[45]

8.3.4 Prevention

Section III of the Protocol enshrines the preventive character of the UN Protocol, primarily contained in Article 9 on prevention and supported by Articles 10 and 11 and 12 on information exchange and training, border measures, and security and control of documents. Article 9 paragraph 1 reads 'States Parties shall establish comprehensive policies, programmes and other measures', and stipulates a general obligation of states to implement a *comprehensive* set of measures to prevent and combat trafficking and protect victims of trafficking from re-victimization.[46] Paragraphs 2–4 lay down more detailed instructions on how to react to trafficking, for instance by 'undertak[ing] measures such as research, information and mass media campaigns and social and economic initiatives ...'[47] This information has proved necessary to establish suitable measures to prevent and react to trafficking.

In light of the comprehensive preventive approach the Protocol represents, its developmental approach should also be considered. Root causes of trafficking are addressed in paragraph 4 of Article 4, where it is upheld that 'State Parties shall take or strengthen measures ... to alleviate the factors that make persons, especially women and children, vulnerable to trafficking, such as poverty, underdevelopment and lack of equal opportunities'. Bi- and multilateral cooperation is therefore required, to 'discourage the demand that fosters all forms of exploitation of persons'.[48] The Protocol, furthermore, entails border measures to prevent trafficking in Article 11, a provision that later was strongly criticized as supporting a restrictive immigration policy rather than preventing trafficking. Since more restrictive immigration policies will increase

[44] UNODC, *Global Report on Trafficking 2012*, cited in note 21 above, p. 85.

[45] UNODC (ed.), 'An introduction to human trafficking: vulnerability, impact and action', Background Paper 2008, p. 12.

[46] Art. 9 para. 1 (a)–(b). [47] Art. 9 para. 2. [48] Art. 9 para. 5.

the efforts needed to enter a country illegally, the measures of Article 11 might run counter to the overall object and purpose of the Trafficking Protocol.[49]

The following Articles, 13 and 14, address handling documentation, on one hand to ensure validity and control of travel or identity documents, and on the other hand, by request of another state, to verify legitimacy and validity of documents.

8.3.5 Cooperation in a common effort: states and NGOs

The transnational character of trafficking is taken up in the Protocol's obligation to cooperate, since without cross-border cooperation any efforts to fight trafficking will most likely fail: 'in short, transnational organised crime transcends cultural, social, linguistic, and geographical borders and must be met with a concerted response'.[50] There is no general provision on assistance and cooperation of states in the Protocol, as this can be found in Article 18 of the Convention on mutual legal assistance. The Protocol entails specific provisions on cooperation including sharing of confidential information and building capacity to combat trafficking. Article 10(I) reads

> law enforcement, immigration or other relevant authorities of States Parties shall, as appropriate, cooperate with one another by exchanging information … [and] States Parties shall provide or strengthen training for law enforcement, immigration and other relevant officials in the prevention of trafficking in persons. The training should focus on methods used in preventing such trafficking, prosecuting the traffickers and protecting the rights of the victims, including protecting the victims from the traffickers. The training should also take into account the need to consider human rights and child- and gender-sensitive issues and it should encourage cooperation with non-governmental organisations, other relevant organisations and other elements of civil society.

Article 9(II) concerns cooperation with NGOs in providing assistance, which is of the essence in this field of organised crime. Victims of trafficking are not always willing or able to cooperate with law enforcement as they fear possible consequences, either retaliation by traffickers or actions by immigration enforcement, such as deportation or prosecution. The benefit of establishing comprehensive state and NGO cooperation is therefore particularly stressed. NGOs often have easier access to victims and information about their experiences. Accordingly, engagement of non-governmental partners 'often serving as a bridge between otherwise-isolated victims and officials'[51] must be considered as key to successfully tackling trafficking. To support the implementation of the provisions, several manuals for law enforcement and prosecution were published by UNODC.

[49] Heintze and Peterke, 'Inhalt und Bedeutung', cited in note 19 above, p. 15.
[50] UNODC, Organized Crime, p. 1, available at: https://www.unodc.org/unodc/de/organized-crime/index.html, accessed 24 March 2016.
[51] UNODC, *Assistance for the Implementation of the ECOWAS Plan of Action*, cited in note 4 above, p. 83.

8.3.6 The UN Protocol and public international law

Other international and regional human rights instruments additionally establish a protection for trafficked persons even if they are not bound by the UN Trafficking Protocol. These include among others the UN Convention and the Supplementary Convention on the Abolition of Slavery, the Slave Trade, and Institutions and Practices Similar to Slavery, the UN Convention on the Rights of the Child, the UN Convention on the Elimination of All Forms of Discrimination Against Women, and the European Convention for the Protection of Human Rights and Other Fundamental Freedoms. Article 14 of the UN Protocol addresses the relationship to these treaties by enshrining the obligation to not impair any rights and duties arising under other instruments of international law, in particular humanitarian law and human rights law. The Statement of Purpose laid down by Article 2 additionally emphasizes adherence and recourse to human rights law, as protection and assistance must be established for trafficked persons in accordance with human rights standards (paragraph b). Contemporary expanding human rights jurisprudence concerning trafficked persons therefore furthers protection, as will be discussed below in section 8.4 of this chapter.

A factor exacerbating the difficulty of promoting trafficking as a crime to be addressed by the international community was the incorporation of trafficking in international criminal law. The Rome Statute of the International Criminal Court codifies trafficking. It does so in relation to the classic crime of slavery under the umbrella of crimes against humanity in Article 7, but adds trafficking as a distinct dimension: '"enslavement" means the exercise of any or all of the powers attaching to the right of ownership over a person and *includes the exercise of such power in the course of trafficking in persons, in particular women and children*'.[52]

8.4 Implementing the Protocol

The Convention against Transnational Organized Crime contains a mechanism for implementation, which consists of periodic Conferences of the Parties. At its fourth session in 2008, the Conference adopted decision 4/4, which established an open-ended interim working group to advise and assist the Conference in the implementation of its mandate with regard to the Trafficking Protocol. Their functions were:

(a) to facilitate implementation of the Trafficking in Persons Protocol through the exchange of experience and practices between experts and practitioners in this area, including by contributing to the identification of weaknesses, gaps, and challenges;

(b) to make recommendations to the Conference on how states parties can better implement the provisions of the Protocol;

[52] Art. 7(II)(c) Rome Statute of the International Criminal Court. For a discussion on trafficking in the Rome Statute see for instance, Clare Frances Moran, 'Human trafficking and the Rome Statute of the International Criminal Court', (2014) 3 *The Age of Human Rights Journal*, 32–45.

(c) to assist the Conference in providing guidance to its secretariat on its activities relating to the implementation of the Protocol; and

(d) to make recommendations to the Conference on how it can better coordinate with the various international bodies combating trafficking in persons with respect to implementing, supporting, and promoting the Protocol.

This implementation mechanism is rather weak; however, the involvement of the different stakeholders and the transparency of the reports enable the public to obtain an overview of the problems at stake. The same is true for other reporting procedures. In its Resolution 63/194, the General Assembly invited the member states and regional and international organisations to submit their views on the full and effective coordination of efforts against trafficking in persons. In 2009, a background paper summarizing the views of the different stakeholders was presented.[53] The background paper contained information on an interactive dialogue 'Taking collective action to end human trafficking', held at the General Assembly on 13 May 2009. The states considered the advisability of a global plan of action to establish a greater political will and commitment to prevent and combat trafficking in persons.

Pushed forward by the international commitment, international bodies, along with civil society groups, are becoming increasingly involved in researching the issue of trafficking and supporting anti-trafficking efforts, and states have begun to introduce new laws and policies aimed at criminalizing trafficking, protecting victims, and preventing future trafficking. One state launched a unilateral monitoring mechanism that began reporting on and evaluating the response of other states to the issue of trafficking in persons.[54]

A more radical means of implementation at the universal level was the establishment by decision 2004/110 of the Commission on Human Rights of the position of a Special Rapporteur, 'whose mandate will focus on the human rights aspects of the victims of trafficking in persons, especially women and children'. In the same decision, the Commission invited the Special Rapporteur to submit annual reports, including recommendations on measures required to uphold and protect the human rights of victims, and to respond effectively to reliable information on possible human rights violations, with a view to protecting the human rights of actual or potential victims of trafficking. The UN considers the establishment of the Special Rapporteur as being a 'critical circuit-breaker'.[55] Indeed, the extension by the Human Rights Council in 2008 of the initial three-year mandate of the Special Rapporteur for a further three years reflects the success of that office.[56] By Decision 2004/110, the mandate became specified because it was requested to contribute to the further improvement of relevant international norms and standards and to integrate a gender and age perspective. Another task was the identification of best practice and the proposing of adequate responses to challenges and obstacles, in order to uphold and protect the human rights of victims. In 2009, the strategic vision was enlarged to:

[53] Cf. UN Doc. A/64/130, 3 February 2010, para. 2.

[54] UN Doc. A/HRC/26/37, 1 April 2014, para. 11.

[55] Ibid, para. 16.

[56] UN Doc. HRC Res. 8/12, 18 June 2008.

(a) criminal justice including punishment of perpetrators/non-punishment for trafficked persons and promotion of international cooperation;
(b) redress, rehabilitate, and reintegrate; and
(c) improve capacity, coordination, and cooperation.[57]

This approach aided the Special Rapporteur in shaping and promoting a coherent and comprehensive vision of an effective and rights-based response to trafficking.

In 2011, the Human Rights Council again extended the mandate of the Special Rapporteur. The modified mandate requested that she 'examine the impact of anti-trafficking measures on the human rights of victims of trafficking in persons with a view to proposing adequate responses to challenges arising in this regard and to avoid re-victimization of victims of trafficking'.[58] The Special Rapporteur is entitled to receive communications on reliable allegations of human rights violations, with a view to protecting the rights of actual or potential victims of trafficking. She is explicitly mandated to respond effectively in accordance with established procedures. Accordingly, she communicates a case to the government concerned, requesting clarification and action, either through an allegation letter or through an urgent appeal where the alleged violation is time-sensitive and/or of a very grave nature. Since the mandate was established, a total of ninety-nine communications have been sent and a total of fifty-four responses received.[59] Taking into consideration that the states are always quite reluctant to accept the involvement of an international body in human rights issues within the state, this number is considerable. Moreover, states were also invited to answer a questionnaire to solicit their views on the achievements of the mandate and its future areas of work.

The Special Rapporteurs now regularly submit annual and thematic reports, country mission reports, communications sent to governments, statements from the mandate holders, research, and reports of meetings. The most recent reports dealt with the identification, protection of and assistance to victims of trafficking,[60] the prevention of trafficking in persons,[61] the right to an effective remedy for trafficked persons,[62] the issue of human trafficking in supply chains,[63] and the issue of trafficking in persons for the removal of organs.[64]

There are other fields of UN activity to aid in the struggle against trafficking of persons for economic and sexual exploitation. In 2002, the issue of such acts during UN peace operations gained considerable attention. The UN High Commissioner for Refugees (UNHCR) accused humanitarian workers and peacekeepers in West Africa of widespread sexual exploitation and abuse of refugees

[57] See UN Doc. A/HRC/10/16, 10 February 2009, section V and the statement made by the Special Rapporteur to the Third Committee on 25 October 2010 during the sixty-fifth session of the General Assembly.
[58] UN Doc. HRC Res. 17/1, 22–3 August 2011.
[59] UN Doc. A/HRC/26/37, cited in note 53 above, para. 32.
[60] UN Doc. A/64/290, 27 July 2010.
[61] UN Doc. A/65/288, 9 August 2010.
[62] UN Doc. A/66/283, 9 August 2011.
[63] UN Doc. A/67/261, 6 June 2013.
[64] UN Doc. A/68/256, 2 August 2013.

and internally displaced women and children.[65] In 2004, Amnesty International published a detailed report about the failure of UN peacekeepers to overcome trafficking in persons and inadequate attempts to assist and protect the victims of that crime.[66] In Liberia in 2003, many victims of trafficking found themselves exploited by peacekeepers.[67] Against this background, legal scholars argue that the means to protect and assist victims (namely law, training, and liaison) must be rights-based and applied in a way 'that ensures peacekeepers do not create more victims of trafficking or further victimize those that are already victims of trafficking'.[68] Such UN reports can be seen also as mechanisms for implementation of international obligations.

The importance of the Palermo Convention and the Trafficking Protocol per se, and as impetus for regional initiatives, is widely acknowledged. 'The conclusion of the Palermo Convention and the Anti-Trafficking Convention demonstrate the increasing recognition at the international level of the prevalence of trafficking and the need to combat it.' This statement was given by the European Court of Human Rights (ECtHR) in its judgment in *Rantsev v Cyprus and Russia* in 2010.[69] The absence of explicit references to trafficking in the European Convention on Human Rights (ECHR) does not surprise because this instrument was inspired by the UN's Universal Declaration of Human Rights. That document, too, made no express mention of trafficking. In Article 4 the ECHR does prohibit slavery and the slave trade in all forms. In assessing this obligation, Article 4 must be interpreted in the light of present-day conditions. Besides, the ECtHR has noted that the growth of trafficking in Europe has been facilitated in part by the collapse of the communist bloc and recognized the need for measures to combat it. Against this background the European human rights protection mechanisms can be seen as a means of implementing the Anti-Trafficking Convention. In *Rantsev v Cyprus and Russia* the Court held that trafficking itself is prohibited under Article 4 ECHR and ruled on one hand that Cyprus had acted in violation of Article 4 because the state did not put in place an appropriate legal and administrative framework to combat trafficking as a consequence of the current regime of artiste visas. On the other hand, Cyprus had failed to enable the police to take operational measures to protect the applicant's daughter from being trafficked, despite circumstances that had given rise to a credible suspicion that she might have been a victim of trafficking. The case and further jurisprudence of the ECtHR on Article 4 proves that the modern interpretation of slave work includes the

[65] UNHCR and Save the Children UK (eds), *Sexual Violence and Exploitation: The Experience of Refugee Children in Guinea, Liberia and Sierra Leone Based on Findings and Recommendations from Assessment Mission 22.10.–30.11.2001*, London, UNHCR and Save the Children UK, 2002.

[66] Amnesty International, 'Kosovo (Serbia and Montenegro), so does that mean I have rights?', 6 May 2004.

[67] Elizabeth M. Bruch, 'Models wanted: the search for an effective response to human trafficking', (2004) 40 *Journal of International Law*, 1.

[68] Bruce Oswald and Sarah Finnin, 'Combatting the trafficking of persons on peace operations', in Harvey Langholtz, Boris Kondoch, and Alan Wells (eds), *International Peacekeeping: The Yearbook of International Peace Operations*, Vol. 10, Dordrecht, Brill/Nijhoff, 2006, p. 32.

[69] The case concerned the death of a young woman that was trafficked to Cyprus. *Rantsev v Cyprus and Russia*, Application 25965/04 (2010), paras 227–78.

prohibition of trafficking.[70] Thus, general human rights enforcement mechanisms deal equally with cases of trafficking. The European Convention on Action against Trafficking in Human Beings of 2005, which entered into force on 1 January 2008, complements the universal anti-trafficking system and can again be considered an expression of the increasing recognition of international condemnation of this modern version of the crime of slavery. It applies to all forms of trafficking, whether national or international, all victims of trafficking, and all forms of exploitation. The Convention is open to ratification by states that are not members of the Council of Europe and the member states are monitored by the Group of Experts on Action against Trafficking in Human Beings.[71] This European mechanism, therefore, contributes to the implementation of the UN Convention. While keeping in mind the still existing flaws,

> there are still noticeable gaps between the obligations of States with regard to trafficking and the extent to which those obligations are met in practice ... [former Special Rapporteur Ezeilo assesses] (but) the protocol has prompted strong political commitment ... (and) has informed regional, subregional and national counter-trafficking legal frameworks. ... The Protocol stands out as an international law intended to advance the global movement through collective action to end human exploitation.[72]

8.5 Conclusions

Practice shows that trafficking is quite a complex international issue. The UN Trafficking Protocol constitutes the first comprehensive instrument to address a broadly defined crime of trafficking and the growing number of ratifications mirrors the still increasing awareness. It reflects the political will and the necessity of states to combat organised crime in its various manifestations, among them human trafficking. The ratification of the Protocol and supplementary legal instruments, however, is only one first step. The practical implementation and cross-border cooperation of all stakeholders involved, including allocation of financial means, still remains a challenge.[73] Restraints identified are the lack of research, the lack of capacity in the countries affected, and the lack of monitoring and evaluation.[74] The Protocol has generated amendments to national legislation, but there has been less evidence of its effective implementation. The majority of states parties have adopted at least a minimal legal framework to enable implementation but the capacities of the member states vary. Thus, development is needed of an effective and multidisciplinary anti-trafficking strategy with sustainable resources.[75]

[70] Cases of further interest on Art. 4 ECHR are *V. F. v France* Application 7196/10 (2011), M. *and Others v Italy and Bulgaria* Application 40020/03 (2012), *F. A. v UK* Application 20658/11 (2013) (these concerning states' obligations).Concerning measures taken by states against traffickers, see *Kaya v Germany* Application 31753/02 (2007), *Tas v Belgium* Application 44614/06 (2009). Concerning domestic workers, see *C. N. and V. v France* Application 67724/09 (2012).

[71] UN Doc. A/HRC/29/38, 31 March 2015, para. 35.

[72] Ezeilo, 'Achievements of the Trafficking Protocol', cited in note 8 above, pp. 144–8.

[73] UNODC, *Global Report on Trafficking 2012*, cited in note 21 above, p. 88.

[74] Ibid, p. 90.

[75] UN Doc. CTOC/COP/2006/6Rev.1, 9 September 2008.

Accordingly, the General Assembly adopted the United Nations Global Plan of Action to Combat Trafficking in Persons.[76] This document endorses a multidisciplinary and integrated approach to end trafficking in human beings by confronting it in the wider setting of development, peace, security, and human rights.[77] It takes into consideration that the victims find themselves being enslaved in forced labour and domestic servitude, sexually exploited, or used as child soldiers. Most trafficked persons cannot be formally identified because they are not able or willing to support the national authorities owing to fear of expulsion. Moreover, the states deny them assistance when they most critically need it. Therefore the UN, in Resolution A/RES/64/293 of 12 August 2010, launched the United Nations Voluntary Trust Fund for Victims of Human Trafficking. The idea is to support actual, on-the-ground humanitarian, legal, and financial aid to victims of trafficking. Most of the victim protection provisions establish minimum standards and are often optional instruments to increase pressure on states. Introduction of stricter border control measures causes states to be asked whether this action contradicts the Protocol's object, purpose, and its effective implementation. The UN underlines several interacting principles in order to address the challenges of implementation.[78] The most important one is that the human rights of trafficked persons should be at the centre of all activities. States parties have to make sure that their measures do not adversely affect the human rights of persons who are victims of trafficking or migrants. The measures should accord with the internationally recognized principles of non-discrimination and should also be gender-sensitive. This approach empowers potential and actual victims to access of information and remedies.

Effective action requires a comprehensive international approach in the states of origin, transit, and destination, which includes the prevention of trafficking as well as the punishment of the traffickers. A coordinated and sustainable policy is required that includes governmental agencies as well as NGOs. Policies and measures should be developed based on data collection, research, and regular monitoring of the anti-trafficking response. Having these principles in mind, the UN developed a Framework of Action, which focuses on five key pillars of intervention needed to ensure an effective anti-trafficking response: prosecution, protection, prevention, and both national and international coordination and cooperation. The Action plan proves that nobody expects an automatic implementation of the Protocol. It deals with many aspects of the national legal order and the strict enforcement of measures against organised crime. Many countries are confronted with weak or absent rule of law and weak legal systems. They are therefore neither able nor willing to implement the Protocol. Against this background, additional actions are needed to make the Protocol a powerful instrument against organised crime. Thus, the activities of the UN are a useful incentive to implement the Protocol and activate an effective protection that the Protocol, as major legal instrument, has founded.

[76] UN Doc. A/Res/64/293, 12 August 2010.

[77] Ibid, Introduction to Annex, p. 1.

[78] UNODC (ed.), *International Framework for Action to Implement the Trafficking in Persons Protocol*, New York, UNODC, 2009, p. 8.

9

The UN Protocol against the Smuggling of Migrants by Land, Sea and Air 2000

Andreas Schloenhardt

9.1 Introduction

The United Nations (UN) Protocol against the Smuggling of Migrants by Land, Sea, and Air seeks 'to prevent and combat the smuggling of migrants, as well as to promote cooperation among States Parties to that end, while protecting the rights of smuggled migrants'.[1] These objectives reflect the inherent complexity of the phenomenon of migrant smuggling and the distinct—and at times conflicting—goals of international efforts in this field.

The Smuggling of Migrants Protocol supplements the UN Convention Against Transnational Organized Crime.[2] This relationship between the Protocol and the Convention squarely places the phenomenon of migrant smuggling in the category of organised crime. Through the Convention, States Parties to the Protocol also gain access to a myriad of investigative, prosecutorial, and judicial tools to combat organised crime, including in cases that require international cooperation.

The Convention and the Protocol were conceived in the late 1990s and, after two years of formal negotiations, opened for signature at a high-level meeting in Palermo, Italy, in December 2000. Since its inception, the Protocol has garnered considerable support: as of 1 January 2015, 141 States were Parties to the Protocol.[3]

9.2 Evolution and Background

9.2.1 Background and settings

Negotiations for the elaboration of an international treaty to combat the smuggling of migrants began in the 1990s amidst growing concerns about irregular and

[1] Opened for signature 15 December 2000, 2241 UNTS 507 (entry into force 28 January 2004) [hereafter Smuggling of Migrants Protocol]. Art. 2 of the Protocol.

[2] Art. 1(1) Smuggling of Migrants Protocol; United Nations Convention Against Transnational Organized Crime, opened for signature 12 December 2000, 2225 UNTS 209 (entry into force 29 September 2003). See generally, Andreas Schloenhardt, 'Transnational organised crime', in Neil Boister and Robert J. Currie (eds), *Routledge Handbook on Transnational Criminal Law*, London, Routledge, 2014, pp. 409–33.

[3] UNODC, *Protocol against the Smuggling of Migrants by Land, Sea and Air* (27 November 2014), Status of Ratification, available at: http://www.unodc.org/unodc/en/treaties/CTOC/signatures.html, accessed 4 February 2016.

uncontrolled migration in the post-Cold War era. The opening of the 'Iron Curtain' that had prevented any siginificant movement of persons between the Western and Eastern blocs was followed by mass migration across the newly opened borders. Taking advantage of routes and transit points that had previously been unavailable, the smuggling of migrants emerged as a growing business to assist those wanting or needing to migrate but not meeting the legal requirements for immigration in transit and destination countries.[4] The smuggling of migrants became a political concern and was viewed as a 'security threat by the preferred destination countries in Europe, North America, and Australia'.[5] The uncontrolled movement of irregular migrants and the involvement of criminal elements in facilitating these movements were seen as threats to state sovereignty over immigration and border control.[6]

9.2.1.1 Early developments

Countries determined to combat the smuggling of migrants and to prosecute and punish migrant smugglers quickly became aware of the fact that international cooperation was essential in their quest. Critical gaps in their ability to cooperate across borders, non-existing anti-migrant smuggling laws in many countries, and fragmented domestic law enforcement efforts, however, meant that governments were not in a position to easily cooperate to prohibit migrant smuggling and prosecute migrant smugglers.

The UN General Assembly first addressed the issue of migrant smuggling in Resolution 48/102 of 20 December 1993, entitled 'Prevention of the smuggling of aliens'. This Resolution 'condemns the practice of smuggling of aliens in violation of international and national law and without regard for the safety, well-being and human rights of the migrants'[7] and calls on Member States to enhance their efforts and cooperate to prevent and combat this phenomenon.[8]

To further advance consultations in this field, the Resolution requested the UN Commission on Crime Prevention and Criminal Justice (CCPCJ) to give special attention to the issue of migrant smuggling at its third session, held in Vienna between 26 April and 6 May 1994. In discussing this issue, the Commission noted that '[a]lien smuggling was considered a matter of grave concern for many Governments' and suggested that '[c]riminal legislation should be enacted and enforced to combat the

[4] Andrée Kirchner and Lorenzo Schiano di Pepe, 'International attempts to conclude a Convention to combat illegal migration', (1998) 10 *International Journal of Refugee Law*, 662, p. 668; Peter Andreas, 'The rise of the American crimefare state', (1997) 14 *World Policy Journal* (3), 37; Susan Martin, 'Global migration trends and asylum', *New Issues in Refugee Research*, UNHCR Working Paper 41, 30 April 2001, pp. 8 and 13.

[5] Anne Gallagher, 'Human rights and human trafficking: quagmire or firm ground? A response to James Hathaway', (2009) 49 *Virginia Journal of International Law*, 789, p. 790.

[6] John Backers-Morrison and Sharone Backers-Morrison, 'The dark side of globalisation: the criminalisation of refugees', (2001) 43 *Race & Class* (1), 71.

[7] UN General Assembly, *Prevention of the Smuggling of Aliens*, UN Doc. A/RES/48/102, 20 December 1993, [1].

[8] Ibid, [3]. See also Anne Gallagher and Fiona David, *The International Law of Migrant Smuggling*, Cambridge, CUP, 2014, pp. 30–31.

abominable practice'.[9] During the meeting, the United States introduced the first draft of a resolution on criminal justice action to combat the organised smuggling of illegal migrants across national boundaries.[10] This draft was slightly revised and later presented as Draft Resolution III for adoption by the UN Economic and Social Council (ECOSOC).[11] This draft specifically

> [c]alls upon all States to take effective and expeditious measures, such as the enactment or amendment if necessary of domestic criminal law, providing appropriate penalties to combat all aspects of organized crime activities constituting the smuggling of illegal migrants, including all elements of the organization of smuggling and transport of illegal migrants, such as the production or distribution of false travel documents, money laundering, systematic extortion and misuse of international commercial aviation and maritime transport, in violation of international standards.[12]

ECOSOC adopted the Commission's proposed resolution on 25 July 1994.[13]

Between 1994 and 1997, the General Assembly,[14] the CCPCJ,[15] and ECOSOC[16] revisited the topic of migrant smuggling several times, thus paving the way for greater international cooperation in this field.

9.2.1.2 Development of the Protocol

In mid-1997, the Government of Italy submitted a proposal for a draft convention to define and target the smuggling of migrants by sea to the International Maritime Organization (IMO).[17] It was at that time that Italy started to become particularly affected by seaborne smuggling from North Africa, the Balkans, and the Eastern Mediterranean—a situation that persists today. In 1997, the primary concern of the

[9] UN Commission on Crime Prevention and Criminal Justice, 'Report of the Commission on Crime Prevention and Criminal Justice on its 3rd session', UN Doc. E/CN.15/1994/12 (1994) 66, [29].

[10] UN CCPCJ, *Criminal Justice Action to Combat the Organized Smuggling of Illegal Migrants Across National Boundaries*, UN Doc. E/CN.15/1994/L.8, 4 May 1994.

[11] UN CCPCJ, *Criminal Justice Action to Combat the Organized Smuggling of Illegal Migrants Across National Boundaries*, UN Doc. E/CN.15/1994/L.8/Rev.1, 6 May 1994.

[12] UN CCPCJ, *Draft Smuggling Resolution*, cited in note 10 above, UN Doc. E/CN.15/1994/12 (1994) 12 [9].

[13] ECOSOC, *Criminal Justice Action to Combat the Organized Smuggling of Illegal Migrants Across National Boundaries*, UN Doc. E/1994/14, 25 July 1994.

[14] UN General Assembly, 'Crime prevention and criminal justice: measures to combat alien smuggling; Report of the Secretary-General', UN Doc. A/49/350, 30 August 1994, 22 [99]; UN General Assembly, *Measures for Prevention of the Smuggling of Aliens*, UN Doc. A/RES/61/62, 28 January 1997, 2 [3].

[15] UN CCPCJ, 'Report of the Commission on Crime Prevention and Criminal Justice on its Fourth Session', UN Doc. E/CN.15/1995/13 (1995), 17–20; UN CCPCJ, 'Measures to combat the smuggling of migrants, Report of the Secretary-General', UN Doc. E/CN.15/1996/4, 21 March 1996, 7 [71]; UN CCPCJ, *International Cooperation in Combatting Transnational Organized Crime: Smuggling of Illegal Migrants*, UN Doc. E/CN.15/1997/8, 18 February 1997 and UN Doc. E/CN.15/1997/8/Add.1, 8 April 1997; UN CCPCJ, 'Report on the Sixth Session', UN Doc. E/CN.15/1997/21 (1997), 130 [74]–[75].

[16] ECOSOC, *Criminal Justice Action to Combat the Organized Smuggling of Illegal Migrants Across National Boundaries*, UN Doc. E/1995/10, 24 July 1995.

[17] IMO Legal Committee, *Proposed Multilateral Convention to Combat Illegal Migration by Sea*, IMO Doc. LEG 76/11/1, 1 August 1997.

Italian Government was the heavy loss of life when crowded, unseaworthy, smuggling vessels sank en route to Italy.[18]

A separate initiative by the Austrian Government pursued a similar goal. On 16 September 1997, Austria submitted a letter to the UN Secretary-General presenting a draft 'International Convention against the Smuggling of Illegal Migrants'.[19] The letter stressed that the 'efforts of the international community to cope in an efficient manner with the phenomenon of smuggling of migrants for criminal purposes' were significantly impeded by a 'legal lacuna under international law'. It was proposed 'that the problem should be dealt with in a special convention' and the letter stressed that

> the action to be undertaken under the aegis of the Commission [CCPCJ] urgently needs to be complemented by the elaboration of an appropriate international instrument ensuring that perpetrators as well as instigators and accomplices of this transnational crime will be effectively brought to justice.[20]

Italy expressed its support of the Austrian proposal and the two governments agreed to combine their initiatives. This was achieved by including special measures relating to the smuggling of migrants by sea into the Austrian draft.[21]

The proposals by the Austrian and Italian governments also found strong support in various UN bodies and coincided with moves by the UN General Assembly to establish an open-ended, intergovernmental Ad Hoc Committee for the Elaboration of a Convention Against Transnational Organized Crime (AC.154).[22] The combined Austrian and Italian proposal formed the basis of the Ad Hoc Committee's deliberations and constitutes the main textual influence on the Smuggling of Migrants Protocol.[23] Over the following two years, the Ad Hoc Committee developed the Convention Against Transnational Organized Crime, along with three supplementing protocols, including the Protocol against the Smuggling of Migrants by Land, Sea, or Air. The Convention and Protocol were opened for signature on 15 December 2000; the Protocol entered into force on 28 January 2004.[24]

[18] See further Patricia Mallia, *Migrant Smuggling by Sea*, Leiden/Boston, Martinus Nijhoff Publishers, 2010, pp. 112–16; Kirchner and Schiano di Pepe, 'International attempts to conclude a Convention', cited in note 4 above, pp. 664–8; Andreas Schloenhardt, *Migrant Smuggling: Illegal Migration and Organized Crime in Australia and the Asia Pacific Region*, Leiden/Boston, Martinus Nijhoff Publishers, 2003, pp. 347–8.

[19] UN General Assembly, 'Letter dated 16 September from the Permanent Representative of Austria to the United Nations addressed to the Secretary-General', UN Doc. A/52/357, 17 September 1997.

[20] Ibid, p. 2 [2], [4]. See further David McClean, *Transnational Organized Crime*, Oxford, OUP, 2007, pp. 21–2; Kirchner and Schiano di Pepe, 'International attempts to conclude a Convention', cited in note 4 above, p. 670.

[21] See also Anne Gallagher, 'Migrant smuggling', in Boister and Currie, *Routledge Handbook on Transnational Organized Crime*, cited in note 2 above, p. 187, pp. 190–91; Gallagher and David, *The International Law of Migrant Smuggling*, cited in note 8 above, p. 33.

[22] UN General Assembly, 'Report of the Ad Hoc Committee on the elaboration of a Convention against Transnational Organized Crime on the work of its first to eleventh sessions; Addendum: Interpretative notes for the official record (*travaux préparatoires*) of the negotiations for the United Nations Convention against Transnational Organized Crime and the Protocols thereto', UN Doc. A/55/383/Add.1, 3 November 2000 [hereafter 'Interpretative Notes'], p. xxv; UN General Assembly, *Resolution on Transnational Organized Crime*, UN Doc. A/RES/53/111, 9 December 1998.

[23] UNODC, *Travaux Préparatoires of the Negotiations of the United Nations Convention against Transnational Organized Crime and the Protocols thereto*, UN Pub. No. E.06.V.5, 2006 [hereafter *Travaux Préparatoires*], p. 451.

[24] See Art. 22, Smuggling of Migrants Protocol.

9.2.2 Outline of the protocol

The Protocol's central feature is the requirement in Article 6(1) to comprehensively criminalize the smuggling of migrants and related conduct. Articles 5 and 6 set out several other requirements relating to these criminal offences. The prevention and suppression of the smuggling of migrants by sea is specifically addressed in Articles 7–9. Articles 10–14 of the Protocol requires the adoption of general prevention measures targeted at improving border control capabilities, information gathering, and law enforcement.

Despite the Protocol's strong criminal justice focus, the stated purpose of protecting the rights of smuggled migrants in Article 2 is reflected in several provisions. Article 4 extends the scope of the Protocol to 'the protection of the rights of persons who have been the object of [migrant smuggling]'. Under Article 9(1), States Parties are obliged to 'ensure the safety and humane treatment of the persons on board' suspected smuggling vessels. Article 16 sets out a number of 'protection and assistance measures'. Article 19 of the Protocol contains a 'saving clause' which obliges States Parties to give deference to the 'other rights, obligations and responsibilities of States and individuals under international law', and to apply the Protocol in a way 'that is not discriminatory to persons on the ground that they are the object of' migrant smuggling. In Article 18, the Protocol also sets out a framework for receiving states to use in the repatriation of smuggled migrants. It concludes with a range of final clauses that are mainly administrative in nature.[25]

9.3 Definitions and Terminology

9.3.1 'Smuggling of migrants'

Article 3(a) of the Protocol defines the term 'smuggling of migrants' to

> mean the procurement, in order to obtain, directly or indirectly, a financial or other material benefit, of the illegal entry of a person into a State Party of which the person is not a national or a permanent resident.[26]

The term 'illegal entry' used in this definition is further defined in Article 3(b) to mean 'crossing borders without complying with the necessary requirements for legal entry into the receiving State'. The illegal border crossing is an essential part of the concept of smuggling of migrants and highlights the transnational nature of this activity. Article 4 of the Protocol further emphasizes that the Protocol will apply 'to the prevention, investigation and prosecution of the offences established in accordance with Article 6 of the Protocol, where the offences are transnational in nature ...'. Article 4 has to be read in conjunction with Article 34(2) of the Convention Against Transnational

[25] Arts 20–25, Smuggling of Migrants Protocol. For an outline of the Protocol, see also Andreas Schloenhardt and Jessica E. Dale, 'Twelve years on: revisiting the UN Protocol against the Smuggling of Migrants by Land, Sea and Air', (2012) 67 *Zeitschrift für öffentliches Recht* 129.

[26] The terms 'smuggling of migrants' and 'migrant smuggling' are used interchangeably throughout this chapter. See also Gallagher and David, *The International Law of Migrant Smuggling*, cited in note 8 above, pp. 44–7.

Organized Crime, which provides that the offences under the Convention and its Protocols will be established in the domestic law of each state party independently of the transnational nature. In other words, while the offences set out in the Protocol apply exclusively to transnational cases, domestic law should not be limited in this way. The 'Interpretative notes for the official record *(travaux préparatoires)* of the negotiations for the United Nations Convention Against Transnational Organized Crime and the Protocols thereto' ('Interpretative Notes') confirm that the purpose of Article 34(2) is to indicate unequivocally that the transnational element is not to be considered elements of those offences for criminalization purposes.[27] The *Legislative Guides for the Implementation of the United Nations Convention Against Transnational Organized Crime and the Protocols thereto* (*Legislative Guides*) further remark that:

> while States Parties should have to establish some degree of transnationality and organized crime with respect to most aspects of the Protocol, their prosecutors should not have to prove either element in order to obtain a conviction for smuggling of migrants or any other offence established in accordance with the Convention or its Protocols. In the case of smuggling of migrants, domestic offences should apply even where transnationality and the involvement of organized criminal groups does not exist or cannot be proved.[28]

9.3.2 'Financial or other material benefit'

A particularly vexing issue during the negotiations of the text of the Smuggling of Migrants Protocol was the term 'financial or other material benefit' that serves as the purposive element in the definition of smuggling of migrants. This was referred to as 'profit' in earlier drafts.[29]

The inclusion of this element articulates clear boundaries about the types of migrant smuggling that are viewed as criminal and makes it clear to states parties what types of circumstance would not—and should not—be criminalized. The Interpretative Notes emphasize that:

> the reference to 'a financial or other material benefit' as an element of the definition in subparagraph (a) was included in order to emphasize that the intention was to include the activities of organized criminal groups acting for profit, but to exclude the activities of those who provided support to migrants for humanitarian reasons or on the basis of close family ties. It was not the intention of the Protocol to criminalize the activities of family members or support groups such as religious or non-governmental organizations.[30]

[27] Interpretative Notes, cited in note 22 above, p. [59].

[28] UNODC, *Legislative Guides for the Implementation of the United Nations Convention Against Transnational Organized Crime and the Protocols thereto* (2004) [hereinafter *Legislative Guides*], p. 334; McClean, *Transnational Organized Crime*, cited in note 20 above, p. 392.

[29] UNODC, *Smuggling of Migrants: A Global Review and Annotated Bibliography of Recent Publications*, New York, United Nations Press, 2011, p. 106. See also Andreas Schloenhardt and Connor Davies, 'Smugglers and Samaritans: defences to people smuggling in Australia', (2013) 36 *University of New South Wales Law Journal* (3), 954, pp. 981–2.

[30] Interpretative Notes, cited in note 22 above, pp. 16 [88], 17 [89].

The Interpretative Notes further indicate that the term 'benefit' 'should be understood broadly, to include, for example, crimes in which the predominant motivation may be sexual gratification, such as the receipt or trade of materials by members of child pornography rings, the trading of children by members of paedophile rings or cost-sharing among right members'.[31] Further clarification from United Nations Office on Drugs and Crime's (UNODC) *Model Law against the Smuggling of Migrants* states that this benefit should be conceived as broadly and inclusively as possible to include 'non-financial inducements, such as a free train or airplane ticket, or property, such as a car'.[32]

9.3.3 Smuggling of migrants vs trafficking in persons

The Smuggling of Migrants Protocol achieved a considerable feat in gaining international consensus on a definition of smuggling of migrants. Article 3(a) serves as a 'common denominator' for national legislation worldwide. This definition, combined with the criminalization requirements set out in Article 6, creates clear parameters for determining the illegality of this crime type.[33] Although the Protocol provides a straightforward and universally accepted definition, confusion of smuggling of migrants with trafficking in persons and other forms of irregular migration persists.

Article 3(a) of the UN Protocol to Prevent, Suppress and Punish Trafficking in Persons, especially Women and Children,[34] which, like the Smuggling of Migrants Protocol, supplements the Convention Against Transnational Organized Crime, defines 'trafficking in persons' to

> mean the recruitment, transportation, transfer, harbouring or receipt of persons, by means of the threat or use of force or other forms of coercion, of abduction, of fraud, of deception, of the abuse of power or of a position of vulnerability or of the giving or receiving of payments or benefits to achieve the consent of a person having control over another person, for the purpose of exploitation.[35]

The term 'exploitation' used in this definition is further defined in Article 3(a) to

> include, at a minimum, the exploitation of the prostitution of others or other forms of sexual exploitation, forced labour or services, slavery or practices similar to slavery, servitude or the removal of organs.

The main point of difference between the way in which smuggling of migrants and trafficking in persons are conceptualized in international law are the different purposes that each offence serve. The offence of trafficking in persons seeks to protect the rights, integrity, and freedoms of the trafficked persons and punish people who force,

[31] Interpretative Notes, cited in note 22 above, p. 2 [3].

[32] UNODC, *Model Law against Smuggling of Migrants*, Vienna, UNODC, 2010, p. 13.

[33] UNODC, *Smuggling of Migrants*, cited in note 29 above, p. 5.

[34] Opened for signature 12 December 2000, 2237 UNTS 319 (entered into force 25 December 2003) [hereafter 'Trafficking in Persons Protocol'].

[35] See further, Andreas Schloenhardt and Jarrod M. Jolly, *Trafficking in Persons in Australia: Myths and Realities*, Chatswood, New South Wales, LexisNexis, 2013, pp. 81–3 [3.10]–[3.11].

threaten, deceive, or otherwise abuse them for exploitative purposes. Because the definition of trafficking does not involve an element of transnationality, this offence does not purport to protect national interests such as border control and national security.

In contrast, the way in which the smuggling of migrants is conceptualized emphasizes the fact that the offence serves to protect national sovereignty and the ability of states to control borders and manage the flow of people across them. The protection of the smuggled migrants and their rights and liberties is, at best, only a secondary goal of the Protocol. It is for this reason that the Protocol does not refer to smuggled migrants as victims.

A further point of difference relates to the intention of the perpetrator. UNODC stresses that 'the primary source of profit and thus also the primary purpose of trafficking in persons is exploitation'.[36] In the case of migrant smuggling, however, there is typically 'no intention to exploit the smuggled migrant after having enabled him or her to irregularly enter or stay in a country'.[37] Rather, migrant smugglers seek payment in advance or upon arrival from the smuggled migrant. In many cases this distinction is not an easy one to draw. For example, a person may agree to be smuggled, unaware that on arrival he/she will be forced to work in poor or restrictive conditions for the smuggler in order to pay off a 'debt' for the service. This situation would be considered an instance of trafficking because of the exploitation of the smuggled person and the deceptions used.

The issue of consent provides a further point of difference.[38] The Trafficking in Persons Protocol is based on the understanding that

> [v]ictims of trafficking have either never consented—for instance if they have been abducted or sold—or, if they have given an initial consent, their initial consent has become void through the means the traffickers have used to gain control over the victim, such as deception or violence.[39]

While the Smuggling of Migrants Protocol does not directly address the issue of consent, in practice the smuggling of migrants involves an agreement whereby a person may pay or give some other benefit to a smuggler in order to facilitate that person's illegal migration. It has been recognized that smuggled migrants might retract their initial consent during a smuggling operation and be forced to continue on the journey.[40] Retracting consent, however, does not automatically denote an instance of trafficking. Other elements of the trafficking definition, such as the purpose of exploitation, would still need to be satisfied.

The Working Group on the Smuggling of Migrants, established by the Conference of States Parties to the UN Convention Against Transnational Organized Crime acknowledges that '[t]here is a need for more clarity regarding the differences between the crimes of trafficking in persons and smuggling of migrants'.[41] The conceptual

36 UNODC, 'A short introduction to smuggling of migrants', Issue Paper, Vienna, UNODC, 2010, p. 10.

37 Ibid, p. 10.

38 Art. 3(b), Trafficking in Persons Protocol.

39 UNODC, 'A short introduction', cited in note 36 above, p. 10.

40 Ibid; *Legislative Guides*, cited in note 28 above, pp. 340–41.

41 UN, Conference of States Parties to the United Nations Convention against Transnational Organized Crime, Working Group on the Smuggling of Migrants, 'Challenges and good practices in

distinction between smuggling of migrants and trafficking in persons is subtle, and sometimes faint, but it is imperative, since separate international legal instruments with vastly different requirements and consequences address the two phenomena. Several commentators have criticized the existing definitions for creating an artificial dichotomy between the experiences of victims of trafficking and those of smuggled migrants.[42] Instead, it has been suggested that a more nuanced approach would acknowledge a single continuum on which the two phenomena are more realistically placed.[43]

9.4 Criminal Offences, Article 6

Article 6 of the Smuggling of Migrants Protocol sets out a comprehensive list of obligations to criminalize the smuggling of migrants.[44] Article 6(1) identifies three offences that must be established in domestic law, including:

- a smuggling of migrants offence, Article 6(1)(a);
- a document fraud offence, Article 6(1)(b); and
- an offence of enabling illegal stay (or harbouring), Article 6(1)(c).

Implementation of the requisite criminalization elements may be achieved through establishing either three separate offences or one 'omnibus offence' that subsumes the three offences.[45]

9.4.1 General requirements for all offences

The obligation in the *châpeau* of Article 6(1) 'when committed intentionally and in order to obtain, directly or indirectly, a financial or other material benefit' applies to all three offences. Article 6(1) is thus limited to 'intentional' offences. Article 34(3) of the Convention Against Transnational Organized Crime, with which the Smuggling of Migrants Protocol must be read, however, provides that 'each State Party may adopt more strict or severe measures'. National legislators are thus free to create offences

the criminalization, investigation and prosecution of the smuggling of migrants', UN Doc. CTOC/COP/WG.7/2012/2, 21 March 2012, 2 [6].

[42] Tom Obokata, 'Smuggling of human beings from a human rights perspective: obligations of non-state and state actors under international human rights law', (2005) 17 *International Journal of Refugee Law* 394, p. 397; John Fitzpatrick, 'Trafficking as a human rights violation: the complex intersection of legal frameworks for conceptualizing and combating trafficking', (2003) 24 *Michigan Journal of International Law* 1143, p. 1150; John Salt, 'Trafficking and human smuggling: a European perspective', (2000) 1 *International Migration*, 3133.

[43] Fitzpatrick, ibid, p. 1143; Erick Gjerdingen, 'Suffocation inside a cold storage truck and other problems with trafficking as "exploitation" and smuggling as "choice" along the Thai–Burmese border', (2009) 26 *Arizona Journal of International and Comparative Law* 699; Hannah Simon, 'Human trafficking from an international protection perspective: probing the meaning of anti-trafficking measures for the protection of trafficking victims, with special regard to the United Kingdom', (2010) 28 *Pennsylvania State International Law Review* 633.

[44] See, generally, Gallagher, 'Migrant smuggling', cited in note 21 above, pp. 192–3.

[45] UNODC, *Model Law*, cited in note 32 above, pp. 28–9; *Legislative Guides*, cited in note 28 above, p. 350.

that require less onerous mental elements than intention, such as recklessness or, perhaps, negligence.

Article 6(1) further provides that the crime of migrant smuggling is present when the act is committed intentionally 'in order to obtain a financial or other material benefit either directly or indirectly' from the smuggled migrant. The *Legislative Guides* stress that Article 6(1) involves a two-pronged intention element: intention to procure illegal entry, and an intention to obtain a financial or other material benefit.[46] To prove the offence, intention may be inferred from objective factual circumstances; a principle that is common to almost every legal system.[47]

9.4.2 Penalties

The Smuggling of Migrants Protocol does not prescribe specific penalties or sanctions.[48] Article 6(4) merely notes that '[n]othing in this Protocol shall prevent a State Party from taking measures against a person whose conduct constitutes an offence under its domestic law'. The Interpretative Notes indicate that the reference to 'measures' is to be interpreted broadly to include both administrative and criminal sanctions. Article 11(1) of the Convention Against Transnational Organized Crime may be relevant in this context since it provides that states parties are required to adopt sanctions within domestic law that take into account and are proportionate to the gravity of the offences.[49]

9.4.3 Offence of smuggling of migrants, Article 6(1)(a)

Article 6(1)(a) of the Smuggling of Migrants Protocol requires the smuggling of migrants to be criminalized, as defined in Article 3(a). Table 9.1 sets out the physical and mental elements (*actus reus* and *mens rea*) of this offence.

The offences that must be criminalized under Article 6(1) include the procurement of illegal entry, 'the actual physical act of smuggling' in paragraph (a),[50] as well as the procurement of legal residence by some illegal means in paragraph (c), 'even if the actual entry that preceded it was legal'.[51] The *Legislative Guides* make an important point about the requirement for 'illegal entry' in this offence by noting that 'the drafters intended that cases in which valid documents were used improperly and the entry was technically legal would be dealt with by the offence of enabling illegal residence' under Article 6(1)(c).[52]

[46] *Legislative Guides*, cited in note 28 above, 342.
[47] McClean, *Transnational Organized Crime*, cited in note 20 above, p. 394.
[48] *Legislative Guides*, cited in note 28 above, 351.
[49] Cf. McClean, *Transnational Organized Crime*, cited in note 20 above, p. 396.
[50] Claire Brolan, 'An analysis of the human smuggling trade and the Protocol against the Smuggling of Migrants by Land, Air and Sea (2000) from a refugee protection perspective', (2002) 14 *International Journal of Refugee Law* (4), 561, p. 584.
[51] *Legislative Guides*, cited in note 28 above, p. 341.
[52] Ibid, p. 342.

Table 9.1 Elements of the offence of smuggling of migrants under Article 6(1)(a), Smuggling of Migrants Protocol

Physical elements	
conduct	procurement
result	illegal entry
object	smuggle a person into a state party of which the person is not a national or a permanent resident
Mental elements	
intention	'when committed intentionally'
purpose	in order to obtain, directly or indirectly, a financial or other material benefit

9.4.4 Producing, procuring, providing, or possessing fraudulent travel or identity documents, Article 6(1)(b)

Article 6(1)(b) of the Smuggling of Migrants Protocol requires that 'producing a fraudulent travel or identity document'[53] and 'procuring, providing or possessing such a document'[54] should be criminalized, when either offence is intentionally committed for the purpose of the smuggling of migrants. The reference to 'smuggling of migrants' means that the document fraud offences must relate to the procurement of illegal entry into a State Party of which that person is neither a national nor a permanent resident.[55] There is also the requirement that the offence be committed for 'financial or other material benefit'.[56] For offences in relation to travel or identity documents, there must be a further 'intention or purpose of enabling the smuggling of migrants'.

Article 3(c) defines 'fraudulent travel or identity document' to mean

> any travel or identity document:
> (i) that has been falsely made or altered in some material way by anyone other than a person or agency lawfully authorized to make or issue the travel or identity document on behalf of a State; or
> (ii) that has been improperly issued or obtained through misrepresentation, corruption or duress or in any other unlawful manner; or
> (iii) that is being used by a person other than the rightful holder.

The Protocol seeks to ensure that countries comprehensively proscribe and criminalize any form of fraud affecting travel and identity documents, ranging from creating new documents, via altering existing documents, to using another person's document, and obtaining documents fraudulently, corruptly, or coercively. To that end, the Interpretative Notes further remark that

> the words 'falsely made or altered' should be interpreted as including not only the creation of false documents, but also the alteration of legitimate documents and the

[53] Art. 6(1)(b)(i), Smuggling of Migrants Protocol.
[54] Art. 6(1)(b)(ii), Smuggling of Migrants Protocol.
[55] Art. 3(a), Smuggling of Migrants Protocol.
[56] Art. 3(a), Smuggling of Migrants Protocol.

filling in of stolen blank documents. They should also indicate that the intention was to include both documents that had been forged and genuine documents that had been validly issued but were being used by a person other than the lawful holder.[57]

The Article 6(1)(b)(i) offence of producing a fraudulent travel or identity document relates to making or creating the fraudulent document, or causing it to be created. For example, a smuggler might obtain an authentic or genuine passport, remove the photograph from it, and substitute a picture of the migrant; or the smuggler might be running a criminal enterprise such as a fraudulent passport factory.[58]

Article 6(1)(b)(ii) criminalizes a range of other of conduct associated with document fraud and smuggling of migrants, such as procuring, providing, or possessing fraudulent travel or identity documents. 'Procuring' means obtaining or causing a result by effort: for example, the smuggler might obtain the document for someone else. 'Providing' means giving: for example, the smuggler might give the document to the migrant or to another smuggler in the smuggling network.[59] The Interpretative Notes stress that Article 6(1)(b)(ii) 'would only apply when the possession in question was for the purpose of smuggling migrants as set forth in subparagraph (a). Thus, a migrant who possesses a fraudulent document to enable his or her own smuggling would not be included.'[60] This is an important aspect of the principle of 'non-criminalization of migrants' enshrined in Article 5 of the Protocol, which is discussed further below.

9.4.5 Enabling illegal stay, Article 6(1)(c)

The offence in Article 6(1)(c) is primarily aimed at criminalizing the harbouring and concealing of persons who reside in the host country illegally. The *Legislative Guides* state that the objective of Article 6(1)(c) is

> to include cases where the smuggling scheme itself consisted of procuring the entry of migrants using legal means, such as the issuance of visitors' permits or visas, but then resorting to illegal means to enable them to remain for reasons other than those used for entry or beyond the length of time covered by their permits or authorizations to enter.[61]

The conduct element of Article 6(1)(c) is cast widely to also capture illegal residence for 'any other illegal means' as defined under domestic law.[62] As with other offences in Article 6(1) there must be an 'intention to commit whatever act is alleged as having enabled illegal residence and the further intent or purpose of obtaining some financial or other material benefit'.[63]

[57] Interpretative Notes, cited in note 22 above, p. 16 [90]; see further, *Legislative Guides*, cited in note 28 above, pp. 343–5.

[58] UNODC, *In-depth Training Manual on Investigating and Prosecuting Smuggling of Migrants*, Vienna, UNODC, 2011, Modules 1 and 8.

[59] Ibid, Modules 1 and 8.

[60] Interpretative Notes, cited in note 22 above, p. 17 [93].

[61] *Legislative Guides*, cited in note 28 above, pp. 342–3.

[62] Interpretative Notes, cited in note 22 above, p. 17 [94]; *Legislative Guides*, cited in note 28 above, p. 343.

[63] Ibid, p. 343.

9.4.6 Extensions to criminal liability, Article 6(2)

9.4.6.1 Attempts, Article 6(2)(a)

Article 6(2)(a) of the Protocol requires states parties to extend criminal liability for the offences established under Article 6(1)(a)–(c) to instances in which an accused attempts any of them. Article 6(2)(a) is not a mandatory provision. This is explained by the fact that 'not all legal systems make for the criminalisation of cases in which an unsuccessful attempt has been made to commit the offence'.[64] The Interpretative Notes add that

> references to attempting to commit the offences established under domestic law in accordance with [Article 6(2)(a)] are understood in some countries to include both acts perpetrated in preparation for a criminal offence and those carried out in an unsuccessful attempt to commit the offence, where those acts are also culpable or punishable under domestic law.[65]

9.4.6.2 Participation, Article 6(2)(b)

Article 6(2)(b) of the Protocol requires States Parties to adopt the necessary legislative and other measures to criminalize participation in the offences under Article 6(1)(a), (b)(i), and (c).

In relation to Article 6(1)(b)(ii) States Parties have discretion whether to extend liability to participants and accomplices. This recognizes that national legal systems may have difficulties in 'in accommodating some aspects of the proposed offence, notably that of "possessing" a fraudulent document'.[66] In some jurisdictions it is not settled 'whether one could be made an accomplice to [an] offence such as possession'.[67]

9.4.6.3 Organising and directing, Article 6(2)(c)

Article 6(2)(c) of the Protocol creates a mandatory obligation for states parties to criminalize the organising or directing of other persons to commit an offence established in accordance with Article 6(1)(a)–(c). The inclusion of this provision serves to criminalize people who occupy more senior roles or are otherwise integral players acting in a 'chain of coordinators'.[68]

9.4.6.4 Corporate liability

Article 10 of the Convention Against Transnational Organized Crime encourages States Parties 'to establish the liability of legal persons'. Article 1(3) of the Protocol establishes the critical link to Article 10 of the Convention, stating that '[t]he offences

64 Ibid, pp. 347–8.

65 Interpretative Notes, cited in note 22 above, p. 17 [95].

66 McClean, *Transnational Organized Crime*, cited in note 20 above, p. 395.

67 *Legislative Guides*, cited in note 28 above, p. 348.

68 Matthias Neske, 'Human smuggling to and through Germany', (2006) 44 *International Migration* (4), 121, p. 156.

established in accordance with Article 6 of the Protocol shall be regarded as offences established in accordance with the Convention'. The *Toolkit to Combat Smuggling of Migrants* notes that the choice between 'criminal, civil, or administrative liability', offered by Article 10(2), seeks to 'acknowledge and accommodate the diversity of approaches adopted by different legal systems with respect to the liability' of a corporation.[69] Article 10(4) of the Convention further emphasizes that states parties 'shall, in particular, ensure that legal persons held liable in accordance with this article are subject to effective, proportionate, and dissuasive criminal or non-criminal sanctions, including monetary sanctions'.[70]

Article 10(3) of the Convention mandates that the liability of legal entities must not affect the liability of natural persons. The *Toolkit to Combat Smuggling of Migrants* adds that 'when an individual commits crimes on behalf of a legal entity, it must be possible to prosecute and sanction both the individual and the legal entity'.[71]

9.4.7 Aggravations, Article 6(3)

Article 6(3) of the Smuggling of Migrants Protocol creates an obligation to incorporate 'aggravating circumstances' into the offences established pursuant to Article 6(1)(a), (b)(i), and (c). These aggravating circumstances need to be connected to the smuggling of migrants offence,[72] the offence of producing a fraudulent travel or identity document to enable the smuggling of migrants,[73] and the offence of enabling illegal residence.[74] This can be achieved by creating parallel offences, such as an aggravated smuggling of migrants offence, or by inserting provisions that require courts to consider more severe penalties where there has been an aggravating circumstance.[75]

9.4.7.1 Endangering the lives or safety of smuggled migrants, Article 6(3)(a)

The aggravation in Article 6(3)(a) relates to circumstances 'that endanger, or are likely to endanger, the lives or safety of the migrants concerned'.[76] This provision seeks to protect the physical integrity and the lives of smuggled migrants by calling on states parties to provide higher penalties for instances that involve particularly dangerous methods of smuggling or circumstances that put the health of smuggled migrants at risk or their lives in jeopardy.

The *Legislative Guides* note that 'the most common occurrence to which this requirement is directed is the use of modes of smuggling, such as shipping containers, that are inherently dangerous to the lives of the migrants' but also call on states

[69] UNODC, *Toolkit to Combat Smuggling of Migrants*, New York, UNODC, 2010, Tool 5: Legislative framework, p. 28.
[70] See further ibid, Tool 5: Legislative framework, p. 29.
[71] Ibid, Tool 5: Legislative framework, p. 28.
[72] Art. 6(1)(a), Smuggling of Migrants Protocol.
[73] Art. 6(1)(b)(i), Smuggling of Migrants Protocol.
[74] Art. 6(1)(c), Smuggling of Migrants Protocol.
[75] *Legislative Guides*, cited in note 28 above, p. 346 [46].
[76] See also UNODC, *Model Law*, cited in note 32 above, p. 41 [Art. 6(a)].

parties to ensure 'that legislation should be broad enough to encompass other circumstances, such as cases where fraudulent documents create danger'.[77] The *Toolkit to Combat Smuggling of Migrants* lists several other examples for situations that may endanger the lives or safety of smuggled migrants, such as 'conditions in which migrants are smuggled if, for example, the boat, bus or car was particularly cold, wet, dry or crowded, or if the current at sea was particularly strong' or if the smuggled migrants sent out are left unattended in a boat that is not seaworthy.[78]

The *Model Law* against the Smuggling of Migrants also suggests the introduction of a separate aggravation status for instances in which 'the offence involves serious injury or death of the smuggled migrant or another person, including death as a result of suicide'.[79]

9.4.7.2 Inhuman or degrading treatment of smuggled migrants, Article 6(3)(b)

The aggravation in Article 6(3)(b) relates to the way in which smugglers treat migrants, which also includes the exploitation of smuggled migrants.[80] The term 'inhuman or degrading treatment' is not further defined in the Protocol but is generally understood to include acts that cause physical or mental suffering.[81] Examples of such treatment include the 'abuse of a child or a position of trust or authority', 'use of violence, threats or intimidation against migrants or their families [such as] hitting migrants to control them during travel', or the use of minors in the commission of offences.[82]

The *Model Law against the Smuggling of Migrants* also proposes the introduction of a separate status of aggravation for instances in which the offender takes advantage of or abuses a 'particular vulnerability or dependency of the smuggled migrant for financial or other material gain'.[83] The *Model Law* provides two examples to illustrate the application of this provision:

> Migrants, abandoned in the desert and with no other option, accept the services of a smuggler who happens to be passing by, but have to pay him or her three times the normally agreed price when departing from the nearest city.
>
> An agent, as part of the smuggling 'package of services', arranges for the migrants to rent a rundown house that he owns in a transit city for a very inflated amount of rent, and to buy packages of food that he provides at greatly inflated prices, while the migrants wait for their next connection.[84]

[77] *Legislative Guides*, cited in note 28 above, p. 346 [48]; see also, UNODC, *Toolkit to Combat Smuggling of Migrants*, cited in note 69 above, pp. 24–5.

[78] UNODC, *Toolkit to Combat Smuggling of Migrants*, cited in note 69 above, pp. 24–26; see also, UNODC, *Model Law*, cited in note 32 above, p. 41.

[79] UNODC, *Model Law*, cited in note 32 above, p. 45 [Art. 6(c)].

[80] The *Legislative Guides* (cited in note 28 above, at 346 [48]) note that this may also include 'cases where fraudulent documents ... lead to inhuman or degrading treatment'.

[81] See further, UNODC, *Model Law*, cited in note 32 above, pp. 42–4.

[82] UNODC, *Toolkit to Combat Smuggling of Migrants*, cited in note 69 above, pp. 24–5.

[83] UNODC, *Model Law*, cited in note 32 above, p. 46 [Art. 6(d)].

[84] Ibid, p. 46.

The Interpretative Notes acknowledge that the aggravation under Article 6(3)(b) overlaps with the concept and offences relating to trafficking in persons under Articles 3(a) and 5 of the Trafficking in Persons Protocol.[85] The *Legislative Guides* further note that, in cases of migrant smuggling in which

> there is no consent or if there is consent that has been vitiated or nullified as provided for in Article 3, subparagraphs (b) or (c) of the Trafficking in Persons Protocol, the presence of exploitation in what would otherwise be a smuggling case will generally make the trafficking offence applicable if the State Party concerned has ratified and implemented that Protocol.[86]

The *Model Law* also proposes the introduction of an aggravating circumstance for cases in which 'the offender used or threatened to use any form of violence against the smuggled migrant or their family'.[87] It further recognizes that a situation of smuggling of migrants may turn into one of trafficking in persons if the smugglers control or confiscate the travel or identity documents of the smuggled migrants, and suggests a particular circumstance of aggravation if 'the offender confiscates, destroys or attempts to destroy the travel or identity documents of the smuggled migrant'.[88]

9.4.7.3 Involvement of an organised criminal group

Article 5 of the Convention Against Transnational Organized Crime requires States Parties to criminalize participation in an organised criminal group. Article 2(a) of the Convention defines the term 'organized criminal group' to mean

> [a] structured group of three or more persons, existing for a period of time and acting in concert with the aim of committing one or more serious crimes or offences established in accordance with this Convention, in order to obtain, directly or indirectly, a financial or other material benefit.

Article 5 of the Convention creates criminal liability for persons who intentionally participate in or contribute to the criminal activities of organized criminal groups. The offence seeks to prevent and pre-empt organised criminal activity by holding those criminally liable who associate for the purpose of criminal offending, even if they have not yet committed any offence.[89]

Articles 1 and 4 of the Smuggling of Migrants Protocol establish the nexus between the criminalization of migrant smuggling and Articles 2(a) and 5 of the Convention. Article 4 of the Protocol states that 'this Protocol shall apply, except as otherwise stated herein, to the prevention, investigation, and prosecution of the offences established

[85] Interpretative Notes, cited in note 22 above, p. 17 [96].

[86] *Legislative Guides*, cited in note 28 above, p. 347 [49]; see also UNODC, *Toolkit to Combat Smuggling of Migrants*, cited in note 69 above, p. 25; see also, UNODC, *Model Law*, cited in note 32 above, pp. 43–4.

[87] UNODC, *Model Law*, cited in note 32 above, p. 50 [Art. 6(o)].

[88] Ibid, p. 50 [Art. 6(p)].

[89] See further, UN Conference of the Parties to the United Nations Convention against Transnational Organized Crime, Working Group of Government Experts on Technical Assistance, 'Criminalization of participation in an organized criminal group (Art. 5 of the Convention Against Transnational Organized Crime)', UN Doc. CTOC/COP/WG.2, 23 May 2014; Schloenhardt, 'Transnational organised crime', cited in note 2 above, pp. 414–33.

in accordance with this Protocol, where the offence … involves an organized criminal group …' Article 1 of the Protocol, as mentioned earlier, also stresses that the Protocol and the Convention must be interpreted together, that the Convention provisions apply *mutatis mutandis* to the Protocol, and that the offences established under Article 6 of the Protocol are to be regarded as offences established in accordance with the Convention. The Interpretative Notes further remark that 'the offences set forth in Article 6 should be seen as being part of the activities of organized criminal groups. In this Article, the Protocol follows the precedent of the Convention (Article 34(2)).'[90]

This nexus between the smuggling of migrants and criminal organisations is not, however, a mandatory requirement in the criminalization of migrant smuggling and Article 34(2) of the Convention expressly requires that liability for domestic offences, including the smuggling of migrants, must not be limited to instances involving organised criminal groups.[91]

The *Model Law against the Smuggling of Migrants* recommends that States Parties to the Protocol treat circumstances in which 'the offence was committed as part of the activity of an organized criminal group' as an aggravation.[92] This aggravation recognizes that the smuggling of migrants involving criminal organisations poses greater challenges to government authorities and is likely to involve greater numbers of smuggled migrants and potentially greater dangers and greater levels of exploitation.[93]

9.4.7.4 Other aggravations

Article 34(3) of the Convention Against Transnational Organized Crime enables States Parties to enact that circumstances beyond those set out in the Protocol might be regarded as aggravations. The Working Group on the Smuggling of Migrants also noted that '[g]ood practice is for States to consider aggravating circumstances that go beyond those set out in the Smuggling of Migrants Protocol'.[94]

The *Model Law against the Smuggling of Migrants* and the *Toolkit to Combat Smuggling of Migrants* set out a range of aggravating circumstances that legislators may wish to consider. Some of these aggravating circumstances relate to instances in which migrants are involved in the smuggling of migrants—as smuggled migrants, or where they are used to support the activities of migrant smugglers. This may also include the 'abuse of a child or abuse of a position of trust or authority', the smuggling

[90] Interpretative Notes, cited in note 22 above, p. 17 [92].

[91] See further, UNODC, *Toolkit to Combat Smuggling of Migrants*, cited in note 69 above, pp. 21–2.

[92] UNODC, *Model Law*, cited in note 32 above, p. 46 [Art. 6(f)].

[93] Cf. Susanne Reindl-Krauskopf and Christian Grafl, *Kriminalität nicht integrierter Ausländer—eine vielfältige Herausforderung für das Strafrecht*, Verhandlungen des Siebzehnten Österreichischen Juristentages Wien 2009, Manzsche Verlags- und Universitätsbuchhandlung, 2009, pp. 56–7.

[94] UN Conference of States Parties to the United Nations Convention against Transnational Organized Crime, Working Group on the Smuggling of Migrants, 'Challenges and good practices in the criminalization, investigation and prosecution of the smuggling of migrants', UN Doc. CTOC/COP/WG.7/2012/2, 21 March 2012, 3 [10]; see also UN Conference of States Parties to the United Nations Convention against Transnational Organized Crime, Working Group on the Smuggling of Migrants, 'Report on the meeting of the Working Group on the Smuggling of Migrants held in Vienna from 30 May to 1 June 2012', UN Doc. CTOC/COP/WG.7/2012/6, 27 June 2012, 3 [15].

of (unaccompanied) minors, and the use of minors in the commission of offences.[95] Aggravations for the smuggling of migrants with other special vulnerabilities, such as pregnant migrants or persons with intellectual or physical disabilities, are also conceivable.[96]

Other suggestions for aggravations relate to the scale of the smuggling operations, such as the smuggling of large numbers of migrants and the size of the profits received.[97] The *Model Law* also proposes aggravated status where offences are repeated and for the use of 'drugs, medications or weapons in the commission of the offence'.[98]

It has also been suggested that an aggravated offence should be committed by public officials who become involved in the smuggling of migrants or abuse their position in the commission of the offence, for example 'by issuing false documents or allowing people through checkpoints without conducting a proper check'.[99]

The migrant-smuggling offences may also be aggravated if they are combined with another offence, for example where smuggled migrants are compelled to carry out other offences when they are smuggled, or where the migrant smugglers commit offences against the migrants, such as assaults, sexual abuse, etc.[100]

9.5 Exemptions and Limitations of Criminal Liability

The definitions and criminalization requirements under the Smuggling of Migrants Protocol provide several parameters that serve to limit the application of criminal offences and exempt certain types of person from criminal liability.[101] These limitations stem from the overall objectives of the Protocol and, in particular, its purpose to protect the rights of smuggled migrants.[102]

9.5.1 Humanitarian smuggling

The Smuggling of Migrants Protocol recognizes that irregular migration, of which migrant smuggling is one form, is frequently connected to situations in which persons flee from persecution, war, torture, discrimination, and severe human rights abuses, or are forced to leave their home countries and seek asylum abroad for other reasons. For many smuggled migrants, the services offered by the smugglers represent the only avenue to escape threats, harm, and death.[103]

[95] UNODC, *Toolkit to Combat Smuggling of Migrants*, cited in note 69 above, pp. 24 and 26; UNODC, *Model Law*, cited in note 32 above, p. 49 [Art. 6(k) and (l)].

[96] UNODC, *Model Law*, cited in note 32 above, p. 49 [Art. 6(m) and (n)].

[97] Ibid, p. 47 [Art. 6(h)]; UNODC, *Toolkit to Combat Smuggling of Migrants*, cited in note 69 above, p. 25.

[98] UNODC, *Model Law*, cited in note 32 above, p. 46 [Art. 6(e) and (g)].

[99] Ibid, p. 47 [Art. 6(i) and (j)].

[100] UNODC, *Toolkit to Combat Smuggling of Migrants*, cited in note 69 above, pp. 24–6.

[101] UN Conference of States Parties to the UNTOC, 'Challenges and good practices', cited in note 94 above, p. 3 [11].

[102] Art. 2, Smuggling of Migrants Protocol.

[103] Cf. UNODC, *Toolkit to Combat Smuggling of Migrants*, cited in note 69 above, Tool 1: Understanding the smuggling of migrants, p. 29. See also Schloenhardt and Davies, 'Smugglers and Samaritans', cited in note 29 above, pp. 976–80.

The Protocol does not intend to criminalize persons who assist others for humanitarian or altruistic reasons in their quest to find safety and a better life abroad. Humanitarian smuggling activities might involve, for instance, providing food, medication, clothing, and temporary accommodation so long as these activities serve to save or protect the life of the smuggled migrant. Activities such as rescuing smuggled migrants from a life-threatening situation also fall into that category. Other measures designed to save or restore the smuggled migrants' lives, health, or physical integrity can also be viewed as humanitarian activities. Whether or not the danger to the smuggled migrants stems from another person (such as the smuggler) or from natural events (such as storms, freezing weather, or extreme heat, etc.) does not matter in these circumstances. In other words, these humanitarian acts resemble situations of emergency or necessity in which a failure to act might result in much greater harm and in which the smuggling of migrants and other acts that facilitate the illegal entry or enable the illegal stay of another person might be justifiable.[104]

It is for this reason that the Protocol limits the definition of smuggling migrants and the criminalization requirement under Article 6(1) to instances in which the offender seeks to obtain, directly or indirectly, a financial or other material benefit. Any act that facilitates the illegal entry or stay of another that is not done for that purpose does not fall within the scope of the Protocol. Similarly, the production, procurement, provision, and possession of fraudulent travel or identity documents for the purpose of migrant smuggling only fall within the scope of the Protocol if these acts are done in order to obtain a financial or other material benefit. The Protocol leaves it open for states parties to criminalize such acts under their domestic laws even where they are not done for profit,[105] but the Protocol does not provide a foundation or justification for such an extension and it would not fall within the definition of smuggling of migrants.

9.5.2 Smuggling of family members

The financial or other material benefit requirement in Articles 3(a) and 6(1) of the Protocol also serves to exempt from criminal liability individuals who are involved in the smuggling of their family members. The Protocol recognizes that it is not uncommon for earlier migrants to support the migration of their relatives, and that irregular migration, such as migrant smuggling, may serve as a way to reunite families or rescue family members from situations of persecution, poverty, or other hardship.

Persons facilitating the illegal entry or enabling the illegal stay of a family member (or indeed any other person), or who produce, provide, or procure fraudulent travel or identity documents to enable their irregular migration, are therefore not criminalized by the Protocol so long as they do not seek to benefit materially from these activities.

[104] Reindl-Krauskopf and Grafl, *Kriminalität nicht integrierter Ausländer* cited in note 93 above, p. 66; see also Schloenhardt and Davies, 'Smugglers and Samaritans', cited in note 29 above, pp. 969–76.

[105] UN Conference of States Parties to the UNTOC, 'Challenges and good practices', cited in note 94 above, p. 4 [12].

The idea here is that no person should have to choose between committing a criminal offence and abandoning his or her closest relative.[106]

9.5.3 Non-criminalization of smuggled migrants, Article 5

Under Article 5 of the Protocol, 'migrants shall not become liable to criminal prosecution under this Protocol for the fact of having been the object of conduct set forth in Article 6 of this Protocol'. The basic effect of this provision is to shield smuggled migrants from criminal prosecution arising from the fact of having been smuggled. The Article seeks to uphold the cardinal principle that irregular migration is not a criminal offence and that smuggled migrants should not be punished for using the services migrant smugglers offer, unlawful as these services may be. On this point, the *Legislative Guides* stress that it

> is the intention of the drafters that the sanctions established in accordance with the Protocol should apply to the smuggling of migrants by organized criminal groups and not to mere migration or migrants, even in cases where it involves entry or residence that is illegal under the laws of the State concerned ...[107]

Consequently, smuggled migrants should not be held criminally liable for being the object of migrant smuggling (Article 6(1)(a)), for offences involving document fraud (Article 6(1)(b)), or for remaining in the host country clandestinely or otherwise illegally (Article 6(1)(c)). The Interpretative Notes add that the offence of procuring, providing, or possessing a fraudulent travel or identity document under Article 6(1)(b)(ii) 'would only apply when the possession in question was for the purpose of smuggling migrants as set forth in subparagraph (a). Thus, a migrant who possessed a fraudulent document to enable his or her own smuggling would not be included.'[108]

Through Article 5, the Protocol recognizes that smuggled migrants are often unable to comply with domestic legal and regulatory requirements relating to immigration and emigration. The *Toolkit to Combat Smuggling of Migrants* emphasizes 'that refugees often have to rely on smugglers to flee persecution, serious human rights violations or conflict. They should not be criminalized for making use of smugglers or for their illegal entry.'[109] In this context, reference is also made to Article 31 of the Convention relating to the Status of Refugees,[110] which imposes a clear obligation on states parties to refrain from penalizing the unauthorized entry or presence of refugees, or applying unnecessary restrictions to their movements. In a similar fashion, Article 5 of the Smuggling of Migrants Protocol operates to protect smuggled migrants from criminalization merely for seeking or gaining illegal entry assisted by migrant smugglers.[111]

[106] Reindl-Krauskopf and Grafl, *Kriminalität nicht integrierter Ausländer* cited in note 93 above, p. 70.
[107] Legislative Guides, cited in note 28 above, p. 340.
[108] Interpretative Notes, cited in note 22 above, p. 17 [93].
[109] UNODC, *Toolkit to Combat Smuggling of Migrants*, cited in note 69 above, p. 29.
[110] Opened for signature 28 July 1951, 189 UNTS 150 (entry into force 22 April 1954) [hereinafter 'Refugee Convention'].
[111] See further, Andreas Schloenhardt and Hadley Hickson, 'Non-criminalization of smuggled migrants: rights, obligations, and Australian practice under Art. 5 of the Protocol against the Smuggling of

Article 5 does not grant blanket immunity to smuggled migrants, however, as they might face criminal prosecution for offences not related to migrant smuggling, and the Article also does not shield them from removal or deportation to another country.[112] The *Legislative Guides* note that

> [t]he Protocol itself takes a neutral position on whether those who migrate illegally should be the subject of any offences: Article 5 ensures that nothing in the Protocol itself can be interpreted as requiring the criminalization of mere migrants or of conduct likely to be engaged in by mere migrants as opposed to members of or those linked to organized criminal groups. At the same time, Article 6, paragraph 4, ensures that nothing in the Protocol limits the existing rights of each State Party to take measures against persons whose conduct constitutes an offence under its domestic law.[113]

Article 5 does not limit a State's ability to control and regulate migration, or to process smuggled migrants according to domestic laws and procedures.[114] Article 16(5) of the Protocol also acknowledges that some States Parties detain persons who are suspected of illegal entry in order to investigate their background, process their claims, or facilitate their removal.

9.6 Smuggling of Migrants by Sea

In Articles 7–9, the Smuggling of Migrants Protocol pays particular attention to the smuggling of migrants by sea.[115] Under Article 7, states parties must mount extensive cooperation efforts to prevent and suppress the smuggling of migrants by sea. Accordingly, in some circumstances, Articles 8 and 9 authorize 'appropriate' action against vessels that are, or are reasonably suspected to be, engaged in the smuggling of migrants by sea.[116] This is especially the case when authorities are concerned 'about the basic safety and security of migrants and others on board such vessels, given the dilapidated conditions of vessels often used by smugglers and the fact that boarding may take place at sea and far from safe harbour conditions'.[117] The term 'engaged' used in Article 8(1), (2), and (7) is to be interpreted broadly to prevent loopholes: in the practical experience of smuggling by sea, vessels can be 'engaged' directly and indirectly in the process.[118] The term 'search' rather than 'inspect' was specifically

Migrants by Land, Sea, and Air', (2013) 25 *International Journal of Refugee Law* (1), 39, pp. 45–7; Mary A. Young, 'The smuggling and trafficking of refugees and asylum seekers: is the international community neglecting the duty to protect the persecuted in the pursuit of transnational organized crime?', (2003) 27 *Suffolk Transnational Law Review* (1), 101, pp. 117–18.

112 See also Art. 18, Smuggling of Migrants Protocol.

113 *Legislative Guides*, cited in note 28 above, p. 347.

114 UN Conference of States Parties to the UNTOC, 'Challenges and good practices', cited in note 94 above, p. 4 [12].

115 See generally, Mallia, *Smuggling by Sea*, cited in note 18 above, pp. 120–26; and Gallagher and David, *The International Law of Migrant Smuggling*, cited in note 6 above, pp. 55–9, pp. 78–86.

116 Arts 7, 8, and 9, Smuggling of Migrants Protocol.

117 According to the *Legislative Guides*, cited in note 28 above, p. 365.

118 Interpretative Notes, cited in note 22 above, para. 100.

included to warrant higher levels of intrusion on vessels suspected of engaging in smuggling activities.[119]

The cooperation regime envisaged by Articles 7–9 is rather extensive. Under Article 8(6) and (4) States must designate an authority or authorities that operate a 24-hour service tasked with ensuring that their requisite obligations are fulfilled expeditiously. Cooperation to combat smuggling of migrants by sea must accord with both customary and conventional international law, including the UN Convention on the Law of the Sea.[120] The measures set forth in Articles 8 and 9 may be exercised in the territorial sea of another State only with the permission or authorization of the State responsible for the coastal sea concerned.[121]

The broad powers under these provisions are mitigated by the extensive dialogue and coordination required between the 'requesting State' and the 'flag State'.[122] Similarly, the safeguards in Article 9 of the Protocol encapsulate the principles of maritime law governing 'the rights and interests of States and shipowners' and 'the detention, boarding and searching of vessels' in sufficient terms.[123] The obligation under Article 9(1)(a) is expressed in absolute terms and extends to ensuring the safety and humane treatment of the persons on board after a vessel has been boarded and smuggled migrants found.[124]

9.7 Prevention, Cooperation, and Other Measures

By signing the Smuggling of Migrants Protocol, states agree to enable and engage in the specific forms of cooperation outlined in Articles 10–18. These include:

- information and intelligence exchange, Article 10;
- strengthening border controls, Article 11(1)–(6);
- verification and control of travel and identity documents, Articles 12–13;
- providing training and technical assistance, particularly to countries of origin or transit, Article 14;[125]
- prevention through raising public awareness and recognition of root causes, Article 15(1)–(3);
- developing bilateral or regional agreements or arrangements to prevent and combat the smuggling of migrants; and
- facilitating the return of smuggled migrants, Article 18.

Most of these provisions serve to restrict the smuggling of migrants so far that smuggling processes can be stopped and smuggled migrants saved before they begin the often dangerous journeys.

[119] See Smuggling of Migrants Protocol, Art 8(7); *Travaux Préparatoires*, cited in note 23 above, p. 503.
[120] *Travaux Préparatoires*, cited in note 23 above, p. 494.
[121] If no flag state is involved then Art. 8(7), Smuggling of Migrants Protocol will apply; McClean, *Transnational Organized Crime*, cited in note 20 above, pp. 405–10.
[122] See Art. 8(2), (3), and (5), Smuggling of Migrants Protocol.
[123] *Legislative Guides*, cited in note 28 above, p. 364.
[124] McClean, *Transnational Organized Crime*, cited in note 20 above, pp. 413–14.
[125] See also Convention Against Transnational Organised Crime, Arts 29 and 30.

Article 10 advocates information exchange between countries about the patterns and methods of migrant smuggling, the individuals and organisations involved, and the authenticity and form of official travel and identity documents. Article 10 reflects the principles contained in Articles 27 and 28 of the Convention against Transnational Organised Crime—which relate to law enforcement cooperation and information exchange—but is tailored to the particular context of exchanging information to target smuggling of migrants.[126]

Articles 11–13 require States Parties to strengthen border controls and enhance the quality, security, and control of travel and identity documents. Article 11(2)–(4) also requires States Parties to hold commercial carriers, such as airlines, bus companies, and shipping lines, responsible if their passengers do not carry the travel documents necessary for entry to the receiving state.

Articles 14 and 15 promote further cooperation and training on the key elements of the Protocol and the establishment of programmes to prevent the smuggling of migrants. Additionally, Article 15(1) and (2) recommends that States Parties conduct awareness-raising programmes and public information campaigns about migrant smuggling and the risks that it poses to migrants. Article 15(3) promotes development programmes and cooperation at the national, regional, and international levels to address the 'root socio-economic causes of smuggling of migrants'. As such, the 'sensitive issues' underlining the migrant-smuggling phenomenon receive brief yet deliberate attention.[127]

While most of these provisions employ mandatory language, the provisions include multiple clauses to accommodate the means and needs of individual States Parties, such that the obligations must be fulfilled 'consistent with their [states parties] domestic legal and administrative systems ... to the extent possible ... in accordance with its domestic law', or 'as may be necessary', or 'within available means'.[128]

9.8 Protection of Smuggled Migrants

The initial drafts of the Smuggling of Migrants Protocol did not contain any reference to protection or assistance for smuggled migrants.[129] In an address to the Ad Hoc Committee developing the Convention and Protocol, the UN High Commissioner for Human Rights (UNHCR) urged the Committee to recognize the vulnerability of irregular migrants and incorporate in the Protocol provisions protecting their human rights.[130] A later note by an 'Inter-Agency Group', comprising the Office of the High Commissioner for Human Rights (OHCHR), the UNHCR, the International Organization for Migration (IOM), and the United Nations Children's Fund

[126] McClean, *Transnational Organized Crime*, cited in note 20 above, p. 416.

[127] Ibid, p. 425; see also, *Travaux Préparatoires*, cited in note 23 above, p. 536.

[128] Arts 10(1), 11, 11(4), 12, and 13, Smuggling of Migrants Protocol.

[129] See UN Ad Hoc Committee on the Elaboration of a Convention against Transnational Organised Crime, 'Draft elements for an international legal instrument against illegal trafficking and transport of migrants', UN Doc. A/AC.254/4/Add.1, 15 December 1998.

[130] UN General Assembly, 'Informal note by the United Nations High Commissioner for Human Rights', 4th sess., UN Doc. A/AC.254/16, 1 June 1999, [1–2].

(UNICEF), called for specific consideration to be given to smuggled migrants who are women and children, as well as recognition of the right of return with respect to the principle of non-refoulement to ensure that migrants who are covered by protection obligations under international refugee law are afforded protection by the state so obliged.[131]

9.8.1 Protection of the rights of smuggled migrants

Article 16 of the Smuggling of Migrants Protocol contains several provisions relating to the protection of smuggled migrants that apply equally to the receiving State and the State where the smuggled migrants have their origin or habitual residence. These 'provisions are intended to set an appropriate standard of conduct for officials who deal with smuggled migrants and illegal residents and to deter conduct on the part of offenders that involves danger or degradation to the migrants'.[132] Article 16(1) contains a general statement to protect the basic human rights of smuggled migrants accorded in relevant international treaties,[133] especially the International Covenant on Civil and Political Rights (ICCPR) and the International Covenant on Economic, Social, and Cultural Rights (ICESCR).[134] Article 16(1) does not create any new obligations for states parties.[135]

Article 16(5) also implies an obligation on States Parties to facilitate communication between smuggled migrants and the relevant consulate, especially in situations in which the receiving country detains smuggled migrants because of their illegal entry or to facilitate their removal. Reflecting provisions under the Vienna Convention on Consular Relations,[136] this encompasses assistance measures such as informing migrants of their right to contact the relevant consulate, notification of a migrant's request to do so, and facilitation of this communication, in person or otherwise.[137]

9.8.2 Assistance to smuggled migrants

Article 16(2) of the Protocol requires states parties to protect smuggled migrants from physical violence, but contains no further detail about the way in which such protection may be provided. Article 16(3) calls on States Parties to 'afford appropriate assistance to migrants whose lives or safety are endangered by reason of being

[131] UN General Assembly, 'Note by the Office of the United Nations High Commissioner for Human Rights, the United Nations Children's Fund and the International Organization for Migration on the draft protocols concerning migrant smuggling and trafficking in persons', 8th sess., UN Doc. A/AC.254/27, 8 February 2000.

[132] *Legislative Guides*, cited in note 28 above, p. 364.

[133] See generally, Gallagher and David, *The International Law of Migrant Smuggling*, cited in note 8 above, pp. 128–151.

[134] ICCPR: opened for signature 16 December 1966, 999 UNTS 171 (entered into force 23 March 1976), Art. 6(1); see also Art. 12(1). ICESCR: opened for signature 16 December 1966, 993 UNTS 3 (entered into force 3 January 1976); cf. Interpretative Notes, cited in note 22 above, p. [108].

[135] Interpretative Notes, cited in note 22 above, p. [109]; *Legislative Guides*, cited in note 28 above, p. 365.

[136] Opened for signature 24 April 1963, 596 UNTS 261 (entered into force 19 March 1967), Art. 36.

[137] Vienna Convention, ibid; UNODC, *Model Law*, cited in note 32 above, p. 73.

[smuggled migrants]'. Article 16(4) recognizes the particular vulnerability of women and children.

Whilst the general content of Article 16 is mandatory, the way and extent to which smuggled migrants are protected remain within the ambit of states parties' discretion.[138] The *Model Law against the Smuggling of Migrants* proposes that smuggled migrants should have the right to receive urgent medical care where their life is at risk or they face irreparable harm to their health.[139] This is drawn from the inherent right to life under the ICCPR.[140] A combined reading of Article 16(1) of the Protocol and provisions under the Convention on the Rights of the Child suggests that assistance measures could also extend to the provision of education to smuggled migrants who are children.[141] International guidelines further suggest that it may be desirable to explore, in conjunction with international organisations and donor countries, the feasibility of offering smuggled migrants temporary protection and basic access to accommodation, food, medical care, and legal assistance.[142] In dealing with smuggled migrants, the special needs of children and persons with disabilities should also be recognized.[143]

9.8.3 Refugee and human rights law

Article 19(1) of the Smuggling of Migrants Protocol draws particular attention to the specific requirements under the Refugee Convention and Protocol that place obligations on states parties to provide refuge for persons who fear persecution in another country. The key aspect of the protection granted under the Refugee Convention is that a refugee must neither be expelled nor returned ('refouled')[144] to 'the frontiers of territories where his [or her] life or freedom would be threatened'.[145] A country is in breach of this non-refoulement obligation if its authorities fail to properly identify and protect persons who are entitled to the benefits of refugee status.[146] Moreover, States Parties are prohibited from penalizing refugees for their illegal entry and presence,[147] and must give them free access to courts of law,[148] as well as assistance in their naturalization.[149] The Convention also requires States Parties to provide refugees with welfare, including housing, public education,[150] and opportunity for employment.[151]

Article 19 of the Smuggling of Migrants Protocol seeks to ensure that the obligations under the Refugee Convention and other relevant international treaties are not

138 See, for example, UNODC, *Model Law*, cited in note 32 above, p. 66. 139 Ibid, pp. 65–6.

140 Cited in note 134 above, Art. 6(1); see also Art. 12(1).

141 Convention: opened for signature 20 November 1989, 1577 UNTS 3 (entered into force 2 September 1990). UNODC, *Model Law*, cited in note 32 above, p. 71.

142 See, for example, UNODC, *Toolkit to Combat Smuggling of Migrants*, cited in note 69 above, Tool 8 Protection and assistance measures; UNODC, *Model Law*, cited in note 32 above.

143 See further, UNODC, *Basic Training Manual on Investigating and Prosecuting the Smuggling of Migrants*, Vienna, UNODC, 2010, Modules 8 and 9.

144 Refugee Convention, Art. 32, 'save on grounds of national security'.

145 Refugee Convention, Art. 33.

146 See further, UNODC, *Basic Training Manual*, cited in note 143 above, Modules 9 and 6.

147 Refugee Convention, Art. 31. 148 Refugee Convention, Art. 16.

149 Refugee Convention, Art. 34. 150 Refugee Convention, Arts 20–24.

151 Refugee Convention, Arts 17–19.

infringed by any provision contained in the Protocol (in countries that are party to the Protocol as well as the international refugee law instruments). In addition, Article 19(2) seeks to ensure that domestic laws pertaining to migrant smuggling are not designed or applied in a manner that discriminates against smuggled migrants or illegal residents by reason of their status as such.[152]

9.9 Observations and Conclusions

The Smuggling of Migrants Protocol is an important milestone in global efforts to prevent and suppress this crime and to protect the rights of smuggled migrants. It has created an international framework for criminalization and cooperation where, up until recently, none existed.

9.9.1 Concepts and criminalization

Through their signature, States Parties express their consent to the definition of smuggling of migrants under Article 3(a) of the Protocol and to the criminalization requirements under Article 6(1). This provides assurance that, at a minimum, States Parties recognize the distinct features and unique criminality of this phenomenon, intend to conceptualize their domestic offences accordingly, and fundamentally understand smuggling of migrants as a distinct form of transnational organised crime.

Although the Smuggling of Migrants Protocol provides a solid foundation on which states parties can build their domestic efforts to criminalize this phenomenon, the *Legislative Guides* concede that the Protocol requirements are only a 'minimum standard'.[153] While domestic offences against the smuggling of migrants must broadly align with the obligations set forth in the Protocol, States Parties have great discretion about how they implement the substance of the obligation; that is, the prescribed range of conduct and what levels of sanctions will be accorded to the offences. This flexibility has been heralded as affording states the ability to adopt further supplementary offences thereby enhancing 'the effectiveness of prevention, investigation and prosecution in cases or smuggling of migrants'.[154] Concerns have been raised, however, over the extent to which states may use their legislative discretion to raise the threshold prescribed by the Protocol.[155] In this context, it should also be noted that the criminalization of migrant smugglers and the detention of smuggled migrants may be a quick, popular, and inexpensive way to be seen as acting against migrant smuggling, but that it has limited impact on the levels of this phenomenon and does nothing to address the root causes of irregular migration.[156]

152 *Legislative Guides*, cited in note 28 above, p. 367.

153 *Legislative Guides*, cited in note 28 above, p. 331.

154 Ibid, p. 323.

155 McClean, *Transnational Organized Crime*, cited in note 20 above, p. 26.

156 See also, Gallagher, 'Migrant smuggling', cited in note 21 above, p. 188.

9.9.2 Cooperation

Considering that one of the primary pillars upon which the Protocol rests is the recognition of the integral role of international cooperation, it may be surprising and concerning that there is no control organ with enforcement or quasi-judicial powers tasked with overseeing the Protocol. UNODC, the 'guardian' of the Convention Against Transnational Organized Crime and its Protocols, promotes the universal adoption of the Smuggling of Migrants Protocol and assists States Parties with the legislative and technical issues involved in implementing the Protocol's provisions. But UNODC has no power to compel states parties to comply with their international obligations or to sanction them in the event of non-compliance. Should disputes over the interpretation or application of a provision arise, the Protocol's jurisdictional clause, Article 20(2), provides for adjudication of intra-country disputes. It outlines measures for recourse to settlement via arbitration and, if this fails, jurisdiction is conferred on the International Court of Justice.[157] In practice, the Court's jurisdiction is rarely, if ever, brought to life. The lack of a control organ speaks to the difficulty of ensuring that the Protocol's provisions are implemented in the spirit within which the Protocol was conceived.

9.9.3 Protection of smuggled migrants

The Smuggling of Migrants Protocol takes a weak approach to the assistance and protection of smuggled migrants, which reflects its criminal justice focus.[158] Significantly, the Protocol does not view smuggled migrants as victims of this crime—and avoids using such language.[159] Despite clearly prioritizing the criminalization of migrant smuggling, there is a growing body of literature that attempts to construe and assess the Protocol against a human rights framework, often drawing on the international protection principles for asylum seekers and refugees, to highlight the Protocol's inadequacies insofar as the assistance and protection of smuggled migrants are concerned.[160]

[157] Seventeen states parties have made a reservation under Art. 20(3) of the Smuggling of Migrants Protocol to giving jurisdiction to the International Court of Justice. The reservations outline that the referral of the dispute to this jurisdiction must be consensual between all states parties involved.

[158] Cf. Sharon Pickering, 'Transnational crime and refugee protection', (2007) 34 *Social Justice* (2), 47, p. 52.

[159] *Travaux Préparatoires*, cited in note 23 above, p. 461; cf. Tom Obokata, 'The legal framework on immigration control at sea', in Bernard Ryan and Valsamis Mitsilegas (eds), *Extraterritorial Immigration Control: Legal Challenges*, Leiden/Boston, Martinus Nijhoff Publishers, 2010, p. 151, p. 164.

[160] See, for example, Anne Gallagher, 'Human rights and the new UN Protocols on trafficking and migrant smuggling: a preliminary analysis', (2001) 23 *Human Rights Quarterly* 975; Brolan, 'An analysis of the human smuggling trade', cited in note 50 above; Erika Feller, 'Asylum, migration and refugee protection: realities, myths and the promise of things to come', (2006) 18 *International Journal of Refugee Law* (3–4), 509; Pickering, 'Transnational crime and refugee protection', cited in note 158 above, p. 47; Obokata, 'Smuggling from a human rights perspective', cited in note 42 above, p. 394; Obokata, 'Immigration control at sea', cited in note 159 above, p. 151; Andreas Schloenhardt and Kate L. Stacey, 'Assistance and protection of smuggled migrants: international law and Australian practice', (2013) 35 *Sydney Law Review*, 53–84.

9.9.4 Non-party states

States that have not, or not yet, become parties to the Smuggling of Migrants Protocol might be reluctant to commit themselves to this body of law because they lack the resources, capacity, or the political will to sign a treaty that they consider unnecessarily burdensome or conflicting with national interests.[161] The smuggling of migrants is a highly complex international problem without a single, standardized, or low-cost solution. If States lack effective governance and institutions to properly implement the Protocol, arguably they are less likely to undertake legal obligations in the first place. Civil conflict and unrest in many countries are further obstacles to the accession to and ratification of international instruments, including the Smuggling of Migrants Protocol. In this context, it should be noted that the lack of any rule of law that occurs during and after an armed conflict in a country or region might expose the population to a particularly high risk of irregular migration and of falling prey to the promises made by migrant smugglers.

Proper implementation of the Protocol's criminalization, cooperation, and protection provisions requires a very substantial financial and material commitment. For this reason, lack of such resources may provide an additional barrier to ratification. The perceived lack of incentives, the view that enough is already done through national laws or non-binding regional initiatives, and a general reluctance to accept binding obligations on issues that traditionally have been matters of national concern are other reasons why some countries might choose not to sign the Protocol.

9.9.5 Concluding remarks

The smuggling of migrants creates a complex national security, international relations, and human rights problem that is the subject of fierce and controversial debate, polarizes public opinion, and features prominently in political contests and media coverage. Combating the smuggling of migrants poses unique challenges to the international community and to national governments. Adding to the complexity is the role many countries play in the web of smuggling routes that connect sending, transit, and destination points by sea, land, and air.

The Smuggling of Migrants Protocol and its extensive explanatory and interpretative materials provide national legislators with a blueprint to combat the smuggling of migrants at domestic levels, which can be integrated bilaterally, regionally, and multilaterally. Moreover, drafters of the Protocol were cognizant of the need for the provisions to be sufficiently malleable to apply to varying legal systems. Despite some weaknesses of the Protocol and the concerns expressed by some scholars, in order to to prevent and combat the smuggling of migrants more effectively and more universally it is important that more states ratify this important treaty.

[161] See further, Andreas Schloenhardt and Hamish Macdonald, 'Barriers to ratification of the United Nations Protocol against the Smuggling of Migrants', research paper, The University of Queensland Migrant Smuggling Working Group, February 2015, available at: http://www.law.uq.edu.au/migrantsmuggling, accessed 29 October 2015.

10

The UN Protocol against the Illicit Manufacturing and Trafficking in Firearms, Their Parts and Components, and Ammunition 2001

Aaron X. Fellmeth

10.1 The Social Problem of Firearms Regulation and the Municipal Criminal Law Response

Organised criminals frequently rely on the threat and use of deadly force both to fund and perpetrate illegal activities. Narcotics and human traffickers, pirates, and terrorists in particular use small arms and light weapons (SALW), such as automatic rifles and handguns, to protect their income sources and leadership, suppress rival groups, kidnap for ransom, and intimidate state law enforcement officers. Every year, at least 7.5 million small arms and light weapons are manufactured and traded globally at a value of some $4 billion to $7 billion. About one-quarter of this trade is illicit and supplies organised criminals.[1] By 2001, there were at least 639 million documented small firearms circulating in the world and an unknown number of undocumented weapons.[2] Most of these by far are manufactured in Europe, the United States, Brazil, Japan, and Russia.[3] The number of small weapons is growing rapidly, not only due to high production, but because firearms tend to have a usable life of twenty years or more. Once on the market, they stay there for a very long time.

All states have organised criminal groups, but some regions suffer chronic disruption by armed bands of *guerrilleros*, religious fanatics, and local warlords. These groups may be involved in theft, the narcotics trade, human trafficking, kidnappings for ransom, money laundering, bribery of public officials, wildlife poaching, and other criminal activities, using SALW both to perpetrate crimes and raise funds to buy more SALW. The contingencies of unlicensed armed trade gives those regions specially affected by criminal organisations a considerable incentive to regulate the cross-border

[1] Aaron Fellmeth, 'The UN Arms Trade Treaty: temporarily holstered', (2012) 16 *ASIL Insights* (30); United Nations Small Arms Review Conference 2006, 'Facts on illegal small arms', Fact Sheet 1, UN Pub. No. DPI/2428A, p. 1.

[2] Graduate Institute of International Studies, *Small Arms Survey 2002, Counting the Human Cost*, Geneva, GIIS, 2002, Ch. 2, p. 63. Today, the number is estimated at 875 million. Small Arms Survey, Weapons and Markets, available at: http://www.smallarmssurvey.org/weapons-and-markets.html, accessed July 2014.

[3] Graduate Institute of International Studies, *Small Arms Survey, Producers of Small Arms, Light Weapons, and Their Ammunition*, No. 4, Geneva, GIIS, 2014, p. 4.

movement of SALW. In Colombia, for example, it was estimated in 2006 that out of 3.1 million guns in circulation, 2.4 million were illegally owned. One in ten homicides there were caused by firearms that year.[4]

Stopping illegal cross-border traffic in small firearms especially has proved extremely challenging because of their portability and the fact that, in most countries, private gun ownership for self-defence, hunting, and sport shooting is legally permitted. Most small arms used by criminal organisations began their product life as legitimate weapons sold to the military, the police, or private citizens. Manufacturing of and trade in SALW for use other than military or police is banned outright in only a few countries, unlike trade in more specialized military munitions, such as landmines and bombs. Small firearms can be manufactured at low cost and with relatively simple technology, and, without strict security on and tracing measures, SALW can be stolen, traded, or purchased by criminal organisations without much difficulty. They can be smuggled by boat or ground transport; in sacks of vegetables on the back of a truck or amid car parts in massive cargo containers on ocean freighters. They have even been sent by express mail, and in at least one case they have been air-dropped from an old Soviet cargo plane. Sometimes they may circulate illicitly for decades before confiscation. In 1997, for example, US government officials intercepted a shipment of unassembled automatic rifles and grenade launchers that had been left in Vietnam by withdrawing American forces in 1975. They had been sold by the Vietnamese government to private purchasers in Singapore and, over a twenty-year period, travelled to Germany, California, and finally Mexico for use by drug cartels.[5]

Official corruption sometimes contributes to firearms smuggling as well, but even when customs and law enforcement officials are upright and properly trained, the resources required to regulate the cross-border flow of firearms and ammunition are considerable, and many countries with diverse demands on limited budgets struggle to provide the necessary funding to the law enforcement agencies. Even the states with the greatest resources cannot hope to inspect every inbound cargo container; in practice, customs agents inspect only a small random sample, with the result that illegal arms shipments inevitably cross borders even at monitored customs ports.

Compounding the problem is the fact that many small arms are inexpensive yet exceedingly lethal. In November 1997, for example, a mere six Muslim terrorists armed with assault rifles and pistols were able to murder sixty-two tourists and guards at Luxor.[6] The combination of lethality, facility of concealment, low cost, durability, and widespread availability makes the regulation of SALW both important and extremely challenging. It is not surprising, therefore, that states plagued by organised crime have sought assistance from the international community in their efforts to manage the traffic in illicit weapons.

[4] UN SARC, 'Facts on illegal small arms', cited in note 1 above.

[5] Anne-Marie O'Connor and Jeff Leeds, 'US agents seize smuggled arms', *L.A. Times*, 15 March 1997, p. 19.

[6] 'Tourists massacred at temple', BBC News, 17 November 1997, available at: http://news.bbc.co.uk/2/hi/32179.stm, accessed 4 February 2016.

10.2 The Movement for International Firearms Regulation

10.2.1 Negotiations for international illicit firearms regulation generally

By the end of the twentieth century, most countries had adopted laws requiring a government-issued licence for the exportation, importation, and sale of SALW, but there was no general international treaty to help states coordinate their cross-border regulation. Before 1994, the international community's attention focused mainly on nuclear disarmament and certain habitually indiscriminate weapons such as chemical weapons and landmines. Yet SALW, especially assault rifles, have caused far more contemporary civilian deaths than any other form of weapon. Municipal measures in many states proved ineffective at controlling the international traffic in firearms by terrorists and other organised criminal groups. According to a 1997 UN Report on SALW, some criminal organizations were even known 'to procure weapons and obtain financial support with the assistance of allied groups and organizations based abroad which act as a front and which illicitly traffic in weapons, ammunition and explosives'.[7]

By the turn of the millennium, no global legal instrument regulated the transfer of firearms that could end up in the hands of criminal organisations. The 1980 Convention on Conventional Weapons (CCW) and its protocols do regulate arms manufacturing, trade, and use by states.[8] However, that Convention does not regulate sales of conventional weapons to private actors unless they fall within one of the proscribed categories, such as incendiary weapons, landmines, or blinding lasers. The CCW leaves the much more lethal trade in conventional firearms untouched.

The closest the international community came to a more comprehensive regulation of transnational arms transfers was through the Coordinating Committee for Multilateral Export Controls (CoCom). The arms manufacturing democracies of Europe and North America established CoCom in 1945 as an informal consultative group to monitor and control the export of all arms and militarily significant technologies to the Soviet bloc and emergent communist revolutionary groups elsewhere.[9] With the fall of the Soviet Union, CoCom was disbanded and reformed in 1996 as the Wassenaar Arrangement on Export Controls for Conventional Arms and Dual-Use Goods and Technologies.[10] The Wassenaar Arrangement covers forty-one states as of 2014, including almost all of the largest arms-exporting states except China and North Korea. Like CoCom before it, the Wassenaar Arrangement is an informal co-ordinating group, but its emphasis has shifted to preventing the transfer of arms that

[7] 'Report of the Panel of Governmental Experts on Small Arms', 7 August 1997, UN Doc. A/52/298, Annex, para. 55.

[8] Convention on Prohibitions or Restrictions on the Use of Certain Conventional Weapons Which May Be Deemed to Be Excessively Injurious or to Have Indiscriminate Effects, 10 October 1980, 1342 UNTS 137, available at: http://www.unog.ch/ccw/, accessed 4 February 2016.

[9] Aaron Fellmeth, 'Cure without a disease: the emerging doctrine of successor liability in international trade regulation', (2006) 31 *Yale Journal of International Law* 125.

[10] Ibid.

would promote terrorism, regional instability, or human rights violations, or that would empower certain aggressive states.

In theory, the Arrangement could offer a useful coordinating tool for arms manufacturing states to deny organised criminal syndicates access to SALW. In particular, the Wassenaar states adopted in 2002 a set of 'best practices' on the air transport of SALW that, if thoroughly implemented, would reduce some risk of diversion to criminal organisations.[11] Most directly, the designation of specific private actors as diversion risks encourages parties to use their domestic administrative and criminal institutions to prevent the transfer of arms and ammunition to individual criminals or criminal organisations. The US export regulatory agencies, for example, have adopted lists of 'denied persons' and organisations to whom exports of arms or dual-use items are prohibited.[12]

In practice, however, the Wassenaar Arrangement guidelines are adopted by consensus and enforced through informal channels of diplomacy rather than international law. The informality of the arrangement, the decentralization of implementation (every state adopts its own export regulations), the absence of certain arms exporters from the membership, and the lack of monitoring or enforcement institutions combine to limit the Arrangement's effectiveness at solving the problem of armed criminal organisations on a global scale. For example, although the Russian Federation is now a member of the Wassenaar Arrangement, Russia has freely allowed the sale of arms to criminal groups in Georgia and Ukraine. It has also allowed the sale of arms to the Assad regime during its assault on the human rights of Syrians. In each case, the Wassenaar Arrangement had no power to intervene formally and took no effective measures through informal channels.

Some progress towards regulating the international illicit traffic in SALW before 2000 came from regional initiatives. Not all were aimed directly at criminal organisations or included concrete regulatory measures. The 1993 Organization for Security and Cooperation in Europe (OSCE) Principles Governing Conventional Arms Transfers, for example, made no mention of crime control and included no concrete cooperation, monitoring, or enforcement measures.[13] The Principles do apply to arms transfers generally but offered little more than a stated commitment to avoid transfers that would be used to violate human rights, prolong or aggravate armed conflicts, or be used for terrorism. The European Union adopted a similar Code of Conduct on Arms Transfers in 1998 with one explicit mention of denying arms exports that might promote organised crime,[14] but its commitments were no more institutionalized than the OSCE's.

[11] Wassenaar Arrangement, 'Best practices to prevent destabilising transfers of small arms and light weapons (SALW) through air transport', adopted at the Plenary Meeting of 11–12 December 2002, revised in December 2007.

[12] The US Department of Commerce and the US Department of the Treasury maintain lists of individuals and organizations involved in arms proliferation and unregulated transfer to whom arms transfers are forbidden. See, e.g. 15 CFR pt 744 supp. (2014).

[13] Special communication of the CSCE Forum for Security Co-operation in Vienna, 49th mtg, Programme for Immediate Action Series, No. 3, OSCE Doc. FSC/3/96, 25 November 1993.

[14] European Union Code of Conduct on Arms Exports, DG E – PESC IV, EU Doc. 8675/2/98, 5 June 1998.

The first binding treaty directly relating to the SALW trade was adopted in 1997 by the Organization of American States.[15] The Inter-American Convention against the Illicit Manufacturing of and Trafficking in Firearms, Ammunition, Explosives, and Other Related Materials requires the adoption of a manufacturing and import–export licensing regime, the marking of firearms, the confiscation of illicitly manufactured firearms and ammunition, and security measures to reduce the incidence of firearm theft. Although some major SALW exporters, such as Canada and the United States, never ratified the Convention, thirty-one states did eventually adopt it, including significant weapons manufacturers Argentina and Brazil. Beginning in the early 1990s, pressure began building in the United Nations for effective international action to regulate the illicit trade in SALW. The scope and severity of illicit SALW trafficking contrasted starkly with the absence of any broad, multilateral initiative to bring it under control. Both civil society and many states severely affected by firearms violence began calling for decisive measures on a global scale to solve a global pathology. UN Secretary-General Kofi Annan's 2005 *Agenda for Peace* had introduced the concept of 'micro-disarmament' to address the problem in West Africa of proliferating, illicit SALW.[16] That same year, the UN Institute for Disarmament Research (UNDIR) produced a report on small arms in non-international conflicts that noted the absence of any general international regime regulating traffic in small arms and recommending the appointment of a panel of experts to study means of addressing the problem.[17] The General Assembly followed UNDIR's recommendation and, in December 1995, requested the Secretary-General to prepare a report, with the assistance of a Panel of Governmental Experts on Small Arms, on the use of SALW in conflicts, with emphasis on their illicit manufacture and trafficking.[18]

In August 1997, the Panel produced a report recommending *inter alia* greater international and regional cooperation to control illicit SALW, UN assistance in regional disarmament efforts, municipal and international measures to prevent the illicit traffic in SALW, and that the 'United Nations should consider the possibility of convening an international conference on the illicit arms trade in all its aspects'.[19] In December of that year, the General Assembly requested the UN Secretary-General to prepare a study on the problems of ammunition and explosives in all their aspects with the assistance of a Group of Governmental Experts.[20] In 1998's Resolution 53/77 E (see later in this section), the General Assembly tasked the Group with assisting the Secretary-General to prepare a report with recommendations on the objective, scope, agenda, and logistics of an international conference on the international trade in illicit firearms in all its aspects. The Secretary-General appointed twenty-three experts to the

[15] Inter-American Convention against the Illicit Manufacturing of and Trafficking in Firearms, Ammunition, Explosives, and Other Related Materials, 14 November 1997, OAS Doc. A/53/78, annex, available at: http://www.oas.org/juridico/english/treaties/a-63.html, accessed 22 March 2016.

[16] UN Secretary-General, *Agenda for Peace 2005*, A/50/60*-S/1995/1*, 25 January 1995, New York, United Nations Press, 1995.

[17] Swadesh Rana, 'Small arms and intra-state conflicts', UNIDIR Research Paper No. 34, New York, United Nations Press, 1995, UN Pub. No. GV.E.95.0.7.

[18] UN GA Res. 50/70 B (1995).

[19] UN Secretary-General, 'Report on small arms', August 1997, UN Doc. A/52/298, Annex, para. 80(k).

[20] UN GA Res. 52/38 J (1997).

Group in April 1998, which began meeting the following month and continued its work into 1999.

At the same time, the UN Development Programme was studying the SALW problem in West Africa in coordination with African and European state officials.[21] In May 1998, the G-8 requested that its Roma-Lyons group of experts on terrorism and transnational crime develop an international firearms treaty. Based on this report, twenty-one states met in Oslo in July 1998 to discuss the outlines of a global treaty regulating firearms manufacturing and trafficking.[22] The exploratory meeting did not produce any consensus document,[23] but the conference reinforced the need for global regulation of SALW trafficking.

The Assembly also adopted three other resolutions on the problem of illicit trade in SALW in 1998,[24] signalling an intensifying interest in a global solution to the small firearms problem. In November 1998, the UN Security Council adopted its own resolution on illicit arms flows,[25] in which it encouraged the Secretary-General to investigate international arms dealers trafficking in illicit arms in Africa in violation of the Council's arms embargoes. The following month, the General Assembly decided to convene an international conference on the illicit arms trade in all its aspects by 2001 at the latest.[26]

The summer of 1999 proved a turning point in international momentum for the regulation of SALW. In late June, the Secretary-General released the Group of Governmental Experts' report on the role of ammunition and explosives in the uncontrolled dissemination and abuse of SALW.[27] The Group noted the lack of reliable information about production and stockpiles of, and trade in, ammunition and explosives, and especially about their illicit trafficking. The Group also noted that the problem of theft, pilferage, and smuggling of ammunition and explosives was evident, however, and it posited a link between narcotics traffickers and other organised criminals as a source of supply to terrorist groups.[28] Finally, it drew attention to the absence of any obligatory universal system for marking and tracing ammunition.[29] In its recommendations, the Group proposed international harmonized regulation of ammunition and explosives and the adoption of international standards for marking.[30]

In August 1999, the Group released its report on firearms, in which it described the progress made towards implementing the recommendations of the Panel of Governmental Experts on Small Arms, and recommended state, regional, and UN measures to contain the threat of illicit SALW.[31] The report elaborated on the objectives, scope, and agenda of the planned international conference on the illicit arms trade planned by the General Assembly. The objectives endorsed by the group were

[21] Raymond Bonner, 'Nations endorse moves to eradicate plague of small arms', *NY Times*, 2 April 1998, p. 113.

[22] Raymond Bonner, '21 nations seek to limit the traffic in light weapons', *NY Times*, 12 July 1998, p. A3.

[23] Raymond Bonner, 'US joins 20 nations in urging controls on spread of small arms', *NY Times*, 15 July 1998, p. A7.

[24] UN GA Res. 53/77B; UN GA Res. 53/77M; UN GA Res. 53/77T.

[25] SCR 1209 (1998).

[26] UN GA Res. 53/77E (1998).

[27] 'Report of the Group of Experts on the problem of ammunition and explosives', UN Doc. A/54/155 (1999).

[28] Ibid, paras 50–51.

[29] Ibid, para. 73.

[30] Ibid, paras 98 and 104–5.

[31] 'Report of the Group of Governmental Experts on small arms', UN Doc. A/54/258 (1999).

significantly broader than facilitating international firearms regulation for crime control purposes:

(a) [To] strengthen or develop norms at the global, regional and national levels that would reinforce and further coordinate efforts to prevent and combat the illicit trade in small arms and light weapons in all its aspects;
(b) [To d]evelop agreed international measures to prevent and combat illicit arms trafficking in and manufacturing of small arms and light weapons and to reduce excessive and destabilizing accumulations and transfers of such weapons throughout the world, with particular emphasis on the regions of the world where conflicts come to an end and where serious problems with the proliferation of small arms and light weapons have to be dealt with urgently;
(c) [To m]obilize the political will throughout the international community to prevent and combat illicit transfers in and manufacturing of small arms and light weapons in all their aspects, and raise awareness of the character and seriousness of the interrelated problems associated with illicit trafficking in and manufacture of small arms and light weapons and the excessive and destabilizing accumulation and spread of these weapons;
(d) [To p]romote responsibility by States with regard to the export, import, transit and retransfer of small arms and light weapons.[32]

The recommended scope was all illicit trade in SALW 'that are manufactured to military specifications', as well as ammunition for such weapons.[33]

The General Assembly endorsed the Group's recommendations, requested the Secretary-General to continue research on illicit trade in SALW, and outlined the preparations for the 2001 Conference on the Illicit Trade in Small Arms and Light Weapons in All Its Aspects.[34] The Preparatory Committee held its first session in early 2000 with the objective of making recommendations to the 2001 Conference for an agenda and background documents. In his report of August 2000, the Secretary-General described a large number of regional conferences on SALW trafficking that had been convened over the summer of 2000 in Asia, Africa, Europe, and the Americas.[35] From this flurry of activity, the Secretary-General concluded:

> The growing attention to small arms issues is, in part, attributable to the momentum building towards the 2001 Conference and the commensurate desire among States and regions to develop common priorities or 'common positions' on issues related to the illicit trade in small arms and light weapons in all its aspects which are to be considered at the Conference. Interest in these matters has also been provoked by the Vienna-based negotiations on the protocol of firearms. The proposed Protocol would be a legally binding instrument establishing standards for, among other things, firearms marking, import–export controls and international cooperation and information exchange, all intended to prevent and combat illicit firearms manufacture and trafficking.[36]

[32] Ibid, para. 126. [33] Ibid, paras 129–30.
[34] UN GA Res. 54/54R (1999); UN GA Res. 54/54V (1999).
[35] 'Report of the Secretary-General on illicit traffic in small arms', 25 August 2000, UN Doc. A/55/323.
[36] Ibid, para. 70.

In its February 2001 report, the Group of Governmental Experts recommended a panoply of international regulatory and coordination measures, including licensing and record-keeping requirements for arms manufacturers, tracing cooperation, national registration of offenders, tighter controls on stockpiles and surplus weapons, import and export controls, fraud-resistant documentation requirements, registration and licensing of arms brokers, and related measures.[37] These recommendations formed the basis of the 2001 conference's negotiations for the planned international treaty regulating illicit SALW generally.

Although the international community's interest in global regulation of the illicit traffic in firearms was clear by this time, the conference led to no legally binding instrument, mainly because some states had concerns about the scope of the treaty, such as the extent of state interdiction obligations and how the treaty would apply to government or military purchases. Progress towards an international legal solution to the problem of illicit traffic in firearms generally remained elusive, but the studies and recommendations coloured the parallel negotiations for a protocol to the United Nations Convention Against Transnational Organised Crime (UNTOC) for the regulation of firearms specifically relating to organised crime.[38]

10.2.2 Regulation of illicit firearms relating to organised crime

The UNTOC effort to regulate illicit firearms trafficking began in parallel with the events leading up to the 2001 SALW conference. The Ninth UN Congress on the Prevention of Crime and the Treatment of Offenders was held in Cairo during the spring of 1995. The Congress adopted a resolution on 'Firearms regulation for purposes of crime prevention and public safety' that, among other things, requested the Economic and Social Council (ECOSOC)'s Commission on Crime Prevention and Criminal Justice (CCPCJ) to 'consider measures to regulate firearms commonly applicable in Member States, such as the prevention of transnational illicit trafficking in firearms, with a view to suppressing the use of firearms in criminal activity'.[39] The Congress further requested that the CCPCJ call on the UN Secretary-General to initiate a study into the uses of firearms in crime, the facts about illicit trafficking, and national and regional measures to control such trafficking. The Congress also asked that the CCPCJ urge the Secretary-General to submit a recommendation 'for further concerted action at the national and transnational levels, including the possibility of seeking views of Member States on the preparation of a declaration'.[40] The Congress stopped short of calling for a treaty on firearms regulation of any kind, however.

[37] 'Report of the Group of Governmental Experts established pursuant to General Assembly Resolution 54/54V of 15 December 1999, entitled "Small arms"', UN Doc. A/CONF.192/2 (2001).

[38] See ibid, para. 71 ('the Vienna negotiations and the work of the Preparatory Committee for the Conference will continue to shape and inform one another'); 'Small Arms Report', cited in note 35 above, para. 9 ('[t]he Group noted the complementarity of its mandate with the work of the Ad Hoc Committee on the Elaboration of a Convention against Transnational Organized Crime ... The Group avoided unnecessary overlap with the work of the Ad Hoc Committee, and noted that the mandates of the Ad Hoc Committee and of the Group were both complementary and mutually reinforcing.').

[39] 'Report of the Ninth United Nations Congress on the prevention of crime and the treatment of offenders', Cairo, 29 April–8 May 1995, A/CONF.169/16/Rev.1, p. 30.

[40] Ibid, p. 31.

In July, ECOSOC passed a resolution to implement the Congress's recommendations and requested the UN Centre for International Crime Prevention to conduct a study on the possibilities for international firearms regulation to better prevent the spread of conflicts and to protect civil society.[41] The resulting International Study on Firearm Regulation surveyed a broad array of data on legal and illegal firearms usage, state regulation of firearms, and regional and international initiatives.[42]

The Secretary-General also formed his own team to work out a methodology for an international study on state regulation of civilian-owned firearms. After ECOSOC approved the study design in 1996,[43] the survey was distributed to UN member states, and the Secretary-General formed a Group of Experts to advise on improving the survey and finalizing the study. Within a few months, the Secretary-General had collected responses from several intergovernmental organisations and forty-six member states, which he took as 'indicative of the strong interest of the international community in the question of firearm regulation'.[44]

The Secretary-General distributed a report on 'Criminal justice reform and strengthening of legal institutions measures to regulate firearms' in March 1997, to which was annexed the conclusions and recommendations of the Group of Experts and a summary of the study to date.[45] Among the notable conclusions of the Group were the following:

(a) import and export controls on firearms are not sufficient by themselves to prevent illicit trafficking in firearms;
(b) the absence of effective firearm regulation in one Member State can undermine not only the regulatory efforts but also the effective governance of other Member States;
(c) the manufacture of and trade in firearms for civilian use require effective domestic regulation and international cooperation and control; [and]
(d) effective domestic regulation of firearms requires cooperation between all levels of government, law enforcement agencies, business, the media and citizens to promote crime prevention, public health and the safety and security of individuals.[46]

The Group also made several recommendations for information gathering, harmonization of national regulations, and coordination, and urged that the Secretariat

> should convene regional workshops to consider, *inter alia*, harmonization of the collection of information on firearm regulation, the provision of technical assistance, including training, the sharing of information and the need for implementing bilateral, regional or multilateral agreements on combating illicit trafficking in firearms,

[41] ECOSOC Res. 1995/27, 50th plenary meeting, 24 July 1995.

[42] UN Pub. Sales No. E.98.IV.2 (1998). See also 'Report of the Secretary-General on measures to regulate firearms', 5th session, UN Doc. E/CN.15/1996/14; 'Report of the Secretary-General on measures to regulate firearms', 6th session, UN Doc. E/CN.15/1997/4.

[43] ECOSOC Res. 1996/28.

[44] 'Report of the Secretary-General on criminal justice reform and strengthening of legal institutions measures to regulate firearms', UN Doc. E/CN.15/1997/4, para. 6.

[45] Ibid. [46] Ibid, Annex I, para. 2.

in order to ensure that all Member States have sufficient capacity in the area of firearm regulation.[47]

The Group did not yet recommend the convening of a conference to consider the adoption of an international treaty regulating firearms trafficking, but its recommendations clearly suggested the utility of international coordination of regulatory measures.

The studies and negotiations leading up to the 2001 SALW conference were accompanied by a good deal of lobbying by non-governmental organisations, coordinated through the International Action Network on Small Arms, to address the problem of firearms trafficking through a legally binding instrument of global scope.

The UN General Assembly resolved in December 1998 to commence negotiations on a draft firearms protocol to the UNTOC, then being drafted by the Ad Hoc Committee on the Elaboration of a Convention against Transnational Organised Crime.[48] The Ad Hoc Committee began its work in Vienna in January 1999 and subsequently held twelve sessions, and in March 2001 it issued a specific report containing a draft Protocol against the Illicit Manufacturing and Trafficking in Firearms, Their Parts and Components and Ammunition.[49] At the final session in 2001, the Committee approved the Firearms Protocol and resolved to submit it to the UN General Assembly for adoption, which the General Assembly did on 31 May 2001.[50] The Firearms Protocol became the first legally binding, global treaty regulating SALW.

10.3 Analysis of the Key Provisions of the Protocol

10.3.1 Preamble

The Protocol begins with a statement of its purpose, 'to prevent, combat and eradicate the illicit manufacturing of and trafficking in firearms, their parts and components and ammunition' through international and regional cooperation.[51] Curiously, the preamble then invokes the principles of equal rights and self-determination of peoples, which suggests a concern either that regional conflicts fuelled by illicit traffic in firearms threaten regional stability and democratic governance, or else that, if the international community does not take effective measures to suppress the international traffic, some states might be tempted to take extra-territorial, unilateral measures to stem the flow of illicit firearms.

10.3.2 Part I—general provisions

Article 1 of the Protocol provides that the Protocol supplements and should be interpreted in conjunction with the UNTOC. Article 3 defines the key terms. The definition

[47] Ibid, Annex I, para. 3(c).
[48] UN GA Res. 53/111 (1998).
[49] UN Doc. A/55/383/Add.2, 2326 UNTS 208.
[50] UN GA Res. 55/255 (2001).
[51] The phrase 'firearms, and their parts and components and ammunition' recurs throughout the Protocol and its *travaux préparatoires*. For brevity, the following text will simply refer to these separate concepts under the combined rubric 'firearms', unless a distinction becomes necessary.

of 'firearm', the most important term of the treaty, is limited to any 'portable barrelled weapon' that expels projectiles 'by the action of explosion'. The definition thus excludes large weapons such as artillery; weapons relying for power on the direct expulsion of air, such as air rifles or pellet guns; and weapons relying on tension release or other kinetic force, such as BB guns or crossbows. Antique firearms and replicas are expressly excluded as well. The definition would seem to include portable mortars and most grenade launchers.

'Parts and components' are defined in Article 3 to mean elements 'specifically designed for a firearm and essential to its operation', including barrels, receivers, and any part of the action. The use of the conjunctive 'and' grammatically indicates that elements *either* not specifically designed for firearms *or* inessential to their operation would not qualify as parts or components. However, the definition specifically includes silencers or mufflers, which do not satisfy its second part, because silencers are not generally essential to the operation of any firearm.

'Ammunition' is defined to include not only a complete round, but its components as well, such as casing or gunpowder. A broad definition of ammunition is necessary because of the ease of manufacturing ammunition with minimal, low-technology equipment from prepared components.

'Illicit manufacturing' includes manufacturing from illicitly trafficked components, manufacturing without a licence in the state of manufacture, or manufacturing without marking as required by Article 8 of the Protocol. Interestingly, Article 3 does not define the term 'manufacturing' itself. The term would obviously include full assembly from components, but it leaves to states parties the option of including major repairs or partial assembly of modular components within the term 'manufacturing'.

'Illicit trafficking' means the importation, exportation, sale, movement, or transfer of the firearms between states parties or across the territory of a state party in transit, if 'any one of the State Parties concerned does not authorize' that traffic. It also includes any traffic of firearms not marked as required by Article 8.

Article 4(1) clarifies that the Protocol applies only to illicit traffic where the offences 'are transnational in nature and involve an organized criminal group', that last term defined in Article 2(a) of UNTOC to mean:

> a structured group of three or more persons, existing for a period of time and acting in concert with the aim of committing one or more serious crimes or offences established in accordance with this Convention, in order to obtain, directly or indirectly, a financial or other material benefit.[52]

Article 4(2) of the Protocol provides that state-to-state arms transfers and state transfers in cases where the application of the Protocol would prejudice the right of self-defence under the UN Charter do not fall within the scope of the Protocol. This qualification would seem unnecessary in light of paragraph 1, unless the state itself is considered an organised criminal group, a possibility that a plain reading of Article 4 intriguingly leaves open.

[52] The term 'serious crime' is further defined in UNTOC Art. 2(b) to mean an offence punishable by a maximum deprivation of liberty of at least four years or some more serious penalty.

Article 5, one of the core substantive provisions of the Protocol, requires states parties to adopt legislative and other measures to establish illicit manufacturing and traffic in firearms as criminal offences. The obliteration or falsification of the marking required in Article 8 must also be criminalized, as well as attempting, organising, aiding, facilitating, and counselling the commission of any of the predicate offences of Article 5. Article 5 leaves to the states parties discretion to define what forms of aiding, organising, etc. qualify as criminal offences. The interpretative note to paragraph 2 indicates that states are at liberty to define 'attempts' to include 'both acts perpetrated in preparation for a criminal offence and those carried out in an unsuccessful attempt to commit the offence, where those acts are also culpable or punishable under domestic law'.[53]

The requirement to establish a criminal offence of 'counselling' the illicit manufacture or traffic in firearms is the most problematic provision, as it might conflict with some interpretations of the human right to freedom of expression. To reconcile the 'counselling' provision with international human rights obligations, it may be necessary to interpret the term to encompass only those acts accompanied by a criminal conspiracy or concrete action by the person doing the counselling. Article 5 also leaves open the penalties for these violations, although presumably the penalties must be sufficiently severe to deter violations in accordance with the purpose of the Protocol.

Article 6 requires states to adopt measures that would lead to confiscation of illegally manufactured or trafficked firearms and to prevent their falling into the hands of 'unauthorized persons' through their seizure and destruction. Other methods of disposal, such as confiscation and use by military or police forces, is also permitted provided the firearms have been marked and their disposition recorded.

10.3.3 Part II—prevention

Part II of the Protocol contains most of its key substantive provisions. Article 8 requires states to adopt regulations requiring each firearm manufactured in or imported into its territory to include a unique marking that includes the name of the manufacturer, country of manufacture, and serial number (or a similar identification scheme). Article 7 obligates parties to maintain records on firearms sufficient to trace and identify them for ten years after manufacture or importation. Article 7 does not specify precisely what information should be maintained other than the marking information. Most obviously, the International Criminal Police Organization (Interpol) Firearms Tracing System criteria could be used, such as barrel length and number of estimated discharges. It also leaves open the possibility of using technological identification measures developed in the future. Article 7 also lacks any provisions for securing these records from destruction or tampering. In any case, the intended records include licensing information and the marking information on each firearm required

[53] 'Report of the Ad Hoc Committee on the elaboration of a Convention Against Transnational Organized Crime on the work of its first to eleventh sessions', 12 March 2001, UN Doc. A/55/383/Add.3, p. 2, para. 6.

by Article 8. Neither provision is very specific about the kind of marking required and what information must be included.[54]

Article 10 imposes an obligation to establish import and export licensing for firearms trade and transit. Firearms may not be exported to a state until the importing state has issued an import licence, and a communication protocol is established for exporting, transit, and importing states to help reduce the probability that licensed exports are diverted in transit from the importing for which the export licence was issued. For example, if Country *X* issues an export license for a shipment of firearms destined for Country *Y*, Country *X* may request that, after the expected period of carriage, Country *Y* verify receipt of the licensed firearms shipment. Article 10 obligates the importing state to verify the receipt (or not) of the shipment to the exporting state. Article 11 further obligates states to take appropriate measures to secure firearms shipments during manufacture, carriage, and border inspections to prevent theft or smuggling.

A further institutionalization of procedures would have been more effective—for example, if the exporting state had been obliged to verify with the importing state receipt of the shipment, and if the importing state had been obligated to report to the exporting state any receipt of a firearm shipment. The Protocol merely makes such verification procedures optional. Article 11 could also be strengthened by adding more institutionalized procedures. It stops short of establishing minimum standards of manufacturing and carriage security, or of training in border inspection and procedures or technologies for detecting pilferage or smuggling. Similarly, Article 15 requires states merely to 'consider' adopting a regulatory system for registering arms brokers and licensing their activities, despite the prominent role brokers play in the international sale and movement of firearms.

Article 12 sets forth important norms for information sharing to prevent and prosecute the illicit manufacturing and trafficking of firearms. These provisions are exceptionally expansive and pragmatic. They include duties to share case-specific facts about firearms shipments as well as more general information relating to organised criminal groups involved in illicit firearms manufacturing and trafficking; techniques of concealment used by such groups; and their customary trafficking routes. The parties also undertake to share their experiences with legislation and regulation to prevent illicit manufacturing and trafficking, law enforcement technologies, and firearms tracing information. Article 14 supplements these obligations by calling for cooperation among the parties and with 'relevant international organisations'—most obviously, Interpol—in law enforcement training and technical assistance.

Articles 13 adds a more general duty of cooperation at bilateral, regional, and global levels, with each party undertaking to designate a single point of contact as an international liaison on illicit firearms manufacturing and trafficking issues.

Article 15 exhorts states that have not adopted a system for regulating arms brokers to do so by requiring registration or licensing of brokers, or at least the disclosure

[54] In contrast, some regional instruments like the Nairobi Protocol and the Southern African Development Community (SADC) Protocol do include specific information requirements in their marking provisions.

of the participation of brokers in export or import transactions. It further encourages states that have adopted brokering regulation to share information on brokers through the Article 7 procedures.

10.3.4 Part III—final provisions

Article 16 of the Protocol includes a dispute settlement clause providing for arbitration or, if the organisation of an arbitral tribunal and agreement on procedures should fail, referral to the International Court of Justice. However, parties are expressly left free to disavow this provision by reservation, and many have done so.

Articles 17 and 18 provide standard terms for signature, ratification, accession, and entry into force. 'Regional economic integration organisations' are authorized to sign or accede if one member state is a party to the Protocol. The Protocol entered into force on 3 July 2005, the ninetieth day after ratification or accession by the fortieth party. Ratifications have rolled in steadily every year, with five more in 2014, and, as of January 2016, the Protocol has 114 parties, including the European Union. However, many major arms manufacturing states, most notably Canada, China, Israel, Japan, the Russian Federation, and the United States, have declined to ratify or accede to the Protocol.

The most common official reason given for rejecting the Protocol has been that existing international law would suffice to control the illicit spread of firearms if it were thoroughly implemented, and therefore the international community's efforts should be directed towards that end. Many states refuted this claim by pointing out the utter absence of a binding treaty on the subject, but thus far this argument has not moved the hold-outs, who insist that no common export and transfer standards for SALW are necessary or advisable. The United States in particular opposed the Protocol on the grounds that it might prevent the sale or transfer of small arms to those rebelling against oppressive regimes; that the regulation of ammunition would be difficult and expensive; and that the Protocol might somehow interfere with the supposed constitutional right of US citizens to own firearms.[55]

10.4 Negotiating History of the Protocol

This part will highlight some interesting and consequential aspects of the negotiations and drafting process. It is far from a complete negotiating history; UNODC has published a much more detailed description of the process in Part IV of the UNTOC *Travaux Préparatoires*.[56] This part instead focuses on specific events during the negotiations that may prove important to the interpretation of the Protocol.

[55] See Robert Joseph, Statement at the 2006 UN Conference to review progress made in the implementation of the program of action to prevent, combat and eradicate the illicit trade in small arms and light weapons in all its aspects, 27 June 2006. This last claim is simply implausible, because the Constitutional right to bear arms, even if it included an individual right to own firearms, would not necessarily encompass the right to import foreign firearms in an unrestricted manner.

[56] UN Office on Drugs and Crime, *Travaux Préparatoires of the negotiations for the elaboration of the United Nations Convention Against Transnational Organized Crime and the Protocols thereto*, UN Pub. No. E.06.V.5, 2006.

10.4.1 Preamble

Preambular language is not intended to be binding, but it does tend to colour the interpretation of the treaty. Most changes to the preamble during the negotiations had no significant impact on the Protocol as finally adopted, but one change was significant. The category of SALW includes explosives such as grenades and small bombs, which are sometimes used by criminal organisations. The preamble of the Protocol originally referred to explosives as well as firearms, but the Office of Legal Affairs interpreted the relevant General Assembly resolutions as not authorizing the inclusion of explosives regulation in the scope of the Protocol. References to explosives were accordingly removed from the entirety of the draft Protocol.

Perhaps the most controversial inclusion was the preambular reference to the self-determination of peoples. The government of Argentina expressed reservations about this inclusion, which it thought inappropriate for a treaty on illicit firearms trafficking. Most probably the concern was that the language could be used to support a claim by rebel militias to the right to manufacture and acquire firearms as part of an effort at secession, which would undermine the basic international legal principles of territorial integrity and non-interference in the political affairs of other states.

10.4.2 Part I—general provisions

In the original draft Protocol put forward by Canada, the definition of 'firearms' included the frame or receiver alone. The reference was deleted on a proposal by the United States and moved to the definition of parts and components. Some participants thought the limitation to barrelled weapons was too specific and should be omitted for added flexibility, but this proposal was not adopted. The United States observed that the definition of parts and components would exclude silencers, and the definition was accordingly amended to include them.[57]

During the negotiations on the scope of the Protocol (Article 4), a proposal was made to limit the Protocol to 'illegally manufactured and traded firearms'. This option was rejected by a majority of delegations on the ground that, in order to control trafficking in firearms, it was thought necessary to regulate all firearms trade. The underlying concern seems to have been that the legality of the manufacturing and trade is a *post hoc* legal determination, and so states need to monitor the production and trafficking of all firearms to detect deviations from private legal obligations. The *travaux* and the interpretative note to Article 4 also make clear that the exemption in paragraph 2 of Article 4 is intended to limit the scope of the Protocol to crime control rather than arms control generally. The delegations generally agreed that 'state-to-state transactions' and 'state transfers' exclude transfers from one government to another 'in a sovereign capacity' but not transfers between entities owned or operated by governments, such as state-owned arms manufacturers.[58]

[57] Ibid, p. 613 n. 44.

[58] 'Report of the Ad Hoc Committee', cited in note 53 above, p. 2, para. 4.

During negotiations on Article 5 (criminal offences), the French delegation proposed limiting the codification obligation to offences 'in connection with a criminal organisation'. The proposal was rejected by the Ad Hoc Committee with the intention of keeping the scope of the Protocol broad, and possibly out of concern about the evidentiary burden the state would have to carry to regulate and prosecute firearms manufacturing and trafficking crimes.

10.4.3 Part II—prevention

During the negotiations, many states considered the tracing provisions of the Protocol to be among the most important for the prevention of illicit trafficking.[59] The vitality of this provision was accordingly an important concern throughout the negotiations. For example, despite the wishes of some delegations to reduce the period for which records should be maintained under Article 8 to five years, most delegations favoured the ultimate choice of ten years on the ground that firearms themselves are very durable. On the specificity of the marking requirement, the *travaux* are worth quoting more extensively:

> On the type of information contained in the marking at the time of manufacture, the United Kingdom proposed to include 'the year of manufacture', and suggested to clarify the meaning of the words 'place of manufacture'. Argentina proposed to include the 'model number', in addition to the serial number. New Zealand proposed to replace the words 'serial number' with 'unique identifier'. China proposed to delete the words 'name of manufacturer'. Switzerland suggested that the marking requirement should not be overloaded.[60]

After unusually extensive discussions, including proposals to include additional information in the marking, such as date of manufacture, or unique identifying information, the delegates agreed upon the more parsimonious option of name and place of manufacture plus serial number.

During negotiations over the Article 10 export, import, and transit licensing of firearms, the representatives generally agreed upon the need for reasonably detailed licence requirements (ultimately adopted as paragraph 3 to Article 10) to avoid uncertainty about the extent of the exporting state's authorization or diversion from the intended state of importation. Finland proposed that the exporting state should refrain from licensing exports without the previous written consent of the importing state's competent authority. This proposal was adopted on the understanding that an import licence qualifies as consent.

It was also proposed that an importing or transit state should obtain the consent of the exporting state before re-exporting or re-transferring the firearms in a manner not authorized by the export licence, to prevent firearms from falling into unauthorized hands. A debate ensued over whether the proposal was feasible and would infringe the

[59] See, e.g. UN GAOR, 55th session, 101st plenary meeting, 31 May 2001, UN Doc. A/55/PV.101, p. 11 (European Union).

[60] Ibid, p. 650 n. 12.

sovereignty of the importing state, and the proposal was ultimately rejected in favour of adopting less stringent requirements in the Article 11 preventive measures.

A proposal by South Africa to reference Interpol's Weapon and Explosives Tracking System as a possible means for cooperation in weapons tracing under Article 12 was rejected without recorded explanation, probably because it was considered unnecessary to name any or all possible means of cooperation in weapons tracing when they might change with new agreements, practices, and technologies.

Article 15 proved one of the more contentious provisions. Early on, the United States, with the support of South Africa and Turkey, had proposed the mandatory regulation of arms brokers through registration in both their country of nationality and the country of operation. Probably the main consideration behind this proposal was the fact that the state of the broker's nationality was likely to have the best information on the broker's reliability, history of compliance with the law, and associations with criminal groups. According to the *travaux*, 'many participants expressed concern with regard to the registration and licensing of brokers in the country of nationality as well as the country of operation'.[61] The main objection expressed related to the difficulty of enforcing registration in the country of nationality. Finland proposed at the fifth session to limit any registration obligation to the state of the broker's operations, in consultation with the state of the broker's nationality.

10.4.4 Deleted provisions

During the spring 1999 negotiations, Mexico proposed including an article entitled 'Sovereignty' in the following terms:

1. States Parties shall fulfil their obligations under this Protocol in a manner consistent with the principles of sovereign equality and territorial integrity of States and that of non-intervention in the domestic affairs of other States.
2. A State Party shall not undertake in the territory of another State Party the exercise of jurisdiction and performance of functions that are exclusively reserved to the authorities of that other State Party by its domestic law.

The most likely motivation was to discourage states from repeating the kinds of extra-territorial law enforcement measures that the United States had undertaken in the *Alvarez-Machain* case, in which US government agents had arranged for the abduction from Mexican territory of a Mexican national allegedly cooperating with a drug syndicate in the torture and murder of a US agent in Mexico,[62] and, still more dramatically, the US invasion of Panama to arrest President Manuel Noriega for drug trafficking. Consideration of this article was deferred until the eleventh session, when the Ad Hoc Committee deleted it without recorded comment. The provision, if included, would not have altered the existing international law on the subject of sovereign equality or intervention in the domestic affairs of other states, however, and so its omission has no significant consequences.

[61] *Travaux*, cited in note 56 above, pp. 701–2.

[62] *United States v Alvarez-Machain*, 504 US 655 (1992).

10.5 Implementation of the Protocol and Subsequent Developments

10.5.1 Impact of the Protocol on international practice

As of 2014, the Protocol boasts ninety-five parties, but only a few of the major firearms manufacturing states subscribe other than Argentina and Brazil. Canada, China, the European Union and its largest arms exporters, Japan, the Russian Federation, South Korea, Switzerland, and the United States have all declined to ratify the Protocol as of 2014. Because of the Wassenaar Arrangement, most of these non-parties already comply with at least some of the main substantive provisions of the Protocol, and others have adopted them *sua sponte*. The United States, for example, requires the marking of a serial number on firearms manufactured in that country, a serial number on some kinds of firearms (e.g. machine guns) imported into the country,[63] and registration of all US firearms importers and manufacturers.[64] It also requires separate import and export licences for each shipment of firearms into and out of the country, respectively.[65] Canada and the European Union have very similar regulations.[66] Nonetheless, few non-parties comply with all of the provisions of the Protocol at present.

After the Protocol's entry into force in July 2005, the Conference of the Parties to the UNTOC (CoPU) decided that, at its third session in 2006, it would review for the first time implementation of the Protocol. It specifically planned:

(i) consideration of the basic adaptation of national legislation in accordance with the Protocol;
(ii) commencement of the examination of criminalization legislation and difficulties encountered in the implementation of Article 5 of the Protocol;
(iii) enhancing international cooperation and developing technical assistance to overcome difficulties identified in the implementation of the Protocol; [and]
(iv) exchange of views and experience regarding record-keeping, marking of firearms and licensing gained in the implementation of Articles 7, 8 and 10 of the Protocol.[67]

The Secretariat accordingly submitted an analytical report to the third and fourth sessions based on the responses of parties to the Protocol.[68] The parties responding generally reported compliance with the Protocol's requirements other than the marking

[63] 18 USC para. 922(k); 26 USC para. 5842; 27 CFR para. 478.92.
[64] 26 USC para. 5802.
[65] 18 USC para. 923 (import licences); 22 USC para. 2778 (export licences).
[66] EU Directive 2008/51/EC; EU Council Directive 91/477/EEC; EU Common Position 2008/944/CFSP; EU Common Position 2003/468/CFSP; Exports and Imports Permits Act, RSC 1985, c. E-19 (Canada).
[67] Conference of the Parties to the United Nations Convention Against Transnational Organized Crime (CoPU), Decision 2/5, 2nd Session, 21 October 2005, UN Doc. CTOC/COP/2005/8, p. 10.
[68] 'Analytical report of the Secretariat on Implementation of the Protocol against the Illicit Manufacturing of and Trafficking in Firearms, Their Parts and Components and Ammunition, supplementing the United Nations Convention against Transnational Organized Crime', 16 August 2006, UN Doc. CTOC/COP/2006/8 [hereafter abbreviated to 'Report on Implementation']; CoPU, 3rd Session, 18 October 2006, UN Doc. CTOC/COP/2006/14.

offences, although this has taken some time to adopt in domestic legislation. However, full implementation has proved a slow process. In 2012, the CoPU felt it necessary to urge parties to adopt legislation to criminalize marking offences, require record keeping, impose effective import and export licensing controls, and other implementing measures.[69]

The CoPU also requested in its fifth session that the UNODC conduct a study 'of the transnational nature of and routes used in trafficking in firearms, based on the analysis of information provided by States on confiscated weapons and ammunition'.[70] UNODC began gathering information through surveys sent to member states in December 2011 and opened a website to allow access by member states to the replies to its survey questionnaires about seizures of illicit firearms.[71] Initial reports indicate a variety of trafficking and concealment methods, and a substantial disparity in reported seizure quantities among states parties to the Protocol.[72] The survey results will inform the discussions of the Working Group on Firearms at future Conferences of the Parties to UNTOC. The challenge of ensuring widespread and effective implementation of the Protocol continues.

In its fourth session, the CoPU had also urged states parties to the Protocol to strengthen their national legislation to conform to the Protocol and requested the Secretariat to facilitate technical assistance to parties facing difficulties in implementation.[73] The UNODC responded in 2011 by publishing a detailed Model Law against the Illicit Manufacturing of and Trafficking in Firearms, Their Parts and Components and Ammunition.[74] The *Model Law* is intended to assist states in implementing the Protocol in their domestic legislation by providing an exemplar of municipal laws that comply with the Protocol's disciplines. As such, the Model Law's provisions track the Protocol's definitions and modalities closely. It also includes provisions that would implement the non-mandatory provisions of the Protocol for regulating brokers, as well as simplified procedures for temporary imports and exports of firearms.

Despite its considerable length, the Model Law disclaims any intention to serve as a pattern for comprehensive national firearms regulation. For example, the Law does not contain general provisions respecting international cooperation in matters commonly integrated with illicit weapons trafficking issues such as anti-money laundering regulations or customs inspection procedures. Nonetheless, the Law concludes with an Annex containing additional provisions that states may wish to include in their domestic legislation for the regulation of firearms more generally, such as licensing requirements for manufacturers, importers, and exporters; detailed marking provisions for firearms and ammunition (the latter of which is not required by the Protocol);

[69] 'Activities of the Working Group on Firearms', report submitted by the Chair of the Working Group, 27 June 2012, UN Doc. CTOC/COP/2012/6.

[70] CoPU, Resolution 5/4, 5th Session, 22 October 2010, para. 7, UN Doc. CTOC/COP/2010/17; see also CoPU, Resolution 6/2, 6th Session, 19 October 2012, para. 7, UN Doc. CTOC/COP/2012/15.

[71] See https://firearmstrafficking.unodc.org/, accessed 5 February 2016.

[72] See Note by the Secretariat, 'Work of the United Nations Office on Drugs and Crime on conducting a study of the transnational nature of and routes used in trafficking of firearms', 8 August 2012, UN Doc. CTOC/COP/2012/12.

[73] CoPU, Decision 4/6, 4th Session, 17 October 2008, CTOC/COP/2008/19.

[74] UN Pub. No. E.11.V.9, 2011.

detailed record-keeping provisions; and penal laws. These were developed based on a variety of international treaties and guidelines, as well as UNODC's experience with national firearms regulation obtained through surveys and fieldwork.

10.5.2 Beyond the Protocol

Immediately following conclusion of the Protocol, the United Nations held its Conference on the Illicit Trade in Small Arms and Light Weapons in All Its Aspects in July 2001, but, as noted, no legally binding treaty resulted. The United States in particular expressed strong reservations about any regulation of private gun ownership,[75] despite the exceptionally high number of murders and accidental deaths caused by ubiquitous privately owned guns in that country.[76] The delegates ultimately issued a non-binding Programme of Action to Prevent, Combat and Eradicate the Illicit Trade in Small Arms and Light Weapons in All Its Aspects in hopes of a stronger future consensus.[77] In the Programme, the states 'undertake' a non-binding commitment to adopt national, regional, and global measures to eradicate the illicit trade in SALW. Many of the Programme's terms echo or replicate provisions of the Protocol, with a scope broadened to include illicit trade in SALW not directly connected to organised criminal groups.

A number of regional instruments and declarations followed the adoption of the Protocol. Four SALW treaties have been adopted in Africa by regional groups. In 2001, the Southern African Development Community (SADC) adopted a Protocol on the Control of Firearms, Ammunition and Other Related Materials. The SADC Protocol is an ambitious treaty. It obligates states parties to criminalize the illicit manufacturing, possession, trafficking, and use of unauthorized firearms and ammunition; to adopt a registration and licensing regime for civilian firearm possession; to implement national training programmes for law enforcement agents; to secure state-owned firearms and ammunition; to ensure marking of and record keeping for firearms; and to coordinate law enforcement and information sharing among states parties regarding firearms.[78] The Protocol entered into force in July 2004 following ratification by Botswana, Lesotho, Malawi, Mauritius, Mozambique, Namibia, South Africa, Swaziland, Tanzania, Zambia, and Zimbabwe.

[75] United Nations Conference on the Illicit Trade in Small Arms and Light Weapons in All Its Aspects, 27 July 2001, UN Doc. A/CONF.192/SR.1, paras 50–55.

[76] In the year of the conference, for example, nearly 30,000 gun deaths occurred in the United States. The number has continued to rise since that time. See Gunpolicy.org, United States, 'Gun facts, figures and the law: death and injury', available at: http://www.gunpolicy.org/firearms/region/united-states, accessed 5 February 2016. Of these, more than one-third were homicides. Also see generally National Center for Injury Prevention & Control and US Centers for Disease Control and Prevention, 'Web-based injury statistics query & reporting system (WISQARS) injury mortality reports, 1999–2010', for national, regional, and states, December 2012, available at: http://webappa.cdc.gov/sasweb/ncipc/dataRestriction_inj.html, accessed 5 February 2016.

[77] UN Doc. No. A/CONF.192/15, 20 July 2001.

[78] 'Protocol on the Control of Firearms, Ammunition and Other Related Materials in the Southern African Development Community (SADC) Region', 14 August 2001, available at: http://www.sadc.int/files/8613/5292/8361/Protocol_on_the_Control_of_Firearms_Ammunition2001.pdf, accessed 22 March 2016.

In addition there are three other African regional treaties: the 2004 Nairobi Protocol for the Prevention, Control and Reduction of Small Arms and Light Weapons in the Great Lakes Region and the Horn of Africa; the 2006 Economic Community of West African States Convention on Small Arms and Light Weapons, their Ammunition and Other Related Materials; and the 2010 Central African (Kinshasa) Convention for the Control of Small Arms and Light Weapons, their Ammunition, Parts and Components that can be used for their Manufacture, Repair and Assembly. Non-binding regional initiatives have abounded since the adoption of the Protocol, especially in Africa, the Middle East, and Latin America.

The major global developments in SALW trafficking regulations since the Protocol are a pair of international instruments dealing directly with the small arms trade. The first is the awkwardly named 2005 International Instrument to Enable States to Identify and Trace, in a Timely and Reliable Manner, Illicit SALW (also known as the International Tracing Instrument, or ITI),[79] which responded to one of the exigencies identified in the 2001 UN Programme of Action. During negotiations for stronger regulation of SALW ownership, significant opposition came from some major small arms exporters, such as China, Russia, and the United States,[80] quite likely motivated in part by an interest in ensuring that democratic-minded rebel groups can effectively oppose authoritarian regimes, but also probably by the desire to avoid the negative publicity that would most likely result when weapons held by criminal groups, terrorists, or child soldiers in Africa are traced back to their arms manufacturers, as they inevitably must be. The resulting 2005 Instrument does not depart significantly from the marking and tracing provisions of Part II of the Protocol, to the disappointment of principled states and those suffering from violence related to illicit SALW proliferation.[81]

The second global development, the UN Arms Trade Treaty (ATT), was adopted by the General Assembly in 2013.[82] The ATT enacts a regime for the regulation of the international arms trade generally, including but not limited to SALW. It imposes disciplines on the trade in SALW and ammunition, but it includes few measures that would lead to the significant protection of persons historically victimized by gun violence. In general, the ATT obligates parties to refuse authorization of arms transfers that would violate UN embargoes or treaty obligations, or that would be used for the commission of atrocities (Article 6). The treaty does not require states to prohibit arms transfers destined for criminal groups, however. It merely urges states to 'tak[e] into account relevant factors', among which are whether the arms export could be used to violate human rights or commit acts 'constituting an offense under international conventions or protocols relating to transnational organized crime to which the exporting State is a Party' (Article 7). States not already a party to the UNTOC Firearms Protocol need

[79] UN GA Res. 60/88 (2005).
[80] Irwin Arieff, 'Paris backs away from mandatory arms marking plan', *Reuters News*, 13 July 2001; Mei-Ling Hopgood, 'Negotiators struggle to reach small-arms pact: complex politics stall agreement', *Toronto Star*, 21 July 2001; Irene Ngoo, 'US wins out but irks 160 nations', *Straits Times*, 23 July 2001.
[81] 'Delegates protest over arms pact: diluted small-arms accord accepted', *Toronto Star*, 22 July 2001.
[82] UN GA Res. 67/234 (2012), UN Doc. A/RES/67/234, 4 January 2013.

not pause to consider whether an arms export is destined for a criminal group under the ATT.

The ATT also requires parties to adopt and maintain a 'national control system to regulate' the exportation of ammunition (Article 3), but it does not impose specific regulatory requirements and includes no provisions for tracing weapons or ammunition. Its record-keeping provisions require parties to maintain national records of export licences for ten years, but 'encourage' parties to maintain records of arms imports (Article 12). There are no provisions for the adoption of record-keeping requirements for private arms exporters, importers, or brokers.

10.5.3 Final observation

The apparent fragmentation of the global arms regulation regimes does not currently pose any significant problem, partly because many major arms manufacturers refuse to be bound by detailed treaties, but partly because the ATT and the UNTOC Protocol adopt different and complementary approaches to international regulation. The ATT takes a more comprehensive view of arms trade regulation, but its monitoring mechanics are fairly sketchy and shallow. In any case it is neither specially focused on SALW and ammunition, nor adapted to interdict shipments to organised criminal groups. The Protocol's disciplines are fully compatible with the ATT, but they expand on them by requiring closer coordination and supervision of SALW with a specific focus on criminal groups.

The frustration of what formerly appeared to be strong international momentum towards a binding international regime for the regulation of SALW reinforces the Firearms Protocol's value as currently the strongest multilateral bulwark against illicit firearms trafficking. Although the international community could renew its push for a strong treaty on general SALW trade sometime in the future, for the time being the Protocol represents the apogee of global regulation of illicit manufacturing of and trafficking in firearms.

11

The United Nations Convention against Corruption and its Criminal Law Provisions

*Michael Kubiciel and Anna Cornelia Rink**

11.1 Origins of the UNCAC

'It has been suggested that as far as transnational financial crime is concerned, national legislation will never be sufficient [and] that some form of multinational securities and exchange commission may well be required. But the prospects for this kind of regulation do not seem good, at least in the near future,' the United Nations found in its Fifth Congress on the prevention of crime in 1975.[1] The changes leading from this set in quicker than could have been predicted: only two years later, investigations following the Watergate Affair disclosed that more than 400 companies had paid bribes of some US$300 billion to foreign public officials.[2] In the course of this, politicians and the wider public became aware of the extent of transnational corruption for the first time. It was conceived as another symptom of the moral decay that was supposed to be widespread among society and its elite. After the first shock had worn off a reaction began, starting with legislation known as the US Foreign Corrupt Practices Act (FCPA) of 1977.[3] This was not the end of the anti-corruption response; in fact, the FCPA was not even the beginning of the end but turned out to be the end of

* Central parts of the text are based on a previously unpublished study that Michael Kubiciel conducted for the United Nations Office on Drugs and Crime (UNODC) in 2005/2006. The text, however, does not reflect the position of the UNODC.

[1] See Fifth United Nations Congress on the Prevention of Crime and the Treatment of Offenders, Toronto, Canada, 1–12 September 1975: report prepared by the Secretariat, UN Pub. A/CONF.56/3, Ch. I, para. 31; on the UN's way to its convention in depth: United Nations, *Travaux Préparatoires of the negotiations for the elaboration of the United Nations Convention against Corruption*, New York, UN, 2010, p. xiiff.

[2] On the Watergate affair: Lewis Chester, Cal McCrystal, Stephen Aris, and William Shawcross, *Watergate. The Full Inside Story*, 1973; President Richard Nixon's speech of 30 April 1973 dealing with the scandal, 'The Watergate affair. The integrity of the White House', in *Vital Speeches of the Day*, 1973, p. 450. House of Representatives Report No. 95-640, p. 1, available at: http://www.justice.gov/criminal/fraud/fcpa/history/1977/houseprt-95-640.pdf, accessed 28 September 1977. On this see also 'Report of the Securities and Exchange Commission (SEC) on questionable and illegal corporate payments and practices', 1976, available at: http://www.sec.gov/spotlight/fcpa/sec-report-questionable-illegal-corporate-payments-practices-1976.pdf, accessed 18 September 2015.

[3] Hartmut Berghoff, 'From the Watergate scandal to the compliance revolution. The fight against corporate corruption in the United States and Germany, 1972–2012', (2013) 53 *Bulletin German Historical Institute*, 6; Mark Pieth, 'Introduction', in Mark Pieth, Lucinda Low, and Nicola Bonucci (eds), *The OECD Convention on Bribery—A Commentary*, 2nd edn, Cambridge, CUP, 2014, p. 8.

the beginning of a development that finally led to the adoption of the United Nations Convention against Corruption (UNCAC).

In the late 1970s there was still a great deal to be achieved. The United States did not enforce the FCPA, while most of the other developed countries simply ignored the problem of transnational corruption. None of them wanted to imperil the business opportunities of its enterprises abroad; and all of them had a strong interest in maintaining their good relations with developing regimes that, to a great extent, gained and sustained their power bases on corrupt practices.[4] Thus, the FCPA remained the only significant legal innovation in the combat against corruption for almost twenty years.[5] The end of the Cold War and the increasing globalization altered the economic and political framework in which corruption could be ignored or tolerated for so long.[6] Economically, the true costs of corruption became apparent as the growth of global competitors drove up bribe levels in international procurement.[7] More and more economic leaders agreed that the costs of corruption had become unacceptably high.[8] The change in economic perception met a changed political situation. The 'post-Cold War' world made Western politics accessible for complaints.[9] Many governments found themselves unable to explain why the interest in stabilizing a political status quo in a country outweighed the support of corruption. Political allies hence became 'corrupt regimes' and corruption was no longer part of an admissible political strategy but became apparent as a crucial cause of global poverty.[10] These alterations were complemented by a significant change in criminal politics: many Western governments came to regard transnational corruption as a danger to their own societies because increased global trade and more frequent international mergers facilitated infection with the virus of corruption.[11] In particular, the eastern expansion of the EU is feared to bear the risk of infecting the western parts of the Union with corruption.[12]

[4] Michael Kubiciel, 'International legal development and national legal change in the fight against corruption', in David Linnan (ed.), *Legitimacy, Legal Development and Change*, Farnham, Ashgate, 2012, p. 419, p. 421; see also Jan Wouters, Cedric Ryngart, and Ann Sofie Cloots, 'The international legal framework against corruption: achievements and challenges', (2013) 14 *Melbourne Journal of International Law*, 1, p. 4.

[5] Kubiciel, 'International legal development and national legal change', cited in note 4 above.

[6] On this, in depth, Michael Kubiciel, 'Core criminal law provisions in the United Nations Convention Against Corruption', (2009) 9 *International Criminal Law Review*, 139, p. 140; the following remarks are partly based on this text.

[7] See Alan Doig and Robin Theobald, *Corruption and Democratization*, Abingdon, Psychology Press, 2000, p. 7; Carolyn Hotchkiss, 'The sleeping dog stirs: new signs of life in efforts to end corruption in international business', (1998) 17 *Journal of Public Policy & Marketing*, 108, p. 110.

[8] See, for example, the International Chamber of Commerce Rules of Conduct to Combat Extortion and Bribery in International Business Transactions from 1996; open letter from European business leaders to OECD Economic ministers from 1997, which is available at: https://www.transparency.org/news/pressrelease/business_leaders_call_on_oecd_ministers_to_act_against_international_corrup, accessed 18 September 2015.

[9] Hotchkiss, 'The sleeping dog stirs', cited in note 7 above, p. 109; Mark Turner and David Hulme, *Governance, Administration & Development: Making the State Work*, Basingstoke, Palgrave Macmillan, 1997, pp. 222–4.

[10] Doig and Theobald, *Corruption and Democratization*, cited in note 7 above, p. 8ff.

[11] Rajib Sanyal, 'Determinants of bribery in international business: the cultural and economic factors', (2005) *Journal of Business Ethics* 59, 139.

[12] Cf. Barbara Crutchfield George, Kathleen A. Lacey, and Jutta Birmele, 'On the threshold of the adoption of global antibribery legislation: a critical analysis of current domestic and international efforts toward the reduction of business corruption', (1999) 32 *Vanderbilt Journal of Transnational Law*, 24.

In this new light, anti-corruption initiatives met an auspicious international policy climate.[13] Transparency International was an early advocate of putting global focus on (foreign) bribery. Founded in 1993, the non-governmental organisation published its Corruption Perceptions' Index and supported the United States in its attempt to convince other states of the necessity to take action against foreign bribery. This work had a first success in 1996 when twenty-three member states of the Organization of American States (OAS)[14] signed the Inter-American Convention against Corruption.[15] This organisation paved the way for gaining the necessary global support for the fight against foreign bribery. Only one year later, the OECD Convention on Combating Bribery of Foreign Public Officials in International Business Transactions became the supra-regional instrument in the fight against corruption.[16] Once the international awareness of foreign bribery had been raised, various international anti-corruption initiatives were launched,[17] e.g. the Council of Europe's (CoE) Criminal Law Convention on Corruption in 1998.[18] In 2003, three decades after the UN published its first rather reserved statement, quoted at the start of this chapter, the international development reached its peak with the adoption of the UNCAC.

11.2 Significance and Scope

Between 2003 and 2015, 140 countries signed the Convention and 176 became states parties.[19] Even the European Union signed (2005) and ratified (2008) the UNCAC. Only six states (Belize, Chad, Eritrea, Equatorial Guninea, North Korea, and Suriname) neither signed nor ratified the UNCAC. Still, two industrialized nations (Japan and New Zealand) have not yet ratified the Convention, lumping them in the same category as Barbados, Bhutan, and Syria. Nevertheless the UNCAC must be called the first truly global anti-corruption treaty.[20]

In contrast to other conventions, the UNCAC is not, and not even foremost, a criminal law convention. Rather, it goes further than the criminalization of corrupt acts and law enforcement (Articles 15 to 42), and includes substantive chapters on prevention,

[13] Cf. for the campaign of the US administration under President Bill Clinton, see Steven Salbu, 'Bribery in the global market: a critical analysis of the Foreign Corrupt Practices Act', (1997) 54 *Washington and Lee Law Review*, 230; Hotchkiss, 'The sleeping dog stirs', cited in note 7 above, p. 111.

[14] See http://www.oas.org/en/default.asp, accessed 18 September 2015.

[15] The OAS Convention is available at: http://www.oas.org/juridico/english/treaties/b-58.html, accessed 18 September 2015.

[16] On this, Kubiciel, 'Core criminal law provisions in UNCAC', cited in note 6 above, p. 140.

[17] For an overview of twenty-one anti-corruption legal instruments, see United Nations Office on Drugs and Crime (UNODC), *The Compendium of International Legal Instruments of Corruption*, 2nd edn, Vienna, 2005.

[18] Criminal Law Convention on Corruption, CM (98) 181/ETS No. 173, available at: http://conventions.coe.int/Treaty/en/Treaties/Html/173.htm, accessed 18 September 2015.

[19] Text of Convention available at: https://www.unodc.org/documents/treaties/UNCAC/Publications/Convention/08-50026_E.pdf, accessed 22 March 2016. UNCAC Signature and Ratification Status as of 1 April 2015, available at: https://www.unodc.org/unodc/en/treaties/CAC/signatories.html, accessed 18 September 2015.

[20] Antonio Argandoña, 'The United Nations Convention against Corruption and its impact on international companies', (2007) 74 *Journal of Business Ethics*, 481, p. 485; Wouters, Ryngaert, and Cloots, 'The international legal framework', cited in note 4 above, p. 216.

international cooperation, asset recovery, technical support, and exchange of information. Thus, the UNCAC is uniquely comprehensive.

This also holds to be true for the scope of criminalization. Since the UNCAC was drafted at a relatively late stage of the international development, its drafters could draw on the approaches of several other international conventions and enhance them.[21] As far as the chapter on criminalization is concerned, the UNCAC carries forward an international tendency of expanding the understanding of corrupt practices to be criminalized. While the OECD Convention had only focused on the active bribery of foreign public officials in international business transactions, the CoE Convention already included a wide range of criminal law provisions: active and passive bribery of domestic and foreign public officials, active and passive bribery of elected public officials, as well as bribery in the private sector, trading in influence, and money laundering. The UNCAC goes even further, as it also includes rather extraordinary provisions such as illicit enrichment, which was first to be found in Article IX OAS Convention and Article 8 African Union Convention on Preventing and Combating Corruption. As the UNCAC covers the broadest range of corruption offences, including obstruction of justice and embezzlement, it is the most comprehensive international anti-corruption convention to date.[22]

The Legislative Guide to the UNCAC points out that the causes of corruption are many and varied. For that reason 'preventive, enforcement and prosecutorial measures that work in some States may not work in others'.[23] Accordingly, the UNCAC includes both mandatory and non-mandatory provisions in order to grant states a margin of appreciation in implementing the UNCAC and adjusting its content to the domestic situation. More importantly, the distinction between mandatory and non-mandatory provisions reflects where a conceded international standard regarding culpability of behaviour exists and where it does not. Even in areas in which such consent does not exist among states the UNCAC does not abstain from submitting a legislative proposal, but rather includes non-mandatory provisions. Therefore, the Convention does not reflect the lowest common denominator but invites states parties to consider the criminalization of certain behaviours.[24]

In contrast to the chapter on preventive measures, which is predominantly phrased in non-mandatory terms, Chapter III includes several mandatory provisions on criminalization and law enforcement. They are 'the most urgent and basic part of a global and coordinated effort to counter corrupt practices'.[25] Of particular importance are the provisions on bribery of national public officials and active bribery of foreign

[21] Cf. Wouters, Ryngaert, and Cloots, 'The international legal framework', cited in note 4 above, p. 218, who refer to Art. 12 UNCAC, which requires tax deductibility of bribes to be prohibited; the OECD Convention on Bribery merely recommends prohibiting such deduction.

[22] OECD, *Corruption—A Glossary of International Standards in Criminal Law*, Paris, OECD Publishing, 2008, p. 14; Wouters, Ryngaert, and Cloots, 'The international legal framework', cited in note 4 above, p. 247: 'most elaborate and most detailed international anti-corruption instrument'.

[23] UNODC, *Legislative Guide for the Implementation of the United Nations Convention against Corruption*, 2nd rev. edn, Vienna, UNODC, 2012, p. V.

[24] Mark Pieth, 'Der Beitrag der UN Konvention zur Bekämpfung der transnationalen Korruption', in Tiziano Balmelli and Bernard Jaggy (eds), *Les traités internationaux contre la corruption*, 2004, p. 7, p. 8.

[25] UNODC, *Legislative Guide*, cited in note 23 above, p. 77, para. 178.

public officials.[26] Apart from them, the other mandatory criminal provisions cover embezzlement of property by a public official, money laundering, and obstruction of justice. Beside these, the UNCAC requires state parties to criminalize participation in corruption offences (Article 27). We also want to shine light on three especially interesting non-mandatory criminal measures, namely trading in influence (Article 18), abuse of functions (Article 19), and bribery in the private sector (Article 21).

11.3 Mandatory Criminal Law Provisions

11.3.1 Bribery of national public officials (Article 15)

11.3.1.1 Background

Article 15 relates to the classic form of corruption: the bribery of national public officials. The statute is no innovation in international law, since several previous regional anti-corruption conventions include equivalents,[27] as does the UN Convention Against Organized Transnational Crime. The criminalization of bribery of national public officials is of paramount importance as bribery in the public sector is limited neither to perverting a single decision nor to causing financial damage to public assets. In fact, bribery in the public sector can wreak havoc on the political architecture as such because it endangers the trust of people in the functioning of proceedings. Consequently, Article 15 includes a mandatory criminal provision, which refers both to the active and passive side of bribery. Article 15(a) refers to active bribery when it criminalizes the promising, offering, or giving of an undue advantage to a public official. Article 15(b) covers passive bribery in making the public official him- or herself who solicits or accepts the undue advantage a criminal. The extent of criminalization for which Article 15 provides can be demonstrated by the following, non-conclusive list of typical phenotypes of bribery of national public officials: facilitating advantages, payments to expedite processes ('speed money'), preventive bribes, procurement fraud, embezzling bribery, nepotism, and political corruption. Compared with several national criminal laws, which opt for a more narrow approach, Article 15 UNCAC facilitates the investigation, the adjudication, and the proof of corrupt behaviour substantially by using relatively wide terms.

11.3.1.2 Scope

Article 2 defines 'public official' as the central term of the statute. According to Article 2(a), a 'public official' encompasses any person holding a legislative, executive, administrative, or judicial office, whether appointed or elected, and—even wider—any person performing a public function. Thus, the Article covers people appointed to public office such as policemen, customs officers, members of the armed forces, judges, public prosecutors, and any other public servant. Moreover, where elected, persons

[26] Kubiciel, 'Core criminal law provisions in UNCAC', cited in note 6 above, p. 141.
[27] Cf. Arts 2 and 3 of the CoE Criminal Law Convention on Corruption.

such as members of parliaments, mayors, public prosecutors, or judges are subject to Article 15. Consequently, party states and their judiciaries have to ensure that the standard of Article 15 applies equally to 'ordinary' public officials and elected persons. Except where granted immunities (cf. Article 30 UNCAC), legal or judicial privileges for elected persons, for example special defences or restrictive interpretations of anti-bribery norms, are thus a violation of the UNCAC. The scope of Article 2(a), however, is even wider. It includes any person who performs a public function, e.g. persons working for a public agency or enterprise, or providing a public service. These people are public officials irrespective of their formal status. With this broad definition of the term 'public official' the UNCAC exceeds the scope of many national criminal codes,[28] as well as that of most of the other international anti-corruption conventions.[29] It reflects the fact that it is the actual power and influence, and not the formal status of an official, that enable corruption.[30]

The second term of central importance—'undue advantage'—is not defined in the UNCAC. Advantage is anything of value to the specific recipient, be it tangible or intangible. This includes, for example, the granting of a post, a career prospect, or a political position. Whether this advantage exceeds propriety and hence has to be called 'undue' depends, primarily, on the national laws. Consequently, every benefit, acceptance of which is allowed by national law, is not 'undue'.[31] In contrast, a benefit must be conceived as undue when the public official obtains a personal benefit. In between these two extreme positions, factors like value, frequency, and (lack of) transparency can serve as indicators for the question whether an advantage is 'undue' or not.[32]

The prohibited behaviour on the active side of bribery encompasses all stages from promising to giving. This comprehensive coverage of possible bribing actions includes unilateral announcement of or bilateral agreement on a future undue advantage (promise), the briber's signal of his or her willingness to grant an undue advantage at any time (offering), and the actual transfer of this benefit (giving). On the passive side, the prohibition covers the solicitation and acceptance of an undue advantage. Thus, a public official is not allowed to, explicitly or implicitly, give it to be understood that their official acts (or refraining from acting) are dependent on the conferment of an undue advantage. Requesting a bribe (solicitation) is an early stage of a corrupt behaviour and, thus, might be difficult to prove. In contrast, it is a lot

[28] For a comparative overview cf. Albin Eser and Michael Kubiciel, *Institutions Against Corruption*, Baden-Baden, Nomos, 2005, pp. 22–5.

[29] See Art. 1(a) CoE Convention on Corruption; Art. 1(c) CoE Convention on the Fight against Corruption; comparable to the scope of Art. 2 UNCAC are Art. 1(1) AU Convention on Preventing and Combating Corruption; Art. 1 OAS Inter-American Convention Against Corruption, and—concerning foreign public officials—Art. 1(4 a) OECD Convention on Combating Bribery.

[30] Eser and Kubiciel, *Institutions Against Corruption*, cited in note 28 above, p. 39; Kubiciel, 'Core criminal law provisions in UNCAC', cited in note 6 above, p. 143.

[31] Kubiciel, 'Core criminal law provisions in UNCAC', cited in note 6 above, p. 145.

[32] However, it is not clear from the wording whether advantages of very low value and socially accepted gifts should be criminalized. Both the EU and the OECD Convention strictly prohibit any advantage whatsoever. In contrast, the CoE Convention excludes 'minimum gifts, gifts of very low value and socially accepted gifts' from criminalization: see Explanatory Report to the Council of Europe's Criminal Law Convention on Corruption (ETS No. 173). Cf Kubiciel, 'Core criminal law provisions in UNCAC', cited in note 6 above, p. 145.

easier to establish the fact that the beneficiary entered into the possession of a bribe (acceptance). It is only necessary to prove that the bribe was related to performance within the beneficiary's sphere of action.[33] The public official's consent to this passing of the bribe might have been at any time. Therefore, if the public official subsequently failed to perform what had been agreed, this will not affect his or her criminal liability.[34]

Whether the briber or the bribed took action themself (directly) or through the use of an intermediary (indirectly), is of no significance for the criminal liability. In order to avoid any legal loopholes, the requirements regarding any intermediary have to be modest: The intermediary might be a natural person or a legal entity, and act in good or in bad faith. The main reason for Article 15 is to criminalize the abuse of public power for private interests; the question whose private interests are served is not of legal significance. Accordingly, any person or legal entity might be the beneficiary. However, the public official must be aware of the fact that the third person is given an advantage.

Article 15 uses the term 'in order that' to refer to an intention rather than to a completion. In other words, it criminalizes the promising, giving, soliciting, or accepting of a bribe with the specific intention that a public official will act or refrain from acting. Accordingly, the Convention does not require it to be proved if or when the act or omission of the public official took place. The mere intention to purchase an official behaviour is criminalized. Therefore, it is irrelevant whether the public official is actually able, competent, or at least willing to perform the official act or to refrain from acting.[35] This covers, for example, off-duty policemen soliciting bribes from speeders for refraining from further action against them.[36] The wording 'in order that' points towards a future act or omission by the official, and hence the Article does not encompass the situation in which an undue advantage is given or accepted after an act or omission by a public official has occurred without a previous offer or solicitation.

Finally, 'in the exercise of his or her official duties' does not require a breach of duty. In order to assure compliance with Article 15, states parties having bribery provisions that require a breach of duty could consider—in lieu of changing their laws—interpreting those clauses in such a way that the connection between an undue advantage and the public act or omission as such constitutes a breach of duty.

Both active and passive bribery require intention, which has to cover all other substantive elements of crime under Article 15. It is important to note that a fraudulent intention is not required. Article 28 specifies that the intent to commit an offence 'may be inferred from objective factual circumstances'. Thus, a perpetrator need not necessarily have knowledge of the specific legal designation as long as he or she has knowledge of the relevant facts and the general meaning of the legal term.

[33] Kubiciel, 'Core criminal law provisions in UNCAC', cited in note 6 above, p. 145.
[34] Ibid, p. 147. [35] Ibid, p. 149. [36] Ibid, p. 150.

11.3.2 Bribery of foreign public officials and officials of public international organisations (Article 16)

11.3.2.1 Background

As the UN had predicted as early as 1975, globalization of the economy in fact led to a globalization of white-collar crime.[37] Several scandals starting in the 1970s (e.g. Lockheed) and continuing to the present (e.g. Siemens) have shown that bribery of foreign public official has been—and remains—a widespread phenomenon, especially in international business transactions.[38] While some political scientists and economists argue that certain forms of corruption at least (e.g. facilitation payments) can be a 'not undue' instrument for opening closed markets and accelerating proceedings in slow bureaucracies,[39] international organisations regard transnational bribery as an obstacle to fair international competition and the economic and social development of the southern hemisphere.[40] Therefore, several precursors of the UNCAC included articles on bribery of foreign public officials. Most prominently, Article 1 OECD Convention on Combating Bribery of Foreign Public Officials in International Business Transactions asks states to criminalize active bribery of foreign public officials, when committed 'in order to obtain or retain business or other improper advantage in the conduct of international business'. According to that approach, states should tackle the 'supply side' of corruption, thereby reducing the influx of bribe money and benefiting international competition by 'levelling the playing field' for those enterprises competing on the world market.[41]

Article 6 CoE Criminal Law Convention opted for a wider approach. It prescribes that each party shall establish as criminal offences both active and passive bribery, when involving any person who is a member of any public assembly exercising legislative or administrative powers in any other state. Under that Article, states parties must criminalize any form of bribery of a public official, whether it has a connection to transnational business or not. The reason for that wide wording lies in the understanding of corruption as an obstacle to economic *and* social development. Accordingly, the CoE aims at safeguarding 'the confidence of citizens in the fairness of Public Administration which would be severely undermined, even if the official would have acted in the same way without the bribe'.[42]

Roughly speaking, the UNCAC follows the OECD approach, leaving the adoption of the wider CoE model to the discretion of states. Article 16 paragraph 1 is a mandatory provision opposing the active bribery of a foreign public official and of officials of public international organisations, done in order to obtain or retain business or

[37] Fifth UN Congress on the Prevention of Crime, cited in note 1 above.

[38] Cf. Pieth, 'Introduction', cited in note 3 above, pp. 8–16.

[39] Samuel Huntington, 'Modernization and corruption', in Arnold J. Heidenheimer and Michael Johnston (eds), *Political Corruption*, 3rd edn, New York, Transaction, 2009, p. 253. Also see Mushfiq Swaleheen and Dean Stansel, 'Economic freedom, corruption and growth', (2007) 27 *Cato Journal*, 343.

[40] Kubiciel, 'Core criminal law provisions in UNCAC', cited in note 6 above, p. 150; Pieth, 'Der Beitrag der UN Konvention', cited in note 24 above. Also see the preambles of both the OCED Convention and the UNCAC.

[41] Pieth, 'Introduction', cited in note 3 above, pp. 30–31.

[42] Explanatory Report, cited in note 32 above, para. 39.

any undue advantage in relation to the conduct of international business. For good reasons, Article 16 paragraph 2, which attacks the passive side of corruption, is non-mandatory.[43] First of all, criminalizing and penalizing a corrupt public official makes this a unique provision, since states used to impose duties solely on their own public officials. Consequently, no international standard or consents govern whether or not foreign public officials may be criminalized, and, if so, to what extent. Second, criminalizing and penalizing foreign public officials may interfere with the principle of sovereign equality of states and the principle of non-intervention, both provided for by Article 4. In fact, the protection of its institutions and proceedings falls within the *domaine réservé* of each state.

As long as a state can claim jurisdiction on the basis of international law, neither criminalizing its officials nor the enforcement of transnational bribery legislation violates the principles of sovereign equality and non-intervention. Under Article 42(1)(a), a state party has jurisdiction when the offence established in accordance with Article 16 was committed within its territory. Moreover, Article 42(2)(b) provides jurisdiction on the basis of the principle of nationality. Article 42(3) grants jurisdiction where an alleged offender is present within the state party's territory and the state party does not extradite solely on the ground that the offender in question is one of its own nationals.

11.3.2.2 Scope

Unlike other conventions, which leave the definition of foreign public officials to the states concerned, Article 2 describes a foreign public official as any 'person holding a legislative, executive, administrative or judicial office of a foreign country, whether appointed or elected', or a 'person exercising a public function for a foreign country, including for a public agency or public enterprise'. Hence, Article 2 provides an autonomous definition of the foreign public official.[44] Therefore, criminalizing foreign bribery does not depend on the classification of the accused by the employing state.

As the importance of international organisations increases constantly, the proceedings within these structures have to be safeguarded against corruption too, in particular when it comes to the funding of major development projects.[45] Article 2(c) defines an official of a public international organisation 'an international civil servant or any person who is authorised by such an organisation to act on behalf of that organisation'. An employment relationship with the organisation is not necessary.[46] 'Public international organisations' are international organisations established by states, governments, or other public international organisations, regardless of their legal form and remit.[47] The term encompasses both classic international organisation and supra-national organisations like the European Union.[48] Whether the state party

[43] Argandoña, 'UNCAC and its impact on international companies', cited in note 20 above, p. 490, criticizes this, seeing a limitation of the UNCAC's effectiveness.
[44] Pieth, 'Der Beitrag der UN Konvention', cited in note 24 above.
[45] Kubiciel, 'Core criminal law provisions in UNCAC', cited in note 6 above, p. 151.
[46] Ibid, p. 152. [47] Ibid, p. 152. [48] Ibid, p. 152.

is a member of the relevant international organisation or not, is not relevant;[49] therefore, a state may even criminalize active or passive bribery within international organisations that it has not joined so far.

Deciding whether an advantage is 'undue' can already be difficult within one jurisdiction. The task becomes even more difficult when the advantage was granted or accepted abroad and hence within different legal and socio-cultural scaffolding. The UNCAC reflects that concern, as it does not specify what has to be considered corrupt, and hence leaves space for interpretation.[50] These judgements must be made by national courts applying criminal law statutes on bribery of foreign public officials, which means that they are not bound by foreign laws and social customs.[51] The mere reference to a 'tradition of gift' does not constitute a defence per se. Instead, courts have to evaluate carefully whether an alleged tradition exists and whether the behaviour matches the tradition. With regard to this, it has to be stressed that one cannot call any widespread behaviour a tradition, since the latter implies the notion of social acceptance. For example, requesting 'commissions' may be widespread in many African countries; behaviour of that kind, however, is not part of any country's 'tradition'. But even if the granting of an advantage is in line with an existing tradition, social contingencies of this kind can be subject to the evaluation whether they are capable of damaging public confidence in the functioning of public services and state proceedings. Aspects like value, frequency, temporal closeness to an official act, lack of transparency, failure to disclose or register can serve as evidence of 'undue' character. Against this background, only the granting or accepting of advantages having a very low value may be exempted from criminalization or adjudication, if such small donations are socially accepted.

Article 16 relates solely to bribes that are granted or accepted in order to obtain or retain business or any other undue advantage in relation to the conduct of international business. This requirement excludes bribery committed for mere private purposes and hence limits the scope of criminalization significantly,[52] although the term 'business' can be understood in a broad sense, covering all commercial activities regardless of their nature.[53] The limitation does not correspond well to the purpose of the UNCAC, which addresses the 'threats posed by corruption to the stability and security of societies, undermining the institutions and values of democracy, ethical values and justice and jeopardizing sustainable development and the rule of law'.[54] As corruption undermines institutions irrespective of their (commercial) context, the wider approach of the CoE Criminal Law Convention would have been preferable, given the ambitions of the UNCAC. For this reason, facilitation payments,[55] which can affect the stability

[49] Ibid, p. 152.

[50] Wouters, Ryngaert, and Cloots, 'The international legal framework', cited in note 4 above, p. 241.

[51] Kubiciel, 'Core criminal law provisions in UNCAC', cited in note 6 above, p. 153.

[52] Ibid, p. 153. [53] Ibid, p. 153. [54] UNCAC, Preamble.

[55] On this term Antonio Argandoña, 'Corruption and companies: the use of facilitating payments', (2005) 60 *Journal of Business Ethics*, 251; Robert Bailes, 'Facilitation payments: culturally acceptable or unacceptably corrupt?', (2006) 15 *Business Ethics: A European Review*, 293; Stuart Deming, *The Foreign Corrupt Practices Act And the New International Norms*, Washington DC, American Bar Association, 2005, p. 15ff.

and integrity of institutions, should not be exempted from criminalization, even if they do not have the potential to hamper competition and hence provide an undue advantage related to business transactions in the circumstances of a concrete case.[56]

11.3.3 Embezzlement of property by a public official (Article 17)

11.3.3.1 Background

The UNCAC does not define the blurry term 'corruption', nor do other conventions explicate their underlying conception of corrupt behaviour.[57] The criminalization of embezzlement, however, suggests that the UNCAC presupposes a broad definition that is not limited to offering or soliciting an undue advantage to improperly influence the actions of a public official, but also encompasses any abuse of public office for private benefit. As the embezzlement or the misappropriation of public assets themselves can threaten the stability of societies by undermining the institutions and the values of democracy, the criminalization of embezzlement is in line with the general aims of the UNCAC mentioned in its Preamble. Accordingly, Article 17 aims at creating, enhancing, and maintaining good governance among public officials. In contrast, Article 22 targets embezzlement in the private sector as a non-mandatory provision. Notwithstanding, states should implement Article 22, since the border between the private and public sectors can sometimes be winding and unclear, especially after a phase of privatization and outsourcing. Not implementing comprehensive legislation that tackles embezzlement in all sectors could prove to be an obstacle to an effective fight against corruption.[58]

Article 17 does not have an exact equivalent in other anti-corruption conventions.[59] Article 4(d) African Union Convention on Preventing and Combating Corruption is comparable, since it tackles 'the diversion by a public official or any other person, for purposes unrelated to those for which they were intended, for his or her own benefit or that of a third party, of any property belonging to the state or its agencies, to an independent agency, or to an individual, that such official has received by virtue of his or her position'. In comparison, Article 17 UNCAC is broader in scope,[60] making it one of the Convention's legal innovations. The provision requires states to criminalize the embezzlement, misappropriation, or other diversion, by a public official for his or her own benefit or for the benefit of another person or entity, of any property, public or private funds or securities, or any other thing of value entrusted to the public official by virtue of his or her position. Even though Article 17 is a mandatory provision,

[56] Michael Kubiciel, 'Facilitation payments: a crime?', Cologne Papers on Criminal Law Policy 2/2015, Cologne, Institute for Criminal Law and Criminal Procedure, 3, pp. 7–8. Also see Wouters, Ryngaert, and Cloots, 'The international legal framework', cited in note 4 above, p. 240.

[57] For the breadth of the term cf. Wouters, Ryngaert, and Cloots, 'The international legal framework', cited in note 4 above, p. 238. Also see Eser and Kubiciel, *Institutions Against Corruption*, cited in note 28 above, pp. 20–21.

[58] Argandoña, 'UNCAC and its impact on international companies', cited in note 20 above, p. 490.

[59] Ibid, p. 489.

[60] Cf. Rajesh Babu, *The United Nations Convention Against Corruption*, 2006, pp. 1 and 11, available at: http://papers.ssrn.com/sol3/papers.cfm?abstract_id=891898, accessed 2 March 2016.

most states parties do not require new legislation, as functionally equivalent offences are widespread. These norms either explicitly designate the offence as embezzlement or include the conduct in the offences of theft, fraudulent conversion, or fraudulent misappropriation.

11.3.3.2 Scope

The scope of Article 17 is wide. It covers the public official who diverts public assets by allowing a contractor to charge an excessive price to the account of his public enterprise, in order to obtain or retain (parts of) the overcharge. The shift of values might benefit public officials themselves, any another person, or an entity. The latter term is to be understood widely, covering private companies and political parties, since the Article does not speak, for example, of 'legal person' or 'private legal entity'. Thus, a public official who unlawfully grants state subsidies to a political party has to be penalized in accordance with the UNCAC. States must provide for criminal law statutes to be applicable to an elected public official, e.g. a city mayor, who has misused tax funds by investing in a project that was doubtful from its beginning. Thus, Article 17 does not allow for political decisions to be generally exempted from criminal sanction.

The Article highlights the examples of funds and securities, thereby reflecting the fact that public officials might not just work in traditional areas of the public service, but perform public functions within institutions administering, for example, public health-care, pension funds, or securities markets. Article 17 does not cover solely the embezzlement of public property, even though this is its main field of application, but also the embezzlement of property, belonging to a private person. The Article 17 requires only that this public official has access to the embezzled property by virtue of their position. So, police officers who divert assets they have seized in the flat of a suspect must be held liable.

The central element of the provision is not the embezzlement, misappropriation, or other diversion, since the Article applies no matter how the public official has diverted alien property; nor is it the property, since under Article 2(d) assets of every kind can be the object of the offence. The crucial element is the normative link between the public official and the property: it must have been entrusted to the public official by virtue of their position. These duties may arise from statutory or case law, legal agreement between the owner and the public official or his/her employing institution, or internal regulations or instructions.

11.3.4 Laundering of the proceeds of crime (Article 23)

11.3.4.1 Background

The UNCAC tackles various forms of laundering (Article 23) and concealing (Article 24) of property that has been derived from acts of corruption.[61] This is of particular importance, since money laundering and concealment are typical by-products of

[61] Babu, *The UNCAC*, cited in note 60 above, p. 13.

corruption, especially as the globalized financial system facilitates capital movements all over the world. Thus, legal disparities between various countries can be exploited in order to hide and legitimize the proceeds of crime.[62] The UN stated in 1975 that 'it can be taken [as] axiomatic that until the regulation of business and financial activities is reasonabl[y] uniform, crime will flow to those countries having the least effective regulation'.[63] Not just crime but also illegal property will flow to such safe havens. To prevent transnational money laundering, international cooperation is crucial. Article 24 deals with the 'concealment or continued retention' of property derived from corrupt activities. States are required to consider criminalizing concealment, when the person involved knows that such property is the result of any of the offences established under the Convention. While Article 24 is non-mandatory, states are obliged to implement the provision on money laundering (Article 23). Both Articles form part of a group of provisions aiming at a similar objective, which includes Article 31 (freezing, seizure, and confiscation of proceeds) and Chapter V (asset recovery).[64]

11.3.4.2 Scope

In order to criminalize money laundering comprehensively, Article 23 provides for a large variety of predicate offences.[65] Moreover, states are obliged to establish four offences as crimes: conversion or transfer of proceeds of crime (Article 23(1)(a)(i)), concealment or disguise of proceeds of crime (Article 23(1)(a)(ii)), acquisition, possession, or use of proceeds of crime (Article 23(1)(b)(i)), and participation in, association with, or conspiracy to commit, attempt to commit, or aid, abet, facilitate, or counsel the commission of, any of the foregoing offences (Article 23(1)(b)(ii)). While states must establish the first two offences as a crime under any circumstances, the establishment of the last two offences is subject to the basic concepts of their legal systems.

11.3.5 Obstruction of justice (Article 25)

11.3.5.1 Background

Simply criminalizing corruption offences in accordance with the UNCAC is insufficient if states parties do not safeguard those persons who obtain crucial roles within proceedings related to the commission of these offences. A consequent enforcement of the anti-corruption norms of the Convention requires the protection of witnesses, victims, and justice and law enforcement officials. Criminalizing the obstruction of justice supports the judicial enforcement of other corruption offences by flanking Article 32, which deals with the protection of witnesses, experts, and victims. In fact, Article 25 itself lays down an offence relating to corruptive behaviour, as it covers the exertion of undue influence on proceedings by means of undue advantages as well as

[62] UNODC, *Legislative Guide*, cited in note 23 above, p. 69, para. 221.
[63] Fifth UN Congress on the Prevention of Crime, cited in note 1 above, p. 15, para. 31.
[64] UNODC, *Legislative Guide*, cited in note 23 above, p. 70ff., para. 228.
[65] This—according to Article 2(h)—means 'any offence as a result of which proceeds have been generated that may become the subject of an offence as defined in article 23 of this Convention'.

physical force, threats, or intimidation. In both dimensions the Article serves the purposes of the Convention as expressed in the Preamble: the protection of the institutions, ethical values, justice, and the rule of law.[66]

Article 25 is a mandatory provision encompassing two types of obstruction of justice. Paragraph 1 relates to efforts to influence potential witnesses, victims, and other persons who can produce testimony in order to provide the authorities with relevant evidence. It encompasses the use of both corrupt means (bribery) and coercive means, such as the use or threat of violence. In contrast, the second offence stated in paragraph 2 only addresses justice and law enforcement officials and it refers solely to the use of physical force, threats, or intimidation. The bribery element is not included in paragraph 2 because this behaviour is already covered by Article 15(1), since justice and law enforcement officials are considered to be public officials (cf. Article 2(a)).

11.3.5.2 Scope

The 'use of physical force, threats, or intimidation' can be understood in its broadest sense. Even the use of a legal instrument such as filing a lawsuit can create a threat or intimidation and has to be penalized if it is used to induce false testimony. Hence, the focus of Article 25(1) lies on the purpose of the act, not on the act itself. Comparably, paragraph 2 primarily tackles a mere intention. Consequently, the intended outcome—the false testimony or the interference—must not be achieved. Rather, the offence is completed simply by the use of a threat or intimidation as long as this has been done with the purpose of inducing false testimony, or interfering with the giving of testimony or the production of evidence in a proceeding.

For the purpose of ensuring substantial protection of proceedings relevant to corruption crimes, states parties must consider interpreting the term 'proceeding' in a broad sense covering all official governmental proceedings, including non-criminal proceedings such as administrative or civil activity, for example extradition proceedings, the recovery of assets, and compensation for damage. In order to protect proceedings comprehensively, it also makes sense to have a broad understanding of the term 'evidence'. For the same reason, it is preferable to interpret the phrase 'interfere with the exercise of official duties' in its widest sense, generally covering any interference whatsoever. The fundamental goals of the Convention are to enhance an impartial and law-abiding exercise of the duties of public officials. This, of course, is of particular importance in the most sensitive context of the judicial enforcement of corruption offences.

[66] UNCAC, Preamble; also see UN GA Res. 58/4 of 31 October 2003, para. 9; criminalizing obstruction of justice is an important tool in the fight against organised crime as a form of crime that is often linked to corruption. For this reason, the offence is also included in the UN's Covention Against Transnational Organized Crime, Art. 23.

11.4 Non-Mandatory Criminal Law Provisions

11.4.1 Trading in influence (Article 18)

11.4.1.1 Background

Article 18 introduces, albeit as a non-mandatory provision, a remedy for a major corruption evil: trading in influence. Generally speaking, trading in influence is the purchase of any influence that a public official or any other person claims to have with a view to obtaining an undue advantage over an administrative or public authority. It can be described as 'background corruption'. Many national criminal law codes do not treat trading in influence as an offence; rather, they try to tackle that sort of behaviour through statutes prohibiting participation in core corruption offences like bribery. The typical constellation for this offence is a trilateral relationship, in which A offers an undue advantage to B (a public official or other person), so that B will abuse his or her real or supposed influence on another person, C, with a view to obtaining from an administration or public authority of the state party an undue advantage for A or for another person. Disrupting these unfair 'client–patron networks', which regularly interlace high-ranking officials and politicians, is the aim of Article 18. This being said, the reason for criminalizing this behaviour is similar to that for establishing other corruption offences such as bribery: to guarantee transparent and impartial decision-making processes in order to provide for the necessary reliance of the public on proceedings as a foundation of societies. In fact, it could be argued that without remedies for trading in influence it is unlikely that a jurisdiction will be able to effectively combat high-level corruption.

11.4.1.2 Scope

Article 18 covers both forms of trading in influence: Article 18(a) requires 'active' trading in influence to be criminalized, while Article 18(b) covers 'passive' trading in influence. Article 18 adopts several terms from other articles, such as 'public official', 'promise, offering, giving', 'solicitation or acceptance', 'directly or indirectly', and 'undue advantage' (although this term is not defined here, either).

The Article's phrase 'in order that the public official or the person abuse his or her real or supposed influence' covers the essence of trading in influence. In the 'triangle' that we described in 11.4.1.1 above, a second person, B, whether public official or not, has to claim influence over an administration, or a public official in the administration, C. It is not necessary to prove that the person in fact possesses the claimed influence because Article 18 covers fraudulent claims of influence, too. Neither do the law enforcement agencies have to give evidence that the influence actually has been exerted as the phrase 'in order to' reveals that a mere proposal to abuse the influence is sufficient. The phrase, therefore, already covers the intent and does not require the desired result to be achieved.

The word 'abuse' introduces a normative element. Thereby, the Article reveals that 'not undue' forms of influence, such as political lobbying or orders within an organisational hierarchy, are generally not covered by the offence of trading in influence. States parties may regard it as an 'abuse' for a person to use their influence in a way that is legal per se, but with a view to an undue advantage.

'With a view to obtaining an undue advantage from an administration or public authority' also points towards an intention rather than to an outcome. Whether the undue advantage has in fact been obtained or not, is irrelevant; in this respect, Article 18 differs from Articles 15 and 16. Second, the phrase does not refer to the 'undue advantage' of the person claiming to have influence, but to the advantage that the instigator wants to obtain. In this regard, the offence parallels the behaviour of the public official described in the bribery offences.[67]

11.4.2 Abuse of functions (Article 19)

11.4.2.1 Background

In order to protect the stability of society by safeguarding its institutions, its values, and the rule of law, special attention has to be paid to public officials who have particular duties in relation to the general public. Accordingly, nations throughout the world have implemented legislation regulating the duties of their public officials. These efforts have been motivated and enhanced by international model codes such as the United Nations International Code of Conduct for Public Officials (see Article 8 UNCAC). These means help to enhance the ethical climate in the public sector and to inform the public about what to expect of public servants.

The abuse of functions is an offence that comprises public officials' most essential breaches of duty. The non-mandatory Article 19 complements the core corruption offences, such as bribery, with the overall objective of providing a comprehensive criminalization of corrupt behaviour.

11.4.2.2 Scope

Article 19 criminalizes an abuse by a public official in the discharge of his or her functions for the purpose of obtaining an undue advantage for themself or for another person or entity. Again, the Article uses several terms from Article 15.

Unlike Article 18, Article 19 specifies 'abuse of functions or position' as 'the performance of or failure to perform an act, in violation of laws'. This means that a mere breach of an employment contract, or of an informal code of ethics, which has not been enacted as law, falls outside the scope of Article 19. In this respect, Article 19 differs from 'breach of duties' in the private sector as described in Article 21. Various ways in which a public official might violate the laws exist: Article 19 covers cases in which the public official is not entitled to act or refrain from acting (at all or in a specific manner) as well as cases in which an illegal outcome is produced.

[67] 'Undue advantage' has already been described in this context; see section 11.3.1.2 of this chapter.

States parties may consider clarifying that the abuse of functions and the violation of laws have to be committed in the discharge of the public official's functions. Thus, a violation of a law that does not have any connection with the position or the function of the public official falls outside of the scope of Article 19.

The phrase 'for the purpose of obtaining an undue advantage' indicates that Article 19 applies to cases in which the public official performs, or fails to perform, in violation of the laws *before* obtaining an undue advantage. This means that the phrase covers an intention rather than an outcome. Moreover, it reveals that Article 19 is intended to close a legal loophole in Article 15, since the latter does not prescribe the penalizing of situations in which an undue advantage is obtained *after* the official's act unless the undue advantage has been offered, promised, or solicited. Comprehensive legislation, however, requires the prohibition of misconduct by a public official that occurs for the purpose of obtaining an undue advantage. Proactive behaviour of public officials for the purpose of obtaining advantages has the potential to endanger the impartiality of proceedings and undermine public trust in the lawful exercise of duties.

11.4.3 Article 21: bribery in the private sector

11.4.3.1 Background

Article 21 is based on the insight that corruption in the private sector is not simply a matter of interpersonal relationships and therefore suitable for regulation by civil or commercial law, but endangers society as a whole: it undermines fair competition and hence is an obstacle to the economic development of a society. Corruption cannot be limited to particular sectors of a given society. In fact, flourishing corruption within the private sector will pervert the public sector as well. In addition, since business and competition are to be understood as processes of coordinating private, economic, and financial interests, corruption in the private sector harms the reliance of market participants on the functioning of these processes. Finally, corruption in the private sector is a threat to a law-abiding society since it undermines common values and standards of 'due' behaviour. In short, since corruption in the public and private sectors evinces similar elements and causes comparable results, criminalization of bribery in the private sector is an essential tool in the fight against corruption. This makes Article 21 one of the most important non-mandatory criminal provisions of the UNCAC.

11.4.3.2 Scope

The Article mirrors both active and passive bribery as described in Article 15 with regard to the public sector. Thus, the conditions for penalty are largely identical to those in Article 15. Attention has to be paid to two differences: Article 21 clarifies that the criminalized conduct has to take place 'in the course of economic, financial or commercial activities', and moreover, that the person has to act or refrain from acting 'in breach of his or her duties'.

The key issue in making bribery in the private sector a crime is the demarcation of delicate advantages in a business context and harmless presents in a personal context. In this regard it is necessary for the behaviour to be embedded 'in the course of economic, financial, or commercial activities', even if a personal component existed. Thus, only the sphere of purely personal and private relations is excluded from criminalization.

The Article addresses any 'person who directs or works, in any capacity, for a private sector entity'. Hence it implies a functional, not a formalistic, status-oriented understanding: it indicates that employment at or another form of contract with the private sector entity is not essential. Even external personnel, such as lawyers and consultants, can be subject to any legislation based on Article 21. The 'private sector entity' need not take any specific legal form. Thus, a one-person business can be regarded as an 'entity'. The term 'private' is the most important word in this phrase as it excludes entities under public law.

The act of the decision maker must breach their duties. These duties might arise from a variety of legal sources: first, statutory law sets a framework for private business and imposes general obligations on the actors. Second, these general statutory obligations are accompanied by specific duties and particular business goals constituted by contracts, instructions, or internal regulatory frameworks such as private codes of ethics. Finally, where no written norms exist, law enforcement bodies and courts have to evaluate whether the conduct complies with good faith as practised within the entity.

11.5 Review Mechanism and Implementation

Implementation always marks a Convention's actual trial by fire. This also holds true for the UNCAC. Thus, it is of value to have a look at the way the Convention aims to assist its own implementation as well as the actual results achieved. Chapter VI deals with 'Technical assistance and information exchange'. According to its Article 60, states parties shall initiate, develop, or improve specific training programmes for personnel responsible for preventing and combating corruption. Article 62 places the states parties under the obligation to collect, exchange, and analyse information on corruption within their territory. In particular, they must consider monitoring their policies and actual measures to combat corruption and making assessments of the effectiveness and efficiency of these (paragraph 3).

Article 63 in Chapter VII 'Mechanisms for implementation' goes beyond this self-assessment by changing the perspective. Paragraph 1 established the UNCAC's Conference of the States Parties especially for the purpose of promoting and reviewing implementation of the Convention. Paragraph 7 puts this in concrete terms by allowing the Conference to establish a mechanism or body to assist in the effective implementation of the UNCAC. The regulation in Article 63 was peculiar because earlier experiences (with the CoE, the EU, OECD) showed that a strict monitoring procedure would be crucial for ratification and enforcement.[68] Only in 2009 did the

[68] Pieth, 'Der Beitrag der UN Konvention', cited in note 24 above, p. 18.

Conference finally instal a review mechanism.[69] By then, some regimes had already misused the Convention rhetorically in favour of their corrupt elites.[70] Studies point to the 'weaknesses of the UNCAC' and reveal that the political will to fully implement the UNCAC is still lacking in those countries with a long history of political and grand corruption.[71] These countries ratified the UNCAC and had a sufficient legal and institutional framework—but they failed to enforce the Convention's rules properly.[72] The corrupt regimes are unlikely to turn in their leaders.[73] Also, some internal reviews made recommendations not specifically tailored to the political realities but remained vague regarding difficult topics.[74] All these circumstances give cause to fear that the UNCAC runs the risk of remaining in a vacuum.

These observations show again that legal norms have to grow alongside social moral standards,[75] and must keep in touch with social realities.[76] The decision to establish the UNCAC was, indeed, a major step in the fight against corruption. So far, it remains the peak of global anti-corruption development. It is now necessary to climb the next, and even higher, mountain: the thorough, successful implementation of these laws. In this context, a great deal of work remains to be done.

[69] Resolution 3/1, available at: https://www.unodc.org/documents/treaties/UNCAC/COSP/session3/V1051985e.pdf, accessed 18 September 2015, printed version: UNODC (ed.), 'Mechanism for the review of implementation of the United Nations Convention against Corruption—basic documents', Vienna, UNODC, 2011, p. iiiff.; on the development of the review mechanism, see 'Report of the Secretary, Work of the Open-ended Intergovernmental Working Group on Review of the Implementation of the United Nations Convention against Corruption', UN Doc. CAC/COSP/2009/2, available at: https://www.unodc.org/documents/treaties/UNCAC/COSP/session3/V0986556e.pdf, accessed 18 September 2015.

[70] Just as Pieth had feared in 2004, 'Der Beitrag der UN Konvention', cited in note 24 above, p. 18.

[71] Hannes Hechler, Gretta Zinkernagel, Lucy Koechlin, and Dominic Morris, *Can UNCAC address grand corruption?—A political analysis of the UN Convention against Corruption and its implementation in three countries*, U4-Report, Bergen, Norway, U4 Anti-Corruption Resource Centre, 2011, p. 2, available at: http://www.u4.no/publications/can-uncac-address-grand-corruption, accessed 18 September 2015/; Tim Daniel and James Maton, 'Is the UNCAC an effective deterrent to grand corruption?', in Jeremy Horder and Peter Alldridge (eds), *Modern Bribery Law—Comparative Perspectives*, 2013, p. 293, p. 305.

[72] Hechler *et al.*, ibid, p. 20.

[73] Daniel and Maton, 'Is the UNCAC effective?', cited in note 71 above, pp. 316ff and 322.

[74] Hechler *et al.*, *Can UNCAC address grand corruption?*, cited in note 71 above, p. 20: 'for example, while the Indonesia and Bangladesh gap analyses acknowledge the problem of enforcement caused by weak judiciaries, they make vague recommendations or none at all about how to remedy this'.

[75] Cornelia Rink, '*Leges sine moribus vanae*', (2016) 17 *German Law Journal* 19.

[76] Kubiciel, 'Core criminal law provisions in UNCAC', cited in note 6 above, p. 155.

PART III

OTHER RELEVANT INTERNATIONAL REGIMES AND ISSUES

12

Transnational Organised Crime and the Anti-Money Laundering Regime

Louis de Koker and Mark Turkington

12.1 Introduction

Since the late 1980s the global community has embraced money laundering control as a means to combat especially organised crime. This chapter reviews the development of the global standards framework relating to money laundering control and the key elements of the anti-money laundering (AML) strategy before closing with perspectives on the effectiveness of this strategy.

In 2001 money laundering control became fused with the combating of financing of terrorism (CFT).[1] Although money laundering and terrorism financing are linked in the global standards and in practice, they are conceptually very different. For example, while money laundering acts can only be committed in respect of proceeds of crime, terrorism can also be funded with legitimately obtained funds.[2] This chapter focuses on money laundering but refers to financing of terrorism where relevant.

12.2 The Money Laundering Concept

The concept of money laundering is defined in a range of ways. Busuioc for example describes money laundering as the process of 'disguising the unlawful source of criminally derived funds to make them appear legal'.[3] Cuellar uses a definition that has two components: first, the money is converted 'into a more desirable medium i.e. a bank balance or equity in a company'; then follows a process to remove or 'erase' its more obvious links to crime.[4] Gilmore describes the laundering of drug money as having three common elements: first, the dealers must conceal the ownership of the funds; second, they must control the flow of funds; and finally, they must change the form of the asset.[5] These factors are evident in the formal definition of the money laundering offence found in the 1988 United Nations Convention Against Illicit Traffic in Narcotics Drugs

[1] Financial Action Task Force, *Annual Report 2001–2002*, FATF, 2002, paras 16–30.

[2] Financial Action Task Force, 'Terrorist financing', FATF, 2008, p. 11.

[3] Elena Madalina Busuioc, 'Defining money laundering', in Brigitte Unger (ed.), *The Scale and Impacts of Money Laundering*, Camberley, Edward Elgar, 2007, p. 15.

[4] Mariano-Florentino Cuellar, 'The tenuous relationship between the fight against money laundering and the disruption of criminal finance', (2002) 93 *JCLC* (2–3), 311, p. 324.

[5] William C. Gilmore, *International Efforts to Combat Money Laundering, Cambridge International Documents* Series Vol. 4, Cambridge, Grotius Publications, 1992, p. x.

and Psychotropic Substances (the Vienna Convention),[6] which requires states parties to criminalize acts to conceal or disguise relevant facts relating to illicit property.[7]

Money laundering is often described as occurring in three stages.[8] The first is where the criminal funds enter the financial system. This *placement* stage can take many forms, although initial concerns dealt with drug money from organised crime, and the depositing or placing of large volumes of cash into the financial system. The second *layering* stage is where criminal funds are converted to appear legitimate while disguising both their origin and ownership. *Integration* is the final stage where funds or assets are accessed and controlled by their criminal owners and are effectively integrated into the mainstream financial system.

The three-stage analysis of money laundering, it is submitted, is of limited value. While these stages may be identifiable in a complex money laundering scheme, they cannot be identified in all schemes. Sometimes cash proceeds are deposited in a bank account and then spent to fund the lifestyle of the criminal. While the depositing and spending of the funds would generally constitute money laundering offences under the national law, it is not easy to fit such spending into layering and integration phases. The stages analysis, of course, also focuses on the formal financial system as placement is absent when criminal proceeds in cash are simply spent in cash without actually entering the formal financial system—a reality of the criminal economy.

12.3 The Global Anti-Money Laundering Framework

12.3.1 The development of international standards

The 1960s and 1970s saw a rise in drug trafficking across many nations. This escalation in criminal activity resulted in a corresponding increase in illicit funds accessing the financial system.[9] An organised trafficking operation for instance could accumulate literally tons of physical currency in small notes each month that somehow needed to be converted into legitimate assets.[10] By the 1970s, the entry of drug-related cash into the financial system was recognized as an international concern—and a crime combating opportunity—that would require collaborative, transnational efforts to address.[11] It is at this point that the origins of an international AML regime can be observed.[12]

[6] United Nations Convention Against Illicit Traffic in Narcotic Drugs and Psychotropic Substances (Vienna, adopted 20 December 1988, entered into force 11 November 1990) 1582 UNTS 95 (Vienna Convention).

[7] Ibid, Art. 3.

[8] The Financial Action Task Force uses these stages in their definitions of 'money laundering'. See Financial Action Task Force, 'Frequently asked questions', available at: http://www.fatf-gafi.org/pages/faq/moneylaundering/#d.en.11223, accessed 24 June 2015.

[9] Peter H. Smith, 'The political economy of drugs: conceptual issues and policy options', in Peter H. Smith (ed.), *Drug Policy in the Americas*, Boulder, Colorado, Westview Press, 1992; Peter Reuter and Edwin M. Truman, *Chasing Dirty Money: The Fight Against Money Laundering*, Washington DC, Institute for International Economics, 2004, p. 41.

[10] Smith, 'The political economy of drugs', cited in note 9 above, p. 11.

[11] Gilmore, *International Efforts*, cited in note 5 above, pp. ix–xix; William C. Gilmore, *Dirty Money*, 3rd edn, Geneva, Council of Europe, 2004, p. 51.

[12] Barry Rider, 'Taking the profit out of crime', in Barry Rider (ed.), *Money Laundering Control*, Dublin, Round Hall Sweet and Maxwell, 1996, p. 1.

The adoption of international Conventions and other agreements restricting the manufacture and sale of illicit drugs reaches back to the 1912 International Opium Convention.[13] Since 1945 the United Nations has taken a lead in addressing the problem on the international front. One aspect of the United Nations strategy had been to target the supply side of the illicit drugs trade from growth and production through to distribution. The 1961 Single United Nations Convention on Narcotic Drugs (as amended by the 1972 Protocol),[14] and the 1971 United Nations Convention on Psychotropic Substances are examples of supply-side-focused actions taken by the international community to control and address the drug problem.[15] The economic theory behind this strategy assumed that a reduction in the supply of a product would correspond to an increase in prices, creating a consequent reduction in demand.[16] This had been a long-standing driver of policy and is an important assumption as it underpins much of the subsequent activity in this area.[17]

The United Nations, however, recognized that existing instruments were inadequate for supply-side control and that more needed to be done.[18] In 1985, the United Nations General Assembly therefore commenced drafting a new Convention. Experts supported the drafting of provisions aimed at reducing both the supply and demand for illicit substances through a combination of initiatives, including targeting the financial operations of those organised crime groups responsible for drug production and distribution, to disrupt the drug supply networks.[19] The new 'going after the money' strategy would not only be aimed at disrupting the criminal business model but also strengthen deterrence of and punishment for organised criminals.[20]

The drafters were not grappling with the proceeds of crime provisions in isolation. By 1986, both the United States and the United Kingdom had adopted legislation targeting the processing of criminal funds,[21] which at this stage was closely associated with the trade in illicit substances. By the late 1980s, the United Nations had released

[13] Convention Relating to the Suppression of the Abuse of Opium and Other Drugs, The Hague, 23 January 1912, 38 Stat 1912, TS No. 612, 1 Bevans 855, 8 LNTS 187. See David Stewart, 'Internationalizing the war on drugs: the UN Convention against Illicit Traffic in Narcotic Drugs and Psychotropic Substances', (1989) 18 *Denver Journal of International Law and Policy* 387, p. 388; Jack Donnelly, 'The United Nations and the global drug control regime', in Smith, *Drug Policy in the Americas*, cited in note 9 above, pp. 284–5.

[14] Single Convention on Narcotic Drugs, New York, adopted 30 March 1961, entered into force 13 December 1964, 520 UNTS 151. Protocol Amending the Single Convention on Narcotic Drugs, 1961 (Geneva adopted 25 March 1972, entered into force 8 August 1975) 976 UNTS 3.

[15] Convention on Psychotropic Substances, Vienna, adopted 21 February 1972, entered into force 16 August 1976, 1019 UNTS 175. See also Gilmore, *Dirty Money*, cited in note 11 above, p. 51.

[16] Smith, 'The political economy of drugs', cited in note 9 above, p. 6; see also United Nations Office on Drugs and Crime, *World Drug Report*, Vienna, UNODC, 2012, p. 89.

[17] Smith, 'The political economy of drugs', cited in note 9 above, p. 6.

[18] Gilmore, *Dirty Money*, cited in note 11 above, pp. 51–2.

[19] Stewart, 'Internationalizing the war on drugs', cited in note 13 above, p. 390.

[20] Ethan A. Nadelmann, 'Unlaundering dirty money abroad: US foreign policy and financial secrecy jurisdictions', (1986) 18 *University of Miami Inter-American Law Review* (1), 33, p. 34; Jeffrey L. Quillen, 'The international attack on money laundering: European initiatives', (1991) 213 *Duke Journal of Comparative and International Law*, p. 213.

[21] In the United States this was the Money Laundering Control Act of 1986, 18 USC 1956 *et seq.* and in the United Kingdom the Drug Trafficking Offences Act 1986 (c. 32). Australia was also developing its Financial Transaction Reports Act 1988 (Cth).

its Convention in 'near record' time,[22] and the G-7 Group of Nations (G-7) had commissioned a Financial Action Task Force (FATF) to look at the issue and make recommendations for the control of this problem. Collectively, these activities established the groundwork for a global AML regime.

The G-7 commissioned the FATF in 1989 as a temporary task force with the mandate 'to assess the results of cooperation already undertaken in order to prevent the utilisation of the banking system and financial institutions for the purpose of money laundering, and to consider additional preventive efforts in this field, including the adaptation of the legal and regulatory systems so as to enhance multilateral judicial assistance'.[23] In addition to the 1989 G-7 summit participants, the group had representatives from Australia, Austria, Belgium, Luxembourg, the Netherlands, Spain, Sweden, and Switzerland.[24] The original task force brought together more than 130 experts from around the world and formulated what became known as the FATF's Forty Recommendations.[25] A task force report containing these recommendations was delivered in February 1990, endorsed at ministerial level and presented to the G-7 Houston Summit in July 1990. It was agreed in Houston that the task force would continue for a further year to explore in more detail how the recommendations could be implemented in the international community.[26]

The original Forty Recommendations were divided into four sections. Section 1 provided a general framework that addressed the ratification of the 1988 UN Vienna Convention, ensuring that financial secrecy laws did not inhibit the implementation of the Recommendations, and provided for an increase in mutual legal assistance and cooperation. Section 2 called for the strengthening of national legal systems to control money laundering. Paramount to this was alignment on the definitions and criminalization of the act of money laundering. The third section provided twenty-one of the Forty Recommendations and required enhancements to the financial system. These recommendations were either directed towards private sector changes or called for the establishment of an appropriate regulatory and supervisory framework to oversee AML activities. The task force also recognized that no country could successfully operate an AML regime in isolation and so Section 4 expanded on actions required to strengthen international cooperation in criminal matters. That this final section occupied ten of the Forty Recommendations demonstrates an important focus on international collaboration.[27]

[22] Gilmore, *Dirty Money*, cited in note 11 above, p. 52.

[23] G-7 Group of Nations, 'Economic Declaration', Paris Summit, 1989, para. 53, available at: http://www.g8.utoronto.ca/summit/1989paris/communique/drug.html, accessed 19 July 2015.

[24] Financial Action Task Force on Money Laundering, *Report*, FATF, 1990, p. 3, available at: http://www.fatf-gafi.org/media/fatf/documents/reports/1990%20ENG.pdf, accessed 20 July 2015.

[25] Gilmore, *Dirty Money*, cited in note 11 above, p. 94. Mark Pieth observes that the 1990 version of the FATF standards 'was written in less than half a year, with no ulterior ambition and very little academic preparation': see Mark Pieth, 'The harmonisation of law against economic crime', (1999) 1 *European Journal of Law Reform* 527, p. 531.

[26] At this time, the task force was joined by a further eight OECD countries (Denmark, Finland, Greece, Ireland, New Zealand, Norway, Portugal, and Turkey) along with Hong Kong and the Gulf Cooperation Council. FATF, Report 1990–91, cited in note 24 above, p. 4.

[27] Financial Action Task Force on Money Laundering, *The Forty Recommendations of the Financial Action Task Force on Money Laundering*, FATF, 1990.

Many of these original Recommendations stand today in one form or another and underpin the current AML/CFT framework. The development of these standards was not an easily achieved task, however. The twenty-one recommendations for the enhancement of the financial sector provide a good example of the negotiation and compromise required to reach a collaborative agreement. US banks had already been living with the requirement to report transactions to the relevant authorities as part of their Bank Secrecy Act 1970 and the more recently introduced Money Laundering Control Act 1986.[28] The global broadening of these reporting obligations within the Recommendations was seen as an 'acceptable price to pay for being involved in the fight against organised crime'.[29] The recording and reporting of transactions is principally a mechanical operation and so was not viewed as difficult to comply with (given appropriate effort to do so). Where the original FATF delegations differed was in the application of customer due-diligence principles, and the requirement for bankers to report their customers on the basis of suspicion. The US banks' view was that costs associated with customer due diligence and the reporting of suspicious transactions were too high to implement and that customers would regard them as an invasion of privacy.[30] These requirements were seen as a European notion that did not reflect the way the US banking system operated.[31] Consequently, the original US delegation to the 1989 FATF meetings was not supportive of customer due-diligence measures, nor of duties to report suspicious transactions. The US intent at the time was to create international control mechanisms on the flow of money. This focus on cash in particular was a direct effort to control the entry points for organised-crime drug money into the international financial system.[32] Underpinning this approach was the assumption that if you control the entry of funds into the financial system, then stringent rules on customer due diligence and the reporting of suspicions become unnecessary.

During the negotiations the US regulators had a change of heart. In particular, the UK, French, and Swiss banking supervisors collaborated with the US Federal Reserve representatives to ensure that customer due-diligence standards were included in the initial Forty Recommendations.[33] According to Pieth and Aiolfi these Recommendations were based on a combination of national strategies, an early international recommendation of the Basel Committee, and the experience and legislative example of Swiss law.[34] In return for this inclusion, the US Federal Reserve wanted the formalization of requirements existing under the Vienna Convention of 1988 for the international criminalization of money laundering, 'to forfeit ill-gotten gains and to share information, even though at that time it was still restricted to the topic of

[28] Money Laundering Control Act 1986, cited in note 21 above. The Currency and Foreign Transactions Reporting Act of 1970 (31 USC 5311 *et seq.*). See also Michael DeFeo, 'Depriving international narcotics traffickers and other organised criminals of illegal proceeds and combatting money laundering', (1989) 18 *Denver Journal of International Law and Policy*, 405.

[29] Mark Pieth and Gemma Aiolfi, 'The private sector becomes active: the Wolfsberg process', (2003) 10 *Journal of Financial Crime* (4), 359; DeFeo, 'Depriving international narcotics traffickers', cited in note 28 above, p. 414. Pieth's observations regarding the early FATF processes are of particular relevance as he was closely involved in the money laundering standard-setting processes.

[30] Pieth and Aiolfi, ibid, p. 359. [31] Ibid. [32] Ibid. [33] Ibid. [34] Ibid.

drugs'.[35] This process of negotiation and trading on ideas provided the foundation for the development of the international standards.

Since the adoption of the first set of Recommendations many important developments have taken place. In 1996 the Recommendations were revised to extend beyond the proceeds of drug offences to proceeds of all serious offences.[36] In 2001 eight Special Recommendations on Terrorist Financing were adopted, later expanded to nine.[37] In 2003 the Recommendations were extensively revised and deepened.[38] They were also extended beyond financial institutions to designated non-financial businesses and professions. These were identified as being at particular risk in relation to money laundering. Another important revision process was concluded in 2012 with the adoption of the current set of revised Recommendations that combine the AML and the CFT standards.[39] This set introduced a mandatory risk-based approach requiring countries and regulated institutions to identify and assess their money laundering and terrorist financing risks and to adjust their counter-measures to address those risks by focusing more attention and resources on higher risks, potentially lowering the level and intensity of controls where the risks are lower.

12.3.2 The international legal framework

At a global level a range of international instruments set out money laundering and terrorist financing obligations. These include the Vienna Convention,[40] the United Nation's International Convention for the Suppression of the Financing of Terrorism,[41] the United Nations Convention Against Transnational Organised Crime (the Palermo Convention),[42] and the United Nations Convention against Corruption.[43]

In addition to these global instruments there are also regional instruments that are relevant. The Council of Europe's 1990 Convention on Laundering, Search, Seizure, and Confiscation of the Proceeds from Crime,[44] for example, was an early regional instrument that shaped the development of European laws on proceeds of crime. In certain cases an aspect that is directly relevant to the AML/CFT framework forms only a sub-part of a broader regional instrument. Article VI of the Organization of American States' Inter-American Convention against Corruption and Article 6 of the African Union Convention on Preventing and Combating Corruption,[45] for example,

[35] Ibid. [36] Pieth, 'Harmonisation of law', cited in note 25 above, p. 533.

[37] Paul Allan Schott, *Reference Guide to Anti-Money Laundering and Combating the Financing of Terrorism*, 2nd edn, New York, World Bank, 2006, p. IX-1.

[38] Financial Action Task Force on Money Laundering, *The Forty Recommendations*, FATF, 2003.

[39] Financial Action Task Force, *International Standards on Combating Money Laundering and the Financing of Terrorism & Proliferation: The FATF Recommendations*, FATF, 2012.

[40] Cited in note 6 above.

[41] New York, adopted 9 December 1999, entered into force 10 April 2002, 2178 UNTS 197.

[42] Adopted 15 November 2000, entered into force 29 September 2003, 2225 UNTS 209 (Palermo Convention).

[43] New York, adopted 31 October 2003, entered into force 14 December 2005, 2349 UNTS 41.

[44] Strasbourg, adopted on 8 November 1990, entered into force 1 September 1993, CETS 141.

[45] Inter-American Convention against Corruption, Caracas, adopted 29 March 1996, entered into force 6 March 1997. African Union Convention on Preventing and Combating Corruption, Maputo, adopted 11 July 2003, entered into force 5 August 2006.

require states parties to criminalize specified laundering acts in relation to the proceeds of corruption.

Since the European Community's 1991 directive on money laundering, the European directive-led anti-money laundering framework has been of particular relevance to the global community.[46] The Fourth European Union Directive on Money Laundering was adopted in May 2015 with implementation envisaged by 2017.[47] As so many global financial institutions are headquartered in Europe, European Directive-led compliance practices influence global practices. The Directives comply with the FATF Standards but often go beyond them and foreshadow amendments to the FATF Recommendations.

12.3.3 The FATF

The FATF's organisational framework today comprises the FATF, FATF-style Regional Bodies (FSRBs), and a range of international observer institutions that partner with the FATF to support the adoption and implementation of global AML/CFT standards.

At the heart of this network lies the FATF, which has developed into an intergovernmental policy-making body that functions as the globally recognized standard-setting body for AML/CFT. The FATF sets standards in the form of the FATF Recommendations and via non-binding guidance. It currently has thirty-seven members, including two regional bodies. According to the FATF it guards its membership and exclusivity to preserve its structures and character as standard setter.[48] Since 1998 it has allowed only nine new members.[49] In 2013, however, the FATF decided to consider a limited expansion of its membership to include a small number of strategically important countries that would enhance FATF's geographic balance.[50]

[46] Council Directive (EEC) 91/308 on prevention of the use of the financial system for the purpose of money laundering [1991] OJ L166/77; Directive (EC) 2001/97 of the European Parliament and of the Council amending Council Directive 91/308/EEC on prevention of the use of the financial system for the purpose of money laundering, [2001] OJ L344/76; Directive (EC) 2005/60 of the European Parliament and of the Council of 26 October 2005 on the prevention of the use of the financial system for the purpose of money laundering and terrorist financing, [2005] OJ L309/15. Commission Directive (EC) 2006/70 of 1 August 2006 laying down implementing measures for Directive 2005/60/EC of the European Parliament and of the Council as regards the definition of politically exposed person and the technical criteria for simplified customer due diligence procedures and for exemption on grounds of a financial activity conducted on an occasional or very limited basis, [2006] OJ L214/29.

[47] Directive (EU) 2015/849 of the European Parliament and of the Council of 20 May 2015 on the prevention of the use of the financial system for the purposes of money laundering or terrorist financing, amending Regulation (EU) No. 648/2012 of the European Parliament and of the Council, and repealing Directive 2005/60/EC of the European Parliament and of the Council and Commission Directive 2006/70/EC, [2015] OJ L141/73. See also European Commission, 'European Parliament backs stronger rules to combat money laundering and terrorism financing', press release, Brussels, 20 May 2015, available at: http://europa.eu/rapid/press-release_IP-15-5001_en.htm, accessed 20 July 2015.

[48] Organization for Economic Development, 'FATF "mandate" renewed for eight years', press release, Paris, 14 May 2004, para. 6: 'however, the FATF has perhaps approached the limit of members if it is to continue to retain its current structure and character'.

[49] Ibid.

[50] Malaysia became a member in 2016 and the Kingdom of Saudi Arabia (2015) and Israel (2016) were given observer status, putting them on track to be considered for FATF membership.

FATF overcomes its lack of international representation through the network of FSRBs. In October 2015 the central African body, the Groupe d'Action Contre le Blanchiment d'Argent en Afrique Centrale (GABAAC—Task Force on Money Laundering in Central Africa), became the latest to be recognized by the FATF as a fully-fledged FSRB. FSRBs enjoy associate membership of FATF, providing their non-FATF members with a voice in the standard-setting and assessment processes. The FATF and FSRB membership currently account for more than 190 jurisdictions globally.[51]

In addition, the FATF has a host of international organisations as observers. These include the World Bank, the International Monetary Fund (IMF), and other financial standard-setting bodies such as the Basel Committee on Banking Supervision. These partner organisations strengthen the global footprint of the FATF, especially by working with the FATF to ensure that AML/CFT measures are appropriately embedded in relevant standards as well as national laws and practices.

The FATF's impact as international standard setter is strengthened through its peer-based compliance assessment processes. Mutual assessments, which can be conducted by the FATF, its FSRBs, the IMF, or the World Bank,[52] use a standard methodology. In the past this methodology focused on country compliance with the FATF Standards. In the Fourth Round of mutual evaluations, following on the revised 2012 FATF Recommendations, however, the focus was broadened to also include the effectiveness of a country's AML/CFT framework.

The outcome of the mutual assessment holds important consequences for countries. Negative findings can impact on the financial standing of the country and in the past this threat has proved to be a powerful tool to move countries to greater compliance with the FATF Standards.[53] Currently the FATF's International Co-operation Review Group (ICRG) uses mutual assessment reports and other sources of information to identify countries and jurisdictions with strategic AML/CFT deficiencies. These countries are identified publicly in statements that reflect the seriousness of the risk that such countries pose to the integrity of the international financial systems. Other countries and their financial institutions are required to take appropriate steps to mitigate the particular risks that may arise from financial dealings with the identified countries, their institutions, and their citizens. In some cases countries have such serious strategic deficiencies that the FATF calls on its members and non-members to apply counter-measures.[54] These counter-measures contain a range of risk mitigation measures that may include limiting dealings with the identified country or persons in that country.[55] Non-compliance with the FATF Standards may therefore increase the costs of doing business and may even exclude a country from some or all international financial transactions.[56]

[51] Financial Action Task Force, *Annual Report 2013–2014*, FATF, 2014, p. 31.

[52] For the history behind the IMF and World Bank involvement in the assessment processes, see Nadim Kyriakos-Saad, 'The methodology for assessing compliance with anti-money laundering and combating the financing of terrorism standard', (2005) 3 *Current Developments in Monetary and Financial Law*, 265–78.

[53] Rainer Hülsse and Dieter Kerwer, 'Global standards in action: insights from anti-money laundering regulation', (2007) 14 *Organisation* (5), 625, pp. 632–4.

[54] FATF, *International Standards*, cited in note 39 above, Rec. 19.

[55] Ibid, INR 19.

[56] For the impact of non-compliance, see International Monetary Fund, *Anti-Money Laundering and Combating the Financing of Terrorism (AML/CoFT)—Report on the Review of the Effectiveness of the Program*, New York, IMF, 2011, pp. 82–4.

12.4 The AML/CFT Strategy

The AML/CFT strategy involves harmonized global action to criminalize money laundering; to employ the private sector to guard the international financial system and to generate financial intelligence to be shared with a specialized government agency (a financial intelligence unit (FIU)); to enable the seizure and forfeiture of proceeds of crime; and to enable law enforcement to collaborate domestically and globally. The following discussion takes a closer look at the elements of this strategy.

12.4.1 The money laundering offence

The relevant United Nations Conventions set out the framework of the key money laundering offences, but this is done in general terms. The FATF Standards on the other hand are more specific, to advance a higher level of consistency in the formulation of money laundering offences in domestic laws globally. The specificity is however limited as the FATF refrains from providing detailed, prescriptive guidance. Its Standards are designed to reflect general principles that countries should implement through measures adapted to, and reflecting, their own, unique circumstances, especially their legal, administrative, and operational frameworks.[57] While leveraging off the key United Nations Conventions, the relevant FATF Standards therefore provide countries with a measure of flexibility.

Recommendation 3 requires countries to criminalize money laundering on the basis of the Vienna Convention and the Palermo Convention.[58] These Conventions require states parties to criminalize:[59]

(a) the conversion or transfer of proceeds of crime; and
(b) concealment or disguise of the nature, source, location, disposition, movement, or ownership of proceeds of crime.

Subject to the basic concepts of their domestic systems, countries must also criminalize:[60]

(c) the acquisition, possession, or use of proceeds of crime and
(d) participation in, association with, or conspiracy to commit, attempts to commit, and aiding, abetting, facilitating, and counselling the commission of, any of the money laundering offences.[61]

[57] FATF, *International Standards*, cited in note 39 above, Rec. 7. [58] Ibid, Rec. 3.

[59] Vienna Convention, cited in note 6 above, Art. 3(1)(b); Palermo Convention, cited in note 42 above, Art. 6(1)(a).

[60] Vienna Convention, cited in note 6 above, Art. 3(1)(c); Palermo Convention, cited in note 42 above, Art. 6(1)(b).

[61] The Vienna Convention, cited in note 6 above, Art. 3(1)(b), does not make the requirement to criminalize 'assisting any person who is involved in the commission of such an offence or offences to evade the legal consequences of his actions' subject to the constitutional principles and the basic concepts of a country's legal system. The FATF standards, on the other hand, mirror the requirements of the Palermo Convention: '[t]here should be appropriate ancillary offences to the offence of money laundering,

The Palermo Convention, the broader of the two Conventions, defines 'proceeds of crime' as meaning 'any property derived from or obtained, directly or indirectly, through the commission of an offence'.[62] This must, however, be read in the context of the nature of the money laundering offence. Money laundering is a secondary offence that requires a prior, primary, or so-called 'predicate offence' to have been committed.[63] This offence in turn would have had to generate proceeds that can form the subject of the laundering acts.

Initially predicate offences were drug offences. In 1996, when the FATF Recommendations were first revised, the concept of 'predicate offence' was broadened to all serious offences.[64] Countries were at liberty to define the level of seriousness required and that led to a range of different approaches, with some countries opting to list specific predicate offences while others extended the concept of 'predicate offence' to all offences that were capable of generating proceeds of crime.[65] Since 2003 the FATF has urged countries to ensure that money laundering offences can be committed in relation to the proceeds of all serious offences, and that they should strive to include the widest range of predicate offences in their definition of a 'serious offence'.[66]

The FATF currently recognizes that country practices in relation to the definition of predicate offences may range from one that includes all proceeds-generating offences to one that lists specific offences, and that some countries may even combine elements of both these approaches.[67] If a country does not extend the concept of 'predicate offence' to all offences the FATF requires it, at a minimum, to include a range of offences within each of the categories of a list of 'designated categories of offences'.[68] These categories cover the offences generally associated with organised crime, including participation in an organised criminal group and racketeering.[69] The Palermo Convention and the FATF Standards furthermore provide that predicate offences must include both offences committed within the jurisdiction and, in the case of dual criminality,[70] offences committed abroad.[71]

including participation in, association with or conspiracy to commit, attempt, aiding and abetting, facilitating, and counselling the commission, unless this is not permitted by fundamental principles of domestic law'. FATF, *International Standards*, cited in note 39 above, INR 3.

[62] Palermo Convention, cited in note 42 above, Art. 2(e).

[63] In Art. 2(h) of the Palermo Convention, cited in note 42 above, 'predicate offence' is defined as 'any offence as a result of which proceeds have been generated that may become the subject of an offence as defined in article 6 of this Convention'.

[64] FinCEN, 'FATF updates anti-money laundering standards', 28 June 1996, available at: http://www.fincen.gov/news_room/nr/html/19960628.html, accessed 20 July 2015.

[65] United Nations Office for Drugs and Crime, *Legislative Guides for the Implementation of the United Nations Convention Against Transnational Organised Crime and the Protocols Thereto*, Vienna, UNODC, 2004, para. 115.

[66] FATF, *International Standards*, cited in note 39 above, Rec. 3. This requirement is mirrored in the Palermo Convention, cited in note 42 above, Art. 6(2)(a).

[67] See FATF, *International Standards*, cited in note 39 above, INR 3, for FATF standards that apply when countries decide not to extend the concept of 'predicate offence' to all offences.

[68] See the glossary to FATF, *International Standards*, cited in note 39 above, 112–13.

[69] See also the Palermo Convention, cited in note 42 above, Art. 2(b).

[70] UNODC, *Legislative Guides*, cited in note 65 above, para. 119.

[71] Palermo Convention, cited in note 42 above, Art. 6(2)(c); FATF, *International Standards*, cited in note 39 above, INR 3(5).

The Palermo Convention and the FATF Standards require countries to criminalize intentional money laundering. The conversion offence under the Palermo Convention, for example, can only be committed by a person who knows that the property is the proceeds of crime and who commits the relevant acts in relation to the property to conceal or disguise its illicit nature or to assist someone involved in the predicate offence to evade the course of justice.[72] The FATF Standards, however, require countries to ensure that the requisite intent and knowledge may be inferred from objective factual circumstances and, for example, not solely from the confessions of offenders.[73] In addition, it is important to appreciate that the FATF Standards are minimum standards. Countries may therefore go beyond them. A number of countries have extended money laundering offences to persons acting negligently who did not know, but should reasonably have known, that they were dealing with proceeds of crime.[74]

Countries are allowed to exclude the perpetrator of the predicate offence from the ambit of the money laundering offence, but only where this is required by fundamental principles of their domestic law. Some countries have fundamental legal principles that do not allow them to prosecute and punish a person for committing a predicate offence as well as for laundering the proceeds of that offence.[75]

A final observation in relation to the design of the money laundering offence relates to corporate criminal liability. Legal persons such as companies and corporations are often abused for criminal purposes. Not all countries allow for corporations to be criminally prosecuted. Germany, for example, does not recognize corporate criminal liability.[76] The Palermo Convention and the FATF Standards recognize these international differences but require states to hold legal persons liable. The Palermo Convention requires states to ensure such liability but allowing that liability to be criminal, civil, or administrative in nature, depending on the legal principles of the state party.[77] The FATF Standards, on the other hand, go somewhat further. They require criminal liability and sanctions, and only where those are not possible, owing to fundamental principles of domestic law, allow for civil or administrative liability and sanctions.[78] Both require that such liability should not preclude the liability of natural persons, for example the directors and employees of the company who were personally involved in the offence. Both also require that all sanctions should be effective, proportionate, and dissuasive.[79]

While the framework created by the relevant Conventions and the FATF Standards ensure a large measure of consistency in the criminalization of money laundering offences globally, the flexibility that they allow does leave significant space for differences

[72] UNODC, *Legislative Guides*, cited in note 65 above, para. 101.

[73] FATF, *International Standards*, cited in note 39 above, INR 3(7)(a).

[74] See e.g. Prevention of Organised Crime Act 121 of 1998, s. 4 (South Africa); Criminal Code Act 1995 (Cth), Div. 400 (Australia).

[75] UNODC, *Legislative Guides*, cited in note 65 above, para. 120. Even where that is not the case, courts might not be prepared to support self-laundering charges when the criminality of the money laundering is completely encompassed in the predicate offence. See *Nahlous v R* [2010] NSWCCA 58; *Thorn v R* [2009] NSWCCA 294.

[76] Guy Stessens, 'Corporate criminal liability: a comparative perspective', (1994) 43 *ICLQ* (3), 493.

[77] Palermo Convention, cited in note 42 above, Art. 10(2).

[78] FATF, *International Standards*, cited in note 39 above, INR 3.

[79] Ibid, INR 3(7)(c).

in national definitions of the key offences, providing gaps that transnational organised crime can exploit.

12.4.2 National and international cooperation

Government action against organised crime requires international cooperation in criminal matters. The ability to render such cooperation depends on the legal mechanisms that are in place to support international collaboration but equally on the quality of national law enforcement cooperation amongst domestic agencies. The FATF Standards address national infrastructure, domestic collaboration, and international cooperation separately. As in practice these elements are so closely linked in relation to the combating of transnational organised crime, it is submitted that they are best considered jointly.

The FATF Standards require each country to establish a Financial Intelligence Unit (FIU) that serves as a national centre receiving and analysing suspicious transaction reports filed by financial institutions. They are also required to collect and analyse other relevant information regarding predicate offences, money laundering, and terrorist financing, and to disseminate the results to domestic law enforcement agencies and international counterparts.[80] FIUs are therefore at the operational centre of domestic and international action against money laundering and terrorist financing. FIUs may also be assigned other AML functions such as policy making, regulation, supervision, and investigation. Given their sensitive roles, the FATF requires FIUs to be operationally independent and autonomous,[81] and to have the resources needed to carry out their functions, free from any undue political, government, or industry influence or interference.[82]

Internationally, in 1995 FIUs joined to form the Egmont Group of Financial Intelligence Units, a global FIU platform that unites more than 150 FIUs.[83] Membership of the Group facilitates collaboration and the exchange of information at an operational level. The FATF Standards require non-members to apply for membership of the Egmont Group.[84]

In the 2003–2012 round of mutual assessments, it was found that the lack of adequate human, technological, and financial resources hampered the ability of some countries to establish and maintain FIUs and competent supervisory authorities to conduct oversight of AML/CFT matters.[85] Twenty-three of the 116 countries that

[80] Ibid, Rec. 29.

[81] Ibid, INR 29(8); Louis de Koker, 'Applying anti-money laundering laws to fight corruption', in Adam Graycar and Russell G. Smith (eds), *Handbook of Global Research and Practice in Corruption*, Camberley, Edward Elgar, 2011, p. 340, pp. 351–2.

[82] FATF, *International Standards*, cited in note 39 above, INR 29(12).

[83] The Egmont Group of Financial Intelligence Units, 'Remarks by the Chair of Egmont Group of Financial Intelligence Units at FATF Plenary', Egmont Group, 2015, available at: http://www.egmontgroup.org/news-and-events/news/2015/02/27/remarks-by-the-chair-of-egmont-group-of-financial-intelligence, accessed 20 July 2015; Munk School of Global Affairs, 'Gap analysis & stakeholder engagement report for the Egmont Group of Financial Intelligence Units', Munk School of Global Affairs, 2014, p. 16.

[84] FATF, *International Standards*, cited in note 39 above, INR 29(13).

[85] Concepcion Verdugu Yepes, 'Compliance with the AML/CoFT International Standard: lessons from a cross-country analysis', IMF Working Paper, WP/11/177, New York, IMF, 2011, p. 67.

were assessed (nearly 20 per cent) had not yet established an FIU in accordance with the Standards.[86] The current Egmont membership reflects a significant improvement in the numbers of FIUs in the past decade.

Lack of coordination between the FIUs and other competent authorities such as regulatory, investigative, and prosecutorial agencies was also identified as a challenge in those assessments.[87] In the 2012 revised Recommendations, domestic coordination was accordingly prioritized. Recommendation 2 requires countries to ensure that their policy makers, FIUs, law enforcement authorities, supervisors, and other relevant competent authorities, at the policy making and operational levels, have effective mechanisms enabling them to cooperate and coordinate their activities relating to money laundering, terrorist financing, and the financing of proliferation of weapons of mass destruction.

Five FATF Recommendations address aspects relevant to international cooperation. Their contents reflect and strengthen the existing international cooperation obligations set out in international instruments. The FATF Standards, for example, require countries to become party to specific international instruments and to implement them in national laws.[88] The Recommendations themselves set out a range of standards relating to international cooperation in criminal matters,[89] and make specific reference to asset freezing and confiscation,[90] and to extradition.[91] The set of Recommendations closes with a general requirement for countries to ensure that 'their competent authorities can rapidly, constructively and effectively provide the widest range of international cooperation in relation to money laundering, associated predicate offences and terrorist financing'.[92] There should be appropriate legal frameworks in place to ensure that the cooperation is rendered spontaneously and when requested, and where specific bilateral or multilateral agreements or arrangements are required, they should be negotiated and signed 'in a timely way with the widest range of foreign counterparts'.[93]

In the 2003–2012 round of mutual assessments, high-income countries were generally found to comply with the international cooperation standards under the 2003 Recommendations. Low-income countries, however, were far less compliant. The most prevalent reason for non-compliance was the absence of clear rules on cooperation and mechanisms to support such cooperation.[94]

The 2012 revised FATF Standards increased the requirements relating to cooperation. Coordination at a national level, for example, must take place within the context of a risk-informed, national, AML/CFT policy. Despite the additional requirements and the use of a new technical compliance and effectiveness assessment methodology—discussed in section 12.5 of this chapter—the first group of countries

[86] Ibid, p. 67. [87] Ibid, pp. 67–8.

[88] FATF, *International Standards*, cited in note 39 above, Rec. 36, refers specifically to the Vienna Convention, 1988; the Palermo Convention; the International Convention for the Suppression of the Financing of Terrorism; and the United Nations Convention against Corruption. It also encourages countries, where applicable, to ratify and implement other relevant international instruments.

[89] Ibid, Rec. 37. [90] Ibid, Rec. 38. [91] Ibid, Rec. 39. [92] Ibid, Rec. 40.

[93] Ibid, Rec. 40.

[94] Yepes, 'Compliance with the International Standard', cited in note 85 above, pp. 74–5.

to be assessed for compliance with the new standards, mostly high-income developed countries, achieved good levels of general compliance with the cooperation requirement. This reflects mainly existing collaboration as the countries had little time to adjust their frameworks to the new standards before their compliance levels were assessed. The following tables summarize the assessment outcomes of these countries on the key domestic and international cooperation standards:

Table 12.1 Selected technical compliance assessments ratings: Fourth Round of mutual evaluations

	Australia	Belgium	Ethiopia	Norway	Spain
Rec. 2: National cooperation and coordination	LC	LC	PC	PC	LC
Rec. 29: Financial Intelligence Unit	C	C	LC	LC	C
Rec. 36: International instruments	LC	C	PC	C	C
Rec. 37: Mutual legal assistance	C	LC	LC	LC	C
Rec. 38: Mutual legal assistance: freezing and confiscation	C	LC	LC	LC	C
Rec. 39: Extradition	C	LC	LC	LC	LC
Rec. 40: Other forms of international cooperation	C	LC	NC	LC	C

Ratings: Compliant (C); Largely Compliant (LC); Partially Compliant (PC); Non-Compliant (NC)

Financial Action Task Force, *Mutual Evaluation Report: Norway*, FATF, 2014; Financial Action Task Force, *Mutual Evaluation Report: Spain*, FATF, 2014; Financial Action Task Force, *Mutual Evaluation Report: Australia*, FATF, 2015; Financial Action Task Force, *Mutual Evaluation Report: Belgium*, FATF, 2015; World Bank and Eastern and Southern Africa Anti-Money Laundering Group, *Mutual Evaluation Report: The Federal Democratic Republic of Ethiopia*, ESAAMLG, 2015.

Table 12.2 Selected effectiveness assessments ratings: Fourth Round of mutual evaluations

	Australia	Belgium	Ethiopia	Norway	Spain
Immediate outcome 1: Risk, policy, and coordination	S	S	L	M	S
Immediate outcome 2: International cooperation	H	S	M	S	M
Immediate outcome 6: Financial intelligence	S	S	L	M	H

Ratings: Low (L); Moderate (M); Substantial (S); High (H)

FATF, *Mutual Evaluation Reports* for *Norway, Spain, Australia*, and *Belgium*, cited in Table 12.1 above; World Bank and ESAAMLG, *Mutual Evaluation Report* for *Ethiopia*, cited in Table 12.1 above.

In this group Norway is the only developed economy that was scored only partially compliant on technical compliance with one of the relevant Recommendations: Recommendation 2 requiring national cooperation and coordination. This is in part owing to its lack of an overarching, risk-informed, AML/CFT policy, a requirement introduced in the standards in 2012. If it had had such a policy it would still have not been rated compliant, since the assessors also found that the country lacked adequate mechanisms to enable its relevant authorities to cooperate and coordinate on AML at an operational level.[95] Not surprisingly in this group, Ethiopia as a resource-challenged developing country has the most 'partially compliant' findings as well as one 'non-compliant' finding on technical compliance. It is, however, important to note that even as the least compliant jurisdiction in this group Ethiopia does have the majority of elements of national and international cooperation in place. It was rated as largely compliant on four of the seven key collaboration standards on technical compliance and its level of effectiveness in international cooperation was rated as moderate. These ratings are indicative of the general level of sound international collaboration on AML that has been established since the late 1980s.

12.4.3 The engagement and role of the private sector

The strategy to pursue criminal funds through the private sector was adopted at a time when commercial links were becoming increasingly complex, especially owing to increasing globalization.[96] In parallel, technological developments enabled the rapid global dissemination of financial products and services and faster international transaction flows. This period also witnessed a growth in the scale, reach, and diversification of criminal behaviour. Given the complexity of the financial system, and the specialization of financial products across a wide range of private sector entities, it is unlikely that such a strategy to target criminal funds could be implemented without the participation of industry.

It is debatable whether enlisting the private sector in AML was wholly or only partially coerced. Spectacular multibillion dollar fines for non-compliance with financial crime control laws have certainly put the focus squarely on the coercive aspect of the framework. This was not always so clear. Levi, for example, argued that an effective AML movement requires an 'active citizenship' on the part of the banks, which presumably includes an element of voluntary participation.[97] There is in fact some suggestion that banks may have worked closely with governments to create early legislation and regulation before the FATF Recommendations were fully implemented. For example, the US Annunzio-Wylie Act of 1992 required the formation of a Bank Secrecy Act (BSA) Advisory Group to act as a conduit between government and private sector agencies.[98] Earlier, the

[95] Financial Action Task Force, *Mutual Evaluation Report: Norway*, FATF, 2014, p. 44:

> In addition, Norway does not have adequate coordination mechanisms at the operational level, particularly in relation to the investigation and prosecution of ML and the implementation of AML/CoFT preventive measures. Cooperation on these issues is undertaken on an informal and ad hoc basis and varies between agencies.

[96] Joseph Stiglitz, *Globalisation and its Discontents*, Harmondsworth, Penguin Books, 2002, pp. 4–5; Michael Levi and Peter Reuter, 'Money laundering: a review of current controls and their consequences', (2006) 34 *Crime and Justice: An Annual Review of Research*, 289, p. 367.

[97] Michael Levi, 'Regulating money laundering: the death of bank secrecy in the UK', (1991) 31 *British Journal of Criminology* (2), 109, p. 110.

[98] Annunzio-Wylie Anti-Money Laundering Act, PL 102-550, para. 1514, 106 Stat 4044. Heba Shams, *Legal Globalisation: Money Laundering Law and Other Cases*, London, British Institute of International and Comparative Law, 2004, p. 184.

Swiss banks had to respond to the Chiasso Affair to address serious criticism that 'rogue' elements had placed the credibility of the sector in jeopardy.[99] The self-regulatory result was an 'Agreement on the Observance of Care by the Banks in Accepting Funds and on the Practice of Banking Secrecy'.[100] These examples are not representative, however, and perhaps indicate an exception rather than a robust engagement model. There is also speculation that elements of the banking industry may simply have not appreciated the potential impact of these new obligations,[101] as they did not appear to be 'unduly alarmed' by measures to control deposits in domestic and retail accounts.[102] Levi recounts that when an official from the British Bankers Association was asked about it at this time (1985–6), he confided that he had to go to the USA to find out what money laundering was all about. In the UK, financial crime was not 'seen as a mainstream source of banking income'. The sector also knew that to raise objections to financial crime legislation would be 'social disaster' in the climate of crime control at the time. Levi notes that concerns were raised over potential breaches of bank customers' privacy, but that these did not influence either the US or UK legislation to any real extent.[103]

Attempting to capture the diversity of financial operations with a single set of standards to be applied consistently by industry across multiple jurisdictions has proved challenging. There are in fact two aspects to this complexity and diversity challenge. First, the same set of standards aimed to capture the many different 'entry points' into and providers in the financial system, such as banks, casinos, and money service businesses. Second, layering and integration activities can include institutions of all kinds, such as retail banks and building societies, commercial banks, private banking services, investment banking, as well as real estate agents, lawyers, and accountants (the financial intermediaries), market traders, and financial planners.[104] To successfully engage the private sector therefore means ensuring the standards are set at a sufficiently general level to cover this diversity, whilst still providing a robust model for conversion to meaningful national legislation and practices. The FATF therefore adopted a risk-based approach in 2012, requiring each country and each financial institution to identify, assess, and mitigate its money laundering risk within the framework of the FATF Standards and domestic law.[105] While at face value this approach

[99] In 1977 Credit Suisse was found to have a major fraudulent banking and foreign exchange trading operation at the bank's Chiasso branch. See Shams, *Legal Globalisation*, cited in note 98 above, p. 22.

[100] Ibid. In the 1990s in South Africa the business community pressured the government to move faster on the implementation of money laundering control legislation: see L. de Koker, 'Money laundering control: the South African model', (2003) 6 *Journal of Money Laundering Control* (2), 166, p. 177.

[101] Pieth and Aiolfi, 'The private sector becomes active', cited in note 29 above.

[102] Michael Levi, *Controlling the International Money Trail: A Multi-Level Cross-National Public Policy Review*, Economic and Social Research Council, 2003, p. 10.

[103] Ibid, p. 10.

[104] Since 2003 participants in many of these industries have been subjected to AML/CFT controls. The FATF Standards broadened to include them as Designated Non-Financial Businesses and Professions (DNFBPs).

[105] While a risk-based approach has been recognized as acceptable since 2003, the 2012 FATF Standards embedded it as mandatory in the design of national and institutional risk-mitigation measures. Louis de Koker, 'The 2012 revised FATF Recommendations: assessing and mitigating mobile money integrity risks within the new standards framework', (2013) 8 *Washington Journal of Law, Technology & Arts* (3), 165, pp. 173–7.

may appear to provide a theoretical solution to the dilemma of ensuring effective individual action by a wide range of institutions, it is submitted that the inability of countries and many institutions to correctly identify, assess, and mitigate their money laundering risks will pose a serious challenge.

This complexity of private sector engagement is also inherent in the role the sector has been assigned. The core of the role currently defined in the AML/CFT standards is for countries to require their financial institutions to undertake due diligence on their customers at the commencement of business activities, and on a periodic basis to identify where customer details or circumstances may change. As the standards evolved, the requirements were extended to include designated non-financial businesses and professions identified as especially vulnerable to money laundering abuse. 'Customer due diligence' (CDD) in this context has three basic components:

(a) identification of the customer and verification of that identity using independent sources;
(b) identification and verification of the beneficial owner of the customer to ensure that the ownership and control structure of the customer are understood; and
(c) understanding the nature and purpose of the intended business relationship.

Having identified and verified the identity of the customer, regulated institutions are also required to monitor the activity of the customer to ensure it aligns with behaviour consistent with the customer's profile and the stated intent of the business. The FATF's Recommendation 10 addresses these CDD requirements and provides for the institutions involved to apply these diligence measures in a manner consistent with their money laundering and terrorist financing risk assessment of the customer.[106]

Finally, having completed adequate CDD and determined an appropriate level of monitoring for the customer based on the assessed risk level, the institutions are obligated to report where they believe the customer activity to be suspicious or unusual.

These obligations, while relatively straightforward to explain, are then applied in the diverse environments of the financial sector. The legislation that creates the private sector obligations is based on domestic understanding of what is required to mitigate the perceived risk from financial criminal activity within that country. While the institutions have license to assess their own exposure to threat and risk of financial crime, it is often informed by guidance from the local authorities and practices of domestic and international peers. This creates a further layer of complexity.

The AML/CFT standards are designed to establish a uniform or comparable system of financial crime control. This is impacted by the many different types of financial institution involved and the variety of services they offer. The variation between jurisdictions in their assessment and treatment of risk, and how this translates into their domestic law (and therefore private sector obligations), means that institutions operate under differing domestic due-diligence requirements. With many of the higher-risk institutions, products, and services operating in an international environment,

[106] FATF, *International Standards*, cited in note 39 above, Rec. 10. See L. de Koker, 'The FATF's customer identification framework: fit for purpose?', (2014) 17 *Journal of Money Laundering Control* (3), 281.

the difficulty compounds. For those entities that are truly international—operating across many jurisdictions—the ability to define and apply an appropriate level of capability across often conflicting jurisdictions is especially challenging.[107]

12.4.4 Asset forfeiture

A discussion of the use of the money laundering controls to combat organised crime would be incomplete without a reference to criminal asset forfeiture. Asset forfeiture is aimed at depriving criminals of their ill-gotten gains, thereby preventing a re-investment of such proceeds in further criminal activities. Asset forfeiture also helps law enforcement to signal that crime is not profitable.[108]

While asset forfeiture and money laundering rules operate separately, they are interlinked at a strategic and operational level: criminals who are concerned about the risk of forfeiture have an additional incentive to hide and disguise their ownership in the assets that are, or that represent, proceeds of crime. Criminalization of such concealment by money laundering laws is therefore required to support asset forfeiture. The intelligence generated by the private sector as part of CDD furthermore facilitates the identification of such assets, thereby supporting asset forfeiture by the state.

While the United States had a comprehensive forfeiture regime and many other countries had schemes allowing for the post-conviction forfeiture of evidence such as weapons used to commit crimes,[109] the Vienna Convention created a broader, global framework for asset confiscation. Article 5 of the Convention requires states parties to adopt the necessary measures to enable confiscation of:

(a) proceeds derived from offences under the Convention or property the value of which corresponds to that of such proceeds; and

(b) any illicit drugs, materials, and equipment or other instrumentalities used or intended to be used for such offences.

To support such confiscation states also had to adopt the necessary measures to enable them to identify, trace, and freeze or seize the relevant property.

These provisions are mirrored in Article 12 of the Palermo Convention. That Convention, however, creates far more detailed and extensive asset forfeiture obligations and extends them to the broader range of relevant offences under that Convention.[110]

[107] Basel Committee on Banking Supervision, *Sound Management of Risks related to Money Laundering and Financing of Terrorism*, Bank for International Settlements, 2014, paras 63–83.

[108] Nadelmann, 'Unlaundering dirty money abroad', cited in note 20 above, p. 33; R. Tom Naylor, 'Wash-out: a critique of follow-the-money methods in crime control policy', (1999) 32 *Crime, Law and Social Change* (1), 1, pp. 11–13; Louis de Koker and Loot Pretorius, 'Confiscation orders in terms of the Proceeds of Crime Act: some constitutional perspectives', 1998 *Journal of South African Law* 39; Chat le Nguyen, 'International anti-money laundering standards and their implementation by Vietnam', PhD thesis, Canterbury University, 2014, pp. 141–2.

[109] Loot Pretorius and Hennie Strydom, 'The constitutionality of civil forfeiture', (1998) 13 *South African Public Law*, 385.

[110] See Palermo Convention, cited in note 42 above, Art. 12 (confiscation and seizure), Art. 13 (international cooperation for purposes of confiscation), and Art. 14 (disposal of confiscated proceeds of crime or property).

Most countries today have asset forfeiture provisions allowing confiscation of proceeds of crime after conviction and sometimes even without conviction. Whether these measures have been implemented appropriately or have made a discernible impact on organised crime is debated. It is argued that a small fraction of criminal profits are confiscated and that the financial costs of confiscation outweigh the value of the confiscated property.[111] Arguments are complicated by a lack of data, however. Nonetheless, McFadden *et al.* argue that the focus should not be on the value of the confiscated assets but rather on the disruptive impact of such forfeiture on the criminal enterprise which far outweighs the costs of the system.[112]

12.5 The Effectiveness of the AML/CFT Strategy

The question whether the AML/CFT strategy is effective is complicated by different views as to what the system attempts to achieve, the interaction between the different elements of the strategy, and the lack of reliable data.[113] The early objectives of the financial crime counter-measures were to make it more difficult and costly for drug gangs to launder the proceeds of crime.[114] Robust anti-money laundering policy could reduce crime levels by disrupting the cash flows of organised crime business, increase the probability of being caught as well as the punishment applied on conviction, and escalate the associated transaction costs for criminal operations.[115] In terms of this linear 'cause-and-effect' logic, targeted action by authorities will produce a reduction in money laundering, thereby resulting in a reduction in underlying (predicate) crime. Criminality, however, is complex. Causality is not always clear and consequences are not always easily measured. It is assumed that by increasing the cost of money laundering the criminal organisations will be deterred—by either the increased financial cost or the personal cost through the likelihood of apprehension and prosecution. It is equally plausible, however, that the strategy might compel ordinary criminals to organise themselves more professionally and encourage criminal operations to resort to more complex and sophisticated methods of moving their illicit funds, thereby increasing organised crime risks.[116] Additionally, criminal enterprises are notoriously secretive and

[111] Peter Sproat, 'Payback time? To what extent has the new policing of assets provided new assets for policing?', (2009) 12 *Journal of Money Laundering Control* (4), 392, p. 402; Michael McFadden, Martin O'Flaherty, Paul Boreham, and Michele Hayne, *Targeting the Profits of Illicit Drug Trafficking through Proceeds of Crime Action*, Monograph series 52, National Drug Law Enforcement Research Fund, 2014.

[112] McFadden, *et al.*, ibid.

[113] Eleni Tsingou, 'Global governance and transnational financial crime: opportunities and tensions in the global anti-money laundering regime', Centre for the Study of Globalisation and Regionalisation, Working Paper 161/05, 2005, pp. 3–4; Louis de Koker and Mark Turkington, 'Anti-money laundering measures and the effectiveness question', in Barry Rider (ed.), *Research Handbook on International Financial Crime*, Cheltenham, Edward Elgar, 2015, p. 520.

[114] Charles Freeland, 'How can sound customer due diligence rules help prevent the misuse of financial institutions in the financing of terrorism?', (2002) 4 *European Journal of Law Reform* (2), 291.

[115] Joras Ferwerda, 'The economics of crime and money laundering: does anti-money laundering policy reduce crime?', (2009) 5 *Review of Law and Economics* (2), 903, p. 923.

[116] Joras Ferwerda, Mark Kattenberg, Han-Hsin Chang, Brigitte Unger, Loek Groot, and Jacob A. Bikker, 'Gravity models of trade based money laundering?', (2013) 45 *Applied Economics* (22), 3170, p. 3178; Brigitte Unger, 'Can money laundering decrease?', (2013) 41 *Public Finance Review* 658, p. 671.

the increasingly complex nature and the variety of their activities complicate attempts to determine activity levels and effective strategies to counter them.[117] In this environment, attempts to measure the size of the financial crime problem have produced 'largely varied estimates, none of which can be irrefutably proven'.[118]

The assessment of the effectiveness of the strategies is also heavily dependent on views regarding the objectives of the strategies. From the 1990s the FATF's focus on combating crime shifted to the global adoption of its standards. In 2003 Levi opined that 'the goal of affecting the organisation and levels of serious crimes has been displaced in practice by the more readily observable goal of enhancing and standardising rules and systems'.[119] The FATF however remained under pressure to respond to questions regarding the effectiveness of its standards. In 2013 it responded by broadening its mutual assessment methodology to address national effectiveness.

The methodology that was adopted to assess jurisdictional compliance with the FATF Standards now consists of two components.[120] The first component mirrors the type of assessment that was undertaken in the past by the FATF and assesses a country's technical compliance with the Recommendations. The second component assesses various aspects relating to the effectiveness of the country's AML/CFT system. The centrality of the second component is new to the assessment methodology. In the previous assessment rounds aspects of effectiveness may have been considered by assessors. A clear lack of effectiveness could have resulted in a lower compliance rating. This was not considered consistently in assessments, however. In the new methodology, though, it is a major, compulsory component.

The effectiveness assessment requires country assessors to judge whether, and to what extent, specific outcomes are being achieved. The FATF identified these outcomes and sorted them into a three-level hierarchy. At the highest level, the outcome of the AML/CFT system is defined as follows: 'financial systems and the broader economy are protected from the threats of money laundering and the financing of terrorism and proliferation, thereby strengthening financial sector integrity and contributing to safety and security'.[121]

Three intermediate outcomes are identified:[122]

(a) policy, coordination, and cooperation mitigate the money laundering and financing of terrorism risks;

[117] Michael Levi and Mike Maguire, 'Reducing and preventing organised crime: an evidence-based critique', (2004) 41 *Crime, Law and Social Change* 397, p. 405; Levi and Reuter, 'Money laundering', cited in note 97 above, p. 312.

[118] Angela S. M. Irwin, Kim-Kwang Raymond Choo, and Lin Liu, 'An analysis of money laundering and terrorism financing typologies', (2011) 15 *Journal of Money Laundering Control* (1), 85, p. 86; Antonello Biagioli, 'Financial crime as a threat to the wealth of nations: a cost-effectiveness approach', (2008) 11 *Journal of Money Laundering Control* (1), 88, p. 94.

[119] Levi, *Controlling the International Money Trail*, cited in note 103 above; Terrence Halliday, Michael Levi, and Peter Reuter, *Global Surveillance of Dirty Money: Assessing Assessments of Regimes to Control Money Laundering and Combat the Financing of Terrorism*, Champaign, Illinois, Center on Law and Globalization, 2014, p. 14.

[120] Financial Action Task Force, *Methodology for Assessing Technical Compliance with the FATF Recommendations and the Effectiveness of AML/CoFT Systems*, FATF, 2014.

[121] Ibid, para. 42. [122] Ibid, para. 43.

(b) proceeds of crime and funds in support of terrorism are prevented from entering the financial and other sectors or are detected and reported by these sectors; or

(c) money laundering threats are detected and disrupted, and criminals are sanctioned and deprived of illicit proceeds. Terrorist financing threats are detected and disrupted, terrorists are deprived of resources, and those who finance terrorism are sanctioned, thereby contributing to the prevention of terrorist acts.

The actual effectiveness assessment focuses mainly on whether and, if so the extent to which, a country meets eleven specified immediate outcomes.[123] The assumption underlying this approach is that a country that achieves the immediate outcomes would be assumed to achieve the three intermediate outcomes and, therefore, would achieve the high-level outcome too.[124]

The design of the effectiveness assessment weakens the usefulness of the assessment outcomes to answer the question whether the strategy is effective in countering organised crime. The assessment assumes that the current elements of the strategy will protect the financial system and the broader economy from the threats of money laundering and the financing of terrorism and proliferation. There is no empirical evidence to show that the existing elements will actually achieve that result if they are all implemented effectively. It assumes that the existing strategy, which still largely reflects its 1980s design,[125] remains suitable to reach that objective, and leaves little room to consider what might be absent and whether some of the elements might actually combine in certain cases to weaken effectiveness.

From a law enforcement perspective it is noticeable, for instance, that the FATF stakeholders have become more focused on protecting the financial system from illicit funds than on using it to monitor such funds. The FATF strategy therefore focuses on keeping dirty money out of the financial system, rather than adopting and processing it to generate crime combating intelligence. The assumption that the former is more effective at contributing to safety and security than the latter is untested. As a result persons may be refused access to the banking system, thereby increasing the risk that they might conclude transactions in the opaque, cash-based, informal economy that is not subject to AML/CFT protection or surveillance.

[123] Ibid. Examples of immediate outcomes include:

(a) 'money laundering and terrorist financing risks are understood and, where appropriate, actions coordinated domestically to combat money laundering and the financing of terrorism and proliferation';

(b) 'international cooperation delivers appropriate information, financial intelligence, and evidence, and facilitates action against criminals and their assets'; and

(c) 'money laundering offences and activities are investigated and offenders are prosecuted and subject to effective, proportionate and dissuasive sanctions.'

[124] Ibid, para. 43.

[125] Pieth, 'Harmonisation of law', cited in note 25 above, and see quotation from p. 531. While this strategy was developed further in revisions of the Standards, the original principles provided a conceptual framework. Even the number of original recommendations—forty—developed into a standard-setting brand for the FATF. Some FATF stakeholders therefore hold the view that new measures should only be accommodated if they fit logically with the existing principles, bearing in mind the need to maintain the number of recommendations at forty.

Since 2010 the FATF has grown more sensitive to the exclusionary impact of AML/CFT controls,[126] but their concern is mainly aimed at lower-risk individuals, especially in developing countries. Higher-risk individuals, which would include those who are of particular interest from an organised crime perspective, are still viewed as persons who may be excluded from the banking systems by banks.[127] Banks have been denying service to a broader range of higher-risk customers, including charitable organisations and small money- and value-transfer service providers, for a number of reasons, including concern that their AML/CFT compliance costs and the AML/CFT-related legal and reputational risks are not justified by the profit generated from the banking services offered.[128] Such service denial weakens the surveillance capacity of the AML/CFT regime and its ability to contribute meaningful intelligence that could support the combating of organised crime and terrorism.

The FATF's primary focus on the formal financial sector also leaves on the periphery significant organised-crime-related economic activity such as trade-based money laundering and the cash economy.[129] According to a 2015 Europol report entitled 'Why is cash still king? A strategic report on the use of cash by criminal groups as a facilitator for money laundering' the criminal abuse of cash is still the major criminal strategy to avoid AML/CFT controls:[130]

> Law Enforcement findings, stemming from operational cases, suspicious transaction reporting and cash detections show that while cash is slowly falling out of favour with consumers, it remains the criminals' instrument of choice to facilitate money laundering.

[126] Louis de Koker, 'Aligning anti-money laundering, combating of financing of terror and financial inclusion: questions to consider when FATF Standards are clarified', (2011) 14 *Journal of Financial Crime* (4), 361; Louis de Koker, 'Money laundering control and suppression of financing of terrorism: some thoughts on the impact of customer due diligence measures on financial exclusion', (2006) 13 *Journal of Financial Crime* (1), 26; Financial Action Task Force, *Anti-Money Laundering and Terrorist Financing Measures and Financial Inclusion*, FATF, 2013.

[127] Financial Action Task Force, 'FATF clarifies risk-based approach: case-by-case, not wholesale de-risking', press statement, 23 October 2014, Paris, available at: http://www.fatf-gafi.org/documents/news/rba-and-de-risking.html, accessed 20 July 2015; Financial Action Task Force, 'Drivers for "de-risking" go beyond anti-money laundering/terrorist financing', press statement, 26 June 2015, Brisbane, available at: http://www.fatf-gafi.org/documents/news/derisking-goes-beyond-amlcft.html, accessed 20 July 2015.

[128] *Dahabshiil Transfer Services Ltd. v Barclays Bank plc* [2013] EWHC 3379 (Ch); Tom Keatinge, 'Uncharitable behaviour', report for Demos, 2014, available at: http://www.demos.co.uk/files/DEMOSuncharitablebehaviourREPORT.pdf?1419986873, accessed 8 February 2016; World Bank, 'Migration and remittances: recent developments and outlook', *Migration and Development Brief* 24, 13 April 2015, p. 11.

[129] Financial Action Task Force, *Best Practices on Trade-Based Money Laundering*, FATF, 2008; Ross Delston and Stephen Walls, 'Reaching beyond banks: how to target trade-based money laundering and terrorist financing outside the financial sector', (2009) 41 *Case Western Reserve Journal of International Law* (8), 85; John Zdanowicz, 'Trade-based money laundering and terrorist financing', (2009) 5 *Review of Law and Economics* (2), 858; Samuel McSkimming, 'Trade-based money laundering: responding to an emerging threat', (2009) 15 *Deakin Law Review* (1), 37; Clare Sullivan and Evan Smith, *Trade-Based Money Laundering: Risks and Regulatory Responses*, Canberra, Australian Institute of Criminology, 2011; Melvin Soudijn, 'A critical approach to trade-based money laundering', (2014) 17 *Journal of Money Laundering Control* (2), 230.

[130] Europol, 'Why is cash still king? a strategic report on the use of cash by criminal groups as a facilitator for money laundering', The Hague, European Police Office, 2015, p. 7.

High-denomination banknotes create a particular vulnerability. The report finds for example that, at the end of 2014, the €500 note alone accounted for more than 30 per cent of the €1 trillion of Euro banknotes in circulation, despite the fact that such a large banknote is not a common means of payment for general consumers and businesses.[131]

Aspects of informal financial services feature in the FATF Standards but in a limited manner.[132] High-denomination banknotes and trade-based laundering did receive some FATF attention in the past. In 1999 the FATF considered the introduction of the €500 note, raised concerns about its potential money laundering abuse, and called on the European Central Bank to thoroughly examine the potential legitimate and illicit uses of large-denomination banknotes.[133] The FATF has also issued a typology and best practices paper on trade-based money laundering.[134] Although these issues are highly relevant to combating crime, the focus on formal financial services meant that their relevance was not adequately reflected in the 2012 Standards.

FATF stakeholders argue that the mandatory risk-based approach incorporated in the 2012 Standards provides a country with the flexibility to address the cash economy and trade-based money laundering where these are found to hold significant risks. Such action would be domestic and unilateral. Unilateral action on generic aspects of transnational organised crime is, however, of limited effect and, where it displaces criminal activity to neighbours, may be counter-productive. The need for consistent, joint action underpins the FATF framework. The possibility of taking national action is not sufficient to address key gaps in the international money laundering strategy, therefore.

12.6 Final Observation

Although many questions remain regarding the effectiveness of the AML/CFT strategy to combat organised crime, it is important to recognize that the strategy resulted in the global community adopting a range of measures to disrupt criminal money flows. The strategy was very ambitious and that makes the level and speed of global adoption remarkable. Organised crime evolved, however, while the FATF standards still reflect the original crime combating strategy. There is therefore no assurance that effective implementation of the FATF Standards will mitigate organised crime risks. Despite the financial war waged on it, organised crime therefore still remains a major threat to national and international security.

[131] Ibid, p. 6; de Koker, 'Questions to consider', cited in note 127 above, p. 367.

[132] See, for example, FATF, *International Standards*, cited in note 39 above, Rec. 14, in relation to the registration of providers of money or value transfer services; for example, registration of remitters.

[133] Financial Action Task Force, *1998–1999 Report on Money Laundering Typologies*, FATF, 1999, paras 13–18.

[134] Financial Action Task Force, *Trade Based Money Laundering*, FATF, 2006; FATF, *Best Practices on Trade Based Money Laundering*, cited in note 130 above.

13

Transnational Organised Crime and the Illegal Trade in Endangered Species of Wild Fauna and Flora

Hennie Strydom

13.1 Introduction

Although the need for a universal international agreement regulating the cross-border trade in wildlife products has been on the rise since the early 1900s, the confluence of a number of factors in the 1960s and 1970s ripened the moment for agreement on an instrument of this kind. By that time states had become acutely aware of the fact that environmental problems could no longer be viewed as primarily a domestic matter; the idea that wild fauna and flora have value as such, as opposed to being mere economic commodities, had taken root by then; the trade in wildlife products was on the rise and with it the concern about some species becoming extinct; and international debates became infused with terminology such as 'sustainable development' and the 'sustainable use of natural resources'. In these moments of growing environmental awareness the 1973 Convention on International Trade in Endangered Species of Wild Fauna and Flora (CITES) was adopted by a relatively small number of plenipotentiaries in Washington at a time when the potential consequences of the 1972 gathering for the landmark Stockholm Declaration were still the subject of much speculation.

With 181 member states today, CITES is the world's most important treaty for conserving wild fauna and flora. Its main objective is the regulation of the international trade in endangered species in a manner that maintains the balance between the preservation of wildlife and the economic interests of states in the use of their natural resources. How CITES sets out to achieve this is dealt with later on in this chapter. Of specific relevance for this chapter is the potential role of CITES in the combating of wildlife crime, which has become a major concern for the international community in recent years. Like the illegal drug and arms trade and human trafficking, the illicit trade in wildlife products has become a major source of income for organised criminal groups and a further opportunity for multiplying their streams of income. From a law enforcement point of view this has become a major concern for the international community and the urgency has increased for states to strengthen international, regional, and bilateral cooperation in combating the illicit trade in wildlife products on the basis that it constitutes a serious crime with major social, political, environmental, and economic consequences for developing countries.

The chapter starts with an overview of the link between organised crime and the illegal trade in endangered species and why this phenomenon has been elevated to a level of international concern. This is followed by a brief description of the treaty developments that preceded CITES as the currently most important, near-universal, wildlife conservation instrument. The main objectives of CITES, the obligations of the states parties, and issues concerning compliance with CITES are dealt with in section 13.4, followed by enforcement problems in section 13.5. The linkage between CITES and other multilateral agreements is dealt with in section 13.6 and in section 13.7 regional initiatives in Africa, the Association of South-East Asian Nations (ASEAN), and the European Union (EU) are briefly explained. Some recent other initiatives are cursorily referred to in section 13.8. Some final observations are covered in section 13.9.

13.2 Transnational Organised Crime and the Illegal Trade in Endangered Species: The Scope of the Problem

In recent years the link between transnational organised crime and the illegal trade in endangered species has been raised in a number of international fora. The message that has emerged is that the states of the world are confronted with an increasing complex and difficult situation in successfully combating wildlife crime, which has the potential to pose a serious threat to the security, political stability, economy, and biological diversity of many countries. Especially at risk are developing countries, in which the regulatory regimes for the protection of natural resources and law enforcement capabilities suffer from a range of deficiencies. These include inadequate legislation; lack of proper training, intelligence gathering and forensic analysis; and poor governance and corruption.

At the outset some of the initiatives taken to raise awareness about the scope of the threat and the kind of action needed should be mentioned. In 2009, the first ever consortium, made up of representatives of CITES, Interpol, the United Nations Office on Drugs and Crime (UNODC), the World Bank, and the World Customs Organization (WCO), held a joint meeting in Vienna to bring together efforts in a coordinated strategy for the prevention and combating of wildlife crime.[1] In the 2012 'Future We Want' outcome document, the economic, social, and environmental impacts of the illicit trafficking in wildlife were duly recognized, coupled with a call for international cooperation in taking firm and strengthened action to deal with both the supply and the demand sides of wildlife crime.[2] One of the largest gatherings on corruption and illegal trade, including the illegal trade in wildlife, took place in September 2013 in Bangkok, Thailand. This initiative, known as the Asia-Pacific Economic Cooperation Pathfinder Dialogue was co-hosted by UNODC, the OECD, and the American Bar Association and focused on the need to combat corrupt activities that play such a large part in facilitating illicit trafficking in today's world.[3]

[1] See https://www.unodc.org/unodc/en/wildlife-and-forest-crime/iccwc.html, accessed 16 October 2015.

[2] UN GA Res. 66/288, 11 September 2012, para. 203.

[3] See http://www.apec.org/~/media/Files/Groups/ACT/20131027_PathfinderDialogue_ChairsSummary_FINAL.pdf, accessed 16 October 2015.

Under CITES, the 16th Conference of the Parties (CoP 16), held in Bangkok in 2013, took decisive action in response to the disturbing rise in the killing of elephants and rhinoceros for their ivory and horn. The decisions taken have implications for specific countries that have been identified as source, transit, and destination countries in the illicit trafficking chain, and will be dealt with later on. At the United Nations General Assembly thematic debate on wildlife and forest crime on 6 March 2015, high-level officials emphasized that this kind of crime has become an urgent and serious transnational organised crime that calls for a coordinated international response involving better law enforcement, community development, and measures to reduce demand.[4]

At the level of the Security Council the illicit exploitation of natural resources including wildlife poaching has received attention in the context of armed conflict situations in Africa. For instance, in the case of the internal armed conflict and widespread breakdown of law and order in the Central African Republic (CAR), the Security Council has expressed its concern with this phenomenon and, acting under Chapter VII of the UN Charter, has imposed obligations on UN member states to take the measures necessary to prevent certain listed individuals and entities from providing support for armed groups or criminal networks through the illicit exploitation of natural resources, including wildlife and wildlife products in the CAR.[5] This followed up an earlier resolution in which the Security Council made it clear that poaching and the trafficking in wildlife are among the factors that fuel the crisis in the CAR.[6]

In the case of the armed conflicts in the Great Lakes Region, the Report of the Expert Group on the Democratic Republic of the Congo has noted that the 'slaughter of elephants in the Democratic Republic of the Congo is one of the most tragic consequences of years of war and poor governance'.[7] Poaching by rebel forces is rife in a number of game parks and transit routes through Uganda and Kenya facilitate the illicit trade in poached animals.[8] In 2014 the Security Council, in response to this situation, drew attention to the linkage between the illicit trade in natural resources, including poaching and illegal trafficking of wildlife, and the proliferation and trafficking of arms. According to the Council this constitutes one of the major factors fuelling the conflict in the Great Lakes region of Africa.[9]

A number of wildlife-crime-specific reports further highlight the scope of the threat posed by the illegal exploitation and trade in wildlife and forest resources. In 2013, the International Fund for Animal Welfare (IFAW) published a report (a sequel to a 2008 report) on the global security implications of the illegal wildlife trade.[10] The report estimates that the trade involves revenue levels that are comparable with drug trafficking and the arms trade, and that enforcement agencies and security analysts have only recently begun to understand the linkages between the different sectors of

[4] See https://www.unodc.org/unodc/en/frontpage/2015/March/un-general-assembly-cooperation-vital-to-combating-organized-wildlife-crime.html, accessed 16 October 2015.

[5] SC Res. 2134, 2014, preamble and para. 37(d).

[6] SC Res. 2127, 2013, preamble.

[7] UN Doc. S/2014/42, 23 January 2014, para. 225.

[8] Ibid, paras 226ff.; and National Geographic, 'Tracking ivory', September 2015, p. 30.

[9] SC Res. 2136, 2014, preamble. See also paras 18 and 24.

[10] IFAW, *Criminal Nature: The Global Security Implications of the Illegal Wildlife Trade*, IFAW, 2013.

the criminal underworld and the threat they pose to global security and stability.[11] The illicit trading in ivory constitutes an important component of the illegal wildlife trade and in Africa this trade is funding a range of destabilizing actors across Africa such as militias, rebel movements, and terrorist organisations.[12]

A 2014 UN Environmental Programme (UNEP) report has also confirmed that wildlife parks, biodiversity hotspots, and other vulnerable habitats are increasingly exploited by militias and other non-state armed groups acting in conjunction with transnational criminal networks. This phenomenon causes ecologically important and sensitive areas to become militarized, which reduces the potential for conservation and contributes to the permanent destruction of natural resources, threatening local populations and their livelihoods. Moreover, at a transnational level the illegal trade in wildlife products to feed demand in foreign markets breeds corruption and undermines the rule of law.[13]

Since the illegal activities that form the subject matter of this chapter involve the illicit trade in endangered species of wild fauna and flora the primary international law instrument of relevance here is CITES, which came into force on 1 July 1975. This instrument and related developments will form the main focus of this chapter but some earlier developments must be highlighted first.

13.3 Some Key Earlier Examples of Conservation-minded International Legal Instruments: A Brief Overview

The use of international instruments for the protection or conservation of natural resources is a phenomenon that dates back to the latter part of the nineteenth century. In no small measure did colonial expansion and the travels of Charles Darwin stimulate interest in the world's wildlife resources during this time and ensuing legal developments in the field were helped along by the threat of industrialization and the growing interconnectedness of communities, coupled with their shared use of natural resources.[14]

In Europe the contemporary regulation of the use of international watercourses, of fishing in rivers, and of control over the spread of plant pests provides us with examples of a gradual internationalization of natural resource protection and management, albeit still motivated by narrow utilitarian objectives.[15] By the turn of the twentieth century

[11] Ibid, pp. 8 and 11–12. See also Mara E. Zimmerman, 'The black market for wildlife: combating transnational organized crime in the illegal wildlife trade', (2003) 36 *Vanderbilt Journal of Transnational Law*, 1657, p. 1667ff.

[12] See Center for Advanced Defense Studies, *Out of Africa: Mapping the Global Trade in Illicit Elephant Ivory*, Washington DC, Center for Advanced Defense Studies, 2014, pp. 8–9; Center for Strategic and International Studies, *Wildlife Poaching and Insecurity in Africa*, 2015, pp. 2–3, available at: http://csis.org, accessed 16 October 2015.

[13] Christian Nellemann, Rune Henriksen, Patricia Raxter, Neville Ash, and Elizabeth Mrema (eds), *The Environmental Crime Crisis: Threats to Sustainable Development from Illegal Exploitation and Trade in Wildlife and Forest Resources*, A UNEP Rapid Response Assessment, Geneva, UNICRI, 2014, pp. 48–9.

[14] Michael Bowman, Peter Davies, and Catherine Redgwell, *Lyster's International Wildlife Law*, 2nd edn, 2010 Cambridge University Press, pp. 3 and 4.

[15] Ibid, p. 5.

a further, still significant, international conservation dispute was the Bering Sea fur seals arbitration between the United States and the United Kingdom.[16] The conservation instrument from which the dispute arose was the bilateral treaty of 1892 between the United States and the United Kingdom relating to the US rights of jurisdiction in the Bering Sea and the preservation of fur seals. Unresolved issues then led to the 1911 Convention for the Preservation and Protection of Fur Seals in the North Pacific Ocean between the United States, Great Britain, Japan, and Russia and a further attempt in 1957 by the adoption of the Interim Convention on Conservation of North Pacific Fur Seals, amended in 1976 and supplemented by two Protocols in 1980 and 1984, respectively.[17] The narrow utilitarian objective of the 1911 Convention's conservation goal is clearly stated in its preamble, namely as 'achieving the maximum sustainable productivity of the fur seal resources of the North Pacific Ocean so that the fur seal population can be brought to and maintained at the levels which will provide the greatest harvest year after year ...'.

The need for the development of special protective regimes for wild fauna and flora resulted in the adoption of two multilateral treaties shortly before and after the outbreak of the Second World War. In 1933, nine states (the (then) Union of South Africa, the United Kingdom, Egypt, Spain, France, Italy, Portugal, and Anglo-Egyptian Sudan)[18] adopted the Convention Relative to the Preservation of Fauna and Flora in their Natural State in response to concerns that in certain parts of the world, particularly Africa, natural fauna and flora were in danger of extinction or permanent injury. A key measure envisaged in the Convention was the establishment of national parks and nature reserves within which hunting, killing, or capturing of fauna, and the collection or destruction of flora, would be limited or prohibited by the national authorities.

This approach was also followed in the second example, namely the 1940 Convention on Nature Protection and Wild Life Preservation in the Western Hemisphere, which counts amongst the first of its kind to conserve habitats as a means of protecting plant and animal species.[19] The initial signatories to this Convention were the United States, Venezuela, Ecuador, Costa Rica, Mexico, Uruguay, Brazil, Colombia, Chile, Guatemala, Haiti, Argentina, and Panama. It is also significant to note that the Convention provided in its Article IX for the regulation of the importation, exportation, and transit of protected fauna and flora. This was to be effected by the issuing of certificates by states parties authorizing the importation, exportation, and transit of such species. It stands to reason that this part of the Convention has now been overtaken by CITES.

[16] *Award between the United States and the United Kingdom relating to the rights of jurisdiction of United States in the Bering's Sea and the preservation of fur seals*, RIAA Vol. XXVII, 15 August 1893, 265.

[17] 1911 Convention, http://iea.uoregon.edu/page.php?query=treaties_lineage&lineage=North%20Pacific%20Fur%20Seals.

[18] Note the prominence of colonial states with possessions in Africa among the signatories. 1933 Convention Relative to the Preservation of Fauna and Flora in their Natural State, http://www.ecolex.org/ecolex/ledge/view/RecordDetails?id=TRE-000069&index=treaties.

[19] For a more extensive account of the Convention see Bowman, Davies, and Redgwell, *Lyster's International Wildlife Law*, cited in note 14 above, p. 241ff. The 1940 Convention on Nature Protection and Wild Life Preservation in the Western Hemisphere, http://www.ecolex.org/ecolex/ledge/view/RecordDetails?id=TRE-000069&index=treaties.

In 1968, the newly independent states in Africa adopted the African Convention on the Conservation of Nature and Natural Resources in Algiers. Subsequent developments, most notably the adoption of the Stockholm and Rio Declarations in 1972 and 1992 respectively, have prompted the African Union to revise certain aspects of the Convention and in 2003 a revised version was adopted during the second ordinary session of the Assembly of Heads and States of Government in Maputo. These and subsequent developments are dealt with in section 13.7.1 of this chapter.

Some ten years after the 1968 African Convention, the Council of Europe laid the foundation for the adoption in 1979 of the Convention on the Conservation of European Wildlife and Natural Habitats, also known as the Bern Convention. The preamble recognizes that wild fauna and flora 'constitute a natural heritage of aesthetic, scientific, cultural, recreational, economic and intrinsic value that needs to be preserved and handed on to future generations', a statement that confirms the value of wild fauna and flora as such, as opposed to the mere utilitarian value that some earlier treaties seem to have taken as a guiding norm. The conservation objective of the treaty was manifested in the obligation of states parties to conserve the habitats of wild fauna and flora, to pay special attention to the habitats of migratory species, and to coordinate efforts for the protection of habitat areas situated in frontier areas.[20]

With the exception of the 2003 version of the 1968 African Convention and the 1979 Bern Convention,[21] a common feature of these early instruments is the absence of institutional mechanisms for ensuring compliance with the provisions of the instruments. With enforcement options rather limited, the delivery of practical contributions to achieving the conservation objectives was destined to fall short of what was needed. However, there were secondary effects in that states parties increasingly resorted to national legislation as a means of regulating interstate commerce in protected species.[22]

13.4 The 1973 Convention on Illegal Trade in Endangered Species of Wild Fauna and Flora (CITES)

As early as 1963, the International Union for the Conservation of Nature (IUCN) campaigned for an international convention on the regulation of export, transit, and import of rare or threatened wildlife species, to address the practical and political problems involved in the illegal export of such species.[23] Successive drafts were prepared,

[20] Bern Convention Art. 4. For a more extensive account of the Convention see Bowman, Davies, and Redgwell, *Lyster's International Wildlife Law*, cited in note 14 above, p. 297ff.

[21] The 2003 version of the African Convention has assigned an enforcement and compliance function to a Conference of the Parties in Art. XXIII while the 1979 Bern Convention provides for a Standing committee to oversee the implementation of the Convention in Arts 13 and 14 (http://www.coe.int/en/web/bern-convention/presentation).

[22] Peter H. Sand 'Whither CITES? The evolution of a treaty regime in the borderland of trade and environment', (1997) 1 *EJIL*, 29, p. 33.

[23] IUCN, *Proceedings of the 8th Session of the General Assembly*, Gland, Switzerland, IUCN, 1963, p. 130 para. 5. This resolution of the IUCN wrongly refers to Res. 1931 of the UN General Assembly on economic development and the conservation of nature, adopted in 1962 during the 17th session of the Assembly. The correct number of the resolution is 1831. On the increase in international wildlife trade in the 1960s and 1970s see Bowman, Davies, and Redgwell, *Lyster's International Wildlife Law*, cited in note 14 above, p. 483.

circulated, and revised between 1963 and 1971 based on the premise that the controlling or banning of wildlife trade would be informed by global lists of threatened species, updated from time to time by an international expert committee. This approach was opposed by developing countries and the United States, which were of the view that the determination of threatened species should reside with individual states. A consolidation of the different views served as part of the draft convention that was submitted to the conference of eighteen plenipotentiaries that met in Washington in February/March 1973 for the adoption of CITES.[24]

13.4.1 Main objectives

Since wild fauna and flora represent irreplaceable elements of the Earth's natural systems, CITES has the objective of protecting particular species against over-exploitation through international trade. The species that are subject to special protective measures are listed in three appendices according to their vulnerability. Roughly 5,600 animal species and 30,000 plant species are listed in the appendices. Appendix I covers all species threatened with extinction and that might be affected by trade. Trade in specimens of these species is therefore subject to particularly strict regulation to prevent further threats to their survival. Hence, trade in them is allowed only in exceptional circumstances.[25]

Appendix II includes species that may become threatened with extinction unless trade in them is strictly regulated to avoid a level of utilization that is incompatible with their survival. It also includes other species that must be subject to regulation to bring under effective control the trade in species mentioned in the previous sentence.[26]

Appendix III lists all species identified by any state party as being subject to national regulation for the purpose of preventing or restricting exploitation and for which co-operation by other states parties is needed in the control of trade.[27]

13.4.2 Obligations of the states parties

This categorization of vulnerable species under three Appendices has the effect that states parties are interdicted from allowing trade in these species that is not in accordance with the provisions of CITES.[28] Thus, the trade in species falling under Appendix I is only lawful on the basis of an export or import permit issued by the relevant authorities once certain conditions have been met.[29] These are: a scientific report advising that the export or import will not be detrimental to the survival of the species; and proof that the specimen was not unlawfully obtained, that shipment, housing, and care will not put the specimen at risk, and that the specimen is not intended to be used primarily for commercial purposes.[30] To the extent relevant, these conditions also apply to trade in Appendix II and III species.[31]

[24] Sand, 'Whither CITES?', cited in note 22 above, p. 34. [25] CITES, Art. II(1).
[26] Ibid, Art. II(2). [27] Ibid, Art. II(3). [28] Ibid, Art. II(4).
[29] A permit must comply with the requirements of CITES, Art. VI.
[30] Ibid, Art. III. [31] Ibid, Arts IV and V.

The requirements and conditions for trade specified in the previous paragraph do not affect the right of states parties to adopt stricter domestic measures for trade, the taking, possession, or transport of specimens of species listed in Appendices I–III, or the complete prohibition thereof. Also not affected are obligations for states parties deriving from other international agreements relating to other aspects of trade, possession, or transport of specimens; or the obligations deriving from regional trade agreements establishing a Customs Union and customs control system.[32]

Apart from permit and authorization requirements, states parties incur certain minimum obligations for the enforcement of CITES and the prohibition of trade in specimens in contravention of CITES. The trade in and possession of specimens covered in the Appendices must be penalized and their confiscation and return to the state of export must be provided for.[33] In case of the latter, a state party may also provide for any method of internal reimbursement for expenses incurred as a result of the confiscation and return.[34]

The passing of specimens through trade formalities must be ensured with a minimum of delay and for that purpose a state party may designate certain ports of exit and entry at which specimens must be presented for clearance. In the case of living specimens, states parties must ensure that these are properly cared for so as to minimize the risk of injury, damage to health, or cruel treatment during transit, holding, or shipment.[35]

When a living specimen is confiscated, it must be entrusted to a Management Authority in the confiscating state.[36] After consultation with the state of export, the Management Authority must return the specimen to that state or to such other place as the Authority deems appropriate and consistent with CITES. In such instances, the Authority may obtain the advice of a Scientific Authority,[37] or the CITES Secretariat.[38]

States parties are further obliged to maintain an inventory of trade in specimens included in the Appendices,[39] and must submit periodic reports to the Secretariat on the measures taken to facilitate the implementation of CITES.[40] The periodic reports take the form of an annual report containing a summary of the information in the specimen inventory and a biennial report on legislative, regulatory, and administrative measures taken to enforce the provisions of CITES.[41]

13.4.3 Compliance, control, and cooperation

The CoP, established under Article XI, is the main body for overseeing the implementation of CITES and for improving compliance with it.[42] The functions assigned to the

[32] Ibid, Art. XIV. [33] Ibid, Art. VIII(1).
[34] Ibid, Art. VIII(2). [35] Ibid, Art. VIII(3)
[36] Ibid, Art. IX provides for the designation by states parties of Management Authorities responsible for the granting of permits or certificates.
[37] See Ibid, Art. IX. [38] Ibid, Art. VIII(4). [39] Ibid, Art. VIII(6).
[40] Ibid, Arts XII (reporting) and VIII(7) (content of report). [41] Ibid, Art. VIII(7).
[42] See also the 'Guide to CITES Compliance Procedures' in Resolution Conf. 14.3 (adopted at the 14th COP, available at https://cites.org/eng/res/14/14-03C15.php).

CoP are performed in conjunction with the Secretariat, established under Article XII. What warrants attention here are some resolutions and recommendations of the CoP aimed at improving compliance with CITES.

In 2010, at CoP 15, states parties noted that, despite the fact that substantial progress had been made with the national implementation of CITES, approximately half of the parties still lack appropriate measures at the national level for the enforcement of the Convention's provisions. It therefore directed the Secretariat to identify the states parties whose domestic measures do not provide them with the authority to comply with their core obligations under CITES and to seek from such states parties information indicating the action and time frames they envisage for adopting, as a matter of the highest priority, the measures required for the effective implementation of the Convention. It was also made clear that defaulting members may face compliance measures, including the suspension of trade in certain species.[43] Information published in 2014 and compiled by the Secretariat showed that 48.3 per cent of states parties had in place legislation that is believed generally to meet the requirements for implementation; 27.2 per cent of states had legislation in place that is believed generally not to meet all the requirements for implementation; and 21.7 per cent of states had legislation in place that is believed generally not to meet the requirements for implementation. At the time 2.8 per cent of the states had legislation pending.[44]

Over the years the CoP has dealt with a number of issues relating to enforcement and compliance, which, by implication, expose the areas where improvement is expected in the performance by states parties if CITES is to become more effective in combating the illegal wildlife trade. The issues include the strengthening of controls over shipments from producing countries; the strict verification of documents originating from producing countries; the raising of the combating of the illegal wildlife trade as a matter of high priority; the proper training and equipping of wildlife law-enforcement officials; the effective punishment of violators; prompt reply to requests for information by the Secretariat; improved cooperation between Management Authorities and governmental agencies responsible for the enforcement of CITES; improved cooperation and coordination between parties and wildlife law-enforcement agencies within the different regions; the nomination of officials for participation in the Interpol Wildlife Crime Working Group; the establishment of mechanisms for monitoring internet-related wildlife trade; and the development of a comprehensive strategy for border controls, audits, and investigations.[45]

The increase in the scale of wildlife crime in recent years and the transnational and organised nature of it have also exposed the urgent need for more effective collaboration and cooperation between intergovernmental organisations and enforcement agencies to combat what has become a serious crime, given the threat it poses

[43] Resolution Conf. 8.4 (Rev. CoP 15). Resolution 8.4 (CoP 1992) (https://cites.org/eng/cop/index.php) provides the basis for the CITES national legislation project and aims at assisting states parties in adopting adequate and up-to-date legislative measures for the effective implementation of CITES.

[44] See https://cites.org/eng/legislation, accessed 1 October 2015.

[45] See Willem Wijnstekers, *The Evolution of CITES*, 9th edn, Budapest, CIC—International Council for Game and Wildlife Conservation, 2011, Ch. 16; and Resolution Conf.11.3 (Rev. CoP 16).

to the security, political stability, and economies of many countries and regions. To bring coordinated support to wildlife law enforcement an International Consortium on Combating Wildlife Crime (ICCWC) was established in 2010. The Consortium is made up of CITES, Interpol, UNODC, and the WCO, and coordinates global, regional, and national responses to critical issues in wildlife crime.[46]

13.5 Enforcement Problems

13.5.1 Reservations and exemptions

CITES disallows general reservations to the Convention.[47] Parties to the Convention are entitled to enter only specific reservations with regard to any of the species in any of the Appendices or to any parts or derivatives in relation to a species in Appendix III. Reservations of this kind must be made at the time of depositing an instrument of ratification, acceptance, approval, or accession by a state party.[48] Until a reserving party has withdrawn its reservation it shall be treated as a non-state party to the Convention with respect to trade in a species, or parts, or derivatives specified in the reservation.[49] The same effect will result from reservations to amendments adopted by parties in respect of Appendices I and II,[50] and in respect of lists submitted under Appendix III and amendments thereto.[51]

It has been suggested that the aim of the inclusion of reservation clauses in CITES was to accommodate two objectives: first, to prevent dissent between parties over the listing and status of species posing an obstacle to ratification of the Convention, and second, to accommodate the objective of CITES, namely to strike a balance between protecting endangered wildlife species on the one hand and the economic interests of states relating to wildlife trade, on the other.[52]

Although a reservation results in the reserving state becoming a non-state party to the Convention to the extent of the reservation, the reserving state seems to be still obliged to at least comply with the Convention's documentation requirements. Article X, for instance, determines that in trade between a non-state party and a state party the latter may accept 'comparable documentation' from the former that 'substantially conforms' to the requirements of the Convention for trade permits and certificates. However, whatever merit this 'safeguard' might hold, it is rendered ineffective in trade between a reserving state and a non-party and between states parties that have entered identical reservations. Since in the latter instance the trade is between non-state parties, reserving states with a large market share in wildlife trade may provide opportunities for illicit trade in endangered species, especially if the reserving states are countries of origin and have fewer resources for effective enforcement.[53]

[46] For more information on the ICCWC see http://www.cites.org/eng/prog/ICCWC.php, accessed 16 October 2015.

[47] CITES, Art. XXIII(1). [48] Ibid, Art. XXIII(2). [49] Ibid, Art. XXIII(3).

[50] Ibid, Art. XV(3). [51] Ibid, Art. XVI(2).

[52] Gwyneth G. Stewart 'Enforcement problems in the endangered species conventions: reservations regarding the reservation clauses', (1981) 14 *Cornell International Law Journal*, 429, p. 436.

[53] Ibid, p. 438.

That the reservation clauses may be contradictory to the general objectives of CITES has been duly noted, with the further observation that there seems to be 'little doubt that their operation has detrimental effects on listed endangered species'.[54] In an apparent attempt to limit the potentially detrimental effects of reservations on the protection of certain endangered species, the fourth CoP meeting recommended that parties having entered a reservation with regard to Appendix I species treat that species as if it were an Appendix II species for all purposes, including documentation and control. The same meeting also called on parties having entered reservations to nevertheless maintain and communicate statistical records on trade affected by the reservation so that international trade in such species may still be properly monitored.[55] At the eleventh meeting it was nevertheless necessary to make states parties again aware of the fact that reservations by importing countries allow loopholes for specimens illegally acquired in countries of origin to find legal markets 'without any control whatsoever'.[56]

In addition to reservations the protective objective of CITES may be further compromised by the exemptions provided for in the Convention. For instance, the Articles III, IV, and V conditions for the regulation of trade in Appendix I, II, and III species do not apply to the transit or trans-shipment of specimens through or in the territory of a party as long as the specimens remain under Customs control.[57] Also exempted from these provisions are specimens acquired before the Convention became applicable to them, provided a Management Authority in the state concerned has issued a certificate to that effect;[58] specimens that are personal, and household effects,[59] although in the case of the latter certain conditions must be fulfilled;[60] and specimens subject to a non-commercial loan, donation, or exchange between scientists or scientific institutions registered by a Management Authority of their state.[61]

A Management Authority of a state is also entitled to waive the requirements of Articles III, IV, and V and to allow the movement without permits or certificates of specimens forming part of a travelling zoo, circus, menagerie, or plant exhibition.[62] However, in these instances the exporter or importer must register full details of the specimens with the Management Authority; the specimens must have been acquired prior to the Convention, or bred in captivity (in the case of an animal), or artificially propagated (in the case of a plant); and the relevant Management Authority must be satisfied that any living specimen will be transported and cared for in a manner that will minimize the risk of injury, damage, harm to health, or cruel treatment.[63]

The above, potentially problematic, features of CITES must be read in conjunction with the concerns expressed by the CoP with regard to the enforcement and evasion of the Convention's provisions. For instance, it has been noted that, in the past in both

[54] Philippe Sands and Jacqueline Peel, *Principles of International Environmental Law*, Cambridge, CUP, 2012, p. 476.
[55] Resolution Conf. 4.25 (Rev. CoP 14).
[56] Resolution Conf. 11.3 (Rev. CoP 16), preamble.
[57] CITES, Art. VII(1).
[58] Ibid, Art. VII(2).
[59] Ibid, Art. VII(3).
[60] Ibid, Art. VII(3)(a) and (b).
[61] Ibid, Art. VII(6).
[62] Ibid, Art. VII(7).
[63] Ibid, Art. VII(7)(a)–(c).

importing and exporting countries, violations have occurred as a result of inadequate or insufficient implementation by Management Authorities,[64] with regard to surveillance and compliance with the issuance of documentation and provisions regulating trade in endangered species.[65] Variations in capacity to implement and to enforce provide further opportunity for exploitation, a factor that is even more disconcerting in developing countries that experience major difficulties in complying with control requirements as a result of their socio-economic, political, and geographic circumstances.[66] Moreover, the extreme implementation and enforcement difficulties faced by producer countries exacerbate enforcement problems in other countries, while consumer countries often allow illegal imports as a result of inadequate CITES control in producer countries and in that way become directly responsible for encouraging illegal trade world-wide.[67]

13.5.2 The complexity and gravity of the problem

The involvement, for some time now, of a number of UN bodies and other international and national organisations and entities in the combating of wildlife crime provides ample evidence that the illegal trade in fauna and flora is no longer considered as an emerging issue. Instead, it has become a massive global industry worth billions of dollars annually and well integrated within the illicit economies that drive organised crime, international terrorism, and violent conflicts.[68] In taking these developments into account, as well as the seriousness of the threat they pose to the security, environment, and sustainable development of many countries, it has been noted that the 'pace, level of sophistication and globalised nature of wildlife and forest crime is beyond the capacity of many countries and individual organisations to address'.[69] As a result there is a gap between commitments and compliance that needs to be narrowed.

The nature of the trafficking supply chain poses serious obstacles for enforcement agencies. Although trafficking organisations must often source, transport, and sell their contraband along a complex supply chain that crosses borders and oceans, from remote corners in Africa to retail markets in Asia, they have succeeded in consolidating and professionalizing their operations. In the illegal ivory trade alone transnational organised crime networks trafficked as much as 170 tons of ivory between 2009 and 2014, which, according to reports, could amount to as many as 229,729 elephants.[70] Studies have shown that networks of this kind are tied together by a large number of facilitators in a global distribution chain made up of an almost infinite number of poachers

[64] To make these authorities more effective practical guidelines were developed to assist them with their verification tasks. See Alison R. Rosser and Mandy J. Haywood, *Guidance for Cites Scientific Authorities: Checklist to assist in making non-detriment findings for Appendix II exports*, Cambridge, IUCN, 2002; and European Community Regs No. 338/97 and 687/2006, agreed on 3 September 2014.

[65] Resolution Conf. 11.3 (Rev. CoP 16), preamble. [66] Ibid. [67] Ibid.

[68] IFAW, *Criminal Nature*, cited in note 10 above, pp. 11–12; *Illegal Wildlife Trade Declaration*, paras 2–4 (https://www.gov.uk/government/publications/declaration-london-conference-on-the-illegal-wildlife-trade).

[69] Nellemann *et al.*, *The Environmental Crime Crisis*, cited in note 13 above, p. 10.

[70] CADC, *Out of Africa*, cited in note 12 above, pp. 3 and 10ff.

in remote areas in Africa, illicit mineral transporters, freight forwarding companies, shipping agents, politicians, and merchants operating mainly in China, Thailand, and Vietnam.[71]

The methods used to facilitate the illicit trade in wildlife products also illustrate the complexity of the problem and the sophistication of the criminal networks. The trade commonly involves the mixing of legal and illegal harvesting of resources, the forgery of documents, the hacking of government websites to obtain forged permits, the establishing of shell companies, the bribing of corrupt government officials, and the laundering of contraband.[72] Corruption seems to be of special concern in that it is considered a 'deeply embedded feature of environmental crime'.[73] At the same time these methods illustrate the wide range of measures member states will have to implement to effectively curb the illegal trade in wildlife products, which raises serious concerns about the capacity of some states to effectively combat wildlife crime, a matter that features frequently in CITES documentation and CoP meetings and that the UNODC is attempting to address with its Wildlife and Forest Crime Analytic Toolkit.[74]

Apart from capacity issues there is also the issue of discrepancies within and among national wildlife, forestry, criminal, and other laws. In this regard, the UNODC has concluded that:

> [m]any countries do not, or do not yet, comprehensively criminalise the many activities involved in illegal trade in wild fauna and flora. In some jurisdictions, the criminal law does not adequately capture attempts at committing offences or participation in these offences. In addition, it may not contain special provisions for corruption and money-laundering in the wildlife and forestry sectors. Consequently, the reform of legal and regulatory systems becomes a prerequisite for combating wildlife and forest crime.[75]

13.6 CITES and the Broader International Treaty Framework

As a result of treaty developments since the adoption of CITES, enforcement measures may be multifaceted because of overlapping treaty membership and states parties may draw inspiration from (mainly) three other multilateral instruments. These are the 1992 Convention on Biological Diversity, the 2000 UN Convention Against Transnational Organized Crime, and the 2003 UN Convention against Corruption. The latter two Conventions entered into force in 2003 and 2005 respectively. Below, the relevance of these instruments for the subject matter of this chapter is cursorily dealt with.

[71] Ibid, 31ff.
[72] Nellemann *et al.*, *The Environmental Crime Crisis*, cited in note 13 above, pp. 13 and 14.
[73] Ibid, p. 14.
[74] Available at https://www.unodc.org/documents/Wildlife/Toolkit_e.pdf, accessed 16 October 2015.
[75] cited in note 73 above, p. 13.

13.6.1 The Convention on Biological Diversity (CBD)

The common objective that CITES shares with the CBD is the conservation of biological diversity and the sustainable use of its components.[76] The difference is that CITES pursues this objective by means of a set of circumscribed trade restrictions and their regulation to protect endangered species of wild fauna and flora, while the CBD envisages the adoption of a wide range of measures for the conservation of biodiversity in general, the form and manner of which is largely left to the discretion of the states parties.[77] CITES also places the emphasis on the adoption of *enforcement* measures as an obligation under the Convention, which include the *penalization* of the trade in or possession of certain specimens and their confiscation and return to the state of export.[78] In the case of the CBD, the emphasis is on the adoption of national strategies, plans, programmes, and management systems for the conservation and sustainable use of biological diversity.[79] However, states remain free after all to provide in their domestic law criminal sanctions to protect their biological resources as a corollary of the sovereignty they exercise over such resources.

13.6.2 UN Convention against Transnational Organised Crime (Palermo Convention)

The Palermo Convention is of direct relevance for the combating of the illicit trade in endangered species in that it provides a new tool for international cooperation in combating organised crime and its globalized, illicit, economic enterprises more effectively.[80] This relevance was recognized by the UN General Assembly on the occasion of the adoption of the text of the Palermo Convention in 2000.[81] Since this Convention is extensively covered in Chapter 7 of this volume, this section will only allude to a few salient aspects.

The Palermo Convention applies to 'serious crimes' committed by 'organised criminal groups'. A serious crime is defined as 'conduct constituting an offence punishable by a maximum deprivation of liberty of at least four years or a more serious penalty'.[82] An 'organised criminal group' means ' a structured group of three or more persons, existing for a period of time and acting in concert with the aim of committing one or more serious crimes or offences established in accordance with this Convention, in order to obtain, directly or indirectly, a financial or other material benefit'.[83] Although the threshold for an offence to qualify as a serious crime is relatively low, the complementary role of the Palermo Convention in combating wildlife crime will very much

[76] The Convention on Biological Diversity. Reprinted in P. Sands and P. Galizzi (eds) *Documents in International Environmental Law*, 2nd edn, 2004, Cambridge University Press, p. 696.

[77] See Convention on Biological Diversity, Arts 6–10.

[78] CITES, Art. VIII(1).

[79] Cited in note 77 above.

[80] Palermo Convention, opened for signature 15 November 2000, 2225 UNTS 209, in force 29 September 2003; Art. 1.

[81] UN GA Res. 55/25 of 15 November 2000.

[82] Palermo Convention, cited in note 80 above, Art. 2(b).

[83] Ibid, Art. 2(a).

depend on national measures for penalizing the trade in and possession of specimens under CITES and the harmonization of such measures with the implementation of the Palermo Convention. The definition of an organised criminal group should be unproblematic in the case of organised criminal activities in wildlife crime. It is uncontested that wildlife crime is facilitated by cross-border networks involving a sophisticated and well-organised chain of persons and entities financially benefiting, directly or indirectly, from the illegal enterprise. Those involved in such enterprises also operate as a 'structured group', meaning 'a group that is not randomly formed for the immediate commission of an offence and that does not need to have formally defined roles for its members, continuity of its membership or a developed structure'.[84] Much of modern-day wildlife crime is also transnational in nature and satisfies Article 3(2) of the Convention.

Other complementary features of the Palermo Convention include the criminalization of corruption,[85] which plays a significant role in the facilitation of organised criminal activities; the criminalization and combating of money-laundering;[86] the criminal liability of legal persons;[87] the confiscation of the proceeds of crime;[88] extradition;[89] and mutual legal assistance in investigations, prosecutions, and judicial proceedings.[90]

Of specific relevance is the offence of participation in the activities of an organised criminal group.[91] Since many forms of wildlife crime are indirectly associated with organised crime, and since organised crime syndicates make use of various forms of assistance in furthering their criminal undertakings, traditional forms of criminal liability may not always be suitable for criminally charging individuals involved with and in a criminal organisation. This is especially the case with large syndicates operating through various subsidiaries in different parts of the world. Those in leadership positions seldom get involved in the actual execution of the criminal act and many individuals, although contributing to the activities of the syndicate in some way or another, might not have specific knowledge about the individual crimes associated with the syndicate.

Article 5 widens the scope of criminal liability by criminalizing participation as an act distinct from the attempt to commit a criminal offence or the completion thereof. Participation can be manifested in agreeing with others to commit a serious crime for the purpose of directly or indirectly obtaining a financial or other material benefit and involving an organised criminal group.[92] Under this provision, knowledge of the activities of the organised criminal group is not a requirement for establishing the criminal liability of the participant.

13.6.3 UN Convention against Corruption

This convention is extensively covered in Chapter 11. What needs to be emphasized here is that corruption has become a transnational phenomenon, as the preamble of

[84] Ibid, Art. 2(c). [85] Ibid, Art. 8. See also Art. 9. [86] Ibid, Arts 6 and 7.
[87] Ibid, Art. 10. [88] Ibid, Arts 12 and 13. [89] Ibid, Art. 16. [90] Ibid, Art. 18.
[91] Ibid, Art. 5. [92] Ibid, Art. 5(1)(a).

the Convention rightly confirms, and it plays a significant role in the chain of events that facilitate cross-border criminal activities. As pointed out earlier in this chapter, corruption of government officials is one of the obstacles in combating wildlife crime effectively. Hence, the use of the Convention to facilitate international cooperation in preventing and combating corrupt activities could be complementary to the combating of the illicit trade in endangered species under CITES and to the international measures for the combating of transnational organised crime under the Palermo Convention, which, as indicated above, also contains anti-corruption measures.

13.6.4 UN Convention Concerning the Protection of the World Cultural and Natural Heritage

This Convention predates CITES by one year and was adopted by the seventeenth session of UNESCO's General Conference on 16 November 1972.[93] Its main objective is to provide for the collective protection of cultural and natural heritage of outstanding universal value on a permanent basis and in accordance with scientific methods. 'Natural heritage' includes natural features consisting of physical and biological formations with an outstanding universal value from an aesthetic or scientific perspective; delineated areas that constitute the habitat of threatened plant and animal species; and natural sites with an outstanding universal value from a science, conservation, or natural beauty perspective.[94]

The Convention recognizes that the cultural and natural heritage that it refers to primarily belong to the territorial state and that the territorial state will do its utmost in taking the necessary protective measures.[95] However, this deferral to national sovereignty is qualified by the recognition that the heritage in question constitutes a world heritage with the result that the international community as a whole must cooperate in achieving the objectives of the Convention.[96] For this purpose the Convention envisages the establishment of a system of international cooperation and assistance to support states parties in their efforts to identify and conserve their heritage.[97] For this purpose a World Heritage Committee has been established, made up of representatives of twenty-one of the states parties.[98]

13.7 Regional Efforts

Over the years various regional initiatives have been taken to supplement and strengthen the enforcement of measures against wildlife and forest crime. This has come about as a result of region-specific issues and the need for greater cooperation between enforcement agencies and other role players at the regional level. Some of the main developments are dealt with below.

[93] UN Convention Concerning the Protection of the World Cultural and Natural Heritage. Reprinted in P. Sands and P. Galizzi (eds) *Documents in International Environmenal Law*, 2nd edn, 2004, Cambridge University Press, p. 644.

[94] Art. 2. [95] Art. 4. [96] Art. 6. [97] Art. 7. [98] Art. 8.

13.7.1 Africa

Earlier, in section 13.3, mention was made of the 1968 African Convention on the Conservation of Nature and Natural Resources (revised in 2003).[99] In this section some elaboration on its scope and its implementation is needed, especially in the context of subsequent developments.

The opening paragraph in the Convention's preamble acknowledges that Africa's natural environment and natural resources 'are an irreplaceable part of the African heritage and constitute a capital of vital importance to the continent and humankind as a whole'. The preamble also affirms that the conservation of the global environment is a common concern of humankind and that the African environment is a *primary* concern of all Africans. Based on this assumption, the Convention aims at the enhancement of environmental protection, the conservation and sustainable use of natural resources, and the harmonization and coordination of policies in these areas.[100] The obligations of states in this regard, interestingly enough, are rights-based in that states are instructed to perform their Convention duties with due regard for the right of all peoples to a satisfactory environment favourable to their development and for ensuring the enjoyment of the right to development.[101] The wording of these rights provisions is taken from Articles 22 and 24 respectively, of the African Charter on Human and Peoples' Rights, which raise, at least in theory, interesting questions about the kinds of remedy available to individuals or communities in the case of non-observation or inadequate observation of the Convention duties.[102] In this regard it must also be noted that under the Convention it is a *fundamental obligation* for states to adopt and implement 'all measures necessary to achieve the objectives of this Convention, in particular through preventive measures and the application of the precautionary principle'.[103] In the context of state responsibility in international law, the duty to adopt preventive measures, in particular to prevent transboundary harm, is now recognized as a fundamental principle of customary international law by the International Court of Justice,[104] and it forms an integral part of the due diligence obligations of governments.[105]

Cooperation between the parties, as a Convention obligation, has the aim of strengthening the implementation of the Convention, but also of dealing with the transboundary consequences of national measures, the enhancement of their effectiveness, and the harmonization of laws and policies adopted at the continental or regional (read: subregional) levels. In particular, cooperation is incumbent upon the parties when a natural resource or ecosystem straddles borders, in which case the cooperation must aim at

[99] African Convention on the Conservation of Nature and Natural Resources. See http://sedac.ciesin.org/entri/texts/african.conv.conserva.1969.html

[100] Art. II. [101] Art. III.

[102] The African Charter on Human and Peoples' Rights, http://www.achpr.org/instruments/achpr/.

[103] Art. IV.

[104] See *Legality of the Threat of Nuclear Weapons*, Advisory Opinion, ICJ Reports 1996(1), para. 29; *Pulp Mills on the River Uruguay (Argentina v Uruguay)*, ICJ Reports 2010(14), para. 193.

[105] See Seabed Disputes Chamber (ITLOS), *Responsibilities and Obligations of States Sponsoring Persons and Entities with Respect to Activities in the Area*, Advisory Opinion, List of Cases no. 17, 1 February 2011, paras 107–16.

the conservation, development, and management of the resource or ecosystem, if need be by means of an interstate commission.[106]

More specifically relevant for CITES is the Lusaka Agreement on Co-Operative Enforcement Operations Directed at Illegal Trade in Wild Fauna and Flora of 1994.[107] Poaching of wild fauna and flora and the illegal trade in these objects have taken on serious proportions in Africa and are a major contributor to the depletion of certain wildlife populations in African states with serious consequences for biodiversity. It therefore makes sense that the Lusaka Agreement finds its orientation in the African Convention on the Conservation of Nature and Natural Resources (1968, revised 2003), CITES, and the CBD.[108] Essentially an enforcement instrument, the areas to which the Agreement applies are those comprising the land, marine, and coastal areas that fall within the limits of national jurisdiction of the states parties, including their air space and internal waters.[109]

In fulfilling their obligations under the Agreement the parties must individually and/or jointly take appropriate measures to investigate and prosecute cases of illegal trade and must also cooperate with one another in reducing, and ultimately eliminating, illegal trade in wild fauna and flora.[110] The main instrument created in pursuit of the Agreement's objectives is the Task Force for Co-operative Enforcement Operations Directed at Illegal Trade in Wild Fauna and Flora.[111] The Task Force possesses international legal personality and has the legal capacity necessary for the performance of its functions in the territories of the member states. Its members also enjoy immunity from legal process in member states.[112]

Governmental entities or national bureaux must be established or designated at the national level through which information sharing will take place and investigations into illegal trade by the Task Force will be coordinated.[113] These activities, as well as the functioning of the Task Force, fall under the supervisory and monitoring powers of a Governing Council comprising delegates from all states parties. The Council is also responsible for keeping under review the overall implementation of the Agreement.[114]

Cooperation in the field of biodiversity, conservation, and management also became the subject of a Memorandum of Understanding (MoU) between South Africa and Mozambique on 17 April 2014. Apart from linking the *ratio* for the MoU to the general obligations of the parties under the CBD and CITES, it is clear from the preamble that a strong motivation for the MoU is the poaching and trafficking of wild animals in the sub-region. It is widely known that this phenomenon has reached critical levels and that poaching syndicates often operate from Mozambican territory, where they enjoy the protection of local communities and of corrupt government officials. In the first four months of 2015 alone, the poaching of rhinoceros in the Kruger National Park,

[106] Art. XXII and especially XXII(2)(e).

[107] The Lusaka Agreement on Co-Operative Enforcement Operations Directed at Illegal Trade in Wild Fauna and Flora, https://treaties.un.org/pages/ViewDetails.aspx?src=TREATY&mtdsg_no=XXVII-11&chapter=27&lang=en.

[108] Lusaka Agreement, preamble. [109] Art. 1, 'agreement area'. [110] Arts 2 and 4(1).

[111] Art. 5(1). [112] Arts 5(8) and (11). [113] Art. 6. [114] Art. 7.

bordering Mozambique, has escalated by 20 per cent, compared with 2014, amounting to 544 rhinos killed. According to reports roughly 'three rhino a day are slaughtered by well-armed poachers who enter the park illegally, many from Mozambique, in small groups'.[115]

Not only does the MoU specifically mention cooperation between the parties for law enforcement purposes, but it also makes reference to the 1999 SADC Protocol on Wildlife Conservation and Law Enforcement, which has the primary objective to establish within the region common approaches to the conservation and sustainable use of wildlife resources and to assist with the effective enforcement of laws applicable to such resources.[116] The Protocol is premised on the principle that states parties have the obligation to ensure that activities within their jurisdiction or control do not cause damage to the wildlife resources of other states or in areas beyond the limits of national jurisdiction.[117] Hence states parties must take the necessary legal, administrative and policy measures to ensure the conservation and sustainable use of wildlife; to enforce national legislation pertaining to wildlife effectively; and to cooperate with one another to manage shared wildlife resources as well as the transfrontier effects of activities within their jurisdiction or control.[118] The harmonization of national laws in the sub-region is also singled out as a matter on which states parties must act. This relates, *inter alia*, to measures governing the taking of wildlife; measures governing the trade in wildlife and wildlife products; measures determining penalties for the illegal taking of and trade in wildlife products; and procedures governing the extradition of offenders.[119]

Measuring these regional treaties together, the MoU between South Africa and Mozambique is the weakest of the three in terms of its law enforcement objective. While cooperation between the parties in the area of law enforcement is listed amongst the instrument's purposes in Article 1, the law enforcement issue is not again specifically listed amongst the priority areas of cooperation in Article 2 of the MoU. Instead, one finds a more general reference to 'compliance with national laws and applicable regional and sub-regional conventions and protocols' (Article 2(e)). Moreover, in the implementation provision (Article 5), the MoU makes use of hortatory language in stating that the parties shall 'encourage' their respective organisations and their law and order institutions 'to interact through their respective ministries in the management, conservation and protection of biodiversity, law enforcement and compliance with CITES and other conventions and relevant legislation'. The forms of cooperation in Article 3 are also couched in vague and open-ended language. It states that the parties 'may' cooperate through the exchange of information; visits of delegations; joint organisation of seminars, etc.; the establishment of an implementation framework; and other forms of cooperation—not exactly the kind of language that will make game poachers quiver in their boots.

[115] *Business Day*, 'Plan B needed to save rhinos', 2 September 2015, p. 11 (Review & Opinion).

[116] The SADC Protocol on Wildlife Conservation and Law Enforcement, http://www.sadc.int/documents-publications/show/Protocol%20on%20Wildlife%20Conservation%20and%20Law%20Enforcement%20%281999%29.

[117] SADC Protocol, Art. 3(1). [118] Ibid, Art. 3(2). [119] Ibid, Art. 6.

13.7.2 ASEAN

During the thirteenth Conference of the Parties to CITES in October 2004, a number of ASEAN countries (Brunei, Cambodia, Indonesia, Thailand, Malaysia, Myanmar, the Philippines, Singapore, and Vietnam) issued a statement, committing themselves, *inter alia*, to further promote regional cooperation through bilateral and multilateral arrangements between enforcement agencies for achieving more effective control of the illegal international trade in endangered wildlife species; to strengthen enforcement efforts along their borders; and to improve law enforcement capacity and capability.[120]

In May 2005 the ASEAN Regional Action Plan on Trade in Wild Fauna and Flora was developed and adopted, and in August of that same year endorsed by the eighth meeting of the ASEAN Senior Officials on Forestry. In December 2005, the ASEAN Wildlife Enforcement Network (ASEAN-WEN) was launched to address the illegal exploitation and trade in CITES-listed species within the ASEAN region. It claims to be the world's largest wildlife-law enforcement network, involving the police, Customs, and environment agencies of all ten ASEAN countries, namely Brunei, Cambodia, Indonesia, Laos, Malaysia, Myanmar, the Philippines, Singapore, Thailand, and Vietnam.[121]

In 2011, this initiative, supported by USAID, was further expanded by the creation of Asia's Regional Response to Endangered Species Trafficking (ARREST), aimed at combating the multimillion dollar wildlife trade in the Lower Mekong Basin, affecting countries such as Cambodia, Laos, Thailand, and Vietnam.[122] This programme follows a three-fold strategy in combating wildlife crime: reduce consumer demand, strengthen law enforcement, and strengthen regional cooperation and anti-trafficking networks.

In 2015, the Environmental Investigation Agency (EIA), a recognized global authority on the illegal timber trade, raised concern about ASEAN's regional rosewood crisis. From an EIA briefing issued at the eleventh meeting of the ASEAN Expert Group on CITES in May 2015 in Brunei, it appeared that the illegal logging and trade in endangered Siamese rosewood, to supply Asia's booming Hongmu furniture markets, has reached critical levels. The violence associated with the trade has also led to the killing of 150 law enforcement officers and, since forested areas where rosewood is found straddle borders, regional stability has also come under threat.[123] The severity of the problem led to the protection of the species under Appendix II of CITES in 2013, but the listing restricts controls to logs, sawn timber, and veneers. What remains unregulated is the growing furniture and components trade that allows legal

[120] Available at: http://www.asean.org/asean-statement-on-cites-on-the-occasion-of-the-thirteenth-meeting-of-the-conference-of-the-parties-to-cites-bangkok/, accessed 16 October 2015.

[121] Available at: http://www.asean-wen.org/index.php/about-us/what-is-asean-wen, accessed 3 September 2015.

[122] Available at: https://www.usaid.gov/asia-regional/fact-sheets/lmi-asias-regional-response-endangered-species-trafficking-arrest, accessed 3 September 2015.

[123] Available at: https://drive.google.com/viewerng/viewer?url=https://eia-international.org/wp-content/uploads/ASEAN-rosewood-briefing-English-FINAL.pdf, accessed 4 September2015.

and illegal products to enter the market. Thus, what the EIA wants to achieve is to have the listing changed from Annotation 5 to Annotation 4 to close existing loopholes.

13.7.3 European Union (EU)

To ensure the uniform implementation of CITES provisions in the single market of the EU, the Union has adopted a range of regulations, known as the EU Wildlife Trade Regulations. The Basic Regulation of 1996 aims at improving the protection of species of threatened wild fauna and flora by means of a set of rules applicable to the introduction of a species into the Community,[124] the export or re-export from the Community, transit through the Community, the movement of live specimens within the Community, the management of scientific authorities, the issuing of certificates, and the monitoring of compliance and investigation of infringements. The Basic Regulation is supplemented by an Implementing Regulation laying down the rules for the design of permits,[125] certificates, and other documents relating to the protection of endangered species and the trade therein; and a Suspension Regulation prohibiting the introduction into the EU of certain species of wild fauna and flora.[126]

In 2007 an EU Commission recommendation was also adopted,[127] identifying a set of actions for the enforcement of the Basic Regulation. The actions identified by the Recommendation are aimed at improving enforcement capacity, cooperation, and information exchange between member states.

13.8 Other Initiatives

Since 2001, regional initiatives on forest law enforcement and governance (FLEG) were put in place in cooperation with governments and consumer countries and coordinated by the World Bank. The objective of these initiatives is to improve governance in the forest sector to prevent illegal logging, the illegal timber trade, and corruption.[128] A notable consequence of this development is the 2003 proposal by the EU Commission for an EU action plan on forest law enforcement, governance, and trade (FLEGT) that became a priority issue for the Commission in the follow-up to the 2002 World Summit on Sustainable Development.[129] One of the essential elements of the action plan is the introduction of a licensing scheme between EU members and partner countries in other regions to ensure that only timber lawfully harvested will be allowed to enter or circulate through the EU.

This led in 2010 to a new EU Regulation providing for obligations applicable to operators (natural or legal persons) placing timber and timber products on the market.[130] Under the Regulation operators have a due diligence obligation,[131] compliance with

[124] Council Regulation (EC) No. 338/97 of 9 December 1996, OJ 1997/L 061, 0001–0069.
[125] Commission Implementing Regulation (EU) No. 792/2012 of 23 August 2012.
[126] Commission Implementing Regulation (EU) No. 2015/736 of 7 May 2015.
[127] Commission Recommendation No. 2007/425/EC, OJ 2007/L 159 of 20 June 2007.
[128] UNODC, 'Wildlife and forest crime analytic toolkit', Vienna, UNODC, 2012, p. 60.
[129] COM (2003) 251 of 21 May 2003.
[130] Regulation (EU) No. 995/2010 of 20 October 2010.
[131] Ibid, Art. 4.

which is measured with reference to the accessibility of information concerning the operator's supply of timber and timber products, and the operator's procedures for assessing the risk of the lawful or unlawful harvesting of the timber or timber products.[132] The Regulation also provides for the establishment of monitoring organisations with the authority to maintain and regularly evaluate due diligence systems used by operators, to verify the proper use of such systems, and to take remedial action in the event of a failure by an operator to properly use the due diligence system.[133]

13.9 Final Observations

The combating of wildlife crime faces the same obstacles as the combating of other forms of transnational organised crime and by now most of the obstacles are well known and repeatedly emphasized in different fora: coordinated enforcement between different enforcement agencies at the national, regional, and international levels often falls short of what is needed; national legislation is often inadequate; criminal laws in different countries lack harmonization; culpability criteria differ from country to country; law enforcement agencies in many countries are under-resourced and inadequately trained; and the aiding and abetting of criminals by corrupt state officials undermine effective law enforcement.

Most of these problems can be solved if there is the requisite political will to do so, if the political will is matched by the required resources, and if there is some level of agreement between states as to the seriousness of the problem. Through improved international enforcement collaboration in recent years, progress has been made in overcoming some of the obstacles mentioned here and strengthening existing initiatives in this regard remains an essential prerequisite for combating wildlife crime more effectively. Hence, states should be reminded about their primary responsibility under the UN Charter, namely to prevent conflict, and about the gap that still exists between rhetoric and reality when it comes to conflict prevention. Since 2001 at the UN level various efforts have been made that aim at bridging this gap, based on the premise that progress in this area is dependent upon actions that effectively reduce the impact of risk factors. And among these factors we find listed natural resource depletion and environmental degradation.[134]

If the threat of organised wildlife crime is approached from a more holistic point of view, addressing certain socio-economic elements like poverty alleviation and unemployment, community involvement and awareness raising are certainly crucial elements in any long-term strategy for removing some of the crime-facilitating factors. However, from an effective law-enforcement perspective there needs to be a clear understanding that the scope, level of sophistication, and globalized nature of wildlife crime have put the combating of this scourge beyond the capacity of many countries and institutions. For this to be remedied international collaboration in development support will have to be scaled up in areas that address the key elements of an effective

[132] Ibid, Art. 6. [133] Ibid, Art. 8.

[134] UN Secretary, 'Progress report of the prevention of armed conflict', UN Doc. A/60/891, 18 July 2006, paras 15ff.

law enforcement strategy. These include, at a minimum, the legislative and administrative framework for effectively addressing wildlife-related offences in accordance with member states' treaty obligations; cooperation between investigators, prosecutors, Customs, and the judiciary, and the institutional capacity for bringing successful prosecutions; and regional and international cooperation between law enforcement agencies and other government institutions in regard to mutual legal assistance in criminal matters and extradition proceedings.

Finally, while we contemplate what needs to be done by states to address the evils of transnational organised crime that feature in this and other chapters, we may recall the opening paragraph in Chapter 34 of Toffler's *Powershift*, which reads as follows:

> Asking which nations will dominate the 21st century is an exciting game. But it is, in fact, the wrong question to ask—or at least the wrong form to ask it—because it overlooks what could turn out to be the biggest change in global affairs since the rise of the nation state: the coming of the Global Gladiators.
>
> A new group of power seekers are leaping onto the world stage and seizing sizeable chunks of the clout once controlled by nations alone. Some are good; some are decidedly evil.[135]

[135] Alvin Toffler, *Powershift: Knowledge, Wealth, and Violence at the Edge of the 21st Century*, Canada, Random House, 1990, p. 456.

14

Transnational Organised Crime and the Sale of Children, Child Prostitution, and Pornography

Thorsten Müller

14.1 Introduction

This chapter will investigate how transnational organised crime affects the most vulnerable and powerless group in society—the children.

Owing to limited experience and reduced physical strength children are easy victims of exploitation for international operating criminal organisations. The sale of children, child prostitution, and the use of children in pornographic performances are deeply linked. To discuss the problem of the sale of children without facing the problem of child prostitution and child pornography is almost impossible. In particular, there is a strong connection between the exploitation of children for prostitution and exploitation for child pornography. Children who have been involved in prostitution are often used for pornographic performances, too. The offenders who make use of child prostitutes often record their activities on film and publish them on the internet. However, these phenomena are also connected with social and economic problems like poverty. The internet allows offenders to operate from the darkest parts of the globe. Thus, the fight against the sale of children, child prostitution, and child pornography is an international one.

14.2 Terminology and Demarcations

The task of defining the terms 'sale of children', 'child prostitution', and 'child pornography' is not an easy one. Different international organisations and protocols use different terminology. This results from the fact that several countries are represented in international institutions. Thus, every country has its own legal traditions and principles. For the purpose of this chapter the author refers to the Optional Protocol to the Convention on the Rights of the Child on the Sale of Children, Child Prostitution, and Pornography (OPSC),[1] because it was drafted especially to fight international crimes involving the sale of children, child prostitution, and child pornography. The term 'sexual exploitation' could be used as a general headline for these three types of crime.

[1] UN GA Res. A/RES/54/263 of 25 May 2000.

14.2.1 Sale of children

Under the OPSC 'sale of children' is defined as 'any act or transaction whereby a child is transferred by any person or group of persons to another for remuneration or any other consideration'.[2] The Protocol delivers a very wide definition. This is because the signatory states discussed whether it should cover the sale of children for sexual exploitation or the sale for any purpose.[3] An 'other purpose' could be to take the child's organs, or to exploit the child for work, or sell it into forced marriage. Moreover, illegal adoption is a well-hidden phenomenon.[4]

A special agenda regarding the sale of children is the transfer of organs. Richer individuals from wealthy countries travel to poor areas where less fortunate people will sell their organs as a survival strategy. The victims are the most vulnerable members of the population—children.[5]

Child marriage can also be 'any other purpose'. Child marriage is rooted in an unequal gender status, power relations in society, and often centuries-old tradition.[6]

14.2.2 Child prostitution

Prostitution is as old as humankind. Article 2(b) of the OPSC states that child prostitution 'means the use of a child in sexual activities for remuneration or any other form of consideration'. The UN uses the term 'any other form of consideration' to cover the possibility that children might be used as prostitutes in exchange for goods, service, food, or drugs. It is not necessary to pay money for child prostitutes. Child prostitution includes all forms of transactional sex involving children. Thus, the Protocol noticed that in some societies the exchange of goods is widespread.

According to the Special Rapporteur on the sale of children, child prostitution and child pornography child prostitution is still an acute problem in many countries. Reasons for the demand for child prostitution are the belief that having sex with a child is 'safer' and issues like power, superiority, and the perception of children as objects. Also, sex tourism is a defining aspect of child prostitution.[7] Customers for child sex tourism favour countries with weak legislation, fewer controls, and impunity gaps.[8] On the other hand affected countries are afraid to report these crimes to the international community because of the attached stigma.

14.2.3 Child pornography

Child pornography is defined as 'any representation, by whatever means, of a child engaged in real or simulated explicit sexual activities or any representation of the sexual parts of a child for primarily sexual purposes'.[9] Pornography can be created

[2] OPSC, Art. 2(a).

[3] UNICEF, *Handbook on the Optional Protocol on the Sale of Children, Child Prostitution and Child Pornography*, Geneva, Innocenti Research Centre, 2009, p. 9.

[4] United Nations General Assembly, 'Report of the Special Rapporteur on the sale of children, child prostitution and child pornography', Najat Maalla M'jid, 23 December 2013, A/HRC/25/48, para. 23.

[5] Ibid, para. 25. [6] Ibid, para. 26. [7] Ibid, para. 15. [8] Ibid, para. 18.

[9] OPSC, Art. 2(c).

in live performances, photographs, motion pictures, video recordings, and digital images.[10] Moreover, child pornographic material is available worldwide through the internet.

14.3 The Regime of International Law

14.3.1 Universal Declaration on Human Rights

Following the atrocities of the Second World War the international community felt the need for a document recognizing the fundamental rights of every human being. In 1948 the General Assembly proclaimed the Universal Declaration on Human Rights.[11] This Declaration is the first document of rights to which every human being is entitled.

The preamble stressed the 'faith in fundamental human rights' and the 'dignity and worth of the human person'. There is no explicit article about the protection of children, nor a provision concerning sexual exploitation. Article 3 deals with the duty of the state to secure the life, liberty, and security of its citizens: it should not infringe these rights.[12] Furthermore Article 4 sets out that 'no one shall be held in slavery or servitude'. There is a close relationship between slavery and human trafficking, especially in women and children.[13]

The Universal Declaration has no binding character because it is not an international public treaty. The obligation of the United Nations member states to respect and protect human rights is set out in the Charter of the United Nations and the Universal Declaration just concretizes these obligations.[14]

14.3.2 UN International Covenant on Civil and Political Rights

In 1966 the International Covenant on Civil and Political Rights (ICCPR) was adopted;[15] it entered into force in 1976. This Covenant obliged the parties to respect civil and political rights, such as the right to life.

Article 24 deals with children's rights. Paragraph 1 says that every child has 'the right to such measures of protection as are required by his status as a minor'. Thus the state is obliged to prevent interferences by its authorities and to secure protection against violation from private parties. The state is also obliged to pass laws or other measures to require special protection for children.[16] It should be noted that Article 24 does not contain a definition of the term 'child'.[17] This means there is no age restriction.

[10] UNICEF, *Handbook on the Optional Protocol*, cited in note 3 above, p. 12.

[11] Universal Declaration on Human Rights, UN GA Res. 217 A (III) of 10 December 1948.

[12] Bardo Fassbender (ed.), *Menschenrechteerklärung*, Munich, Sellier European Law Publishers, 2009, p. 81.

[13] Ibid, p. 85. [14] Ibid, pp. 16–18.

[15] International Covenant on Civil and Political Rights, UN GA Res. 2200A (XXI) of 16 December 1966.

[16] Manfred Nowak (ed.), *UN Covenant on Civil and Political Rights Commentary*, Kehl, Engel Publishers, 1993, Art. 24 para. 5.

[17] Ibid, para. 12.

14.3.3 UN International Covenant on Economic, Social, and Cultural Rights

In the year 1966 the International Covenant on Economic, Social and Cultural Rights (ICESCR) was opened for signature.[18] Unlike the ICCPR, this document deals with 'second generation' rights.

Article 2(1) of the Covenant obliges every state party 'to take steps, individually and through international assistance and co-operation' to achieve the full realization of the rights in the ICESCR. To reach this goal, states parties should adopt 'legislative measures'. Article 2(1) recognized the problem of economic differences and limitations by obliging the parties to cooperate internationally.[19]

Article 10(3) deals with children's rights stating:

> special measures of protection and assistance should be taken on behalf of all children and young persons without any discrimination for reasons of parentage or other conditions. Children and young persons should be protected from economic and social exploitation. Their employment in work harmful to their morals or health or dangerous to life or likely to hamper their normal development should be punishable by law.

The ICCPR and the ICESCR are legally binding sources of law. Together with the Universal Declaration, the ICCPR and ICESCR have come to be known as an 'International Bill of Rights'.[20]

14.3.4 UN Convention on the Rights of the Child

The United Nations is the largest existing international organisation and its objective is to 'achieve international co-operation'.[21] Therefore it is the optimal political platform on which to establish children's rights.[22] In 1989 the United Nations Convention on the Rights of the Child (CRC) came into force.[23] The CRC is the most celebrated human rights document in history and it has been ratified by 195 countries: all except Somalia and the United States. The essential theme of the Convention is that children need special protection and priority care, because they are a vulnerable group during the developmental phase of their lives.[24] Furthermore, they cannot negotiate their interests in political decisions in parliament. The CRC covers civil, political, economic,

[18] International Covenant on Economic, Social, and Cultural Rights, UN GA Res. 2200A (XXI) of 16 December 1966.

[19] Eibe Riedel, 'International Covenant on Economic, Social, Cultural Rights', in Rüdiger Wolfrum (ed.), *Max Planck Encyclopaedia on Public International Law*, available at: http://www.mpepil.com, accessed 29 October 2015, para. 7.

[20] Thomas Buergenthal, 'Human rights', in Wolfrum, *Max Planck Encyclopaedia*, cited in note 19 above, para. 9.

[21] United Nations Charter of 26 June 1945, Art. 1(3).

[22] Yaman Akdeniz (ed.), *Internet Child Pornography and the Law, National and International Response*, Aldershot, Ashgate, 2008, p. 209.

[23] United Nations Convention on the Rights of the Child, UN GA Res. 44/25 of 20 November 1989.

[24] Solange Rosa and Mira Dutschke, 'Child rights at the core: the use of international law in South African cases on children's socio-economic rights', (2006) *SAJHR*, 224, 230.

and social and cultural rights. This is a novelty among human rights treaties.[25] The Committee on the Rights of the Child (hereafter 'Committee') has identified four general principles enshrined in the CRC that are fundamental:

- non-discrimination (Article 2);
- the best interest of the child (Article 3);
- the right to life, survival, and development (Article 6); and
- respect for the views of the child (Article 12).[26]

Article 12 is more idealistic than realistic.[27] In developing its jurisprudence around the application of all the general principles the Committee applies them in different contexts in its General Comments.[28]

The CRC contains basic rights that are also classified as the four 'P's:

- 'provision rights'—rights for children to realize their basic needs (Articles 24, 26, and 28);
- protection of children from violence, abuse, against discrimination, and against all forms of torture, cruel, inhuman, and degrading treatment (Articles 19, 37, 34, and 36);
- prevention of harm to children, the development of health-care, and prevention of child abduction (Articles 23, 24, 32, and 35); and
- 'participation rights'—these rights enable children to express their views in all matters affecting them (Article 12).[29]

The roots of the CRC lie in the Declaration of the Rights of the Child from 1924.[30] This Declaration was drafted by the League of Nations. The document set out five principles and required the protection of children against 'every form of exploitation' in Principle 4.[31] It should be remembered that this early Declaration had no binding force for the signatory parties.

Thirty years later the United Nations, the successor organisation to the League of the Nations, drafted a new Declaration of the Rights of the Child in 1959.[32] Like the 1924 Declaration, the new Declaration of 1959 is set out in principles, and contains ten. Principle 9 stresses that the child should be protected against all forms of

[25] Geraldine van Bueren, 'The United Nations Convention on the Rights of the Child: an evolutionary revolution', in C. J. Davel (ed.), *Introduction to Child Law in South Africa*, Claremont, Juta, 2000, p. 202.

[26] See Prinslean Mahery, 'The United Nations Convention on the Rights of the Child: Maintaining its value in international and South African child law', in Trynie Boezaart (ed.), *Child Law in South Africa*, Juta Publishing, Cape Town, 2009, 315; Cris R. Revaz, 'An introduction to the UN Convention on the Rights of the Child', in Jonathan Todres, Mark E. Wojcik, and Cris R. Revaz (eds), *The UN Convention on the Rights of the Child*, Ardsley, New York, Transnational Publishers, 2006, p. 9; Evarist Baimu, 'Children, international protection', in Wolfrum, *Max Planck Encyclopaedia*, cited in note 19 above, para. 7.

[27] Jane Fortin (ed.), *Children's Rights and the Developing Law*, 3rd edn, Cambridge, CUP, 2009, p. 40.

[28] Mahery, cited in note 26 above, p. 315.

[29] Ibid, p. 314; van Bueren, 'An evolutionary revolution', cited in note 25 above, p. 203.

[30] Geneva Declaration of the Rights of the Child, 26 September 1924.

[31] 'Principle 4: The child must be put in a position to earn a livelihood, and must be protected against every form of exploitation.'

[32] Declaration of the Rights of the Child, UN GA Res. 1386 (XIV) of 10 December 1959.

exploitation.[33] The Declaration of 1959 introduced the principle of 'the best interest of the child'.[34] Once again, this Declaration had no binding force.

14.3.4.1 Article 19 CRC

Article 19 deals explicitly with exploitation and sexual abuse of children. This Article is a core provision for discussions and strategies to face and eliminate all forms of violence against children.[35] It states that all 'States Parties shall take all appropriate legislative, administrative, social and educational measures to protect the child from all forms of physical or mental violence, injury or abuse, neglect or negligent treatment, maltreatment or exploitation, including sexual abuse, while in the care of parent(s), legal guardian(s) or any other person who has the care of the child.'

'All forms of … violence' includes sexual abuse and exploitation. The Committee recognized the commercial sexual exploitation and the use of children in audio or visual images of sexual abuse as a form of sexual abuse and exploitation.[36] Moreover, sexual abuse and exploitation includes 'child prostitution, sexual slavery, sexual exploitation in travel and tourism, trafficking and sale of children for sexual purposes and forced marriage'. The Committee was concerned that many children become victims of sexual abuse that is not accompanied by physical force or restraint but that is also psychologically intrusive, exploitative, and traumatic.[37] The Committee stressed that children could experience violence through information and communications technologies. Child abuse images are facilitated by the internet or other information and communication technologies.[38]

14.3.4.2 Article 32 CRC

The text of Article 32(1) CRC states that 'State Parties recognise the right of the child to be protected from economic exploitation and from performing any work that is likely to be hazardous or to interfere with the child's education, or to be harmful to the child's health or physical, mental, spiritual, moral or social development'. This Article is closely related to Articles 34 and 35, which deal with specific forms of exploitation. The sale of children, child prostitution, and child pornography are forms of economic exploitation. The child is used as a 'product'. It is moreover indisputable that child prostitution and child pornography are especially likely to be hazardous or to interfere with the child's upbringing. Under subsection 2 of Article 32 CRC 'State Parties shall take legislative, administrative, social and educational measures' to pursue the fight against economic exploitation set out in subsection 1.

[33] 'Principle 9: The child shall be protected against all forms of neglect, cruelty and exploitation. He shall not be the subject of traffic, in any form.

The child shall not be admitted to employment before an appropriate minimum age; he shall in no case be caused or permitted to engage in any occupation or employment which would prejudice his health or education, or interfere with his physical, mental or moral development.'

[34] Jörg Maywald, 'UN-Kinderechtskonvention: Bilanz und Ausblick', (2010) 38 *APuZ*, 8, p. 10.

[35] Committee, General comment No. 13, 21 March 2011, para. 7(a).

[36] Ibid, para. 25(b) and (c). [37] See ibid, para. 25(d). [38] Ibid, para. 31(a).

14.3.4.3 *Article 34 CRC*

Article 34 of the CRC is the main provision against sexual exploitation and reads as follows:

> State Parties undertake to protect the child from all forms of sexual exploitation and sexual abuse. For these purpose, State Parties shall in particular take all appropriate national, bilateral and multilateral measures to prevent:
> (a) the inducement or coercion of a child to engage in any unlawful sexual activity;
> (b) the exploitative use of children in prostitution or other unlawful sexual practices;
> (c) the exploitative use of children in pornographic performances and materials.

This Article obliges states parties to protect the child against all forms of sexual exploitation and sexual abuse. To meet the obligations in subsections (a) to (c) Article 34 states parties must take 'appropriate national, bilateral and multilateral measures'.[39] This provision gives countries from the developing world, which cannot fight sexual exploitation themselves, the possibility to utilize the help of more developed countries. On the other hand, the developed world is obliged to help other countries with their means and experience.

Article 34 gives greater stress to the fight against sexual exploitation than to the fight against sexual abuse, because sexual abuse is mentioned in Articles 19 and 39.[40] Sexual exploitation includes three possibilities: child prostitution, child pornography, and child trafficking for sexual purposes.

A pure definition of the term 'sexual exploitation' remains non-existent in the CRC. A few important international developments have clarified the meaning of this term.[41] No General Comment from the Committee deals with Article 34.

14.3.4.4 *Article 35 CRC*

Article 35 CRC obligates the states parties to 'take all appropriate national, bilateral and multilateral measures to prevent the abduction of, the sale of or traffic in children for any purpose or in any form'. This Article is closely related to Articles 32 and 34, which also address specific forms of exploitation. The drafters of the CRC felt that the abduction of, sale of, or traffic in children should be covered by a specific article. A separate article dealing with sale of or traffic in children was necessary because this problem is wider in scope than sexual exploitation. Children may be subjected to sale and trafficking for the purpose of sexual exploitation and abuse, but also for the purposes of economic exploitation, commercial adoption, or e.g. sale for marriage (bride-price).[42]

[39] Sharon Detrick (ed.), *A Commentary on the United Nations Convention on the Rights of the Child*, The Hague, Kluwer Law International, 1999, p. 592.

[40] Vitit Muntarbhorn, 'Article 34: sexual exploitation and sexual abuse of children', in André Alen, Johan Vande Lanotte, Eugeen Verhellen, Fiona Ang, Eva Berghmans, and Mieke Verheyde (eds), *A Commentary on the United Nations Convention on the Rights of the Child*, Leiden, Martinus Njhoff, 2007, p. 22, para. 38.

[41] Ibid, p. 1, para. 2.

[42] See Detrick, *A Commentary on the CRC*, cited in note 39 above, p. 599.

14.3.4.5 Committee on the Rights of the Child

The CRC also establishes a Committee on the Rights of the Child, as mentioned in section 14.3.4 above.[43] The main functions of the Committee are the examination of measures taken by states that aim to give effect to the obligations in the CRC and assisting and advising states.

14.3.5 World Congress against Commercial Sexual Exploitation

The First World Congress against Commercial Sexual Exploitation was held in 1996 in Stockholm, Sweden. The Congress was proposed by the *End* Child Prostitution in Asia Tourism campaign in cooperation with United Nations International Children's Emergency Fund (UNICEF) and other non-governmental organisations. The outcome was the Stockholm Declaration and Agenda of Action which defines sexual exploitation on page 1 at point 5 as follows:

> sexual exploitation of children is a fundamental violation of children's rights. It comprises sexual abuse by the adult and remuneration in cash or kind to the child or a third person or persons.

The Agenda of Action also stresses the protection of children against child prostitution and child pornography. In Point 3 under the topic 'Agenda for Action against Commercial Sexual Exploitation of Children' the paper implores governments to

> (h) develop or strengthen, implement and publicise relevant laws, policies and programmes, to prevent the commercial sexual exploitation of children, bearing in mind the Convention on the Rights of the Child;
> (i) review laws, policies, programmes and practices which lead to or facilitate the commercial sexual exploitation of children and adopt effective reforms;
> (j) mobilise the business sector, including the tourism industry, against the use of its networks and establishments for the commercial sexual exploitation of children;
> (k) encourage media professionals to develop strategies which strengthen the role of the media in providing information of the highest quality, reliability and ethical standards concerning all aspects of commercial sexual exploitation of children; and
> (l) target those involved with commercial sexual exploitation of children with information, education and outreach campaigns and programmes to promote behavioural changes to counter the practice.

Moreover point 4(b) of the Agenda requires the state to

> develop or strengthen and implement national laws to establish the criminal responsibility of service providers, customers and intermediaries in child prostitution, child trafficking, child pornography, including possession of child pornography, and other unlawful sexual activity.

[43] CRC, Art. 43.

This World Congress was followed by two others. The Second World Congress against Commercial Sexual Exploitation was held in 2001 in Yokohama, Japan. One of the major themes of this Congress was child pornography; another was the trafficking of children for sexual purposes; both were mentioned in the theme papers.[44] The World Congress in Japan reaffirmed the primary consideration of the First World Congress, the protection and promotion of the interests and rights of the child to be protected from all forms of sexual exploitation.[45]

The Third World Congress was held in Rio de Janeiro, Brazil in 2008. This Congress focused on five main themes and issues related to these themes. The first theme was forms of sexual exploitation and its new pictures; what trafficking in children for sexual exploitation means; sexual exploitation of children in prostitution and tourism; paedophilia and pornography; and internet crimes and new technologies. Additionally the legal framework and liability for these problems was discussed. Moreover, the participants talked about mechanisms to integrate interagency policies and the initiatives of social responsibility. The Congress also stressed strategies for international cooperation.[46]

14.3.6 Worst Forms of Child Labour Convention

The Convention concerning the Prohibition and Immediate Action for the Elimination of the Worst Forms of Child Labour (known as the Worst Forms of Child Labour Convention) was adopted in 1999 by the General Conference of the International Labour Organization (ILO).[47]

Article 3(a) states that 'all forms of slavery ... such as the sale and trafficking of children', to which Article 3(b) adds 'the use, procuring or offering of a child for prostitution for the production of pornography or for pornographic performances', are defined as the worst forms of child labour. Thus, the Convention regards the sale and trafficking of children as a form of slavery. Furthermore, it includes articles giving effect to the following provisions. Article 6(1) requires member states to eliminate, as a priority, the worst forms of child labour through 'design[ing] and implement[ing] programmes of action'. Moreover, Article 7 obliges every member state to 'take all necessary measures to ensure the effective implementation and enforcement of the provisions' of the Convention.

14.3.7 International Conference on Combating Child Pornography on the Internet

The International Conference on Combating Child Pornography on the Internet was held in Vienna in 1999. This conference mentioned the widespread access to the

[44] Theme papers available at: http://www.csecworldcongress.org/en/yokohama/Background/Theme_papers.htm, accessed 16 January 2014.

[45] See http://www.ecpat.net/sites/default/files/the_yokohama_global_commitment_2001.pdf, accessed 28 October 2014.

[46] See http://resources.ecpat.net/worldcongressIII/thematic2.php, accessed 28 October 2014.

[47] ILO Convention No. 182 of 17 June 1999.

internet and its increasing importance. The conference ended with several recommendations that have no binding force. It called for a policy of zero tolerance for child pornography on the internet and stressed the need for global partnership and worldwide criminalization of child pornography. It also called for the strengthening of law enforcement and closer cooperation and partnership between governments and the internet industry.[48]

Moreover it should be noted that this conference was held when the World Wide Web was still in its infancy.

14.3.8 Convention on Cybercrime

The Council of Europe's Convention on Cybercrime opened for signature on 23 November 2001 in Budapest, Hungary and came into force on 1 July 2004[49]. The Council of Europe (CoE) is an international organisation founded in 1949 with forty-seven members.[50] It is important to note that the CoE is independent of the European Union (EU). The members of the CoE are not necessarily members of the EU. The objects of the CoE are to protect human rights and fundamental freedoms, the rule of law, and democratic principles. To achieve this objective the CoE drafts conventions.[51] These conventions are also open for non-member states that actively participated in the elaboration of the Convention. This is to enable as many interested states as possible to become parties to the Convention.[52]

The primary objective of the Cybercrime Convention is 'a common criminal policy aimed at the protection of society against cybercrime ... by adopting appropriate legislation and fostering international co-operation'.[53] Furthermore member states and other states must consider ratifying the CRC and the ILO Worst Forms of Child Labour Convention. Also, the drafters are 'concerned by the risk that computer networks ... may also be used for committing criminal offences' as today it is known that computer networks are used widely to commit crimes.[54]

The Convention deals (in Chapter 2, section 1) with substantive criminal law. Child pornography is explicitly covered in Article 9. It is appropriate to interpret the Convention on Cybercrime in line with the Explanatory Report issued by the CoE.[55]

[48] See http://textus.diplomacy.edu/thina/txGetXDoc.asp?IDconv=3193, accessed 28 October 2014.

[49] Convention on Cybercrime, CETS No. 185 of 23 November 2001.

[50] See: http://www.coe.int/en/web/portal/47-members-states, accessed 04 June 2015.

[51] See Matthias Herdegen, *Europarecht*, 16th edn, Munich, C. H. Beck, 2014, §2, pp. 1–3; Aphrodite Smagadi (ed.), *Sourcebook of International Human Rights Materials*, London, British Institute of International and Comparative Law, 2008, p. 46; Rudolf Streinz, *Europarecht*, 9th edn, Heidelberg, Müller, 2012, p. 28.

[52] European Treaty Service, *Explanatory Report on the Convention on Cybercrime*, ETS No. 185, available at http://conventions.coe.int/Treaty/EN/Reports/Html/185.htm, accessed 4 November 2015, para. 304.

[53] Convention on Cybercrime, cited in note 49 above, preamble.

[54] Ibid, preamble.

[55] *Explanatory Report*, cited in note 52 above.

14.3.8.1 *Article 9(1)*

Each Party shall adopt such legislative and other measures as may be necessary to establish as criminal offences under its domestic law, when committed intentionally and without right, the following conduct:

(a) producing child pornography for the purpose of its distribution through a computer system;
(b) offering or making available child pornography through a computer system;
(c) distributing or transmitting child pornography through a computer system;
(d) procuring child pornography through a computer system for oneself or for another person;
(e) possessing child pornography in a computer system or on a computer-data storage medium.

Article 9 criminalizes aspects of the electronic production, possession, and distribution of child pornography. The traditional production and physical distribution methods are already criminalized in many states. Owing to the increasing use of the internet as a primary instrument for trading pornographic material, the state community saw the need for specific provisions in an international legal instrument to combat internet child pornography as a new form of sexual exploitation of children.[56] The Convention protects children against sexual exploitation and not potential consumers against pornographic material.[57]

Paragraph 1 describes five activities that are penalized. Subsection (a) simply criminalizes the production of child pornography. Subsection (b) penalizes the offering of child pornography through a computer system. In this context the term 'offering' means 'soliciting others to obtain child pornography'. This implies that the person who offers pornography can also provide it. The term 'making available' is intended to cover 'the placing of child pornography online for the use of others'.[58] Distribution and transmission are criminalized in subsection (c): 'distribution' is the active dissemination of child pornography; 'transmitting' means to send material from one person to another through a computer system.[59] Paragraph (d) seeks to prevent the active obtaining of child pornography, e.g. by downloading it.[60] Last, subsection (e) penalizes the possession of child pornography in a computer system or on a computer data-storage medium. The drafters are of the opinion that the possession of child pornography stimulates the demand for such material. Therefore, it is useful to punish every participant in the chain from production to possession.[61]

According to the drafters of the Cybercrime Convention, the term 'without right' allows each member state to take into account fundamental rights like freedom of expression or privacy. It is also possible that artistic, medical, scientific, or similar merit

[56] Ibid, para. 93.

[57] Christian Spannbrucker, 'Convention on Cybercrime (ETS 185): ein Vergleich mit dem deutschen Computerstrafrecht in materiell- und verfahrensrechtlicher Hinsicht', university dissertation, Regensburg, 2004, p. 101.

[58] *Explanatory Report*, cited in note 52 above, para. 95.

[59] Ibid, para. 96.

[60] Ibid, para. 97.

[61] Ibid, para. 98.

could be grounds for defence. Each state can define that a person is not responsible if the person depicted is not a minor under the Convention.[62]

14.3.8.2 Article 9(2)

Subsection 2 clarifies that

> the term 'child pornography' shall include pornographic material that visually depicts:
> (a) minor engaged in sexually explicit conduct;
> (b) a person appearing to be a minor engaged in sexually explicit conduct;
> (c) realistic images representing a minor engaged in sexually explicit conduct.

For the term 'realistic', it is not necessary that a real child is engaged in sexually explicit conduct. This will cover pictures that are altered or even generated completely by a computer.[63] It is possible to replace images of adults with images of children by using computer techniques: this process is known as 'morphing'. These pictures can be posted on the internet without the knowledge of the victim.[64] Subsection (a) seeks to protect children directly against abuse. The objectives of subsection (b) and (c) are to provide protection against conduct that might be used to encourage or seduce children into participating in child pornography and therefore protect them from becoming part of a subculture that favours child abuse.[65]

'Pornographic material' is determined by national standards regarding the classification of material as obscene, inconsistent with public morals, or just corrupt. Material that has artistic, medical, scientific, or similar merit could be considered to be not pornographic by the state authorities.[66] The term 'sexually explicit conduct' covers a lot of possibilities: real or simulated sexual intercourse, including genital–genital, oral–genital, anal–genital, or oral–anal, between minors, or between an adult and a minor, of the same or opposite sex. It also includes bestiality, masturbation, sadistic or masochistic abuse in a sexual context, and lascivious exhibition of the genitals or the pubic area of a minor.[67] Paragraph 2 fails to define 'pornography'. It simply includes the phrase 'pornographic material that visually depicts ...', because it is up to national courts to define the term 'pornographic'. One reason is national sovereignty. Criminal law and jurisprudence are the power of a governing body. By avoiding definition in the Convention, the national court can take into account domestic values and law traditions.[68] Another reason is that defining 'pornography' is not easy at all.

[62] Ibid, para. 103; Spannbrucker, 'Convention on Cybercrime', cited in note 57 above, p. 103.

[63] *Explanatory Report*, cited in note 52 above, para. 101.

[64] Martin C. Calder, 'The internet: potential, problems and pathways to hands-on sexual offending', in Martin C. Calder (ed.), *Child Sexual Abuse and the Internet: Tackling the New Frontier*, Dorset, Russell House, 2004, pp. 1–23, pp. 7 and 8.

[65] *Explanatory Report*, cited in note 52 above, para. 102.

[66] Ibid, para. 99.

[67] Ibid, para. 100; Spannbrucker, 'Convention on Cybercrime', cited in note 57 above, p. 102.

[68] Helmut Baier, 'Die Bekämpfung der Kinderpornografie auf der Ebene von Europäischer Union und Europarat', in (2004) *Zeitschrift für Urheber- und Medienrecht*, 39, pp. 42 and 43.

14.3.8.3 Article 9(3)

'For the purpose of paragraph 2 above, the term "minor" shall include all persons under 18 years of age. A Party may, however, require a lower age-limit, which shall be not less than 16 years.'

In accordance with the definition of 'child' in Article 1 of the CRC,[69] the Cybercrime Convention defines the term 'minor' in general as all persons younger than 18 years of age. It is important that the drafters set a uniform international standard regarding age. This standard applies to the use of children as sexual objects, and is separate from the age of consent to sexual activity. The last phrase of paragraph 3 allows each state party to set a different age limit, but not below 16 years of age.[70]

14.3.9 Optional Protocol to the Convention on the Rights of the Child on the Sale of Children, Child Prostitution, and Child Pornography

In 2002 the OPSC came into force.[71] It is the first international document that deals explicitly with the fight against the sale of children, child prostitution, and child pornography. The aim of the OPSC is to achieve the implementation of the CRC in relation to sexual exploitation.[72] The reason why this document names the 'sale of children, child prostitution, and child pornography' is because of the strong link between these three phenomena.[73] Children are often sold for the purpose of prostitution and they are also used as actors in pornographic performances. This is lucrative for the exploiters because they can 'use' the children twice, once for prostitution and once for pornographic material.

The drafting process was promoted by an increasing international concern about the sexual exploitation of children.[74] The OPSC aims to improve the protection of children all over the world. The preamble sets out that the OPSC should achieve the purposes of the CRC, *inter alia* Article 34.[75] The states parties to the Protocol are gravely concerned at the significant and increasing international traffic in children for sale, prostitution, and pornography, along with the widespread and continuing practice of sex tourism, to which children are especially vulnerable as it directly promotes those three evils.[76] The drafters of the OPSC were also concerned about the simple and growing availability of child pornography on the internet. Accordingly, they referred to the International Conference on Combating Child Pornography on the Internet,[77] and stressed a worldwide criminalization of the production, distribution, exportation, transmission, importation, intentional possession, and advertising of child pornography.[78] This Protocol also stresses a solution for the elimination of the sale of

[69] 'For the purposes of the present Convention, a child means every human being below the age of eighteen years unless under the law applicable to the child, majority is attained earlier.'

[70] *Explanatory Report*, cited in note 52 above, para. 104.

[71] Cited in note 1 above.

[72] Trevor Buck (ed.), *International Child Law*, 3rd edn, New York, Routledge, 2014, p. 108.

[73] Cf. Theme Paper 'Child pornography' for the Second World Congress against Sexual Exploitation, p. 18, available at: http://csecworldcongress.org, accessed 05 March 2012.

[74] Buck, *International Child Law*, cited in note 72 above.

[75] OPSC, preamble, para. 1.

[76] Cf. ibid, paras 3 and 4.

[77] Ibid, para. 5.

[78] Ibid, para. 6.

children, child prostitution, and child pornography: fighting underdevelopment, poverty, economic disparities, inequitable socio-economic structure, dysfunctional families, lack of education, rural–urban migration, gender discrimination, irresponsible adult sexual behaviour, harmful traditional practices, armed conflicts, and trafficking in children.[79] Moreover, the states parties believe that it is necessary to raise public awareness to reduce consumer demand for the sale of children, child prostitution, and child pornography.[80] The Protocol also aims to strengthen global partnership and to improve law enforcement at the international level.[81]

It should be noted that the OPSC was developed in parallel with the Protocol to Prevent, Suppress and Punish Trafficking in Persons, Especially Women and Children,[82] which should complement the UN Convention Against Transnational Organised Crime.[83]

Article 1 obliges states parties to prohibit the sale of children, child prostitution, and child pornography.

Article 2 delivers definitions:

(a) sale of children means any act or transaction whereby a child is transferred by any person or group of persons to another for remuneration or any other consideration;
(b) child prostitution means the use of a child in sexual activities for remuneration or any other form of consideration;
(c) child pornography means any representation, by whatever means, of a child engaged in real or simulated explicit sexual activities or any representation of the sexual parts of a child for primarily sexual purposes.

Furthermore, Article 3(1) OPSC states quite clearly that 'each State Party shall ensure that, as a minimum, the following acts and activities are fully covered under its criminal or penal law'. In the context of sale of children these acts are offering, delivering, or accepting, by whatever means, a child for the purpose of sexual exploitation, transfer of organs for profit, and engagement in forced labour. The Protocol also obliges states parties to criminalize the offering, obtaining, procuring, or providing of a child for prostitution. With regard to child pornography the activities criminalized are the producing, distributing, disseminating, importing, exporting, offering, and selling of child pornographic material. In addition, the possessing of child pornographic material is punished when this possession is for the above purposes, whereas the Convention on Cybercrime prohibits possession of child pornography in a computer system or on a computer data-storage medium.[84] Moreover, the state has to ensure that such offences are penalized, whether they are committed domestically or transnationally; on an individual or on a gang-structured base. The domestic law of the participating states should also apply to attempt at, complicity in, or participation

[79] Ibid, para. 7. [80] Ibid, para. 8.
[81] Ibid, para. 8. [82] A/55/383, 15 November 2000, 2237 UNTS 319.
[83] UNCAC: A/55/383, 15 November 2000, 2225 UNTS 209. Buck, *International Child Law*, cited in note 72 above.
[84] See UNICEF, *Handbook on the Optional Protocol*, cited in note 3 above, p. 12.

in any of the criminalized activities.[85] Article 3(4) of the Protocol states that states parties should establish the liability of legal entities, although such liability could be criminal, civil, or administrative.

Article 4(1) is a clear illustration of the territoriality principle. Under Article 4(2), every state should establish jurisdiction in cases where the offender is a national of the state in question, or a person with habitual residence in the state's territory, and also when the victim of child pornography is a national. These are the principles of active and passive personality. Article 4(3) states that every state must bring to justice offender(s) who are present in its territory, if such person(s) commit a crime under the Protocol.

In the view of van Bueren, the OPSC makes 'significant improvements in the enforcement of law'.[86] Under Article 5(1), offences of selling children, child prostitution, and child pornography are deemed extraditable. Where no extradition treaty exists between states parties, the state seeking extradition may consider the OPSC as a legal basis for this.[87]

Article 7 deals with the seizure and confiscation of goods and other instrumentalities used to commit or facilitate the offences.

The OPSC is not concerned only with dealing with criminal conduct. On the contrary, it also protects the rights and interests of child victims and witnesses in Article 8. Article 8(1)(d) obliges states parties to provide 'appropriate support service to child victims throughout the legal process'. Furthermore, the state should protect the 'privacy and identity of child victims'.[88] Provisions to protect victims are present in the OPSC. Article 9 states that governments must introduce programmes to prevent offences of sale of children, child prostitution, and child pornography.

14.4 Enforcement

The primary function of criminal law is the sanctioning of unlawful behaviour by the legislature.[89]

International documents provide provisions dealing with the enforcement of the obligations mentioned in them.

The International Criminal Court (ICC) deals with individual criminal responsibility in relation to war crimes, genocide, and crimes against humanity. The Statute of the International Criminal Court (Rome Statute) states explicitly that 'sexual slavery, enforced prostitution ... or any other form of sexual violence of comparable gravity' is a form of 'crime against humanity'.[90] These crimes must be committed as part of a widespread or systematic attack directed against any civilian population to be within the jurisdiction of the ICC. An attack by state authorities is needed to meet these criteria. Transnational organised and operating gangs (mostly) form no part of state authorities; hence, these offenders are not within the jurisdiction of the ICC.

Nearly every international document deals with implementation of its provisions. Law enforcement is the core element in the combat against sexual exploitation of

[85] Art. 3(2). [86] van Bueren, 'An evolutionary revolution', cited in note 25 above, p. 209.

[87] Art. 5(2). [88] Art. 8(1)(e).

[89] Kai Ambos, *Treatise on International Criminal Law*, Vol. II, *The Crimes and Sentencing*, Oxford, OUP, 2014, p. 60.

[90] Art. 7(1)(g) of the Rome Statute.

children. According to the Report of the UN Special Rapporteur, weak law enforcement leads to a 'culture of impunity' that is the main cause of sexual exploitation. This 'culture of impunity' encourages the demand for sexually exploitative services like child prostitution. The main problem is a gap in implementation. Effective law-enforcement measures and the possibility to report crimes to authorities are core elements in fighting sexually motivated crimes. Effective law enforcement needs effective resources, both human and technical. Another important measure is also to raise awareness through the law enforcement authorities.[91]

In 2013 the UN Special Rapporteur on the sale of children, child prostitution, and child pornography presented a new Report. The Rapporteur stated that there has been a significant change in the extent and nature of sale and sexual exploitation since 2008. The report names the progression of globalization, the continued expansion of the use of the internet, including in developing countries, increased migration, urbanization, the economic and financial crisis, natural disasters, conflicts, and climate-related changes as all affecting children's vulnerability.[92]

14.5 Performance

There is a deep link between child prostitution and poverty. Adult prostitution is motivated by poverty; unlike child prostitution, adult prostitution is mainly self-determined. The self-determination of children is not well developed. Thus, child prostitution could not be covered by the child's self-determination. Information and education of children in their rights and self-determination are fundamental steps in raising a child to be a responsible person.

To fight poverty in developing countries it is best to fight child prostitution. Many factors are linked to sexual exploitation of children.

Three factors could break the vicious circle:

1. *Education* Schooling builds the foundation of a prosperous future. Educated people are less affected by poverty and social exclusion than illiterate people.
2. *The fight against parental abuse* It is widely known that children who experience abuse during childhood are easy victims for sexual abuse.
3. *The fight against violence* A society that is dominated by violence and abuse will be harmful for the growth of children.

The Special Rapporteur Najat Maalla M'jid mentioned in 2013 the strong links between economic, social, and political development, and child protection issues.[93] It is also important to take a closer look at the factors that cause or increase the demand for sexual exploitation. In his 2006 Report, the Special Rapporteur Juan Miguel Petit pointed out that the factors can be grouped into five main different categories.[94]

[91] United Nations General Assembly, 'Report of the Special Rapporteur on the sale of children, child prostitution and child pornography', Juan Miguel Petit, 12 January 2006, E/CN.4/2006/67, para. 43.
[92] Report of the Special Rapporteur 2013, cited in note 4 above, para. 6.
[93] Ibid, para. 116. [94] Report of the Special Rapporteur 2006, cited in note 91 above.

1. *Culture of impunity* A culture of social and legal impunity motivates demand for sexual exploitation. The majority of countries have sufficient legal provisions criminalizing such exploitation. The problem arises with the implementation of these provisions: the lack of effective law enforcement measures, difficulties in reporting crimes to police authorities, and ensuring their effective investigation. Additionally, the lack of technical and human resources to fight sexual exploitation encourages sexual exploitation. In some states the problem of corruption and the complicity of police and officials in cases of trafficking have exacerbated the problem of impunity. Lastly, a failure of adequate assistance to and protection of victims is detrimental to the criminal processes.[95]
2. *Client demand for prostitution* It is questionable whether legal (adult) prostitution and men's demand for prostitution in general are linked with sexual exploitation.[96] On one hand it is argued that prostitution reduces women to bought objects and is degrading. Prostitution is never a free choice as woman and girls were either coerced by compelling circumstances like poverty, discrimination, or childhood trauma, or by other persons, into the sex industry.[97] Sex exploiters use the legal framework as a facade for sexual exploitation.[98] On the other hand there is no scientific proof that legalization of prostitution leads to more cases of trafficking into prostitution.[99]
3. *Demand for cheap prostitution and migration* Because of globalization and the free market economy the demand for cheap labour and services (including sexual services) has increased. Also economic divides between countries and irregular migration and demand for cheap labour have led to commercial sexual exploitation.[100]
4. *Discriminatory attitudes and client prejudices* Another factor in the exploitation of children is the attitude that they might be 'exploitable' in the eyes of the criminals. Such discriminatory attitudes make victims—especially girl-child victims of commercial sexual exploitation—invisible.[101] Adults who 'use' child prostitutes think that those prostitutes descended from marginalized families and that these families put their children in situations of vulnerability.[102] Moreover, ethnic and racial identity is used to excuse sexual exploitation. Offenders often exploit children whose race or ethnicity is different from their own. Accordingly, criminals define these children as 'others' and thus as 'natural' prostitutes.[103]
5. *Armed conflicts and political instability* During an armed conflict or a period of political instability, military demand for prostitution is often met through trafficking and coercion. This follows from the rule of law being weak or often non-existent in these situations. Social structures have been debilitated and women and children are particularly vulnerable.[104] Moreover, military personal

[95] Ibid, para. 43. [96] Ibid, para. 44. [97] Ibid, para. 45. [98] Ibid, para. 47.
[99] Ibid, para. 48. [100] Ibid, para. 49. [101] Ibid, para. 55. [102] Ibid, para. 57.
[103] Ibid, paras 59 and 60. [104] Ibid, para. 62.

are trained to 'dehumanize' the enemy.[105] This ability cannot be 'switched off' after battle. The soldiers also accept prostitutes as a kind of 'reward' for their deadly commitment. A lack of understanding of the given culture and population in the country of duty can also contribute heartlessness towards sexual exploitation.[106] Furthermore, it is known that systematic and organised violence against women, especially rape, trafficking, and forced prostitution, are used as a strategy in armed conflicts to humiliate the enemy.[107]

14.6 Analysis

The international community has adopted instruments to fight the sexual exploitation of children. Sexual exploitation of children includes sex tourism, child prostitution, and child pornography. Beside others, the most important instruments in fighting this are the UN Convention on the Rights of the Child, the CoE Convention on Cybercrime, and the OPSC, which was drafted by the UN. Among these, the CRC is the most widely ratified and accepted piece of legislation in the world. It mostly obliges states parties to adopt a special aim. These obligations, however, are less absolute than they seem because they are mostly restricted by vague terms like 'appropriate' and 'maximum extent of their available resources'. The OPSC and the Convention on Cybercrime deal with substantive criminal law. They contain special definitions and spell out the norms of criminal behaviour that should be punished. A more specific treaty would be more helpful, because it would contain provisions referring to substantive criminal laws that define legal terms and legislate against special kinds of criminal behaviour. It would set out international common standards and treaties seeking to close gaps in criminal liability. States hesitate to sign such treaties, because criminal law is at the core of the state's sovereignty. For this reason, international documents use terms like 'appropriate' or 'necessary' measures to give the ratifying states the opportunity to implement the provisions in line with their own legal tradition and culture.

It is very important to include those states where e.g. child prostitution is widespread. There must be a monitoring system and an exchange of data. The destination countries for child sex tourism should be informed if a potential offender crosses their border. Moreover, the state of origin should aid in the prevention of these crimes. There should be the possibility to address potential offenders before they leave the country to abuse children in a developing country.

Another important fact is regional cooperation, as the European Union offers 'its citizens an area of freedom, security and justice' and the 'prevention and combating of crime'.[108] This is a fundamental promise by the Union and part of its goals. Accordingly, the European Parliament and the Council can 'establish minimum rules concerning the definition of criminal offences and sanctions in the area of particularly serious crime with cross-border dimension'.[109]

[105] Ibid, para. 64. [106] Ibid, para. 64. [107] Ibid, para. 63.

[108] Treaty of Lisbon, 2007/C306/1, Art. 2(2).

[109] Treaty on the Functioning on the European Union, 2010/C83/47, Art. 83(1).

The European Union acknowledged the rights of children in Article 24 of the Charter of Fundamental Rights of the European Union.[110] This scope is also recognized in Article 83(1) of the Treaty on the Functioning of the European Union (TFEU), which states that the EU should prevent and combat sexual exploitation. Moreover, Article 29 of the Treaty on the European Union states that the Union's objectives are to prevent and to combat offences against children, which includes child pornography.[111]

The Treaty of Lisbon ensures the consistency of the European Union's security policy.[112] Article 67(1) TFEU states '[t]he Union shall constitute an area of freedom, security and justice with respect for fundamental rights and the different legal systems and traditions of the Member States'. The measures for achieving this objective are laid out in subsection (3). The Union shall ensure security within its area 'through measures of coordination and cooperation between police and judicial authorities ... and, if necessary, through the approximation of criminal laws'.

Criminal law is the monopoly of lawful violence by the state. The state has the powers of detention, coercion, and surveillance. The citizens are normally not allowed to secure order or to enforce judicial decisions. This power is fundamental to every sovereign state.[113] To exercise its competence the institutions of the EU can adopt legal acts. These legal acts are regulations, directives, decisions, recommendations, and opinions.[114] Recommendations and opinions do not have binding force,[115] while regulations have general application and are binding on all member states.[116] Under Article 288 paragraph 3, directives bind each member state to the subject matter they address. The national authorities can choose the form and method by which they implement the aims of a directive. A decision binds only those to whom it is addressed.[117]

Countries in Asia established the Association of South-East Asian Nations (ASEAN). This association drafted the Declaration Against Trafficking in Persons Particularly Women and Children of 29 November 2004.[118] The members agreed to 'undertake concerted efforts to effectively address an emerging regional problem, namely the trafficking in persons, particularly women and children' through different measures. These measures are set out in eight points. However, these points do not refer to substantive criminal law.

14.7 Final Observations

To enforce the obligations mentioned in this chapter it is necessary to set out uniform standards. The most widely ratified international document obliges states parties to define 'necessary' or 'appropriate' measures. Thus, it is in the sphere of the national

[110] 2000/364/01. [111] 2006/C 321 E/1.

[112] Art. 3(2) Treaty of Lisbon, cited in note 108 above.

[113] See Damian Chalmers, Gareth Davies, and Giorgio Monti (eds), *European Union Law*, 2nd edn, Cambridge, CUP, 2010, p. 584.

[114] TFEU, Art. 288. [115] TFEU, Art. 288 para. 5. [116] TFEU, Art. 288 para. 2.

[117] TFEU, Art. 288 para. 4.

[118] See https://www1.umn.edu/humanrts/research/Philippines/ASEAN%20Declaration%20Against%20Trafficking%20in%20Persons%20Particularly%20Women%20and%20Children.pdf, accessed 4 March 2016.

government to implement the standards set out in the international document. This leads to the problem that every participating country has its own unique legal tradition and culture. Some societies have very different traditions to others, e.g. to give one's daughter to another family for a 'good price'. Such forced marriages and sales for marriage are a form of exploitation and trafficking. The offenders (in this case: the parents of the child) would not be liable because these acts are not forbidden, but the government may sign the CRC. Another problem rises through differences in wealth between states or regions. People from poor areas would more readily sell their children than parents from the richer world. And people from rich countries visit poor countries to satisfy their sexual desires with children. These symptoms could not be fought just by international agreements. These phenomena can be combated only with international support and cooperation. It is necessary to raise awareness within society about the issue and crimes of sexual exploitation whether in the developed or developing world.

In any case, every international treaty and obligation can only be enforced by a national government. But what if there is no government, or a government in name only that condemns international statutes as 'Western propaganda'? Since the rise of the 'Islamic State' and other terror organisations not a day goes by without horrible news from the war zone in Iraq or Syria. Mostly women and children get kidnapped by rebels. Women and young girls are often used as slaves to 'supply' the warriors of terror organisations with sex, or left to suffer in refugee camps.

As we can see, during the last twenty years the international community has stressed the fight against child pornography. This is attributable to the increasing spread of the internet.

There are also historical reasons why the international community drafted so many human rights treaties during the last twenty years. With the fall of the Berlin Wall and the collapse of the Eastern bloc many differences began to harmonize. In the past the East and West mostly blocked each other in drafting human rights treaties. Now, they seek mutual cooperation.

As mentioned above, in this context the CRC is the most widely ratified and accepted document in the world. This might be a great step towards protecting children's rights and the prevention of sexual exploitation. A closer look at the ratification process leads to another point of view. Although the CRC mostly obliges states parties to aim to enact a special objective, these obligations are less absolute than they seem because they get restricted by vague terms like 'appropriate' or 'maximum extent of their available resources'. In addition the CRC does not provide an appropriate monitoring system. The Committee on the Rights of the Child can recommend measures to states parties. Like other human rights treaties, the CRC has no individual or collective complaint system.[119]

Both the OPSC and the Convention on Cybercrime contain provisions with regard to substantive criminal law. They contain special definitions and spell out the norms

[119] Thilo Marauhn, 'Schutz von Kindern gegen sexuelle Ausbeutung und Gewalt: Das Fakultativprotokoll zum Übereinkommen über die Rechte des Kindes betreffend den Verkauf von Kindern, die Kinderprostitution und die Kinderpornographie', in Sabin von Schorlemer and Elena Schulte-Herbrüggen (eds), [*1989-2009: 20 Jahre Kinderrechtskonvention. Erfahrungen und Perspektiven*, Dresdener Schriften zu Recht und Politik der Vereinten Nationen, Band 15, Peter Lang Verlag, Frankfurt am Main, 2010.], pp. 146, 147.

of criminal behaviour that should be punished. Other human rights treaties just provide common measures for the protection of children.[120]

As mentioned earlier, some international documents use terms such as 'appropriate' or 'necessary' to give signing states the opportunity to implement the provisions in line with their legal tradition and culture. A more specific treaty would have a great impact if it contained provisions referring to substantive criminal laws, defined legal terms, and legislated against special types of criminal behaviour. Such a treaty could set out international common standards and treaties seeking to close gaps in the criminalization of such acts. States are hesitant to sign such treaties as criminal law plays a critical role at the core of a state's sovereignty. The authority of the state to prosecute criminal offenders is one of its highest powers and it should therefore be left to the state to choose the conditions and definitions under which to prosecute its inhabitants. We live in a mobilized and globalized world and international offences need an international reaction.

Every international document is based on the principle that a state party enforces the given obligations or that the infringement of rights is passed to government authorities to deal with. The ICC was established to fight fundamental crimes like genocide and offences against humanity. Its roots lie in the period after the Second World War and the Nuremberg trials. The ICC is based on the idea that horrible crimes will be committed by state authorities and should therefore be punished by the international community. In today's globalized and highly networked world offenders can commit crimes around the world; therefore law enforcement must globalize in order to enforce the rule of law and prosecute offenders.

[120] Ibid, p. 152.

15

Transnational Organised Crime and Cultural Property

Bernhard Kretschmer

15.1 Preliminary Observations

What distinguishes human beings most of all is their unique inclination as a species towards culture. This encompasses an ability to create culture as well as perceiving, applying, or simply enjoying it. This drive is directed not just to their own art and to the works that emerge from that art, but also in no lesser capacity to artefacts from humanity's past. Of course, these artefacts usually do not become of interest until a long time has passed, so that until then the ground is their curator (a situation that is not limited to antiquities only). While the collector is attracted to recovered objects primarily by their quality, aesthetics, or historical dignity, the archæologist or monument curator might be interested even more in the situational context of the find, although such contextual information is often lost in unprofessional excavations.

The strong appreciation that people have for cultural goods is presumably based on the fact that these objects, in their own way, are a reflection of the peoples, cultures, and epochs from which they emerged. Although those cultures may be long gone, having left behind little more than these very relics, nearly all modern states consider themselves to be the custodians and administrators of the objects left behind by the peoples and cultures that once lived in their territory. The cultural objects in question often have the function of forging a certain identity, which explains the vital interest that states assert in 'their' cultural property. The attraction of cultural achievements is not limited by national boundaries. After all, in many cases cultural property is not just national heritage, but the heritage of all humanity (well beyond the objects designated by UNESCO as world heritage).[1] In this spirit, numerous museums have collected innumerable artefacts from all over the world for the enjoyment of their visitors. A similar passion drives private individuals, depending on their interest and financial capacity, to acquire certain items or even to put together whole collections (which are then often lent out to public museums or, at some point, bequeathed entirely to them). This reveals a form of cultural tourism that can be experienced without actual travel, creating strong demand for art and antiquities from all over the world. Since the laws of power and the market economy apply here as well, cultural property tends to make its way to places where people can afford it.

[1] Based on the Convention Concerning the Protection of the World Cultural and Natural Heritage, adopted 16 November 1972. To date, 191 states have ratified the Convention.

15.2 Art and Cultural Objects in Transnational Crime

The promise of lucrative profits from art, antiquities, and other cultural objects has attracted criminals, as is the case elsewhere as well, and the lines between the legal and illegal markets are often blurred as the two are more intertwined than in other segments.[2] Criminal behaviour in the art and antiquities market can take a wide variety of shapes. For the most part, the types of offence concerned are property and financial offences, namely the theft and robbery of cultural property from museums, collections, and private homes, as well as the appropriation of cultural property from illicit excavations, the illicit transport of cultural property across national boundaries, and not to forget the forgery of art and antiquities, all of these associated with receiving stolen property, fraud, extortion, bogus or forged certificates of authenticity and export certificates, infringement of tariff laws, tax evasion, and more. If we were to trace the long history of this form of crime (of which only a few examples can be given below), we would find that the market, with its preferences and opportunities, has always set the tune. We need only be reminded of the lively market in medieval days for supposedly sacred relics—*mundus vult decipi*.[3]

15.2.1 The criminology of offences relating to art and cultural objects

The actual extent of the illegal trade in cultural objects is largely unclear. It is repeatedly stated that the volume of the global market is from €5 billion to €8 billion, or even €10 billion and more per year; and is exceeded in size only by the illegal drug and weapons trade; or is even larger than the latter.[4] In fact, sensational classifications of this kind should be treated with caution, since they are hardly based on reliable data, but rather on estimates by law enforcement agencies. Constant repetition, simply accepting claims, and mutual citation may be able to drive politics and public opinion, but they do not meet the standards of criminology.[5] The high-profile cases may illustrate the situation, but are poorly suited for scientifically useful generalizations. It should be noted, from a criminological perspective, that even the known cases of this segment of the criminal world have been inadequately studied:

For example, German data (the Police Crime Statistics for 2014) show 2,106 cases of theft of antiquities, art, and sacred objects (2013: 2,561). It should be recognized, of

[2] Neil Brodie and Jennifer Doole, 'Illicit antiquities', in Neil Brodie *et al.* (eds), *Trade in Illicit Antiquities: The Destruction of the World's Archæological Heritage*, Cambridge, McDonald Institute, 2001, pp. 1, 2; Frank Wehinger, 'Illegale Märkte', MPIfG Working Paper 11/6, Max Planck Institute for the Study of Societies, Cologne, 2011, p. 51.

[3] For details, see Patrick J. Geary, *Furta Sacra: Thefts of Relics in the Central Middle Ages*, rev. edn, Princeton, New Jersey, Princeton University Press, 1990; Bernhard Kretschmer, *Der Grab- und Leichenfrevel als strafwürdige Missetat*, Baden-Baden, Nomos, 2002, p. 187ff.

[4] Cf. for the various estimates, Wehinger, 'Illegale Märkte', cited in note 2 above, p. 50. As an example, see the flyer from the German Federal Foreign Office, 'Illegaler Kulturguthandel bedroht das Kulturerbe der Menschheit' [Illegal trade in cultural goods threatens the cultural heritage of humanity] of April 2014, referring to estimates by the US security agency ICE from 2012.

[5] Rightfully criticized by Wehinger, 'Illegale Märkte', cited in note 2 above, p. 50. Accordingly, it is not surprising that associations of art and antiquities dealers cite figures that are drastically lower.

course, that thefts of this kind rarely target specific art and cultural objects, but are rather directed in general towards any object worth stealing. This is evident from the fact that, in most cases, the figures for the amounts of loss were low: according to the Police Crime Statistics, only 265 cases in 2013 involved losses of more than €5,000, and losses in excess of €50,000 were caused in only 42 cases (total losses: €9,096,429). A statistical breakdown of the stolen objects is not provided in the Police Crime Statistics; rather, the crimes are merely broken down by type of complaint (namely, theft from residences or thefts from office, industrial, and storage space). Moreover, a suspect was identified in only 19.2 per cent of the cases in 2014 and 22.2 per cent of cases in 2013. With regard to embezzlement and receiving stolen property, a relevant breakdown is entirely missing from the Police Crime Statistics.

Even less helpful are the law enforcement data dealing with convictions, as the extent to which the acts in question related to art or cultural objects is not evident from the data. It is only possible to discern that, in 2013, a single conviction was handed down for violation of the Act to Prevent the Exodus of German Cultural Property (Kulturgutschutzgesetz). This single conviction, sentencing the defendant to a monetary penalty, does not really tell us very much, since it can be interpreted at will as a sign either of the effectiveness or of the ineffectiveness of the statute.

We have even less knowledge with regard to the dark side of the illegal trade in art and antiquities. This may have to do with the fact that there are often criminal players on both sides of the trade. This and the highly conspiratorial nature of the crime make it difficult even to design an investigative approach that could help illuminate the situation. This is certainly true insofar as gangs of perpetrators become integrated into organised crime, although this organisation is more likely to take the form of a network than of a vertically integrated structure; this is clearly the case often, although there are substantial gaps in our knowledge.[6] In any case, auction houses, galleries, and dealers who are caught almost always seek to present themselves as victims. Confessions can be found in the revelations by alleged insiders from the 'art mafia', but these confessions are often overly sensationalized, which is good for book sales, but bad when it comes to providing convincing data. As far as illicit excavations are concerned, local excavation sites can be identified as such if an expert observer is aware of their presence, but even then it can hardly be said whether any objects were found at these sites and sold to (illegal) dealers, and if so which.

Despite the difficult research conditions, criminologists are attempting to validate existing presumptions and permanently illuminate the realities of this form of crime. Particular mention should be made in this regard of the International Observatory on Illicit Traffic in Cultural Goods project, initiated by the International Council of Museums (ICOM), which has been active since 2013 and is already compiling interesting facts. We should also point out ILLICID,[7] a multidisciplinary

[6] Cf. Antonius J. G. Tijhuis, *Transnational Crime and the Interface between Legal and Illegal Actors: The Case of the Illicit Art and Antiquities Trade*, Nijmwegen, Wolf Legal Publishers, 2006, p. 140; for further information on network structure in illegal markets, Wehinger, 'Illegale Märkte', cited in note 2 above, p. 104ff.

[7] ILLICID is the Procedure for illuminating the unknown as the basis for fighting and preventing crime, using the example of antique cultural objects. The project was initiated by the Prussian Cultural

project that has adopted the goal, since spring 2015, of collecting reliable criminological data on crimes relating to cultural objects. The aim is to develop and test efficient methods and tools for data collection, documentation, and analysis with respect to the illegal trade of cultural objects in Germany, with a focus on artefacts from the Eastern Mediterranean. Systematic documentation of the legal and illegal trade in cultural objects is to be achieved by creating a database that will include information about suspicious auctions. Especially given the fact that the project aims to develop better tools and measures to fight and prevent crime, the plan is for investigators to be able to access this information through an app in the future. The success of this project, which is (so far) scheduled to take place over three years, is to be awaited anxiously.

15.2.2 Investigation of crimes relating to art and cultural objects

Investigating crimes relating to art and cultural objects poses unique requirements, since highly specific expertise is called for. Crimes of this nature require a knowledge of art history, archæology, ancient and early history, numismatic expertise, and/or expertise with regard to other art and cultural objects, ideally relating to all world cultures, past and present. Because no one can even come close to doing all this alone, the investigative work in this area must be concentrated in specialized authorities or departments, the resources of which vary widely from state to state.[8] Even so, the use of internal and external experts, as well as professional support from authorities specializing in the protection of cultural property, is indispensable. Moreover, given the fact that the scale of this kind of criminal activity is very much global in nature, there is a need for international cooperation in order to fight crime. It is therefore consistent that the UN Convention Against Transnational Organised Crime of 15 November 2000 expressly includes offences against cultural heritage within its scope.[9]

High-profile roles in the international effort to fight this form of crime are played above all by Interpol, the UN Office on Drugs and Crime (UNODC), and the World Customs Organization (WCO). Interpol has maintained a separate (albeit small) department for this form of crime since 1947 and regularly organises conferences at which experts in the field engage in exchanges with regard to new developments, criminal structures, methods, and investigative approaches. Also of importance in this context is the Stolen Works of Art Database, introduced by Interpol, which lists stolen artworks in cooperation with UNESCO, ICOM, and other organisations. This database is supplemented in some states by national registers, as well as by the private Art Loss Register, in which lost and stolen art can be registered for a fee, and art

Heritage Foundation, the Fraunhofer Institute for Secure Information Technology, and the GESIS—Leibniz-Institute for the Social Sciences. Associated project partners are the Federal Foreign Office, the Federal Government Commissioner for Culture and Media, the Federal Criminal Police Office, and the Cologne Customs Investigation Office.

[8] The German agency, for example, has scant resources while the Carabinieri Art Squad in Italy (Comando Carabinieri per la Tutela del Patrimonio Culturale) is much better equipped.

[9] See UN GA Res. 55/25 of 15 November 2000, which adopted the Convention.

objects can be searched for cases of theft.[10] These services are provided free of charge to law enforcement agencies. It should also be mentioned that the European Union has initiated an informal network of law enforcement authorities and expertise competent in the field of cultural goods (EU CULTNET).[11]

15.2.3 Phenomenology of the theft of art and cultural objects

We have seen that the motives for the criminal seizure of cultural objects are very diverse, so that the perpetrators of such acts are a very heterogeneous group: buyers of stolen cultural objects become perpetrators themselves if they act in bad faith and with malicious intent (otherwise they become possible fraud victims). When cultural objects are stolen from private collections, these are usually opportunistic thefts carried out by more-or-less professional thieves, who then seek to sell the stolen property via fences. Thefts and robberies from museums and collections, on the other hand, are directed at cultural objects from the start, and in many cases actually target a specific object. In those cases, however, the stolen objects, given their significance, can no longer find their way into the legal art trade (which applies even to works whose degree of recognition is far lower than that of Edvard Munch's *The Scream*).[12] As a result, these thefts serve either, as in the case of the theft of *Saliera* from the Kunsthistorisches Museum in Vienna (2003), as a means of extracting ransoms from the museum or the insurance company ('art napping')[13] or the stolen objects find their way into the hands of a malicious art lover, who may even have ordered the theft in the first place and will continue to enjoy the stolen masterpiece unnoticed.[14] This explains, among other things, why stolen art and cultural objects often do not resurface until decades later, after the perpetrator's heirs, less passionate about art, have decided to cut the stolen objects loose. In any case, a good number of cases have been unsolved to this day and the stolen paintings remain lost, although it is unlikely that they have been destroyed. Significant examples of such cases include the art thefts in Gotha on 14 December 1979 and at the Isabella Stewart Gardner Museum in Boston on 18 March 1990. How complex all this can be is illustrated by perhaps the most famous

[10] Cf. in this regard James Ratcliffe, 'The Art Loss Register and due diligence in the trade in cultural property', in Stefano Manacorda and Arianna Visconti (eds), *Protecting Cultural Heritage as a Common Good of Humanity: A Challenge for Criminal Justice*, Milan, ISPAC, 2014, pp. 191–201.

[11] Based on the Council Resolution of 4 October 2012 (Council Document No. 14232/12).

[12] The 1893 tempera version of *The Scream* from 1893 was stolen on 12 February 1994 from the Norwegian National Gallery in a futile attempt to extract a ransom; the painting was recovered three months later. The 1910 tempera version and a version of Munch's *Madonna* were stolen from the Munch Museum in Oslo on 22 August 2004 by a band affiliated with organised crime; these paintings were not recovered until 2006 (and even then, not without damage).

[13] Cf. R. Thomas Naylor, 'The underworld of art', (2008) 50 *Crime, Law and Social Change*, 263, p. 273; Wehinger, 'Illegale Märkte', cited in note 2 above, p. 52. Many museums choose not to insure their works, a choice that often serves not only to save on premiums but also to avoid giving an incentive to thieves (also see Antonio Nicita and Matteo Rizzoli, 'The economics of art thefts: too much screaming over Munch's *The Scream*?', (2009) 28 *Economic Papers*, 291, p. 302.

[14] Little is known about such contracted thefts; they are considered rare (Lauren Bernick, 'Art and antiquities theft', (1998) 4 *Transnational Organized Crime*, 91, p. 104; also Wehinger, 'Illegale Märkte', cited in note 2 above, p. 53.

of all art thefts, namely that of the *Mona Lisa*, which disappeared from the Louvre on 21 August 1911.

After the loss of the painting, investigations were made in many different directions, including looking at international gangs of thieves and asking other countries for help. Two years after the theft, a certain Vincenzo Perugia was identified as the main culprit when he was caught trying to sell the work in Florence.[15] He stated that his principal motive was to bring the *Mona Lisa* back home to Italy, which quite likely explains the light prison sentence handed down (after appeal: seven months and eight days), so that the thief left the court a free man, thanks to time served, and continued to be celebrated as a national hero by many Italians (although it should be remarked that the *Gioconda* was not among the art stolen by Napoleon, as the thief mistakenly believed; in fact, Leonardo da Vinci had taken it with him to Clos Lucé). It is highly likely that there were other people behind the theft. Suspicious above all is the extremely shady Otto Rosenberg, who would pop up at art auctions all over Europe (the art market was lucrative even then, with art by the shipload being sold to *nouveau riche* Americans).

Probably invented, but still fascinating (inspiring books and films), is the charade that apparently was devised by an Argentinean would-be marquis.[16] This person claims that he used the actual thief to steal the painting after previously forging six copies of the *Mona Lisa* and shipping them to the USA before the suspicions of law enforcement were aroused. After the painting was stolen, he claims that he sold the forgeries to rich and malicious buyers (primarily American industrialists) for a great deal of money. That these copies, if they ever existed, have yet to surface to this day is not an effective argument against this story, given that a defrauded tycoon who thought that he was actually dealing in stolen property is not likely to reveal the truth. And who knows: given that conspiracy theorists are unfazed in their belief that the *Gioconda* that was returned to the Louvre in 1913–14 was not the original, but rather a copy, it may be that one family of billionaires or another believes to this day that it is in possession of the authentic work.[17] It is speculation to be sure, but in the art market nothing should be ruled out, certainly after the reappearance of the Gurlitt collection (2012–13). As a side note: following the theft of the *Mona Lisa*, suspicion fell on a certain Pablo Picasso, who clearly had nothing to do with the theft, but was found in possession of some stone masks that had been stolen from the Louvre (he was not convicted of the theft because intent could not be proved).

[15] Cf. in this regard, and for a detailed examination of the whole subject, Jérôme Coignard, *Une femme disparaît. Le vol de La Joconde au Louvre en 1911*, Paris/New York, LePassage, 2010; Jérôme Coignard, *'On a volé la Joconde'*, Paris, Adam Biro, 1990.

[16] Cf. in this regard and below, Coignard, *Une femme disparaît*, cited in note 15; for a novelistic treatment: Martín Caparrós and Jasper Reid, *Valfierno: The Man Who Stole the Mona Lisa*, New York, Atria, 2008, p. 159. The thesis is traced back to a report published in 1932 by the American journalist Karl Decker in the *Saturday Evening Post*, allegedly as the confession of the said marquis after his death.

[17] Cf. in this regard Manfred Reitz, *Die geraubte Mona Lisa*, Frankfurt/Leipzig, Suhrkamp, 2001, p. 148ff.

15.2.4 Phenomenology of the illegal handling of archæological cultural objects

When archæological objects are sold illegally, the objects in question were typically plundered or illegally excavated from sites all over the world. In the past, those guilty of this practice even included American and European museums, which were interested less in legitimate origin than in building up their own collections.[18] In the same way, neither are scientists innocent of taking home foreign cultural objects in violation of local law, for which we once again see the suppression mechanisms that are typically found in criminology to keep scruples from arising in the first place and to suppress them if they do (the scientists might reason, for example, that the work in question is far too unsafe in its home country). Owing to international legal developments in recent decades, most museums have begun to rethink this practice so there have been a large number of restitutions recently. Nevertheless, the litigation that has been triggered in this regard has yet to be resolved; probably the most famous conflict involves the Elgin Marbles, which have stood in the British Museum since 1816 after being removed from the Acropolis (although this was done with the approval of the Ottoman Sultan, in the interest of preserving them).[19]

The looting of museums and cultural sites is usually carried out by indigenous people, and frequently by locals. Archæological objects are especially at risk if an adequate security structure does not exist, or no longer exists, as is the case during armed conflicts, through inadequate staffing, or as a result of corruption. The situation today differs little from earlier times in this regard: graves have been robbed for as long as people have been buried along with their valuables.[20] Some cultural objects, after being dug up, find their way into the local markets and may be sold to travellers, who then take the objects with them out of the country, illegally. The majority of these objects cross national borders through dark channels, and it is presumed that well-organised gangs, or rather networks of criminals, arrange to channel the stolen goods into the antiquities market.[21] While the actual excavations may typically be performed by small-time and occasional criminals who aim to do no more than support their families, the distribution chain, with all of its members, is composed of professional criminals. It is here that the real profits are earned, as the artefacts are often shipped to multiple countries, making it difficult to investigate the crime. Investigations are already impeded by the high degree of corruption in many places, as was reported in Twentieth Dynasty tomb-robber papyri.[22]

[18] For example, the J. Paul Getty Museum, cf. Peter Watson and Cecial Todeschini, *The Medici Conspiracy: the Illicit Journey of Looted Antiquities from Italy's Tomb Raiders to the World's Greatest Museums*, New York, Public Affairs, 2006.

[19] Also to be mentioned is the dispute between Egypt and Germany concerning the bust of Nefertiti, with regard to which there are recurring allegations, which appear to be unjustified, that the arrangement made at the time to divide the finds has not been honoured.

[20] Cf. for details Kretschmer, *Der Grab- und Leichenfrevel*, cited in note 3 above, p. 105ff. and *passim*.

[21] Cf. the case studies of Simon Mackenzie and Tess Davis, 'Cambodian statue trafficking networks', in Manacorda and Visconti, *Protecting Cultural Heritage*, cited in note 10 above, pp. 149–64, and Jason Felch, 'Case studies involving antiquities trafficking networks', in ibid, pp. 177–88.

[22] Cf. in this regard Kretschmer, *Der Grab- und Leichenfrevel*, cited in note 3 above, pp. 124ff. and 702ff.; Thomas Eric Peet, *The Great Tomb-Robberies of the Twentieth Egyptian Dynasty*, Oxford, Clarendon Press, 1930.

A prime annoyance for those charged with protecting historical monuments in Europe are detectorists, who go searching for metallic objects without permission. The criminal damage they cause consists not so much in the theft of arrowheads or horseshoe nails, as in the damaging and destruction of monuments themselves. Nevertheless, such actions often uncover objects of both cultural and material value, including objects of outstanding significance: one need only think of the Kalkriese area (the presumed scene of the Varus battle) or the Nebra Sky Disc (with regard to which there were convictions for embezzlement and trading in stolen property).[23] Organised gangs are rarely engaged in this practice, so that grave robbers of this kind hardly have access to firm distribution structures. As a result, the internet has established itself as the key border-crossing medium for distribution in this regard. Of course, law enforcement officers know this too, and they are often able to identify and solve thefts in this way. It should be mentioned that the auction platform eBay has responded to these developments and its terms of sale now exclude known antiquities without certificate of origin.

15.2.5 Phenomenology of the forgery of art and cultural objects

The art and cultural markets are contaminated to a substantial extent by forgeries. This should come as no surprise, as nearly anything of value will be forged and sold. Art and cultural objects are no different in this respect from money, precious metals, jewellery, pharmaceuticals, wine, automotive spare parts, and many more. Once again, the market sets the tune in this regard, which is why even mummies were forged once, back when buying them was considered an appropriate thing to do. The current size of the market for forged paintings, sculptures, graphic works, manuscripts, antiquities, stamps, rugs, and other cultural objects is largely unclear. It is repeatedly asserted that forged works make up a substantial 40–60 per cent of the market (or, in the case of the graphic works of Dalí, even 90 per cent). Of course, this market too is diverse, and cases of fraud can be found by measurement and by classification. The copying of a well-known original is rare; it is more common to copy the work of a popular artist, an act that involves fraud and document forgery. Similar problems are raised with regard to the fraudulent forgery of antiquities (even the authenticity of the Nefertiti bust is repeatedly questioned).

The more highly regarded the artist and his/her works, the more painstaking the authenticity inspections can be expected to be, raising the cost of forgeries. In this case, it is not enough to fool the art experts alone, it is also necessary to fool the materials testers with their high-tech analytical methods.[24] Of course, close inspections are costly and generally done in the high-price segment of the market

[23] District Court of Halle/S., Judgment of 26 September 2005, Case No. 26 Ns 33/2004.

[24] Han van Meegeren, who felt misunderstood as a painter, was able to fool many experts with imitations, e.g. of Vermeer, extracting high prices from the Dutch government and Hermann Göring (cf. Georg Kretschmann, *Faszination Fälschung*, Berlin, Parthas Verlag, 2001, p. 57ff.). These forgeries would be unable to stand up to modern-day analysis since the lead compounds and isotopes used in the colours would betray them.

only, both for artworks and for antiquities. The truth that forgeries are still possible with the right finesse and criminal energy has been demonstrated by a variety of art forgers in the recent past.[25] After all, Beltracchi was able to sell an untold number of his forgeries, several of them for prices in the millions, until he was betrayed by a careless mistake.[26] Apparently, dozens or even hundreds of the forgeries he made over decades of work still exist as supposed originals. A similar situation is that of the imitation Giacometti sculptures, more than a thousand of which have been made by the Dutchman Robert Driessen, who was convicted in July 2015 by the District Court of Stuttgart, and who claims to have forged other art as well for decades.

Little is known, in general, about the structures and networks used by art forgers, especially since perpetrators, once they are caught, tend not to make any specific statements in this regard. In most of the cases that have been uncovered, the criminal initiative came from the outside, so that the forger is often not even at the centre of the actual criminal activity. For works that sell for a few thousand euros, the risk of discovery is in any case low, because the inspections of these works are less intensive, for obvious reasons. Talented painters who have become involved in the criminal forgery scene can be found at relatively small prices in Eastern Europe and elsewhere. The works are then sold via criminal networks, in which legal and illegal art sales seem to overlap. Innumerable art and cultural objects have found their way into living rooms and other chambers in this way, even though they are nothing more than overpriced copies or other forgeries. Of course, the loss is only felt when the whistle is blown, which rarely happens. Still, one-of-a-kind in the world is the Database of Critical Works initiated in 2005 by the Federal Association of German Art Auctioneers, which serves to facilitate exchanges between honest auction houses and art dealers in order to protect against forgeries.[27]

Unmasked art forgers almost always attract sympathy among the public at large because they are seen less as common criminals than as tricky hoaxers. Sympathy for the deceived victims is rare, because they are almost always too wealthy to attract much. People are amazed (and often jealous as well) of the high degree of artistic skill needed to craft a work of such quality as to be mistaken for the original.[28] In order to earn high prices at auctions, it is necessary to convince well-known experts of the work's authenticity, as well as assigning the work a credible origin. In this sense, as in others, the Beltracchi case proves to be a textbook example of international art traders deliberately

[25] Cf. further, with numerous examples, Noah Charney, *The Art of Forgery*, London, Phaidon, 2015; Rolf-Bernhard Essig and Gudrun Schury, *Schlimme Finger: Eine Kriminalgeschichte der Künste von Villon bis Beltracchi*, Munich, C. H. Beck, 2015; Henry Keazor, *Täuschend echt! Eine Geschichte der Kunstfälschung*, Darmstadt, Theiss, 2015.

[26] Out of carelessness, Beltracchi overlooked the fact that the colours in one batch included titanium white, which was not available in Campendonck's time (cf. in the liability proceedings against the auctioneer, District Court of Cologne, Judgment of 28 September 2012, Case No. 2 O 457/08, ZUM 2013, 332, p. 333f.).

[27] Areas of concern in data protection law have been reported to Jörg Wünschel, 'Die Datenbank kritischer Werke im Lichte des Datenschutzes', (2015) *Kunst und Recht*, 49.

[28] Also see Frank Arnau, *Kunst der Fälscher, Fälscher der Kunst*, 2nd edn, Düsseldorf/Vienna, Econ, 1969, p. 43ff.

ignoring the warning signs.[29] For buyers, this can be explained by lack of expertise, but when it comes to auction houses and galleries, the explanation is, at best, carelessness. Deliberately looking the other way in order to earn commission from the auction sale is a criminal practice that is often suspected, but can hardly be proved. And the expert who confirmed the authenticity of an Ernst forgery was not even penalized, even though financial connections and other grounds for suspicion existed (however, recourse claims were filed under civil law, as they were against the auction houses).

Finding an expert to confirm authenticity often seems to be no more than a question of price, which has the potential to destroy confidence in the entire art market. The false expert opinion need not even be based on an express arrangement, if the wrong incentives are set (e.g. in the form of a percentage of the sale proceeds, or in the expectation of more jobs to provide an expert opinion in the future). Since many experts who have falsely confirmed the authenticity of forged works were or are above all suspicion (e.g. when purchasing works for their own museum),[30] proof that experts attesting to the authenticity of a work are actually convinced otherwise (which constitutes fraud) is difficult to furnish (at worst, the expert's reputation will suffer from having been fooled). We have seen that, for example, the market for works of the Russian avant garde, for which top prices are paid, is full of forgeries because an expert can usually be found to certify that a work is authentic, and that an expert's expertise can itself be fabricated.[31]

15.2.6 Phenomenology of crimes involving cultural objects in armed conflict

As mentioned above, the protection of cultural objects is especially fragile when state security structures are weakened, which may be the case in wars or after natural disasters. Under such conditions, it is easier to plunder museums and other cultural sites, as occurred in the course of the Gulf Wars of 1991 and 2003 in Iraq.[32] Furthermore,

[29] Cf. also Henry Keazor and Tina Öcal, *Der Fall Beltracchi und die Folgen. Interdisziplinäre Fälschungsforschung heute*, Berlin, De Gruyter, 2014; Jörg Kinzig, 'Kunstfälschung—eine Skizze anhand des Falles "Sammlung Werner Jägers"', in Eric Hilgendorf and Rudolf Rengier (eds), *Festschrift für Wolfgang Heinz*, Baden-Baden, Nomos, 2012, pp. 124–40; for the case itself see Stefan Koldehoff and Tobias Timm, *Falsche Bilder, Echtes Geld*, Berlin, Kiepenheuer & Witsch, 2012; for an autobiographical view, Helene and Wolfgang Beltracchi, *Selbstporträt*, Reinbek, Rowohlt, 2014.

[30] One need only think of Shaun Greenhalgh, who fooled even the most famous museums with attention-grabbing works like the allegedly Egyptian 'Amarna Princess' and the sculpture 'The Faun', supposedly by Gauguin. The swindles were discovered when spelling mistakes were found on the inscription of the Assyrian stone frieze that was offered for sale to the British Museum. Mention should also be made of John Myatt, whose forgeries were accepted by major auction houses.

[31] Origin is relatively easy to invent in the case of these works because avant garde art was rejected by Stalinism and Social Realism, and confined to storage at best. The Beltracchis invented the 'Werner Jägers' and 'Knop' collections in order to demonstrate 'proper' origin. With the Giacometti forgeries, the story was that the brother's artist had hidden away sculptures that the master wanted to melt down in a perfectionist craze. To back up this story, one of the perpetrators, an art dealer, actually wrote a book under the aristocratic pseudonym of another perpetrator, titled *Diegos Rache* (2004) [Diego's Revenge].

[32] Further, Milbry Polk and Angela M. H. Schuster, *The Looting of the Iraq Museum, Baghdad: the Lost Legacy of Ancient Mesopotamia*, New York, Harry N. Abrams, 2005; Lawrence Rothfield, *The Rape of Mesopotamia behind the Looting of the Iraq Museum*, Chicago, University of Chicago Press, 2009.

the victors and occupiers in such conflicts have long since laid their hands on the cultural treasures of the other party. Art and cultural objects have been appropriated—potentially as trophies—or served as an object of assault, as collateral, or in an effort to weaken the enemy symbolically. Beyond the self-serving mentality of the colonial powers, in recent times dictatorships have proved especially eager to seize the cultural treasures of other countries: Napoleonic France in Egypt, Italy, and Germany;[33] Nazism, with the help of the Rosenberg Task Force, wherever it could;[34] and Stalinism, which seized cultural objects above all as the spoils of victory.[35] While even before the First World War the Hague Conventions dealt with the protection of cultural objects (see below), the derailments of the Second World War provided greater cause for international attention to the subjects of art theft, looted art, and the destruction of cultural objects.

International treaties distinguish between the protection of cultural objects in armed conflicts and in illegal commercial transactions. That a clear separation between the two is not possible has been evident since long before present-day armed conflicts. Recently, the militias of the Islamic State have acted in a highly iconoclastic manner in destroying pre-Islamic statues and other world-class cultural objects in Nineveh, Palmyra, and elsewhere. Surely, they did so for fundamentalist religious motives, motives that were shared by the iconoclasts of the Christian West. Really the only new aspect is the filming of these acts for the internet, as propaganda for the Western world, as the Taliban did earlier with the destruction of the Buddha statues of Bamiyan in 2001. The extent to which Islamic radical troops are involved in the very large-scale plundering of pre-Islamic cultural objects and the sale of these objects on the global antiquities market is far from clear. This kind of involvement would not be ideologically consistent, but a different argument can be made for the taxation of grave robbers and plunderers (which might be declared as protection money).[36] It becomes

[33] Cf. e.g. Bénédicte Savoy, *'Patrimoine annexé. Les biens culturels saisis par la France en Allemagne autour de 1800'*, Paris, Éditions de la Maison des Sciences de l'Homme, 2003; Bénédicte Savoy, *'Kunstraub. Napoleons Konfiszierungen in Deutschland und die europäischen Folgen'*, Cologne/Weimar/Vienna, Böhlau, 2010.

[34] See e.g. Hector Feliciano, *The Lost Museum: The Nazi Conspiracy to Steal the World's Greatest Works of Art*, New York, Basic Books, 1997 (German version: *Das verlorene Museum. Vom Kunstraub der Nazis*, Berlin, Aufbau Verlag, 1998); Günther Haase, *Kunstraub und Kunstschutz*, Hildesheim, self-published, 1991; Lynn H. Nicholas, *The Rape of Europa. The Fate of Europe's Treasures in the Third Reich and the Second World War*, New York, Vintage, 1994 (German version: *Der Raub der Europa*, Munich, Kindler Verlag, 1995).

[35] Probably the most famous example is Priam's Treasure, which was illegally removed from Troy by Schliemann in 1873. For more on this whole subject, see Konstantin Akinsha *et al.*, *Beautiful Loot: The Soviet Plunder of Europe's Art Treasures*, New York, Random House, 1995. The Western Allies, on the other hand, made more of an effort towards restitution, although American officers above all engaged in theft, of which the most significant example is the theft from the Quedlinburg Cathedral (cf. Reinhard Heydenreuter, *Kunstraub. Die Geschichte des Quedlinburger Stiftsschatzes*, Munich, Bechtle, 1993; William H. Honan, *Treasure Hunt. A New York Times Reporter Tracks the Quedlinburg Hoard*, New York, Fromm International, 1997; Siegfried Kogelfranz and Willi A. Korte, *Quedlinburg—Texas und zurück. Schwarzhandel mit geraubter Kunst*, Munich, Knaur, 1994); cf. for a comprehensive account, Kenneth D. Alford, *The Spoils of World War II: The American Military's Role in the Stealing of Europe's Treasures*, New York, Birch Lane Press, 1994.

[36] For comments on this subject, Alexander Bühler, 'Antiken für die Kriegskasse (Antiquities for the war chest)', (2015) *SPK-Magazin* (1), 38, p. 40f.

clear, in any case, that the armed conflict in Syria and Iraq goes hand in hand with civilian trade once the plundered treasures are taken out of the country and sold in Europe and other largely peaceful areas.

15.3 International Law on the Protection of Cultural Property

That states have reached agreements on binding standards is a very recent achievement that did not gather momentum until the nineteenth century. This was the beginning of international humanitarian law, focusing on the protection of vulnerable groups of people in times of armed conflict (in the Geneva Conventions) and seeking to place limitations on and establish rules for the conduct of war (in the Hague Conventions). Also included is the protection of cultural objects, although initially this protection only applied during military conflicts. Only later did international treaties extend their scope to fighting illegal sales and transfers as well.

15.3.1 Protection of cultural property in armed conflict

The core instrument in international law for the protection of cultural objects during armed conflict was the Hague Convention of 1954 and its (subsequent) protocols (see section 15.3.1.1 of this chapter). The central goal of this and other legal texts was to protect cultural objects from destruction as far as possible and to prohibit their plunder and other forms of removal. This represents a more in-depth formulation of the rules that first took on written form with the Lieber Code of 1863,[37] and that acquired universal significance somewhat later with the Hague Regulations Respecting the Laws and Customs of War on Land of 1899 and 1907 (see section 15.3.1.2 of this chapter), culminating in the Roerich Pact (1935), the first international treaty devoted entirely to the protection of cultural objects.[38]

15.3.1.1 The Hague Convention of 1954 and its supplements

The Hague Convention for the Protection of Cultural Property in the Event of Armed Conflict of 14 May 1954 relates to all movable and immovable property of great importance to the cultural heritage of every people, regardless of origin and ownership (Article 1).[39] The guideline to be followed by the parties to any conflict is to safeguard

[37] Instructions for the Government of Armies of the United States in the Field, 24 April 1863. This Code, which was formulated during the American Civil War, was to apply to all American troops but initially applied just to the Union army (cf. in this regard John Fabian Witt, *Lincoln's Code*, New York, Free Press, 2012).

[38] Treaty on the Protection of Artistic and Scientific Institutions and Historic Monuments of 15 April 1935. This treaty, initiated by Russian artist and philosopher Nicholas Roerich (also called *Pax cultura*) was subsequently ratified by only ten American states (including the USA). It forms the nucleus of the Hague Convention of 1954.

[39] For example, it relates to monuments of architecture, art, or history, archaeological sites, groups of buildings of historical or artistic interest, works of art, manuscripts, books and other objects of artistic, historical, or archæological interest, scientific collections and important collections of books, archives,

and respect cultural property (Article 2). The Convention therefore requires the contracting parties to prohibit, prevent, and, if necessary, put a stop to any form of theft, pillage, or unlawful misappropriation of cultural objects, as well as vandalism against those objects (Article 4(3)). Reprisals against cultural objects are wholly excluded (Article 4(4)). Moreover, the defending party in a conflict is required to keep its distance from cultural property, subject to overriding military necessity, in order to avoid provoking attacks (Article 4 (1)). Members of the military are to be instructed with regard to all of these requirements (Article 7). In addition, those who violate the Convention or order acts that violate the Convention are to be penalized or disciplined (Article 28). These requirements apply regardless of a formal declaration of war and remain in effect even in cases of uncontested occupation (Article 18). Cultural property is to be respected even in armed conflicts that are not of an international nature (Article 19(1)), a rule that deserves attention now because Iraq and Syria are both signatories of the Convention.[40]

No less important for the debate on the protection of cultural objects is the First Protocol, which was negotiated at the same time and was separated only for tactical reasons. By ratifying this Protocol, the contracting states agreed to prevent the exportation of cultural property from occupied territories, to take into custody any cultural objects that nevertheless make their way into their sovereign territory, to refrain from using such goods for purposes of reparations, and to return such property once hostilities have closed (Additional Protocol (AP) I Articles 1–4).[41] Important supplements to the Hague Convention are provided by the two Additional Protocols of 8 June 1977 to the Geneva Conventions. These Protocols prohibit hostile actions against historical monuments, artworks, and places of worship that constitute the cultural or spiritual heritage of peoples (Article 53 AP I, Article 16 AP II). Moreover, they may not be used in support of military efforts or made the subject of reprisals. These Protocols were attached to the Geneva Convention because a larger number of states could be expected to ratify that Convention. In fact, the two Additional Protocols have been ratified by 174 (AP I) and 168 states (AP II) while the Hague Convention has now been ratified by 127 states, and the First Protocol to the Hague Convention by 104 states.[42]

The Convention is completed by the Second Protocol of 26 March 1999, which has been ratified by just sixty-eight states (none of them a major military power). Of

or reproductions, to buildings preserving and exhibiting such cultural assets, such as museums and archives, and to monument centres.

[40] Moreover, the Convention deals to a great extent with special protection zones and the safe transport and identification of cultural objects, which are addressed in the Regulations for the Execution of the Convention. This was done in light of the experiences from the Second World War, with warfare in extended areas in mind.

[41] Of course, the situation remains fragile: in the course of the Turkish invasion of Cyprus (1974), for example, Orthodox cultural objects were destroyed and plundered in a highly systematic fashion and brought to the world market via middlemen, even though Turkey has been a member of both the Convention and the Protocol since 1965.

[42] Upon the signing of the Additional Protocols to the Geneva Conventions, only sixty-four states became a party to the Hague Convention and only fifty-five states acceded to its Protocol. It should be pointed out that, of these four texts, only the Convention of 1954 has been ratified by the USA (and only in 2009, as until then accession to this widely respected Convention was rejected in order to keep open the nuclear option).

substantive importance are the definition of military objectives (Article 1(f)) and the detailing of imperative military necessity (Article 6), with the goal of affording the highest possible degree of protection.[43] The Protocol prohibits the illicit export, other removal, or transfer of ownership of cultural property, as well as archæological excavations (except in cases of emergency) and any alteration to or change of use of cultural property intended to conceal or destroy cultural, historical, or scientific evidence (Article 9(1)). The Protocol also applies to armed conflicts that are not of an international character (Article 22(1) and (2)).

Of interest from the point of view of criminal law is the fact that, under the Protocol, a person commits an offence by making cultural property under enhanced protection the object of attack or using cultural property under enhanced protection or its immediate surroundings in support of military action (Article 15(1)(a) and (b)).[44] The same applies to those who engage in extensive destruction or appropriation of protected cultural property (15(1)(c)), who make protected cultural property the object of an attack (15(1)(d)), or engage in theft, pillage, or misappropriation, or acts of vandalism directed against cultural property protected under the Convention (15(1)(e)). When it comes to implementing these enforcement obligations, the contracting states must keep in mind the principles of international law (Article 15(2)). The contracting states are to have jurisdiction at least over offences that are committed in their territory and where the alleged offender is a national of that state, as well as over the acts mentioned above within sub-paragraphs (a)–(c), in which case extradition is to be facilitated as well (Article 18), even where the offender is a national of the state in question (Article 16(1)). In addition, any intentional use of cultural property in violation of the Convention and the Protocol, as well as any illicit export, other removal, or transfer of ownership of cultural property from occupied territories is to be penalized (Article 21).

15.3.1.2 The Hague Regulations Respecting the Laws and Customs of War on Land

Also of importance with regard to the protection of cultural property are the Regulations Respecting the Laws and Customs of War on Land, which were adopted at the Hague Conferences of 1899 and 1907 and have since been ratified by nearly all civilized states.[45] Even where states have not adopted these Regulations, their content

[43] The Protocol only deems an act of hostility against cultural property to be in conformance with the Convention if such an act brings a clear military advantage and if there is no other way of achieving a comparable result (Art. 6(a)); furthermore, cultural property may only be used for purposes that are likely to expose it to destruction or damage when and for as long as no other feasible method exists to achieve a similar military advantage (6(b)), in addition, the decision to invoke imperative military necessity is reserved to officers commanding a force the equivalent of a battalion in size or larger (6(c)) and effective advance warning must be given whenever circumstances permit (6(d)). During an attack, all feasible precautions should be taken to ensure that protected cultural property is not the subject of attack and to avoid or minimize damage to cultural property; under certain circumstances, the attack must be suspended or cancelled entirely (for details, see Article 7).

[44] This is in view of the fact that, under certain circumstances, cultural heritage of the greatest importance may be afforded enhanced protection (Art. 10ff.), in order to ensure immunity (Art. 12).

[45] The Regulations were attached to the Convention (II) of 1899 (Hague Convention with Respect to the Laws and Customs of War on Land) and the Convention (IV) of 1907 (Hague Convention respecting the Laws and Customs of War on Land). Most of the states that ratified the 1899 Convention also ratified

has long been considered international custom (as the Tribunals in Nuremberg and Tokyo assumed).[46] The Regulations afford special protection to certain buildings, including museums, churches, and universities. Buildings that are devoted to higher purposes must be spared as far as possible, unless they are also used for military purposes (Article 27).[47] The seizure, destruction, or wilful damaging of such institutions, historic monuments, and works of art and science are forbidden, and must (as stated in the 1899 version) or should (as in the 1907 version) be made the subject of legal proceedings (Article 56).[48] Pillage is formally forbidden (Article 47), which protects art and cultural objects as well. Of course, one need only look at the subsequent world wars to see that there are limits to the effective power of the Regulations.

15.3.1.3 International criminal law with regard to cultural property

Since Article 56 of the Regulations Respecting the Laws and Customs of War on Land already called for penalties for the prohibited seizure, destruction, or damaging of cultural property protected by international law, the Nuremberg and Tokyo Tribunals regarded the pillage and destruction of foreign property, including cultural objects, as a war crime. Following the Cold War, which interrupted all efforts to enforce international criminal law, these efforts continued as both the ICTY and the ICTR have convicted some defendants for the destruction of cultural property.[49] The Statutes of the two ad hoc tribunals of 1993 and 1994 were able to base their provisions in this regard (Articles 3 and 4) on the fact that the Hague Convention of 1954 contains an express duty to impose sanctions (Article 28), although this duty was originally intended for states. Since then, these rules have been supplemented by the enforcement obligations in the Second Protocol to the Hague Convention.

The quasi-codified present status of international criminal law is reflected by the Rome Statute of 17 July 1998, although the agreement is involved in a continuing ratification crisis.[50] Subject to prosecution under this Statute, within the context of international or non-international armed conflict, are intentional attacks against buildings

the 1907 Convention. Although some states failed to accede to the Convention adopted at the Second Hague Conference, this is of no material importance here.

[46] For customary international law with regard to the protection of cultural objects, cf. Jean-Marie Henckaerts, Louise Doswald-Beck, Carolin Alvermann, International Committee of the Red Cross, *Customary International Humanitarian Law*, Cambridge, CUP, 2005, Chapter 12: Cultural Property, Rules 38–41.

[47] Also Art. 5 of the IX. Hague Convention concerning Bombardment by Naval Forces in Time of War.

[48] Property of this kind must be generally respected and may not be confiscated (Art. 46). Even prior to occupation, the destruction or seizure of enemy property is in any case prohibited, except in case of urgent military necessity (Art. 23(g)).

[49] For details, see Hirad Abtahi, 'The protection of cultural property in times of armed conflict. The practice of the International Criminal Tribunal for the Former Yugoslavia', (2001) 14 *Harvard Human Rights Journal*, 1; specifically, the proceedings to be mentioned are those against *Kordić and Čerkez* (Lašva Valley), *Jokić* (Dubrovnik), *Martić* (RSK) and *Prlić et al.*

[50] The major powers China, India, Russia, and the USA have not ratified the Statute and are not expected to do so in the foreseeable future. Those who have failed to ratify also include Turkey and nearly all states in the Arab world, the Middle and Near East, and Indochina, including Malaysia and Indonesia. The next-to-last of the 124 contracting states was Palestine, which ratified at the start of 2015 (to put pressure on Israel); El Salvador was following on 3 March 2016.

subject to special protection (which include those dedicated to art and science), or on historic monuments (Article 8(2)(b)(ix) and (e)(iv)).[51] In addition, any destruction, pillaging, or seizure of enemy property (including cultural property) is subject to prosecution unless imperatively demanded by the necessities of war (8(2)(b)(xiii) and (e)(xii)).[52] The Statute does not cover damage to cultural property outside armed conflicts (e.g. internal disturbances and tensions such as riots), isolated and sporadic acts of violence or other acts of a similar nature (8(2)(f); also Article 22(2) of the Second Protocol to the Hague Convention). Moreover, if a controlling power destroys the cultural objects of an enemy group, such an act may be considered a crime against humanity (at times referred to boldly as 'cultural genocide').

Once again, the limited jurisdiction of the International Criminal Court (ICC) poses a serious problem when it comes to enforcing these elements. Insofar as the court has operated up to this point, it has focused above all on crimes against humanity and other war crimes. The conflicts in Syria and Iraq, in which cultural property has been violated in a high-profile fashion, are not subject to the jurisdiction of the ICC, in the absence of an assignment of jurisdiction by the UN Security Council, since neither country is a contracting state. But that is not true of Mali, where fundamentalist militias engaged in iconoclastic destruction of cultural property, above all in 2012. Headlines worldwide reported the destruction of the Islamic shrines in Timbuktu, which have been a Cultural World Heritage Site since 1988. Between May and July of 2012, apparently, at least nine mausoleums, two mosques, and two historical monuments were attacked and destroyed by members of the Islamist group Ansar Dine (and possibly also AQIM and MUJAO).[53] Religious and historical sites outside Timbuktu were also reported destroyed.[54] Mali referred the situation to the ICC Prosecutor (Article 14 Rome Statute), which has been investigating all acts committed since January 2012. This includes intentionally directing attacks against protected objects, since such attacks may constitute war crimes.[55]

Aside from sanctions imposed by the ICC or an ad hoc tribunal, as was created in the case of the ICTY and ICTR (followed by the IRMCT), war crimes may also be prosecuted under national criminal law (and not just if the offence occurred in the state or if the offender is a national of the state in question). We have seen that many states have imposed penalties of their own for core crimes in international criminal law. This is the case, for example, in Germany, where war crimes are included in

[51] Also prohibited in international armed conflict, subject to penalty, are all intentional attacks against civilian objects (Art. 8(2)(b)(ii)) and disproportionate damage to civilian objects ((b)(iv)). This also applies for violations of the Geneva Convention through the extensive destruction and appropriation of property not justified by military necessity and carried out unlawfully and wantonly (Art. 8(2)(a)(iv)).

[52] Cf. the specification in Art. 6 of the Second Protocol to the Hague Convention (see section 15.3.1.1 of this chapter).

[53] This also constitutes a violation of the Geneva Additional Protocol (cf. above, section 15.3.1.2 of this chapter). However, Mali did not accede to the Second Protocol to the Hague Convention of 1954 until after the acts in question.

[54] The Office of the Prosecutor of the ICC, 'Situation in Mali, Article 53(1) Report of 16 January 2013', pp. 24 and 31–2.

[55] In these terms, the acts of destruction are also considered to be a war and international crime by the UN Security Council (UNSC Res. 2056 (2012)—5 July 2012, para. 18), the African Union (AU), and the ECOWAS Contact Group of Mali.

the elements of offences in §§8ff. of the Code of Crimes against International Law (Völkerstrafgesetzbuch). This statute makes launching a military attack against objects that are protected by international humanitarian law liable to prosecution; once again, these objects include historical monuments and buildings that are devoted to religious worship, education, art, science, and charitable activities (§11(1) No. 2 of the Code). Also subject to prosecution are those who destroy, appropriate, or seize objects of an enemy party to a substantial extent in violation of international law (§9(1) of the Code). In accordance with substantive law, universal jurisdiction should exist in this regard, even if there is no point of connection to Germany (§1 of the Code). This (apparent) extension of jurisdiction is lessened on the procedural side (§153f. of the Criminal Procedure Code [Strafprozessordnung]) for as long as alleged destroyers of cultural property do not travel to Germany, they have no need to expect an investigation.

15.3.2 Protection of cultural objects from illegal sale

For a long time, efforts to afford protection to cultural property in international law have focused on the side of conflict and the duties of the belligerent parties, as devastating wars and government-directed looting gave sufficient cause for this focus. It is certainly true that, in times of crisis such as these, cultural property is at its greatest risk of being plundered from museums and other cultural sites to be sold in the art and antiquities markets. This also occurs in times of peace, as demonstrated by innumerable acts of theft and illegal excavations. Accordingly, cultural property absolutely requires protection on the supply and demand side as well. In a global market, international cooperation is indispensable, with stronger inspections of imports and exports of art objects and artefacts. We have seen, however, that inspections in many states increased only in the post-colonial period, once nations' own museums had already been filled, with more objects in storage than in the exhibition spaces.

15.3.2.1 The UNESCO Convention of 1970

The key instrument of international law on this issue is the UNESCO Convention on the Means of Prohibiting and Preventing the Illicit Import, Export and Transfer of Ownership of Cultural Property of 14 November 1970.[56] It counts cultural property among the cultural heritage of a state if this was/is created by the individual or collective genius of the state's nationals (or persons residing within its territory) or if it was found within the state's territory (Article 4(a) and (b)). Yet, it also includes cultural property that, with the consent of the country of origin, was received free of charge, lawfully purchased, or acquired by archæological, ethnological, or natural science

[56] Currently, the last of the 131 states parties is Ghana (effective 20 January 2016). On the other hand, the approximately twenty-five resolutions of the UN General Assembly on the return or restitution of cultural property to the countries of origin, most recently that of 5 December 2012 (A/RES/67/L.34) have more the character of an appeal, rather than law.

missions, thus securing the status of possessions of European and American museums (Article 4(c) through (e)). The actual determination of protected cultural property is left by the Convention to the individual states, which themselves are to designate, on religious or secular grounds, items of importance for them for archæology, prehistory, history, literature, art, or science (Article 1). This determination is to be based on a list citing a large number of categories (sub-paragraphs (a)–(k)).[57]

The state parties are required to prevent museums and similar institutions within their territories from acquiring cultural property originating in another state party that has been illegally exported after the entry into force of the Convention (24 April 1972; Article7(a)), i.e. cultural goods without an export certificate (Article 6(b)). Even more, they are required to prohibit the import of cultural property stolen from a museum or a religious or secular public monument or similar institution in another state party after the entry into force of the Convention for the states concerned, provided that such property is documented as belonging to the inventory of that institution (Article 7(b)(i)). At the request of the state of origin, cultural property stolen and exported after the mutual validity of the Convention for both involved states must be returned, although just compensation is to be paid to bona fide buyers (Article 7(b)(ii); cf. also Article 13).[58] The illegal import and export of protected cultural property as described above is to be subjected to penalties (Article 8).

The Convention suffers from the fact that it can be understood to mean that it only covers cultural property that is specifically designated by the state of origin. If, upon implementing the Convention in national law, a state party stipulates that the objects have to be specifically listed or itemized and, moreover, specifies short periods in which to request the restitution of cultural property, the protection afforded by the Convention may be largely hollow (as was the case until now in Germany). Another tricky aspect is that the cultural object in question has to have been exported after the Convention entered into force, which is not always easy to prove in view of the fact that antiquities have been sold and assembled in private collections for a long time. This is also problematic in view of the fact that past cultures did not conform to present-day national boundaries. If the precise location of the find is unknown it may therefore be unclear to which state the artefact in question even belongs. As a result, objects have been claimed at times by multiple states (although in practice, it has often proved to be the case that the antiquities in question are forgeries). All of these factors affect the results of the assessment in public, civil, and criminal law.

[57] Namely: rare collections and examples of natural science, property relating to history, products of archæological excavations or of archæological discoveries, elements of artistic or historical monuments or archæological sites, antiquities more than one hundred years old (such as inscriptions, coins, and seals), objects of ethnological interest, property of artistic interest (such as pictures, paintings, and drawings produced entirely by hand, original works of statuary art and sculpture, original artistic assemblages and montages), rare manuscripts and incunabula, old books, documents, and publications of special interest, postage, revenue, and similar stamps, archives, including sound, photographic, and cinematographic archives, articles of furniture more than one hundred years old, and old musical instruments.

[58] The export and transfer of ownership of cultural property under compulsion attributable to the occupation of a country by a foreign power is also regarded as illicit (Art. 11), a rule that is based on the Hague Convention and was then specified in greater detail in the Second Protocol to that Convention.

15.3.2.2 *The UNIDROIT Convention of 1995*

Because the UNESCO Convention leaves the states parties a considerable amount of flexibility, the laws differ from country to country, making them substantially less effective. The UNIDROIT Convention on Stolen or Illegally Exported Cultural Objects of 24 June 1995 aims to eliminate this defect. The Convention wants to be understood as complementary and therefore adopts the previous definition of cultural objects, broken down into categories (Article 2 with Annex).[59] As the directly applicable law of the states parties, the Convention formulates a claim for restitution against the possessors of stolen cultural objects (Article 3(1)), although certain periods exist for the assertion of such a claim. Going beyond the 1970 Convention, objects that are found in the course of illegal excavations are generally considered to be stolen (cf. more precisely, Article 3(2)).[60] Possessors who acquired the object in good faith must be paid fair compensation (Article 4), although the possessor bears the burden of proof as to the exercise of due diligence (with specific criteria defined for the examination of this question), a point with significant ramifications. The Convention also establishes rules for the return of illegally exported cultural objects (Articles 5 and 7), for which, in turn, specific periods apply, as well as a duty to compensate good-faith possessors (Article 6). These articles only apply to cultural objects that are stolen or exported after the state party in question accedes to the Convention (for details, Article 10). As a result, the effective force of the Convention is curtailed even further because the states with the most important markets are not yet parties to the Convention.[61]

15.3.2.3 *Resolutions of the UN Security Council*

The fact that the protection of cultural property during armed conflicts and the fight against the illegal sale of cultural property are often two sides of the same coin has already been mentioned; the conflicts in Syria and Iraq and the associated sell-off of cultural objects are prime examples. Given that the existing instruments of international law have proved inadequate for the international community to combat these practices, the UN Security Council has adopted two Resolutions to counteract the illegal sale of cultural objects from Syria and Iraq. The first of these is the Iraq Resolution, S/RES/1483 (2003) of 22 May 2003 (para. 7), under which the member states

[59] Explanatory report, (2001) *Uniform Law Review* 6, 476–581; Lyndel Prott, 'UNESCO and UNIDROIT: a partnership against trafficking in cultural objects', in Norman Palmer (ed.), *The Recovery of Stolen Art*, London, Kluwer Law International, 1998, pp. 205–15; for a comprehensive view, Bettina Thorn, *Internationaler Kulturgüterschutz nach der UNIDROIT-Konvention*, Berlin, De Gruyter, 2005.

[60] Cf. for more details, Kurt Siehr, 'Das UNIDROIT-Übereinkommen von 1995 und Staatseigentum an archäologischen Kulturgütern', in Aldo Ligustro and Giorgio Sacerdoti (eds), *Problemi e tendenze del diritto internazionale dell'economia*, Naples, Editoriale Scientifica, 2011, pp. 983–97.

[61] Only a few European states have acceded to the Convention so far (mostly in Southern Europe), particularly Spain, Italy, and Greece, but not Germany, France, the Benelux states, and the United Kingdom, and also not the USA, Canada, or Japan. Nevertheless, casting the Convention in a kind light is Lyndel Prott, 'The UNIDROIT Convention on Stolen or Illegally Exported Cultural Objects—ten years on', (2009) *Uniform Law Review*, 215–37.

shall take appropriate steps to facilitate the safe return to Iraqi institutions of Iraqi cultural property and other items of archæological, historical, cultural, rare scientific, and religious importance illegally removed from the Iraq National Museum, the National Library, and other locations in Iraq since the adoption of resolution 661 (1990) of 6 August 1990, including by establishing a prohibition on trade in or transfer of such items and items with respect to which reasonable suspicion exists that they have been illegally removed, and calls upon the United Nations Educational, Scientific, and Cultural Organisation, Interpol, and other international organisations, as appropriate, to assist in the implementation of this paragraph.

Resolution S/RES/2199 (2015) of 12 February 2015 is a subsequent response to the events in Syria and Iraq, and once again concerns the protection of world cultural heritage (paras 15–17).[62] The Resolution condemns the destruction of cultural heritage and states with concern that Islamist groups are probably earning direct or indirect profits from the looting and smuggling of cultural heritage items and using these funds to recruit new members, strengthen their operational capacities, and undertake terrorist attacks. Following upon the Iraq Resolution, this Resolution accordingly seeks to prohibit the purchase and sale of Syrian cultural objects exported since 15 March 2011.

To implement the Iraq Resolution, the European Union has prohibited the import and export, the bringing into or removing from the territory of the Community, and all dealing in the cultural property in question, unless it can be shown that the cultural items were exported from Iraq prior to the date on which the embargo against Iraq was imposed.[63] Violations are to be penalized in accordance with national law and are subject to prosecution in Germany under the Foreign Trade and Payments Act (Außenwirtschaftsgesetz). As a preventative measure, the European Union promptly enacted the same rules for Syria.[64]

15.3.2.4 Other international law

The Convention on the Protection of the Underwater Cultural Heritage of 2 November 2001, which was adopted following the UN Convention on the Law of the Sea, deals with the protection of underwater cultural heritage.[65] It aims above all to secure the relevant cultural heritage, which includes prohibiting looting (cf. Articles 10(4) and 12(3)). The states parties are to prevent the dealing in and taking possession of underwater cultural heritage that is illicitly exported and/or recovered contrary to the

[62] Affirmative: Resolution of the General Assembly A/RES/69/281 'Saving the cultural heritage of Iraq'.

[63] Art. 3 of Council Regulation (EC) No. 1210/2003 of 7 July 2003 concerning certain specific restrictions on economic and financial relations with Iraq, OJ L 169/6.

[64] Art. 11c of Council Regulation (EU) No. 1332/2013 of 13 December 2013 amending Regulation (EU) No 36/2012 concerning restrictive measures in view of the situation in Syria, OJ L 335/3.

[65] See Sarah Dromgoole, *The Protection of the Underwater Cultural Heritage*, 2nd edn, Leiden/ Boston, Martinus Nijhoff Publishers, 2006; Ronald Herzog, *Kulturgut unter Wasser*, Aachen, Shaker Verlag, 2002; K. Siehr, 'Die UN-Konvention über den Schutz des kulturellen Erbes unter Wasser und das Internationale Sachenrecht', in Michaela Wittinger, Rudolf Wendt, and Georg Ress (eds), *Verfassung—Völkerrecht—Kulturgüterschutz. Festschrift für Wilfried Fiedler zum 70. Geburtstag*, Berlin, Duncker & Humblot, 2011, pp. 447–60.

Convention (Article 14). Any commercial exploitation of such heritage is fundamentally incompatible with its protection (for details, see Annex, Rule 2). The Convention is to be enforced through sanctions of adequate severity and deterrent effect, depriving offenders of the benefits of unlawful activity (Article 17). Objects that were recovered in a manner contrary to the Convention are to be seized and used for public benefit (Article 18). Acceptance of the Convention has been modest so far, as key markets have yet to ratify it (e.g. the USA, the United Kingdom, and Germany).

Especially owing to the fact that European states are among the key markets for the sale of legal and illegal art and antiquities, we will now briefly list the applicable Conventions of the Council of Europe as well as the relevant legal acts of the European Union:

1. The European Convention on the Protection of the Archæological Heritage of 16 January 1992 describes e.g. duties of an administrative and qualitative nature (Article 2ff.).[66] For example, museums and similar institutions are to refrain from acquiring objects that have been illicitly excavated or stolen (Article 10).
2. The Convention for the Protection of the Architectural Heritage of Europe of 3 October 1985 deals with the preservation of Europe's architectural heritage (monuments, buildings, and other sites), but is hardly relevant in the area of transnational crime.[67]
3. The situation might have been different in the case of the European Convention on Offences relating to Cultural Property of 23 June 1985.[68] Offences relating to cultural property under the Convention include at least the theft of cultural property, appropriating cultural property with violence or menaces, and receiving cultural property acquired in this manner (Article 3(1), with Appendix III (1) (a)–(c)). The Convention also cites many other acts and omissions in this regard which the state parties may regard as offences, although this is not intended to be an exhaustive list (Article 3(2), with Appendix III (2)). No further details are required in this regard, since the Convention has not been accepted by any state.
4. Council Regulation (EC) No. 116/2009 of 18 December 2008 on the export of cultural goods serves to prevent the export of significant cultural objects from the European Union.[69] The classification of cultural goods that may not be exported from the European single market without official approval (Article 2) is made using detailed, largely age-based categories (Article 1 with Annex I A(1)–(15)) and based on value categories (B). The member states are required to ensure effective, proportionate and dissuasive sanctions in order to ensure enforcement of the Regulation.

[66] ETS No. 143. Now that Italy has joined (effective 31 December 2015), forty-four of the forty-seven member states of the Council of Europe have accepted the Convention or switched over to it (plus the Holy See). Cf. the forerunner to the Convention: the European Convention for the Protection of the Archæological Heritage, 6 May 1969 (ETS No. 66; two of the three remaining Council of Europe states are still members of this Convention).

[67] ETS No. 121, accepted by nearly all Council of Europe states.

[68] ETS No. 119.

[69] OJ 2009 L 39/1. The regulation in effect before this one was the often-amended European Council Regulation (EEC) No. 3911/92 of 9 December 1992 on the export of cultural goods, OJ L 395/1.

5. Directive 2014/60/EU of 15 May 2014 on the return of cultural objects unlawfully removed from the territory of a member state deals with claims for the return of cultural goods between EU member states.[70] If a state asserts such a claim, it is required to pay the good-faith possessor fair compensation, unless that possessor (or the person who gave or bequeathed the object to that possessor) failed to demonstrate the exercise of due diligence in making the acquisition (Article 10(1)). In accordance with the UNIDROIT Convention of 1995, the possessor bears the burden of proof in this regard, and all circumstances relating to the acquisition are to be taken into account (documentation of provenance, necessary export licences, the character of the parties, the price paid, consultation of accessible registers of stolen cultural objects, other available information, etc.).[71] Implementation in national law may involve the imposition of criminal penalties, as is the case with Section 20 of Germany's Act on the Return of Cultural Property (as of 2007, this Act also serves to implement the UNESCO Convention of 1970).[72]

15.4 Protection of Art and Cultural Objects in Criminal Law

International criminal law may be applied for the protection of cultural objects in order to impose penalties for offences committed in the context of armed conflicts (see section 15.3.1.1 of this chapter). Aside from this case, the imposition of criminal penalties remains in the hands of individual states, which can support each other through law enforcement cooperation and by way of mutual assistance (and should do so, depending on the treaty status). In an individual case the criminal law of any state might have jurisdiction to prosecute crimes relating to art and cultural objects, although of course this is most common in states with rich cultures, perhaps as the state of origin, and the state where the trading or purchase takes place. With regard to the interactions between national laws it must be said that, of course, no criminal law of a state is congruent with the criminal law of another state.

When treating the forgery of art and antiquities, criminal law has focused on the offence of fraud, but also on document forgery, copyright infringements, in some states conspiracy, and many more.[73] While the elements of these offences differ from state to state, this does not hinder enforcement very much since the criminal statutes in

[70] OJ L 159/1. Such a system already existed before this, based on European Council Directive No. 93/7/EEC of 15 March 1993 on the return of cultural objects unlawfully removed from the territory of a member state, OJ L 74/74.

[71] Cf. the comparison by K. Siehr, 'The protection of cultural property: the 1995 UNIDROIT Convention and the EEC Instruments of 1992/93 compared', (1998) *Uniform Law Review* (2/3), 671–83.

[72] Kulturgüterrückgabegesetz, BGBl. 2007 I 757, 2547. The illicit transfer of national cultural heritage is subject to separate penalties in Germany in the Act to Prevent the Exodus of German Cultural Property (Kulturgutschutzgesetz). Under existing law, however, and unlike in other legal systems, this is only the case if the object in question is included in a list (this is set to change).

[73] Cf. Joachim Löffler, 'Künstlersignatur und Kunstfälschung', (1993) *NJW*, 1421–9; Claudia and Dirk von Selle, 'Illegaler Kunsthandel—Teil 1', (2008) *Kultur und Recht*, L 3.7, p. 14ff.; for basic principles, Thomas Würtenberger, *Der Kampf gegen das Kunstfälschertum in der deutschen und schweizerischen Strafrechtspflege*, Wiesbaden, F. Steiner, 1951, p. 83ff.

the various states, especially with respect to fraud, are sufficiently consistent for the provision of mutual assistance, with a view to double criminality as well.[74] The biggest problem with regard to the forgery of art and cultural objects continues to be furnishing actual evidence. After all, it is necessary to prove that the object in question is a forgery in the first place. Actually ascertaining the identity of the forger and, even more, proving intentional misconduct on the part of experts, auction houses, or dealers, continues to be a tricky proposition, especially since offenders who are caught committing crimes of this nature tend to be cautious in making statements about the other persons involved.

The legal assessment of illicitly obtained art and cultural objects is on solid ground as long as the case concerns theft or robbery from museums or other collections. In that case, the state with criminal jurisdiction is typically the state where the offence was committed, or possibly the state of which the offender is a national if the offender is a foreigner, and states tend to provide mutual support in the investigation and prosecution of such offences. The legal assessment of illicit excavations is less consistent. States having soil rich in historical artefacts tend to include highly specific elements in their laws aiming to criminalize the plunder of archæological sites. But in other states, this is not the case, and the only possible offence is a property offence, e.g. misappropriation or unlawful acquisition (and possibly damage to property as well). This is possible only if, by removing the artefacts, the offender trespasses on foreign property or violates laws relating to land ownership. We have seen that most states have adopted the 'treasure trove' principle, assigning ownership of new finds to the state. But independently removing finds is typically a criminal offence even if the state law stipulates that ownership is to be shared between the finder and the property owner ('Hadrian's division').[75] Unlike the treasure trove rule, in this case an offence is not committed if the property owner is a participant (let alone if the property owner is the person who conducted the excavation).

A legal assessment is more difficult with regard to the illegal transfer of art and cultural objects. The task of detecting and preventing such offences falls primarily to the Customs authorities of the various states, but in view of the actual shipping volume of goods of all kinds, these authorities generally have to hope for a lucky find, unless they are supplied with specific information or a background investigation has been conducted. In cases involving the illicit removal from a state of its own cultural heritage, there is a strong global tendency towards nationalist protectionism (even within the European Single Market). For the identification of cultural heritage, most states classify relevant objects by categories, under threat of punishment, through the use of an official licence. Far rarer is the list principle according to which cultural property is only considered as national heritage if it is listed as such (as is currently the case in

[74] In the European Union, moreover, fraud is a catalogued offence for many legal instruments, so that it need not be an offence under the law of the state itself for mutual assistance to be rendered.

[75] Referring to the Roman Emperor of that name, Inst. 2.1.39 in *Corpus Iuris Civilis*, still in effect, e.g. in Art. 716 of the French Civil Code and Art. 351 of the Spanish Civil Code. German law has adopted the principle of 'Hadrian's division' in §984 of the Civil Code, but this is deceptive since the laws of fifteen of the sixteen German States deviate from this principle, decreeing a treasure trove rule instead (which is allowed by Art. 73 of the Introductory Act to the Civil Code; the sole exception is Bavaria).

Germany). Additional criminal provisions can typically be found in the laws relating to cultural property and/or export law.

The legal situation is complicated in cases involving the import and export of art and artefacts that do not belong to a state's own cultural heritage, but rather to that of another state. It is not a matter of course for a state to show solidarity with another state, rather than allowing the cultural property to enter the country to raise the prestige of its museums. This is also true of situations in which a country makes the application of its own legal instruments, including instruments of criminal law, contingent upon whether the foreign state has officially approved the export. The grounds for such thinking can be found in international law, and are not limited to the Hague Convention of 1954, the UNESCO Convention of 1970, and the two Resolutions of the UN Security Council with regard to Iraq and Syria. The decisive question is whether and when the states in question accepted the relevant instrument of international law as binding (insofar as they do not in any case have bilateral arrangements, which is often the case). In general, the cultural objects that a state recognizes as subject to protection, and the point from which this occurs, depend on this question. Moreover, the restitution of cultural property and the enforcement of the rules by national law are arranged in a highly complex and heterogeneous matter, resulting in a true flood of literature on the subject. All of this has an impact on the accompanying rules with regard to criminal penalties and other sanctions, the substance and content of which are based on these legal structures.

The legal difficulties become even more complex in cases involving the possession and trade of art and cultural objects that have been stolen, misappropriated, or illegally exported. Such cases relate to civil law, specifically if the (former) owner seeks to recover the property from the current possessor. The examination of the case under civil law is significant regardless of whether the state of origin can obtain restitution of its cultural property under administrative law, since this may require the state to pay compensation to a possessor who exercised due diligence. Depending on the legal situation, however, the latter is not the case, if a claim exists for absolute surrender. Accordingly, the decisive aspect for these claims is the legal status of the current possessor. In particular, the question is raised as to whether the possessor has become the owner, or whether the unlawful situation has been remedied in another way. The answer to this question is decisive for the purposes of civil law, but it affects criminal law as well: after all, misappropriation is no longer a possibility if the former owner has since lost this legal status. In the same way, prosecuting for receiving stolen property is excluded if the unlawful possession/assets position no longer exists, as would be the case if the current possessor has acquired ownership.

The associated problems are the subject of intense discussion both in the laws of individual states and in international civil procedure and cultural property law. The discussions concern the questions whether it is even possible to acquire ownership of the objects in question, whether good-faith acquisition of property is possible and which requirements apply, whether this may even apply for property that is stolen or otherwise lost (or whether a cancellation right exists), whether less stringent conditions apply for purchases made at auctions, whether different rules apply for private and commercial dealings, whether the absence of approval (particularly of an import or export licence, in the absence of which the transfer might be illicit) constitutes a legal prohibition preventing the acquisition of ownership, whether ownership can be acquired by adverse possession (and if so, after what time and under which conditions), whether a surrender claim can expire (and if so, after how many years and under which conditions), whether an acquisition of ownership is recognized in a state of transit (and if so, whether the case is to be evaluated exclusively in accordance with the foreign law), which law applies (*lex situs* or *lex originis*), and others. All of these questions are answered and handled very differently by the laws of various states, which may result in considerable procedural difficulties.[76]

If the legal situation is already complicated in the laws of individual states, it becomes entirely unmanageable in cases of an international nature. The flood of scientific publications is overwhelming and the presence of loopholes is not to be denied (although it takes considerable expertise to find these loopholes and use them in a plausible manner).[77] Because prosecutors and judges have other cases to try, the high complexity of these matters may mean that the proceedings will be aborted if it is somehow possible to believe the contention of the accused that they acted without intent and in the belief that the objects in question were their own property. Mere negligence in this area typically does not constitute conduct liability for prosecution (which may not be the case for the trade in precious metals and gems).[78]

Somewhat idealistically, UNESCO attacks the legal fragmentation problem using a Database of national cultural heritage laws, which it launched in 2005. Available in six languages, the database now contains more than 2,500 legal texts from more than 180 countries having national cultural heritage laws dealing with the protection of cultural objects. Certainly, a state might find in this database a model for how its own law could be better formulated. It would be naive to assume that legal practitioners in any country could acquire an accurate understanding of foreign law just by reading their legal texts. While mere approximation may be acceptable in cases of civil law (e.g. upon the application of matrimonial or family law for foreign spouses), this is not sufficient for criminal law, which is bound by constitutional principles.

15.5 Final Observations

People have long been fascinated by crimes involving art and cultural objects, which usually find broad attention in the media (and therefore are often the subject of novels and feature films). One consequence of the worldwide interest in art and cultural

[76] Illustrative is the Gotha Case, adjudicated before the English High Court of Justice, in which the City of Gotha and the Federal Republic of Germany successfully sued the auction house Sotheby's for the return of looted art, and the case was decided in accordance with German law (Judgment of 9 September 1998, in Michael H. Carl, *'Kunstdiebstahl vor Gericht'*, Berlin/New York, De Gruyter, 2001, p. 77; also see articles assessing the case by Herbert Güttler, in ibid, pp. 7–32; see ibid, pp. 33–52 and Kurt Siehr, in ibid, pp. 53–75.

[77] Cf., e.g. Michael Anton, *Handbuch Kulturgüterschutz und Kunstrestitutionsrecht*, Berlin/New York, De Gruyter, with three volumes in 2010 and around 4,000 pages (and three additional volumes have been announced).

[78] In Germany, e.g. in accordance with §148b of the Industrial Code (Gewerbeordnung).

objects is that we are dealing with an international crime *par excellence*: on one hand in the sense of international criminal law in cases of armed conflict, and on the other hand in the transnational sense, when dealing with cross-border crime that has long been globalized. Contractual and other instruments of international law can certainly be helpful in protecting cultural property. The impact of such instruments in raising awareness is illusory, as has been shown most recently by the events in Iraq, Mali, and Syria. Also, the wide diversity of legal norms does not contribute to solving global crime. The situation can be lamented, but can hardly be undone.

The method of choice for the protection of cultural property remains international cooperation, although this can still be intensified. The organisations named above (Interpol, UNESCO, UNODC, WCO) play a key coordinating and driving role in this regard. Moreover, positive mention should be made of the ethical commitments that have been undertaken by various organisations and associations of museums, as well as art and antiquities dealers. These include, for example, the Code of Ethics for Museums (ICOM), the Ethical Code of Conduct (Confédération Internationale des Négociants en Oeuvres d'Art, CINOA), and the International code of ethics for traders in cultural property (UNESCO). Of course, the direct impact of voluntary commitments is limited, even if we can hope for broad compliance. In view of the fact that such codes formulate principles of compliance and due diligence within the profession, they may acquire significance as 'soft law', so that failure to comply with these rules would indicate that the offender is acting in bad faith, or even justify the assumption of malicious intent.[79] This also includes searches of available databases of lost and stolen art and cultural objects. Aside from these efforts, UNESCO has been advocating an OBJECT-ID Standard for Cultural Objects since 1997, which may prove to be an important element for the protection of valuable cultural objects.

Expectations for these measures should not be set too high: art-related crime will continue in the future as, all too much, human beings are also cultural beings.

[79] Cf. in this context, von Selle, 'Illegaler Kunsthandel', cited in note 73 above, p. 11; for details, M. Anton, 'Neuer Schutz archäologischer Kulturgüter', in Wittinger *et al.*, *Festschrift Fiedler*, cited in note 65 above, pp. 319–51.

16

Transnational Organised Crime and Cybercrime

*Dominik Brodowski**

16.1 On the Phenomenology of Cybercrime

16.1.1 Introduction

Information and communication technology (ICT) is, above all, a powerful tool, but not an end in itself. Its widespread—in ever more areas of the world: ubiquitous—use has shaped the world of today and continues to transform not only the economy, but also society, the political sphere, and the interaction between people.

For these reasons, ICT has become a tool that is also regularly being used by criminals (including those involved in organised crime (OC)) and thus provides valuable information for the investigation and prosecution of crimes—for instance if drug dealers keep a record of business dealings on a computer, or if the location of a kidnapper may be determined by tracking a cell phone. Beyond such neutral use of ICT by criminals, most conventional crimes can be committed today using ICT—ranging from the dissemination of child pornography on the internet, over defrauding someone in a business transaction, to even murdering someone by interfering with the ICT embedded in a car. Last but not least, the ubiquity and power of ICT as well as the dependence on ICT means that it has become a target for criminals itself.

16.1.2 Definition and scope

While the origin of the term *cybercrime* can easily be linked to the concept of *cyberspace* first coined in science fiction,[1] no clear legal definition of the term exists as of today.[2] While some authors specifically focus on the criminal misuse of a *networked* computer system or the data located within those networks,[3] others focus on the means of perpetration being computers.[4] The most current usage of the term may

* The research for this publication was partly supported by the German Federal Ministry of Education and Research in the Project 'Open Competence Center for Cyber Security (OpenC3S)'. The author expresses his gratitude to Laura Zander and Magdalena Muttenthaler for their valuable input in furtherance of this chapter.

[1] Cf. Stein Schjolberg, *The History of Cybercrime, 1976–2014*, Norderstedt, Books on Demand, 2014, p. 12 fn. 1; David S. Wall, *Cybercrime: the Transformation of Crime in the Information Age*, Cambridge, Polity Press, 2007, p. 10.

[2] Cf. Nir Kshetri, *The Global Cybercrime Industry*, Berlin, Springer, 2010, p. 3.

[3] Wall, *Cybercrime*, cited in note 1 above, p. 10; Ulrich Sieber, 'Mastering complexity in the global cyberspace', in Miereille Delmas-Marty, Mark Pieth, and Ulrich Sieber (eds), *Les chemins de l'harmonisation pénale*, Paris, Société de Législation Comparée, 2008, pp. 127, 131.

[4] Cf. Kshetri, *Global Cybercrime Industry*, cited in note 2 above, p. 3.

be seen as a '*collection* of acts or conduct':[5] under such a concept, cybercrime is understood as all criminal activity in which ICT is used as a tool to commit a crime and/or in which ICT is a target of a crime.[6]

Such a broad understanding of cybercrime is also in line with international legal instruments in this field,[7] and especially with the landmark Council of Europe Convention on Cybercrime (see section 16.3.2 of this chapter), which does not define cybercrime (not even in its Explanatory Report) but contains substantive criminal provisions regarding a wide range of conduct relating to ICT as well as provisions concerning the investigation and international cooperation and the specific requirements of *electronic evidence*.

To summarize, cybercrime is best understood not as a *legal concept* but as a *regulatory challenge*: the transformation of our lives and our societies by ICT poses new challenges to the sphere of criminal justice. Some criminal laws of previous days may need to be adapted to also cover activity for which ICT is used as a *means*; new crimes may be needed to cover harmful activity against ICT; and most importantly the investigation and prosecution of crimes need to adapt to the challenges caused by the widespread use of ICT.

This broad and regulatory understanding of cybercrime provides for the scope of the following analysis: concerning substantive criminal law, I will focus on crimes specifically *targeting* ICT or crimes in which ICT poses a specific challenge (see section 16.3). Concerning the evolution of cybercrime (see 16.2), jurisdiction (see 16.4), and the investigation and prosecution of cybercrime (see 16.5), however, one cannot limit the discussion to specific types of crime, since—as outlined in the introduction (see 16.1.1)—electronic evidence may nowadays be found in relation to *any* crime. In order to focus on *Transnational Organised Crime (TOC)*, questions on cyberterrorism, cyberspionage, and cyberwar will need to be excluded.

16.1.3 Core challenges of cybercrime

For a better understanding of the regulatory frameworks against cybercrime of today and tomorrow, it is important to take into account the five core challenges of cybercrime.[8]

A first challenge, which is often at the core of discussions on cybercrime, is the inherent *transnationality* of the internet:[9] from a technical and historical perspective,

[5] UNODC (United Nations Office on Drugs and Crime), *Comprehensive Study on Cybercrime*, New York, United Nations, 2013, p. 11.

[6] Mohamed Chawki, Ashraf Darwish, Mohammad Ayoub Khan, and Sapna Tyagi, *Cybercrime, Digital Forensics and Jurisdiction*, Cham, Springer, 2015, p. 3; Joachim Vogel, 'Towards a global Convention against cybercrime', (2008) *Revue électronique de l'AIDP* C-07:1, p. 1f.

[7] UNODC, *Comprehensive Study*, cited in note 5 above, p. 12.

[8] See also, with partly different emphases, Dominik Brodowski and Felix Freiling, *Cyberkriminalität, Computerstrafrecht und die digitale Schattenwirtschaft*, Berlin, Forschungsforum Öffentliche Sicherheit, 2011, p. 53; Marco Gercke, 'Die Bekämpfung der Internetkriminalität als Herausforderung für die Strafverfolgungsbehörden', (2008) 11 *Multimedia und Recht* (5), 291ff.; Sieber, 'Mastering complexity', cited in note 3 above, pp. 132ff.; Wall, *Cybercrime*, cited in note 1 above, pp. 34ff.

[9] Sieber, 'Mastering complexity', cited in note 3 above, p. 134.

the computer networks that create the internet tend to allow for a free and rapid flow of data between *all* end points, independent of their geographic location. Thus, the geographic borders between nation-states seem to lose their importance in the context of criminal justice: a criminal in one state can easily access and attack computers located in another state, he or she can transfer incriminating data to a third state providing a safe haven. Nonetheless, there *is* a geographic location of each end point, and technical means can provide—at either a micro level (for instance by GPS sensors embedded into smartphones), a local level (for instance a 'firewall' in a company, or geolocation techniques based on the IP address), or a regional level (e.g. the so-called 'Great Firewall of China')[10]—for some (but circumventable) geographic differentiation. Therefore, cyber*space* can hardly be conceived as a fifth common space.[11]

A second challenge is the assumed *anonymity* of the internet:[12] the basic identification of each end point (an IP address) is, for most common customers, dynamically assigned and may easily be used by several if not thousands of users at the same time; not all Internet Service Providers (ISP) require a valid identification of their customers. From a purely technical perspective, therefore, the partners in an internet-based communication at first only know their (inconstant) IP address, but not their real identity. With the help of the ISPs that allocate the IP addresses it is (in many cases) possible to narrow down the possible participants in a communication. Users often identify themselves—sometimes also through reliable external means—and may thereby be identified by their communication partners. Finally, by using *data mining* techniques and by matching data from multiple sources, large internet sites may be able to profile persons and their behaviour—and thereby pinpoint an individual, even though they might not know the real name. Therefore, the anonymity of the internet is in many cases only *assumed*, but not asserted.

Computers and ICT networks of today provide for an unbelievably quick speed of transactions; if data storage is overwritten just once, the previous data is lost—this *volatility* is seen as a third challenge, since incriminatory evidence may easily be lost.[13] On the other hand, digital forensics excel in preserving and analysing data currently stored on computer systems. The vast amount of data stored permanently in computer systems—who deletes his or her e-mails any longer?—constitutes a 'data trail' and provides an incredible source for investigating people's lives and behaviour, and thereby also for investigating any criminal behaviour.

A major, fourth, challenge is caused by the widespread use of *cryptography*, which is enabled by the vast processing speed of current ICT systems. Properly

[10] Jyh-An Lee and Ching-Yi Liu, 'Forbidden City enclosed by the Great Firewall: the law and power of internet filtering in China', (2012) 13 *Minnesota Journal of Law, Science & Technology*, 125.

[11] Contrary to Schjolberg, *History of Cybercrime*, cited in note 1 above, p. 12, who considers cyberspace to be the fifth common space besides land, sea, air, and outer space.

[12] Cf. Phillip W. Brunst, *Anonymität im Internet—rechtliche und tatsächliche Rahmenbedingungen: zum Spannungsfeld zwischen einem Recht auf Anonymität bei der elektronischen Kommunikation und den Möglichkeiten zur Identifizierung und Strafverfolgung*, Berlin, Duncker & Humblot, 2009; Brodowski and Freiling, *Cyberkriminalität, etc.*, cited in note 8 above, pp. 54ff.

[13] Sieber, 'Mastering complexity', cited in note 3 above, p. 133.

implemented and used cryptography is hard or even impossible to decrypt by the authorities. Often meta-data is *not* protected and provides first useful clues; securely transmitted data is decrypted and may be stored at the end points and be accessed there (covertly or openly) by authorities. Finally, weaknesses in the implementation of cryptography are widespread, leading to further vectors by which seemingly encrypted communication may be intercepted by the authorities—but also by criminals.

Last but not least, the automation enabled by ICT provides strong *multiplier effects*.[14] Defrauding many thousand people of a fraction of a Euro may lead to a high gain for the criminal and high damages in total, but to minimal individual damages. As a result, there may be low incentives for the individual to initiate a criminal prosecution. Furthermore, the authorities may need to investigate and prove thousands of identical cases, which is a challenge on its own.

16.2 The Evolution of Transnational Organised Cybercrime

While the empirics of cybercrime still are not well known—owing to numerous factors such as the low incentives of individuals to report their victimization[15]—and the types of damage caused by cybercrime are hard to measure,[16] some general trends or 'generations' of cybercrime can be discerned (see section 16.2.1 of this chapter). The newest—or fourth—generation may be described as an interlinking between TOC and cybercrime (see 16.2.2).

16.2.1 From the lonely hacker to a market of cybercrime services

In the shift from industrial to information societies, at least some decision making has been and is being transferred from humans to ICT systems (such as automated teller machines (ATM) 'deciding' about handing out money instead of a cashier); *information* has surpassed *tangible goods of value* in economic importance.[17] A first generation of cybercrime may then be seen in the exploitation of ICT systems and the data located therein at a *local* level, committed largely for economic purposes.[18] As conventional substantive criminal laws were often founded on human decision making and tangible goods, however, this first generation of cybercrime already led to a necessity to extend the substantive criminal law provisions to cover conduct such as *computer fraud* or *computer manipulation*, as well as to a necessity to protect the *confidentiality, integrity*, and *availability* of computer systems ('CIA offences').[19]

[14] Ibid, p. 132; Brodowski and Freiling, *Cyberkriminalität, etc.*, cited in note 8 above, pp. 57f.

[15] Cf. Wall, *Cybercrime*, cited in note 1 above, p. 20; Brodowski and Freiling, *Cyberkriminalität, etc.*, cited in note 8 above, pp. 72ff.

[16] Cf. Kshetri, *Global Cybercrime Industry*, cited in note 2 above, p. 7.

[17] Dominik Brodowski, 'Preparatory colloquium for the XIXth International Congress of Penal Law (Moscow, 24–27 April 2013)', (2013) 1 *Russian Law Review*, 94, p. 94f.

[18] Cf. Sieber, 'Mastering complexity', cited in note 3 above, p. 129; Wall, *Cybercrime*, cited in note 1 above, p. 44.

[19] Cf. Sieber, 'Mastering complexity', cited in note 3 above, p. 129.

With knowledge on and access to ICT systems only to be found in a comparatively small group of people, the stereotype of a 'lonely hacker' as the typical cybercriminal was born.[20]

A second generation of cybercrime was enabled by the building of networks of ICT systems, especially the internet. This technical trend expedited many of the challenges already described (see section 16.1.3) and is linked, from the perspective of substantive criminal law, to the protection of computer networks (such as against *Denial of Service attacks)* and the fight against incriminated information (such as child pornography) and information sharing (such as the unlawful distribution of copyright-protected material).[21]

With the ubiquity of ICT systems and increased protection against the first two generations of cybercrime, the incentive structures shifted towards a third and economically driven generation of cybercrime—a model that Wall labelled as a 'flat e-commerce business model',[22] that has been described by several authors in a similar manner: several highly specialized perpetrators only focus on their specific technical skill-set (such as the infiltration of an ICT system, the exploitation of such systems, or the misuse of credit card data). In loose and case-by-case collaboration with co-perpetrators (such as money mules), a specific criminal activity is committed for the economic gain of each participant in the crime.[23] Over time, this differentiation of skills has led to some (particularly highly skilled) cybercriminals becoming mere 'service providers' for other perpetrators: for example, they sell 'malware' toolkits, attack vectors, or sell or lend to other perpetrators access to large-scale botnets (networks of infected and exploitable computers of victims).[24]

16.2.2 Organised crime meets cybercrime

While this third generation of cybercrime is, by itself, highly *organised* by means of a market business-model, it lacks certain features typically found in OC: its 'flat model' especially lacks any (enforced) hierarchy, its loose affiliation lacks the

[20] Cf. Wall, *Cybercrime*, cited in note 1 above, pp. 15f.

[21] Cf. Sieber, 'Mastering complexity', cited in note 3 above, pp. 129f.; Wall, *Cybercrime*, cited in note 1 above, p. 45; Murugesan Srinivasan, Solomon Raja Pandian, and Arockiasamy Enoch, 'International crimes: cyber crime, crimes against cultural heritage, environmental crimes, and money laundering', in Sesha Kethineni (ed.), *Comparative and International Policing, Justice, and Transnational Crime*, Durham, North Carolina, Carolina Academic Press, 2010, p. 390ff.

[22] David S. Wall, 'The organization of cybercrime and organized cybercrime', in Marcello Bellini, Phillip Brunst, and Jochen Jähnke (eds), *Current Issues in IT Security*, Berlin, Duncker & Humblot, 2010, p. 51, p. 54.

[23] See, e.g. Susan W. Brenner, 'Organized cybercrime? How cyberspace may affect the structure of criminal relationships', (2002) 4 *North Carolina Journal of Law & Technology*, 1ff.; Brian Krebs, *Spam Nation*, Naperville, Illinois, Sourcebooks, 2014, p. 113ff.; Dmitry Samosseiko, 'The *partnerka* what is it, and why should you care?', Technical Paper, SophosLabs Canada, 2009, available at: https://www.sophos.com/security/technical-papers/samosseiko-vb2009-paper.pdf, accessed 1 March 2016; Jan Spoenle, 'Underground economy', in Bellini *et al.*, *Current Issues in IT Security*, cited in note 22 above, p. 67.

[24] See, e.g. Erika Kraemer-Mbula, Puay Tang, and Howard Rush, 'The cybercrime ecosystem: online innovation in the shadows?', (2013) 80 *Technological Forecasting & Social Change* (3), 541, p. 550.

internal stability and continuity of OC groups as well as an internal bond between the co-perpetrators.[25]

In recent years, however, closer links between (classic) OC and cybercrime have been reported:[26] first, some high-profile actors in the field of cybercrime have built a sustainable organisation around their activities, and reportedly engage not only in 'classic' cybercrime but also in (not only virtual, but also physical) turf wars with competing cybercriminals.[27] Second, OC groups have been noted as buying services from cybercriminals, such as to interfere with police operations.[28] Third, the sophisticated features of modern cybercrime—such as using money mules to transfer money,[29] its new forms of interacting with customers (e.g. in the 'darknet'),[30] and the reportedly high yield of cybercrime—have attracted the interest of classic OC groups.[31] Combined with the ease of crossing the borders of nation-states on the internet, any involvement of OC groups in cybercrime easily gains an international dimension *and* requires an international response.

Therefore, TOC itself is transformed by cyberspace and is transforming itself in the field of cybercrime: it nowadays features an increased (case-by-case) cooperation of an OC group with highly skilled but group-external criminals, modifications in its business models, and an increased awareness of the risk of electronic evidence to its criminal activities.

16.3 International Law and Substantive Criminal Law against Transnational Organised Cybercrime

As of today, no legally binding, hard-law instrument exists on a global level that specifically addresses the challenges of cybercrime.[32] While the landmark Council of Europe Convention on Cybercrime of 2001 (CCC, the so-called 'Budapest Convention', see section 16.3.2) is still highly influential far beyond Europe and open to signature by any state under a special accession regime (Article 37 CCC), it has not gained worldwide acceptance but instead receives continuing resistance. Accordingly, it becomes ever more important to look at the soft law on a global level and at initiatives in furtherance of a truly global convention against cybercrime (see section 16.3.1), and at other regional initiatives besides the Budapest Convention (see section 16.3.3).

[25] Cf. Brenner, 'Organized cybercrime?', cited in note 23 above, p. 1; Brodowski and Freiling, *Cyberkriminalität, etc.*, cited in note 8 above, p. 64; Jonathan Lusthaus, 'How organised is organised cybercrime?', (2013) 14 *Global Crime* (1), 52, p. 53ff.

[26] Lusthaus, 'How organised is organised cybercrime?', cited in note 25 above, p. 57ff.; see also Europol, *The Internet Organised Crime Threat Assessment (iOCTA)*, The Hague, Europol Police Office, 2014—which must, however, be seen as a position paper of an involved actor instead of a scientific publication.

[27] Krebs, *Spam Nation*, cited in note 23 above.

[28] Cf. Kshetri, *Global Cybercrime Industry*, cited in note 2 above, p. 14.

[29] Cf. ibid, p. 14.

[30] Cf. Kyle Soska and Nicolas Christin, 'Measuring the longitudinal evolution of the online anonymous marketplace ecosystem', in *Proceedings of the 24th USENIX Security Symposium*, 2015, p. 33.

[31] Roderic Broadhurst, Peter Grabosky, Mamoun Alazab, and Steve Chon, 'Organizations and cyber crime: an analysis of the nature of groups engaged in cyber crime', (2014) 8 *International Journal of Cyber Criminology* (1), 1.

[32] But see, concerning the specific aspect of child pornography, the Optional Protocol to the [United Nations] Convention on the Rights of the Child on the Sale of Children, Child Prostitution, and Child Pornography, New York, 25 May 2000, 2171 UNTS 227.

16.3.1 Selected initiatives on a global level on substantive cybercrime law

16.3.1.1 United Nations

Since 1990, a number of resolutions by the United Nations (UN) and its institutions call for a concerted approach in addressing cybersecurity and cybercrime issues, albeit mostly in very general terms.[33] Of particular importance is UN General Assembly (GA) Resolution A/RES/55/63 of 22 January 2001 which sets out that the 'confidentiality, integrity and availability of data and computer systems' should be protected 'from unauthorized impairment' by means of criminal laws (Resolution 1(e)), and that any 'safe havens for those who criminally misuse information technologies' should be eliminated (Resolution 1(a)). UN GA Resolution A/RES/56/261 of 15 April 2002 and its annexed action plan put particular emphasis on computer-related fraud and the commitment of offences by means of ICT (annex, part XI, Resolution 35(a)). Furthermore, on the basis of UN GA Resolution A/RES/65/230 UNODC (Resolution 9), an open-ended, intergovernmental, expert group with the UN Office on Drugs and Crime (UNODC) conducted a comprehensive study on the problem of cybercrime and extensively reported on its comparative analysis on cybercrime laws in 2013. Therein, it mentions an 'insufficient harmonization of "core" cybercrime offences' in national legislation and therefore calls for action on (soft) convergence or (hard) harmonization.[34] Attempts—especially by Russia—to use these findings as a basis for a global convention against cybercrime have not materialized so far.[35]

16.3.1.2 International Telecommunication Union

Despite strong efforts by some of its member states, the International Telecommunication Union (ITU) has not yet gained a central role in the governance of the internet. For instance, calls for a universal cybersecurity treaty under the auspices of the ITU were struck down from a 2014 resolution draft,[36] and another ITU resolution of 2014 specifically excludes cybercrime matters from its scope of applicability.[37]

[33] See the overview in ITU (International Telecommunication Union) and Marco Gercke, *Understanding Cybercrime: Phenomena, Challenges and Legal Responses*, ITU, 2012, p. 115ff., Schjolberg, *History of Cybercrime*, cited in note 1 above, pp. 56ff. and especially UN GA Res. A/RES/45/121 of 14 December 1990 (s. C Res. 9), UN GA Res. A/RES/68/243 of 27 December 2013 as well as, most recently, the Doha Declaration on integrating crime prevention and criminal justice into the wider United Nations agenda to address social and economic challenges and to promote the rule of law at the national and international levels and public participation, adopted at the Thirteenth United Nations Congress of Crime Prevention and Criminal Justice, A/CONF.222/L.6, Res. 9(b).

[34] UNODC, *Comprehensive Study*, cited in note 5 above, pp. xiiff., but see also pp. 77f., noting a 'baseline consensus on culpable cybercrime conduct'.

[35] See, e.g. UN/A/69/723 (letter dated 9 January 2015 from the Permanent Representatives of China, Kazakhstan, Kyrgyzstan, the Russian Federation, Tajikistan, and Uzbekistan to the United Nations addressed to the Secretary-General).

[36] Cf. ITU Resolution 174 (rev. Busan, 2014) (ITU's role with regard to international public policy issues relating to the risk of illicit use of information and communication technologies).

[37] ITU Resolution 130 (rev. Busan, 2014) (Strengthening the role of ITU in building confidence and security in the use of information and communication technologies).

16.3.1.3 *Academia*

A landmark 'Stanford Draft International Convention to Enhance Protection from Cyber Crime and Terrorism of 2000' published by the American Hoover Institution included far-sighted demands not only for the criminalization of interference with or intrusion of 'cyber systems',[38] intercepting or interfering with computer data, and the trafficking in cybercrime tools (Article 3(a) to (e)), but also for the specific protection of critical infrastructure (Article 3(g)). Another novel approach of this Stanford Draft Convention is the creation of an International Agency for Information Infrastructure Protection:[39] to address the quickly changing phenomenology of cybercrime, its Council would be able to adopt amendments of conduct that states have to criminalize in their national laws.[40]

In 2014, the International Association of Penal Law (AIDP) focused on the topic of 'Information Society and Penal Law' in its XIXth International Congress. In the final resolutions, it did not call for a global treaty on (substantive) cybercrime law, but instead pointed out specific issues to be addressed also by means of criminal law, such as identity theft and the 'grossly negligent management of critical ICT infrastructure and of large amounts of sensitive data',[41] as such behaviour facilitates the commission of cybercrimes.

Academic proposals that call for an international tribunal on the most serious forms of cybercrime and include definitions of such conduct have, so far, not gained notable attraction.[42]

16.3.2 The Council of Europe Convention on Cybercrime

16.3.2.1 *Historical overview, applicability, and scope*

The Convention on Cybercrime (Budapest, 23 November 2001, ETS 185; hereafter: CCC) was drafted in the framework of the Council of Europe and was able to build upon previous soft-law work by the same international organisation.[43] Having entered into force on 1 July 2004, the CCC still is the most influential and most widely applicable international instrument concerning cybercrime. As of March 2016, forty-eight states have ratified or acceded to the CCC,[44] including eight states that are not members of the Council of Europe, most notably the

[38] Abraham D. Sofaer and Seymour E. Goodman (eds), *The Transnational Dimension of Cyber Crime and Terrorism*, Stanford, California, Hoover Institution Press, 2001.

[39] In contrast to the global area, such an approach has been well known in EU criminal law since 1997.

[40] Cf. Vogel, 'Towards a global Convention', cited in note 6 above, C-07:9.

[41] AIDP (International Association of Penal Law), 'Resolutions of the XIXth International Congress of Penal Law. Information Society and Penal Law', (2014) 85 *Revue International de Droit Pénal* (3–4), 607 (French), 629 (English), 649 (Spanish), resolutions 8 and 11.

[42] See, most recently, Schjolberg, *History of Cybercrime*, cited in note 1 above, Annex 1.

[43] In particular, Recommendation No. R (89) 9 on computer-related crime of 13 September 1989 and Recommendation No. R (95) 13 of 11 September 1995; see the overview in Schjolberg, *History of Cybercrime*, cited in note 1 above, pp. 38ff.

[44] All members of the Council of Europe *except* Russia and San Marino have signed the CCC.

United States of America.[45] Six further states have signed but not yet ratified the Convention. Beyond this direct and binding force of the CCC, it has also shown a strong indirect influence on other multinational instruments and on national legislation,[46] which is in line with the G-8 and the European Union (EU) endorsing the CCC.[47]

Russia, among other states, objected to the CCC and is unlikely to accept its legal standards in the foreseeable future. The most prominent reason for such objections relates to an aspect of jurisdiction and investigation (Article 32(b) CCC; see section 16.5.2 of this chapter); others point to the CCC being partly outdated owing to subsequent developments in ICT and cybercrime.[48] Beyond these substantive matters, some states lament their non-participation in the drafting process and the cumbersome accession process (Article 37 CCC), especially in comparison to UN conventions.[49] Notwithstanding these concerns, the CCC entered into force in five states in 2015, underlining that it still serves as an important baseline in the international fight against cybercrime.

The scope of the CCC is broad and covers 'measures to be taken at the national level' (Chapter II) in matters of substantive criminal law, procedural criminal law (see section 16.4 of this chapter), and jurisdiction (see 16.5), and provisions enhancing international cooperation (Chapter III). Instead of defining cybercrime (see 16.1.2), it focuses on specific types of behaviour relating to computer systems and computer data. These terms, legally defined in Article 1 CCC, need to be interpreted broadly and include—also according to a common understanding of all states parties assembled in the Cybercrime Convention Committee (T-CY)—'developing forms of technology that go beyond traditional mainframe or desktop computer systems, such as modern mobile phones, smart phones, PDAs, tablets or similar', since such devices do perform the automatic processing of data pursuant to a program.[50] In other Guidance Notes, the T-CY has shown that the approach taken by the CCC to 'use ... technology-neutral language so that the substantive criminal law offences may be applied to both current and future technologies involved'[51] provides a sufficient basis to address modern forms of cybercrime, such as botnets,[52] identity theft,[53] and new forms of malware.[54]

[45] In order of ratification or accession: United States of America, Japan, Australia, Dominican Republic, Mauritius, Panama, Sri Lanka, and Canada.

[46] Cf. UNODC, *Comprehensive Study*, cited in note 5 above, pp. 74ff.

[47] Communiqué, Meeting of G-8 Justice and Home Affairs Ministers (Washington, 11 May 2004), p. 10, available at: http://www.justice.gov/sites/default/files/ag/legacy/2004/05/13/Communique_2004_G8_JHA_Ministerial_051204.pdf, accessed 1 March 2016. EU: see, e.g. COM (2014) 365 final of 20 June 2014, p. 8.

[48] Cf., e.g. Schjolberg, *History of Cybercrime*, cited in note 1 above, pp. 76ff.; ITU and Gercke, *Understanding Cybercrime*, cited in note 33 above, p. 126.

[49] Cf. Marco Gercke, '10 years Convention on Cybercrime', (2011) 12 *Computer Law Review International* (5), 142.

[50] Cybercrime Convention Committee, Report T-CY (2012) 21, p. 4.

[51] Convention on Cybercrime, Budapest, 23 November 2001, ETS 185, Explanatory Report, §36.

[52] Cybercrime Convention Committee, Report T-CY (2013) 6E.

[53] Cybercrime Convention Committee, Report T-CY (2013) 8E.

[54] Cybercrime Convention Committee, Report T-CY (2013) 12E.

16.3.2.2 *Offences against ICT systems*

The first cornerstone of substantive cybercrime laws that states parties are to implement deals with 'offences against the confidentiality, integrity and availability of computer data and systems' (Article 2ff. CCC). All these offences—including the aiding or abetting of them—are to be made punishable 'by effective, proportionate and dissuasive sanctions, which include deprivation of liberty' (Article 13 para. 1 CCC) for natural persons as well as 'by effective, proportionate and dissuasive criminal or non-criminal sanctions or measures, including monetary sanctions' for legal persons (Article 12, Article 13 para. 2 CCC).

16.3.2.2.1 Illegal access (Article 2 CCC)

The CCC seeks to protect the integrity of computer systems by calling for the criminalization of the intentional *accessing of computer systems* without right (Article 2 CCC).[55] Accessing a system means to successfully establish an (offline or online) interaction with a system so that it is reacting to (further) commands or requests;[56] this element is not fulfilled if someone merely sends data (such as an e-mail) *to* a computer system.[57] A right to access a system may be given explicitly by the owner or others holding rights in the computer system,[58] but it also exists for 'legitimate and common activities inherent in the design of networks, or legitimate and common operating or commercial practices' and therefore may also be implied, e.g. when accessing a website using commonly applied communication protocols and programs.[59]

The rationale behind criminalizing the access to a *computer system* without right—and not just the access to data stored therein—is that gaining access to a computer system is often the decisive obstacle in the furtherance of a cybercriminal activity.[60] The low threshold required to commit such an offence explains why several states, in accordance with Article 2 sentence 2 CCC, include additional requirements in their legislation, e.g. an intent to (unlawfully) obtain computer data, or to circumvent security measures.[61] This low threshold also explains why illegally *remaining* in a computer system, after having accessed it *with* right or unintentionally, is reasonably not included in the CCC as behaviour to be criminalized.[62]

16.3.2.2.2 Data interference (Article 4 CCC)

The integrity—but not the confidentiality—of computer data is the *ratio* behind the requirement to criminalize the intentional 'damaging, deletion, deterioration, alteration or suppression of computer data without right' (Article 4 para. 1 CCC),[63] including the

[55] UNODC, *Comprehensive Study*, cited in note 5 above, p. 82.

[56] State parties are not required to criminalize the attempt at such conduct: cf. Art. 11 para. 2 CCC. The coverage of offline and online interaction follows *e contrario* from Art. 2 sentence 2 alternative 3 CCC.

[57] Cf. CCC, cited in note 51 above, Explanatory Report, §46.

[58] Cf. ibid, Explanatory Report, §47.

[59] Cf. ibid, Explanatory Report, §§38 and 48.

[60] Cf. UNODC, *Comprehensive Study*, cited in note 5 above, p. 82.

[61] Other states may refer to procedural means to avoid the prosecution of such minor cases.

[62] But see ITU and Gercke, *Understanding Cybercrime*, cited in note 33 above, p. 181.

[63] For an explanation of the various forms of data interference, cf. CCC, cited in note 51 above, Explanatory Report, §61.

attempt to do any of those things (Article 11 para. 2 CCC). The mere *adding* of data is not covered, however, unless it changes the content of the existing data (e.g. when adding a transaction to a database). Not all data are required for the regular operation of a computer system, and not all data are of importance to the owner or operator of a computer system. Accordingly, Article 4 para. 2 CCC offers states parties the opportunity to limit the criminalization of data interference to cases where the conduct resulted in serious harm.

16.3.2.2.3 System interference (Article 5 CCC)

In a similar vein, only the intentionally *serious* interference with the operation of a computer system is covered by Article 5 CCC, which means that receiving a few unsolicited messages ('spam') and the nuisance they cause are not covered. Article 5 CCC is further limited to specific data-related actions such as inputting, deleting, or altering computer data. Therefore, this provision (which is, however, only a minimum standard for criminalization) only partly covers the functionality of computer systems and only partly addresses *computer sabotage*: if such sabotage is achieved through other, 'offline' means such as cutting off network or electrical connections, this does not constitute conduct within the scope of Article 5 CCC. An attempted system interference should suffice for criminal punishment (Article 11 para. 2 CCC). As already mentioned concerning Article 2 CCC, 'common activities inherent in the design of networks, or common operational or commercial practices' such as the 'testing of the security of a computer system, or its protection, authorised by its owner or operator' are with right, and therefore not to be criminalized under Article 5 CCC.[64]

16.3.2.2.4 Illegal interception (Article 3 CCC)

Article 3 CCC addresses the confidentiality of information being transferred *between* computer systems or processed within one computer system: intentionally intercepting non-public data by technical means without right must be penalized, as must an attempt to do so (Article 11 para. 2 CCC). However, the Article neither covers the confidentiality of information stored *in* a computer system,[65] nor the inadvertent transmission of sensitive data to an unintended party, e.g. if users are lured to enter their password and access data on a criminal's website instead of on the intended online banking site.

16.3.2.2.5 Misuse of devices/'hacking tools' (Article 6 CCC)

Possibly the most controversial criminalization requirement of the CCC may be found in Article 6: the handling of *devices* and especially *computer programs* 'designed or adapted primarily for the purpose of committing' the 'CIA offences' (see section 16.2.1 of this chapter) above, as well as of *access codes* such as *passwords*, is to be curtailed by means of criminal law. More specifically their production and distribution is to be

[64] Cf. ibid, Explanatory Report, §68.

[65] Cf. ITU and Gercke, *Understanding Cybercrime*, cited in note 33 above, p. 185.

criminalized, as is the mere possession of such tools 'with intent that it be used for the purpose of committing' one of the CIA offences. Besides dogmatic controversies regarding the early stage at which a perpetrator becomes criminally liable, the main dispute relates to the aspect that IT security specialists require the same or similar ('dual-use') tools as cybercriminals in order to analyse computer systems for weaknesses.[66] Therefore, particular emphasis has to be put on the *mens rea* requirements, which relate both to the object of the crime *and* to the future commission of a specific crime against the confidentiality, integrity, and availability of a computer system or computer data. Concerning the illicit trafficking in password data, however, strict subjective requirements have turned out to be highly problematic.[67]

16.3.2.2.6 *Lacunae*

The most notable omission concerning the confidentiality, integrity, and availability of computer systems and data is that the CCC, as noted above, does not contain a provision regarding the confidentiality of data as such. Therefore, it does not cover *data espionage* as a distinct offence. As a preparatory step, however, it is likely that the perpetrator committed (at least) an illegal access within the meaning of Article 2 CCC, at least in those circumstances where criminal punishment actually seems adequate. Moreover, it is important to remember that the CCC only contains a *minimum standard of criminalization:* states parties are able to criminalize further types of behaviour within the limits that follow from human rights, constitutional law, and other obligations.

16.3.2.3 Computer-related and content-related offences

16.3.2.3.1 Computer-related forgery (Article 7 CCC)

The first offence under the title of computer-related offences does not protect the integrity of computer systems or computer data as such, but only insofar as it is a requirement for the *authenticity* of data with a specific legal relevance. Any intentional or attempted (Article 11 para. 2 CCC) input, alteration, deletion, or suppression of computer data that results in inauthentic data, is to be penalized. To further distinguish the fraudulent character of the offence covered in Article 7 CCC from the ICT-related offence in Article 4 CCC, states may need to include a further element of specific intent in their penal codes.

16.3.2.3.2 Computer-related fraud (Article 8 CCC)

An obvious economic link is present in the provision regarding computer-related fraud (Article 8 CCC), which is therefore of more direct importance for the fight against OC: it relates to a '*direct* economic or possessory loss of another person's property'[68] caused by a manipulation of computer data or an interference with the functioning of a computer system. Besides intended achievement of these ends,

[66] Cf. CCC, cited in note 51 above, Explanatory Report, §73.
[67] Cf. Sieber, 'Mastering complexity', cited in note 3 above, p. 146.
[68] Cf. CCC, cited in note 51 above, Explanatory Report, §88 (emphasis added).

the provision calls for a specific, 'fraudulent or dishonest intent of procuring, without right, an economic benefit for oneself or for another person'. In general terms, therefore, this provision—and the attempt at such conduct (Article 11 para. 2 CCC)—addresses the automation of economic decision-making. The CCC does not address the *unauthorized* use of (valid) data, however, and therefore does not cover all cases of illicit enrichment by means of a computer.[69] Furthermore, the CCC does not extend the misuse of devices (Article 6 CCC) to computer-related offences.[70]

16.3.2.3.3 Child pornography (Article 9 CCC)

The intentional production, transfer, and possession of child pornography without right and by use of ICT is regulated in Article 9 para. 1 CCC. The age limit for the determination of child pornography was set comparatively high at 18 years (but is derogable to 16 years under Article 9 para. 3 CCC), and (realistic) pornography in which—contrary to the appearance—no child was involved is to be covered in criminal statutes by the states parties (Article 9 para. 2(b) and (c) CCC, derogable according to Article 9 para. 4 CCC). Since procurement, one of the alternative transfer methods mentioned in Article 9 para. 1 CCC, requires a transfer or copy of control over the incriminated data, the mere *viewing* of child pornography by ICT—without downloading and storing it locally—is not covered by this provision.[71]

16.3.2.3.4 Infringements of copyright and related rights (Article 10 CCC)

The CCC refers to other international legal frameworks for determining the states parties' obligations to protect copyright and related rights in general. The CCC only requires states to penalize wilful infringements—or 'piracy'—'on a commercial scale and by means of a computer system' (Article 10 paras 1 and 2 CCC).[72] It therefore contains a strong link to the economically highly interesting *disseminating* side. For the *consumer* side, though, the usefulness of a criminal approach—which is not required but allowed by the CCC[73]—remains doubtful in any case.

16.3.2.3.5 *Lacunae*

As mentioned above, almost all crimes can be committed using ICT as a means; therefore, the aspect that the CCC only covers a handful of content-related offences is per se not a surprise. The challenges of cyberspace—and especially its transnationality and (assumed) anonymity—may require an additional international response for other types of cyberspace conduct, especially in the following areas:

[69] Cf. UNODC, *Comprehensive Study*, cited in note 5 above, p. 98.
[70] Sieber, 'Mastering complexity', cited in note 3 above, pp. 145f.
[71] See the example mentioned in CCC, cited in note 51 above, Explanatory Report, §97.
[72] The change to 'wilful'—other provisions in the CCC use the term 'intentional[ly]'—seeks to align the provision to Art. 61 Agreement on Trade-Related Aspects of Intellectual Property Rights (TRIPS), Marrakesh, 15 April 1994, 1869 UNTS 299. For the questionable term 'piracy' see: CCC, cited in note 51 above, Explanatory Report, §114.
[73] Cf. ibid, Explanatory Report, §114.

- the unauthorized use or processing of *personal data*, including but not limited to the phenomenon of identity theft, that is indirectly but not directly addressed by the provisions of the CCC;[74]
- illegal pornography, gambling, and the dissemination of regulated substances such as medicine (an economically highly profitable business that profits from the transnationality and from the availability of virtual currencies);
- further forms of sexual exploitation of children (see Chapter 14 in this book); and
- hate speech, libel, and defamation (see section 16.3.2.4).

16.3.2.4 Additional Protocol (acts of a racist and xenophobic nature)

An Additional Protocol to the CCC, concerning the criminalization of acts of a racist and xenophobic nature committed through computer systems, addresses one of these *lacunae*.[75] It calls for the criminalization of dissemination of racist and xenophobic material through computer systems (Article 3), associated threats (Article 4) and insults (Article 5), as well as the denial, gross minimization, approval, or justification of genocide or crimes against humanity (Article 6). As such behaviour only has a limited link to TOC, it will not be analysed in further detail in this chapter.

16.3.3 Further selected initiatives at a regional level on substantive cybercrime law

16.3.3.1 European Union

In the EU, three legal instruments contain requirements for member states to penalize certain conduct specifically related to cybercrimes.

The oldest instrument still in force, Framework Decision 2001/413/JHA, addresses the misuse of non-cash and electronic means of payment in particular:[76] Article 3 contains a provision highly similar to Article 8 CCC (see section 16.3.2.3.2), albeit limited to 'performing or causing a transfer of money or monetary value' but extended to the unauthorized use of valid identification data. Furthermore, Article 4 of the Framework Decision requires the introduction of criminal provisions to address the 'making, receiving, obtaining, sale or transfer to another person or possession ... [of] computer programmes the purpose of which is the commission of any of the offences described under Article 3' of the Framework Decision.

On the topic of combating the sexual abuse and sexual exploitation of children, and child pornography, Directive 2011/93/EU calls for extensive criminalization of all interaction with child pornography (Article 5),[77] including 'knowingly obtaining access

[74] Cf. Cybercrime Convention Committee, Report T-CY (2013) 8E.

[75] Strasbourg, 28 January 2003, ETS No. 189. The Additional Protocol entered into force on 1 March 2006 and has, so far, been ratified by twenty-four CoE member states and not by any non-member state.

[76] Council Framework Decision 2001/413/JHA of 28 May 2001 on combating fraud and counterfeiting of non-cash means of payment [2001] OJ L149/1.

[77] Directive 2011/93/EU of the European Parliament and of the Council of 13 December 2011 on combating the sexual abuse and sexual exploitation of children and child pornography, and replacing Council Framework Decision 2004/68/JHA [2011] OJ L335/1, as corrected [2012] OJ L18/7.

to [it], by means of information and communication technology' (para. 3), as well as the solicitation of children for sexual purposes, again by means of ICT (Article 6).[78]

The newest instrument particular on cybercrime, Directive 2013/40/EU,[79] as well as its predecessor, Framework Decision 2005/222/JHA,[80] show a strong similarity to the offences against ICT systems included in the CCC (see section 16.3.2.1 of this chapter), but explicitly allow for the exclusion of minor cases.[81] Article 3 of the Directive concerns illegal access to information systems in similar words to Article 2 CCC, but is limited to acts where security measures are infringed. Compared to Article 5 CCC, the provision against illegal system interference (Article 4 Directive) is extended to the 'interruption' of computer systems. Both system and data interference (Articles 4 and 5 Directive) may also occur by rendering computer data inaccessible. The provisions against illegal interception (Article 6 Directive) and concerning tools used for committing offences (Article 7 Directive) are—with the exception of *not* providing opportunities for derogation—identical to the provisions in the CCC.

In any case, the reason for these EU instruments must not be seen in the small differences relating to the description of acts to be prohibited by criminal laws. Instead, first, EU criminal law has a stronger binding effect than standard international law. Second, the instruments contain minimum requirements concerning the sanctions (Article 6 of the Framework Decision; Articles 5 and 6 of Directive 2011/93/EU; Article 9 of Directive 2013/40/EU—with a specific sanctioning level for cybercrimes committed within a criminal organisation in para 4(a)). Third, they lay the groundwork for other, especially procedural, provisions in the same or other EU legal instruments. Last but not least, the political symbol attached to such action must not be underestimated.

16.3.3.2 Commonwealth of Independent States

The Agreement on cooperation among the Member States of the Commonwealth of Independent States (CIS) in combating offences relating to computer information (Minsk, 1 June 2001; hereafter: CIS-CI)[82] contains an ambiguous but far-reaching requirement for states parties to criminalize the 'illegal accessing of computer information' and the 'violation of regulations governing the use' of ICT, insofar as such conduct 'results in the destruction, blocking, modification or copying of information or in the disruption of the functioning of the computer, the computer system or related networks' (Article 3 para. 1(a) and (c) CIS-CI). Thereby, it mixes the phenomena of illegal access, data, and system interference. Any 'creation, use or distribution of

[78] For a further discussion of this topic, see Chapter 14 in this book.

[79] Directive 2013/40/EU of the European Parliament and of the Council of 12 August 2013 on attacks against information systems and replacing Council Framework Decision 2005/222/JHA [2013] OJ L218/8.

[80] Council Framework Decision 2005/222/JHA of 24 February 2005 on attacks against information systems [2005] OJ L69/67.

[81] But see CCC, cited in note 51 above, Explanatory Report, §37, according to which 'the drafters of the Convention understood that Parties may exclude petty or insignificant misconduct from implementation of the offences defined in Articles 2–10' CCC.

[82] Unofficial English translation available at: https://cms.unov.org/LLSULinkBase/ContentTree.aspx?nodeID=5958, accessed 1 March 2016. According to this site, the CIS-CI entered into force in Armenia, Azerbaijan, Belarus, Kazakhstan, Moldova, and Tajikistan up to 2008.

malicious software'—which is not defined any further—is to be criminalized (Article 3 para. 1(b) CIS-CI), as well as the 'illegal use of computer and database software protected by copyright' causing 'significant damage' (Article 3 para. 1(d) CIS-CI).

16.3.3.3 Shanghai Cooperation Organisation

The Agreement among the Governments of the Member States of the Shanghai Cooperation Organisation on Cooperation in the Field of Ensuring International Information Security (Yekaterinburg, 16 June 2009)[83] only calls in broad terms for co-operation in countering 'information crime', which is defined in Annex I as the usage or attack on ICT systems and data for *any* illegal purposes, and further explained in Annex II to also include any unlawful use of ICT systems or data. The Agreement does not require specific substantive criminal law provisions, however.

16.3.3.4 League of Arab States

The Arab Convention on Combating Information Technology Offences (Cairo, 21 December 2010; hereafter: Arab ITO Convention) has gained quick adoption and support in the Arab region.[84] It calls for the criminalization of a multitude of acts (Article 5ff. Arab ITO Convention) in a much more far-reaching way than the CCC and also calls for 'increasing the punishment for traditional crimes when they are committed by means of information technology' (Article 21 Arab ITO Convention). In particular, *any* illicit access to ICT is to be criminalized (Article 6 Arab ITO Convention), as well as the production or dissemination of *any* 'pornographic material or material that constitutes outrage of modesty' (Article 12 Arab ITO Convention), raising questions, for example, regarding the *ultima ratio* limit to criminal justice. Of particular interest with regard to TOC is Article 16 Arab ITO Convention, which requires the criminalization of typical OC conduct committed by means of ICT, namely money laundering, trafficking in drugs and psychotropic substances, trafficking of people, of human organs, and of arms.

16.3.3.5 Economic Community of West African States

The Economic Community of West African States (ECOWAS) Directive C/DIR. 1/08/11 on Fighting Cyber Crime within ECOWAS of 19 August 2011 (hereafter: ECOWAS-Cybercrime), to be implemented by ECOWAS member states by 1 January 2014,[85]

[83] Unofficial English translation available at <https://ccdcoe.org/sco.html> accessed 1 March 2016.

[84] Cf. ESCWA (Economic and Social Commission for Western Asia), *Policy recommendations on cyber-safety and combating cybercrime in the Arab region: Summary*, New York, United Nations, 2015, p. 3, p. 14. The text of the Arab ITO Convention is available at https://cms.unov.org/DocumentRepositoryIndexer/GetDocInOriginalFormat.drsx?DocID=3dbe778b-7b3a-4af0-95ce-a8bbd1ecd6dd, accessed 1 March 2016.

[85] Directive on Fighting Cyber Crime within ECOWAS, unofficially available at: https://ccdcoe.org/sites/default/files/documents/ECOWAS-110819-FightingCybercrime.pdf, accessed 1 March 2016. For the status of the implementation, see UNCTAD (United Nations Conference on Trade and Development), *Review of e-commerce Legislation Harmonization in the Economic Community of West African States*, New York, United Nations, 2015, available at: https://tft.unctad.org/wp-content/uploads/2014/03/ECOWAS-study-on-cyberlaws.pdf, accessed 1 March 2016.

requires them to criminalize fraudulent access to (Article 4 ECOWAS-Cybercrime) and—remarkably—fraudulently remaining in (Article 5 ECOWAS-Cybercrime) ICT systems. Further ICT-related offences relate to the intercepting (Article 8 ECOWAS-Cybercrime), inputting (Article 7 ECOWAS-Cybercrime), and manipulation (Article 8 ECOWAS-Cybercrime) of data as well as interference with the operation of a computer system (Article 6 ECOWAS-Cybercrime), which notably and in distinction to Article 5 CCC, is not limited to interference by electronic means. Computer-related offences include computer-related fraud (Article 11 ECOWAS-Cybercrime) and forgery (Article 10 ECOWAS-Cybercrime), but also the mere knowing use of forged data (Article 13 ECOWAS-Cybercrime). Article 14 ECOWAS-Cybercrime calls for penalizing acts in relation to the preparatory stage of 'hacking tools', but does not require a specific intent and instead refers to the—ambiguous—element of whether the perpetrator acted 'without any legitimate reason'. The Directive also includes a provision regarding the illicit processing of personal data, 'even through negligence' (Article 12 ECOWAS-Cybercrime), as well as offences regarding pornography, including child pornography (Article 16ff. ECOWAS-Cybercrime). Further content-related offences address discriminatory threats (Article 21 ECOWAS-Cybercrime) and abuses (Article 22 ECOWAS-Cybercrime) committed by means of ICT, as well as denying or justifying acts or crimes against humanity by such means (Article 23 ECOWAS-Cybercrime).

Remarkably, Article 25 ECOWAS-Cybercrime transfers some offences traditionally linked to tangible goods to the virtual sphere: for instance, theft, possession of stolen goods, and counterfeiting must also constitute an offence relating to computer data.

16.3.3.6 African Union

As of September 2015, the African Union (AU) Convention on Cyber Security and Personal Data Protection (Malobo, 27 June 2014; hereafter: AU-CS)[86] has not yet entered into force. While Article 25 para. 1 AU-CS only calls in general terms for legislation regarding 'acts which affect the confidentiality, integrity, availability and survival of information and communication technology systems, the data they process and the underlying network infrastructure', Article 29ff. AU-CS contain specific—and rather extensive—provisions relating to *unauthorized access*, including exceeding authorized access and remaining fraudulently in a computer system, and extending to any hindering or distortion of the functioning of ICT systems (not only by means of data input or data manipulation), and to any fraudulent entering or manipulation of data (Article 29 para. 1 AU-CS). The definition of computer-related and content-related offences (Article 29 paras 2 and 3 AU-CS) and the extension of 'traditional' offences (Article 30 para. 1 AU-CS) are similar to those of the ECOWAS-Cybercrime Directive described above (see section 16.3.3.5), but are limited to child pornography instead of all forms of pornography (Article 29 para. 3 AU-CS).

[86] Available at: http://pages.au.int/sites/default/files/en_AU%20Convention%20on%20CyberSecurity%20Pers%20Data%20Protec%20AUCyC%20adopted%20Malabo.pdf, accessed 1 March 2016.

16.3.3.7 *Model Laws*

Besides the aforementioned international and supranational instruments that are legally binding to the signatory states or the member states of the respective regional organisations, a multitude of model laws has been developed.[87] These might serve as an additional source of inspiration to states adapting or modifying their cybercrime laws.[88]

16.4 International Law and the Coordinated and Cooperative Investigation and Prosecution of Transnational Organised Cybercrime

To successfully investigate cybercrimes and to bring such cases to judgment, capacity building still is of the utmost importance, especially in the field of digital forensics. Beside the technical and analytical capabilities, the normative framework to enable the investigation and prosecution of *all* crimes in which ICT plays a role needs to be adapted to meet the challenges outlined above. Alongside the legally binding international instruments, which the following analysis will focus on, model rules might again provide another useful source for states when adapting their codes of criminal procedure.[89]

16.4.1 Requirements on investigatory powers in international law on cybercrime

16.4.1.1 *Coercive measures in general*

One of the classic coercive powers known in criminal procedure is the *search* for and *seizure* of tangible objects. With ICT systems and in particular data storage devices being tangible objects, evidence that may then be analysed by means of digital forensics is accessible to the authorities using classic means. Nonetheless, several international agreements call for national legislation to enable the search and seizure of computer data (Article 19 CCC, Articles 26 and 27 Arab ITO Convention, Article 30 ECOWAS-Cybercrime, Article 31 para. 3(a) and (b) AU-CS), at least for the crimes covered by these instruments. This enables the access to ICT systems on site to pre-select and pre-analyse computer data ('live forensics'), and to access remotely attached

[87] See, e.g. UN Commission on International Trade Law (UNCITRAL) Model Law on Electronic Commerce (1996); Commonwealth Model Laws on Computer and Computer-related Crime (2002); East African Community Draft Legal Framework for Cyberlaws (2008); ITU/Caribbean Community (CARICOM)/Caribbean Telecommunications Union (CTU) Model Legislative Texts on Cybercrime, e-Crime, and Electronic Evidence (2010); Common Market for Eastern and Southern Africa (COMESA) Cybersecurity Draft Model Bill (2011); ITU/Secretariat of the Pacific Community Model Law on Cybercrime (2011); Southern African Development Community (SADC) Model Law on Computer Crime and Cybercrime (2012).

[88] Cf. the review by Zahid Jamil, 'Cybercrime model laws: discussion paper prepared for the Cybercrime Convention Committee (T-CY)', 2014, available at: http://www.coe.int/t/dghl/cooperation/economic-crime/Source/Cybercrime/TCY/2014/3021_model_law_study_v15.pdf, accessed 1 March 2016.

[89] See section 16.3.3.7 and additionally the Commonwealth Model Laws on Electronic Evidence (2002).

storage devices during an open search-and-seizure operation. In general, these new provisions allow investigators to focus on the information sought—which may be the *data*, which can be duplicated without loss, but not the *tangible object*.

When the data are located with a (natural or legal) person not implicated with the crime, it may be more efficient and less invasive to merely require production of the data sought by the authorities (Article 18 CCC, Article 25 Arab ITO Convention).[90] This only relates to data that were located *within* the territory of the state issuing the production order and not data located outside it.[91] Neither provision is clear on the issue whether a third party—or even suspects themselves, which would raise serious *nemo tenetur* implications (see, e.g. Article 15 CCC)—may also be required to *decrypt* the data if so required by the authorities.

As both mutual legal assistance (see section 16.4.2.2) and normal search-and-seizure operations may take some time, but data may be highly volatile (see section 16.1.3), many international legal instruments on cybercrime call for a preliminary, expedited preservation of data (Article 16 CCC, Article 23 Arab ITO Convention, Article 31 ECOWAS-Cybercrime, Article 31 para. 3(d) AU-CS). The preserved data then must generally be acquired under standard investigatory proceedings.

As the interception of content data (telecommunication surveillance) constitutes a very severe infringement of privacy, international legal instruments defer largely to national law to define the scope of applicability of this investigation technique (Article 21 CCC, Article 29 Arab ITO Convention, Article 31 para. 3(e) AU-CS).

No international legal instrument to date contains requirements regarding new forms of covert investigation techniques such as the installation of keyloggers or the use of remote forensic software. Such software may be used to intercept encrypted telecommunication at a stage prior to encryption, to covertly search the data of a suspect, or to survey their actions for a longer period.[92]

16.4.1.2 Identification of subscribers; retention of traffic and identification data

Some international and supranational legal instruments also require an expedited procedure to compel an ISP to identify the subscriber based on their telephone number or the currently assigned IP address (Articles 16 and 17 CCC, Article 24 Arab ITO Convention). Other provisions require it to be possible to collect and preserve traffic data in real time, meaning information on which ICT system contacted which other ICT system at what time and for what duration (Articles 20 and 28 CCC). Neither instrument, however, requires ISPs to collect, preserve, and verify the identification information that links subscriber data (such as an IP address or a telephone number) to one individual owning the respective ICT system,[93] nor do they require the *retention* of all traffic data in the absence of a specific preservation order.

[90] Cf. CCC, cited in note 51 above, Explanatory Report, §§170f.
[91] Cf. ibid, Explanatory Report, §§173.
[92] Sieber, 'Mastering complexity', cited in note 3 above, p. 161.
[93] Cf. CCC, cited in note 51 above, Explanatory Report, §§150, 153, and 181.

Such requirements, however, may stem from other supranational or national legal instruments. In particular, EU Directive 2006/24/EC required member states to prescribe the retention of traffic data related to the assignment of IP addresses,[94] to telephone communications (including SMS), and to e-mail communications, for a period of between six months and two years, depending on national legislation. This retained data could then be used at a later time not only to retroactively identify which customer had used a specific IP address at a specific date and time, but also to analyse their communications for the previous months or even years. Owing to a lack of specific safeguards of data protection and no clear rules on the circumstances under which the retained data might be accessed by authorities, the Directive was struck down by the European Court of Justice in 2014.[95] The general concept, however, has prevailed; national laws in several member states continue to demand such a retention of traffic data.

16.4.2 International cooperation in the investigation and prosecution of transnational organised cybercrime

16.4.2.1 Traditional modes of cooperation extended to transnational organised cybercrime

As is common for international legal instruments addressing certain phenomena of crime, many of the instruments on cybercrime include provisions requiring the cooperation (typically: 'to the widest extent possible', Article 23 CCC) of the states parties in requests for extradition and mutual legal assistance (MLA) concerning cybercrime offences (Article 23ff. CCC, Article 10f. FD 2001/413/JHA, Article 5(b) CIS-CI, Article 31f. Arab ITO Convention, Article 33 ECOWAS-Cybercrime; see also Article 28 para. 2 AU-CS). Some partly include a detailed regime on the handling of these modes of cooperation (Article 27f. CCC, Article 6ff. CIS-CI, Article 34ff. Arab ITO Convention). Of particular importance are provisions calling for the spontaneous exchange of information—which may be helpful for *shadow investigations and proceedings* in several jurisdictions (Article 26 CCC, Article 5(a) CIS-CI, Article 33 Arab ITO Convention). Furthermore, some instruments of international law on cybercrime clarify that MLA may in general also relate to stored computer data (Article 31 CCC, Article 39 Arab ITO Convention), to the real-time collection of traffic data (Article 33 CCC, Article 41 Arab ITO Convention), and to the interception of content data (Article 34 CCC, Article 42 Arab ITO Convention), albeit each dependent on the specific MLA regime provided for by national law and other legal regimes.

Besides these international and supranational instruments specific to cybercrime, several other cooperation instruments are most useful also in assisting transnational

[94] Directive 2006/24/EC of the European Parliament and of the Council of 15 March 2006 on the retention of data generated or processed in connection with the provision of publicly available electronic communications services or of public communications networks and amending Directive 2002/58/EC [2006] OJ L105/54.

[95] Joined Cases C-293/12 *Digital Rights Ireland* and C-594/12 *Kärntner Landesregierung, Michael Seitlinger, Christof Tschohl et al.* [2014], OJ C175/6.

cooperation against cybercrime and against other forms of crime committed by means of ICT. Notably, the EU instruments based on the principle of mutual recognition, such as the European Arrest Warrant and the European Investigation Order (EIO),[96] abrogate the double criminality requirement for cybercrimes (in the meaning of Directive 2013/40/EU). Furthermore, by means of its Article 10 para. 2(e), the EIO provides for an expedited and simple procedure to determine the customer to whom an IP address was allocated at a certain time. Article 30(f) EIO and the preceding Article 17ff. EU 2000 MLA Convention contain specific rules on the transnational interception of telecommunications.[97]

16.4.2.2 Addressing the volatility of computer data

The cumbersome and often lengthy process of traditional MLA requests would mean that, in several cases, volatile computer data and therefore evidence useful for the investigation and prosecution of cybercrimes would be lost.

This leads, firstly, to a need for an expedited, but only *preliminary* preservation of data in one state—the transfer of the data, then, may be delayed until the normal proceedings have been concluded, without the risk that the data are lost in the meantime. To address this need, Article 29 CCC and Article 37 Arab ITO Convention provide for a procedure for expeditious preservation of data, with limited grounds for refusal.

Secondly, in case it is determined that some communication to be preserved preliminarily involves yet another state besides the requesting and the executing states, it is of the utmost importance to share this information as quickly as possible. Therefore, this information—but not any information relating directly to the suspect—can be expeditiously shared, under Article 30 CCC and Article 38 Arab ITO Convention.

Thirdly and most importantly, communications between states parties need to be accelerated, to facilitate the preliminary measures described above, and to particularly facilitate the initiation of *shadow proceedings* in all states that have jurisdiction over a specific cybercrime—thus enabling each state to use its own investigatory powers and, at a later stage, to share any information gained with the other states involved. For these reasons, the G-8 created in 1998 a 24/7 network for high-tech crime,[98] which since then has expanded to cover more than seventy states world-wide. In a similar vein, Article 35 CCC, Article 13 Directive 2011/93/EU, and Article 43 Arab ITO Convention call for the creation of such a network of contact points, to be available around the clock. To meet these requirements of international law, states parties regularly join the G-8 24/7 network, which therefore has become the focal point for a coordinated transnational fight against cybercrime, including TOC.

[96] Council Framework Decision of 13 June 2002 on the European arrest warrant and the surrender procedures between Member States (2002/584/JHA) [2002] OJ L190/1, as amended [2009] OJ L81/24. Directive 2014/41/EU of the European Parliament and of the Council of 3 April 2014 regarding the European Investigation Order in criminal matters [2014] OJ L130/1.

[97] Convention established by the Council in accordance with Article 34 of the Treaty on European Union, on Mutual Assistance in Criminal Matters between the Member States of the European Union [2000] OJ C197/3.

[98] Cf. Schjolberg, *History of Cybercrime*, cited in note 1 above, pp. 43ff.

16.5 Jurisdiction on Transnational Organised Cybercrime

16.5.1 Jurisdiction to prescribe and to adjudicate

The requirements in Article 22 CCC, Article 9 FD 2001/413/JHA, Article 17 Directive 2011/93/EU, Article 12 Directive 2013/40/EU, and Article 30 Arab ITO Convention to establish and extend states' jurisdiction on certain cybercrimes,[99] particularly outside their territory,[100] are a common theme of international legal instruments addressing certain phenomena of crime. Such an extension of the *jurisdiction to prescribe and to adjudicate* can be helpful in the fight against cybercrime in multiple ways. In particular, it enables the initiation of shadow proceedings (see sections 16.4.2.1 and 16.4.2.2) and minimizes safe havens for cybercriminals.[101] On the other hand the risk of positive conflicts of jurisdiction and of forum shopping detrimental to the rights of the defendant increase with such an approach.

16.5.2 Jurisdiction to enforce

The most problematic jurisdictional aspect relates to the jurisdiction to enforce. In general, the jurisdiction to enforce does not extend into the territory of a foreign state. This means that coercive measures, such as search-and-seizure operations, may only be conducted in another jurisdiction in accordance with the authorities of the territorial state; one traditional mode to achieve this is MLA. In cyberspace, it is not only unprecedentedly easy to (deliberately, unwarily, or accidentally) cross territorial borders—e.g. if authorities access and analyse an ICT system over the internet but do not know it is located abroad—but there may often also be a need for quick and decisive action to preserve volatile data. Five major aspects may be discerned concerning this topic, at least some of which still need more clarification by jurisprudence and by future international legal instruments.

First, it seems a widely accepted practice that *publicly available information* on the internet is also lawfully available to authorities in foreign countries. This is underlined by Article 32(a) CCC, Article 40(1) Arab ITO Convention, but may nowadays also be considered an international custom, even beyond the states parties to these Conventions.[102]

Second, it is clear that—in accordance with its domestic law—the territorial state may *consent to coercive actions* by other states within its territory. In line with such an approach are the rules on preliminary cross-border telecommunication surveillance

[99] Cf. Cristos Velasco, 'Cybercrime jurisdiction: past, present and future', *ERA Forum*, 24 June 2015, p. 6ff.

[100] Moreover, in cybercrimes, the location of the perpetrator's action often differs from the location where his/her action takes effect.

[101] In a similar vein, W. Joseph Salvador, 'Dismantling the internet mafia: RICO's applicability to cyber crime', (2015) 41 *Rutgers Computer and Technology Law Journal*, 268 proposes an extensive interpretation of RICO, the US landmark law to fight OC.

[102] Cf. Ulrich Sieber, *Straftaten und Strafverfolgung im Internet, Gutachten C zum 69. Deutschen Juristentag*, Munich, Beck, 2012, pp. C 144f.

in Article 20 EU 2000 MLA Convention and Article 31 EIO. These provisions, however, only allow for a temporary interception and preservation of ongoing telecommunications; the territorial state must generally consent to the later use of the data, e.g. as evidence in criminal proceedings.

Third, two international legal instruments against cybercrime accept the access to ICT systems located in one state party by the authorities of another state party if the latter 'obtains the *lawful and voluntary consent of the person* who has the lawful authority to disclose the data' (Article 32(b) CCC, emphasis added; similarly, Article 40(2) Arab ITO Convention). This provision, which is at the centre of the Russian criticism of the CCC, is ambiguous concerning the person who may consent, and does not require the notification of the other state party.[103] A guidance note by the T-CY at least clarifies that ISPs 'are unlikely to be able to consent validly and voluntarily' to the disclosure of users' data, since they 'will only be holders of such data' but not 'control or own the data'.[104]

Fourth, nonetheless, some authorities attempt to use their jurisdiction to compel natural and legal persons in their territory—especially ISPs—to transfer data inland, thereby laying the ground for authorities' access to those data.[105] In light of the limited applicability of Article 32(b) CCC and the implications for the sovereignty of the territorial state,[106] it seems quite doubtful whether such action is lawful under current international law.

Fifth, it has to be noted that accidental or unwary cross-border access of data is becoming more and more common, as the physical location where the data are stored is often neither known nor determined ("loss of location"). The legality of such action is doubtful but as yet undetermined in terms of international law.[107] Moreover, this question must be distinguished from whether evidence obtained through such means—or even the mere fruits of such evidence—may be used in criminal proceedings. The answer to the latter question depends on domestic evidence laws, which may come to different conclusions than international law.

16.6 Final Observations

To address TOC of today and tomorrow as it becomes increasingly interlinked with organised cybercrime a first, basic building block is ensuring the alignment of the

[103] Cf. ibid, pp. C 78f.

[104] T-CY (2013) 7 E, p. 7; but see Swiss Bundesgericht, Judgment of 14 January 2015, 1 B_344/2014, para. 5.10.

[105] Cf. *In the Matter of a Warrant to Search a Certain E-Mail Account Controlled and Maintained by Microsoft Corporation*, United States District Court (SDNY) Memorandum and Order of 25 April 2014, 13-Mag-2814, upheld by Order of the United States District Court (SDNY) of 11 August 2014. Appeal (pending, with remarkable Brief for the Appellee of 9 March 2015, Document 212, p. 45): *Microsoft Corporation v United States of America*, United States Court of Appeals (2nd Cir.) 14-2985-CV. Cf. further Velasco, 'Cybercrime jurisdiction', cited in note 99 above, pp. 9f.

[106] Cf. Sieber, *Straftaten und Strafverfolgung im Internet*, cited in note 102 above, pp. C 78f.; Swiss Bundesgericht, cited in note 104 above, para. 5.12.

[107] But see, e.g. Magda Wicker, 'Durchsuchung in der Cloud. Nutzung von Cloud-Speichern und der strafprozessuale Zugriff deutscher Ermittlungsbehörden', (2013) 16 *Multimedia und Recht* (12), 765, p. 768f., who considers the physical location of the police officer to be decisive, even if he or she accesses ICT systems abroad.

substantive criminal laws to the virtualization and automation enabled by ICT. In accordance with not only the CCC but also further instruments of international law on cybercrime, the confidentiality, integrity, and availability of ICT systems and the data stored requires protection, by means of criminal law as well as technological means. Additional focus needs to be placed, however, on computer-related and especially content-related offences. Concerning all these cybercrime offences, it is of the utmost importance to carefully limit their scope in order to protect human rights (such as freedom of expression), but also to protect all the useful features the internet and ICT in general provide for society.

The major challenges in addressing Transnational Organised Cybercrime lie, however, in criminal procedure, three of which I will briefly highlight here. First, the use of encryption may mean that some digital evidence is inaccessible to the authorities; on the other hand, however, the use of encryption technology is one of the very best methods to secure ICT against cybercrime and thus to prevent such crime. Second, to address the volatility of data, the issue of whether to introduce requirements on the retention of (mostly: traffic) data, which would lessen the confidentiality of communications, is ongoing. Third, the transnational investigation and prosecution of cybercrime—especially in terms of the jurisdiction to enforce—is perhaps *the* major open question under international law on cybercrime.

PART IV

TRANSNATIONAL ORGANISED CRIME AS MATTER OF CERTAIN BRANCHES OF INTERNATIONAL LAW

17

The International Law of the Use of Force and Transnational Organised Crime

*Pierre Thielbörger**

17.1 Introduction

Although the prohibition on the use of force is in many ways crucial to the issue of fighting transnational organised crime, many questions surrounding the relationship of the two have not yet been answered.[1] The basic dilemma is clear: the prohibition on the use of force (Article 2(4) UN Charter (UNC)) is the product of a state-centred legal order and directed at states, not at non-state actors—as organised criminal groups certainly are. Philip Alston once explained international law through a metaphor about his young, cat-loving daughter. For her, there were only two categories of pets: 'cat' and 'not-a-cat'.[2] Similarly, international law knows states but is rather blind towards other entities. As a consequence, international law often is not in a position to deliver adequate solutions for problems caused by 'not-a-state' actors that, in one way or another, play an ever more important role in today's international relations.

One of the most dramatic recent problems caused by transnational organised crime is that of gangs smuggling (illegal) immigrants into the European Union (EU) over the Mediterranean Sea. Human trafficking has become one of the world's most lucrative and fastest-growing criminal enterprises.[3] In the first six months of 2015, some 150,000 people reached Europe by sea while almost 1,900 persons lost their lives in the Mediterranean Sea trying to migrate from the African to the European continent in the same time frame.[4] This number of lost lives is twice as high as the figure

* The author holds a chair for German Public Law and Public International Law, in particular the International Law of Peace and Armed Conflict, at the law faculty of Ruhr University Bochum. He is also Executive Director of the Institute for the International Law of Peace and Armed Conflict (IFHV) at that university. Thanks to Tobias Ackermann, Theresa Stollmann, Benedikt Behlert, and Thea Coventry for assistance with research and language refining.

[1] Pierre Hauck and Sven Peterke, 'Organized crime and gang violence in national and international law', (2010) 92 *IRRC*, 407, p. 429.

[2] Philip Alston, 'The "not-a-cat" syndrome: can the international human rights regime accommodate non-state actors?' in Philip Alston (ed.), *Non-State Actors and Human Rights*, Oxford, OUP, 2005, pp. 3–36.

[3] Jennifer L. Enck, 'The United Nations Convention Against Transnational Organized Crime: is it all that it is cracked up to be? Problems posed by the Russian mafia in the trafficking of humans', (2003) 30 *Syracuse Journal of International Law & Commerce* (2), 369, p. 370 referring to the US Department of State's 'Asian Regional Initiative Against Trafficking (ARIAT) Country Plan of the United States'. See also Louise I. Shelley, *Human Trafficking: A Global Perspective*, New York, CUP, 2010, pp. 1–17.

[4] 'Migrant boat arrivals in Europe top 150,000 in 2015', *International Organization for Migration*, 10 July 2015, available at: http://www.iom.int/news/migrant-boat-arrivals-europe-top-150000-2015, accessed 15 July 2015.

for the same period in 2014.[5] These figures show how dramatic the problem has recently become. The African migrants are often 'helped' by gangs that falsely promise safe transit to Europe while in reality placing hundreds or thousands of humans in an inescapable death trap on the open sea. The EU has miserably failed to react to this humanitarian catastrophe, focusing on physically preventing the migration rather than fighting its causes or offering humanitarian shelter for the victims arriving on European shores. The European leaders even discussed the absurd option of destroying the vessels with military force in early 2015.[6] Attempts to establish a legally binding quota for the fair distribution of the migrants between the different member states of the Union, as suggested by some states like Germany and France,[7] have so far failed.[8] Until now, under the Dublin Regulation,[9] the burden lies mainly on the state of first entry, thus currently mainly on southern European states such as Italy, Spain, and Greece. This provides another example of the unfitness (in many ways) of international and European law for dealing with the problems that transnational organised crime poses today.

This chapter seeks to answer some of the most important legal questions relating to the interplay of transnational organised crime on one hand and the use of force in international law on the other. After briefly introducing the concepts of 'the prohibition on the use of force' and 'transnational organised crime', two separate questions will be addressed. These two questions speak to different ways of how to fight transnational organised crime: first, whether the use of force against foreign territory from which organised criminal groups operate can be justified as self-defence (Article 51 UNC); and second, whether addressing the problem of organised crime lies within the competence of the UN Security Council under Chapter VII UNC.

[5] Ibid.

[6] See European Council, 'Special meeting of the European Council, 23 April 2015—statement', available at: http://www.consilium.europa.eu/en/press/press-releases/2015/04/23-special-euco-statement/, accessed 15 July 2015. In it, the member states commit, *inter alia*, to 'undertake systematic efforts to identify, capture and destroy vessels before they are used by traffickers'. See, on those plans, Ian Traynor, 'EU draws up plans for military attacks on Libya targets to stop migrant boats', *The Guardian*, London, 10 May 2015, available at: http://www.theguardian.com/world/2015/may/10/eu-considers-military-attacks-on-targets-in-libya-to-stop-migrant-boats, accessed 15 July 2015.

[7] See, for example, Ian Traynor, 'Germany presses for quota system for EU migrant distribution', *The Guardian*, London, 29 April 2015, available at: http://www.theguardian.com/world/2015/apr/29/germany-quota-system-eu-migrant-distribution, accessed 15 July 2015; Matthias Galante, Astrid Wendlandt, and Tom Heneghan, 'France calls for fairer asylum seeker distribution within EU', *Reuters*, London, 16 May 2015, available at: http://www.uk.reuters.com/article/2015/05/16/uk-france-immigration-idUKKBN0O10Q320150516, accessed 15 July 2015.

[8] Ullrich Fichtner, Maximilian Popp, Cristoph Schult, and Alexander Smoltczyk, 'Migration crisis: the EU's shipwrecked refugee plan', *Der Spiegel Online*, Hamburg, 23 June 2015, available at: http://www.spiegel.de/international/europe/how-eu-promises-to-introduce-refugee-quotas-failed-a-1040226.html, accessed 15 July 2015; Andrew Higgins, 'In testy debate, EU leaders fail to agree on quotas to spread migrants across bloc', *New York Times*, New York, 26 June 2015, available at: http://www.nytimes.com/2015/06/27/world/europe/european-union-migrant-crisis-quotas-italy-greece.html, accessed 15 July 2015.

[9] Regulation 604/2013 of the European Parliament and of the Council of 26 June 2013 establishing the criteria and mechanisms for determining the Member State responsible for examining an application for international protection lodged in one of the Member States by a third-country national or a stateless person, OJ 2013/L 180/13 (Dublin III Regulation), Arts 7–15.

Taking together the findings on these questions, the chapter offers several lessons that can be drawn for international law when dealing with transnational organised crime in the future.

17.2 An Introduction to the Threat and Use of Force in International Law

The prohibition on the use of force is one of the cornerstones of international law today. International law's attitude towards the legality of the use of force in international relations has significantly evolved over recent centuries. In traditional international law until the twentieth century, *ius ad bellum* ('the right to go to war') was widely accepted.[10] War was seen as a legitimate means of international politics,[11] albeit nevertheless monarchs often felt the need to rhetorically justify their belligerent actions.[12] Even the 1919 Covenant of the League of Nations did not manage to significantly alter that mind-set.[13] The Covenant contained no general prohibition on the use of force in international relations, even though a superficial reading of Article 10 of the Covenant might suggest this.[14] The failure to contain the threats to international peace and security in a legally binding manner was certainly one, if not the primary, reason for the failure of the League of Nations.

It was famously the Briand-Kellogg Pact, concluded in 1928 and named after US American Secretary of State Frank. B. Kellogg and French Foreign Minister Aristide Briand, in which the contracting parties for the first time condemned recourse to war as a solution for their controversies.[15] Initially intended as a bilateral treaty between France and the USA, fifteen states joined the Pact in 1928 and renounced war as an instrument of international politics in a legally binding way. By 1938, the number of

[10] Paul Heilborn, *Grundbegriffe des Völkerrechts*, Berlin, Kohlhammer, 1912, p. 23; Wolff Heintschel von Heinegg, 'Vom *ius ad bellum* zum *ius contra bellum* (Kriegsverbot, Gewaltverbot und Interventionsverbot)', in Knut Ipsen (ed.), *Völkerrecht*, 6th edn, C. H. Beck, 2014, p. 1055; Randall Lesaffer, 'Too much history: from war as sanction to the sanctioning of war', in Marc Weller (ed.), *The Oxford Handbook of the Use of Force in International Law*, Oxford, OUP, 2015, p. 36. See, for an extensive historical analysis of war as state policy in the period between 1815 and 1919, Stephen C. Neff, *War and the Law of Nations: A General History*, Cambridge, CUP, 2005, pp. 159–275.

[11] Carl von Clausewitz famously understood war as 'merely the continuation of policy by other means': see Clausewitz, *On War* (first published 1832), Oxford, OUP, 2007, p. 28.

[12] Heintschel von Heinegg, 'Vom *ius ad bellum*', cited in note 10 above, p. 1055.

[13] Covenant of the League of Nations, adopted 28 June 1919, entered into force 10 January 1920, 225 CTS 188.

[14] Art. 10 emphasizes that '[t]he Members of the League undertake to respect and preserve as against external aggression the territorial integrity and existing political independence of all Members of the League. In case of any such aggression or in case of any threat or danger of such aggression the Council shall advise upon the means by which this obligation shall be fulfilled.' Heintschel von Heinegg, 'Vom *ius ad bellum*', cited in note 10 above, p. 1059. It is noteworthy, however, that member states of the League of Nations agreed to submit any dispute arising between them to arbitral or judicial settlement (see Arts 12 and 13 Covenant of the League of Nations).

[15] Art. I General Treaty for Renunciation of War as an Instrument of National Policy, adopted 27 August 1928, entered into force 24 July 1929, 94 LNTS 57 (Kellogg-Briand Pact) states: 'The High Contracting Parties solemnly declare in the names of their respective peoples that they condemn recourse to war for the solution of international controversies, and renounce it, as an instrument of national policy in their relations with one another.'

signatory states had risen to more than sixty.[16] As the outbreak of the Second World War proved, however, that Pact suffered from a mayor weakness: it had no enforcement mechanisms to sanction breaches of the newly established prohibition on the use of force.

Article 1(1) UNC emphasises the foremost goal of the UN as being 'to maintain international peace and security … and to bring about by peaceful means … adjustment or settlement of international disputes or situations which might lead to a breach of the peace'. Article 2(4) UNC adds even more explicitly that all UN members 'shall refrain in their international relations from the threat or use of force against the territorial integrity or political independence of any state, or in any other manner inconsistent with the Purposes of the United Nations'.

Despite the terminological vagueness of the term 'force', Article 2(4) UNC is generally understood to have a low threshold. The prohibition on the threat or use of force is thus interpreted very broadly. The Friendly Relations Declaration of the UN General Assembly names as examples of 'force' not only a war of aggression, but also less intensive conflicts such as, *inter alia*, problems concerning frontiers or supporting irregular forces or armed bands including mercenaries in an incursion onto the territory of another state, or participating in acts of already existent civil strife or terrorist acts within another state.[17] However, 'force' under Article 2(4) UNC is always understood to be military in nature. Economic or political pressure might instead be a violation of Article 2(1) UNC, which establishes the sovereign equality of states and the prohibition of intervention. Non-military support, such as financial or political aid for rebels, does not, as the International Court of Justice (ICJ) has emphasized, amount to a violation of Article 2(4) UNC.[18]

The prohibition on use of force also forms part of customary law.[19] Most authors even see it as part of *ius cogens*—thus as one of those rare norms in international law from which no derogation is permitted and which can be modified only by a subsequent norm of general international law having the same character (Article 53 sentence 2 Vienna Convention on the Law of Treaties (VCLT)).[20]

[16] Randall Lesaffer, 'Kellogg-Briand Pact (1928)', in Rüdiger Wolfrum (ed.), *Max Planck Encyclopedia of Public International Law*, last updated October 2010, para. 2, available at: http://opil.ouplaw.com/view/10.1093/law:epil/9780199231690/law-9780199231690-e320?rskey=ADfWXL&result=1&prd=EPIL, accessed 15 July 2015.

[17] UN GA Res. 2626 (XXV) 'Declaration on Principles of International Law concerning Friendly Relations and Co-operation among States in accordance with the Charter of the United Nations', 24 October 1970, UN Doc. A/RES/25/2625, annex, first principle.

[18] *Military and Paramilitary Activities in and against Nicaragua (Nicaragua v USA)*, Judgment (Merits) [1986] ICJ Rep 14, para. 228 ('… the Court considers that the mere supply of funds to the contras, while undoubtedly an act of intervention in the internal affairs of Nicaragua …, does not in itself amount to a use of force'.)

[19] Ibid, para. 188; Heintschel von Heinegg, 'Vom *ius ad bellum*', cited in note 10 above, pp. 1072–3. Critical of this assessment (in particular as the element of state practice was not sufficiently assessed) Frederick L. Kirgis Jr, 'Custom on a sliding scale', (1987) 81 *AJIL* (1), 146, p. 147.

[20] Vienna Convention on the Law of Treaties, adopted 23 May 1969, entered into force 27 January 1980, 1155 UNTS 331. When commenting on the draft of Art. 53 VCLT, the International Law Commission (ILC) pointed out that Art. 2(4) UNC 'constitutes a conspicuous example' of a *ius cogens* norm, and some members of the ILC even considered explicitly mentioning the prohibition of the use of force as one example

Distinctly different from the term 'threat' or 'use' of force in Article 2(4) UNC is the notion of 'armed attack', which is the primary precondition to trigger the exceptional right of self-defence (Article 51 UNC). Article 51 UNC states that '[n]othing in the present Charter shall impair the inherent right of individual or collective self-defence if an armed attack occurs against a Member of the United Nations ...'. An armed attack can only be assumed if a significantly higher threshold, a military conflict, is crossed.[21] The UN General Assembly lists as examples of an armed attack, which it uses more or less synonymously with the notion of 'aggression',[22] *inter alia*, an invasion, a military occupation, bombardments, the blockade of ports or coasts, or the sending of armed bands, groups, irregulars, or mercenaries into another country.[23] Thus, while every case of an armed attack constitutes at the same time a use of force, the opposite is certainly not true.[24]

Other exceptions to the prohibition on the threat or use of force include the possibility of the Security Council acting under Article 42 UNC, if it deems military action necessary in order to address a threat to international peace and security (Article 39 UNC). An unwritten exception, 'humanitarian intervention', has been promoted by quite a few scholars,[25] in particular following the non-intervention in the genocide in Rwanda. However states, many of which do not regard there to be sufficient state practice and *opinio juris* for such an unwritten rule to form part of customary law, have criticized this perception.[26]

of Art. 53 VCLT; see ILC, *Yearbook of the International Law Commission*, Vol. II, New York, UN, 1966, pp. 247–8. See, also, Nico Schrijver, 'The ban on the use of force in the UNC', in Weller, *Oxford Handbook of the Use of Force*, cited in note 10 above, p. 484.

[21] *Nicaragua*, cited in note 18 above, para. 191 (distinguishing 'the most grave forms of the use of force (those constituting an armed attack) from other less grave forms'). This was confirmed in *Oil Platforms (Islamic Republic of Iran v United States of America)*, Judgment [2003] ICJ Rep. 161, para. 51. However, this rather cloudy distinction has received some criticism; see, out of many, Tom Ruys, *'Armed Attack' and Article 51 of the UNC: Evolutions in Customary Law and Practice*, Cambridge, CUP, 2010, pp. 143–9 with further references.

[22] Yoram Dinstein, 'Aggression', last updated May 2009, in Wolfrum, *Max Planck Encyclopedia of Public International Law*, cited in note 16 above, para. 33; available at: http://opil.ouplaw.com/view/10.1093/law:epil/9780199231690/law-9780199231690-e236?rskey=w8XaQ1&result=1&prd=EPIL, accessed 15 July 2015.

[23] UN GA Res. 3314 (XXIX) 'Definition of Aggression', 14 December 1974, UN Doc. A/RES/3314 (XXIX), annex, Art. 3.

[24] See, on the relation between an armed attack and the use of force, James A. Green, *The International Court of Justice and Self-Defence in International Law*, Oxford, Hart, 2009, pp. 25–32.

[25] See, for example, Barry M. Benjamin, 'Note: unilateral humanitarian intervention: legalizing the use of force to prevent human rights atrocities', (1992–3) 16 *Fordham International Law Journal*, 120; Thomas M. Franck, *Recourse to Force: State Action Against Threats and Armed Attacks*, Cambridge, CUP, 2002, pp. 135–73; Ryan Goodman, 'Humanitarian intervention and pretexts for war', (2006) 100 *AJIL* (1), 107. See, further, Albrecht Randelzhofer and Oliver Dörr, 'Article 2(4)', in Bruno Simma, Daniel-Erasmus Khan, Georg Nolte, and Andreas Paulus (eds), *The Charter of the United Nations: A Commentary*, Vol. I, 3rd edn, Oxford, OUP, 2012, paras 52–7 with further references.

[26] Most prominently, the Group of 77, comprising 133 (developing) states, adopted two declarations in which it 'rejected the so-called right of humanitarian intervention, which has no basis in the UNC or in international law'; see Ministerial Declaration of the Ministers for Foreign Affairs of the Group of 77 at the 23rd Annual Meeting (24 September 1999), para. 69, available at: http://www.g77.org/doc/Decl1999.html, accessed 16 July 2015, and the Declaration of the Group of 77 South Summit (10–14 April 2000), para. 54, available at: http://www.g77.org/summit/Declaration_G77Summit.htm, accessed 16 July 2015.

17.3 On the Notion of Transnational Organised Crime

There is no accepted definition of transnational organised crime in international law.[27] Given that several authors in this book address the struggle for a definition,[28] I will not explore the notion of transnational organised crime in great detail, but rather emphasize those elements of the definition that are relevant for the argument put forward here.

The notion certainly covers a variety of illegal activities,[29] including, in particular, the trafficking of firearms and of human beings. The literature distinguishes primary criminal activities, which include those crimes that are typically committed in an organised form, from secondary criminal activities, which make the committing of these primary crimes possible,[30] typically corruption or money laundering.[31] While organised crime often yields high profits for the perpetrators, it carries fatal risks for the victims.

The relationship between terrorism and organised crime is highly contested amongst scholars. One way to look at it is to understand terrorism as a special sub-category of organised crime;[32] another way is to see both terms as distinctly different in that, very simply put, terrorism is a politically motivated criminal activity while organised crime is largely driven by materialistic motivation.[33] But even if one follows the latter approach, this does not necessarily exclude the possibility that terrorist groups also engage in organised crime in order to generate the financial basis for their terrorist activities, or that, vice versa, criminal groups at times employ terrorist methods,[34] so that in effect we often see a mixture of the two phenomena.

Organised crime is certainly becoming increasingly transnational in nature. The condition of 'transnationality' describes activities that are planned or carried out in more than one state. Today, borders no longer constitute a serious obstacle for organised crime. Sometimes the criminal activity even directly relates to the illegal crossing of borders, be it smuggling illicit goods or human beings without

[27] See—for the matter of definition—Arndt Sinn, Chapter 2, sections 2.1.1 and 2.3.2; and Pierre Hauck, Chapter 21 of this book. Cyrille Fijnaut, 'Transnational crime and the role of the United Nations in its containment through international cooperation: a challenge for the 21st century', (2000) 8 *EJCCLCJ* (2), 119; Thomas Feltes, 'Organized crime—sleeping with the enemy?', (2007) 2 *Panóptica* (7), 152, p. 153; Frank G. Madsen, 'Transnational organized crime' in Thomas G. Weiss and Sam Daws (eds), *The Oxford Handbook on the United Nations*, Oxford, OUP, 2007, p. 612; Sven Peterke, 'Völkerrechtliche Selbstverteidigung gegen transnationales organisiertes Verbrechen?', (2011) 24 *Humanitäres Völkerrech t: Informationsschriften* (4), 202.

[28] See, above all, Arndt Sinn, Chapter 1; and Pierre Hauck, Chapter 21, section 2.1.

[29] Rensselaer W. Lee III, 'Transnational organized crime: an overview', in Tom Farer (ed.), *Transnational Crime in the Americas: An Inter-American Dialogue Book*, New York, Routledge, 1999, p. 1ff.

[30] Alan Wright, *Organised Crime*, Portland, Oregon, Willan Publishing, 2006, p. 49; Peterke, 'Völkerrechtliche Selbstverteidigung', cited in note 27 above, p. 204.

[31] UN Convention Against Transnational Organized Crime, adopted 15 November 2000, entered into force 29 September 2003, 2225 UNTS 209, Arts 6 and 8.

[32] Angela Veng Mei Leong, *The Disruption of International Organised Crime: An Analysis of Legal and Non-Legal Strategies*, Aldershot, Ashgate, 2007, pp. 22–5.

[33] Peterke, 'Völkerrechtliche Selbstverteidigung', cited in note 27 above, p. 202. See also Ulrich Schneckener, *Transnationaler Terrorismus: Charakter und Hintergründe des 'neuen' Terrorismus* Frankfurt am Main, Suhrkamp, 2006, pp. 36–7.

[34] Peterke, 'Völkerrechtliche Selbstverteidigung', cited in note 27 above, p. 203.

permission to enter the other state. Having observed this trend, the international community agreed in 2000 upon the UN Convention Against Transnational Organised Crime (Palermo Convention) and three protocols thereto—on trafficking in persons,[35] smuggling of migrants,[36] and trafficking of firearms.[37] The Convention has by now been ratified by 185 states, with only a few, like Iran or Japan, missing.[38] With this high ratification rate, the Palermo Convention can certainly be regarded as a great political achievement and a milestone in the fight against transnational organised crime.

The Convention mirrors a minimal consensus over transnational organised crime,[39] although, interestingly enough, it employs the term 'transnational organised crime' itself solely in its title without offering an explicit definition. Most importantly, however, Article 2(a) Palermo Convention defines an 'organised criminal group' as 'a structured group of three or more persons, existing for a period of time and acting in concert with the aim of committing one or more serious crimes or offences established in accordance with this Convention, in order to obtain, directly or indirectly, a financial or other material benefit'.

While some aspects of the definition merit criticism,[40] the offered definition is altogether a balanced compromise. On one hand, it fulfils the desire to identify a broad term that is capable of including new forms of transnational organised crime, if and once they occur. And on the other, it meets the need to distinguish transnational organised crime from other phenomena such as terrorism[41] (if one understands these two to be different in the first place)[42] or from activities carried out by other forms of gang.[43]

17.4 Self-Defence against Transnational Organised Crime

As initially hinted, the prohibition on the use of force and combating transnational organised crime do not easily go together. International law is a highly state-centred field of law. Different from international relations theory, which takes different international 'actors' into its focus, the primary subjects of international law are states, which means they are the ones that are—as the ICJ phrased it in its *Reparation for Injuries* opinion—'capable of possessing international rights and duties, and ... ha[ve]

[35] Protocol to Prevent, Suppress, and Punish Trafficking in Persons, Especially Women and Children, adopted 15 November 2000, entered into force 25 December 2003, 2237 UNTS 319.

[36] Protocol against the Smuggling of Migrants by Land, Sea, and Air, adopted 15 November 2000, entered into force 28 January 2004, 2241 UNTS 507.

[37] Protocol against the Illicit Manufacturing of and Trafficking in Firearms, Their Parts and Components, and Ammunition, adopted 31 May 2001, entered into force 3 July 2005, 2326 UNTS 208.

[38] The status is available at: <https:// treaties.un.org/pages/viewdetails.aspx?src=ind&mtdsg_no=xviii-12&chapter=18&lang=en>, accessed 16 July 2015.

[39] Peterke, 'Völkerrechtliche Selbstverteidigung', cited in note 27 above, p. 203.

[40] Out of many, see Alexandra V. Orlova and James W. Moore, '"Umbrellas" or "building blocks"?: Defining international terrorism and transnational organized crime in international law', (2005) 27 *Houston Journal of International Law* (2), 267, p. 282.

[41] Peterke, 'Völkerrechtliche Selbstverteidigung', cited in note 27 above, p. 203.

[42] See Schneckener, *Transnationaler Terrorismus*, cited in note 33 above.

[43] Ulrich Eisenberg, *Kriminologie*, 6th edn, Munich, C. H. Beck, 2005, p. 920.

capacity to maintain [their] rights by bringing international claims'.[44] In this way, the prohibition of the threat and use of force—just like any norm of international law that is not human rights or international criminal law[45]—binds primarily states, not 'non-state actors', i.e. peoples, groups, or individuals.

Organised criminal groups (Article 2(a) Palermo Convention) certainly constitute such non-state actors. In order to create liability for transnational organised crime, one must either argue for the accountability of the state from the territory or jurisdiction of which the criminal activity emanates, or emphasize the exceptional subjectivity of transnational organised crime gangs themselves. Of course, both responsibilities—that of the state and that of the non-state actor—can coexist, so that no exclusivity between both options exists.[46] The debate about how to establish responsibility for armed attacks emanating from groups engaging in transnational organised crime resembles the discussion that has been held with regard to terrorist groups ever since the attacks of 11 September 2001.

17.4.1 Organised criminal groups as *de facto* regimes

An approach to establish the responsibility of organised criminal groups without altering existing parameters of international law would be to emphasize their status as (stabilized) *de facto* regimes. *De facto* regimes describe entities that exercise effective control over a given territory for a given period of time.[47] Thus, they generally meet the criteria for statehood or are on the way to doing so,[48] even if other states might not (yet) have recognized them as states (be it for political or other reasons).[49] These stabilized *de facto* regimes are generally understood to be partially subject to international law and thus bound by a basic set of international legal norms,[50] which would include the prohibition on the use of

[44] *Reparation for Injuries Suffered in the Service of the United Nations*, Advisory Opinion [1949] ICJ Rep 174, p. 179. For a critique of this definition of a 'subject' in international law, see Roland Portmann, *Legal Personality in International Law*, Cambridge, CUP, 2010, pp. 9–10 (calling the ICJ's definition 'not very illuminating' and 'tautological'); James Crawford, *Brownlie's Principles of Public International Law*, 8th edn, Oxford, OUP, 2012, p. 115 (calling this traditional definition 'unfortunately circular').

[45] Rosalyn Higgins, 'Conceptual thinking about the individual in international law', (1978) 4 *British Journal of International Studies* (1), 1, pp. 1–2; Andrew Clapham, 'The role of the individual in international law', (2010) 21 *EJIL* (1), 25.

[46] Peterke, 'Völkerrechtliche Selbstverteidigung', cited in note 27 above, p. 207.

[47] Jonte van Essen, '*De facto* regimes in international law', (2012) 28 *Utrecht Journal of International European Law* (74), 31, pp. 32–3; Jochen A. Frowein, '*De facto* regime', last updated March 2013, in Wolfrum, *Max Planck Encyclopedia of Public International Law*, cited in note 16 above, para. 2, available at: http://opil.ouplaw.com/view/10.1093/law:epil/9780199231690/law-9780199231690-e1395?rskey=nUgHc0&result=1&prd=EPIL, accessed 15 July 2015.

[48] See, on the criteria for statehood, Art. 1 Montevideo Convention on the Rights and Duties of States, adopted 26 December 1933, entered into force 26 December 1934, 165 LNTS 19. See, further, James Crawford, 'The criteria for statehood in international law', (1978) 48 *BYBIL*, 93; Martti Koskenniemi, 'The future of statehood', (1991) 32 *Harvard International Law Journal* (2), 397; Thomas D. Grant, 'Defining statehood: the Montevideo Convention and its discontents', (1999) 37 *Columbia Journal of Transnational Law* (2), 403.

[49] See, on the (mostly viewed as declaratory) recognition of states and governments, Hersch Lauterpacht, *Recognition in International Law*, Cambridge, CUP, 1947; Crawford, *Brownlie's Principles*, cited in note 4a above, pp. 143–65; van Essen, '*De facto* regimes', cited in note 47 above, pp. 39–48.

[50] van Essen, '*De facto* regimes', cited in note 47 above, pp. 34–9.

force.[51] If assuming that under certain circumstances terrorist groups can be considered as *de facto* regimes, there is also room, theoretically speaking, for the parallel assumption that the same is possible for organised criminal groups.[52] Some authors have shown that in specific situations organised criminal groups indeed have achieved control over a specific territory and maintained it over a certain period of time.[53] If they do this, it is to shield the established criminal structures or to further enable new crimes.[54] However, different from terrorist groups, organised criminal groups are not mainly politically motivated: by establishing control; they do not seek either recognition or statehood. Thus, often, treating organised criminal groups as *de facto* regimes will not be a suitable approach,[55] at least much less suitable than such an approach might be for terrorist groups.

17.4.2 State responsibility for organised criminal groups

The second option would be to attach the legal responsibility to the state from which the criminal activity emanates. The ICJ originally established quite a high threshold (the 'effective control' test) for holding states responsible for the actions of a group of individuals. The Court stated in its 1986 *Nicaragua* judgment, in which it decided on the USA's responsibility for the Nicaraguan guerrilla group the 'Contras', that:

> [p]articipation, even if preponderant or decisive, in the financing, organizing, training, supplying and equipping of the contras, the selection of its military or paramilitary targets, and the planning of the whole of its operation, is still insufficient in itself … for the purpose of attributing to the United States the acts committed by the contras in the course of their military or paramilitary operations in Nicaragua. All the forms of United States participation mentioned above, and even the general control by the respondent state over a force with a high degree of dependency on it, would not in themselves mean, without further evidence, that the United States directed or enforced the perpetration of the acts contrary to human rights and humanitarian law alleged by the applicant state. … For this conduct to give rise to legal responsibility of the United States, it would in principle have to be proved that that state had effective control of the military or paramilitary operations in the course of which the alleged violations were committed.[56]

This ambitious test of 'effective control' would certainly not have been met by Afghanistan in relation to Al-Qaeda's attack in 2001,[57] and is even less likely to be

[51] Christian Selter, *Gewaltanwendung unter und neben der UN-Charta*, Berlin, Duncker & Humblot, 2007, p. 122; van Essen, '*De facto* regimes', cited in note 47 above, pp. 37–8; Frowein, '*De facto* regime', cited in note 47 above, paras 4–5.

[52] Peterke, 'Völkerrechtliche Selbstverteidigung', cited in note 27 above, p. 208.

[53] For the case of Rio de Janeiro, see Sven Peterke, *Rio de Janeiros 'Drogenkrieg' im Lichte der Konfliktforschung und des Völkerrechts: Eine Fallstudie zur Behandlung organisierter bewaffneter Gewalt*, Berlin, Berliner Wissenschafts-Verlag, 2009, p. 5ff. Steven Haines observes that drug gangs in Mexico 'are in effective control of significant areas of territory and pursue "dual sovereignty"': see Steven Haines, 'The nature of war and the character of contemporary armed conflict', in Elizabeth Wilmshurst (ed.), *International Law and the Classification of Conflicts*, Oxford, OUP, 2012, pp. 25–6.

[54] Peterke, 'Völkerrechtliche Selbstverteidigung', cited in note 27 above, p. 208.

[55] Ibid, p. 208. [56] *Nicaragua*, cited in note 18 above, para. 115.

[57] Michael N. Schmitt, *Essays on Law and War at the Fault Lines*, The Hague, T. M. C. Asser Press, 2012, p. 77; Vincent-Joël Proulx, *Transnational Terrorism and State Accountability: A New Theory of*

satisfied in the cases of most organised criminal groups. These groups are typically not (effectively) controlled by a state, but rather are often in conflict with that state's domestic legal system.

The Appeals Chamber of the International Criminal Tribunal for the Former Yugoslavia (ICTY) established an alternative test for attributing state responsibility for group action (the 'overall control' test), thereby disagreeing explicitly with the ICJ's 'effective control' approach.[58] It argued in the *Tadić* case that '[f]or the attribution to a state of acts of … groups it is sufficient to require that the group as a whole [is] under the overall control of the state'.[59]

To establish such responsibility, it must thus be shown that a state holds overall control over the respective group not only through equipping and financing, but also by coordinating or helping to plan its military activity.[60] Whether or not the group's activities are specifically imposed, requested, or directed by the state would, however, be irrelevant for the establishment of state responsibility under the 'overall control' test.[61]

This approach indeed broadens the scope of acts for which states are held responsible.[62] The ICJ commented in its *Bosnian Genocide* judgment that the ICTY's approach even broadens the scope of state responsibility 'well beyond the fundamental principle governing the law of international responsibility' and rejected this approach altogether.[63] It has equally been rejected by most scholars.[64]

When, nevertheless, applying this alternative test to the case of organised criminal groups, one has to conclude that in most cases states do not even hold 'overall control' over organised criminal groups. Again, this is mainly because such groups find themselves regularly in conflict with the legal system of the state from which they operate. In most cases they do not cooperate with these states, but are, at most, tolerated by the respective governments that often find themselves incapable (rather than unwilling) to address the problem.

States that sought military action against Afghanistan following the attack of 11 September 2011 promoted a third approach, the 'safe haven' doctrine.[65] This doctrine,

Prevention, Oxford, Hart, 2012, pp. 48–9; James Crawford, *State Responsibility: The General Part*, Cambridge, CUP, 2013, p. 156.

[58] *Prosecutor v Duško Tadić*, Appeals Judgment, (1999) 38 *ILM* 1518, paras 115ff. ('the Appeals Chamber, with respect, does not hold the *Nicaragua* test to be persuasive'). The third very prominent test is that one of 'effective overall control' that the European Court of Human Rights employs, most prominently in *Loizidou v Turkey*, App No. 15318/89 (Preliminary Objections), (1995) ECHR Ser. A, No. 310, para. 56. It is not discussed separately here, as first it is rather similar to the 'overall control' test of the ICTY and second it has not received much support from other courts or scholars.

[59] *Prosecutor v Duško Tadić*, cited in note 58 above, para. 120.

[60] Ibid, para. 131.

[61] Ibid, para. 122.

[62] Antonio Cassese, 'The *Nicaragua* and *Tadić* tests revisited in light of the ICJ judgment on genocide in Bosnia', (2007) 18 *EJIL* (4), 649.

[63] *Application of the Convention on the Prevention and Punishment of the Crime of Genocide (Bosnia and Herzegovina v Serbia and Montenegro)*, [2007] ICJ Rep. 43, para. 406.

[64] Out of many, Marko Milanovic, *Extraterritorial Application of Human Rights Treaties: Law, Principles, and Policy*, Oxford, OUP, 2011, p. 48. For a fervent defence of the 'overall control' approach, see Cassese, 'The *Nicaragua* and *Tadić* tests revisited', cited in note 62 above. For a more nuanced approach, see Stefan Talmon, 'The responsibility of outside powers for acts of secessionist entities', (2009) 58 *ICLQ* (3), 493.

[65] Sonja Cenic, 'State responsibility and self-defence in international law post 9/11: has the scope of Article 51 of the United Nations Charter been widened as a result of the US response to 9/11?', (2007) 14 *Australian International Law Journal*, 201, pp. 208–16; Helmut Philipp Aust, 'The normative environment

in quite clear contrast to the ICJ's *Nicaragua* decision and the ICTY's *Tadić* judgment, finds the fact that a state harbours a group sufficient to hold that state liable for the group's activities. Thus, a state would already be liable for a group's action, if it has in one way or another supported that group's criminal activities at home and has merely hosted the group on its territory.[66] It goes much further even than the 'overall control' approach of the ICTY.

Some scholars have argued that a new state practice has arisen in reaction to the attacks of 11 September 2001 to support this 'safe haven' doctrine.[67] However, in truth, it appears that there is clearly insufficient evidence of state practice and *opinio juris* to assume such a new custom. Given this finding, the ICJ is unlikely to follow this line of argument and lower its previously established and repeatedly confirmed threshold for creating state responsibility for groups operating out of their territory. Another significant problem with this approach is that its potential for abuse is high. The 'safe haven' doctrine is also very unlikely to be supported by states when determining responsibility for international criminal activity. In that regard, the 'war on terror' following the attacks of 11 September 2001 must be considered as a unique situation. A new custom (which would additionally be a form of 'instant' custom that the ICJ has previously ruled out)[68] should not be assumed.

Thus, we have found that in most cases both approaches suggested by international courts—the 'effective control' test by the ICJ and the 'overall control' test by the ICTY—would fail to attach responsibility to the state from the territory or jurisdiction of which the criminal activity emanates. The 'safe haven' doctrine, on the contrary, would in many instances be sufficient to hold states responsible for criminal activity originating from their territory or jurisdiction. However, this doctrine does not currently form part of customary international law.

17.4.3 Organised criminal groups as new subjects of international law

One can also consider the direct responsibility of the criminal group under international law.[69] This line of argument is less common than the previously introduced one as it not only alters the parameters of state responsibility attached to an existing subject of international law, but also suggests in some ways criminal organised groups to be new (partial) subjects of that legal order.

for peace—on the contribution of the ILC's Articles on State Responsibility' in Georg Nolte (ed.), *Peace through International Law: The Role of the International Law Commission*, Dordrecht, Springer, 2009, pp. 41–3.

[66] Michael Byers, 'Terrorism, the use of force and international law after 11 September 2001', (2002) 51 *ICLQ* (2), 401, p. 409; Rüdiger Wolfrum, 'The attack of September 11, 2001, the wars against the Taliban and Iraq: is there a need to reconsider international law on the recourse to force and the rules in armed conflict?' (2003) 7 *Max Planck Yearbook of UN Law*, 1, p. 34.

[67] Benjamin Langille, 'It's "instant custom": how the Bush Doctrine became law after the terrorist attacks of September 11, 2001', (2003) 26 *Boston College International Comparative Law Review* (1), 145.

[68] *Nicaragua*, cited in note 18 above, para. 97. But see Bin Cheng, 'United Nations Resolutions on outer space: "instant" international customary law', (1965) 5 *Indian Journal of International Law*, 23.

[69] Ruth Wedgewood, 'Responding to terrorism: the strikes against bin Laden', (1999) 24 *Yale Journal of International Law* (2), 559, p. 564; T. M. Franck, 'Terrorism and the right to self-defense', (2001) 95 *AJIL* (4), 839, p. 840.

While the potential for misuse of this approach through state interventionism is not negligible,[70] and while in practice it might be difficult to hold organised criminal groups liable for their potential violations of international law given that they operate largely 'from the underground',[71] there are significant reasons that speak in favour of such an approach.

The anchor of this approach is rooted in the wording of the UNC itself. While Article 2(4) UNC explicitly addresses states,[72] Article 51 UNC is more openly phrased. It allows states a right to self-defence 'if an armed attack occurs against a Member of the United Nations'. The UNC, when using the term 'occurs', is thus neutral as to the possible source of such an armed attack.[73] The Charter only specifies that the armed attack must be directed against a member state of the UN. It does not equally establish that the initiator of that armed attack has to be also a member state.

This line of argument creates another interesting legal fact: if one assumes that armed attacks can also be launched by non-state actors, this means in turn that violations of the prohibition on the use of force (Article 2(4) UNC) by non-state actors must be also possible. This is logically cogent because it is almost universally assumed that all armed attacks constitute at the same time a 'use of force'. This assumption, however, cannot be squared with the clear wording of Article 2(4) UNC, which states that 'all Members' shall refrain from the threat or use of force. Article 2(4) UNC is thus exclusively addressed to states; it cannot cover the use of force by non-state actors. If every armed attack is simultaneously a use of force, this can only be true in the case of non-state actors if one includes the customary norm of the prohibition on the use of force. In other words, while it may be true that all cases of an armed attack constitute at the same time a use of force, it is not true that all cases under Article 51 UNC are at the same time cases under Article 2(4) UNC. Violent criminal activity can be subsumed under Article 51 UNC, while remaining excluded from Article 2(4) UNC—owing to the latter's more restrictive wording.

What is more, Article 51 UNC refers to a state's 'inherent' right to self-defence. This should be understood to signify the right's parallel existence in customary international law.[74] Even if one understood Article 51 UNC to be restricted to armed attacks by states—for which the wording of the Article gives no reason—this customary right could include a right to self-defence also against attacks by non-state actors.

Some authors assume that such a customary right to self-defence against non-state actors pre-dates the UNC system.[75] The most prominent example would be the famous *Caroline* affair of the mid-nineteenth century, well before the establishment of the UN: after the destruction by British forces of the US-owned steamboat *Caroline*,

[70] Peterke, 'Völkerrechtliche Selbstverteidigung', cited in note 27 above, p. 207.

[71] Oliver Dörr, 'Gewalt und Gewaltverbot im modernen Völkerrecht', (2004) 43 *Aus Politik und Zeitgeschichte*, 14, p. 16; Peterke, 'Völkerrechtliche Selbstverteidigung', cited in note 27 above, p. 207.

[72] Art. 2(4) UNC addresses '[a]ll Members' and thereby only states, as only states may become members of the UN; cf. Art. 4(1) UNC.

[73] Peterke, 'Völkerrechtliche Selbstverteidigung', cited in note 27 above, p. 207.

[74] *Nicaragua*, cited in note 18 above, para. 193; Albrecht Randelzhofer and Georg Nolte, 'Article 51' in Simma *et al.*, *The Charter of the United Nations*, cited in note 25 above, Vol. 2, para. 63.

[75] Raphaël van Steenberghe, 'Self-defence in response to attacks by non-state actors in the light of recent state practice: a step forward?', (2010) 23 *LJIL* (1), 183, p. 198.

which was used by Canadian rebels for smuggling weapons, US Secretary of State Daniel Webster argued that pre-emptive self-defence was possible if 'the necessity of that self-defence is instant, overwhelming, and leaving no choice of means, and no moment of deliberation'.[76] This standard, later on referred to as the '*Caroline* test', is considered to reflect customary law.[77] The ICJ later on added in its *Nicaragua* decision that 'self-defence would warrant only measures which are proportional to the armed attack and necessary to respond to it'.[78] Other authors have argued that even if such a right of self-defence might not have existed at the time of the creation of the UN system in 1945, it has arisen in the meantime as part of customary international law.[79]

Some authors have also pointed out that the ICJ has not explicitly positioned itself against an approach to broaden the addressees of Article 51 UNC.[80] This is different from the case of lowering the criteria for state responsibility where the Court has explicitly refused to adopt the ICTY's 'overall control' test and insisted on its own formula of 'effective control'. Instead, in its 2005 judgment in the *Armed Activities on the Territory of the Congo* case, the ICJ left the question of a right of self-defence against non-state actors explicitly open,[81] although the case presented a prime opportunity to clarify this highly contested issue.

In separate opinions—for instance in the aforementioned case of 2005—some judges of the ICJ have supported an approach to broaden the scope of the addresses of international law and, while concurring with the Court's eventual finding, criticized the Court for having evaded this highly important question.[82] The judges, Pieter Hendrik Kooijmans and Bruno Simma, both expressed regret that the ICJ 'missed a chance to fine-tune the position it took 20 years ago' in the *Nicaragua* case.[83] Kooijmans argued in his separate opinion that armed attacks carried out by non-state actors 'are still armed attacks even if they cannot be attributed to the territorial state. It would be unreasonable to deny the attacked state the right to self-defence merely because there is no attacker state, and the [UN] Charter does not so require.'[84] Kooijmans had

[76] Letter from Daniel Webster to Henry Stephen Fox (24 April 1841), available at: http://avalon.law.yale.edu/19th_century/br-1842d.asp, accessed 16 July 2015.

[77] Cf. David Kretzmer, 'The inherent right to self-defence and proportionality in "*jus ad bellum*"', (2013) 24 *EJIL* (1), 235, pp. 247–50. See, also on the difference between pre-emptive and preventive self-defence in the case of the 2003 invasion of Iraq, John F. Murphy, 'Is US adherence to the rule of law in international affairs feasible?', in Michael N. Schmitt and Jelena Pejic (eds), *International Law and Armed Conflict: Exploring the Faultlines. Essays in Honour of Yoram Dinstein*, Leiden/Boston, Martinus Nijhoff Publishers, 2007, pp. 207–8.

[78] *Nicaragua*, cited in note 18 above, para. 176.

[79] Claus Kreß, 'Die Rettungsoperation der Bundeswehr in Albanien am 14. März 1997 aus völker- und verfassungsrechtlicher Sicht', (1997) 57 *Zeitschrift für ausländisches öffentliches Recht und Völkerrecht*, 329, p. 346.

[80] Kimberley N. Trapp, 'Back to basics: necessity, proportionality, and the right of self-defence against non-state terrorist actors', (2007) 56 *ICLQ* (1), 141, p. 142; Peterke, 'Völkerrechtliche Selbstverteidigung', cited in note 27 above, p. 207.

[81] *Armed Activities on the Territory of the Congo (Democratic Republic of the Congo v Uganda)*, Judgment [2005] ICJ Rep. 168, para. 147: 'accordingly, the Court has no need to respond to the contentions of the Parties as to whether and under what conditions contemporary international law provides for a right of self-defence against large-scale attacks by irregular forces'.

[82] Ibid, Separate Opinion of Judge Pieter Hendrik Kooijmans [2005] ICJ Rep. 306, pp. 312–15; and Separate Opinion of Judge Bruno Simma [2005] ICJ Rep. 334, pp. 335–8.

[83] Ibid, Kooijmans, para. 25; and ibid, Simma, para. 8.

[84] Ibid, Kooijmans, para. 30.

already emphasized in his separate opinion to the ICJ's *Advisory Opinion on the Legal Consequences of the Construction of a Wall in the Occupied Palestinian Territory* in 2004 that Article 51 UNC 'conditions the exercise of the inherent right to self-defence on a previous armed attack without saying that this armed attack must come from another state even if this has been the generally accepted interpretation for more than 50 years'.[85]

Bruno Simma adds in his separate opinion to the *Armed Activities on the Territory of the Congo* case that the international community, including the UN Security Council,[86] accepted in the aftermath of the attacks on 11 September 2001 that 'large-scale attacks by non-state actors can qualify as "armed attacks" within the meaning of Article 51 [UNC]'.[87] In Resolutions 1368 of 12 September 2001 and 1373 of 28 September 2001, the Security Council recognized—as Koojimans puts it—'the inherent right of individual or collective self-defence without making any reference to an armed attack by a state. In these Resolutions the Council called acts of international terrorism, without any further qualification and without ascribing them to a particular state, a threat to international peace and security.'[88]

The logic of this line of argument is irresistible. There is no state practice standing against an interpretation of Article 51 UNC that includes armed attacks of non-state actors on the contrary; from the *Caroline* affair in the mid-nineteenth century to the attacks of 11 September 2001, states have always claimed for themselves a right to self-defence against non-state military action. This is by no means a surprise given that the physical effects the attacked state experiences are often the same regardless of whether the attack is carried out by another state or by a non-state actor such as a terrorist or organised criminal group. In some cases, attacks by non-state actors might even have worse effects, as these groups operate underground and often act particularly perfidiously, disregarding even the basic laws of armed conflict. Of course, the state the territory of which is targeted by the criminal group will often suffer a non-negligible infringement of its sovereignty. In many cases, however, states might even give their consent and regard the stroke of self-defence as a welcome help in fighting organised crime in their own territory. While the risk of abuse for state activism is not deniable, it can be sufficiently addressed by strictly applying the measures of necessity and proportionality when assessing the legality of self-defence. In that way, if we compare two possible actions—an attack on the government's headquarters in order to create regime change, and where measures of self-defence target the bases of organised criminal groups and are carried out after notifying the government concerned of the planned attack—the second action is much more likely to meet the test of necessity and proportionality than ever would the first.

[85] *Legal Consequences of the Construction of a Wall in the Occupied Palestinian Territory*, Separate Opinion of Judge P. H. Kooijmans [2004] ICJ Rep. 219, para. 35, repeated in *Armed Activities*, cited in note 82 above, Kooijmans, para. 28.

[86] Both, Kooijmans and Simma, refer to UN SC Res. 1368, 12 September 2001, UN Doc. S/RES/1368; and UN SC Res. 1373, 28 September 2001, UN Doc. S/RES/1373.

[87] *Armed Activities*, cited in note 82 above, Simma, para. 11.

[88] *Armed Activities*, cited in note 82 above, Kooijmans, para. 28.

In 2015 the UNC celebrated its 70th birthday. It has not lost any of its relevance, and, in most parts, still presents adequate solutions for the world's most pressing problems. Some of these problems, however, were not sufficiently foreseen in 1945. Amongst them is the dimension that transnational organised crime would take in the twenty-first century. Where the wording allows it, the Charter should be understood in a way to best address the problems of the present, not the problems of the past. Article 51 UNC is a prime example of such an open-worded norm. It allows for a contemporary interpretation that includes armed attacks by non-state actors such as organised criminal groups. This approach serves best the overall purpose of the Charter, namely the maintenance of international peace and security against threats that look different today from how they appeared in 1945.

17.5 Transnational Organised Crime and the Security Council

The previous part of this chapter dealt with the possibility of justifying the use of force against organised criminal groups by the means of self-defence. A second way of justifying the use of force against organised criminal groups is to seek such justification through the Security Council.

17.5.1 Limitations of competence when dealing with transnational organised crime

Following Article 39 of the UNC, the Security Council can act under Chapter VII if it finds a threat to the peace, a breach of the peace, or an act of aggression. In most cases, the Council limits itself to establishing whether a 'threat to the peace' has been made.[89] This way, it does not have to identify an 'aggressor' or prove that the peace has already been broken (rather than only threatened, which is much easier to show). The Charter's preamble, Article 24 UNC, and the second part of Article 39 UNC emphasize that the Council's primary responsibility lies in the maintenance and restoring of *international* peace and security. Purely internal conflicts are exempted from its competence. This is coherent, given that Article 2(4) UNC also only applies to inter-state affairs, which clarifies that states are not allowed to use force 'in their international relations' against 'the territorial integrity or political independence of any state'. In other words, a state's *domaine réservé* is to remain sacrosanct from the Council's grasp.[90]

Deviating from this original concept of the Charter, the Council has given its own task under Article 39 UNC a much more extensive interpretation over the course of recent years. It has also addressed several (rather clear-cut) internal conflicts in which

[89] Nico Krisch, 'Article 39', in Simma *et al.*, *The Charter of the United Nations*, cited in note 25 above, p. 1278; Christine Gray, 'The use of force and the international legal order', in Malcom D. Evans (ed.), *International Law*, 4th edn, Oxford, OUP, 2014, p. 634; Malcolm N. Shaw, *International Law*, 7th edn, Cambridge, CUP, 2014, pp. 898–9.

[90] Jochen A. Frowein, 'Article 39', in Bruno Simma and Hermann Mosler (eds), *The Charter of the United Nations: A Commentary*, 1st edn, Oxford, OUP, 1994, pp. 608–9.

it deemed its own involvement necessary.[91] This 'activism'[92] of the Council was not met with enthusiasm, with some observers claiming that the Council at times overstepped its own competence.[93]

One indeed has to be careful to accept ever-expanding competences for the Security Council in order to safeguard its political acceptance and legitimacy in the eyes of the UN member states. It is thus important to emphasize that the Security Council is not omni-competent for all kinds of intra-state criminal activity that reach a particular severity. The competence of the Council is only given for cases of *transnational* organised crime.

Exceptions to this rule can only be assumed, if at all, where national organised crime causes particularly serious human rights violations. Under Article 55(c) UNC, the UN promotes universal respect for human rights and fundamental freedoms. Today, this must be considered as one of the UN's prime *raisons d'être*. In exceptional circumstances, gross human rights violations have been considered as amounting to a threat to international peace and security, thus to triggering the competence of the Security Council under Article 39 UNC.[94] This is so because human rights create so-called obligations *erga omnes*,[95] i.e. obligations that exist not only towards a state's own people, but towards the international community as a whole. Owing to the increasing importance of human rights, the *domaine réservé* of states is shrinking;[96] it ends where particularly serious human rights violations occur, be they through positive state action or through persistent state inaction against violence caused by organised criminal groups. However, the Council's competence to address human rights violations has been assumed only in truly exceptional circumstances in the past—such as genocide or crimes against humanity. This threshold is reached only rarely through transnational organised crime. But in light of recent developments—in particular the recent cruel practice of mass human smuggling—one might certainly assume that the threshold can indeed *be* reached.

[91] Michael Wood, 'United Nations, Security Council', last updated July 2007, in Wolfrum, *Max Planck Encyclopedia of Public International Law*, cited in note 16 above, para. 26, available at: http://opil.ouplaw.com/view/10.1093/law:epil/9780199231690/law-9780199231690-e561?rskey=vL1T1x&result=1&prd=EPIL, accessed 15 July 2015; Georg Nolte, 'Article 2(7)' in Simma *et al.*, *The Charter of the United Nations*, cited in note 25 above, p. 301; Gray, 'The use of force', cited in note 89 above; Shaw, *International Law*, cited in note 89 above, pp. 889–91.

[92] E.g. Alexandra Knight, 'Global environmental threats: can the Security Council protect our earth?', (2005) 80 *NYULR* (5), 1549, p. 1566.

[93] In favour of such extended competence: *Prosecutor v Duško Tadić*, Establishment of the International Tribunal, (1996) 35 *ILM* 32, p. 43; Nolte, 'Article 2(7)' cited in note 91 above, p. 301; critical of such extension: Frowein, 'Article 39', cited in note 90 above, p. 609; Björn Elberling, 'The *ultra vires* character of legislative action by the Security Council', (2005) 2 *International Organizations Law Review* (2), 337.

[94] Most importantly UN SC Res. 688, 5 April 1999, UN Doc. S/RES/0688. On this issue, out of many, see Antonio Cassese, *International Law*, 2nd edn, Oxford, OUP, 2005, pp. 347–8.

[95] *Barcelona Traction, Light and Power Company, Limited (Belgium v Spain)*, Judgment [1970] ICJ Rep. 3, para. 33. See, e.g. Maurizio Ragazzi, *The Concept of International Obligations Erga Omnes*, Oxford, Clarendon Press, 2000.

[96] Katja S. Ziegler, 'Domaine réservé', last updated April 2013, in Wolfrum, *Max Planck Encyclopedia of Public International Law*, cited in note 16 above, paras 30–2, available at: http://opil.ouplaw.com/search?sfam=&q=Domaine+r%C3%A9serv%C3%A9&prd=EPIL&searchBtn=Search, accessed 1 September 2015; Andreas von Arnauld, *Völkerrecht*, 2nd edn, Heidelberg, C. F. Müller, 2014, p. 148.

A second legal concern regarding the Council's competence lies in the fact that at the bottom of the phenomenon of transnational organised crime are not states, but organised criminal groups. The Security Council was designed, however, to be a platform to solve inter-state problems—problems like the ones of transnational organised crime were not the reason why the Council was created in 1945.

Nonetheless, in a similar manner to what has been argued before with regard to Article 51 UNC, one must note here the wording of Articles 39 and 42 UNC. Article 39 UNC tasks the Council to determine 'the existence of any threat to the peace, breach of the peace, or act of aggression' and to 'make recommendations, or decide what measures shall be taken … to maintain or restore international peace and security'. Article 42 UNC states that the Security Council 'may take … action as may be necessary to maintain or restore international peace and security'. Neither Article suggests that such threat to international peace and security must be caused by state action. The wording, just as in Article 51 UNC for the case of an armed attack, is open as to what causes the threat to international peace and security. There is, in fact, a tendency to increasingly understand transnational organised crime as just such a threat to international peace and security.[97]

17.5.2 Practice of the Security Council

In its 2004 report, the UN's High-Level Panel on Threats, Challenges, and Change identified particularly urgent threats for international peace and security, amongst them transnational organised crime,[98] addressing in particular the need for improved international regulatory frameworks and better capacity building by states. Consequently, over the last decade, the Security Council's involvement with transnational organised crime has steadily increased: while the year 2004 saw only one Resolution and one Presidential statement by the Security Council referencing organised crime, the year 2014 was marked by more than thirty of such Resolutions and Presidential statements of the Council.[99]

The Resolutions and statements by the Security Council can be classified in three categories: some addressing transnational organised crime or aspects of it in a general manner; some targeting a concrete threat posed in a specific region; and some giving UN peacekeeping or peacebuilding forces the explicit mandate to deal with transnational organised crime.

As for the first category, in February 2010 the Security Council discussed organised crime as a threat to international peace and security in a general manner. The

[97] Peterke, 'Völkerrechtliche Selbstverteidigung', cited in note 27 above, p. 215.

[98] UN High-level Panel on Threats, Challenges and Change, 'A more secure world: our shared responsibility', New York, UN, 2004, paras 165–77.

[99] The Global Initiative against Transnational Organized Crime, 'Reinforcing multilateral approaches to transnational organized crime by strengthening local ownership and accountability', 2015, p. 3, available at: http://www.globalinitiative.net/download/global-initiative/Global%20Initiative%20-%20Input%20to%20the%20High%20Level%20Panel%20on%20Peacekeeping%20Operations%20-%20Feb%202015.pdf, accessed 31 August 2015. Given this long list, I will focus in the following only on some particularly important Resolutions and use a few to exemplify the practice of the Security Council.

President, on behalf of the Council, noted in his statement the serious and growing threat posed by transnational organised crime to international security in different regions of the world.[100] The statement further requested the UN Secretary-General to consider transnational organised crime in his strategies of conflict prevention and analysis and when planning and assessing UN missions.[101] In December 2014, the Security Council emphasized the special connection between transnational organised crime and terrorism and urged that the link between the two be broken. In particular, the Council expressed concern about terrorists benefiting from transnational organised crime in some regions, including from the trafficking of arms, persons, drugs, and artefacts, from the illicit trade in natural resources, and from kidnapping for ransom and other crimes including extortion and bank robbery.[102]

In some other Resolutions, the Council focused on specific regions being particularly affected by transnational organised crime. For instance, in 2012 the President, on behalf of the Security Council, warned against the influence of transnational organised crime in Western Africa.[103] The Council expressed concern about the serious threats transnational organised crime posed to international peace and stability in West Africa and the Sahel Region. These threats contributed to undermining governance, social and economic development, and stability in the region, so it was argued, making the delivery of humanitarian assistance difficult and threatening to reverse peacebuilding advances in the region.[104]

With regard to peacekeeping and peacebuilding missions, one must assert that an increasing number of these are given the particular task of combating transnational organised crime within their mandate. After having previously encouraged Guinea-Bissau's government to fully implement the UN Programme of Action to Prevent, Combat, and Eradicate the Illicit Trade in Small Arms and Light Weapons in All Its Aspects,[105] the Council explicitly tasked the UN Integrated Peacebuilding Office in Guinea-Bissau [group] to assist national authorities to fight organised crime.[106] In Haiti, the UN Stabilization Mission was mandated in 2006 to assist the authorities in initiatives to strengthen the rule of law and to provide employment opportunities for former gang members.[107]

Seen together, such initiatives show that the Security Council has started to comprehensively address the problem of transnational organised crime: on a universal level; for specific regions; and when mandating peacebuilding missions. The role of the Security Council in contributing to the fight against transnational organised crime can thus be considered twofold. The Council, like the UN as a whole, must first help to define the problem better, since the contours of the phenomenon of transnational

[100] UN SC, Statement by the President of the Security Council, 24 February 2010, UN Doc. S/PRST/2010/4, para. 2.

[101] Ibid, para. 13.

[102] UN SC Res. 2195, 19 December 2014, UN Doc. S/RES/2195, preamble, para. 7.

[103] UN SC, Statement by the President of the Security Council, 21 February 2012, UN Doc. S/PRST/2012/2.

[104] Ibid, para. 2.

[105] UN SC Res. 1580, 22 December 2004, UN Doc. S/RES/1580, para. 2(f).

[106] UN SC Res. 1876, 26 June 2009, UN Doc. S/RES/1876, para. 3(f).

[107] UN SC Res. 1702, 15 August 2006, UN Doc. S/RES/1702, para. 11.

organised crime are still contested. It must then identify concrete steps and approaches to fight transnational organised crime,[108] as many of them can only be found on the international plane. As always, the Security Council can only be as successful in this endeavour as its members, in particular those with veto power, allow it to be.

17.6 Conclusion

The phenomenon of transnational organised crime does not sit easily with international law. The main reason for this is that the international legal order—including the prohibition on the use of force—was created as a legal relationship between states. In many ways this order is not sufficiently equipped for addressing problems that non-state actors, such as organised criminal groups, pose today.

I have highlighted in this chapter the two main ways military strikes against organised criminal groups can be justified. I have not expressed an opinion whether further unwritten exceptions, including a 'humanitarian' intervention, might also exist or not. If one assumes this to be the case, one can certainly consider whether recent, ruthless forms of transnational organised crime, including the mass smuggling of (illegal) immigrants by organised gangs condoning the death of the transported people in large numbers, reaches the severity of gross human rights violations sufficient to trigger such an exceptional use of force via the means of humanitarian intervention.

A more accepted way of justifying the use of force is self-defence (Article 51 UNC). Owing to the open wording of Article 51 UNC, I have argued that organised criminal groups can commit 'armed attacks' (just like states) and thus trigger the right to self-defence by another state. This makes them indeed partial subjects of the international legal order. Of course, the high threshold of what constitutes an 'armed attack' must be met before triggering such an exceptional right to self-defence. Additionally, the act of self-defence itself must meet the strict measures of necessity and proportionality—which are two important safeguards to prevent the abuse of that right, including the right to pre-emptive self-defence, in the future.

The second option justifying military strikes against organised criminal groups in another country is to seek permission to use that force via the means of a Security Council Resolution (Articles 39 and 42 UNC). The Security Council is not supposed to deal with issues surrounding national security, but rather to focus on international matters. For this reason, not every criminal activity that reaches a certain severity within a state is automatically a case for the Security Council. *Transnational* organised crime, however, always is. Furthermore, Articles 39 and 42 UNC do not require that such a threat to international peace and security must be caused by state action. Consequently, the Council has already dealt with transnational organised crime in the past, as a threat to international peace and security. It has done so not only on a case-by-case basis, but also addressed the problem as a whole (trying to help to further define the contours of the phenomenon). Additionally, in certain Resolutions it has focused on specific regions and mandated UN peacebuilding missions to assist national

[108] Fijnaut, 'Transnational crime and the role of the United Nations', cited in note 27 above, p. 126.

authorities in their fight against organised crime (attempting to offer concrete solutions for specific regions). Given the increasing importance of the topic, the Security Council would indeed be well advised to continue to put transnational organised crime on its own agenda, just as it has started to do in recent years.

Altogether, this chapter has shown that the use of force against organised criminal groups can be justified, either by relying on states' right to self-defence or by turning to the UN Security Council and seeking its action under Chapter VII of the UNC. If they make use of these two options, states are not after all quite so ill-equipped in their fight against transnational organised crime as is sometimes assumed.

18

International Humanitarian Law and Transnational Organised Crime

Sven Peterke and Joachim Wolf

18.1 Introduction

International humanitarian law (IHL), also known as the law of armed conflict, aims to mitigate human suffering in times of war.[1] It consists of principles and rules specifically designed to protect persons who do not or who no longer directly participate in the hostilities, above all, the civil population and fighters, i.e. those who are wounded, shipwrecked, sick, or detained (*hors de combat*). In addition, IHL unfolds its humanizing effects through prohibiting and restricting certain methods and means of warfare.

Historically, the process of IHL's codification began in Europe in the second half of the nineteenth century. Since then, it has been continuously developed. The most important documents are the four Geneva Conventions (GC I–IV) of 1949,[2] and the two Additional Protocols (AP I and II) of 1977.[3] They date from a time when phenomena today labelled as transnational organised crime (TOC) were not yet considered as a threat to peace and international security. However, even at the time of negotiating the GCs states expressed the concern that the violence of criminal groups could be (mis)understood as triggering the applicability of the law of non-international armed conflict.[4] As a matter of fact, no attempt has been made since 1977 to alter or extend the existing concepts of armed conflict to address the violence of non-state actors more accurately. Up to the present, there has not been a single norm in IHL that explicitly refers to the ambiguous concept of TOC.

[1] However, IHL can also be taken more narrowly or more broadly. See Robert Kolb and Richard Hyde, *An Introduction to the International Law of Armed Conflicts*, Oxford, Hart Publishing, 2008, p. 17; Gary D. Solis, *The Law of Armed Conflict. International Humanitarian Law in War*, Cambridge, CUP, 2010, p. 22.

[2] Convention (I) for the Amelioration of the Condition of the Wounded and Sick in Armed Forces in the Field, Geneva, 12 August 1949, 75 UNTS 31; Convention (II) for the Amelioration of the Condition of Wounded, Sick and Shipwrecked Members of Armed Forces at Sea, Geneva, 12 August 1949, 75 UNTS 85; Convention (III) Relative to the Treatment of Prisoners of War, Geneva, 12 August 1949, 75 UNTS 135; Convention (IV) Relative to the Protection of Civilian Persons in Time of War, Geneva, 12 August 1949, 75 UNTS 287.

[3] Protocol Additional to the Geneva Conventions of 12 August 1949, and Relating to the Protection of Victims of International Armed Conflicts (Protocol I), Geneva, 8 June 1977, 1125 UNTS 3; Protocol Additional to the Geneva Conventions of 12 August 1949, and Relating to the Protection of Victims of Non-International Armed Conflicts (Protocol II), Geneva, 8 June 1977, 1125 UNTS 609.

[4] Jean S. Pictet, *The Geneva Conventions of 12 August 1949, Commentary*, Vol. I, Geneva, ICRC, 1952, p. 49.

Despite all the hype over TOC, it is a disturbing reality in the beginning of the twenty-first century that criminal groups not only try to profit financially from armed conflicts, but take up arms against the state or rival groups if such interfere in their illicit businesses such as arms, drugs, or human trafficking. On occasion they are also contracted by parties to an armed conflict or create paramilitary units themselves. Such armed violence has become astoundingly professional, causing death and destruction that, in extreme cases, is statistically on an equal footing with international armed conflicts (IAC). Thus, it is of great importance to consider whether such hybrid groups could become parties to an armed conflict and what the consequences are should they qualify as an organised armed group under IHL. Since TOC is interwoven with war economies and the political interests of actors with a legitimate conflict status, this is a sensitive matter analysis of which is often complicated by a lack of reliable information about such alliances and settings. Consequently, this contribution can at most focus on some of the issues relating to the intersections of IHL and TOC.

18.2 Warfare as Transnational Organised Crime

It has been said that 'war making and state making—quintessential protection rackets with the advantage of legitimacy—qualify as our largest examples of organised crime'.[5] Even though some parallels could be drawn between these phenomena international doctrine tends to be extremely cautious with such statements. It takes a rather state-centric approach. With regard to organised crime, this approach is embodied in the United Nations Convention Against TOC (UNTOC) of 2000 and its three Additional Protocols.[6] These international documents criminalize certain activities as particularly serious, as well as participation in an 'organised criminal group'. Article 2(a) UNTOC defines the term as 'a structured group of three or more persons, existing for a period of time and acting in concert with the aim of committing one or more serious crimes or offences established in accordance with this Convention, in order to obtain, directly or indirectly, a financial or other material benefit'. Although this definition has suffered criticism for being too vague, it might also be considered as too narrow. The term excludes politically motivated groups, especially terrorists, whose principal activities are subjects of other international treaties.[7] Furthermore, insurgents and guerrilla fighters do not fall into the category of organised criminal groups. The same is true for mercenaries and private military and security corporations. They might be

[5] See e.g. Charles Tilly, 'War making and state making as organised crime', in Peter B. Evans *et al.* (eds), *From Bringing the State Back In*, Cambridge, CUP, 1985, p. 169.

[6] United Nations Convention Against Transnational Organized Crime, Palermo, 15 November 2000, 2225 UNTS 209; Protocol to Prevent, Suppress, and Punish Trafficking in Persons, especially Women and Children, Supplementing the United Nations Convention Against Transnational Organized Crime, Palermo, 15 November 2000, 2237 UNTS 319; Protocol against the Smuggling of Migrants by Land, Sea, and Air, Supplementing the United Nations Convention Against Transnational Organized Crime, Palermo, 15 November 2000, 2241 UNTS 507; Protocol against the Illicit Manufacturing of and Trafficking in Firearms, Their Parts and Components, and Ammunition, Supplementing the United Nations Convention Against Transnational Organized Crime, New York, 31 May 2001, 2326 UNTS 208.

[7] David McClean, *Transnational Organized Crime: A Commentary on the UN Convention and its Protocols*, Oxford, OUP, 2007, p. 40.

inspired by the prospect of making profits, yet it cannot be said that they always do so by committing serious crimes. Of course the reality is often more complex. As social phenomena, such groups undergo permanent processes of transformation in both their motivation and organisation.

It therefore could be said that the UNTOC encourages a micro-perspective that obfuscates the embeddedness of TOC in today's conflicts. If ties develop between organised crime groups and public authorities such constellations are generally appreciated by international lawyers from a state responsibility perspective. However, as will be set out later in this chapter, the standards of attribution are quite demanding. Thus it is unlikely that such a responsibility can be established in practice.

On the other hand, international law prohibits the use of force in international relations and treats the crime of aggression, together with genocide, war crimes and crimes against humanity, as macro-criminality that entails direct individual responsibility.[8] Accordingly, states have agreed upon a partial criminalization of war and its conduct. How far this will in fact deter the world's most powerful 'white-collar criminals' from resorting to the most uncivilized means remains to be seen.

IHL does not legitimize armed conflicts at all; it merely seeks to establish limits for warfare to avoid unnecessary human suffering. Nevertheless, it legalizes a series of acts of violence that are prohibited under 'normal circumstances', i.e. in peace time. In other words, states have recognized 'privileges' for themselves that are not always justified by purely humanitarian needs. Thus they have a vested interest that non-state actors should rarely benefit from these privileges.

18.3 The Legal Status of Organised Crime Groups and their Members during Armed Conflicts

The applicability of IHL to TOC can be analysed from very different angles. One option is to distinguish between the collective status of organised crime groups and the individual status of their members. With the former, the crucial point is whether and under which circumstances they could become parties to an armed conflict. One might find that criminals should never be attributed the legitimacy of a warring party, because this would imply treating them on an equal footing with states and resistance movements fighting for self-determination. It will be shown that such considerations have found their way into IHL, although states have left some 'loopholes'.

18.3.1 International armed conflicts

Codified IHL is based on a 'two box approach' that distinguishes between international and non-international armed conflicts. Despite a considerable merger of the standards of these regimes under customary law, important differences persist. For this reason, the two regimes will be discussed separately.

[8] United Nations Charter (UNC), San Francisco, 26 June 1945, UNCIO XV, 335, Art. 2 para. 4.

18.3.1.1 Organised crime groups as parties to an international armed conflict

In principle, only states can be parties to an IAC. This follows from Article 2 para. 1, common to the GC I–IV of 1949. According to this provision, the Conventions 'apply to all cases of declared war or of any other armed conflict which may arise between two or more of the High Contracting Parties, even if state of war is not recognized by them'. In addition, cases of partial or total occupation of the territory of a high contracting party are covered by the GCs, 'even if the said occupation meets no armed resistance'. So far, no one has ever dared to interpret the regime of military occupation as being applicable in cases of territorial control through transnational non-state actors. This is not to say that this might not be an interesting task.[9]

The same is true with regard to AP I of 1977, under Article 2 para. 4 of which the notion of an IAC is extended. It stipulates that the Protocol also applies to 'peoples fighting against colonial domination and alien occupation and against racist regimes in the exercise of their right to self-determination, as enshrined in the UN Charter (UNC) and the Declaration on the Principles of International Law concerning Friendly Relations and Co-operation among States'. The basic idea was to extend the status of a party to an IAC to organised resistance movements, thus submitting wars of liberation to what, in comparison with non-international armed conflicts (NIACs), is a more elaborate legal regime. An important legal consequence is that the fighting members of such movements can claim 'combatant immunity' or 'privilege': they have the 'licence to kill' other combatants within the limits of IHL without being held responsible for such acts.[10] Moreover, if captured by the adversary, combatants enjoy status of prisoners of war (PoW) as regulated in GC III. In turn, they represent legitimate objectives of military operations.[11]

One of the most fascinating facets of AP I is that its states parties recognize that the 'authorities representing a people' can unilaterally declare that they assume the rights and obligations of the GCs and the Protocol. Thereafter, they become 'equally binding upon all Parties to the conflict' (Article 96 para. 3(c)). The declaration must be sent to the depositary of the Protocol—the Swiss Federal Council—which has to verify whether the prequisites are met. The Council must examine whether there is in fact a situation as foreseen in Article 1 para. 4 AP I. The problem is that there are no clear-cut criteria that should be applied. The same is true with regard to the concept of liberation movements. So far no non-state actor has ever been recognized by the Swiss Federal Council under AP I. On the other hand, one must bear in mind that the interpretation of IHL is not static, but dynamic, so that terms such as 'colonial domination', 'alien occupation', and 'right to self-determination' may have a post-colonial meaning that originally was not assigned to them.[12]

It was certainly not the intention of states to authorize leaders of transnational criminal organisations to unilaterally 'upgrade' their status to that of a party to an IAC.

[9] See, however, the reflections of Sandesh Sivakumaran, *The Law of Non-International Armed Conflict*, Oxford, OUP, 2012, pp. 529–32.

[10] AP I, cited in note 3 above, Art. 43 para. 2.

[11] Ibid, Art. 48.

[12] Christopher Greenwood, 'Scope of application of humanitarian law', in Dieter Fleck (ed.), *The Handbook of International Humanitarian Law*, 2nd edn, Oxford/New York, OUP, 2008, para. 202.4.

Nor are there currently any attempts to do this, although some particularly powerful drug cartels or other mafia-like entities have declared and, to some extent, waged 'war' against a state.

Such organisations usually avail themselves of a kind of pseudo-ideology to gain support and legitimacy among the population under their control. Pablo Escobar, the famous leader of the Medellín cartel who declared 'war' against the government in Bogotá in 1989, claimed that his drugs, exported to the USA, would help to fight the hated 'imperialistic hegemon' and that the Colombian people would profit from his 'narco dollars'. This legend was relatively easy to decode. This point is, however, that there are many hybrid organisations such as the Fuerzas Armadas Revolucionarias de Columbia (FARC) in which criminal activities, such as drug trafficking and extortion, are launched with an anti-capitalistic surface, claiming that colonialism's basic features still persist. This point of view is shared by critical approaches to international law that oppose the formalist narrative of decolonization that succeeded in the UN.[13]

As a matter of fact, the FARC considers itself a liberation movement. Hence, the problem outlined here may become relevant in the future when groups generally classified as 'criminal' or 'terrorist organisations' take up arms against (supposedly) oppressive governments and dare to send a corresponding declaration to the Swiss Federal Council. Some states are aware of this—in their opinion—'dangerous loophole' and have therefore submitted reservations or interpreting declarations to AP I. In this spirit, the United Kingdom has declared that

> the term 'armed conflict' of itself and in its context denotes a situation of a kind which is not constituted by commission of ordinary crimes including acts of terrorism whether concerted or in isolation. The United Kingdom will not, in relation to any situation in which it is itself involved, consider itself bound in consequence of any declaration purporting to be made under paragraph 3 of Article 96 unless the United Kingdom shall have expressly recognised that it has been made by a body which is genuinely an authority representing a people engaged in an armed conflict of the type to which Article 1, paragraph 4, applies.[14]

Other states, like the USA and Israel, have abstained from ratifying the Protocol.

Under international law, 'declarations of war' by non-state actors have no legal significance. Conversely, if governments officially declare war on non-state actors such as drug trafficking organisations, it cannot be categorically excluded that this has no legal effect at all. In general, such a declaration of war is merely rhetorical and serves as political propaganda. Nonetheless, states are free to recognize insurgents as belligerents. Such recognition would trigger the applicability of the law of IAC. This means that, in theory, international law may come into play in cases of 'criminal insurgency/rebellion'. This would in particular be the case where there is sustained control of a certain territory by a criminal organisation that the government is not capable of

[13] This is particularly true for so-called 'third world approaches to international law'.

[14] United Kingdom of Great Britain and Northern Ireland, Declaration of 2 June 2002, available at: https://www.icrc.org/ihl/NORM/0A9E03F0F2EE757CC1256402003FB6D2?OpenDocument, accessed 1 June 2015.

dismantling, despite the help of armed forces. In practice, it is extremely unlikely that states would recognize such situations as triggering IHL. Most governments fear that this would confer political legitimacy on criminals and give them a privileged legal status under international law.

To summarize, one can conclude that organised crime groups are generally excluded from becoming party to an IAC. It is not to say, however, that this is completely impossible.

18.3.1.2 Individual status of members of organised crime groups

The law of IAC draws a distinction between combatants and civilians. The fact that organised crime groups are not parties to such conflict does not necessarily imply that their members cannot obtain the privileged status of the first category, nor that they are protected because they are civilians.

18.3.1.2.1 Combatant status

According to Article 43 AP I combatants are all regular members of the armed forces as well as of a 'paramilitary or armed law enforcement agency' provided that it was formally incorporated into the armed forces. Article 4 A No. 1 GC III extends PoW status, which derives from combatant status, to 'militias or volunteer corps forming part of such armed forces'. The requirement of a formal link with this state organ is waived in No. 2, which deals with 'members of other militias and members of other volunteer corps, including those of organised resistance movements, belonging to a Party to the conflict'. Such a factual link only results in PoW status if these groups act under a responsible command, wear a fixed distinctive sign that is recognizable at a distance, carry their arms openly and respect the laws and customs of war during their operations. The first sentence of Article 44 para. 3, AP I explains that the obligation of combatants to distinguish themselves from the civilian population applies 'while they are engaged in an attack or in a military operation preparatory to an attack'. In the following sentence, it is recognized 'that there are situations in armed conflicts where, owing to the nature of the hostilities an armed combatant cannot so distinguish himself'. Nevertheless, he may retain this status if he carries his arms openly '(a) during each military engagement, and (b) during such time as he is visible to the adversary while his is engaged in a military deployment preceding the launching of an attack in which he is to participate'.

In other words, members of organised armed groups are treated as combatants or PoWs provided that they legally or factually belong to a state party to an IAC. While the first alternative has no practical relevance, the second at least inspires some reflection on wars in which governments make use of militias and volunteer corps with a dubious reputation because of their reckless violence and involvement in TOC. These might be referred to as 'dual purpose-groups'.[15]

[15] M. Cherif Bassiouni, 'The new wars and the crisis of compliance with the law of armed conflict by non-state actors', (2008) 98 *Journal of Criminal Law and Criminology* (3), 711, p. 716.

A good example in this regard was the Serb Volunteer Guard (SVG), also known as 'Arkan Tigers'. In the 1970s and 1980s, Zeljk o Raznatovic alias 'Arkan' robbed and murdered several persons in various European countries, thus becoming one of the world's most wanted criminals. As leader of the SVG, which was formed in 1990 and consisted of nationalistic hooligans who supported the soccer team Red Star Belgrade, Arkan loved to pose with a baby tiger in his arms. Under his command, the paramilitary unit committed cruel human rights violations in Croatia and Bosnia-Herzegovina. He was accused by the International Tribunal for the former Yugoslavia (ICTY) of war crimes and crimes against humanity. However, in 2000, before the Tribunal could arrest him, he was murdered in a Belgrade hotel.[16] An important file on this 'dirty war' had to be closed.

It would amount to speculation to assume that his potential evidence would have impacted on the ICJ's findings in the *Genocide* case of 2007, in which the state responsibility of Serbia and Montenegro for this international crime was considered.[17] The ICJ dealt with the question whether the 'Tigers' and other paramilitary groups *de facto* belonged to the armed forces.[18] In the end, there was insufficient proof to establish that Serbia had *effective control* over these groups.

The 'effective control' test was first applied in the *Nicaragua* case (1986), in which the attribution of the right-wing Contras to the USA was considered.[19] The USA not only supported this paramilitary group financially, but also armed and trained them. A handbook on guerrilla warfare was handed out to them in which it was advised that '[if] possible, professional criminals will be hired to carry out specific selective "jobs"'.[20] In the end, the court was unable to determine who exactly in the Federal Bureau of Investigation was responsible for distributing the handbook. For this reason, the ICJ held that effective control over the Contras did not exist. As in the *Genocide* case of 2007, it could not attribute acts by a dubious paramilitary group to the state supporting it, although it was salient that it had been used for indirect warfare.

In the *Tadić* case, the ICTY held that 'overall control' over non-state actors would suffice, for example the existence of a relation of dependency that manifests itself in the organisation, coordination, and planning of military operations.[21] This interpretation was based on Article 4 A No. 2 GC III. With the aid of the lower standard of attribution the Tribunal could conclude that there was an international armed conflict between Serbia-Montenegro and Bosnia-Herzegovina. It is not surprising that this judgment was well received by international law experts who argued that such a standard would lead to more adequate solutions.[22] Some maintained that the ICJ had fixed a

[16] Nemanja Mladenovic, 'Transnational organised crime: the failed divorce of Serbia's government and organised crime', (2012) 66 *Journal of International Affairs* (1), 195, p. 199.

[17] *Application of the Convention on the Prevention and Punishment of the Crime of Genocide*, 26 February 2007, ICJ Rep. 2007, para. 390.

[18] Ibid, para. 400.

[19] *Case Concerning Military and Paramilitary Activities in and against Nicaragua*, Merits, Decision of 27 June 1986, ICJ Rep. 1986, para. 115.

[20] Ibid, para. 122.

[21] ICTY, *Tadić*, Case IT-94-1-A, Appeals Judgment, 15 July 1999, para. 146.

[22] See e.g. Marco Sassòli, 'State responsibility for violations of international humanitarian law', (2002) 84 *IRRC* (846), 401, p. 408.

standard of attribution for state responsibility without addressing the issue whether it also applies to determining the existence of an international armed conflict. The fact is that in 2001 the International Law Commission (ILC) incorporated the effective control criterion as a standard of attribution into the Draft Articles on the International Responsibility of States.[23]

Notwithstanding the controversy, it should always be demonstrated in each individual case that the members of an armed group meet all the requirements of Article 4 A No. 2 GC III. Where the applicability of this provision is in doubt, fighters benefit from the GC III 'until such time as their status has been determined by a competent tribunal'.[24] Of course, the combatant/PoW status does not exclude individual responsibility for war crimes or for other criminal acts that were committed outside the context of hostilities. Thus, if a party to an IAC pays mafia groups for the clandestine execution of certain orders such as assassinations of political adversaries, there is no justification for the protection of these henchmen as combatants.

18.3.1.2.2 Status as civilians

Vice versa, one might conclude that members of transnational criminal organisations have to be treated as civilians. This implies that they cannot become targets of military operations.[25] An exception is only made if the person participates directly (actively)[26] in the hostilities. The effect of such participation is not the loss of civilian status but merely of the protection afforded. Hence, treating fighting civilians as 'unprivileged combatants' and arguing that they enjoy no protection at all under IHL—as done by the USA in the context of the 'war on terrorism'—constitutes an abusive practice.[27] Even as civilians involved in serious criminality these persons have a right to humane treatment after their arrest. They benefit in particular from the 'fundamental guarantees' foreseen in Article 75 AP I, which, for example, recognizes the human rights standards of a fair trial and due process of law.

A provision that could be susceptible to misinterpretation is Article 5 para.1 GC IV. It stipulates that:

> [w]here in the territory of a Party to the conflict, the latter is satisfied that an individual protected person is definitely suspected of or engaged in activities hostile to the security of the State, such individual person shall not be entitled to claim such rights and privileges under the present Convention as would, if exercised in the favour of such individual person, be prejudicial to the security of such State.

[23] See Art. 8 of the ILC Draft Articles on Responsibility of States for Internationally Wrongful Acts, UN Doc. A/Res/56/83, 12 December 2001.

[24] GC III, cited in note 2 above, Art. 5 para. 2.

[25] For details concerning the protection conferred upon civilians during international armed conflicts, see e.g. GC IV, cited in note 2 above and AP I, Chapter VI, cited in note 3 above.

[26] The dominant position treats the two terms as synonyms: see ICTR, *Akayesu*, Case No. ICTR-96-4-T, Trial Judgment, 2 September 1998, para. 629.

[27] Knut Dörrmann, 'The legal situation of "unlawful/unprivileged" combatants', (2003) 85 *IRRC* (848), 45, p. 73.

This derogation clause may have some practical relevance on how to treat members of organised armed groups, provided that they are in the hands of a party to an IAC and qualify as 'enemy nationals'. The provision confers exceptional competences upon states under which fundamental rights could be restricted, and should be interpreted restrictively. The vagueness of crucial terms, in particular 'activities hostile to the security of the State', causes difficulties. If one looks at the following paragraph of the Article, it appears that its main purpose is to restrict the freedoms of speech and communication of spies and saboteurs, so that they can be held *incommunicado*.[28] Despite frequent objections concerning the compatibility of this measure with human rights, a number of states invoke it even in peace time to isolate very dangerous criminals, who otherwise might continue their activities from prison cells. In times of war, Article 5 para. 1 GC IV could be invoked to justify such measures. Unlike para. 2, it is not limited in its personal scope to spies and saboteurs.

The phrase 'not be entitled to claim such rights and privileges under the present Convention' is also ambiguous. Nonetheless, it is difficult to justify an interpretation that it should be permissible to use military force against persons 'suspected of or engaged in activities hostile to the security of the State'.[29] The provision deals with rights of detained individuals and cannot suspend the fundamental principle that civilians may not be the object of attacks 'unless and for such time as they take direct part in hostilities'.[30]

In the absence of a legal definition of what exactly is meant by 'direct participation in hostilities', the interpretation of this concept is controversial among states and scholars.[31] The matter is of great relevance, because a broad interpretation could serve to legitimize alarming state practices such as 'targeted killings' of defenceless terror suspects. It has been argued that international terrorists are not protected as civilians owing to their permanent readiness to take up arms.[32]

To start with, the term 'hostilities' is not precise enough: when interpreted in a narrow manner, it would only include the actual engagement in fighting; when a broader interpretation is followed, it could also cover certain preparatory operations. Nils Melzer's definition of the concept appears to be accepted in general. He defines it as follows:[33]

> [T]he concept of 'hostilities' comprises all violent and non-violent activities specifically designed to support one party to an armed conflict by directly causing harm of any quantitative degree to the military operations or military capacity of another.

[28] Yves Sandoz, Christophe Swinarski, and Bruno Zimmermann (eds), *Commentary on the Additional Protocols of 8 June 1977 to the Geneva Conventions of 12 August 1949*, Dordrecht, Martinus Nijhoff Publishers, 1987, p. 56.

[29] See Roland Otto, *Targeted Killings and International Law*, Heidelberg, Springer, 2011, p. 300.

[30] AP I, cited in note 3 above, Art. 51 para. 3.

[31] See e.g. Michael N. Schmitt, 'The interpretative guidance on the notion of direct participation in hostilities: a critical analysis', (2010) 1 *Harvard National Security Journal*, pp. 5–44.

[32] For details see David Kretzmer, 'Targeted killing of suspected terrorists: extrajudicial executions or legitimate self-defence?', (2005) 16 *EJIL* (2), 171, p. 192.

[33] Nils Melzer, *Targeted Killing in International Law*, Oxford/New York, OUP, 2008, p. 275.

Whether such support is financially or ideologically motivated is of no significance since objective criteria are applied. Hence, the activities referred to could be committed by members of organised crime groups as well. The crucial question therefore is what exactly constitutes a 'direct' participation in hostilities. The current discussion concentrates on three features that have been proposed by the International Committee of the Red Cross (ICRC) as 'constitutive elements':[34] first, the act must be likely to affect the military operations or military capacity of a party to an armed conflict, for example inflicting death or injury on combatants (threshold of harm). Second, there must be a direct causal link between the act and the harm to be expected (direct causation). Third, the act must be specifically designed to directly cause the required threshold of harm in support of a party to the conflict and to the detriment of another (belligerent nexus).

It would go beyond the limits of this chapter to discuss potential scenarios and criticism of the ICRC's proposal. It is clear, however, that the selling of illegal drugs to combatants, for example, would have a detrimental effect on their physical fighting conditions but does not qualify as direct participation in the hostilities. To quote Patrick Gallahue: '[i]t would require an absurdly broad reading of the threshold of harm to conclude that trafficking in narcotics presents such a threat to a rival party to the conflict that it makes the trafficker a legitimate target'.[35] The problem is that the US Pentagon put fifty Afghan drug traffickers who have contacts with the Taliban, as 'nexus targets', on a 'killing list' in 2009.[36] The episode illustrates how the 'war on terror' has been merged with the 'war on organised crime'. It also shows that the question of the legal status of members of organised crime groups in armed conflicts is not merely a theoretical one.

18.3.2 Non-international armed conflict

In the context of NIACs organised crime groups and their members supposedly represent a more visible and virulent problem. In general such settings are characterized by the fact that 'organised armed groups' oppose the government of a state. The ICTY held that hostilities between two organised armed groups may also qualify as NIAC.[37] This position was confirmed by the states parties to the Rome Statute of the International Criminal Court (ICC), which 'applies to armed conflicts that take place in the territory of a State when there is protracted armed

[34] ICRC, 'Interpretative guidance on the notion of direct participation in hostilities under international humanitarian law', (2009) 90 *IRRC* (872), 991, p. 995.

[35] Patrick Gallahue, 'Targeted killing of drug lords: traffickers as members of armed opposition groups and/or direct participants in hostilities', (2010) *International Journal on Human Rights and Drug Policy* 1, 15, p. 25.

[36] Report to the Committee on Foreign Relations, United States Senate, 'Afghanistan's narco war: breaking the link between drug traffickers and insurgents', 10 August 2009, Washington, DC, US Government Printing, 2009, p. 1.

[37] ICTY, *Tadić*, Case IT-94-1-AR72, Appeals Chamber Decision, 2 October 1995, para. 70: 'an armed conflict exists whenever there is a resort to armed force between States or protracted armed violence between governmental authorities and organised armed groups or between such groups'.

conflict between governmental authorities and organised armed groups or between such groups'.[38]

18.3.2.1 Organised crime groups as parties to an internal armed conflict

In contrast to Article 3 common to the GC, which represents a 'mini convention' for NIACs, under AP II states parties have avoided referring to non-state actors explicitly as parties to such a conflict. Instead, such status is paraphrased by the term 'organised armed group'. Evidently, such collectives should not be recognized as having a status under international law that would imply a degree of political legitimation, too. For this reason, there is also no combatant status available for the fighting members of organised armed groups. Such status is seen as a privilege that can be claimed only by a subject of international law.

In principle, organised crime groups only qualify as organised armed groups under IHL in exceptional circumstances. One might recall the extremely violent and highly diffuse situation in Mexico and other Latin American countries where the state's security forces—including the armed forces—become frequently involved in combat with heavily armed units of transnational criminal organisations.[39] The horrific pictures and statistics associated with these battles are often regarded as a new kind of 'civil war'.

IHL requires a more sophisticated test for qualifying such situations as NIAC. The criteria applicable are commonly divided into two elements: the intensity of the armed conflict and the organisational requirement. With regard to the former, consensus exists that the intensity has to reach a minimum threshold. What this means exactly is difficult to say. The primary function of this criterion is to exclude 'situations of internal disturbances and tensions, such as riots, isolated and sporadic acts of violence or other act of similar nature'.[40] Over the years, a series of more or less objective indicators have been developed in jurisprudence and international law doctrine that are applied on a case-by-case basis. This was necessary since the opinion of state governments involved in the armed conflict cannot be regarded as decisive for determining the existence of a NIAC. The indicators include 'the number, duration and intensity of individual confrontations; the type of weapons and other military equipment used; the number of [and] calibre of munitions fired; the number of persons and type of forces taking part in the fighting; the number of casualties; extent of material destruction; and the number of civilians fleeing combat zones'.[41] Since these criteria are neither binding nor precise, states have some leeway to decide whether the situation is an

[38] Art. 8, para. 2(f), second sentence ICC Statute, Rome, 17 July 1998, 2187 UNTS 90. This definition is generally assumed to be in line with the scope of application of Article 3 common to the GC. Anthony Cullen, 'The definition of non-international armed conflict in the Rome Statute of the International Criminal Court: An analysis of the threshold of application of Article 8(2)(f)', (2008) 12 *Journal of Conflict & Security Law* (3), pp. 419–45.

[39] See e.g. Sven Peterke, 'Urban insurgency, "drug war" and international humanitarian law: the case of Rio de Janeiro', (2010) 1 *JIHLS* (1). 165.

[40] Art. 8 para. 2(f) first sentence ICC Statute, cited in note 38 above; AP II, cited in note 3 above, Art. 1 para. 2.

[41] ICTY, *Ramush Haradinaj et al.*, Case IT-04-84-T, Trial Judgment, 3 April 2008, para. 49.

armed conflict under IHL. The situation is exacerbated by the fact that there is no international monitoring body authorized to decide within a reasonable period after the outbreak of hostilities whether this is the case. Frequently, clarity is only reached after the recognition of the NIAC by the affected state itself or by the UN Security Council. Human rights courts and the International Criminal Tribunal could also play an important role although, in practice, their opinion is often only available after the termination of the hostilities.

In organisational terms, the non-state party to the armed conflict has to meet the criteria established for identifying 'organised armed groups'. Important guidance is given by Article 1 para. 1 AP II, which codified the criteria for recognizing insurgents as belligerents once these had been developed. According to this provision, an organised armed group needs to have a responsible command structure and must exercise control over a part of the state's territory 'as to enable [it] to carry out sustained and concerted military operations and to implement this Protocol'. There is consensus among scholars that these criteria do not apply cumulatively in cases where Article 3 common to the GCs applies. In particular, the exercise of territorial control is not a prerequisite.[42]

A characteristic of a 'responsible command' appears to be the capability to impose discipline on the group.[43] Command structures comparable to those of regular armed forces are not required. However, since non-state parties to an NIAC should be capable of conducting sustained and concerted military operations, they need to be organised in a paramilitary way; otherwise they cannot openly confront the state's security forces. Criminal associations seldom preside over such structures and capabilities. Yet it must not be ignored that in some countries they have left the 'underworld' and do in fact control and defend certain territories and their populations against the state with their own 'foot soldiers'. Nevertheless, it would be difficult to attest that they have the capability to conduct military operations.

For this reason, few international law scholars would be willing to classify the situation in Mexico as NIAC despite the fact that the armed violence has reached a considerable intensity and that paramilitary criminal groups such as *Los Zetas*, a highly organised group made up of ex-members of the Mexican armed forces, are involved.[44] Whether the classification as NIAC would serve any humanitarian purpose is another controversial issue. The main problems with it are the application of a legal regime that was not designed to regulate 'wars on organised crime', which generally lack any conventional conduct of hostilities; non-state actors not interested in or not in a position to meet the most basic standards; the artificial creation of a state of exception for suspending human rights obligations; and the labelling of lawbreakers as 'public enemies' merely for political purposes, having the potential of weakening democracy and the rule of law.

[42] See e.g. Lindsay Moir, *The Law of Internal Armed Conflict*, Cambridge, CUP, 2002, p. 38.

[43] Anne-Marie La Rosa and Carolin Wuerzner, 'Armed groups, sanctions and the implementation of international humanitarian law', (2008) 90 *IRRC* (870), 327, p. 329.

[44] Cf. Carina Bergal,'The Mexican drug war: the case for a non-international armed conflict', (2011) *Fordham International Law Journal* 34, 1042 p. 1048.

18.3.2.2 *Individual status of members of organised crime groups*

Since members of organised armed groups do not enjoy any combatant privileges in NIAC, they can be prosecuted and punished without restrictions for all their criminal activities. One might criticize this legal position since it does not offer any positive incentives for non-state actors to comply with IHL. On the other hand, it is understandable that states have no motivation to grant immunity to individuals that vigorously challenge their monopoly of violence. If such persons were treated more favourably than 'ordinary criminals' this could be a dangerous incentive for armed insurgency. The general principle that even lawbreakers may not become the object of attacks 'unless and for such time as they take a direct part in hostilities'[45] must nevertheless be respected.

18.3.2.2.1 Status as fighters

This does not mean that members of organised armed groups not involved in the fighting always have to be treated as civilians, nor that they are automatically excluded from protected status. The ICRC has taken the position that the crucial criterion for determining status as fighter (not: combatant) is whether the individual has assumed a *continuous combat function* in the group.[46] This is not the case if the person is responsible for recruiting new members, the trafficking of arms or executing financial responsibilities.[47]

Despite giving some useful guidance about what exactly constitutes a 'continuous combat function', the functional approach does not convincingly prevent the illegal employing of lethal force against persons merely suspected of taking part in hostilities. Above all, it is difficult to check and control whether the information used is sufficient to justify the operation against the human target. On the other hand, the criterion has been criticized—especially in the USA[48]—as too lax: through hiding among the population over a longer period of time or assuming non-combat functions within the organised armed group, the fighter could obtain by trickery a protected status, which is not even granted to combatants.[49] The ICRC counters that a return to civilian status must be possible, because it is an important incentive to give up the combat function, but insists that it must be done in a transparent manner. With regard to the committing of crimes by civilians it is stressed that 'loss of protection against direct attack within the meaning of IHL, however, is not a sanction for criminal behaviour but a consequence of military necessity in the conduct of hostilities'.[50]

Although the current legal framework is unsatisfactory because there are no binding criteria for determining direct participation in hostilities, it must not be forgotten that Article 3 common to the GCs guarantees all fighters *hors de combat* a right

[45] AP II, cited in note 3 above, Art. 13, para. 3; GC I–IV, cited in note 2 above, Art. 3(1).

[46] ICRC, 'Interpretative guidance', cited in note 34 above. [47] Ibid, p. 1008.

[48] See Edward C. Linneweber 'To target, or not to target: why 'tis nobler to thwart the Afghan narcotics trade with nonlethal means', (2011) *Military Law Review* 207, 155, p. 166.

[49] Bill Boothby '"And for such time as": the time dimension to direct participation in hostilities', (2010) 42 *International Law and Politics*, 741, p. 743.

[50] ICRC, 'Interpretative guidance', cited in note 34 above, p. 1029.

to humane treatment. The provision establishes a series of prohibitions such as protection against 'outrages upon personal dignity, in particular humiliating and degrading treatment', as well as 'the passing of sentences and the carrying out of executions without previous judgment pronounced by a regularly constituted court, affording all judicial guarantees which are recognized as indispensable by civilized peoples'. In addition, the state party to the NIAC may unilaterally grant such individuals a treatment that goes beyond the pertinent international obligations. By doing this, it might wish to de-escalate a continuing conflict.

18.3.2.2.2 Status as civilians

Against this backdrop, one can formulate the rebuttable presumption that members of organised crime groups generally qualify as civilians in NIAC. Notwithstanding their potential attribution to organised armed groups, they can only lose this protected status if they directly participate in hostilities. In all other cases, the rules on the protection of the civilian population are applicable. These include the prohibition of hostage taking, acts of terrorism, pillage, and slavery and the slave trade in all its forms.[51] One might find it inconsistent that members of criminal associations are protected in relation to activities which they employ, too. Yet, it must be stressed that the protected status as a civilian does not imply impunity against criminal sanction. Crime can always be prosecuted.

18.3.3 The discussion on transnational armed conflicts: an overview

Article 3 common to the GCs and AP II speaks of armed conflicts 'occurring in the territory of one of the High Contracting Parties'. This has posed the question whether these rules also apply to cross-border hostilities between states and non-state actors. It was the government of the USA that argued in 2002 that the 'war on terrorism' (with al-Qaeda) would be a new type of armed conflict so far unregulated by IHL: a transnational armed conflict.[52] Although this position had certain repercussions in international legal doctrine, the majority opinion holds that such constellations only represent a subcategory of NIAC; governed, however, by the same material requirements.[53] As shown above, this means that transnational conflicts with non-state actors rarely qualify as NIAC.

Nonetheless, the way in which organised crime syndicates operate affects the structure and form of hostilities and the outcome of such 'armed conflicts'. A feature point of such impacts by organised crime are transborder spill-over effects of hostilities that can be traced back to a transnational character of organised crime and organised criminal activities.

[51] See AP II, cited in note 3 above, Art. 4(c), (d), (f) and (g).

[52] US Department of Justice, Office of Legal Counsel, Memorandum for Alberto R Gonzales Counsel to the President, and William J Haynes II General Counsel of the Department of Defense, 'Re: Application of treaties and laws to al Qaeda and Taliban detainees', 22 January 2002, printed in K. J. Greenberg and J. L. Daniel (eds), *The Torture Papers*, Cambridge, CUP, 2005, p. 81.

[53] See e.g. Sivakumaran, *The Law of NIAC*, cited in note 9 above, p. 229; *Hamdan v Rumsfeld*, 29 June 2006, 126 S Ct 2479, p. 2757.

It has become common to speak of organised crime in relation to criminal groups that are not syndicates concentrating on illicit trade in all its forms. The first step in broadening this understanding was made by the US administration under President George W. Bush after the coordinated terror attacks on 11 September 2001. According to President Bush, the attacks have placed the United States in a state of armed conflict.[54] On 7 October 2001 the USA started its military operation 'Enduring Freedom' against the Islamist terror network al-Qaeda. The US administration held that group, and the Afghan Taliban government in Kabul hosting them, responsible for the terror attacks on 9/11 and claimed the right to self-defence under Article 51 of the UNC. This position was joined by NATO, the OAS, and the ANZUS Pact states.[55]

It was the first time in state practice that non-state actors such as the Islamic terrorist network al Qaida were regarded as having executed an armed attack against a state that triggered the right of self-defence under Article 51 UNC. However, neither the USA nor any of its allies or international security organisations went so far as to equate the 'war on terror' with an armed conflict under IHL. As a consequence, 'Enduring Freedom' was in legal Limbo right from the beginning. This confirms that a 'transnational armed conflict' between state armies and security forces, on one hand, and armed forces with an organised crime background, on the other, have not yet been typified as a new type of armed conflict under international humanitarian law.

18.3.3.1 The transnational character of conflicts with organised crime

A characteristic of any form of transnational organised crime is that it breaks through the barriers of the traditional hierarchic structures of nation-state systems in the globalized world.[56] Parties involved are non-state actors at a horizontal level. State authorities are usually not involved in this kind of transborder conflict. The classic form of hierarchic state representation, which uses diplomatic channels, is absent in these conflicts. A dominant feature of such conflicts is that the actors involved act in a private and not in a state capacity.[57] The cross-border activities of criminal syndicates are typified by networking and not formal procedures to represent a state as a whole. The unifying factor of such networks in a conflict is the leadership structure that is able to coordinate diverse local groups in a single operational context.

It is interesting to note that all key elements of economic globalization described above that are conducive for transnational corporations (TCs) are correspondingly also favourable for TOC. This follows from the liberalization of transborder movements and investments in goods, in people, in commodities, in communication

[54] Military Order para. 1(a), 66 Fed. Reg. 57, p. 833.

[55] Public Law No. 107-40, 115 Stat. 224; North Atlantic Treaty, 4 April 1949, Art. 5, 63, Stat. 2244, 34 UNTS 243, p. 246; Inter-American Treaty of Reciprocal Assistance, 2 September 1947, Art. 3(1), 6b2 Stat. 1681, p. 1700, 21 UNTS 77, p. 95; Security Treaty between Australia, New Zealand, and the United States of America, 1 September 1951, Art. IV, 3 UST 23420, 3423, 131 UNTS 83, p. 86; John C. Yoo and James C. Ho, 'International law and the war on terrorism', (2003) *Yoo NYU Combatants.Doc*, 1.

[56] Reinhard Meyers, 'Krieg und Kriegsentwicklung in der wissenschaftlichen Diskussion', in Johannes Varwick (ed.), *Krieg und Frieden*, Schwalbuch/Ts., Wochenschau Verlag, 2014, p. 57.

[57] Ludger Pries, *Die Transnationalisierung der sozialen Welt*, Frankfurt am Main, Suhrkamp, 2008, p. 210.

systems, in information, on money and other financial transactions, and in logistics and traffic connections. TOC groups are beneficiaries of this globalization in a two-fold sense. First, it is the structural similarity with TCs and their legal business activities that make transnational liberalization favourable for both of them. Second, TOC groups take additional advantage from the reduction of national border controls and other state security measures that are part of global liberalization policy and therefore also given up by states.

Cross-border military operations could be coordinated with the goal of outmanoeuvring law enforcement agencies in one state when members of organised crime syndicates are relocated to a different state in order to escape prosecution.[58] However, the benefits in practice of such organised crime strategies are limited. Experience shows that the more successful state security and law enforcement agencies are in fighting organised crime, the more violent become the reactions of targeted organised crime groups. Leaders of drug cartels who are under pressure to find replacements for incarcerated gang members or to find logistic solutions for destroyed transport routes are often prepared to resort to violence even if this would harm the effectiveness of the protection for their illegal transactions. At the same time, the transnational dimension of organised criminal activities, both in terms of illicit trade transactions and in terms of employing armed groups to secure these, are step by step changing the character of the armed violence resorted to by these groups. The insecurities of illicit transborder activities, violent confrontations with state security forces abroad, attacks by competing drug cartels and other organised crime groups against transborder transport routes, and other factors contribute to enormously rising levels of armed violence in transborder areas. It has rightly been observed that sometimes,[59] owing to these factors, the use of excessive armed violence by drug cartels and other armed organised crime groups has lost its instrumental character. In those cases violence has become a means in itself that can no longer be controlled either by the security authorities of states or by the drug barons.

One cannot yet speak of a new, clear-cut, legal or political category of 'transnational armed conflicts', but the structure of transborder effects as described here can be used to analyse relevant transnational manifestations of armed conflict in order to determine their meaning under IHL. The scope and intensity of the paramilitary force of drug cartels would qualify the cartels as potential parties to conflict even though they do not resemble the typical conflict parties under IHL. What is decisive for these forces, to bring them close to the realm of IHL, is their attitude as possible parties to conflict owing to their organisation and their paramilitary power. A suitable description of transborder armed confrontations in this context seems to be to speak of new 'transnational armed conflicts in progress'. The remaining legal difference between transborder paramilitary activities of organised crime groups and armed conflicts under IHL is explained less by armed force capacity and organisation, which are more or less the same on both sides

[58] See the description of TOC in the US 'Strategy to combat transnational organized crime. Addressing converging threats to national security' from 2011, p. 5ff.

[59] Peter Waldmann, 'Is there a culture of violence in Colombia?', (2007) 1 *International Journal of Politics* (1), 61.

when it comes to transborder violent clashes. The legally relevant difference is more to be seen in the intentions held by organised crime groups: making profits and gaining the control necessary for all forms of their illicit trade business. From this it follows that, if such armed and paramilitary transborder violence should become inevitable for organised crime groups, we will be faced with different structures of armed violence. To typify this new form of transborder conflict one must realize that some of the classic elements of war and armed conflict have been replaced by features of organised crime. In the Central American context armed violence is more a survival strategy for drug cartels and less the consequence of the political collapse of state institutions. The drug barons are in a position comparable to that of warlords in other parts of the world. They need armed violence to protect and to develop the economic bases of their 'businesses'. Owing to the criminal character of the transborder trade in drugs and other illicit goods the permanent preparedness for armed violence and involvement in actual armed conflict has become part of the survival strategy. This contributes to transnational armed conflicts becoming a hybrid between armed gangs fighting for drug cartels on one hand and the regular armed forces and law enforcement agencies of states on the other hand. It is because of this hybrid character that such transnational conflicts still overlap in many respects with armed conflicts under IHL. However, a comparison between the situations in Colombia, in Guatemala, in El Salvador, in Mexico, and in the border areas between Mexico and the USA shows that ongoing transnational armed conflicts that have an organised crime background are different in many ways. As a result, one could describe these conflicts as different settings of components partly derived from IHL, partly from organised crime. A consolidated, new type of transnational armed conflict still needs definition in international law.

18.3.3.2 The potential for armed conflict created by organised crime

Organised crime groups are not eager to get involved in armed conflicts and would rather protect their illegal trade routes and business transactions. That is not to say, though, that organised crime syndicates would not be prepared to get involved in extensive armed conflict if that should be required to protect their illegal business interests. This is clear from the enormous security capacity that organised crime syndicates build against the need to use force. Foot soldiers are equipped, paid, and deployed by drug barons. The two most important drug cartels in Mexico—the 'Federation' or Sinaloa Cartel and the 'Los Zetas'—alone have an estimated 100,000 foot soldiers and they are militarily far better equipped and trained than the 130,000 soldiers of the Mexican government armed forces. An important component of the transnational paramilitary capacity of the Mexican drug cartels is street and prison gangs in many Latin American cities and in American cities along the Mexican border. These gangs are controlled by the cartels and can be readily brought in by the drug barons for whatever purposes or goals that need to be accomplished.

Organised crime, especially drug trafficking, has become one of the most serious challenges to state security in Latin American countries, including Mexico, and in the United States. The shift in emphasis can also be gleaned from the National Security Strategy Reports of the US Administration since 2011: before then, the emphasis was on threats from the 'war on terror', but from 2011 it has been extended to include threats from organised crime. This blend of transborder security threats has led to new intergovernmental arrangements between the US administration and neighbouring countries to fight TOC. The most important regional security programmes, which are based on similar political and tactical concepts, are the Plan Colombia of 1999, the Mérida Initiative of 2007, and the CARSI Initiative of 2010.

18.3.3.2.1 Regional security policies to fight TOC and to prevent transnational conflicts

Plan Colombia combines a peace initiative of the Colombian government from September 1999 that focused on development projects and a bilateral agreement between the US Administration under President Clinton and Colombia's President Pastrana that was concluded in July 2000. Pastrana's Plan Colombia, as originally presented, did not focus on drug trafficking, military aid, or crop fumigation, but instead emphasized the manual eradication of drug crops as a better initiative.[60]

During a meeting in August 1998, Pastrana and Clinton discussed the possibility of securing an increase in US aid for counter-narcotic projects, sustainable economic development, the protection of human rights, humanitarian aid, stimulating private investment, and joining other donors and international financial institutions to promote Colombia's economic growth—a type of Marshall Plan.

The US input in drafting Plan Colombia was extensive. Observers have noted that, originally, the focus was on achieving peace and ending violence between Pastrana's government and the FARC guerrillas. The final version of Plan Colombia was seen as considerably different, since its main focus was now on combating drug trafficking and strengthening the military and police forces.[61] From the US perspective Plan Colombia is an extensive security concept for the American continent that encompasses armed operations against drug cartels and neoliberal development aid. Under Plan Colombia's security policy, Colombia agreed that the USA could make use of seven military bases in the country and converted considerable parts of its armed forces into police units. The Colombian police force was restructured and parts of the central police force of Colombia were deployed to all municipalities in the country.[62] This contributed to a drastic drop in homicides and forced disappearances.[63] The USA

[60] Grace Livingstone, *Inside Colombia: Drugs, Democracy, and War*, New Brunswick, New Jersey, Rutgers University Press, 2004, pp. 123–30.

[61] Ibid, pp. 123–6; Russel Crandall, *Driven by Drugs: US Policy Toward Colombia*, Boulder, Colorado, Lynne Rienner Publishers, 2002; Martin Hodgson, 'The coca leaf war: a report from Colombia', (2000) 56 *Bulletin of the Atomic Scientists* (3), 36.

[62] In 1997 the US Congress approved an Amendment to the Foreign Operations Appropriations Act that banned the USA from giving anti-narcotics aid to any foreign military unit whose members have violated human rights. The Amendment was referred to as the 'Leahy Provision' (after Senator Patrick Leahy who proposed it). Partially because of this measure and the reasoning behind it, anti-narcotics aid to Colombia was only provided to police units and not to the military during much of the 1990s.

[63] Attacks conducted by illegally armed groups against rural towns decreased by 91 per cent from 2002 to 2005. Between 2002 and 2008, Colombia saw homicides decrease by 44 per cent, kidnappings by 88 per cent, terrorist attacks by 79 per cent, and attacks on the country's infrastructure by 60 per cent. See the website of the US Embassy in Bogota on 'Plan Colombia': http://bogota.usembassy.gov/plancolombia.html, accessed 15 July 2015.

originally committed US$7.5 billion to the project, mainly for institutional and social development. In practice, the balance of the aid tipped towards military investment in the Colombian armed forces.[64] Social development and humanitarian assistance programmes included in the Plan could not disguise its essentially military character.[65]

With the help of the CIA, the DEA, and the US Defense Intelligence Agency (DIA), the Colombian armed forces became one of the most powerful military forces in Central America. The extent of US involvement is reflected by the size of the US embassy in Colombia, which has 3,500 employees. It is one of the biggest US embassies in the world.[66]

The Mérida Initiative is a security cooperation between the USA, Mexico, and other Central American governments that came into being in October 2007. Unlike Plan Colombia the Initiative is not playing the military card so directly. It is a partnership programme based on the principle of shared responsibility to fight organised drug criminality. The US administration made US$2.3 billion available to Mexico to arm Mexican military and the police.[67] In return, Mexico conceded far-reaching competencies for the US armed forces, the DEA, and US intelligence on Mexican territory.[68] Shared institutions were created in northern Mexico that are run on an equal footing by US and Mexican police and intelligence experts. The rationale behind the Initiative is to close loopholes in border security attributable to the fact that the North American Free Trade Agreement (NAFTA) regulates neither the problem of illegal immigration nor the fighting of the illicit transborder drug trade. In this context a high-ranking US State Department official stated that the three North American governments have found it necessary to invent a mechanism to protect their shared economic space and are implementing this goal by armouring NAFTA.[69] The security philosophy underlying the Mérida Initiative contributed to the militarization of the 'drug war' in Central America and its spill-over into the United States.

Critics of the Mérida Initiative argue that militarizing the fight against the illicit drug trade is not a suitable instrument to root out the real causes of the problem.

[64] In 2000, the Clinton administration in the United States supported the initiative by committing $1.3 billion in foreign aid and up to five hundred military personnel to train local forces. An additional three hundred civilian personnel were allowed to assist in the eradication of coca. This aid was in addition to US$330 million of previously approved US aid to Colombia. US$818 million was earmarked for 2000, with US$256 million for 2001. These appropriations for the plan made Colombia the third largest recipient of US foreign aid at the time.

[65] Military/police aid made up the lion's share compared to social/economic aid. Between 1996 and 2006 the share of US aid for the military/police varied between 78.12 per cent and 99.88 per cent of the total.

[66] See Nazih Richani, *The Peace Process in Colombia and US Foreign Policy: Plan Colombia II*, 2013, available at: https://nacla.blog/2013/6/3/peace-process-colombia-and-us-foreign-policy-plan-colombia-ii, accessed 29 March 2016.

[67] Of the assistance, 59 per cent went to civil agencies responsible for law enforcement and 41 per cent to operational cost for the army and navy. A quarter of the money went into justice reform, institution building, human rights, and rule of law. This proportion was set by statutes adopted in the USA.

[68] US Department of State, 'Diplomacy in action: Mérida Initiative', available at: http://www.state.gov/j/inl/merida, accessed 30 June 2015; Laura Carlsen, 'A primer on Plan Mexico', *Counter Punch*, 8 May 2008.

[69] See Laura Carlsen, 'Armouring NAFTA: the battleground for Mexico's future', *NACLA*, 27 August 2008, available at: http://nacla.org/node/4958, accessed 30 June 2015.

Continued support for combating the supply of drugs rather than focusing on prevention, treatment, and education programmes to curb demand is also criticized. During the early to mid-1990s, the Clinton administration ordered and funded a major cocaine policy study by the Rand Drug Policy Research Center; the study concluded that US$3 billion should be switched from federal and local law enforcement to treatment. The report said that treatment is the cheapest and most effective way to cut drug use. However, US administrations have mostly preferred not to cut law enforcement spending and have even cut back on drug treatment and prevention programmes.[70]

As of 2010 the Obama administration separated the Central America portion of the Mérida Initiative and renamed it the Central America Regional Security Initiative (CARSI).[71] Like Plan Colombia and the Mérida Initiative CARSI is designed as a collaborative partnership between the United States and the Central American region. Up to the present, the United States has provided US$640 million assistance to Central American countries for the project. With the emphasis on funding capacity building for law enforcement and the justice sector in these countries CARSI includes military cooperation in the form of acquisition of US defence equipment, services, and training.

18.3.3.2.2 Towards a 'transnational humanitarian law'?

It is interesting to note that the USA view activities of drug cartels in Central America and in the US–Mexican border area as part of a regional insurgency that has to be fought with military means.[72] This US legal evaluation has become a common denominator underlying all three regional security initiatives. It is highly questionable whether, under public international law, this conflict characterization is correct since the drug cartels have no sort of internal or external political enemy. To name armed parts of drug cartels and other armed organised crime groups 'insurgents' seems rather motivated by creating a possible entrance card for US armed forces if adding transnational use of military forces to the armed DEA units already operating in Central America should be deemed appropriate.

All three partnership initiatives are based on the concept of shared responsibility and competences in fighting organised crime in the region even though the emphasis of each is different and topics of cooperation may vary. Apart from these initiatives, a

[70] President Clinton's administration rejected slashing law enforcement spending. The Bush administration proposed cutting spending on drug treatment and prevention programs by $73 million, or 1.5 per cent, in the 2009 budget. The Fiscal Year 2011 National Drug Control Budget proposed by the Obama administration devoted significant new resources to the prevention and treatment of drug abuse.

[71] US Department of State, 'Diplomacy in action: Central America Regional Security Initiative', available at: http://www.state.gov/p/wha/rt/carsi/, accessed 15 July 2015; see also United States Government Accountability Office (GAO), Washington DC 20548, 30 January 2013—'Subject: Status of funding for the Central America Regional Security Initiative'.

[72] This was the view expressed by the US Minister for Foreign Affairs Hillary Clinton in September 2010—see http://fpif.org/a_plan_colombia_for_mexico/, accessed 30 June 2015; Hillary Clinton, 'Remarks on the Obama administration's national security strategy', Washington DC, Brookings Institution, 2010, available at: http://www.state.gov/secretary/20092013clinton/rm/2010/05/142312.htm, accessed 30 June 2015; William Booth, 'Secretary of State Clinton compares Mexico's drug violence to Colombia's', *Washington Post*, 8 September 2010, available at: http://www.washingtonpost.com/wp-dyn/content/article/2010/09/08/AR2010090806882.html, accessed 30 June 2015.

further thirty units of the US armed forces and DEA are operating in Latin American countries, officially under the banner of fighting drug gangs and disrupting drug transport routes into the United States. A lesser known part of DEA activities is the covert cooperation with right-wing governments in Central America.[73] These armed activities of DEA units in the drug wars of the region contribute substantially to such conflicts becoming international ones.

Both Plan Colombia and the Mérida Initiative have been shaped by successive US administrations to assign specific tasks and responsibilities in the fight against organised crime to armed forces and the police. The shared responsibility between the parties to the agreements involve steady enlargement of the geographical area of operations of the US armed forces and DEA units, while the Latin American partners are reducing their armed forces in favour of enlarging police units. This is not a one-way development but a complex strategy. At the same time, the police forces of the USA have been adopting military training and equipment. In effect, this strategy contributes a lot to militarizing the fight against organised crime in all its forms. It is undisputed that, as a result of the drug war in Mexico, which President Calderón initiated in 2006 as part of a bilateral understanding with the US administration under President George W. Bush, the quantity of illegal drug trafficking in both Mexico and the United States increased considerably. There was a rise in transborder armed incidents and a rise in violence and unrest in big US cities. It is difficult to explain why a strategy that fails to effectively combat organised crime was nevertheless retained.

If one looks at the whole picture, taking into account how deregulation and privatization policies of the United States were also embraced by Mexico via NAFTA during the last five decades, it would not be false to conclude that Plan Colombia, the Mérida Initiative, and CARSI have served the USA's neoliberal globalization politics. Part of this politics is to give up transborder security mechanisms, which are inseparably linked to the classic nation-state idea. However, although border controls were given up, comparable security mechanisms were not introduced in their stead. There are obviously many advantages to the globalization of international trade, such as improved living conditions for many people and freedom of movement for those who can make use of it. Yet, it has not adequately addressed security issues. It is evident that Plan Colombia, the Mérida Initiative, and the CARSI Initiative were conceived to fill this gap. Meanwhile, the strategy and the security instruments implemented have turned out to be ineffective. The main reason is the lack of a strategy to prevent Mexico, Costa Rica, Guatemala, El Salvador, and other states in Central America becoming 'narco-states'. This is Washington's Central American dilemma.[74] The development and security initiatives failed to create economic growth (apart

[73] DEA's enforcement arm abroad—FAST (Foreign-deployed Advisory and Support Team)—cooperated with US Special Operations Forces; see American Special Ops at: http://www.americanspecialops.com/photos/law-enforcement/foreign-deployed-advisory-support-team.php, accessed 2 July 2015.

[74] Peter Gärtner, 'Washingtons zentralamerikanisches Dilemma', April 2015, available at: http://www.quetzal-leipzig.de/lateinamerika/costa-rica/usa-zentralamerika-gewalt-sicherheit-allianz-fuer-den-wohlstand-19093.html, accessed 29 March 2016.

from the illicit trade in drugs), or increase safety. Little progress was made in fighting the impunity of organised crime and in managing border areas effectively. It seems that the initiatives have also facilitated a geopolitical rift between Central American countries south of the Isthmus of Tehuantepec, and Mexico and the North American countries.

Apart from fighting regional insurgencies, a second common denominator of these security initiatives of Northern and Central American states could be to close loopholes in the Geneva Conventions and Protocols with regard to IHL issues in transnational armed conflicts. This is not explicit in the language of these security agreements. It is reflected, however, by their common aims and instruments. These aims, instruments, and shared responsibilities are part of the regional cooperative security framework intended to prevent transborder armed conflicts with an organised crime background. All three agreements include provisions to strengthen the military and police forces of these countries and to coordinate their fight against transborder organised crime better. Transborder armed conflict between regular armed forces and law enforcement agencies of the state, and organised crime groups with paramilitary capacities, are a worst case scenario for all these states. Another common denominator is that all the instruments, shared responsibilities, common institutions, privileges, and supportive measures are shaped in a way that could easily be developed into regional strategies to prevent TOC.

The suitability of the North and Central American security agreements to complement the Geneva Conventions and Protocols for transborder armed conflicts is not acknowledged formally by regulating a legal hierarchy between the agreements and humanitarian law or by similar regulation. Such an understanding will depend on political practice by states concerned in the region. If preventive strategies that are made possible by these agreements should fail, as some critics predict, the remaining option would be that the affected states engage in transborder military action.

18.4 Transnational Organised Crime and 'Failing States'

It is believed that *failed states* and *failing states* are a hotbed for all sorts of TOC. This appears to be the prevailing perspective in political and legal literature in relation to states such as Somalia, Chad, Zimbabwe, Sierra Leone, Ivory Coast, Malawi, Eritrea, Yemen, Bangladesh, and Nepal. This view may be justified for all of these states. However, the position in some Latin American countries, which are often found on the list of failed or failing states, is very different. This is specifically true for some of the drug-transit countries, in particular Mexico. The economic success of transnational organised crime syndicates involved in illicit trade in drugs, weapons, cigarettes, and human beings depends on well-organised logistics and infrastructure for the transnational transport of such goods. These syndicates use modern communication facilities, effectively recruit foot soldiers, and operate in a highly developed economic and political environment. Systematic corruption is a successful investment. It is interesting to note that Mexico has one of the most developed and modern traffic networks in the world. Mexico is also well connected to all its neighbouring countries, which makes it attractive for efficient drug trafficking. The job opportunities for drug dealers, killers, and people with military experience appear to be inexhaustible in Mexico and the neighbouring Latin American countries.

Well-organised and efficiently run state institutions, where the law is properly enforced by independent courts and the criminal justice system is supported by an untainted police force, are the greatest anathema of organised crime cartels. Thus, it comes as no surprise that part of the strategy of organised crime is to target these institutions. In such an environment it is not the situation that a state has failed or is failing that attracts organised crime. It is the other way round: the organised crime approach of undermining state institutions has a corrosive effect. The influence of organised crime is certainly not the only factor that causes states to fail. Yet, it is a dominant factor in why even states that are highly developed in a political and economic sense are not immune to being side-tracked on to the slippery slope of failure.

18.5 'War among People': The Rules of IHL have Come to their Limits

Starting in December 2006, President Calderón deployed the army, and lethal violence in Mexico exploded. He said he was fighting drug trafficking in a 'war on drugs', but the flow of drugs and money continued unimpeded. The violence was justified as a 'crusade for public safety'. The official number of victims is about 50,000, but human rights groups have estimated it to be at least 130,000 Mexicans killed. Another 27,000 have officially disappeared.[75] Civil society at all socio-economic levels is plagued by kidnapping, extortion, and murder. There have been serious allegations of police torture and of 'social cleansing' aimed at those deemed worthless to society: *los malandros*. Most of the victims were unarmed. Medical and social rehabilitation centres for drug addicts have also been targeted.[76] It appears that the 'war on drugs' has become a multifaceted conflict: it includes elements of civil war, insurgencies, ethnic cleansing by powerful elites of the socio-economically weak parts of their own population, and transborder armed conflicts.[77]

In reaction to this disastrous development, civil society initiatives were formed. The 'vigilantes', an armed militia backed by growing parts of the Mexican population, are armed and have taken control over certain areas in which they have taken over state functions to protect people, and handed over arrested people to the authorities for prosecution. Meanwhile the remarkable success of these spontaneous security

[75] See Molly Molloy, 'The Mexican undead: toward a new history of the "drug war" killing fields', *Small Wars Journal*, 21 August 2013.

[76] The estimates vary between 40,000 and more than 130,000 casualties for the period 2009–2012 alone. See ibid; see also 'The dead women of Ciudad Juarez', *Frankfurter Allgemeine Sonntagszeitung*, 20 January 2013.

[77] Tom Burghardt, 'Drugs, terror and the militarization of Mexican society', *Global Research*, 4 May 2012, available at: http://www.globalresearch.ca/drugs-terror-and-the-militarization-of-mexican-society/30833, accessed 30 June 2015; Amrai Coen and Fabian Brenneke, 'Die Zeugen von Iguala', *Die Zeit*, 26 March 2015.

initiatives has led to informal as well as formal arrangements between the vigilantes, the federal government, and the police at a local and regional level.[78]

A tendency can be observed that where urbanization and population growth spin out of control and lead to sprawling slums and desolate poverty among the lower social classes, this often goes hand in hand with drug addiction and a sharp rise in the crime rate. To counter this development, many states are issuing their police forces with heavy weapons and training them in military tactics. An IMI study done in 2007 came to the conclusion that states are increasingly upgrading their armed forces, for wars not against other states but against their own populations.[79] Such 'wars against the people' are fought by powerful elites in society to protect their interests against impoverished and helpless sections of the population who are inadequately protected by state authorities. Sometimes these vulnerable people spontaneously defend themselves against such aggression. As a consequence, violent self-defence and criminal violence, including mass murder, can hardly be distinguished any more.

Such a disastrous scenario of dismembering and partly collapsing societies can still be governed by rules of IHL only in a very limited sense. Such chaos as described above is too complex to qualify as an 'armed conflict' under the Geneva Conventions and Protocols. A precondition for the application of the rules of international humanitarian law is that a state must regain control over non-state actors. A common feature of all the conflicts in the Central and Northern American region is a deep-rooted divide between powerful political elites and socio-economically weak sections of society. Similar constellations can be found in Northern Africa, the Middle East, and Central Asia. This constellation is not a basis for peaceful and sustainable development. Whether these countries will be able to turn around conditions that resemble a civil war, to eliminate dictatorships, and to find ways to secure internal peace and social justice will substantially depend on powerful third parties, first of all the United States. Military expeditions by the USA and its Western allies in various parts of the world can help to keep legitimate governments in power and to protect them against political and religious extremists. Such undertakings, however, might also have adverse effects and could just as well keep illegitimate governments and dictators in power and exacerbate the social and economic plight of people living in these countries. If this should happen, as it did in Central American countries after US intervention, preventive regional security programmes such as Plan Colombia and the Mérida and CARSI initiatives are doomed to fail. To avoid this is a matter of national politics and of regional cooperation, not a matter to which public international law applies.

18.6 Final Considerations

As stated in the beginning, IHL was not developed to deal with phenomena that are currently considered as TOC. On the contrary, states were and still are reluctant to

[78] 'Pistolero im Kleiderschrank', *Neue Züricher Zeitung*, 30 January 2014; 'Wir werden dieses Land säubern', *Neue Züricher Zeitung*, 25 January 2014.

[79] Christoph Marischka, 'Rüsten für den globalen Bürgerkrieg', Informationsstelle Militarisierung, IMI Paper No. 2007/08, 6 October 2007, p. 2.

classify its violent manifestations as 'acts of war' or to accord the status of a warring party to such perpetrators. Nonetheless, the barring of organised crime from the ambit of IHL is not of a categorical nature since some IHL rules may be interpreted more broadly than originally envisaged. The laws of both IAC and NIAC have loopholes under which, in extreme cases of open clashes with the state security forces or paramilitary rivals, perpetrators of TOC might enjoy a collective or individual status under IHL. Unfortunately, it often falls within the discretion of the state party to a conflict to decide whether this legal regime will come into play under such circumstances. This is primarily attributable to the vagueness of the criteria established for verifying the applicability of the GCs and their APs.

There are many legal and political risks involved in regard to the applicability of IHL to TOC, which should be considered carefully. If one goes beyond the state-centric perspective that is embodied by codified IHL and considers violent conflicts of TOC groups with state and non-state actors, like that in Mexico, which resembles a NIAC, it appears that a new type of armed conflict is emerging and that international legal doctrine is not yet able to address that satisfactorily.

19

Transnational Criminal Organisations and Human Rights

Math Noortmann and Dawn Sedman

19.1 Introduction

When we reflect on 'crimes' and 'human rights', we enter different conceptual and normative traditions in (international) legal scholarship with respect to the authority of the state and the position of natural and legal persons. Where criminal law routinely revolves around the idea of the state as the (collective) victim, and the individual/organisation as the offender, human rights law habitually focuses on the state as the wrongdoer and the individual/organisation as the victim. That traditional distinction, however, is increasingly blurring as—on one hand—the pursuit and prosecution of criminal organisations is subjected to a growing set of human rights, and—on the other hand—the activities of a variety of 'non-state actors' have 'horizontalized' human rights, i.e. human rights violations can be attributed to such non-state actors as businesses, armed opposition groups, non-governmental organisations, and indeed organisations that are rightfully or wrongfully labelled as 'criminal', such as terrorist organisations, mafias, bikers, and gangs.

The relationship between criminal organisation and the transnationalization of organised criminal activities on one side and human rights on the other raises two pertinent questions, which feature prominently in the debates on the responsibility of businesses and armed opposition groups for example,[1] but which are under-explored with respect to criminal organisations.[2] The first one is based on the idea that the (transnational) activities of criminal organisations violate human rights and asks whether the labelling of transnational criminal offences as human rights violations is useful.[3] The second question relates to the holding of human rights by (criminal) organisations and their members and queries the means and methods of criminal pursuit and prosecution. The two questions are clearly interlinked as organisations may at the

[1] See e.g. Andrew Clapham, *Human Rights Obligations of Non-State Actors*, Oxford, OUP, 2006; Philip Alston (ed.), *Non-State Actors and Human Rights, Collected Courses of the Academy of European Law*, Vol. 13/3, Oxford, New York, OUP, 2005; M. T. Kamminga and Saman Zia-Zarifi (eds), *Liability of Multinational Corporations under International Law*, Vol. 7, Studies and Materials on the Settlement of International Disputes (SMSID), The Hague, Kluwer Law International, 2000.

[2] To the extent that criminal organisations are included as 'powerful groups within a state' that enjoy '*de facto* immunity from prosecution' reference is generally made to the developments in international criminal law, in particular the establishment of the International Criminal Court (ICC), whose jurisdiction is rather limited in terms of 'ordinary' crimes. See Thomas Buergenthal, 'The normative and institutional evolution of international human rights', (1997) 19 *Human Rights Quarterly* (4), 703, p. 718.

[3] See Arthur Veno, *The Mammoth Book of Bikers*, New York, Carroll & Graf Publishers, 2007, pp. 323–414; Cas Mudde (ed.), *Racist Extremism in Central and Eastern Europe*, Abingdon, Routledge, 2005.

same time be accused of having violated human rights and/or committed a crime, and claim that their activities or the organisation is protected by human rights, most importantly such rights as freedom of speech or association.

The question what constitutes a criminal organisation is a vexed one and runs as much through this chapter as it runs through many of the other chapters, and we will not attempt to solve that question right here and now. What is particularly relevant for this chapter, however, is that there is a socio-political trend to explicitly criminalize organisations such as biker groups, and radical political and religious organisations, thereby *de facto* outlawing their members who become criminal by association, as Peterke and Noortmann argued.[4]

In this chapter we will address both questions by first looking at the general discourse as it emerges from academic literature, policy debates, and jurisprudence (section 19.2 of this chapter). After this general exposé, we conceptually juxtapose criminal offences and human rights violations in order to argue that the difference between a criminal law approach and a human rights approach is one of substance, but that the dividing line is vague. The discourses on criminal law and human rights law seem to focus on the different ends of the perpetrator—victim equation (section 19.3). After arguing for a clearer, distinctive conception of criminal law and human rights law, we discuss the role of state responsibility *versus* different schemes of individual/organisational criminal accountability. Based on the 'horizontalization' of human rights, corporate actors increasingly face (civil) law suits. That trend seems to have found little resonance in the field of activities that are associated with criminal organisations and seems to revamp the traditional notions of the role of the state in criminal law enforcement (section 19.4). Section 19.5 addresses the potential danger that lies in the disregard for human rights in the so-called wars against different types of organised crime such as the war on drugs,[5] the war on terrorism,[6] or the war on trafficking.[7] The danger lies inherently in the labelling of the counter-measures against these forms of organised crime as 'wars'. The balance between the policing and prosecution of transnational crimes and the upholding of human rights is a precarious one and subject to abuse. Finally, we draw some conclusions on the relationship between the activities of transnational criminal organisations and human rights and the danger that the balance tips towards law enforcement, and argue that transnational criminal law enforcement and the prosecution of transnational criminal

[4] Sven Peterke and Math Noortmann, 'Transnationale kriminelle Organisationen im Völkerrecht: mehr als Outlaws?', (2015) *Archive des Völkerrechts* 53.

[5] Bruce L. Benson, David W. Rasmussen, and David L. Sollars, 'Police bureaucracies, their incentives, and the war on drugs', (1995) 83 *Public Choice* (1–2), 21; David P. Stewart, 'Internationalizing the war on drugs: the UN Convention against Illicit Traffic in Narcotic Drugs and Psychotropic Substances', (1989) *Denver Journal of International Law & Policy* 18, 387; Daniel Heilmann, 'The international control of illegal drugs and the UN treaty regime: preventing or causing human rights violations?.', available at: http://works.bepress.com/cgi/viewcontent.cgi?article=1000&context=daniel_heilmann, accessed 26 January 2016.

[6] David Luban, 'The war on terrorism and the end of human rights', Washington DC, Georgetown University Law Center, 2002; Ruth Reitan, 'Human rights in US policy: a casualty of the "war on terrorism"?', (2003) 7 *International Journal of Human Rights* (4); Joan Fitzpatrick, 'Speaking law to power: the war against terrorism and human rights', (2003) 14 *EJIL* (2), 241.

[7] Catherine Dauvergne, *And Yet We Are Not Saved: Hegemony and the Global War on Human Trafficking*, Faculty of Law, University of Toronto, 2005; Valerie Payne, 'On the road to victory in America's war on human trafficking: landmarks, landmines, and the need for centralized strategy', paper presented at the First Annual Interdisciplinary Conference on Human Trafficking, 2009; Kamala Kempadoo, 'The war on human trafficking in the Caribbean', (2007) 49 *Race & Class* (2), 79.

organisations requires a robust and rigorous supervision mechanism that secures the rights of individuals and organisations engaged in transnational criminal activities.

19.2 The State of the Art: Publications, Policies, and Legal Practices

The discourses on transnational crimes and human rights are disconnected for reasons mentioned in the introduction. In this section of this chapter we describe how that disconnect is reflected in literature, policy documents, and court decisions.

19.2.1 Literature review

The relationship between transnational criminal organisations and human rights does not feature well in our academic literatures. Indeed, titles of publications, tables of contents, and indexes do not reveal a sense of an intrinsic link between (organised) criminal activities and human rights.[8] Olivier de Schutter's most comprehensive *International Human Rights Law* is exemplary. Except for explicit reference to the 'crime against humanity', the topics 'slavery', 'terrorism', and 'torture' are not conceptualized as crimes but treated as *erga omnes* violations of human rights.[9] According to August Reinisch, criminal law becomes applicable to human rights violations when these violations are considered to be 'grave', but '[t]he considerable barriers to enforcing the criminal liability of corporations in a domestic context are compounded internationally'.[10] The problem then is twofold. First of all, the absence of an international criminal law catalogue that corresponds to ordinary human rights created a systemic problem that suggests that most human right violations do not constitute a criminal offence. It is telling in this respect that most 'human rights-relevant national legislation'—as August Reinisch calls it—is based on tort claims.[11] Second, on a more practical level, the criminal prosecution of organisations faces the problem of attribution, i.e. the difficulty of identifying acts of the individual with the organisation, which according to Celia Wells and Juanita Elias is first of all a criminal law problem expressed in terms of 'complicity'.[12]

The publications on human rights and corporate responsibility/crime reveal the literature's blindness for transnational criminal organisations. The reasons for not

[8] Overall, one has to conclude that the literature dealing with non-state actors in international law, international relations, and/or human rights tends to generally neglect transnational criminal organisations as subjects of research and discussion. For examples that demonstrate this opinion see: Bob Reinalda, *The Ashgate Research Companion to Non-state Actors*, Aldershot, Ashgate, 2010; Alston, *Non-State Actors and Human Rights*, cited in note 1 above.

[9] Olivier de Schutter, *International Human Rights Law*, Cambridge, CUP, 2010.

[10] August Reinisch, 'The changing international legal framework for dealing with non-state actors', in Alston, *Non-State Actors and Human Rights*, cited in note 1 above, p. 33.

[11] Ibid, p. 55. On human rights litigation and tort claims see also Douglas M. Branson, 'Holding multinational corporations accountable—Achilles' heels in Alien Tort Claims Act litigation', (2011) *Santa Clara Journal of International Law* 9, 227; Eric De Brabandere, 'Human rights and transnational corporations: the limits of direct corporate responsibility', (2010) *Human Rights & International Legal Discourse* 4, 66.

[12] Celia Wells and Juanita Elias, 'Catching the conscience of the king: corporate players on the international stage', in Alston, *Non-State Actors and Human Rights*, cited in note 1 above, pp. 141–75.

investigating mafias, gangs, and drugs cartels can only be guessed, but the absence of a transparent structure and public corporate identity of criminal organisations might hamper lawyers and activists from going after such organisations. The difference between corporate crime and organised crime is not just a conceptual one. The latter is considered to be 'serious but limited' and 'in most cases the victims were more or less shady entrepreneurs'.[13] In the field of corporate crime, the victims are considered to be innocent and uninvolved. The 'quality' of the victim might be taken as an explanation for the distinctive approaches to transnational criminal organisations and their relevance to human rights. Where one would expect more attention for criminal organisations (however defined) in international criminal law literature, the latter branch of international law is narrowly oriented towards the individual criminal actor.[14] Such can be explained by the fact that states have ruled out the possibility of the International Criminal Court (ICC) engaging in cases of corporate crime.[15]

19.2.2 Policy and law

The United Nations Convention Against Transnational Organised Crime (UNTOC)[16] is the most authoritative international legal document on the issue and constitutes an excellent starting point for investigating the international community's stance on the relationship between transnational organised crime and human rights.

The most important conclusion that one can draw from reading the Convention itself is that it does not mention 'human rights' at all. All of its articles are virtually silent on human rights. Only in the Preamble and Articles 2(b), 10(2), and 14(1) of the Protocol to Prevent, Suppress, and Punish Trafficking in Persons, Especially Women and Children, and Article 19 of the Protocol against the Smuggling of Migrants by Land, Sea, and Air are 'human rights' mentioned. The inclusion of 'human rights' performs no specific substantial function other than securing that

> [n]othing in this Protocol shall affect the other rights, obligations and responsibilities of States and individuals under international law, including international humanitarian law and international human rights law ... [17]

[13] Anton Weenink, 'The Russian mafiya: a private actor in international relations', in Bas Arts, Math Noortmann, and Bob Reinalda (eds), *Non-State Actors in International Relations*, Aldershot, Ashgate, 2001, pp. 179–98.

[14] See, for example, Cassandra Steer, 'Non-state actors in international criminal law', in Jean d'Aspremont (ed.), *Participants in the International Legal System: Multiple Perspectives on Non-State Actors in International Law*, Abingdon, Routledge, 2011.

[15] For a discussion of the ICC and corporate crime see Joanna Kyriakakis, 'Corporate criminal liability and the ICC Statute: the comparative law challenge', (2009) 56 *Netherlands International Law Review* (3), 333; Nora Gotzmann, 'Legal personality of the corporation and international criminal law: globalisation, corporate human rights abuses and the Rome Statute', (2008) 1 *Queensland Law Student Review* (1), 38; Harmen van der Wilt, 'Corporate criminal responsibility for international crimes: exploring the possibilities', (2013) 12 *Chinese J L* (1), 43.

[16] UN GA Res. 55/25, New York, 8 January 2001; available at: http://www.unodc.org/pdf/crime/a_res_55/res5525e.pdf, accessed 12 February 2016.

[17] For the text of the Convention and the Protocols see UNODC, *United Nations Convention Against Transnational Crime and the Protocols Thereto*, New York, UN, 2004, available at: http://www.unodc.

Kofi Annan's foreword also seems to understand the relationship between transnational crimes and human rights to be a rather particular one that applies to such criminal activities as the 'trafficking of persons, ... forced labour and sexual exploitation ...'[18] In the Report of the First Conference of the Parties it was concluded that 'trafficking in persons constituted a *grave* violation of human rights',[19] which recalls the idea that human rights have to be severe to cross the criminal law threshold.

A 2013 thematic paper on 'Exploitation and abuse of international migrants, particularly those in an irregular situation: a human rights approach' by the Global Migration Group provides us with a clearer understanding of the relationship between crimes/criminal organisations and abuses or violations of human rights. The best example is provided by the concept of 'exploitation', the definition of which is not only unclear according to the thematic paper, but also lacks an international legal definition.[20] The United Nations Office on Drugs and Crime (UNODC) Model law against Trafficking in Persons, on the other hand, understands 'exploitation' as 'conditions of work inconsistent with human dignity'; not 'inconsistent with human rights', which might be explained by the fact that the Trafficking in Persons Protocol does not criminalize exploitation in and of itself: it is the form of exploitation that determines whether exploitation would be a criminal act, or a violation of one's human rights, or both. Exploitative labour, exploitative traditional practices, and exploitation en route are three examples of exploitative acts that are covered by human rights law, but not by criminal law.[21]

Like the literature, international legal documents and policies seem to reveal a confused relationship between organised crime and human rights, and underpin the suggestion that these two issues sit in different policy areas.

19.2.3 Jurisprudence

Last but not least, one can look at how national and international courts understand the relationship between organised crime and human rights. At the international level, courts clearly differ along the lines of subject matter and jurisdiction, which are predominantly determined by their Statutes. For the present discussion, the distinction between human rights courts and international criminal courts at the international level is most important. At the national level it is not so much the court, as the

org/documents/middleeastandnorthafrica/organised-crime/UNITED_NATIONS_CONVENTION_AGAINST_TRANSNATIONAL_ORGANIZED_CRIME_AND_THE_PROTOCOLS_THERETO.pdf, accessed 12 February 2016.

[18] Ibid, p. iv.

[19] Report of the Conference of the Parties to the United Nations Convention Against Transnational Organised Crime on its first session, held in Vienna from 28 June to 8 July 2004, UN Doc. CTOC/COP/2004/6, p. 19.

[20] Global Migration Group, 'Exploitation and abuse of international migrants, particularly those in an irregular situation: a human rights approach', UNODC, 2013, p. 5, available at: https://www.unodc.org/documents/human-trafficking/2013/2013_GMG_Thematic_Paper.pdf, accessed 29 February 2016.

[21] Available at: https://www.unodc.org/documents/human-trafficking/UNODC_Model_Law_on_Trafficking_in_Persons.pdf, p. 9, accessed 23 March 2016.

question who brings which claim to the court, i.e. is the case against the organisation brought as a civil case or as a criminal case?

The problem—as Clapham rightly asserts—is not whether organisations can violate international criminal laws or engage in transnational activities that are otherwise labelled as criminal, but whether these organisations can be the subject of proper international adjudication.[22] The answer to the latter question tends to be negative. International Criminal Tribunals, human rights courts, and committees are generally precluded from engaging cases in which organisations are the 'defendant'.[23] To the extent that the possibility of bringing cases against organisations has been discussed, these organisations have a legal status, at least under national law. Organisations with criminal intent generally do not have that explicit legal status. Many of the organisations that we identify with criminal activities would not have the explicit legal personality that would enable prosecutors and courts to move against the organisations rather than their members.

19.3 TCOs' Crimes and Human Rights

We move now from the examination of general discourse on literature, policy, and jurisprudence that suggests an absence of focus on transnational criminal organisations (TCOs), to the latter's engagement with the two branches of law. There are two clear intersections between TCOs' crimes and human rights. The first is in the crimes themselves: when the criminal act takes place it will impact on a right of the victim; for example, the trafficking of a person would engage with Article 9 of the International Covenant on Civil and Political Rights (ICCPR), which recognizes the right of each individual to liberty and security. The second intersection would be at the prosecution stage, when the perpetrator of the crime faces a court: regardless of how heinous the offence might be, under Article 14 of the ICCPR a fair trial should follow. There is however a third relationship (less intersection, more dichotomy) and that stems from the branch of law used to remedy the harm caused by the act of the TCO: criminal law or human rights law? What follows is an examination of the intersections and their effects through, first, a brief identification of the crimes under review and the rights engaged, followed by examination of the—argued here—dichotomous struggle between the two branches.

19.3.1 Crimes

What would fall under the definition of a transnational organised crime?[24] As Hauck and Peterke's survey concluded, it is 'very difficult to reach a consensus on the

[22] Andrew Clapham, 'The question of jurisdiction under international criminal law over legal persons: lessons from the Rome Conference on an International Criminal Court', in Kamminga and Zia-Zarifi, *Liability of Multinational Corporations*, cited in note 1 above. For a discussion of 'The question of jurisdiction over legal persons' in the ICC Statute see in particular pp. 143–55.

[23] Ibid.

[24] See—for the matter of definition—Ch. 2 of this book, sections 2.1.1 and 2.3.2, and Ch. 21.

appropriate use and meaning of the term "organised crime"'.[25] The principal international instrument—the UNTOC—itself offers no definition but instead a range of criteria under which Transnational Organised Crime (TOC) would fall.[26] Examples that could come under the Convention would include drug and people trafficking, the illegal arms trade, money laundering, and potentially (depending on organisation structure and transborder nature) terrorism and piracy. Inherent in all these examples is criminal behaviour that impacts the human rights of individuals directly and indirectly affected. Whilst some of the criminal behaviour might be prohibited in part or in whole under international laws, domestic law—of sender states, destination states, or transfer states—would criminalize the underlying acts that combine to result in a TOC, and a key motivation of the Palermo Convention (as explained in Article 1) was to 'promote cooperation [between states parties] to prevent and combat transnational organised crime more effectively' through national criminalization, mutual legal and technical assistance, joint investigations, and preventative policies.[27] An example of this would be the UK's human trafficking law that states 'a person commits an offence if the person arranges or facilitates the travel of another person ("V") with a view to V being exploited'.[28] Whether the listed TOCs above amount to stand-alone crimes under international (criminal) law is less clear.[29] Whilst there is clearly a potential overlap with crimes against humanity (CAH) (for example, a systematic terrorist attack killing a number of civilians or the widespread trafficking of women and girls within conflict for the purposes of sexual exploitation), and the International Criminal Tribunal for the former Yugoslavia (ICTY) has recognized that international crimes need not be committed by state actors,[30] there is debate within academic literature as to whether TOC can be interpreted—yet—to fall under a CAH category.[31]

19.3.2 Human rights

The range of rights engaged by the actions of the TCOs is wide. Given their variety, it would be ill-advised to try to compile a definitive list; however, for illustrative purposes, here is an indicative one to demonstrate the huge potential for a range of rights to be impacted by these types of offence. With regards to people trafficking, there are potential violations of rights protected under the ICCPR, such

[25] Pierre Hauck and Sven Peterke, 'Organised crime and gang violence in national and international law', (2010) 92 *IR RC*, 407, p. 410.

[26] Specifically, Arts 2 and 3.

[27] Arts 7–9 criminalize money laundering and corruption; Arts 16–18 enable extradition and mutual legal assistance; Arts 19–21 encourage transnational investigation and prosecution; Arts 29–31 promote mutual technical assistance, training, and shared best practice.

[28] Modern Slavery Act 2015, Art. 2(1). Note, it is a *person* who can be held accountable, not an *organisation*.

[29] Neil Boister, 'Transnational criminal law?', (2003) 14 *EJIL* (5), 953.

[30] *Prosecutor v Limaj*, Judgment, ICTY-06-66-T, 30 November 2005, examined in Tilman Rodenhauser, 'Beyond state crimes: non-state entities and crimes against humanity', (2014) 27 *Leiden Journal of International Law* 913.

[31] Neil Boister, 'Treaty crimes, International Criminal Court?' (2009) 12 *New Criminal Law Review* 341.

as freedom from cruel, inhuman, or degrading treatment, freedom from slavery, right to liberty and security, right to privacy, protection of family and children.[32] Alternatively, under the International Covenant on Economic, Social, and Cultural Rights (ICESCR), a counterfeiting organisation would encroach upon the intellectual property protections recognized there.[33] Beyond these two foundational and widely ratified international human rights treaties there are many specialized international and regional codifications of human rights: trafficking in children would clearly engage with the rights recognized under the Convention on the Rights of the Child and protection against counterfeiting in the Americas has special recognition under the Salvador Protocol.[34]

These relate to the first kind of intersection between TCO crimes and human rights; the second kind—procedural guarantees when the crimes are investigated and prosecuted—would impact on rights relating to fair trial.[35] In essence, the accused is given the opportunity to defend themselves against clear and unambiguous charges, in a public and impartial hearing, in a timely and equitable fashion. Inevitably, these expectations were devised with an individual rights holder in mind but can still be applied to a legal person defendant in a practical sense (for example, a lawyer appointed to represent the TCO), although some who raise objections to the analogous idea of corporate criminal liability question whether criminal law (particularly the element of *mens rea*) fits to a defendant who does not have the natural person's ability to act wilfully or negligently.[36]

Also, the blunt instrument that criminalizes groups can impact on human rights. An illustrative example would be the criminalization of groups determined as terrorist under UK law. Under the UK Terrorism Act 2000, the Secretary of State has the power to proscribe an organisation she believes is concerned with terrorism (broadly, the commission, preparation, promotion, or encouragement of terrorism);[37] it is then an offence to be a member (or supporter) of the proscribed organisation.[38] Whilst this prohibition of association directly conflicts with the corresponding right to freedom of association under Article 11 of the European Convention on Human Rights, because the Article's clawback provision allows a state party to proportionately restrict this right under law for a legitimate aim such as in the interests of national security, the proscription of suspected terrorist organisations would not violate the state's human rights obligations.[39] The concerns with this piece of legislation have related to the fairness of the procedure to review a decision to proscribe an organisation (tied to

[32] Arts 6–12, 17 ICCPR. [33] Art. 15, ICESCR.

[34] Re child trafficking—Art. 35, Convention on the Rights of the Child, agreed 20 November 1989, entered into force 2 September 1990, 1577 UNTS 3 (this article expressly but many other rights are affected by child trafficking); also additional protection under the Optional Protocol to the Convention on the Rights of Child on the sale of children, child prostitution, and child pornography, agreed 25 May 2000, entered into force 18 January 2002, 2171 UNTS 227; re intellectual property—Art. 14, Additional Protocol to the American Convention on Human Rights in the Area of Economic, Social, and Cultural Rights, agreed 17 November 1988, entered into force 16 November 1999, OAS TS 69.

[35] Arts 9, 10, 14, 15, and 16, ICCPR.

[36] Weenink, 'The Russian mafiya', cited in note 13 above; Wells and Elias, 'Catching the conscience of the king', cited in note 12 above, pp. 141–75.

[37] Terrorism Act 2000, p. 3. [38] Terrorism Act 2000, pp. 11–13. [39] Art. 11(2), ECHR.

the underlying criticism of the wide nature of the definition of terrorism under UK law)[40] as well as to the individual's procedural rights: when accused of membership of a proscribed organisation, the defences available to the individual arguably reverse the burden of proof.[41] Wherever possible, the minister responsible for legislation introduced after the Human Rights Act 1998 (HRA), on its introduction to Parliament must make a declaration as to its compatibility with the rights incorporated under the HRA. This is a conscious public statement considering human rights implications; subsequent to the bill's enactment, further human rights review might occur through judicial review. Should the legislation be found lacking then there can be a judicial 'declaration of incompatibility', and an invitation to amend the legislation (the court cannot strike it down); this 'enact, review, amend' cycle has led to notable revisions of UK anti-terrorism legislation, to increase compatibility with the UK's human rights obligations.

The criminalization of a group or collective is echoed in the UN's use of sanctions related to Al-Qaeda when individuals, groups, undertakings, or entities can be placed on the UN Security Council's Al-Qaeda Sanctions Committee List (also called the 1267 Sanctions Committee).[42] The review of this list is undertaken by an Independent Ombudsperson (created a decade after the Sanctions List itself) who investigates and sends a recommendation back to the Committee.[43] Interestingly, a search of the 1267 Sanctions Committee guidelines offered no consideration of the rights of those on the List (except the similar 'humanitarian consideration' in urgent or emergency situations); the Ombudsperson's Approaches to her review does contain reference to the rights of those under the sanctions.[44] There is noticeably an ambivalent human rights approach and lack of (judicial) review of decisions made in the UN system, compared with the UK example.[45]

Which is to be the model, when considering TCOs? If they are to be criminalized, and membership made illegal, then there needs to be consideration of the human rights impact of this, both on the individual affected and on the organisation itself. Whilst rights may not yet attach to an organisation, those individuals affected would expect their rights to be complied with, and any interference introduced

[40] Colin Warbrick, 'The European response to terrorism in an age of human rights', (2004) 15 *EJIL*, 989, p. 1009; Clive Walker, 'Clamping down on terrorism in the UK', (2006) 4 *JICJ*, 1137, p. 1146.

[41] Andrew Ashworth, 'Four threats to the presumption of innocence', (2006) 10 *International Journal of Evidence and Proof*, 241; Nicola Padfield, 'The burden of proof unresolved', (2005) 64 *Cambridge Law Journal* 17.

[42] UN SC Res. 1267, 15 October 1999, UN Doc. S/RES/1267.

[43] UN SC Res. 1904, 17 December 2009, UN Doc. S/RES/1904. The current (and only) Ombudsperson is Kimberley Prost.

[44] Office of the Ombudsperson of the Security Council's 1267 Committee, 'Approach to and standard for analysis, observations, principal arguments and recommendation', August 2011, available at: http://www.un.org/en/sc/ombudsperson/approach.shtml, accessed 29 September 2015.

[45] Erika de Wet, 'From *Kadi* to *Nada*: judicial techniques favouring human rights over United Nations Security Council sanctions', (2013) 12 *Chinese JIL*, 787. In a prescient observation, Boister warned of the absence of human rights within multiple international treaties that seek to criminalize behaviour: 'human rights obligations should be included ... because international law is still "constitutionally" weak' (Neil Boister, 'Human rights protections in the suppression conventions', (2002) 2 *Human Rights Law Review*, 199, p. 224).

according to international human rights law (IHRL) with the opportunity of independent review. The advantage to a criminal prosecution is that established procedural safeguards exist within a criminal justice process to protect the rights of those involved. The disadvantage to this system would be in how well an organisational defendant might 'fit' in a system designed for adjudicating individual responsibility. Is it fit for purpose? Why is a criminal process prioritized, even? When addressing the question of accountability for TCOs, *who* is being held accountable and under *what* system of law, is important to critically consider, to determine the fairest and most appropriate system to use.

19.3.3 Moving beyond the dichotomy or not?

Two avenues therefore are open: to use criminal law to prosecute the TCO or, where there is no willingness on the part of the state or an inability owing to lack of law, a rights violation can be identified through tort law or specialized committee. Recent examples illustrate this. In 2002, the African Commission on Human and Peoples' Rights decided whether Nigeria had violated various rights, protected under the African Charter on Human and Peoples' Rights, of members of the Ogoni people through the operations of its national oil company in partnership with a multinational oil company.[46] The rights engaged were the right to the best attainable state of physical and mental health, to a generally satisfactory environment favourable to their development, to freely dispose of their wealth and natural resources, to property, and to family.[47] As the Commission found in considering the Merits, a state has a duty under IHRL to respect, protect, promote, and fulfil the rights contained within a human rights treaty, and under the African Charter those include under Article 2(1) the taking of 'steps ... by all appropriate means, including particularly the adoption of legislative measures'.[48] The Commission found Nigeria wanting in all respects of its duty; the absence of national legal options in this instance meant the alternative avenue of a specialized human rights committee was needed. A second example would be the cases brought under the Alien Tort Statute in the USA: where local jurisdictions have not been able or willing to prosecute human rights violations, victims have brought suit in a foreign jurisdiction to seek accountability.[49]

The vanguard case under this law, *Filartaga v Pena-Irala*, concerning the torture and death of a member of the complainants' family by a local police captain in Paraguay; when attempts at criminal prosecution in Paraguay itself were corrupted, and the accused moved to New York, the Filartagas brought a wrongful death action against the

[46] *Social and Economic Action Rights Centre and Centre for Economic and Social Rights v Nigeria*, African Commission on Human and Peoples' Rights, ACHPR/COMM/155/96, Decision on 13–27 October 2001 [Ogoni Decision].

[47] Respectively Arts 16, 24, 21, 14, and 18(1), African Charter of Human and Peoples' Rights.

[48] Ogoni Decision, cited in note 46 above, paras 43–8.

[49] Judiciary Act of 1789, Ch. 20, p. 9(b), 1 Stat. 73, 77 (1789), codified at 28 USC s. 1350 ('all causes where an alien sues for a tort only (committed) in violation of the law of nations'). *Kiobel v Royal Dutch Petroleum Co.*, 133 S.Ct 1659 (2013).

Pena-Irala.[50] The success of this case—holding to account a state official for a violation under IHRL that took place extra-territorially—led to a steady stream of similar actions, and whilst some may criticize this on the grounds of forum shopping, it is an unfair accusation when the alternative is no accountability owing to inadequate, non-existent, or corrupt local laws or processes.[51]

19.4 Holding TCOs Accountable: International State Responsibility vs International Criminal Law

19.4.1 The concept of state responsibility

The concepts of state responsibility and criminal responsibility are conceived fundamentally differently by the International Law Commission (ILC), as Math Noortmann argues in *Enforcing International Law.*[52] According to Noortmann, 'State crimes constitute a specific form of organised crime' and should be treated accordingly.[53] Special Rapporteur James Crawford, however, advised the ILC to reject the concept of 'international crimes' as adopted on First Reading and instead to adopt the notion of 'a serious breach' of an obligation held by states.[54] Underlying that terminological change, according to Crawford, 'was the fundamental doubt over what it means to say a State has committed a "crime", especially now that international law has developed that notion of *criminal responsibility of individuals* to such an extent'.[55]

If we do not know 'what it means to say a state has committed a crime', we must admit that we do not know 'what it means to say an organisation has committed a crime'. And that is precisely where the political problem merges; organisations, to the extent that they are constituted as legal persons according to either national or international law seek to avoid criminal accountability and divert the prosecuting attention to natural persons that represent the organisation. And international tribunals concur as seen from the following:

> Crimes against International Law are committed by men not by abstract entities and only by punishing individuals who commit such crimes can the provision of International law be enforced.[56]

[50] *Filartaga and Filartaga v Pena Irala*, US Court of Appeals, Second Cir. (No. 191, Docket 79-6090), Decision 30 June 1980.

[51] The recent case under the Alien Tort Statute—*Kiobel*—suggests a more limited use of this piece of legislation in the future, after the court interpreted its jurisdiction towards a 'presumption against extra-territoriality'. See Ingrid Wuerth, '*Kiobel v Royal Dutch Petroleum Co.*: the Supreme Court and the Alien Tort Statute', (2013) 107 *AJIL* 601; Sarah Cleveland, 'After *Kiobel*', (2014) 12 *JICJ*, 551.

[52] Math Noortmann, *Enforcing International Law: From Self-Help to Self-Contained Regimes*, Aldershot, Ashgate, 2005.

[53] Ibid.

[54] Compare Art. 19 of the 1996 draft and Art. 40 of the 2001 draft. ILC Yearbook (1976), Vol. II, pp. 95–122 and Crawford Third Report, A/CN.4/507/Add. 4, para. 412. See also James Crawford, *The International Law Commission's Articles on State Responsibility: Introduction, Text, and Commentaries*, Cambridge, CUP, 2005.

[55] ILC Yearbook 1976, cited in note 54 above, p. 17 (emphasis added).

[56] Quoted from Joanna Kyriakakis, 'International legal personality, collective entities and international crimes', in Noemi Gal-Or, Cedric Ryngaert, and Math Noortmann (eds), *Responsibilities of the Non-State*

The trend to prosecute individuals rather than organisations has become the default line in international (criminal) law ever since the post-Second World War military tribunals, up and until the constitution of the ICC.[57] It must therefore be seriously questioned whether international law does not inherently 'draw any categorical distinction between responsibility *ex delicto* and *ex contractu*' as Crawford claims.[58] The categorical distinction between civil and criminal responsibility has traditionally been applied, in such historical cases, against Karl Krauch, Alfred Krupp, and Friedrich Flick who were criminally indicted as CEOs and/or owners of their respective companies: IG Farben, Krupp, and Flick. The corporations, however, were at the most subjected to reparation payments but not legally dissolved as the result of a criminal investigation. A clear distinction is apparently made between organisations involved in activities that have subsequently been labelled as criminal, and organisations that are intentionally criminal. That distinction is of importance for the question whether a state can be held responsible for the actions of TCOs, which must be answered on the basis of the rules of attribution and due diligence.[59]

19.4.2 Attribution and due diligence

The 2001 ILC Articles on State Responsibility include eight Articles on attribution, but are virtually silent on due diligence. The latter principle applies in relation to private persons, the conduct of which 'is not as such' attributable to the state, according to the ILC.[60] In underpinning its opinion the Commission cites the 1923 *Tellini* case:

> The responsibility of a State is only involved by the commission in its territory of a political crime against the persons of foreigners if the State has neglected to take all reasonable measures for the prevention of the crime and the pursuit, arrest and bringing to justice of the criminal.[61]

In its comments to the Articles on attribution, the ILC states that

> [i]n theory, the conduct of all human beings, corporations or collectivities linked to the State by nationality, habitual residence or incorporation might be attributed to the State, whether or not they have any connection to the Government. In international law, such an approach is avoided, both with a view to limiting responsibility to conduct which engages the State as an organization, and also so as to recognize

Actor in Armed Conflict and the Market Place, Heidelberg, Brill, 2015, p. 98. See also International Military Tribunal (Nuremberg), judgment of 1 October 1946, reprinted in (1947) 41 *AJIL* (1), 221.

[57] Cristina Chiomenti, 'Corporations and the International Criminal Court', in Olivier de Schutter (ed.), *Transnational Corporations and Human Rights*, Oxford, Hart, 2006; van der Wilt, 'Corporate criminal responsibility for international crimes', cited in note 15 above.

[58] Crawford, *The ILC Articles*, cited in note 54 above, p. 11.

[59] The question whether organisations can be held responsible for the criminal offences of their employees/officers hinges on the applicability of the same two legal concepts.

[60] See 2001 Draft articles on Responsibility of States for Internationally Wrongful Acts, with commentaries, UN Doc. A/56/10, p. 38.

[61] Ibid.

> the autonomy of persons acting on their own account and not at the instigation of a public authority. Thus, the general rule is that the only conduct attributed to the State at the international level is that of its organs of government, or of others who have acted under the direction, instigation or control of those organs, i.e. as agents of the State.[62]

The combined application of the principles of attribution and due diligence rules out the responsibility of states for acts of TCOs, other than those they direct, or fail to pursue and prosecute. But even if that intent or unwillingness could be established, it would only provide other states with the right to make a claim under the law of international state responsibility, or file individual indictments with the ICC.[63]

19.5 The Fight against TCOs as a Threat to Human Rights

19.5.1 General human rights restrictions by states

Rights fall into categories that differentiate the level of permissible state interference: absolute *versus* qualified rights, derogable *versus* non-derogable rights.[64] Human rights treaties distinguish the rights within, identifying some that are unimpeachable regardless of whether a public emergency befalls a state, some that from which derogation is permissible in a time of public emergency, and others that can have restrictions placed upon them under law and for a specific, listed purpose, in circumstances other than a public emergency. For example, under the ICCPR, in times of public emergency under Article 4 derogation from rights relating to life, torture, and slavery is not permissible, but within those rights' articles there is scope to lawfully interfere with the rights to life (i.e. impose the death penalty)[65] and to freedom from slavery (through the exception for 'forced or compulsory labour' as part of a prison sentence).[66] The right to freedom of association with others is an example of a qualified right, that is a right that can be interfered with under legal prescription, when necessary in a democratic society and for one of the listed legitimate aims such as national security or public safety.[67] Who would decide as to the existence of a public emergency or necessity in a democratic society? Respectively, the executive or legislature of the state. For example, the case of *A & Others* in the UK provides a good illustration of this: the highest court in the UK was faced with the question whether an anti-terrorism statute (enabling the indefinite detention of suspected international terrorists) complied with the UK's obligations under the European Convention on Human Rights.[68] The first question the judges answered was whether there existed a public emergency that could be invoked by the executive to encroach

[62] Ibid, p. 38.

[63] It is to be noted here that the ICC has no jurisdiction over legal persons.

[64] The ICESCR has a different approach owing to the unique nature of its obligation: these rights are 'progressively realized' (ICESCR, Art. 2(1)) rather than instantly recognized on ratification or incorporation into domestic law, allowing states parties to particularize their compliance.

[65] Art. 6, ICCPR.

[66] Art. 8, ICCPR.

[67] Art. 22, ICCPR.

[68] *A and Others v Secretary of State for the Home Department*, [2004] UKHL 56.

on the suspects' rights; the majority of judges declined to be drawn into this question, deeming the determination of a public emergency a question for politicians privy to security and intelligence information.[69] Their second question—whether the indefinite detention provision satisfied the conditions of necessary in a democratic society and for a legitimate aim—was one they could examine, focusing on justiciable appraisals of proportionality.[70] This example shows government and judiciary having particular roles regarding the parameters of derogable and qualified rights, and the principle of the rule of law assisting in correctly assigning those roles; an example of the application of international human rights law to domestic law, and how it can lawfully have restrictions.

19.5.2 Specific human rights violations by states *vis-à-vis* legal and illegal corporate entities

19.5.2.1 The problem of 'criminalization'

The 'criminalization' of organisations that have a licit status under the law serves a political purpose and takes place at both the international and the national level. No organisation is immune from (inter)governmental efforts to label organisations as criminal—whether that organisation be legally established as a cooperative, a charity, a foundation, or an association—or enact criminal laws that would restrict non-governmental and corporate activities. Examples include such actions as the criminal charges (piracy) brought against Greenpeace by Russian investigators, the acceptance of the 1267/1999 Al-Qaeda Sanctions List by the UN Security Council,[71] or the enactment of counter-terrorism and organised crime laws that enable the taking of legal action against biker groups.

'Outlaw' motorcycle clubs have acquired a considerable criminal reputation since US clubs distanced themselves from the official American Motorcyclists Association, which was established in 1924. Many members of outlaw motorcycle clubs have been subjected to legal proceedings and initiatives to restrict their entrance into public and private buildings. While entrance may not be restricted on grounds of public appearance and/or membership, members of motorcycle clubs may be obliged to remove their colours, because of the twin assumptions of provocation and violence.[72] Similar cases are reported from Australia and Canada.

The efforts of national governments to ban outlaw biker clubs has not as yet been very successful. In 2007, the Dutch Ministry of Justice was rebuffed by the court in Amsterdam. In the words of the court, 'the case transcends the violation [of] the rights of the individual suspects in a criminal case, but affects public trust in the rule

[69] Ibid, paras 27–9. [70] Ibid, paras 43–4.

[71] The list was established on the basis of UN SC Resolution 1267 of 15 October 1999. See http://unscr.com/en/resolutions/doc/1267, accessed 29 February 2016.

[72] Cf. the Unruh Civil Rights Act, California Civil Code, p. 51, available at: http://law.onecle.com/california/civil/51.html, with *Cohen v California*, 403 US 15 (1971) and *Hessians Motorcycle Club v J. C. Flanagans*, Court of Appeal, Fourth Dist., Div. 3, California, available at: http://caselaw.findlaw.com/ca-court-of-appeal/1464906.html, both accessed 12 February 2016.

of law in general'.[73] The position of the Dutch government with respect to what they call 'outlaw bikers' is exemplary. In a letter to the Dutch Parliament, the Minister of Justice and Security refers to 'signals' that 'particular motorclubs are obtaining positions in organised crime'.[74] The main problem according to the Minister is the 'gathering of legal proof'. The 'integrated approach' that the Ministry adopted combines administrative law, tax law, and criminal law instruments that affect both members and the clubs. The Minister ends his letter with the following paragraph:

> In addition, we cooperate sometimes with Europol. Europol actively promotes expertise and information exchange, and transnational cooperation, such as Joint Investigation teams (JITs). The engagement with outlaw bikers is the longest running project of Europol. … A number of other European countries have intensified their action against outlaw bikers.[75]

In his letter, human rights and global initiatives against organised crime are ignored. While most of the outlaw biker groups have a well-known global network of local 'chapters', the transnational element of this alleged form of organised crime is overlooked. In particular, where these organisations are considered to be involved in drugs trafficking, money laundering, the arms trade, and prostitution, maintaining links with other criminal organisations, the main investigative focus seems to revolve around intimidation, extortion, violence, and gun possession, i.e. crimes that would require less transnational organisation. Criminalizing these organisations seems to have a predominantly national political purpose and has no wider transnational policy implications.

19.6 Final Conclusions: Criminal Offences or Human Rights Violations: What is the Difference?

On a simple level, there is little difference between 'crimes' and infringements of 'human rights'. In both regards a harm or injury is recognized and whether it is labelled a criminal offence or a human rights violation is secondary to the recognition itself. The way in which the harm or injury is classified becomes much more pertinent when considering how to respond to it. Should criminal justice prevail, so also do procedural frameworks, legal definitions, and a clearly delineated impartial court identifying an individual or organisation responsible, locating an appropriate punishment. Alternatively, should a human rights violation be found, a more political, systematic response is made within a discursive report or decision. In a victim-centred approach, how you categorize can make little difference as long as the harm ends, responsibility is apportioned, and (perhaps) compensation occurs. There may be a normative aspect

[73] Cited from NRC 20 December 2007, available at: http://vorige.nrc.nl/nieuwsthema/hellsangels/article1853741.ece, accessed 12 February 2016.

[74] Letter of the Minister of Justice and Security to the Chair of the Second Chamber of the Dutch Parliament, 25 January 2012, available at: http://1percent.nl/PDF/20120125BriefGeintegreerdeAanpakOutlawbikers.pdf, accessed 12 February 2016.

[75] Ibid, p. 6.

too: once this historic harm is recognized, prevention of future harms might ensue through deterrence and/or informed reform of policy or law, and both a criminal justice process and a human rights adjudication could achieve this. What needs to not occur is for one branch to be prioritized or suppress the other, where the criminalization of an organisation stemming from frustration at an inability to reach the individuals involved results in a curtailment of rights, a lack of judicial oversight, or a failure to fit an (individual) norm to a (collective) defendant.

20

Law of the Sea and Transnational Organised Crime

Alexander Proelss and Tobias Hofmann

20.1 Introduction

In its 2004 report 'A more secured world: our shared responsibility'[1] the High Level Panel on Threats, Challenges and Change identified transnational organised crime as one of the six clusters of threats that the international community has to face in the twenty-first century.[2] It described transnational organised crime as 'a menace to States and society, eroding human security',[3] as something that 'facilitates many of the most serious threats to international peace and security', and that creates a 'permissive environment for civil conflict'.[4] Prior to the 1980s, organised crime was more or less considered to be an internal problem of a few states like Italy (Cosa Nostra, Camorra, and 'Ndrangheta), Japan (Yakuza) or China (Triads), but with ongoing globalization it has more and more developed into a transnational challenge. In light of this development, states started to recognize that an international approach based on cooperation was necessary in order to effectively combat and prevent transnational organised crime.[5] In this respect, the former Secretary-General of the United Nations (UN), Kofi Annan, once stated: 'if crime crosses borders, so must law enforcement. If the rule of law is undermined not only in one country, but in many, then those who defend it cannot limit themselves to purely national means.'[6]

Although no precise and comprehensive definition of the concept of transnational organised crime exists, it can be said that it refers to acts committed by an

[1] UN Doc. A/59/565 of 2 December 2004, 'A more secure world: our shared responsibility—Report of the High Level Panel on Threats, Challenges and Change.'

[2] The High Level Panel on Threats, Challenges, and Change was appointed by the then Secretary-General Kofi Annan in November 2003. It was asked to assess the threats that the international community will face in the twenty-first century and to make recommendations how to deal with them. For more information, see: http://www.un.org/en/events/pastevents/a_more_secure_world.shtml, accessed 10 October 2015. The other threats identified by the Panel were: (1) economic and social threats, including poverty, infectious disease and environmental degradation, (2) inter-state conflict, (3) internal conflict, including civil war, genocide, and other large-scale atrocities, (4) nuclear, radiological, chemical, and biological weapons, and (5) terrorism.

[3] HL Panel, 'A more secure world', cited in note 1 above, para. 165.

[4] Ibid, para. 23.

[5] Naples Political Declaration and Global Action Plan against Organized Transnational Crime, UN Doc. A/RES/49/159 of 23 December 1994.

[6] United Nations Office on Drugs and Crime, *United Nations Convention Against Transnational Organized Crime and the Protocols Thereto*, New York, UN, 2004, p. iii (foreword by Kofi A. Annan).

organised criminal group in order to obtain a financial or other material benefit, and that it is characterized by a transboundary element.[7] It can furthermore be asserted that the concept of transnational organised crime is not *a priori* limited to a few particular crimes, but rather that any crime can principally fall within its scope.[8] While it thus constitutes an evolutionary concept that, as a matter of principle, is capable of encompassing all (future) manifestations of transnational organised crime, some crimes, including drug trafficking, migrant smuggling, and human trafficking, are generally recognized as its typical manifestations. These crimes have in common that their commission presupposes successful transportation.[9] Measures taken to prevent the transport of, say, illegal goods, weapons, or persons are thus particularly important for effectively fighting transnational organised crime. This is where the international law of the sea comes into play, taking into account that shipping represents a centrally important mode of transport in the era of globalization.

Against this background, this chapter attempts to analyse how the international law of the sea contributes to the prevention of and fight against transnational organised crime. In particular, it sets out conditions and circumstances under which states may interdict foreign ships engaged in transnational organised crime. In doing so, it recognizes that the concept of interdiction describes a two-step process: it includes, 'first, the boarding, inspection and search of a ship at sea suspected of prohibited conduct; [and] second, where such suspicions prove justified, taking measures including any combination of arresting the vessel, arresting persons aboard or seizing cargo'.[10] It is not possible here, for reasons of limited space, to assess all potentially relevant activities. Theoretically, the field of transnational organised crime in relation to the international law of the sea is as broad as its terrestrial counterpart. This is why this chapter, following an introduction to the maritime zones and jurisdiction under the international law of the sea (section 20.2), focuses on the exercise of jurisdiction over ships suspected of being involved in the most relevant crimes (section 20.3), including piracy, human trafficking, drug trafficking, and transport of weapons of mass destruction (WMD).[11] It does not address other pertinent issues such as illegal, unreported, and unregulated fisheries (though the potential of such activity for

[7] See—for the matter of definition—Ch. 2 of this book, sections 2.1.1 and 2.3.2 and Ch. 21. Art. 2(a) of the United Nations Convention Against Transnational Organized Crime (UNTOC) of 15 November 2000, 2225 UNTS 209, defines 'organised criminal group' as a 'structured group of three or more persons, existing for a period of time and acting in concert with the aim of committing one or more serious crimes or offences established in accordance with this Convention, in order to obtain, directly or indirectly, a financial or other material benefit'. Cf. also Art. 3(2) UNTOC stipulating that an offence is transnational in nature, if '(a) it is committed in more than one State, or (b) it is committed in one State but substantial parts of its preparation, planning, direction and control takes place in another State, or (c) it is committed in one State but involves an organized criminal group that engages in criminal activities in more than one State, or (d) it is committed in one State but has substantial effects in another State'.

[8] Ibid, Art. 2(b).

[9] Cyrille Fijnaut and Letizia Paoli, 'Transnational organized crime', in Rüdiger Wolfrum (ed.), *Max Planck Encyclopedia of Public International Law*, Vol. IX, Oxford, OUP, 2012, p. 1049, p. 1051.

[10] Douglas Guilfoyle, *Shipping Interdiction and the Law of the Sea*, Cambridge, CUP, 2009, p. 4.

[11] Note that Guilfoyle, ibid, p. 180 considers only migrant smuggling and human trafficking as 'transnational crimes'.

transnational organised crime is, at least theoretically, considerable) or recent controversial activities such as sand smuggling.[12]

20.2 Maritime Zones and Jurisdiction under the International Law of the Sea

The international law of the sea as it stands today is the result of a compromise that reconciles vital (security) interests of coastal states on one hand with the interest of other states, whether coastal or not, in using the seas to the fullest possible extent on the other.[13] Since the entry into force of the United Nations Convention on the Law of the Sea (UNCLOS) on 16 November 1994,[14] it is generally accepted that the sea is divided into several maritime zones. These include:

(1) the internal waters which encompass all waters on the landward side of the baseline,[15]

(2) the territorial sea with a maximum breath of 12 nautical miles (nm) measured from the baseline,[16]

(3) the contiguous zone with a maximum breadth of 24 nm measured from the baseline,[17] and

(4) the Exclusive Economic Zone (EEZ) with a maximum breath of 200 nm measured from the baseline.[18]

Those parts of the sea that are not included in the internal waters, the territorial sea, the contiguous zone, and the EEZ form part of the regime of the high seas.[19] In all these zones, states, whether coastal or not, have different rights and duties. It can be said that the competence and authority of coastal states decrease and the rights of 'using' states increase with growing distance to the coastline. In this respect, while the coastal state exercises sovereignty over its internal waters (including ports) and the territorial sea,[20] on the high seas it is only entitled to exercise jurisdiction over ships flying its flag.[21] This is the reason why in the majority of cases the international law of the sea in general and the UNCLOS in particular do not provide a single and simple answer to whether a given conduct is in conformity with them or not. Rather, in many instances a particular conduct is lawful in one part of the sea while it is at least subject to legal limitations in another part of the ocean.

Taking into account that every interdiction operation ought to be considered as an exercise of jurisdiction, it seems appropriate here to give a short introduction to the

[12] For a report on accusations that ships flying the flag of Singapore are allegedly involved in sand smuggling activities see: http://foreignpolicy.com/2010/08/04/the-sand-smugglers/, accessed 10 October 2015.

[13] Myres S. McDougal and William T. Burke, *The Public Order of the Oceans*, Montreal, McGill University Press, 1962, p. 51ff.

[14] United Nations Convention on the Law of the Sea of 10 December 1982, 1833 UNTS 3.

[15] Cf. Art. 8(1) UNCLOS. [16] Cf. Art. 3 UNCLOS. [17] Cf. Art. 33(2) UNCLOS.

[18] Cf. Art. 57 UNCLOS. Note that the concept of the continental shelf is not mentioned here due to the fact that it only covers certain areas of the seabed and the subsoil thereof and thus is not relevant in the context of transnational organised crime.

[19] Cf. Art. 86 UNCLOS. [20] See Art. 2(1) UNCLOS. [21] Cf. Art. 92(1) 1 UNCLOS.

concept of jurisdiction, in particular as it is generally acknowledged that the term 'jurisdiction' can have many and different meanings in international law.[22] Sometimes the term is used simply to describe the power of an (international) court or tribunal to hear and decide a particular case,[23] whereas in the context of human rights law, 'jurisdiction' refers to a situation where a state, through its officials, exercises a certain degree of control over persons or territory.[24] Under general international law, the concept of jurisdiction describes the extent of a state's competence to govern persons and property by its laws.[25] In essence, two forms of jurisdiction exist: jurisdiction to prescribe, or 'legislative jurisdiction', on one hand and jurisdiction to enforce, or 'executive jurisdiction', on the other.[26] The term legislative jurisdiction refers to a state's competence under international law to adopt, alter, and abandon laws, whereas the latter term addresses a state's power to enforce the laws that it previously prescribed.[27]

It is important to note that jurisdiction in terms of the aforementioned clarifications is not synonymous with sovereignty, but rather that the former is an aspect or central feature of the latter.[28] As the Permanent Court of International Justice (PCIJ) stated, jurisdiction 'is one of the most obvious forms of the exercise of sovereign power'.[29] It should further be noted that jurisdiction is, as was recently emphasized by the International Court of Justice (ICJ) in its *Palestinian Wall* Advisory Opinion, 'primarily territorial'.[30] The same conclusion had already been drawn by the PCIJ in its famous *Lotus* judgment in 1927 where it stated that

> the first and foremost restriction imposed by international law upon a State is that—failing the existence of a permissive rule to the contrary—it may not exercise its power in any form in the territory of another State. In this sense jurisdiction is certainly territorial; it cannot be exercised by a State outside its territory except by virtue of a permissive rule derived from international custom or from a convention.[31]

[22] Robert Jennings, 'The limits of state jurisdiction', (1962) 32 *Nordic Journal of International Law*, 209, p. 212.

[23] Christopher Staker, 'Jurisdiction', in Malcolm Evans (ed.), *International Law*, 4th edn, Oxford, OUP, 2014, p. 309, p. 310.

[24] Marko Milanovic, 'From compromise to principle: clarifying the concept of state jurisdiction in human rights treaties', (2008) 8 *Human Rights Law Review*, 411, p. 417.

[25] Robert Jennings and Arthur Watts, *Oppenheim's International Law*, 9th edn, Oxford, OUP, 1992, p. 456ff.; James Crawford, *Brownlie's Principles of Public International Law*, 8th edn, Oxford, OUP, 2012, p. 456; Frederick A. Mann, 'The doctrine of jurisdiction in international law', (1964) 111 *Recueil de Cours* (I), 9, p. 13; Malcolm N. Shaw, *International Law*, 7th edn, Cambridge, CUP, 2014, p. 469; Roger O'Keefe, 'Universal jurisdiction—clarifying the basic concept', (2004) 2 *JICJ* (3), 735, p. 736; Staker, 'Jurisdiction', cited in note 23 above, p. 309.

[26] Crawford, *Brownlie's Principles*, cited in note 25 above, p. 456.

[27] Cedric Ryngaert, *Jurisdiction in International Law*, Oxford, OUP, 2008, p. 9; Shaw, *International Law*, cited in note 25 above, p. 472; Staker, 'Jurisdiction', cited in note 23 above, p. 312.

[28] Crawford, *Brownlie's Principles*, cited in note 25 above, p. 456; O'Keefe, 'Universal jurisdiction', cited in note 25 above, p. 735, p. 736; Milanovic, 'From compromise to principle', cited in note 24 above, p. 411, p. 420; Haijiang Yang, *Jurisdiction of the Coastal State over Foreign Merchant Ships in Internal Waters and the Territorial Sea*, Berlin, Springer, 2005, p. 31.

[29] *Legal Status of Eastern Greenland (Norway v Denmark)*, Judgment of 5 April 1933, Ser. A/B, No. 53, p. 22, p. 48.

[30] *Legal Consequences of the Construction of a Wall in the Occupied Palestinian Territories*, Advisory Opinion of 9 July 2004, ICJ Rep. 2004, p. 136, at para. 109.

[31] *The Case of the SS 'Lotus' (France v Turkey)*, Judgment of 7 September 1927, Ser. A, No. 10, p. 1, pp. 18–19.

Surprisingly, the *Lotus* judgment is the only decision of an international court or tribunal that has so far addressed the spatial scope and limits of the jurisdiction of states under international law. Regarding prescriptive jurisdiction, the PCIJ held that no rule exists under international law that would generally prohibit a state from extending the application of its domestic laws to acts committed outside its territory.[32] Whether or not this dictum still reflects international law as its stands today is a matter of controversy. Most scholars agree that in light of the development of international law from a system of mere coordination into a cooperative and partly constitutionalized legal order, any lawful exercise of extra-territorial prescriptive jurisdiction today presupposes the existence of a specific link between the subject matter and the state that exercises jurisdiction.[33]

Concerning enforcement jurisdiction, it is generally recognized that a state is not competent to enforce its rules unless it is not entitled to exercise prescriptive jurisdiction,[34] and that enforcement jurisdiction is in principle limited to the territory of the state concerned[35]—a notion that, even though not directly included in the concept of territory, would also cover jurisdiction over the ships flying the flag of the state concerned.[36] While Section 6 of the UNCLOS stipulates special rules concerning enforcement jurisdiction (with Article 218(1) UNCLOS entitling port states even to exercise extra-territorial enforcement powers),[37] these provisions only deal with the sanctioning of different categories of pollution of the marine environment, in particular from ships. They are not applicable to the issue of transnational organised crime that is relevant here.

20.3 Exercise of Jurisdiction over Ships involved in Transnational Organised Crime

For an analysis of the circumstances under which a state may exercise jurisdiction over ships, it is important to distinguish three different scenarios:

(1) the coastal state exercises jurisdiction over a ship that flies its flag ('flag-state jurisdiction'),

[32] Ibid, p. 19.

[33] Ryngaert, *Jurisdiction in International Law*, cited in note 27 above, p. 85; Staker, 'Jurisdiction', cited in note 23 above, p. 315; Crawford, *Brownlie's Principles*, cited in note 25 above, p. 457.

[34] See Bernard Oxman, 'Jurisdiction of states', in Wolfrum, *Max Planck Encyclopedia of Public International Law*, Vol. VI, cited in note 9 above, p. 546, p. 547.

[35] Staker, 'Jurisdiction', cited in note 23 above, p. 331.

[36] Note that the PCIJ had acted on the assumption that 'a ship on the high seas is assimilated to the territory of the State the flag of which it flies, for, just as in its own territory, that State exercises its authority upon it, and no other State may do so'; see *Lotus* Judgment, cited in note 31 above, p. 25. With the advent of flag-state jurisdiction as the third original type of jurisdiction, this assumption was no longer adhered to. It has correctly been noted that the regime resulting from this development is lacking specificity: 'one particular state is granted exclusive jurisdiction; but the jurisdictional link justifying this exclusive regulatory authority is neither linked to tangible factors … , nor is it normatively specified through internationally agreed standards' (Robin Geiß and Christian Tams, 'Non-flag states as guardians of the maritime order', in Henrik Ringbom [ed.], *Jurisdiction Over Ships*, Leiden/Boston, Brill, 2015, p. 19, p. 23).

[37] See Doris König, *Durchsetzung internationaler Bestands- und Umweltschutzvorschriften auf Hoher See im Interesse der Staatengemeinschaft*, Berlin, Duncker & Humblot, 1990, p. 227ff.

(2) the coastal states exercises jurisdiction over a foreign ship within one of its maritime zones, and

(3) a state exercises jurisdiction over a ship, whether flying its flag or not, that is situated in the maritime zone of another state.

Taking into account that a state is not only entitled but, according to Article 94(1) UNCLOS, under a duty to 'effectively exercise its jurisdiction and control in administrative, technical and social matters over ships flying its flag',[38] and that, as a matter of principle, all laws and regulations of the flag state are applicable to its ships, this chapter focuses on the second and third scenarios.

20.3.1 Exercise of jurisdiction over foreign ships situated in the internal waters

As stated, the internal waters encompass all waters on the landward side of the baseline from which the breath of the territorial sea is measured.[39] According to Article 2(1) UNCLOS, coastal states enjoy full sovereignty over their internal waters. This was confirmed to also be valid under customary international law by the ICJ in its *Nicaragua* judgment where it held that '[t]he basic legal concept of State sovereignty in customary international law ... extends to the internal waters ... of every State.'[40] Therefore, if a foreign ship voluntarily enters the internal waters of a state, it places itself under the territorial sovereignty of that state and is thus, as a matter of principle, subject to all of its laws.[41]

That said, notwithstanding the rule, mentioned earlier, according to which enforcement jurisdiction generally follows prescriptive jurisdiction, there is still a certain degree of controversy regarding the question whether and to what extent coastal states may exercise their enforcement jurisdiction over foreign ships situated in their internal waters. While some scholars take the position that coastal states may not exercise their jurisdiction over foreign ships unless the peace and good order of the port is affected, other sources argue that no restriction to the jurisdiction of the coastal state exists, but that, as a matter of comity, the coastal state may simply choose to not exercise its

[38] See also Art. 94(2)(b) UNCLOS, according to which every state shall 'assume jurisdiction under its internal law over each ship flying its flag and its master, officers and crew in respect of administrative, technical and social matters concerning the ship.' Note that in its recent Advisory Opinion of 2 April 2015 rendered upon the request of the Sub-regional Fisheries Commission (available at: www.itlos.org/fileadmin/itlos/documents/cases/case_no.21/advisory_opinion/C21_AdvOp_02.04.pdf, accessed 8 October 2015), the International Tribunal for the Law of the Sea (ITLOS) followed from Art. 94 UNCLOS by way of dynamic interpretation that 'as far as fishing activities are concerned, the flag State, in fulfilment of its responsibility to exercise effective jurisdiction and control in administrative matters, must adopt the necessary administrative measures to ensure that fishing vessels flying its flag are not involved in activities which will undermine the flag State's responsibilities under the Convention in respect of the conservation and management of marine living resources. If such violations nevertheless occur and are reported by other States, the flag State is obliged to investigate and, if appropriate, take any action necessary to remedy the situation.' See Advisory Opinion, para. 119.

[39] Cf. Art. 8(1) UNCLOS.

[40] *Military and Paramilitary Activities in and against Nicaragua (Nicaragua v United States of America)* (Merits), Judgment of 27 June 1986, ICJ Rep. 1986, p. 14, at para. 212.

[41] Yang, *Jurisdiction of the Coastal State*, cited in note 28 above, p. 83; Robin R. Churchill and Vaughan A. Lowe, *The Law of the Sea*, 3rd edn, Manchester, Manchester University Press, 1999, p. 65; McDougal and Burke, *The Public Order of the Oceans*, cited in note 13 above, p. 156.

jurisdiction over the foreign ship.[42] It is submitted that the latter view better reflects the attitude of states concerning this issue,[43] and that Article 27(2) UNCLOS also supports this view. This provision empowers the coastal state to take enforcement measures in its territorial sea against a foreign ship after it has left the internal waters of that state. However, if the coastal state is entitled to exercise enforcement jurisdiction in the territorial sea after the ship has left its internal waters, the state must *a fortiori* be competent to take the same enforcement measures within its internal waters against the foreign ship.[44] In any case, the issue addressed here is one of minor practical relevance since states have concluded numerous similar bilateral agreements prescribing the circumstances under which the coastal state may exercise its criminal enforcement jurisdiction over a foreign ship flying the flag of the other party. These agreements uniformly stipulate that the coastal state will not exercise its jurisdiction over foreign ships if only the internal discipline of the ship is concerned, but that it will enforce its laws and regulations in cases (1) where the offence affects its vital interests, (2) when the intervention of the coastal state is requested by the master of the ship, or the consul of the flag state respectively, (3) when a crew member with a nationality different to the flag state is involved, or (4) when the offence committed is of serious character or of a certain gravity.[45] It can thus be concluded that, unless an international treaty provides otherwise, coastal states are generally entitled to interdict foreign ships present in their internal waters to enforce their criminal laws.[46]

Since the coastal state exercises full sovereignty over its ports and internal waters, states other than the coastal state may not interdict ships in the internal waters of the coastal state, not even those flying the flag of the interdicting state, unless the coastal state has given its consent to the interdiction.

20.3.2 Exercise of jurisdiction over foreign ships situated in the territorial sea

20.3.2.1 Exercise of prescriptive jurisdiction

Similar to the situation in the internal waters, the coastal state exercises sovereignty over its territorial sea, but this sovereignty is *a priori* limited as it must

[42] See US Supreme Court, *Mali v Keeper of the Common Jail (Wildenhus's Case)*, 120 US 1, 12 (1887); *Spector v Norwegian Cruise Line Ltd.*, 545 US 119, 127 (2005). For further reading cf. Yang, *Jurisdiction of the Coastal State*, cited in note 28 above, pp. 90–92; Yoshifumi Tanaka, *The International Law of the Sea*, 2nd edn, Cambridge, CUP, 2015, p. 79ff.

[43] For example, §153c(1) No. 2 of the German Code of Criminal Procedure (Strafprozessordnung) stipulates that the public prosecutor may forgo the prosecution when the criminal act was committed within the territory of Germany ('Inland') by an alien aboard a foreign ship.

[44] Vladimir D. Degan, 'Internal waters', (1986) 17 *Netherlands Yearbook of International Law*, 3, p. 25.

[45] Tanaka, *The International Law of the Sea*, cited in note 42 above, p. 80; Churchill and Lowe, *The Law of the Sea*, cited in note 41 above, p. 66ff. seem to share this view when stating that '[d]espite any difference between the theoretical bases of French and Anglo-American practice, it is clear that the practice of these States, and of States in general, is remarkably consistent'.

[46] Rüdiger Wolfrum, 'Freedom of navigation: new challenges', in Myron H. Nordquist, Tommy T. B. Koh, and John Norton Moore (eds), *Freedoms of the Sea, Passage Rights and the 1982 Law of the Sea Convention*, Leiden, Brill, 2009, p. 79, p. 90.

be exercised 'subject to this Convention and to other rules of international law' (Article 2(3) UNCLOS). The coastal state is thus free to enact laws which are applicable to its territorial sea only if and to the extent to which neither the UNCLOS in particular nor international law in general provide for special rules to the contrary. One of the most important restrictions in this regard is prescribed in Article 21 UNCLOS which limits the coastal state's legislative power to regulate innocent passage of foreign ships through its territorial sea.[47] However, no such limitation exists with regard to the state's competence to adopt criminal laws that are (also) applicable in its territorial sea. As stated by O'Connell, '(s)ince international law concedes that States may exercise sovereignty over their territorial waters there is no theoretical impediment to their power to extend their criminal law to passing ships, of whatever flag'.[48]

20.3.2.2 Exercise of enforcement jurisdiction

In 1933, the US–Panama Claims Commission held in the *David* case that '[t]here is a clear preponderance of authority to the effect that this sovereignty [over the territorial sea] is qualified by what is known as the right of innocent passage'.[49] It may be questioned whether this dictum was correct in 1933, but it perfectly reflects the law as it stands today.[50] The right of innocent passage in its present shape is the outcome of a long-lasting controversy between coastal and shipping states that reconciles the security interests of the former with the navigational interests of the latter.[51] According to Article 19 UNCLOS, 'passage is innocent so long as it is not prejudicial to the peace, good order or security of the coastal State'. Article 19(2) UNCLOS then sets out under which circumstances passage ought to be considered to be prejudicial to the peace, good order, or security of the coastal state. Article 19(2)(g) UNCLOS, stipulating that 'the loading or unloading of any commodity, currency or person contrary to the customs, fiscal, immigration or sanitary laws and regulations of the coastal State', is particularly relevant in the present context. The provision only covers cases where the loading and unloading takes place within the territorial sea of the coastal state, though, which is why the transportation of goods, weapons, or persons through the territorial sea of another state contrary to that state's customs or immigration laws does not render passage non-innocent. Provided that Article 19(2)(g) UNCLOS is applicable, passage of the suspected ship is considered as being non-innocent, a fact that results in the ship being no longer immune from the coastal state's enforcement jurisdiction.[52] That said, as long as the passage of a ship has to be considered as being innocent, coastal

[47] For a brief overview on the meaning of innocent passage see the following section 20.3.2.2.

[48] Daniel Patrick O'Connell, *The International Law of the Sea*, Vol. II, Oxford, Clarendon Press, 1984, p. 919.

[49] *The Republic of Panama, on behalf of the Compañia de Navigatión Nacional v The United States of America*, Judgment of 29 June 1933, (1934) 28 *AJIL*, 596, p. 599.

[50] Cf. Natalie Klein, *Maritime Security and the Law of the Sea*, Oxford, OUP, 2011, p. 75.

[51] Karin M. Burke and Deborah A. DeLeo, 'Innocent passage and transit passage in the United Nations Convention on the Law of the Seas', (1982–3) 9 *Yale Journal of World Public Order*, 389, p. 390ff.

[52] O'Connell, *The International Law of the Sea*, cited in note 48 above, p. 919.

states are under the duty not to hamper passage through its territorial sea.[53] This duty includes an obligation to not interdict the ship.

Despite this, the coastal state has, under Article 27 UNCLOS, the competence to exercise criminal (i.e. enforcement) jurisdiction on board a foreign ship present in its territorial sea. This provision distinguishes three types of passage, namely passage by ships that are inward-bound, by ships that are outward-bound, and by ships in lateral passage.[54] In light of Article 27(2) UNCLOS, no doubt exists that the coastal state is entitled to exercise its criminal jurisdiction aboard outward-bound foreign ships. It is noteworthy that Article 27(2) UNCLOS does not even require that the offence was committed while the ship was present in port or elsewhere in the internal waters of the coastal state.[55] In contrast, the situation regarding inward-bound ships is not that clear, taking into account that Article 27 UNCLOS does not contain any express rule on the matter. Some sources assert that it could be inferred from the Article's paragraph 5 (prohibiting the exercise of criminal jurisdiction over ships in lateral passage for cases where the offence was committed before the suspected ship had entered the territorial sea) that enforcement of antecedent crimes is permitted while a ship is in the territorial sea, and that the same must thus apply if the crime is committed while in the ship is in the territorial sea.[56]

Regarding ships in lateral passage, Article 27(1) UNCLOS stipulates that coastal states 'should not' exercise their criminal jurisdiction aboard a foreign ship 'save only in the following cases'. In light of this, Klein seems to take the view that coastal states are not allowed to interdict foreign ships unless one or more of the exceptions set out in Article 27 (1)(a)–(d) UNLCOS are applicable, but no legal reasoning is provided for this conclusion.[57] *Prima facie*, the phrase 'save only in the following cases' seems to support that view, but such an understanding of Article 27 UNCLOS would be difficult to reconcile with the fact that paragraph 1 of this provision only requires that coastal states 'should not' exercise their criminal jurisdiction on board foreign ships. Relying on the drafting history of Article 19 of the 1958 Geneva Convention on the Territorial Sea and the Contiguous Zone (TSC),[58] the dominant view is that this formula implies that Article 27(1) UNCLOS cannot be read in terms of a hard-law obligation.[59] During

[53] Cf. Art. 24(1) UNCLOS.

[54] Cf. Richard Barnes, 'Article 27', in Alexander Proelss (ed.), *United Nations Convention on the Law of the Sea—A Commentary*, Oxford, Hart Publishing, Munich, C. H. Beck and Nomos, 2016, mn. 2 (available to the authors); Ivan A. Shearer, 'Problems of jurisdiction and law enforcement against delinquent vessels', (1986) 35 *ICLQ*, 320, p. 326; O'Connell, *The International Law of the Sea*, cited in note 48 above, p. 958ff.

[55] Shearer, 'Problems of jurisdiction and law enforcement', cited in note 54 above, p. 326.

[56] See O'Connell, *The International Law of the Sea*, cited in note 48 above, p. 958; see also Luke T. Lee, 'Jurisdiction over foreign merchant ships in the territorial sea: an analysis of the Geneva Convention on the Law of the Sea', (1961) 55 *AJIL*, 77, p. 81; Shearer, 'Problems of jurisdiction and law enforcement', cited in note 54 above, p. 326.

[57] Klein, *Maritime Security and the Law of the Sea*, cited in note 50 above, p. 75.

[58] To refer to the drafting history of Art. 19 TSC is justified in light of the fact that the text of Art. 27 UNCLOS is almost identical with that Article. See also Churchill and Lowe, *The Law of the Sea*, cited in note 41 above, p. 98, according to whom '(t)he 1982 Law of the Sea Convention took over, almost verbatim and without any serious debate on their substance, the 1958 provisions'.

[59] Cf. Churchill and Lowe, *The Law of the Sea*, cited in note 41 above, p. 97; Shearer, 'Problems of jurisdiction and law enforcement', cited in note 54 above, p. 327; Guilfoyle, *Shipping Interdiction*, cited in note 10 above, p. 11; O'Connell, *The International Law of the Sea*, cited in note 48 above, p. 960ff.

the negotiations, the original wording (using the words 'may not') of what later became Article 19 TSC, suggested by the International Law Commission (ILC), was replaced by the less strict phrase 'should not'. In particular the US delegation, in full agreement with the statement made by the US–Panama Claims Commission in *David*,[60] insisted that the formulation proposed by the ILC would not take sufficient account of the sovereignty that coastal states enjoy over their territorial sea.[61] Sir Gerald Fitzmaurice shared the view that '(t)he somewhat unfortunate term "should not" in the first line of this provision is intended to reflect the fact that the rule enunciated represents standard international practice rather than strict international law'.[62] It may thus be concluded that Article 27(1) UNCLOS does not preclude the coastal state from exercising its criminal jurisdiction aboard foreign ships in lateral passage through its territorial sea.[63] As stated by Guilfoyle,

> (t)he law has, then, historically rejected a general prohibition over criminal enforcement jurisdiction subject to exceptions, and has deliberately adopted permissive language exhorting restraint. The only absolute exclusion of enforcement jurisdiction is in the case of a crime 'committed before the ship entered the territorial sea' where that merchant vessel is simply passing through territorial waters without entering port.[64]

The view advocated here has been criticized by Wolfrum, arguing that it would ignore the inherent limits of Article 27 UNCLOS and essentially undermine the right of innocent passage.[65] It is true that Article 27(1) UNLCOS must be exercised in a reasonable, non-abusive manner, but this does not necessarily imply the conclusion that the right of innocent passage limits the exercise of the powers conferred on the coastal state by the Article. It should be noted that the UNCLOS itself recognizes that ships in innocent passage may be interdicted, taking into account that Article 24(1) stipulates that '(t)he coastal State shall not hamper the innocent passage of foreign ships through the territorial sea *except in accordance with this Convention*'.[66] Arguably, Article 27 UNCLOS is one of the provisions containing such exceptions. As was stated by Jessup as early as 1927 'the right of innocent passage does not guarantee to the vessel exercising it a total immunity from the processes of the local laws. Only where the littoral sovereign's conduct amounts to an unreasonable interference with navigation can the flag state protest.'[67]

[60] *David* Judgment, cited in note 49 above, p. 599: 'there is no clear preponderance of authority to the effect that such vessels when passing through territorial waters are exempt from civil arrest. In the absence of such authority, the Commission cannot say that a country may not, under the rules of international law, assert the right to arrest on civil process merchant ships passing through its territorial waters.'

[61] Shearer, 'Problems of jurisdiction and law enforcement', cited in note 54 above, p. 327.

[62] Sir Gerald Fitzmaurice, 'Some results of the Geneva Conference on the Law of the Sea', (1959) 8 *ICLQ*, 73, p. 104.

[63] Cf. Churchill and Lowe, *The Law of the Sea*, cited in note 41 above, p. 98; O'Connell, *The International Law of the Sea*, cited in note 48 above, p. 961.

[64] Guilfoyle, *Shipping Interdiction*, cited in note 10 above, p. 12.

[65] Wolfrum, 'Freedom of navigation', cited in note 46 above, p. 91.

[66] Italics added.

[67] Philip C. Jessup, *The Law of Territorial Waters and Maritime Jurisdiction*, New York, G.A. Jennings, 1927, p. 122ff.

As with the situation in internal waters, states other than the coastal state are not entitled to interdict ships situated in the territorial sea of another state without the consent of that state. The situation changes, however, if the UN Security Council empowers states to interdict ships in the territorial sea of another state,[68] or where the coastal state has authorized foreign states to intercept certain ships situated within its territorial sea by treaty or otherwise. In this respect, several treaties concluded between the USA and some Caribbean states to suppress drug trafficking in the Caribbean Sea entitle US officials to board suspected ships within the territorial sea of the respective state without previous consent.[69] That said, most treaties concluded in order to facilitate the interdiction of foreign ships leave the sovereignty of the coastal state untouched. For example, Article 2(2) of the UN Convention against Illicit Traffic in Narcotic Drugs and Psychotropic Substances obliges the states parties not to carry out their obligations in a manner inconsistent with the principles of sovereign equality and territorial integrity of states and that of non-intervention in the domestic affairs of other states.[70] The conventional regulations regarding the suppression of migrant smuggling go even further: Article 4(2) UNTOC, which applies to migrant smuggling according to Article 1 of the First Protocol thereto,[71] states that '[n]othing in this Convention entitles a State Party to undertake in the territory of another State the exercise of jurisdiction and performance of functions that are reserved exclusively for the authorities of that other State by its domestic law'.

20.3.3 Exercise of enforcement jurisdiction over foreign ships situated in the contiguous zone

The contiguous zone is a boundary control zone of up to 24 nm measured from the baselines (cf. Article 33(2) UNCLOS) that partially overlaps with the territorial sea and the regime of the EEZ, or that of the high seas respectively.[72] In this zone, the coastal state enjoys limited control and enforcement powers (only) in regard to the areas listed in Article 33(1) UNCLOS ('customs, fiscal, immigration or sanitary laws'), but it does not have prescriptive jurisdiction. According to the wording of this provision, the control and enforcement measures conducted by the coastal state must be necessary in order to prevent or punish infringements of its laws and regulations on the aforementioned sectors '*within* its territory or territorial sea'.[73] Consequently, a literal understanding of Article 33 UNCLOS would imply that (1) the coastal state may not enact laws at all to apply in the contiguous zone, not even on the fields expressly mentioned, and (2) that enforcement is limited to

[68] Geiß and Tams, 'Non-flag states as guardians', cited in note 36 above, pp. 28–9.

[69] For references see Guilfoyle, *Shipping Interdiction*, cited in note 10 above, p. 94.

[70] UN Convention against Illicit Traffic in Narcotic Drugs and Psychotropic Substances of 20 December 1988 (1582 UNTS 95).

[71] Protocol to Prevent, Suppress, and Punish Trafficking in Persons, Especially Women and Children, supplementing the United Nations Convention Against Transnational Organized Crime of 15 November 2000, 2237 UNTS 319.

[72] Accordingly, the contiguous zone does not have its own territorial legal status.

[73] Italics added.

situations where the effect of the foreign activity concerned on the territory of the coastal state either has already occurred (sub-paragraph (b)) or is imminent (sub-paragraph (a)).[74] It has convincingly been stated that Article 33(1)(b) UNCLOS can only apply to outgoing ships, whereas Article 33(1)(a) UNCLOS is exclusively applicable to incoming ships, taking into account that prevention cannot arise if the ship concerned is in the process of leaving the areas over which the coastal state exercises territorial sovereignty.[75] Article 111(1) and (8) UNCLOS furthermore clarify that the right of hot pursuit covers the contiguous zone, and that the enforcement jurisdiction that the coastal state is entitled to exercise in that zone includes the right to stop and arrest a foreign ship.

The fact that Article 33(1) UNCLOS does not cover security issues that are not related to customs, fiscal, immigration, or sanitary laws prompts the question whether the Interdiction Principles of the US Proliferation Security Initiative (PSI) are compatible with this provision.[76] According to paragraph 4(d) of these Principles, States are called, *inter alia*,

> [t]o take appropriate actions to (1) stop and/or search in their internal waters, territorial seas, or contiguous zones (when declared) vessels that are reasonably suspected of carrying such cargoes to or from states or non-state actors of proliferation concern and to seize such cargoes that are identified; and (2) to enforce conditions on vessels entering or leaving their ports, internal waters or territorial seas that are reasonably suspected of carrying such cargoes, such as requiring that such vessels be subject to boarding, search, and seizure of such cargoes prior to entry.

A literal reading of Article 33(1) UNCLOS would suggest that the shipment of WMD cannot be relied upon in order to stop and arrest a suspected vessel situated in the contiguous zone, provided that the interdiction is not conducted with the sole aim of preventing a violation of the coastal state's customs laws.[77] Arguably, a dynamic interpretation of this provision in terms of Article 31(3)(b) of the Vienna Convention

[74] See Fitzmaurice, 'Some results of the Geneva Conference', cited in note 62 above, p. 114. A more liberal view is taken by O'Connell, *The International Law of the Sea*, cited in note 48 above, p. 1060; Guilfoyle, *Shipping Interdiction*, cited in note 10 above, p. 13. State practice does not seem to be sufficiently uniform to come to a clear conclusion.

[75] O'Connell, *The International Law of the Sea*, cited in note 48 above, p. 1059; Tanaka, *The International Law of the Sea*, cited in note 42 above, p. 125.

[76] The Interdiction Principles form the core of the PSI, a US-led initiative attempting to respond to the growing challenge posed by the proliferation of WMD, their delivery systems, and related materials world-wide. According to a fact sheet of 4 September 2003 made available by the US Department of State, the 'PSI builds on efforts by the international community to prevent proliferation of such items, including existing treaties and regimes' and 'seeks to involve in some capacity all states that have a stake in nonproliferation and the ability and willingness to take steps to stop the flow of such items at sea, in the air, or on land'. In doing this, the PSI 'also seeks cooperation from any state whose vessels, flags, ports, territorial waters, airspace, or land might be used for proliferation purposes by states and non-state actors of proliferation concern'. See http://www.state.gov/t/isn/c27726.htm, accessed 10 October 2015.

[77] Stuart M. Kaye, 'The Proliferation Security Initiative in the maritime domain', in Thomas McK. Sparks and Glenn M. Sulmasy (eds), *International Law Challenges: Homeland Security and Combating Terrorism*, Newport, Rhode Island, Naval War College, 2006, p. 141, p. 150; Tanaka, *The International Law of the Sea*, cited in note 42 above, p. 393; in contrast, Geiß and Tams, 'Non-flag states as guardians', cited in note 36 above, p. 46 argue that the PSI 'has not brought about any substantive changes in the law applicable to maritime interdictions'.

on the Law of Treaties (VCLT) is not possible owing to the lack of sufficiently uniform state practice.[78]

20.3.4 Exercise of jurisdiction over foreign ships situated on the high seas

The high seas are international waters. The legal regime codified in Part VII UNCLOS covers all waters that are not included in one of the other maritime zones mentioned above.[79] Under Article 89 UNCLOS, '[n]o State may validly purport to subject any part of the high seas to its sovereignty'. Thus, states are not authorized to extend their laws and regulations into this space. Rather, the regime of the high seas has always been dominated by the principles of freedom of navigation and exclusive flag-state jurisdiction. Since the one principle logically implies the other, one might say that the principles are two sides of the same coin. The principle of freedom of navigation guarantees to every state, whether land-locked or coastal, that the ships flying its flag are free to navigate on the high seas without any interference from other states.[80] The principle of exclusive flag-state jurisdiction, in turn, makes it clear that only the state the flag of which the ship flies is entitled to exercise (prescriptive as well as enforcement) jurisdiction over that ship on the high seas.[81] Concerning the scope of this jurisdiction, the International Tribunal for the Law of the Sea (ITLOS) clarified in the *M/V Saiga* case that '[t]he ship, every thing on it, and every person involved or interested in its operations are treated as an entity linked to the flag State. The nationalities of these persons are not relevant.'[82]

As with any principle, the principles of freedom of navigation and exclusive flag-state jurisdiction are not absolute. Article 92(1) UNCLOS perfectly mirrors this assumption by stipulating that '[s]hips shall sail under the flag of one State only and, save in exceptional cases expressly provided for in international treaties or in this Convention, shall be subject to its exclusive jurisdiction on the high seas'. In the present context, Article 110 UNCLOS is particularly important. In its relevant parts, this provision states:

> (1) Except where acts of interference derive from powers conferred by treaty, a warship which encounters on the high seas a foreign ship, other than a ship entitled to complete immunity in accordance with articles 95 and 96, is not justified in boarding it unless there is reasonable ground for suspecting that: (a) the ship is engaged in piracy; (b) the ship is engaged in the slave trade; …

[78] Vienna Convention on the Law of Treaties of 23 May 1969, 1155 UNTS 331. Art. 31(3)(b) requires that '[a]ny subsequent practice in the application of the treaty which establishes the agreement of the parties regarding its interpretation' ought to be taken into account when interpreting a treaty.

[79] Cf. Art. 86 UNCLOS. [80] Cf. Art. 90 UNCLOS.

[81] This is not a violation of the general principles regarding the exercise of jurisdiction set out above. In the *Lotus* case, the PCIJ explicitly recognized that a state may exercise enforcement jurisdiction outside its territory in cases where either a conventional or a customary rule confers such a competence on that state. See *Lotus* Judgment, cited in note 31 above, pp. 18–19.

[82] *The M/V 'Saiga' (No. 2) (St. Vincent and the Grenadines v Guinea)*, Judgment of 1 July 1999, ITLOS Rep. 1999, 10, para. 106.

(2) In the cases provided for in paragraph 1, the warship may proceed to verify the ship's right to fly its flag. To this end, it may send a boat under the command of an officer to the suspected ship. If suspicion remains after the documents have been checked, it may proceed to a further examination on board the ship, which must be carried out with all possible consideration.

Article 110 UNCLOS thus entitles warships and other ships on governmental service to board a ship suspected of being engaged in piracy or the slave trade,[83] and, provided that the suspicion remains after the boarding, to search that ship without previous consent by the flag state.

It should be noted that Article 110 UNCLOS confers on third states only a right to board and to search a foreign-flagged ship. It does not confer any further rights, such as the right to seize cargo or to arrest persons, on the third states concerned. Thus, these measures can only be exercised if the flag state has granted its authorization. Notwithstanding this, Syrigos seems to argue that states other than the flag state are entitled to confiscate the ship and to seize its cargo if there is sufficient evidence that 'the ship is engaged in one of the activities punishable on the high sea'.[84] With the exception of the matter regulated by Article 105 UNCLOS, this view conflicts with the clear wording of Article 110 UNCLOS, does not find any support in other provisions of the UNCLOS, and cannot be based on state practice. It ought thus to be rejected.

It should furthermore be noted that the list of activities contained in Article 110(1) UNCLOS is exhaustive. Therefore, as a matter of principle, the provision cannot justify the interdiction of a foreign-flagged ship suspected of, say, drug trafficking, migrant or human trafficking, or other serious crimes without the previous consent of the flag state. The existence of this gap in the regime established by Part VII UNCLOS has recently prompted some scholars to propose to amend Article 110(1) UNCLOS by adding a reference to drug trafficking[85]—a proposal that arguably falls short, though, of meeting in their entirety the challenges that the international community faces today. In all that, despite its exhaustive character, Article 110 UNCLOS does not completely exclude the opportunity for a state other than the flag state to interdict shipping

[83] Cf. Art. 111(5) UNCLOS.

[84] Angelos Syrigos, 'Interdiction of vessels on the high seas', in Anastasia Strati, Maria Gavouneli, and Nikos Skourtos (eds), *Unresolved Issues and New Challenges to the Law of the Sea*, Leiden/Boston, Martinus Nijhoff Publishers, 2006, p. 149, p. 155.

[85] Anatolij L. Kolodkin, Yulia V. Bobrova, and Galina G. Shinkaretskaia, 'Peaceful uses of the seas in the light of new challenges and threats', in Tafsir Malik Ndiaye and Rüdiger Wolfrum (eds), *Law of the Sea, Environmental Law and Settlement of Disputes, Liber Amicorum Judge Thomas M. Mensah*, Leiden/Boston, Martinus Nijhoff Publishers, 2007, p. 437, p. 442. See also European Court of Human Rights (ECtHR), *Case of Medvedyev and Others v France*, Application No. 3394/03, Judgment of 29 March 2010, para. 101:

> it is regrettable, in the Court's view, that the international effort to combat drug trafficking on the high seas is not better coordinated bearing in mind the increasingly global dimension of the problem. The fact remains that when a flag State ... is not a party to the Montego Bay or Vienna Conventions, the insufficiency of such legal instruments, for want of regional or bilateral initiatives, is of no real consequence. ... Having regard to the gravity and enormity of the problem posed by illegal drug trafficking, developments in public international law which embraced the principle that all States have jurisdiction as an exception to the law of the flag State would be a significant step in the fight against illegal trade in narcotics. This would bring international law on drug trafficking into line with what has already existed for many years now in respect of piracy.

on the high seas. It rather recognizes that interdiction powers can be conferred on third states by treaty,[86] and states have extensively made use of this opportunity.

20.3.4.1 *Interdiction of ships suspected of being engaged in piracy*

The most prominent and certainly the most traditional of the instances mentioned in Article 110 UNCLOS is the interdiction of ships suspected of being engaged in piracy.[87] Piracy is the only (potentially but not necessarily transnational) organised crime regulated in the UNCLOS under which states have expressly been authorized to seize ships and aircraft on the high seas, to seize the property, and to arrest the persons on board.[88] Since, as far as its territorial status and the navigation rights of third states are concerned, the EEZ is in essence subject to the regime of the high seas,[89] the rights codified in Articles 105 and 110 UNCLOS also apply within a foreign EEZ. Notwithstanding that piracy in its present form can be regarded as the prototype of transnational organised crime, the legal requirements governing its repression are still far from clear. The continuing controversies range from how to interpret the element 'committed for private ends' of the definition of piracy that is contained in Article 101 UNCLOS and the legal rules and principles that must be observed with regard to the seizure of pirates, to the scope of the duty to cooperate in the repression of piracy codified in Article 100 UNCLOS, to name just a few.

These issues cannot be discussed in detail here.[90] What should be noted at this stage is that the UNCLOS does not provide for a comprehensive regulation of the repression of piracy, but that, depending on individual circumstances such as the scope of the activities concerned, piracy can also be covered by the UNTOC (even though the underlying concept is nowhere expressly mentioned in the Convention)[91] and influenced by resolutions and recommendations adopted by international organisations such as the UN. Particular attention should also be paid to the question of reconciling the repression of piracy with the need to treat suspected pirates in a manner compatible with international human rights law.[92] The recent debate seems to have focused more on these issues that go beyond the international law of the sea *sensu stricto* than on attempting

[86] Taking into account that consent has been accepted by the ILC as constituting an element precluding wrongfulness (see UN Doc. A/RES/56/83 of 28 January 2002, Annex, Responsibility of States for Internationally Wrongful Acts, Art. 20), it is submitted that no reason exists why a flag state should be precluded from authorising another state to inspect and board a ship flying its flag on an ad hoc basis.

[87] Geiß and Tams, 'Non-flag states as guardians', cited in note 36 above, p. 26: 'piracy has come to be seen as the model exception to flag State jurisdiction'.

[88] Cf. Art. 105 UNCLOS.

[89] See Art. 58(1) UNCLOS. For a detailed assessment of the legal status of the EEZ see Alexander Proelss, 'The law on the Exclusive Economic Zone in perspective: legal status and resolution of user conflicts revisited', (2012) 26 *Ocean Yearbook*, 87–112.

[90] For an overview see Tanaka, *The International Law of the Sea*, cited in note 42 above, pp. 378–88. A detailed analysis of the definition of piracy is provided by Guilfoyle, *Shipping Interdiction*, cited in note 10 above, pp. 29–53. See also the collection of contributions published in Panos Koutrakos and Achilles Skordas (eds), *The Law and Practice of Piracy at Sea*, Oxford, Hart Publishing, 2014.

[91] Ricardo Gosalbo-Bono and Sonja Boelaert, 'The European Union's comprehensive approach to combating piracy at sea: legal aspects', in Koutrakos and Skordas, *Piracy at Sea*, cited in note 90 above, p. 81, p. 100.

[92] See section 20.3.4.7 of this chapter.

to clarify the persisting uncertainties concerning the scope of existing non-flag-state enforcement powers *vis-à-vis* piracy under the UNCLOS. That the developments surrounding the law applicable to the repression of piracy have allegedly been subject to a paradigm shift is often deduced from the activities of the UN Security Council in respect of the situation off the coast of Somalia. However, one might well question whether the Security Council should really be referred to as the 'main driver of the expansion of counter-piracy enforcement powers',[93] taking into account that the pertinent resolutions adopted by the Security Council do not seem to contain any 'constitutive' authorization to use force, or to interdict foreign ships in the territorial sea of Somalia respectively.[94] It has rather been argued that '[n]o evidence exists that the Security Council intended to widen the scope of powers of the states participating in anti-piratical operations in relation to what is already recognized under the LOS Convention and general international law'.[95]

20.3.4.2 Interdiction of ships suspected of being engaged in the slave trade

Article 110(1)(b) UNCLOS prescribes that a warship which encounters a foreign ship on the high seas may board that ship when 'there is reasonable ground for suspecting that … the ship is engaged in the slave trade'. In contrast to the case of piracy, however, the UNCLOS does not contain any definition of the terms 'slavery' or 'slave trade'. It thus seems justified to interpret these terms in line with the 1926 Slavery Convention.[96] According to its Article 1(1), slavery is 'the status or condition of a person over whom any or all of the powers attaching to the right of ownership are exercised', with 'slave trade' including 'all acts involved in the capture, acquisition or disposal of a person with intent to reduce him to slavery; all acts involved in the acquisition of a slave with a view to selling or exchanging him; all acts of disposal by sale or exchange of a slave acquired with a view to being sold or exchanged, and, in general, every act of trade or transport in slaves' (Article 1(2) Slavery Convention). Cases of slavery or slave trading are rare today, though, if not non-existent, which is why the pertinent right of non-flag states to interdict suspected vessels on the high seas is hardly practically relevant any more. Whether or not human trafficking, which is commonly described as the modern form of slavery, can be subsumed under the instance codified in Article 110(1)

[93] Geiß and Tams, 'Non-flag states as guardians', cited in note 36 above, p. 41.

[94] Cf. UN Doc. S/RES/1838 (2008) of 7 October 2008, para. 7; S/RES/1846 (2008) of 2 December 2008, para. 10; S/RES/1897 (2009) of 30 November 2009, para. 7; S/RES/1950 (2010) of 27 November 2010, para. 7; S/RES/2020 (2011) of 22 November 2011, para. 9; S/RES/2077 (2012) of 22 November 2012, para. 12. Reference being made in these documents to piracy as well as to the notion 'armed robbery at sea' implies that the latter covers unlawful acts of violence or detention, or acts of depredation, or threat thereof, other than acts of piracy; cf. IMO Doc. A 22/Res. 922 of 22 January 2002, Annex, para. 2.2. The difference between piracy on one hand and armed robbery at sea on the other thus seems to be that armed robbery at sea covers piratical activities in waters under the jurisdiction of the coastal state.

[95] Alexander Proelss, 'Piracy and the use of force', in Koutrakos and Skordas, *Piracy at Sea*, cited in note 90 above, p. 53, p. 159; see also Douglas Guilfoyle, 'Counter-piracy law enforcement and human rights', (2010) 59 *ICLQ*, 141, p. 145; Tullio Treves, 'Piracy, law of the sea, and use of force: developments off the coast of Somalia', (2009) 20 *EJIL*, 399, p. 407.

[96] Slavery Convention of 25 September 1926, available at: http://www.ohchr.org/EN/ProfessionalInterest/Pages/SlaveryConvention.aspx, accessed 10 October 2015.

(b) UNCLOS is a matter for debate. A reasonable answer that takes into account recent developments in treaty practice would suggest that particularly grave forms of human trafficking may be considered as 'slavery'.[97] It should be noted, though, that neither the UNCLOS nor customary international law confer on states a right to confiscate a ship engaged in the slave trade, nor a right to arrest the persons aboard such a ship.[98] Accordingly, states that intend to arrest persons that are suspected of being engaged in slave trading have to seek the consent of the flag state.

20.3.4.3 Interdiction of ships suspected of being engaged in human trafficking

The fact that doubts exist whether the right to interdict under Article 110(1)(b) UNCLOS is applicable to human trafficking and/or migrant smuggling raises the question whether any other international agreement provides for a right to intervene to be given to non-flag states. As stated above, if applied only between the states parties to the agreement, such a right would be perfectly compatible with Article 110(1) UNCLOS, taking into account that this provision contains an express reservation concerning acts of interference deriving from powers conferred by treaty. While numerous treaties exist that address the issues of human trafficking and smuggling of migrants, the most important of which are the First and the Second Protocol to the UNTOC and the United Nations Convention for the Suppression of the Traffic in Persons and of the Exploitation of the Prostitution of Others,[99] none of these agreements assigns any specific intervention rights to non-flag states. In particular, the Second Protocol to the UNTOC, dedicated, *inter alia*, to the Smuggling of Migrants by Sea, does not authorize non-flag states to interdict and board vessels suspected of being engaged in human trafficking, or migrant smuggling, without the consent of the flag state. The general duty to cooperate with non-flag-state enforcement contained in Article 7 is substantiated by Article 8(2), which states that:

> [a] State Party that has reasonable grounds to suspect that a vessel exercising freedom of navigation in accordance with international law and flying the flag or displaying the marks of registry of another State Party is engaged in the smuggling of migrants by sea may so *notify the flag State, request confirmation of registry and, if confirmed, request authorization from the flag State to take appropriate measures with regard to that vessel.* The flag State may authorize the requesting State, *inter alia*: (a) to board the vessel; (b) to search the vessel; and (c) if evidence is found that the vessel is engaged in the smuggling of migrants by sea, to take appropriate

[97] See Preamble and Art. 4(a) of the Council of Europe Convention on Action against Trafficking in Human Beings of 16 May 2005, CETS No. 197. See also Tanaka, *The International Law of the Sea*, cited in note 42 above, pp. 166–7; Guilfoyle, *Shipping Interdiction*, cited in note 10 above, p. 76; and see further Efthymios Papastavridis, *The Interception of Vessels on the High Seas*, Oxford and Portland, Oregon, Hart Publishing, 2013, p. 278.

[98] Churchill and Lowe, *The Law of the Sea*, cited in note 41 above, p. 212; Tanaka, *The International Law of the Sea*, cited in note 42 above, p. 166; Guilfoyle, *Shipping Interdiction*, cited in note 10 above, p. 76.

[99] Trafficking Protocol, cited in note 71 above. Protocol Against the Smuggling of Migrants by Land, Sea, and Air, Supplementing the United Nations Convention Against Transnational Organized Crime of 15 November 2000, 2241 UNTS 507. United Nations Convention for the Suppression of the Traffic in Persons and of the Exploitation of the Prostitution of Others of 21 March 1950, 96 UNTS 271.

measures with respect to the vessel and persons and cargo on board, as authorized by the flag State.[100]

Paragraphs 3 to 6 of Article 8, and Article 9, of the Second Protocol to the UNTOC prescribe further safeguards in favour of the flag state, the most important one being that '[a] State Party shall take no additional measures without the express authorisation of the flag State, except those necessary to relieve imminent danger to the lives of persons or those which derive from relevant bilateral or multilateral agreements'.[101] Thus, apart from the possibility of concluding bilateral agreements, international law does not envisage autonomous rights for non-flag states to interdict ships suspected of human trafficking or the smuggling of migrants.

20.3.4.4 Interdiction of ships suspected of being engaged in drug trafficking

Since the 1980s, drug cartels have increasingly used the oceans to transport drugs to other states. In order to eradicate and suppress drug trafficking, numerous multi- and bilateral agreements have been concluded.[102] As far as interdiction on the high seas or in the EEZ is concerned, these agreements are based on Article 108(1) UNCLOS, which states that '[a]ll States shall cooperate in the suppression of illicit traffic in narcotic drugs and psychotropic substances engaged in by ships on the high seas contrary to international conventions', and can be categorized into three groups:

(1) treaties that insist on the need to request the previous consent of the flag state if interdiction is intended;
(2) treaties that contain the permission to interdict the ship of the other party on the high seas without previous authorization; and
(3) hybrid treaties that on one hand require previous authorization by the flag state but also contain provisions stipulating that consent is presumed to have been given after a certain period of time on the other.

This analysis has convincingly been referred to the statement in Article 108(2) UNCLOS that '[a]ny State which has reasonable grounds for believing that a ship flying its flag is engaged in illicit traffic in narcotic drugs or psychotropic substances may request the cooperation of other States to suppress such traffic', on the basis that this shows 'how firmly anchored the flag state principle still was at the time of the UNCLOS' drafting'.[103] This view is also reflected in the judgment of the European Court of Human Rights (ECtHR) in the *Medvedyev* case, where the Court held that:

[100] Italics added. [101] Art. 8(5)(2) Second Protocol to the UNCTOC.

[102] Probably the first agreement in this regard was the Convention between the United Kingdom and the United States of America Respecting the Regulation of the Liquor Traffic of 23 January 1924, UKTS No. 22 [1924]. This treaty was the result of a dispute between the USA and the UK regarding the lawfulness of US measures taken against ships that were suspected of smuggling rum, but that were situated in international waters. While the USA claimed to protect its national interests, the UK regarded these activities as being in clear violation of international law. By concluding the treaty, the UK agreed not to protest against the boarding of ships flying the British flag outside the territorial waters of the USA where these ships were suspected of being engaged in liquor smuggling. Cf. Guilfoyle, *Shipping Interdiction*, cited in note 10 above, p. 81.

[103] Geiß and Tams, 'Non-flag states as guardians', cited in note 36 above, p. 35.

> not only are the provisions concerning the fight against drug trafficking [contained in the UNCLOS] minimal—in comparison with those concerning piracy, for example, on which there are eight Articles, which lay down, *inter alia*, the principle of universal jurisdiction as an exception to the rule of the exclusive jurisdiction of the flag State—but fighting drug trafficking is not among the offences, listed in Article 110, suspicion of which gives rise to the right to board and inspect foreign vessels.[104]

The United Nations Convention against Illicit Traffic in Narcotic Drugs and Psychotropic Substance,[105] probably the most important multilateral treaty in this regard, can be ascribed to the first category of agreements. Article 17 of the Convention prescribes the precise circumstances under which a state may interdict a foreign-flagged vessel and largely corresponds, as far as its substance is concerned, to what has later been accepted as Article 8 of the Second Protocol to the UNTOC. It demands in its paragraph 3 that whenever a state has 'reasonable grounds' to believe that a ship is engaged in illicit drug trafficking, it must seek the flag state's consent prior to any interdiction. That said, Article 17(7) of the Convention obliges the flag state to 'respond expeditiously to a request', and a breach of this procedural duty entails the international responsibility of the flag state. Taking into account that arguably such a breach can only be assumed in situations of clearly abusive behaviour, it seems difficult to justify an interdiction operation undertaken without permission of the flag state as a counter-measure under Article 49 of the Articles on Responsibility of States for Internationally Wrongful Acts.[106] Furthermore, one might well question whether the condition set out in paragraph 1 of this provision, namely that the counter-measure concerned may only be taken in order to induce the responsible state to comply with its obligations, is fulfilled in situations of non-flag-state enforcement. Despite this, the fact that Article 17(1) of the Convention prescribes a duty to cooperate 'to the fullest extent possible' suggests that it is not in the flag state's sole discretion as to whether it responds positively to a request or not. Rather, the requested state is arguably under a duty not to abusively withhold the requested permissions and authorization.

An example of the second category of treaties is the Treaty to Combat Illicit Drug Trafficking at Sea concluded between Spain and Italy (Spanish-Italian Treaty) in 1990.[107] In contrast to the UN Convention against Illicit Traffic in Narcotic Drugs and Psychotropic Substances, in its Article 5(2) the Spanish-Italian Treaty recognizes one party's right to interdict a ship flying the other party's flag in international waters.[108] The numerous bilateral treaties concluded between the United States and several Caribbean and South American states are typical examples of the third category of

[104] *Medvedyev* Judgment, cited in note 85 above, para. 85.

[105] Drug Trafficking Convention, cited in note 70 above. For a discussion of the impact of this Convention, concerning the approach pursued by the USA to conclude bilateral shipboarding agreements (see section 20.3.4.5 of this chapter) see Henning Jessen, 'United States' bilateral shipboarding agreements—upholding law of the sea principles while updating state practice', in Henrik Ringbom (ed.), *Jurisdiction Over Ships*, Leiden/Boston, Brill, 2015, p. 50, pp. 61–4.

[106] Responsibility of States, cited in note 86 above.

[107] 23 March 1990, 1776 UNTS 242.

[108] Art. 5(2)(1) reads '[s]hould there be reasonable grounds to suspect that offences covered by article 2 are being committed, each Party recognizes the other's right to intervene as its agent in waters outside its own territorial limits, in respect of ships displaying the flag of the other State'.

agreements. These treaties make the interdiction of a ship flying the flag of another party on the high seas in principle subject to that state's consent. However, consent of the flag state is presumed after a stated period of time.[109]

20.3.4.5 *Interdiction of ships suspected of being engaged in the transport of WMD*

Closely related to the war against terror proclaimed by the US government following the terrorist attacks on 11 September 2001, the transport of WMD by ships has started to attract particular attention. As with human trafficking, the UNCLOS is silent on the issue, which is why first and foremost reference ought to be made to the Convention for the suppression of Unlawful Acts against the Safety of Maritime Navigation (SUA Convention).[110] This multilateral agreement was adopted in direct response to the *Achille Lauro* incident and establishes a legal framework applicable to the suppression of unlawful acts at sea that go beyond piracy. It was revised after 11 September 2001 by way of a Protocol (SUA Protocol 2005).[111] The Convention is applicable to a broad range of crimes, many of which have potentially transboundary character, including: (1) seizure and destruction of a ship, (2) destruction or serious damaging of maritime navigational facilities, and (3) measures that are capable of endangering the safety of navigation. With the entry into force of the SUA Protocol 2005, it also covers, *inter alia*, the transport of biological, chemical, and nuclear weapons and the uses against or on a ship or discharges from a ship of any explosive, radioactive material, or biological, chemical, or nuclear weapon in a manner that causes or is likely to cause death, or serious injury, or damage.[112] Its relevance concerning the transport of WMD on the oceans is thus obvious.[113]

With regard to the question whether the revised SUA Convention ought to be regarded as an agreement under Article 110(1) UNCLOS, Article 8*bis* of the Convention has introduced a general duty to cooperate 'to the fullest extent possible to prevent and suppress unlawful acts covered by this Convention, in conformity with international law, and [to] respond to requests pursuant to this article as expeditiously as possible'. Concerning enforcement by non-flag states, this obligation is substantiated

[109] See, e.g. Art. 7(3)(d) of the Agreement between the Government of the United States of America and the Government of the Republic of Guatemala Concerning Cooperation to Suppress Illicit Traffic in Narcotic Substances and by Sea and Air of 19 June 2003, available at: http://guatemala.usembassy.gov/uploads/images/COB7Udl1HS7y04mWhEcLNg/usguatmaritimeagreemente.pdf, accessed 10 October 2015: 'if there is no response … within two (2) hours …, the requesting Party will be deemed to have been authorized to board the suspect vessel … '. For further examples see Guilfoyle, *Shipping Interdiction*, cited in note 10 above, pp. 89–94; Geiß and Tams, 'Non-flag states as guardians', cited in note 36 above, pp. 39–40.

[110] Convention for the Suppression of Unlawful Acts against the Safety of Maritime Navigation of 10 March 1988, 1678 UNTS 221.

[111] IMO Doc. LEG/CONF.15/21, Protocol of 14 October 2005 to the Convention for the Suppression of Unlawful Acts of Violence against the Safety of Maritime Navigation (SUA Convention). The Protocol (and thus the revised SUA Convention) entered into force on 28 July 2010.

[112] Cf. Art. 3*bis* of the revised SUA Convention.

[113] Note that, so far as its geographical scope is concerned, the revised SUA Convention is applicable whenever a 'ship is navigating or is scheduled to navigate into, through or from waters beyond the outer limit of the territorial sea of a single State, or the lateral limits of its territorial sea with adjacent States' (Art. 4(1)).

by paragraph 5, which prohibits the boarding of a ship flying the flag of another state party without the express authorization of the flag state. Taking into account that Article 8*bis*(6) of the revised SUA Convention likewise makes detention of a ship, its cargo, and the persons on board subject to the authorization of the flag state, it must be concluded that the SUA Convention does not grant autonomous interdiction rights to non-flag states.[114]

Article 8*bis*(13) of the revised SUA Convention prescribes that 'States Parties may conclude agreements or arrangements between them to facilitate law-enforcement operations carried out in accordance with this article'. This is where the PSI announced by former US President Bush in 2003 comes into play.[115] Not only did the USA launch this political initiative to aim at an enhancement of existing law-enforcement cooperation,[116] but it also concluded bilateral ship-boarding agreements with eleven states (including Liberia, Panama, and St. Vincent and the Grenadines, flag states that are amongst the largest shipping registers in the world).[117] These agreements vary in scope and content but generally adhere to the primacy of flag-state authorization prior to the boarding of a vessel suspected of being involved in the transport of WMD. However, in line with the third category of treaties identified in the context of enforcement measures against ships engaged in drug trafficking,[118] some of these treaties presume the consent of the flag state after a given period of time (usually two or four hours) has passed since authorization was requested by the USA.

As in the case of piracy, there is a debate on whether the UN Security Council has taken the role of a world legislator on the field of anti-terrorist counter-proliferation at sea, thereby giving substance to the UNCLOS in this area, as well as to the revised SUA Convention. Indeed, Resolution 1540 (2004) condemns the proliferation of nuclear, chemical, and biological weapons,[119] as well as their means of delivery, as constituting a threat to international peace and security, and its paragraph 10 requires that 'cooperative action to prevent illicit trafficking in nuclear, chemical or biological weapons, their means of delivery, and related material' is taken. However, it is not possible to interpret this Resolution as imposing an obligation on flag states to grant other states authorization to board and search a ship flying their flag whenever the ship concerned is suspected of being involved in the transport of WMD. Paragraph 10 of the Resolution makes this sufficiently clear by rendering any measures taken by non-flag states subject to the condition that it is 'in accordance with their national legal authorities and legislation and consistent with international law'.

[114] It should be noted that mechanisms codified in Art. 8*bis*(5)(d)(e) revised SUA Convention attempt to further facilitate interdictions by non-flag states through advance opting-in. These logically presuppose the consent of the flag state.

[115] See, however, Jessen, 'US bilateral shipboarding agreements', cited in note 105 above, pp. 65–8, arguing that during the last decade the 2005 SUA Protocol has had only indirect and limited effects on the development of US bilateral ship-boarding agreements. The coincidence of time and content is nevertheless striking.

[116] PSI Interdiction Principles, cited in note 76 above.

[117] The list and content of the agreements is available at: http://www.state.gov/t/isn/c27733.htm, accessed 10 October 2015. For an in-depth analysis of the issue see Jessen, 'US bilateral shipboarding agreements', cited in note 105 above, pp. 56–61 and 68–72.

[118] See section 20.3.4.4 of this chapter.

[119] UN Doc. S/RES/1540 (2004) of 28 April 2004.

It is also difficult to defend the existence of a possible obligation of flag states, alleged to stem from the general duty codified in paragraph 1 of the Resolution, to 'refrain from providing any form of support to non-State actors that attempt to develop, acquire, manufacture, possess, transport, transfer or use nuclear, chemical or biological weapons and their means of delivery'. From a methodological viewpoint, it should be noted that a duty to refrain from doing something has a completely different quality from an obligation to tolerate interferences with flag state jurisdiction, which is directly linked to the sovereignty of the state.[120] Furthermore, Resolution 1540 has not been applied in state practice in a manner that would oblige flag states to grant authorization to board suspected vessels flying their flag. Thus, unlike what has been suggested in legal literature, it is submitted here that the fact that flag states are indeed under a duty to effectively control their own ships (and if this duty is not carried out, are in breach of Resolution 1540) is not equivalent to a duty to tolerate control by other states.[121]

20.4 Scope of Interdiction Measures

Provided that one of the aforementioned documents provides a legal basis for the taking of enforcement measures by a non-flag state on the high seas or in an EEZ, the question arises whether the ship conducting the interdiction is entitled to use force against the ship that is suspected of being involved in transnational organised crime. The UNCLOS contains no provision that authorizes the use of force against pirates, smugglers, terrorists, or the like, or that would set out the precise requirements that ought to be observed by the interdicting state. *Prima facie*, this fact seems to suggest that any use of force during interdiction operations is against international law. However, one of the present authors has argued that the exercise of military force has always been considered as legitimate in order to safeguard the freedom of commerce on the high seas.[122] The use of force in international relations does not seem to be exclusively governed by Article 2(4) UN Charter, but can be legally justified beyond the

[120] See also Resolution 1874, UN Doc. S/RES/1540 (2009) of 12 June 2009, by which the Security Council reacted to a nuclear test conducted by the Democratic People's Republic of Korea, prescribing that 'if the flag State does not consent to inspection on the high seas, ... the flag State shall direct the vessel to proceed to an appropriate and convenient port for the required inspection by the local authorities pursuant to paragraph 1'. Even in this instance the UN Security Council thus refrained from imposing a duty on the flag state to tolerate inspection of its vessels by third states on the high seas. In 2013, it then decided that 'if any vessel has refused to allow an inspection after such an inspection has been authorized by the vessel's flag State, or if any DPRK-flagged vessel has refused to be inspected pursuant to paragraph 12 of resolution 1874 (2009), all States shall deny such a vessel entry to their ports, unless entry is required for the purpose of an inspection, in the case of emergency or in the case of return to its port of origination ...', UN Doc. S/RES/2094 (2013) of 7 March 2013, para. 17.

[121] See also Geiß and Tams, 'Non-flag states as guardians', cited in note 36 above, p. 45, concluding that Resolution 1540 'abstained from creating an additional boarding regime'. *Contra* Rüdiger Wolfrum, 'Fighting terrorism at sea: options and limitations under international law', in Jochen A. Frowein (ed.), *Verhandeln für den Frieden—Negotiating for Peace, Liber Amicorum Tono Eitel*, Berlin, Springer, 2003, p. 649, p. 666.

[122] The following assessment is based on Proelss, 'Piracy and the use of force', cited in note 95 above, pp. 63–5.

scope of the prohibition contained in that norm.[123] For example, Article 22(1)(f) of the UN Fish Stocks Agreement,[124] which deals with basic procedures for boarding and inspection of fishing vessels in order to ensure compliance with and enforcement of subregional and regional conservation and management measures for straddling fish stocks and highly migratory fish stocks, states that:

> the inspecting State shall ensure that its duly authorized inspectors … shall avoid the use of force except when and to the degree necessary to ensure the safety of the inspectors and where the inspectors are obstructed in the execution of their duties.

Similarly, Article 8*bis*(9) of the 2005 Protocol to the SUA Convention prescribes:

> When carrying out the authorized actions under this article, the use of force shall be avoided except when necessary to ensure the safety of its officials and persons on board, or where the officials are obstructed in the execution of the authorized actions. Any use of force pursuant to this article shall not exceed the minimum degree of force which is necessary and reasonable in the circumstances.[125]

In the *M/V Saiga* case, the ITLOS confirmed that 'international law … requires that the use of force must be avoided as far as possible and, where force is inevitable, it must not go beyond what is reasonable and necessary in the circumstances'.[126]

These sources address law-enforcement measures against private actors (respecting ships) in areas both within and outside the limits of national jurisdiction, and uniformly emphasize that in principle force may be used to enforce nationally or regionally binding standards, provided that these standards have been enacted in accordance with international law. Thus, even aside from the undisputed general principle of law that an individual may act in self-defence in order to protect his/her own life or the lives of others (and so may a single vessel) (provided that the exercise of force is not disproportionate),[127] international law does not absolutely prohibit recourse to military force. Rather, enforcement measures against private actors may lawfully involve the exercise of force, subject to the legal limits expressed by the Arbitral Tribunal in the *Guyana v Suriname* case (unavoidability, reasonability, and necessity),[128] that ultimately result from the requirements of international human rights law.[129]

[123] Cf. Douglas Guilfoyle, 'Human rights issues and non-flag state boarding of suspect ships', in Clive Symmons (ed.), *Selected Contemporary Issues in the Law of the Sea*, Leiden/Boston, Martinus Nijhoff Publishers, 2011, p. 83, p. 92; Treves, 'Piracy, law of the sea, and use of force', cited in note 95 above, p. 412.

[124] Agreement for the Implementation of the Provisions of the United Nations Convention on the Law of the Sea of 10 December 1982 relating to the Conservation and Management of Straddling Fish Stocks and Highly Migratory Fish Stocks of 4 December 1995, 2167 UNTS 3.

[125] 2005 Protocol, cited in note 111 above; see also note 114 above.

[126] *M/V Saiga* Judgment, cited in note 82 above, para. 155.

[127] Wolff Heintschel von Heinegg, 'Repressing piracy and armed robbery at sea—towards a new international regime?,' (2010) 40 *Israel Yearbook of Human Rights*, 219, p. 228; Treves, 'Piracy, law of the sea, and use of force', cited in note 95 above, p. 412. Note that this individual right of self-defence ought to be distinguished from the right of self-defence held by states under Article 51 UN Charter, or corresponding customary international law respectively.

[128] Arbitral Tribunal constituted pursuant to Article 287, and in accordance with Annex VII, of the United Nations Convention on the Law of the Sea, *Guyana v Suriname*, Award of 17 September 2007, (2008) 47 *ILM*, 166, para. 445.

[129] The ITLOS referred to 'considerations of humanity'; see *M/V Saiga* Judgment, cited in note 82 above, para. 155.

20.5 Enforcement Measures and Human Rights

As demonstratively stated by Treves, '[t]he Law of the Sea and the law of human rights are not separate planets rotating in different orbits. Instead, they meet in many situations.'[130] It is beyond serious argument that states conducting interdiction operations are not released from their human rights obligations. Despite this, the precise relationship and possible interactions between the international law of the sea and human rights law are still surrounded by a considerable degree of uncertainty. One particularly important question is whether the persons aboard an interdicted ship may also rely on their human rights if the ship concerned is situated on the high seas.[131] Whether or not the existing human rights treaties, in particular the International Covenant on Civil and Political Rights (ICCPR)[132] and the European Convention for the Protection of Human Rights and Fundamental Freedoms (ECHR),[133] may unfold extra-territorial effects is a matter of interpretation and has been extensively discussed by the dispute settlement mechanisms established by these treaties. The predominant view is that individuals are protected by the human rights codified in the ICCPR and the ECHR even if the potential violation has taken place outside the territory of the state, so long as that state exercises effective or *de facto* control over the territory or persons concerned.[134] In the *Medvedyev* case, the ECtHR was recently called upon to adjudicate on a situation that was directly related to the matter relevant here. It held that persons aboard a ship flying the flag of Cambodia were effectively within the jurisdiction of France because France 'exercised full and exclusive control over the *Winner* and its crew, at least *de facto*, from the time of its interception'.[135] It can thus be concluded that the ICCPR and the ECHR will usually apply in the context of interdiction operations, even if conducted on the high seas.

Concerning maritime enforcement operations, particular challenges may arise with regard to Article 9(3) ICCPR and Article 5(3) ECHR, under which persons arrested or detained 'shall be brought promptly before a judge or other officer authorized by law to exercise judicial power and shall be entitled to trial within a reasonable time or to release'. In the *Medvedyev* and *Rigopoulos* cases, the interdicting ships of France and Spain needed thirteen and sixteen days respectively to escort the boarded vessels suspected of drug smuggling to French and Spanish ports. In both cases the

[130] Tullio Treves, 'Human rights and the law of the sea', (2010) 28 *Berkeley Journal of International Law*, 1, p. 12.

[131] It is beyond doubt that if an interdiction or policing operation takes place on the territory of the interdicting state, human rights law applies. See Guilfoyle, 'Human rights issues and non-flag state boarding', cited in note 123 above, p. 84.

[132] International Covenant on Civil and Political Rights of 19 December 1966, 999 UNTS 172.

[133] European Convention for the Protection of Human Rights and Fundamental Freedoms of 4 November 1950, 213 UNTS 222.

[134] See, e.g. European Court of Human Rights, *Al-Skeini and Others v UK*, Application No. 55721/07, Judgment of 7 July 2011, paras 135–6; *Öcalan v Turkey*, Application No. 46221/99, Judgment of 12 May 2005, para. 9.

[135] *Medvedyev* Judgment, cited in note 85 above, para. 67 (italics in original). But see the critical analysis submitted by Marta Szuniewicz, 'Problems and challenges of the ECHR's extraterritorial application to law-enforcement operations at sea', (2015) 17 *International Community Law Review*, 445, p. 450ff.

ECtHR decided that the respective periods were not incompatible with the notion of 'promptness' required under Article 5(3) ECHR, taking into account the considerable distances to be covered and that it had been 'materially impossible to bring the applicant physically before the investigating judge any sooner'.[136] One might ask, though, whether Article 9(3) ICCPR and Article 5(3) ECHR should not rather be interpreted as requiring that a 'judge or other officer authorized by law to exercise judicial power' ought to be present aboard ships that are involved in interdiction operations on the high seas.

Human rights law is also relevant with regard to the fact that persons on board intercepted vessels will often be forced to return to their home countries. Under the principle of non-*refoulement* codified in Article 33(1) of the Geneva Convention Relating to the Status of Refugees,[137] Article 3(1) of the Convention Against Torture and Other Cruel, Inhuman, or Degrading Treatment or Punishment,[138] and Article 3 ECHR, person(s) shall not be expelled, returned, or extradited to another state where there are substantial grounds for believing that they would be in danger of being subjected to torture, or where their life or freedom would be threatened on account of their race, religion, nationality, membership of a particular social group, or political opinion. The ECtHR has recognized that the principle of non-*refoulement* also covers persons aboard vessels that are intercepted in areas beyond national territory,[139] and it seems difficult to argue that *a priori* the obligation contained therein is not applicable to persons suspected of being involved in transnational organised crime.

20.6 Conclusion

The international law of the sea and transnational organised crime are closely related to each other owing to the great importance of shipping and navigation as means of international transport. This fact renders particularly important the question which state is entitled to exercise jurisdiction over ships suspected of being involved in crimes such as piracy, human trafficking, drug trafficking, and transport of WMD. This chapter has shown that while the coastal state may lawfully exercise criminal enforcement jurisdiction in its internal waters and territorial sea, the situation is different on the high seas and in the EEZ, where the principle of flag-state jurisdiction has turned out to be almost as relevant today as in the past. In this respect, the international law of the sea establishes a legal framework for cooperation that sets, on one hand, comparatively narrow limits for unilateral enforcement measures, but at the same time leaves sufficient room for flexibility in respect of bilateral and multilateral approaches addressing the interdiction of suspected vessels. The question whether

[136] *Case of Rigopoulos v Spain*, Application No. 37388/97, Judgment of 12 January 1999; see also *Medvedyev*, cited in note 85 above, paras 130–1 and Szuniewicz, 'Problems and challenges', cited in note 135 above, p. 452ff.

[137] Convention Relating to the Status of Refugees of 28 July 1951, 189 UNTS 137.

[138] Convention against Torture and Other Cruel, Inhuman, or Degrading Treatment or Punishment of 10 December 1984, 1465 UNTS 112.

[139] *Case of Hirsi Jamaa and Others v Italy*, Application No. 27765/09, Judgment of 23 February 2012, para. 114.

there is a need for reform of the existing legal regime in light of the present challenges has been put up for discussion in the context of Article 110 UNCLOS, which essentially limits the grounds for the unilateral right to board a suspected ship to piracy and the slave trade, but taking into account that this provision contains an 'opening clause' in favour of the conclusion of other treaties, this chapter submits that particular attention should rather be paid to amending, or in some cases updating, the more specific agreements with the aim of widening the scope of the broad legal framework accepted with the adoption of the UNCLOS. In this context, the category of agreements that has been referred to here as 'hybrid treaties', i.e. treaties that on one hand require advance authorization of interdiction by the flag state, but contain provisions stipulating that consent is presumed to have been given after a given period of time on the other, may serve as a model for the underlying approach to balance the sovereignty of the flag state against the legitimate interest of the international community in combating transnational organised crime. Future research should thus subject these agreements to a practicability test by way of analysis of existing state practice. From an actor's perspective, while the UN Security Council has started to become involved in issues such as piracy and maritime terrorism, it has so far refrained from accepting the role of a world legislature. The field of transnational organised crime in the law of the sea may therefore be described as one of the areas of international law that demonstrates that, notwithstanding all prophecies of doom, the principle of sovereignty is still more or less in good health.

21

Transnational Organised Crime and International Criminal Law

Pierre Hauck

21.1 Introduction

When in 1989 diplomats of Trinidad and Tobago promoted their proposal to establish an International Criminal Court (ICC) in order to gain control over the problem of drug trafficking across the borders in the Caribbean,[1] they probably did not expect two features of the further development: firstly, that the international community indeed managed to establish the Rome Statute in less than a decade, and secondly, that the type of criminality that gave rise to their primary intention obviously did not make its way into this statute.[2] This fairly surprising fact points to the issue of which impediments hamper the inclusion of transnational organised crime in the Rome Statute and, moreover, what it does take in general to elevate these offences onto the level of international jurisdiction and to make them part of international criminal law.

Approaching this topic, one imperatively has to distinguish between three questions: the first, whether a competence of the ICC for transnational offences is *politically* wanted, the second, if such a competence is needed *factually* in the sense of judicial coping with such big calibres of deviance, and the third concerning the question whether on the whole we can afford it *legally* to expand the ICC's jurisdiction towards transnational organised crime. There exists a reciprocal action between these single problems:[3] we cannot seriously canvass a competence of the ICC for transnational organised crime when there is no factual need or legal possibility to do so. Presupposing that there are states that cannot master transnational organised crime for the lack of appropriate personnel, technical means, or other resources in their criminal justice systems, it is now possible to concentrate on the question whether we can afford legally to expand the ICC's competences towards transnational organised crime.

This chapter is organised as follows: First of all, defining transnational organised crime leads to obtaining a reference point for further analysis. The next step will be to describe the notion which sees transnational organised crime already dealt with as one

[1] UN Doc. A/44/195, 21 August 1989; UN Doc. A/44/694, 31 October 1989; UN Doc. A/C.6/44/L.18, 20 November 1989; UN Doc. A/44/770, 24 November 1989; UN Doc. A/RES/44/49, 8 December 1989; UN Doc. A/RES/44/39, 4 December 1989.

[2] Cf. Neil Boister, 'The exclusion of treaty crimes from the jurisdiction of the proposed International Criminal Court: law, pragmatism, politics', (1998) 3 *JCSL* (1) 27, 27.

[3] Also Hans-Peter Kaul, 'Preconditions to the exercise of jurisdiction', in Antonio Cassese *et al.* (eds), *The Rome Statute of the International Criminal Court. A Commentary.* Volume I, Oxford, OUP, 2002, p. 586.

of the core crimes within the jurisdiction of the ICC, and to argue that this path is fallacious (21.3). Then it is necessary to demonstrate the requirements that transnational offences have to fulfil in order to be raised onto an international level of jurisdiction (21.4). For this purpose all of the different methodical ways in which we are able to establish international crimes will be dealt with. It will be shown that the first method is the codification of customary international law (21.4.2). Consequently, the analysis of the elements of customary international law will be explored through cases. As a second requirement in addition to the establishment of 'new international crimes', we will question the principle of universality as a necessary and suitable means of supranational jurisdiction for these crimes (21.4.2.2). After that, a second and a third method will be applied and it will be asked whether such international crimes can be established by virtue of treaties or according to other institutions. We will leave the single stage of international law at that point and will also imply the effects and influence of the discipline of international relations. The different jurisdiction principles will be scrutinized at the same time. Finally, the preconditions that have to be fulfilled in order to establish supranational jurisdiction over transnational organised crime will be soundly established.

The main argument put forth will be that some transnational offences can be named as international crimes by virtue of customary international law, and that they experience universal jurisdiction on a supranational stage since the principle of universality is derived from customary international law itself. Further, it will be demonstrated that other offences fail to be covered by customary international law, for either they lack a commonly accepted definition, so run counter to the principle of certainty, or there is plainly no uniform state practice to be proved.

21.2 Narrowing the Scope and Defining Transnational Organised Crime

'Organised crime' is a very pithy term that is often applied without a clear reference point and, in fact, is highly indeterminate and vague.[4] Despite this there are good reasons to deem a definition of organised crime desirable and necessary. It is therefore very difficult to reach a consensus on the appropriate use and meaning of the term 'organised crime'.[5] Obviously the dilemma is that if 'organised crime' is defined too broadly, the steps taken may be ineffective or incompatible with the rules and principles of the constitutional state, and might even become abusive. However, if 'organised crime' is defined too narrowly important developments and events that could have been prevented may be left out of range.

On one hand, the term can be used to refer to certain types of more sophisticated or even professional criminal activities embedded,[6] in one form or another, in complex

[4] See—for the matter of definition—Chapter 2, sections 2.1.1, 2.3.2. See also Michael Woodiwiss and Dick Hobbs, 'Organized evil and the Atlantic Alliance: moral panics and the rhetoric of organized crime policing in America and Britain', in *British Journal of Criminology*, Vol. 49, 2009, pp. 106–28.

[5] For a comprehensive list of definitions see Klaus von Lampe's compilation, available at http://www.organized-crime.de/OCDEF1.htm (last visited 13 July 2015).

[6] Edwin H. Sutherland, *The Professional Thief*, Chicago, University of Chicago Press, 1937; further, Mary McIntosh, *The Organisation of Crime*, London, Macmillan, 1975, p. 9.

illicit markets. Arms, drug, and human trafficking are often correlated with a set of 'enabling activities' such as (the threat of) violence, corruption, and money-laundering.[7] Some assume that the former constitute core activities of organised crime,[8] others refer to the latter.[9] In both cases the offences can usually be categorized as 'serious crimes'. It may be more accurate to use the term 'organised criminality'. However, this approach based on indicator criminality is problematic since violence against persons, for instance, may be an important means for and characteristic of some illegal activities, but is not necessarily such.[10] '[A] simple listing of crimes does not tell us much about organised crime.'[11]

On the other hand, 'organised crime' may be referred to in the sense of criminal organizations,[12] such as the Colombian and Mexican 'drug cartels', the Japanese 'yakuza', the Chinese 'triads', or the Italian and US-American 'mafia'.[13] The illicit markets are as complex and different as the defining characteristics of the groups that supply them. They vary from small, loosely connected networks, comprising a handful of persons, to large, hierarchical organizations.[14]

The focus on illegal activities is clearly favoured by the fact that modern criminal law primarily does not punish individuals for what they are (e.g. members of a criminal organization) but rather for what they do (e.g. application of violence). Also, using 'indicator activities' may be helpful in detecting 'organised crime' as clandestine criminality that only becomes evident upon further investigation.

[7] Alan Wright, *Organised Crime*, Portland, Oregon, Willan Publishing, 2006, p. 49.

[8] See Jan van Dijk, 'Mafia markers: assessing organized crime and its impact on societies', in *Trends in Organized Crime*, Vol. 10, Heidelberg, Springer, 2007, p. 40; Allan Castle, 'Transnational organized crime and international security', Institute of International Relations, University of British Columbia, Working Paper No. 19, 1997, p. 2; Stefan Mair, 'The world of privatized violence', in Alfred Pfaller and Marika Lerch (eds), *Challenges of Globalization: New Trends in International Politics and Society*, New Brunswick, Transaction Publishers, 2005, p. 54.

[9] Edgardo Buscaglia and Jan Van Dijk, 'Controlling organized crime and corruption in the public sector', in *Forum on Crime and Society*, Vol. 3, Nos 1 and 2, Vienna, UN, 2003, p. 6; Donald Cressy, *The Theft of the Nation*, New York, Harper and Row, 1969, p. 1.

[10] R. Thomas Naylor, 'Violence and illegal economic activity: a deconstruction', in *Crime, Law & Social Change*, Vol. 52, Heidelberg, Springer, 2009, pp. 231–42; H. Richard Friman, 'Drug markets and the selective use of violence', in *Crime, Law & Social Change*, Vol. 52, Heidelberg, Springer, 2009, pp. 285–95.

[11] James O. Finckenauer, 'Problems of definition: what is organized crime?', in *Trends in Organized Crime*, Vol. 8, No. 3, Heidelberg, Springer, 2005, p. 75.

[12] Hagan proposes 'that "Organized Crime" be used to refer to crime organizations, while "organized crime" will refer to activities, crimes that often require a degree of organization on the part of those committing them', and notes that '[n]ot all "organized crime" is committed by "Organized Crime" groups'. Frank E. Hagan, '"Organized Crime" and "organized crime": Indeterminate problems of definition', in *Trends in Organized Crime*, Vol. 9, No. 4, Heidelberg, Springer, 2006, p. 134.

[13] Whether the Italian mafias can be classified as organised crime is controversial. Against that classification see Mario Bezotti, 'Organisierte Kriminalität: zur sozialen Konstruktion einer Gefahr', in *Angewandte Sozialforschung*, Vol. 22, Nos 3 and 4, Hamburg, WiSo, 2002, p. 136. Also Douglas Meagher, *Organised Crime: Papers presented by Mr Douglas Meagher, QC, to the 53rd ANZAAS Congress, Perth, Western Australia, 16–20 May 1983*, Canberra, Australian Government Publishing Service, 1983, p. 3.

[14] Phil Williams, 'Transnational criminal networks', in John Aquilla and David F. Ronfeld (eds), *Netwars and Networks: The Future of Terror, Crime and Militancy*, Santa Monica, California, RAND, 2001, p. 65; *Global Programme against Transnational Organized Crime: Results of a Pilot Survey of Forty Selected Organized Criminal Groups in Sixteen Countries*, Geneva, United Nations Office on Drugs and Crime, 2002, p. 30.

Accordingly, a criminological approach that exemplifies crime by its actual character rather than its legal classification will be pursued here. Within this concept, crimes like trafficking in illicit drugs, arms, explosives, obscene literature, or women or children, torture, smuggling, currency offences, international terrorism, mercenarism, IT- and cybercrimes, wilful and severe damage to the environment, international economic crimes, transnational speech offences, slavery, or piracy—to be understood as a non-conclusive list—can be elements of 'organised crime'.[15]

Likewise, a definition of *transnational* offences has to be flexible in order to cover new phenomena of deviance in a factual and less normative way. Thus, at that early stage, efforts to define them by referring to their criminalization by international law or by more than one domestic jurisdiction will not be followed, because this indirect comprehension causes limitations of the scope and is likely to water down the unadulterated focus on the various kinds of misconduct.[16] But comprehending transnational crime too widely and vaguely will also lead to uncertainties in the endeavour to analyse the possibility of international jurisdiction. Therefore, transnational offending will be understood as deviant behaviour on a level of criminality that by its nature involves either passing state frontiers, transgressing the laws of several states, or evading a state's jurisdiction by being not attributable to a particular state territory.[17]

21.3 Transnational Organised Crime and International Criminal Law *de lege lata*

21.3.1 Transnational organised crimes as core crimes under the Rome Statute

21.3.1.1 The metamorphosis of apartheid, the attack against UN personnel, and torture

As a matter of fact, some crimes that had formerly been considered as independent transnational offences, namely 'apartheid', an 'attack against UN personnel', and 'torture', have been reorganised during the process of negotiation—starting with the ILC works and ending with the Rome Statute—into elements of two of the core crimes:[18] Apartheid now shapes one element of the *actus reus* of a crime against humanity according to Article 7(1)(j) of the Rome Statute (ICCSt), attacks against UN personnel were included in the possibility of committing a war crime under Article 8(2)(b)(iii) and (e)(iii) ICCSt, and torture constitutes either a variant of a crime against humanity under Article 7(1)(f), or a war crime under Article 8(2)(a)(ii). Owing to the fact that these formerly independent kinds of deviance had been considered as genuine crimes

[15] Cf. the content of Donal E. J. MacNamara and Philip John Stead, *New Dimensions in Transnational Crime*, New York, John Jay Press, 1982, p. 5; Nikos Passas (ed.), *Transnational Crime*, Aldershot, Ashgate, 1999, pp. 7–8, 13; Philip Reichel (ed.), *Handbook of Transnational Crime & Justice*, London, Sage, 2014, pp. v–vii.

[16] Passas, ibid, p. 13.

[17] N. Boister, 'Transnational criminal law?', (2003) 14 *EJIL* (5) 953, 954; Passas, ibid, pp. 13–14.

[18] Patrick Robinson, 'The missing crimes', in Cassese *et al.*, *The Rome Statute*, vol. 1, cited in note 3 above, p. 498.

we have to assert that the Rome Conference simply did not acknowledge them as further core crimes having the same value as genocide, crimes against humanity, war crimes, or aggression.

21.3.1.2 Transnational offences covered by the core crimes in general?

Despite a notion holding that it is already possible to try offenders for transnational organised crime before the ICC, the *lex lata* brings us down to the fact that only in special cases transnational offences show such heinous misconduct that they may even fit the definition of a core crime.[19] A current example is violent trafficking in women including rape: this can be proved to be a crime against humanity as long as all the other requirements of Article 7(1)(g) ICCSt are met. But apparently—as in the case of the remodelled crimes mentioned in section 21.3.1.1 of this chapter—by itself transnational deviance without further elements is not sufficient to be tried by the ICC. Trying only the grave cases as core crimes covers nothing but a small percentage of the whole range, similar to the tip of an iceberg. So, as such international jurisdiction by the ICC over transnational organised crime does not exist *de lege lata*. Accordingly, the case law of the IMT, the ICC, and the ICTY/ICTR deals with 'organised crime' in other contexts.[20]

[19] Andreas Schloenhardt, 'Transnational organised crime and the International Criminal Court. Towards global criminal justice', in 'Crime in Australia: International Connections', Australian Institute of Criminology International Conference, Melbourne, 29–30 November 2004, p. 4, http://www.aic.gov.au/media_library/conferences/2004/schloenhardt.pdf, accessed 13 July 2015.

[20] Only allusively did the International Military Tribunal (IMT) touch on the term 'organised crime' when distinguishing between 'groups' and 'organizations' in its case law: cf. *IMT v Martin Bormann et al.*, final arguments by groups and organizations, 212th day (27 August 1946), p. 48. The IMT also mentioned 'organised terror' in order to characterize the Nazi crimes: cf. *IMT v Bormann*, final arguments by prosecution, 215th day (30 August 1946), *passim; IMT v Bormann*, judgment (1 October 1946), *passim*.

The International Criminal Tribunal for the former Yugoslavia (ICTY) and the International Criminal Tribunal for Rwanda (ICTR) referred to 'organised crime' with reference to the concept of indirect participation in German law ('mittelbare Täterschaft'): cf. ICTY, *Prosecutor v Vladimir Lazarevic et al.*, decision on Ojdanic's motion challenging jurisdiction: indirect co-penetration, IT-05-87, para. 30, and ICTR, *Prosecutor v Sylvestre Gacumbitsi*, judgment, ICTR-01-64, para. 19. The ICTY also referred to 'organised crime' in reference to a report of the Mostar CPD, remarking that statistics demonstrated a wave of organised crime with groups of criminals falsely portraying themselves as members of police or military groups: cf. ICTY, *Prosecutor v Valentin Coric et al.*, Coric's final brief, IT-04-74, para. 289.

The ICC referred to the term 'organised crime' mostly in the context of the Kenya riots of 2007 and 2008 in order to characterize illegal action by gangs like the Mungiki in the slums of Nairobi: cf. ICC, *The Prosecutor v Uhuru Muigai Kenyatta and Mohammed Hussein Ali*, ICC-01/09-02/11, decision on the confirmation of charges pursuant to Art. 61(7)(a) and (b) of the Rome Statute, para. 15 *et seq.*; submission by Ali Defence (open session), ICC-01/09-02/11-T-13-ENG ET WT 03-10-2011 1-190 NB PT (3 October 2011), p. 44ff.; ICC-01/09-02/11-T-12-Red-ENG WT 30-09-2011 1-98 SZ PT (30 September 2011), pp. 42, 55, 58; opening statement by Ali Defence, ICC-01/09-02/11-T-4-ENG ET WT 21-09-2011 1-121 PV PT (21 September 2011), p. 116ff.; Annex B: Prosecution's first communication of the disclosure of incriminating evidence and rule 77 materials to Defence, ICC-01/09-02/11-100-Anx B, p. 389; dissenting opinion by Judge H.-P. Kaul to Pre-Trial Chamber II's 'Decision on the Prosecutor's application for summonses to appear for Francis Kirimi Muthaura *et al.*', ICC-01/09-02/11-3, para. 29.

The ICC also referred to the term 'organised crime' with reference to the Palermo Convention and the UN Convention against Transnational Organised Crime in order to define the concept of a 'group': cf. ICC, *The Prosecutor v Callixte Mbarushimana*, ICC-01/04-01/10-T-6-Red2-ENG, submissions by the Defence (open session, 16 September 2011), p. 13ff.

21.3.1.3 Organised crime as subject matter of the Rome Statute

As certain organised criminal groups may qualify as organised armed groups, they might be held responsible for committing international crimes. Therefore, although proposals to establish an international tribunal for the prosecution of terrorism and drug trafficking did not succeed,[21] such groups' conduct might fall within the scope of international criminal law and in particular the Rome Statute.

21.3.1.3.1 Genocide

21.3.1.3.1.1 Special intent

On the face of it, as with terrorism,[22] organised criminal or gang conduct does not usually amount to the crime of *genocide* under Article 6 ICCSt by itself, unless the conduct is undertaken with the specific ('genocidal') 'intent to destroy, in whole or in part, a national, ethnical, racial or religious group'.[23] It is this intent 'which makes genocide an international crime'.[24] To be proved, this intent must manifest several elements:

1. *Quantity*: the perpetrator must intend to destroy a considerable number of members of the group; however, as 'his intent to destroy ... will always be limited by the opportunity presented to him',[25] '[i]t is not necessary to intend to achieve the complete annihilation of a group from every corner of the globe'.[26]
2. *Quality*: it is sufficient to intend to destroy not the whole group but a substantial part of it, most notably its leadership.[27] But regardless of this restriction, the intent ultimately has to entail consequences for the group as such.[28]
3. Finally, breaking down the targeted *group* to *parts of a group* is highly questionable. The International Criminal Tribunal for the former Yugoslavia (ICTY) did just that within its jurisdiction and thus considerably broadened the scope of the crime.[29] It is clear, though, that the perpetrator's intent must always be directed against a group as such, within which individuals may be targeted because of their membership of that group.[30]

[21] See Kai Ambos, *Internationales Strafrecht, Strafanwendungsrecht, Völkerstrafrecht, Europäisches Strafrecht, Rechtshilfe*, Munich, Beck, 2014, p. 301.

[22] See, with special reference to that subject, Claus Kress, 'Völkerstrafrecht der dritten Generation gegen transnationale Gewalt Privater?', in Gerd Hankel (ed.), *Die Macht und das Recht: Beiträge zum Völkerrecht und Völkerstrafrecht zu Beginn des 21. Jahrhunderts*, Hamburg, Hamburger Edition, 2008, p. 323.

[23] For further analysis, see K. Ambos, 'What does "intent to destroy" in genocide mean?', (2009) 91 *IRRC* (876) 833ff.

[24] K. Ambos, *Treatise on International Criminal Law*, Vol. II, Oxford, OUP, 2014, p. 21.

[25] ICTY, Appeals Chamber, *Krstić*, judgment of 19 April 2004, IT-98-33-A, para. 13.

[26] Quotation from ILC Draft Code 1996, UN-YB ILC 1996 II, Art. 17 commentary no. 8 (p. 45). See also Ambos, *Treatise*, pp. 41–2, cited in note 24.

[27] Cf., for example, ICTY, *Sikirica et al.*, Trial Chamber, judgment of 3 September 2001, IT-95-8-T, paras 65, 76.

[28] Ambos, *Treatise*, pp. 42–3, cited in note 24.

[29] ICTY, Trial Chamber, *Krstić*, judgment of 2 August 2001, IT-98-33-T, paras 581, 591, 595.

[30] Ambos, *Treatise*, p. 44, cited in note 24.

Only when these requirements are met can organised crime indeed result in genocide: for instance when criminal collectives engaging in illicit trafficking activities in remote places like the Amazon rain forest may deliberately expel or eliminate groups such as indigenous peoples defending their territory against the intruders.

21.3.1.3.1.2 Contextual element

Interestingly, two German courts have restricted the scope of the crime of genocide by including an unwritten contextual element: only when the genocidal conduct is carried out under 'structurally organized and centralized guidance' is the *actus reus* of genocide accomplished.[31] This opinion has clearly been outnumbered by verdicts from both the ICTY and the International Criminal Tribunal for Rwanda (ICTR),[32] and when applied as a means of demarcation in our context of organised crime this restriction is naturally of no avail.

21.3.1.3.2 Crimes against humanity

Under Article 7(1) ICCSt, in order to constitute a *crime against humanity* certain 'acts [must be] committed as part of a widespread or systematic attack directed against any civilian population'. The acts listed include several crimes typically also committed by representatives of organised crime: murder, extermination, enslavement, deprivation of physical liberty, torture, rape, etc. Interestingly, in the light of the international fight against human trafficking, the term 'enslavement' is defined by the Rome Statute as 'the exercise of any or all of the powers attaching to the right of ownership over a person and includes the exercise of such power in the course of trafficking in persons, in particular women and children'.[33]

Yet two reasons militate against the inclusion of organised crime as a crime against humanity under the Rome Statute.

First, Article 7(2) states that for the purpose of paragraph 1, an '"[a]ttack directed against any civilian population" means a course of conduct involving the multiple commission of acts referred to in paragraph 1 against any civilian population, *pursuant to or in furtherance of a State or organizational policy* to commit such attack'. The provision makes it clear that crimes against humanity can indeed be committed by non-state entities.[34] It is not surprising in this regard that in 1991 the International Law Commission (ILC) listed persons with '*de facto* power or organised in criminal gangs or groups'[35] as possible perpetrators. But in the current debate there is mutual consent that this entity must be 'holding *de facto* authority over a territory',[36] 'should

[31] OLG Düsseldorf, judgment of 26 September 1997, IV-26/96, 2 StE 8/96, p. 162; BVerfG NJW 2001, 1848 (1850) Rn. 20, 23.

[32] See, for example, ICTY, Appeals Chamber, *Jelisić*, judgment of 5 July 2001, IT-95-10-A, para. 48 ('the existence of a plan or policy is not a legal ingredient of the crime'), and Ambos, *Treatise*, p. 17 n. 113, cited in note 24, for further references.

[33] Art. 7(2)(c) ICCSt.

[34] Also ICTY, *Prosecutor v Tadić*, decision on the Defence motion to interlocutory appeal on jurisdiction (Appeals Chamber), Case No. IT–94–1-AR72, 2 October 1995, paras 654–5.

[35] ILC Draft Code 1991, UN-YB ILC 1991 II/2, Art. 21 (systematic or mass violations of human rights), commentary no. 5 (p. 103).

[36] ICTY, *Kupreškić et al.*, judgment of 14 January 2000, IT-95-16-T, para. 552.

partake of some characteristics of a State',[37] or must show power and use of force comparable to those of state institutions.[38] Only exceptionally do criminal organisations meet this criterion of 'a state-like organization'.[39] For example, the Cosa Nostra in the province of Palermo can aspire to this status and consequently raises protection money like a tax.[40] But it should be clear that states and organised groups of criminals are not congruent concepts.

Second, the attack must be directed against a *civilian* population, implying that this crime may only be carried out in the *military* context of an armed conflict where a clear demarcation can be drawn between combatants and non- or at least 'no-longer'-combatants.[41] Although the scope of Article 7(1) ICCSt has been escalated in recent years,[42] such a situation does not occur in the course of ordinary transnational organised crime: victims of such crime do not need special protection by international human rights law (of war) but ordinary protection by regular criminal law.

21.3.1.3.3 War crimes

Basically, war crimes are breaches of the laws and customs of war within an international armed conflict, cf. Article 8(1) and (2) ICCSt.

Under Article 8(2)(f) of the Rome Statute, however, other serious violations of the laws and customs applicable to armed conflicts constitute war crimes. These are not of an international character, but are committed in the territory of a state while there is protracted armed conflict between governmental authorities and organised armed groups, or between such groups.[43] What is required for a group to be considered party to an armed conflict has been discussed earlier.[44]

21.3.1.3.4 Aggression

After the Kampala Conference in 2009, the necessary act of aggression within the concept of this crime must always feature the use of armed force by a state against

[37] ICC, PTC II, *Situation in the Republic of Kenya*, decision of 31 March 2010, ICC-01/09-19, dissenting opinion of Judge H.-P. Kaul, para. 51.

[38] See M. Cherif Bassiouni, *Crimes against Humanity in International Criminal Law*, The Hague, Martinus Nijhoff Publishers, 1999, p. 275; Alicia G. Gil, 'Die Tatbestände der Verbrechen gegen die Menschlichkeit und des Völkermordes im Römischen Statut des Internationalen Strafgerichtshofs', (2000) 112 *ZStW* (2), 391–3.

[39] Ambos, *Treatise*, p. 74, cited in note 24, with reference to C. Kress, LJIL 23 (2010), 867–71.

[40] 'Le mani della criminalità sulle imprese, XI Rapporto SOS Impresa—Confesercenti', Rome, 11 November 2008, p. 13ff.; Diego Gambetta, *The Sicilian Mafia: The Business of Private Protection*, Cambridge, Massachusetts, Harvard University Press, 1996, pp. 138, 186.

[41] Cf. Ambos, *Treatise*, pp. 64, 66, cited in note 24. [42] Cf. ibid, p. 64.

[43] See Gerhard Werle and Florian Jeßberger, *Principles of International Criminal Law*, Oxford, OUP, 2014, marginal no. 982.

[44] Whether Art. 8(2)(e) establishes a threshold that differs from that of Art. 3 (common to the four 1949 Geneva Conventions) has been subject to discussion in legal literature. See Dieter Fleck, 'The law of non-international armed conflicts', in D. Fleck (ed.), *The Handbook of International Humanitarian Law*, Oxford, OUP, 2008, p. 610. That discussion is of no relevance for the purposes of the present analysis.

For earlier discussion, see section 21.3.1.3.2., and Sven Peterke and Joachim Wolf, Chapter 18 of this book.

another state.[45] Therefore, organised crime can only amount to aggression when a valid state representative is acting as the perpetrator. This is only the case in exceptional circumstances.

But, as with every core crime, states might also utilize organised groups to commit such crimes. This is a question of attribution, the attribution to states of crimes committed by organised private individuals, a notorious interface between organised crime and state crime.

21.3.2 Transnational organised crime as crimes under the jurisdiction of national courts but triggered by international law

21.3.2.1 The 'next generation' of international criminal law

As this analysis has shown so far, in exceptional circumstances international criminal law may apply to conduct by organised criminal groups as crimes being tried before the ICC or other national or international tribunals. It is interesting to note that nowadays there is even a third way in which organised crime falls within the reach of international criminal law. In the wake of the Yugoslav wars of the 1990s and despite the ICTY's ongoing jurisdiction, the international community took steps both to recover and to extend international judicial authority in nation-states after periods of transition. Thus the Court of Bosnia and Herzegovina, for example, was founded by the High Representative of the UN in 2000 and mainly has jurisdiction over war crimes, but also—and very decisively for the present analysis—over organised crime.[46] This new mechanism clearly shows the close link between international criminal law and the establishment of new judicial competences relating to organised crime. Indeed, violence by gangs or any other organised group conduct incurs individual criminal responsibility by virtue of national jurisdiction, but essentially this is triggered by international criminal law.

Within this framework of an 'international criminal law of a *new* generation',[47] combating organised crime is also a matter of constituting the appropriate judicial authority and competence at the national level, mindful of the prerequisites for any criminalization of gang violence or organised criminal conduct in public international law: due allowance must be made for a framework of normative boundaries set by international humanitarian law, the law of peace and armed conflict, the protection of human rights, and the rule of law.[48]

[45] Ambos, *Treatise*, pp. 186–90, cited in note 24.

[46] For further details see the court's website: http://www.sudbih.gov.ba/?opcija=sadrzaj&kat=3&id=3&jezik=e, accessed 13 July 2015.

[47] Freely adapted from Kress, 'Völkerstrafrecht', p. 323, cited in note 22 above, who speaks of an 'international criminal law of the *third* generation' [emphasis added]; for further details see K. Ambos, 'International criminal law at the crossroads: from ad hoc imposition to treaty-based universal jurisdiction', in Carsten Stahn and Larissa van den Herik (eds), *Future Perspectives on International Criminal Justice*, Leiden, Asser, 2010, pp. 161–77.

[48] See Kress, ibid, p. 411.

21.3.2.2 The Court of Bosnia and Herzegovina

21.3.2.2.1 General remarks

International criminal law not only appeals to international courts and tribunals but also affects national courts. Especially for the prosecution of organised crime there exist national competences that are both initiated and justified by international criminal law. The first example is the fight against organised crime in Bosnia and Herzegovina. In order to cope judicially with the Yugoslav Civil War *after* the end of the temporary ICTY mandate, and in order to relieve this tribunal by taking over the prosecution of lower-rank defendants *during* its mandatory period, a national criminal court with corresponding competences was established in Bosnia and Herzegovina.[49] It is exceptional that this court's jurisdiction also covers organised crime alongside the four international core crimes.[50] We may use the example of this Court of Bosnia and Herzegovina (hereinafter referred to as SBiH for SudBosneiHercegovine, СудБоснеиХерцеговине),[51] to outline the jurisdictional establishment of international criminal law for the prosecution of organised crime, and go further into the question whether there are any, and if so, what kinds of solution designated by this internationally initiated criminal legal system to solve possible conflicts of competence.

21.3.2.2.2 Regulations governing the establishment of the court

The SBiH was established in order to relieve the ICTY in prosecuting war crimes. Only high-rank representatives were supposed to be tried in The Hague, whereas hierarchically inferior defendants should be taken to a regional criminal court.[52] Article 24(2) of the Law on SBiH requires the court's panel to contain both domestic and international judges,[53] and therefore the SBiH could be classed as a 'hybrid' tribunal.[54] Even so, the panel now consists of domestic judges only.[55]

Ratione materiae the jurisdiction did not stay restricted to war crimes, however. The court was initially established by the Law on the Court of Bosnia and Herzegovina, enacted by the High Representative of the UN on 12 November 2000.[56] Under Article 7(1) of the latest version of this law, its jurisdiction extends *ratione materiae* to all crimes defined by the domestic criminal code of Bosnia and Herzegovina (ccBH).[57]

[49] Cf. introductory and extensively William W. Burke-White, 'The domestic influence of International Criminal Tribunals: The International Criminal Tribunal for the Former Yugoslavia and the creation of the State Court of Bosnia & Herzegovina', (2008) 46 *CJTL* 279–350.

[50] See section 21.3.1 of this chapter.

[51] Cf. the homepage of the Court http://www.sudbih.gov.ba/?jezik=e, accessed 13 July 2015.

[52] Cf. Burke-White, 'Domestic influence', pp. 281ff., 288ff., cited in note 49 above.

[53] Law SBiH available via http://www.sudbih.gov.ba/files/docs/zakoni/en/Law_on_Court_BiH_-_Consolidated_text_-_49_09.pdf, accessed 13 July 2015.

[54] Fidelma Donlon, 'Hybrid tribunals', in William A. Schabas (ed.), *Routledge Handbook of International Criminal Law*, London, Routledge, 2011, pp. 85, 96.

[55] See http://www.sudbih.gov.ba/?opcija=bio&jezik=e, accessed 13 July 2015, for the composition of the court.

[56] Decision of the High Representative: http://www.sudbih.gov.ba/files/docs/zakoni/en/Zakon_o_sudu_-_eng.pdf, accessed 13 July 2015.

[57] 'The Court has jurisdiction over criminal offences defined in the Criminal Code of Bosnia and Herzegovina and other laws of Bosnia and Herzegovina.' The version of Law SBiH current at the date of writing, cited in note 53 above.

In 2002 the High Representative recommended the establishment of a specialized section in the court to deal with war crimes.[58] Implementing this intention the panels were divided into three sections having jurisdiction over war crimes (section I), organised crime, economic crime, and corruption (section II) and all other general crimes (section III).[59]

This is a fundamental feature that distinguishes the genesis of the organised crime-related jurisdiction of the SBiH from other domestic jurisdictions: admittedly, national jurisdiction always arises out of the state's monopoly on the use of force.[60] However, never before were an international initiative and an international legal agreement required in order to assign a domestic court jurisdiction, not only in terms of organization to set up a specialized department, but also *ratione materiae*.

The jurisdiction over organised crime is primarily determined by Article 250 ccBH;[61] it is dominated by the principles of territoriality, flags, and nationality without any identifiable priority for or against one or the other area of operation.[62]

21.3.2.2.3 Case law

In view of this explicit jurisdiction, the SBiH has been concerned with many cases of organised crime in recent years: it has dealt with a range of charges, such as the offence of organised crime in violation of Article 250(1) ccBH, in conjunction with the criminal offence of smuggling of persons in violation of Article 189(1) and (2) ccBH and the criminal offence of illicit trafficking in narcotic drugs in violation of Article 195(2) ccBH.[63]

[58] Cf. the Statement by the President of the Security Council, UN Sec Council S/PRST/2002/21 available from http://www.un.org/en/ga/search/view_doc.asp?symbol=S/PRST/2002/21, accessed 13 July 2015.

[59] See Art. 14(1) Law SBiH and also the 'Registry Agreement' of the SBiH available from http://www.sudbih.gov.ba/files/docs/zakoni/en/Registry_Agreement_English_version.pdf, accessed 13 July 2015.

[60] Albin Eser, in *Schönke/Schröder, Strafgesetzbuch*, 29. Aufl. (Munich 2014), Vor §§ 3–9 Rn. 5, 8ff.

[61] '(1) Whoever perpetrates a criminal offence prescribed by the law of Bosnia and Herzegovina as a member of an organized criminal group, unless a heavier punishment is foreseen for a particular criminal offence, shall be punished by imprisonment for a term not less than three years.

(2) Whoever as a member of an organized criminal group perpetrates a criminal offence prescribed by the law of Bosnia and Herzegovina, for which a punishment of imprisonment of three years or a more severe punishment may be imposed, unless a heavier punishment is foreseen for a particular criminal offence, shall be punished by imprisonment for a term not less than five years.

(3) Whoever organizes or directs at any level an organized criminal group which by joint action perpetrates or attempts to perpetrate [a] criminal offence prescribed by the law of Bosnia and Herzegovina, shall be punished by imprisonment for a term not less than ten years or a long-term imprisonment.

(4) Whoever becomes a member of an organized criminal group which by joint action perpetrates or attempts to perpetrate [a] criminal offence prescribed by the law of Bosnia and Herzegovina, unless a heavier punishment is foreseen for a particular criminal offence, shall be punished by imprisonment for a term not less than one year.

(5) A member of an organized criminal group referred to in paragraph 1 through 4 of this Article, who exposes the organized criminal group, may be released from punishment.'

[62] However, exactly this discussion characterizes the present-day development in Germany, cf. Bernd Hecker, 'Die rechtlichen Möglichkeiten der Europäischen Union zur Lösung von Kompetenzkonflikten', in A. Sinn (ed.), *Conflicts of Jurisdiction in Cross-border Crime Situations*, Osnabrück, Universitätsverlag Osnabrück, 2012, pp. 97–8 ('Hierarchisierung'); A. Eser, in *Schönke/Schröder*, Rn. 11, cited in note 60 above; AnwK-StGB/Mark A. Zöller, Vor § 3 Rn. 9.

[63] Cf. SBiH, No. S1 2 K 002587 11 K (Ref. No. X-K-09/719; 17 June 2011), p. 12; S1 2 K 005325 11 K (12 April 2011), pp. 13, 16ff., 22; S 1 2 K 002500 10 Ko (Ref. No. X-KRN-10/1036, 25 February 2011), p. 2ff., 6;

21.3.2.2.4 Conflicts concerning jurisdiction

Against this background, in the case of cross-border organised crime,[64] conflicts of jurisdiction *stricto sensu*, that is to say the concurrent applicability of more than one national or supranational jurisdiction without any direct rule of priority,[65] are possible in two ways: firstly, through the applicability of the international law of the ICTY or the ICC; secondly, through the applicability of the national law of a neighbouring state.

As far as the jurisdictions of the ICTY and the ICC are concerned, I would first observe that intersections between the offence of organised crime subject to Article 250 ccBH and the four core crimes laid down in Articles 6ff. ICCSt and Articles 2ff. of the Statute of the ICTY can only be possible fragmentarily. Therefore, *ratione materiae*, the conflict can only relate to a (small) scope of intersection. In addition to that, the principle of complementarity explicitly declares national law superior to that of the ICC,[66] and the nature of the subject matter introduces a clear distinction between organized crime and the four core crimes under the ICTY (see 21.3.1.3).

Hence jurisdictional conflicts only arise in relation to other domestic jurisdictions of neighbouring states such as Croatia or Serbia. In the cross-border setting it is easy to imagine case scenarios in which Bosnian gangs importing drugs or exporting prostitutes find themselves responsible not only under Article 250 ccBH but also under a neighbouring state's law because of the victim's nationality or because the crime contravenes that state's legitimate protective interests.

21.3.2.3 How Sierra Leone differs

Sierra Leone provides another good example in criminological terms, showing how close classic war crimes committed by war lords can be to organised crime:[67] as President of Liberia, Charles Taylor supported the Revolutionary United Front (RUF) rebels in Sierra Leone for ideological or economic reasons. He not only used crime middlemen in order to cloak his activities and allow corrupt elites to benefit from the transaction directly or indirectly, he also harboured Al-Qaeda members that had come

S1 2 K 00 3595 10 K (2 December 2010), p. 2ff.; No. X-K-10/889-1 (27 August 2010); No. S1 2 K 3356 10 K (11 May 2011); No. X-K-10/872 (5 August 2010); No. X-K-10/889 (1 September 2010); No. X-K-08/645-2 (9 February 2010); No. X-K-08/638-2 (8 February 2010); No. X-K-08/638-3 (8 February 2010); No. X-K-08/645-1 (26 January 2010); No. X-KZ-08/645-1 (21 May 2010); No. X-K-08/638-1 (14 January 2010); No. S1 2 K 003350 11 Kz (20 June 2011).

The SBiH also referred to the UN Convention against Transnational Organised Crime: cf. SBiH, No. X-K/07/486-2 (15 May 2008), p. 1.

[64] This term should not be confused with transnational (organised) crime; see Reichel, *Handbook of Transnational Crime & Justice*, p. xiii, cited in note 15 above.

[65] On the definition of the conflict of jurisdictions, see Arndt Sinn, *Conflicts of Jurisdiction in Cross-border Crime Situations*, Göttingen, V&R, 2012, p. 598; on the differentiation between conflicts of jurisdictions in the broader and narrower sense, see AnwK-StGB/Zöller, Rn. 10ff., cited in note 62 above.

[66] Cf. Art. 17(1)(a) ICCSt: 'unless the State is unwilling or unable genuinely to carry out the investigation or prosecution'.

[67] Gail Wannenburg, 'Organized crime and terrorism', (2003) 10 *South African Institute of International Affairs Journal* (2), Winter/Spring 2003, pp. 77–90.

to trade in diamonds from Sierra Leone.[68] Two known Al-Qaeda members bought diamonds and tried to buy surface-to-air missiles in Liberia.[69]

On 18 May 2012 the Special Court for Sierra Leone convicted Charles Taylor of all of the eleven charges he faced. Five of these counts charged the accused with crimes against humanity punishable under Article 2 of the Court's Statute, in particular murder (Count 2), rape (Count 4), sexual slavery (Count 5), other inhumane acts (Count 8), and enslavement (Count 10). Five additional counts charged the accused with violations of Article 3 (common to the Geneva Conventions) and of Additional Protocol II, punishable under Article 3 of the Statute, in particular acts of terrorism (Count 1), violence to life, health, and physical or mental well-being of persons, in particular murder (Count 3), outrages upon personal dignity (Count 6), violence to life, health, and physical or mental well-being of persons, in particular cruel treatment (Count 7), and pillage (Count 11). The remaining count charged Taylor with conscripting or enlisting children under the age of 15 years into armed forces or groups, or using them to participate actively in hostilities (Count 9), a serious violation of international humanitarian law punishable under Article 4 of the Statute.

Nevertheless, despite all similarities, the *Taylor* case in Sierra Leone was tried by an ad hoc special court as part of an armed conflict within a civil war setting, so cannot really be compared to the reported cases of organised crime in Bosnia and Herzegovina tried by a national court.

21.4 Transnational Organised Crime and International Criminal Law *de lege ferenda*—TOC as Future Core Crimes

21.4.1 The method of establishing international crimes

Now we have to consider suggestions *de lege ferenda*. This term, the difference between the present, given law and the desirable, wished-for law, leads us to the issue of method: how can international crimes be established and how does international jurisdiction cope with them? Here, different ways are possible. The first possibility—preferred by many delegations at the Ad Hoc Committee,[70] and held to be the method of the Rome Conference[71]—is to codify the given and present *customary* international law.[72] Thus far, we would have to examine carefully the current extent of customary international law concerning transnational crime. And in so doing,

[68] Douglas Farah, 'Liberian is accused of harboring Al-Qaeda', *Washington Post*, 15 May 2003, https://www.washingtonpost.com/archive/politics/2003/05/15/liberian-is-accused-of-harboring-al-qaeda/96f69a3c-31b2-48fe-ad22-33c792129e11/, accessed 23 March 2016.

[69] D. Farah, 'Report says Africans harbored Al-Qaeda', *Washington Post*, 29 December 2002, www.washingtonpost.com. The Al-Qaeda operatives were Ahmed Khalfan Ghailani and Fazul Abdullah Diam.

[70] Adriaan Bos, 'From the International Law Commission to the Rome Conference (1994–1998)', in Cassese *et al.*, *The Rome Statute*, vol. 1, pp. 35, 41, cited in note 3.

[71] Andreas Zimmermann, 'Article 5. Crimes within the jurisdiction of the Court', in Otto Triffterer (ed.), *Commentary on the Rome Statute of the International Criminal Court. Observers' Notes, Article by Article*, Munich, Beck, 2008, pp. 97, 99.

[72] Kriangsak Kittichaisaree, *International Criminal Law*, Oxford, OUP, 2001, p. 55; Leslie C. Green, 'International crimes and the legal process', (1980) 29 *ICLQ* (4) 567, 569.

we would also have to consider that our efforts will reflect *present* customary law and that is why this method is actually misplaced under the heading *lex ferenda*.[73] The second possibility is based on treaty law, where two categories are acknowledged: the first category, self-executing treaties, labels even a mere misconduct as an 'international' or 'universal crime'; the second, suppression treaties, omits this designation, but implies other indications of an internationalization of the crimes (e.g. by referring to the *aut dedere aut iudicare* principle or by providing a clear classification of deviance as an offence under domestic jurisdiction).[74] The third possibility does not depend on any preceding law or norm. Here, initial plain consent by legal discourse and agreement is decisive. This method bypasses given customary law and so questions more conservative currents within public international law.[75] A fourth way, the Security Council's extension of the ICC's jurisdiction *ratione materiae*, grounding on Chapter VII of the UN Charter, has turned out to be impossible and will therefore be ignored in this chapter.[76] So let us now have a look at these different mechanisms.

21.4.2 International jurisdiction over transnational offences by codifying customary international law (method 1)

21.4.2.1 The establishment of crimes

21.4.2.1.1 *Repetitio facti/consuetudo* and *opinio iuris*—observations on some crimes

The first method mentioned, codification of customary international law, has to consider whether transnational offences are already covered as international crimes and whether they can be tried on the international stage. For this, we will concentrate on three crimes: illicit drug trafficking,[77] the trafficking in women,[78] and terrorism.[79] Commonly, customary international law consists of two elements, the objective state practice (*repetitio facti*) and the belief that a particular practice is accepted as law (*opinio iuris sive necessitatis*).[80] By preference, state practice may consist of any act or statement by a state and includes also its non-physical policies. Judicative and legislative acts have to be considered as well as statements at international meetings and

[73] Michael Byers, *Custom, Power and the Power of Rules. International Relations and Customary International Law*, Cambridge, CUP, 1999, pp. 130–32, calls this the 'chronological paradox'.

[74] Ilias Bantekas, Susan Nash, and Mark Mackerel, *International Criminal Law*, London, Routledge-Cavendish, 2010, p. 5; William C. Gilmore, 'The proposed International Criminal Court: recent developments', (1995) 5 *TLCP* (2) 266, 272ff.

[75] Bantekas *et al.*, *ibid*, p. 4.

[76] Cf. Santiago Villalpando and Luigi Condorelli, 'Can the Security Council extend the ICC's jurisdiction?', in Cassese *et al.*, *The Rome Statute*, vol. 1, pp. 571–82, cited in note 3.

[77] See Richard R. Vogler and Shahrzad Fouladvand, Chapter 6 of this book, for details.

[78] See Hans-Joachim Heintze and Charlotte Lülf, Chapter 8 of this book, for details.

[79] See Bettina Weißer, Chapter 5 of this book, for details.

[80] Anthony Aust, *Handbook of International Law*, Cambridge, CUP, 2005, pp. 6–8; J. Craig Barker, *International Law and International Relations*, London, Bloomsbury, 2000, p. 55; for a similar argument, Antonio Cassese, *International Law*, Oxford, OUP, 2005, p. 157; Ian Brownlie and James Crawford, *Principles of Public International Law*, Oxford, OUP, 2012, pp. 24–7; John O'Brien, *International Law*, London, Routledge-Cavendish, 2002, pp. 71–6.

during visits;[81] even international treaties aiming at domestic measures can evidence state practice, when national measures are negotiated internationally.[82] This practice has to show at least some duration and—more important—it has to prove a general and uniform practice, especially in relation to those states being particularly affected by the subject matter of that use.[83] *Opinio iuris* requires the states' intention to be legally bound by a certain practice; it is the belief that a state practice is rendered obligatory by the existence of a rule or law.[84]

21.4.2.1.1.1 Illicit drug trafficking

Does customary international law consequently establish illicit drug trafficking as an international crime?[85] International state practice concerning illicit drug trafficking can be traced back to the Convention of 1936 for the Suppression of the Illicit Traffic in Dangerous Drugs.[86] Already present in its Article 2, state parties were required 'to make the necessary legislative provisions for severely punishing' acts like '... possession, offering (for sale), distribution, purchase, sale, delivery ..., brokerage, despatch (in transit), transport, importation, and exportation of narcotic drugs'. Hence, trafficking in illicit drugs had to be established as a criminal offence on a domestic stage, even though by means of an international agreement. In addition, the *aut dedere aut iudicare* principle was included (Articles 7, 8, 9(1–3)) with an exception for 'not sufficiently serious' crimes (Article 9(4)). This convention—as well as many others—was signed in 1936 by those more or less majorly affected states such as China, Colombia, Cuba, Ecuador, Honduras, Mexico, Panama, Uruguay, and Venezuela.

Only from a superficial point of view does it subsequently seem to be a step back that the Single Convention on Narcotic Drugs of 1961 mainly deals with the legal control of narcotics in terms of administrative law rather than providing criminal offences; but the Convention nevertheless contains some interesting provisions referring to criminal law. Article 4 lays down 'general obligations' including domestic measures and international cooperation in the execution of the convention. Article 35(a) provides for 'arrangements at the national level for coordination of preventive and repressive action against the illicit traffic' and Article 36(1)(a) even stipulates a duty to ensure that all the discrete acts listed in the 1936 convention 'shall be punishable offences when committed intentionally'.[87] So, this convention goes beyond its predecessor,

[81] Aust, *Handbook of International Law*, p. 7 and Barker, *International Law*, pp. 56–57, both cited in note 80 above; Martin Dixon, *Textbook on International Law*, Oxford, OUP, 2005, p. 29; O'Brien, *International Law*, cited in note 80 above, pp. 71–3.

[82] Bantekas *et al.*, *International Criminal Law*, cited in note 74 above, p. 5; Malcolm N. Shaw, *International Law*, Cambridge, CUP, 2008, p. 82; dissenting Michael P. Scharf, 'International criminal jurisdiction', (1993) 87 *AJIL* 604, 606.

[83] Aust, *Handbook of International Law*, pp. 6, 7; Barker, *International Law*, pp. 57–60; Brownlie and Crawford, *Principles*, pp. 24–5, all three cited in note 80 above.

[84] *North Sea Continental Shelf Cases* (1969), International Court of Justice, ICJ Reports 3, pp. 42, 44; Aust, *Handbook of International Law*, pp. 7, 8; Barker, *International Law*, p. 61; Brownlie and Crawford, *Principles*, pp. 25–7, all three cited in note 80 above.

[85] See Vogler and Shahrzad Fouladvand, Chapter 6 of this book, for details.

[86] Cf. Robinson, 'The missing crimes', cited in note 18 above, pp. 497, 498–9 and 523–4, listing the thirteen most important conventions.

[87] Arts 21 and 22 of the Convention on Psychotropic Substances 1971 share the same content.

extending the criminalization of drug trafficking by relating it to an international dimension. The Convention was signed and ratified (year of ratification in brackets) by—among others—Bolivia (accession 1976), Chile (1975), Dominican Republic (1993), Iran (2001), Pakistan (1999), Peru (1977), Thailand (1975), and Vietnam (1997), and had reached a status of 184 state parties by June 2014.[88]

Article 3(1)(a)(i) of the UN Convention against Illicit Traffic in Narcotic Drugs and Psychotropic Substances of 1988 repeats all of these acts of misconduct literally, but to this convention's merit are the provisions of Articles 4 (jurisdiction), 6 (extradition), 7 (mutual legal assistance), and 8 (transfer of proceedings) which together ground on a hitherto unknown understanding of international universal jurisdiction.[89] It was, for example, signed and ratified by Afghanistan (1992), China (1989), Colombia (1994), Ecuador (1990), the European Community (1990), Iraq (1998), Laos (2004), Paraguay (1990), Syria (1991), Trinidad and Tobago (1995), as well as the USA (1990), and had reached the status of 189 state parties by June 2014.[90]

At least since the 1961 Convention, that for the first time included explicit provisions for international cooperation, international state practice has moved in a global direction. The main purpose of fulfilling the convention gradually became accompanied by a belief that the fight against drug trafficking could only be successful when this crime were understood as an international phenomenon. The ratified measures included special provisions aiming at the transgressive character of international trafficking on a domestic scale. This view is reflected in the provisions of the 1988 Conventions establishing universal jurisdiction. Furthermore, these conventions encountered neither any opposing state practice nor any kind of secret reservation. Reservations to the 1961 Convention do not relate to drug trafficking,[91] and reservations to Article 3 of the 1988 Convention that were advanced by Bolivia, Colombia, and Peru seek to ensure impunity for the cultivation of coca leaves for personal consumption on traditional-historical grounds.[92] Since then, the development has not stopped: the UN produced widely accepted resolutions covering illicit drug trafficking as a worldwide problem that needs to be fought by domestic and international strategies.[93] Action plans were drawn up and the year 2008 was set as a target date for all states to eliminate illicit trafficking.[94] Subsequently, state treatment of drug trafficking as an international crime by virtue of customary international law has been a proven fact.

Against this, it has been argued that a wide range of conduct, including contentious matters like money laundering, would hamper *opinio iuris*, since criminalization of such behaviours would not arise from a sense of legal obligation, but from the convention itself.[95] Be that as it may: in all these conventions, it is the specific single act of trafficking in a drug that had formerly been positioned as a criminal offence in most of the

[88] Status of Convention adherence: https://www.unodc.org/unodc/en/treaties/single-convention.html, accessed 22 July 2015.

[89] Similarly Robinson, 'The missing crimes', pp. 497, 499, cited in note 18 above.

[90] Status of Convention Adherence: https://www.unodc.org/unodc/en/treaties/illicit-trafficking.html, accessed 13 July 2015.

[91] Status of Convention Adherence, see note 88 above.

[92] Status of Convention Adherence, see note 90 above.

[93] UN GA A/RES/S-20/2 (1998).

[94] Ibid, paras 13–14.

[95] Robinson, 'The missing crimes', pp. 497, 507, cited in note 18 above.

states, and has then become covered by international state agreements that simultaneously exposed this misconduct as a global threat. At least for the core conduct of trafficking, states are nowadays convinced that this crime has reached a global scale making it necessary to fight it internationally (*opinio necessitatis*) and they also intend to be legally bound by their previous practice, by treaty provisions, and—decisively—by the existence of a rule of law overriding the hitherto existing physical agreements (*opinio iuris*).

21.4.2.1.1.2 Trafficking in persons

Trafficking in persons may be regarded as an international crime subject to Article 7(1)(g) ICCSt,[96] but just like torture, apartheid, and attacks against personnel of the UN this misconduct alone has not reached the status of a core crime (21.3.1.1); further criminal elements are needed to raise it to that level. Although trafficking in persons appears to be punishable, the reasons for its international disregard are obvious: while the misconduct can be defined clearly in line with Article 3 of the Protocol to Prevent, Suppress, and Punish Trafficking in Persons, and while many countries provide for this offence in their domestic jurisdictions, a general and uniform international state practice cannot be detected. Too many countries continue to refuse to adopt suitable provisions in their domestic criminal law, for example the enforcement of laws to combat trafficking in Eastern Europe, or against the *Trokosi* custom in Africa that allows girls to be enslaved for sexual services, remains lax and ineffective. Further, only a few of the relevant international conventions are legally binding, while others have not been ratified or contain throttling reservations.

21.4.2.1.1.3 Terrorism

Attempts to define and establish terrorism as an international crime have been unsuccessful as they lack international acceptance.[97] State practice once seemed to ground on the 1937 League of Nations Convention, but only India eventually ratified the treaty.[98] Since then, one cannot seriously speak of a general and uniform state practice, when all efforts to negotiate treaties and conventions have resulted in nothing but piecemeal, patchwork agreements simply reacting to recent terrorist acts.[99] So, neither can this phenomenon of deviance derive characterization as an international crime from customary international law.

21.4.2.1.2 Additional requirements?

At present, we can indeed note that customary international law treats trafficking in illicit drugs as an international crime. Moreover, there is a strong current in the debate demanding more presuppositions in order to declare the misconduct an international offence. This is remarkable, because one might assert that—as defined in the conventions—trafficking

[96] See Heintze and Lülf, Chapter 8 of this book, for details.

[97] For this subject in general, see Weißer, Chapter 5 of this book. For attempts to define terrorism, see Aaron Fichtelberg, 'Adjudicating international crimes', in Reichel, *Handbook of Transnational Crime & Justice*, cited in note 15 above, p. 321; Green, 'International crimes', cited in note 72 above, p. 576.

[98] Green, 'International crimes', cited in note 72 above, p. 572.

[99] This character of states' practice is neglected by Craig Silverman, 'An appeal to the United Nations: terrorism must come within the jurisdiction of an international criminal court', (1998) *New England International and Comparative Law Annual* 4, 3.

in illicit drugs is already sufficiently deviant. This problem can be solved by looking at the origin of those claims. First and foremost, guided by the idea of a conceptual definition of a crime against the peace and security of mankind, delegations at the UN conferences called for the crimes to show a certain *level of gravity*.[100] Accordingly, Article 5(1) ICCSt limits the subject matter jurisdiction of the ICC to 'the most serious crimes of concern to the international community as a whole'. It is true that without concentrating on the most serious offences there is a danger of overburdening the court and trivializing its role.[101] But in the light of this internationalization of the crime, the definition of the term 'trafficking in illicit drugs' in the conventions we have discussed, which also assign discretion in minor cases, already limits the archetype of transnational drug trade. Hence, it can be guaranteed that in future the *ratione materiae* of the ICC will also be restricted to crimes that pose a threat to the constitutional order of states and to basic human rights.[102] The same argument, the genesis of that crime, counters the reproach that international crimes are only *definable* in cases of genocide, crimes against humanity, and war crimes.[103] This is a fairly spurious reproach, because international law—if applied thoroughly—already defines the international crime of illicit drug trafficking with the necessary precision. It is only those strict assumptions of customary international law that need to be fulfilled in order to establish an international crime which seem to be confounded with an asserted lack of determination. A further pleaded exigency—the *political independence* of an international crime[104]—does not apply to the so far quite neutral offence of illicit drug trafficking, but may be valid for more likely crimes such as terrorism.

21.4.2.2 International jurisdiction for these crimes: universality by virtue of public international law

How does an international crime that is derived from customary international law, like trafficking in illicit drugs, now experience international jurisdiction? A strong notion holds that it is the principle of universality that is automatically applied to crimes prescribed by public international law.[105] In support of that assertion, we have to define jurisdiction as the authority to engage in activities of control or regulation within a certain geographic area.[106] However, if the crimes to be controlled do not occur solely in a

[100] UN GA A/46/10, Report ILC (1991), para. 119: 'extreme gravity'; para. 121: 'sufficiently serious'; UN GA A/C.6/44/SR.38, para. 4 (French delegation); UN GA A/51/22, Report PrepCom Vol I (1996), para. 51.

[101] UN GA A/50/22, Report Ad Hoc Com (1995), para. 81; John Dugard, 'Obstacles in the way of an International Criminal Court', (1997) 56 *CLJ* (2), 329, 334.

[102] UN GA A/RES/44/39, 4 December 1989; UN GA A/44/770, 24 November 1989.

[103] UN GA A/46/10, Report ILC (1991), para. 121; UN GA A/49/10, Report ILC (1994), para. 60.

[104] Fichtelberg, 'Adjudicating international crimes', cited in note 97 above, p. 321.

[105] L. C. Green, 'International crimes', cited in note 72 above, p. 569; Christopher Staker, 'Jurisdiction', in Malcom D. Evans (ed.), *International Law*, Oxford, OUP, 2014, pp. 329, 343; Theodor Meron, 'International criminalization of internal atrocities', (1995) 89 *AJIL* 554, 570; Brownlie and Crawford, *Principles*, cited in note 80 above, pp. 467–71; A. Cassese, 'Is the bell tolling for universality? A plea for a sensible notion of universal jurisdiction', (2003) 1 *JICJ* (3) 589, 591–2; Peter Malanczuk, *Akehurst's Modern Introduction to International Law*, London, Routledge, 1997, pp. 112–13; Shaw, *International Law*, cited in note 82 above, p. 668.

[106] Aust, *Handbook of International Law*, p. 43, and Brownlie and Crawford, *Principles*, pp. 456–7, both cited in note 80 above; Kenneth C. Randall, 'Universal jurisdiction under international law', (1988) 66 *TLR* 785, 786; Shaw, *International Law*, cited in note 82 above, pp. 645–7.

given territory, why should their control be restricted territorially? And if jurisdiction is always bound to a legal system, then it necessarily has to share its character. By looking at the principle of jurisdiction more carefully, we are led to discover that its judicial, reactive element of adjudication just reflects its law-making, proactive element of prescribing crimes.[107] Therefore, jurisdiction over offences established by international law has to be international or—to put it in other terms—universal. Nevertheless, this does not mean that international crimes of universal jurisdiction always have to be tried by a universal body; indeed, jurisdictional competences of prescription, adjudication, and enforcement may be performed by different bodies, which themselves are derived from different jurisdictions and thus fall apart in application.[108] This realization does not detract from the possibility of leaving a jurisdictional competence within its original jurisdictional system: international crimes can always be tried by an international body.

Objections against the principle of universality can be deactivated. Firstly, in cases of double jeopardy violating *ne bis in idem*,[109] the reproach of injustice does not apply when we place the adjudicating competence with a universal body like the ICC, so that it is impossible for different jurisdictional bodies to try the same offender for the same offence. Secondly, abridgements of the principle (set out in Lord Millett's two additional criteria) of being 'contrary to a peremptory norm of international law so as to infringe a *jus cogens*' and a gravity that makes the crime an attack on the international legal order,[110] confound the conditions for establishing an international offence with the requirements that have to be met in order to adjudicate it. Thirdly, the ICJ's judgments only attack universality when applied extensively by *national* courts,[111] and in fact one rule mitigating the application of this principle, as it is supposed to in this context, is to apply it via the ICC.[112] International jurisdiction over international crimes that are derived from customary international law can therefore be based on the principle of universality without reservation.

21.4.3 International jurisdiction over transnational offences by treaties (method 2)

The treaty-based method of qualifying transnational offences as international crimes has to face the problem of being binding on states.[113] Since transnational offences are

[107] Aust, *Handbook of International Law*, cited in note 80 above, p. 43; Byers, *Custom, Power*, cited in note 73 above, p. 54; Dixon, *Textbook on International Law*, cited in note 81 above, p. 133; Shaw, *International Law*, cited in note 82 above, pp. 645–6.

[108] Byers, *Custom, Power*, cited in note 73 above, pp. 54–5; Shaw, *International Law*, p. 668, cited in note 82 above.

[109] Malanczuk, *Akehurst's Modern Introduction*, cited in note 105 above, p. 112.

[110] *R v Bow Street Metropolitan Stipendiary Magistrate, ex parte Pinochet Ugarte (No 3)* [2000] 1 AC 147 HL, pp. 269–79 (Lord Millett at 275); Shaw, *International Law*, cited in note 82 above, p. 673.

[111] *Case Concerning the Arrest Warrant of 11 April 2000 (Democratic Republic of the Congo v Belgium)*, International Court of Justice, 14 February 2002, available from http://www.icj-cij.org/docket/index.php?p1=3&p2=3&case=121&p3=4 (last visited 22 July 2015).

[112] Cassese *et al.*, *The Rome Statute*, cited in note 3 above, pp. 589–90; Dixon, *Textbook on International Law*, cited in note 81 above, p. 138.

[113] Barker, *International Law*, pp. 55, 64–8 and Brownlie and Crawford, *Principles*, pp. 469–71, both cited in note 80 above; Cassese, *International Law*, cited in note 80 above, pp. 170–75; Shaw, *International Law*, cited in note 82 above, pp. 673–90.

often denoted as 'treaty crimes', this is astonishing. However, treaties always have a lateral character that depends on the participating state parties, so that by its nature their content is indeed multinational, yet hardly universal.[114] Even self-executing treaties can only establish international crimes with universal jurisdiction if all states have signed up both to the relevant treaty and to the ICCSt.[115] Legal consent is dependent on political will. That is the reason why particularly powerful states prefer less binding agreements to strong, self-executing treaties that establish international crimes.[116] Thus, treaties are more helpful in discovering state practice in terms of custom than in providing a genuine, but troublesome source of public international law.

21.4.4 International jurisdiction over transnational offences by virtue of plain international consent (method 3)

21.4.4.1 The establishment of crimes

The discipline of international relations has made the third method, the idea of universal jurisdiction over transnational offences by plain international consent, fit for good society. As the role of treaties as primary norms has diminished, international consent could be founded on other factors. As early as 1994, the ILC Report on the Draft Code of Crimes against the Peace and Security of Mankind considered a method that based the finding of international crimes on treaties and intended to found universal jurisdiction for these offences on plain state consent.[117] In order to create an equivalent regulation of international law that might lead to state obedience, the theory of constructivism or other interdisciplinary approaches could be the incentive to establish trafficking in women or terrorism as international crimes and assign them universal jurisdiction. States as social entities could achieve binding norms that provide for international crimes and their jurisdiction by legal discourse and agreement. This method does not have to prove any stable previous state practice nor is it restricted to a single written document like a treaty; nevertheless, without any preceding norm, it undeniably has to consider the demands of legal certainty and foreseeability.[118]

21.4.4.2 International jurisdiction for such crimes: no automatism

International jurisdiction over these crimes that are not rooted in customary law cannot follow the universality/automatism discussed earlier (21.4.2.2), so we have to consider wherefrom their international adjudication could be derived. For various reasons, the opinion of Lord Millett in *Pinochet No 3*, that universal jurisdiction over

[114] Aust, *Handbook of International Law*, cited in note 80 above, pp. 45, 46; Shaw, *International Law*, cited in note 82 above, p. 673; A. Zimmermann, 'The creation of a permanent International Criminal Court', (1998) *Max Planck Yearbook of United Nations Law* 2, 169, 204–5.

[115] Cf. Daniel H. Derby, 'Symposium: international criminal law: an International Criminal Court for the future', (1995) 5 *TLCP* (2) 307, 311.

[116] Dugard, 'Obstacles', cited in note 101 above, p. 334.

[117] UN GA A/49/10, Report ILC (1994), p. 66.

[118] Cf. A. Cassese, 'International criminal law', in Evans, *International Law*, cited in note 105 above, p. 726.

international crimes requires the crimes to be 'contrary to a peremptory norm of international law so as to infringe a *jus cogens*',[119] can neither seriously introduce the *ius cogens* principle as a mechanism for classifying a crime 'international', nor lead to international jurisdiction over such a crime: Article 53 of the 1969 Vienna Convention on the Law of Treaties historically provided for *ius cogens*, as weaker countries demanded its introduction in order to avoid material discrimination by means of treaties and custom.[120] So, for traditional reasons alone, this installation has no point of contact with the formal law of procedure and adjudication competences. Further, the unwritten customary rule on *ius cogens* has to be understood as an exceptional principle that methodically needs to show state practice declaring the rule as non-derogable with peremptory effect;[121] an absurd demand for these offences that on one hand cannot be derived from customary law, but which ought to show all the requirements of custom on the other.[122]

However, as shown, even in the case of establishing crimes beyond customs and treaties universality remains a matter of international law; and 'if universal [prescriptive] jurisdiction is permissible, then its exercise ... is logically permissible also'.[123] The reservations and objectives to the principle of universality that I mentioned earlier do not harm the principle's application to international crimes as much as they do its application to domestic criminal offences.[124] Universality is mostly attacked when applied by domestic courts trying offences that have been committed abroad ('universality *in absentia*') or by foreigners. Nevertheless, aspects of territoriality or state sovereignty cannot hinder jurisdiction over international crimes tried on an international stage. Of course, international crimes can also be defined in terms of the place they were committed. Nonetheless, the purpose of territorial attribution in helping to establish a domestic jurisdictional competence to try an offence has lost its sense as soon as an international body has become responsible.[125] Therefore, we do not even have to rely on recent attempts to harmonize the principle of universality,[126] and neither do we have to trouble other currents in setting up jurisdictional principles.[127]

[119] Cf. *Pinochet (No. 3)*, cited in note 110 above.

[120] Aust, *Handbook of International Law*, cited in note 80 above, p. 11; Cassese, *International Law*, cited in note 80 above, pp. 138–9; Malanczuk, *Akehurst's Modern Introduction*, cited in note 105 above, pp. 57, 58.

[121] Byers, *Custom, Power*, cited in note 73 above, p. 192; Malanczuk, *Akehurst's Modern Introduction*, cited in note 105 above, pp. 57, 58.

[122] This anchorage of *ius cogens* is overlooked by Christopher C. Joyner, 'Arresting impunity: the case for universal jurisdiction in bringing war criminals to accountability', (1996) 59 *LCP* 152, 165–7.

[123] Roger O'Keefe, 'Universal jurisdiction. Clarifying the basic concept', (2004) 2 *CICJ* (3) 735, 750; similarly, Matthieu J. L. Decroos, 'Criminal jurisdiction over transnational speech offences', (2005) 13 *EJCCLCJ* (3) 365, 373–4.

[124] Amnesty International, *Universal Jurisdiction: The Duty of States to Enact and Implement Legislation* (2001), p. 3, available from https://www.amnesty.org/download/Documents/32000/ior530042011en.pdf, accessed 23 July 2015.

[125] See for this old meaning Geoff Gilbert, 'Who has jurisdiction for cross-frontier financial crimes?', (1995) *Web Journal of Current Legal Issues* 2.

[126] Like the Princeton Principles on Universal Jurisdiction, available from https://lapa.princeton.edu/publications.php, accessed 22 July 2015.

[127] Cf. C. Staker, 'Jurisdiction', cited in note 105 above, pp. 343–51; further, see the idea of the ILC to transfer the principles of territory or nationality onto an international level, UN GA A/46/10, Report ILC (1991), para. 117.

Further, other recent movements can uphold universal jurisdiction over these crimes. Within that context, it is possible to ground jurisdiction on international agreements that might find their expression in treaties or other sources. Here, the arrangement of jurisdiction, i.e. the negotiation of universal adjudication, has to be classed as corresponding to the third method of establishing the crimes, by virtue of plain international consent (21.4.4.1). In addition, it could be worthwhile to mitigate the impact of such a categorical approach on state sovereignty and to apply universal jurisdiction in each single case. According to the *travaux préparatoires* of the ICCSt this concept is already known: it calls for the installation of an 'opt-in' system to allow universal jurisdiction to be delegated to the ICC in individual cases,[128] and can be corroborated by an additional conferment as a separate expression of consent to universal jurisdiction.[129]

21.5 Conclusion

This analysis has shown that TOC as such does not fall under the jurisdiction of the Rome Statute *de lege lata*, but that the Statute may at least allude to the core crimes where clear intersections occur, especially in cases of crimes against humanity (section 21.3.1 above).

TOC can be an offence explicitly triable *de lege lata* on the basis of international law by some national courts, such as the Bosnian SBiH (section 21.3.2 above).

TOC often forms an international crime *de lege ferenda*: jurisdiction of the ICC over transnational offences can be derived either (insofar as they represent international crimes) from customary international law, or from other state consent (which cannot be based purely on treaties: section 21.4 above).

In all cases international jurisdiction over these offences can be founded on the principle of universality, the recent limitations of which do not affect international crimes.

Indeed, one can and should 'see the ICCSt as a transformative instrument that must respond to the need to change international law progressively to meet international needs'.[130] From a legal point of view, combating TOC does not have to be ceded to regional endeavours.

[128] Sharon A. Williams, 'Article 12. Preconditions to the exercise of jurisdiction', in O. Triffterer, *Commentary on the Rome Statute*, cited in note 71 above, pp. 329, 337.

[129] UN GA A/46/10, Report ILC (1991), para. 123.

[130] Boister, 'The exclusion of treaty crimes from ICC jurisdiction', cited in note 2 above, p. 34.

PART V

PROCEDURAL AND TECHNOLOGICAL CHALLENGES FOR THE INVESTIGATION OF TOC—POLICING, TECHNOLOGICAL ASPECTS, EFFICIENCY, EXCHANGE OF INFORMATION, ABUSE OF POWER, AND TACTICS FOR CONDUCTING INVESTIGATIONS

22

Policing TOC—The National Perspective

Challenges, Strategies, Tactics

Sheelagh Brady

22.1 Introduction

Globalization has contributed to the growth of transnational organised crime. That said, transnational organised crime (TOC) is not new, but what is new is the scope and magnitude of the problem.[1] Greater ease of access across physical borders through less restrictive visa regimes, cheaper airfares, and increased connectivity, compounded by improvements in telecommunications, technology, the growth of international commerce through enhanced flows of goods and services, and improvements in global banking have facilitated a greater level of accessibility.[2] Many of these factors have been exploited by criminals to build increasingly sustainable illicit trades, in a broad range of commodities, services, and goods. Globalization has empowered criminals with the necessary environment and tools to operate across borders more easily, thereby allowing them to capitalize on new opportunities available to them.[3] These factors have, in part, contributed to the creation of a vacuum for TOC to thrive where it is often difficult for policing agencies to distinguish between illicit and licit economies both within and across countries.[4] Despite considerable improvements in international enforcement responses, global governance and national policing responses to TOC have not kept pace with these developments.

22.2 Traditional Organised Crime and Transnational Organised Crime

Globalization has impacted traditional organised crime (OC), which has also been revolutionized by the increasingly global dimension of TOC. That said, TOC should not be viewed purely as an evolution of OC and, as such, tools used by national law

[1] Caliber Associates, *State and Local Law Enforcement Response to Transnational Crime*, 2005, available at: https://www.ncjrs.gov/pdffiles1/nij/grants/209521.pdf, accessed 1 September 2015.

[2] UNODC, *The Globalization of Crime: A Transnational Organised Crime Threat Assessment*, 2010, available at: https://www.unodc.org/documents/data-and-analysis/tocta/TOCTA_Report_2010_low_res.pdf, accessed 28 August 2015.

[3] Vy Le, Peter Bell, and Mark Lauchs, 'Elements of best practice in policing transnational organized crime: critical success factors for international cooperation', (2013) 2 *International Journal of Management and Administrative Sciences* (3), 24.

[4] UNODC, *Globalization of Crime*, cited in note 2 above.

enforcement to tackle OC do not necessarily transfer across to best tackle TOC. Historically, the image of OC has been influenced by the American concept, heavily portrayed by hierarchical 'mafia-style' groups, associated with relatively strict geographical coverage, be it community or region.[5] This image was imported into Europe and beyond, despite the fact that these criminal groups appeared to be less hierarchical. As a result, response strategies that demonstrated more success in tackling 'mafia-style' OC, failed to have a significant impact when targeted against less structured OC in other countries. It is important to note, however, that some academics argue that these differences in OC structure were attributable to positive policing strategies against hierarchical groups, resulting in a reduction in the number of such groups in operation and their ultimate replacement by less structured alternatives. Others argued that there was always a presence of looser networked criminals, just ignored or less studied given their more flexible and less easily explained structure.

The structure of groups conducting TOC remains relatively distinct from the hierarchical and loosely structured groups involved in traditional OC. TOC is said to be conducted by loose, dynamic, agile networks, which are very flexible in nature, innovative, and resilient, and more driven by market motives and profit.[6] For the most part, these networks straddle geographical borders, economies, and trades. While much of their business is of a clandestine nature in the grey and black economies, the use of facilitators also helps them to infiltrate the legal economy, with a view to laundering assets and penetrating licit markets.[7] In many cases these actors straddle the illicit and licit worlds with distorted views of where their illegal activities begin and the legal ones end. Some of the differences between OC and TOC structure may have been influenced by elements of globalization, thereby influencing the growth in TOC nationally as well as internationally, whilst reducing the influence of traditional OC groups. Irrespective of the exact motivation, the differences in structure has significantly contributed to the need for a change in the traditional national policing approach to TOC.

The dynamics and growth of TOC have brought about the need for a change in policing perspective, from one which focuses on traditional OC to one which challenges traditional policing methods and policing ideology.[8] Before the acknowledgement of TOC's presence, policing responses to OC were traditionally viewed as an issue of national sovereignty, with a nation's criminal justice system (CJS) being viewed as having the primary responsibility for internal stability.[9] Now, the growth in TOC has resulted in the recognition of a need for a two-pronged approach from law enforcement, an international and a national response. While there has been little resistance in accepting the need for a shared, cohesive, collaborative, international response, the shift in national responses appears to have been less consistent from country to country. An

[5] Ibid. [6] Ibid.

[7] Australian Government, Commonwealth Organised Crime Strategic Framework: Overview, 2009, available at: https://www.ag.gov.au/CrimeAndCorruption/OrganisedCrime/Documents/OrganisedCrimeStrategicFrameworkOverview.pdf, accessed 3 September 2015.

[8] Bruce Ohr, 'Effective methods to combat transnational organised crime in criminal justice processes', Resource Material Series No. 58, 116th International Training Course visiting expert papers, UNAFEI, 2001, pp. 40–60.

[9] Le, Bell, and Lauchs, 'Elements of best practice', cited in note 3 above.

integrated national and international response has provoked resistance by many law enforcement agencies as it represents a significant challenge to traditional approaches by which OC is viewed and policed. There are a number of potential reasons for this, including differing availability of resources, skills, experiences, and knowledge. In addition, the level of political will and commitment to tackling TOC differs considerably from country to country.

Such resistance to change is dangerous, given the extent of the damage TOC can do to a nation. TOCs are diverse and require considerable, complex responses. For example, TOCs include but are not limited to illicit drug trafficking, illegal firearms trafficking, human trafficking, sale and supply of stolen vehicles and parts, fraud, money laundering, smuggling stolen antiques or artworks, sale and supply of animal products, counterfeiting, and the illegal trade of legal commodities.[10] Such criminality can permeate and weaken a country's political, economic, social, and security structures. As a result, some nations have realized that TOC has the ability to expose a range of vulnerabilities in their traditional policing response to OC.[11] The acknowledgement of the potential impact of TOC has resulted in some shifting their view of TOC to one in which TOC is viewed as a national security threat. Tackling TOC at the national level is difficult and complex, especially with regard to investigation, prosecution, and understanding. Whilst policing OC at the national level was never easy, the developments within TOC have resulted in the fight becoming increasingly harder. The clandestine nature of these activities, in conjunction with the growing use of modern technology and telecommunications, and the cross-border or commodity elements, makes it increasingly difficult for law enforcement to fully understand.[12]

22.2.1 Challenges for policing TOC *versus* OC

The level of complexity that the fight against TOC presents for law enforcement is exacerbated by a number of other factors. For example, national legislation provides the basis for prosecuting TOC in most countries, but legislation has not been always been amended to reflect the growing changes in technology and communications, resulting in loopholes for knowledgeable criminals to exploit. In addition, legislation often restricts the flexibility with which law enforcement can respond to TOC. Traditional laws and procedures tend to slow down responses and the CJS itself is often slow and bureaucratic in its response. This can severely hamper the ability of many forces to respond effectively to TOC. Restrictive legislative practices at the national level have made many nations look to the international policing environment for better laws that are more easily applied. However, although TOC is an international issue it demands

[10] Ngor Ngor and Awunah Donald, 'Effective methods to combat transnational organised crime in criminal justice processes: the Nigerian perspective', Resource Material Series No. 58, 116th International Training Course visiting expert papers, UNAFEI, 2001, pp. 171–82.

[11] Saša Đorđević, 'Understanding transnational organised crime as a security threat and security theories', (2009) *Western Balkans Security Observer* 13.

[12] Karen Kramer, 'Witness protection as a key tool in addressing serious and organised crime', UNAFEI, 2012, available at: http://www.unafei.or.jp/english/pdf/PDF_GG4_Seminar/Fourth_GGSeminar_P3-19.pdf, accessed 1 September 2015.

both international- and national-level responses involving effective domestic tools, including more flexible legislation, for national law enforcement agencies. While it is acknowledged that TOC is unlikely to be contained without an international response, national law enforcement is likely to remain the primary actor in the fight against TOC for some time to come. That said, many nations fail to respond accordingly, leaving law enforcement to respond within the restrictions imposed on it by national legislation and statute, often not designed for tackling TOC. Many nations have yet to acknowledge that the complexity surrounding TOC has resulted in the need for the CJS to be more flexible, adaptive, and less bureaucratic, like the networks it polices.[13] Nonetheless, legislation can only be effective if law enforcement has the capacity, power, and training to investigate crimes and identify suspects and offenders.[14] The necessary resources have not always been put in place at the national level to allow law enforcement to evolve with these changing needs.

There is also a need for national law enforcement to take a more active and strategic approach to tackling TOC, but it too has its own obstacles. The traditional perspective of OC criminal groups results in law enforcement primarily trained to investigate and apply policing strategies to people and groups, without addressing the dynamics of markets and profit, characteristics of TOC. As such, traditional strategies aimed at TOC will not be as effective.[15] In addition, current national policing responses and practices often remain shaped by historical, national, cultural norms, resulting in approaches that fail to evolve and adapt to changes in societal norms and culture brought about by globalization. Investigations need to move beyond having a good knowledge of criminal profiles, to an improved understanding of the relationships, networks, and organisations involved, transport, financial infrastructure, logistics, knowledge of existing law, and knowledge of illicit markets.[16] Many national police forces recognize a lack of expertise in these specific areas that makes it difficult to respond and fully understand the extent to which criminals conduct their business.[17] In an environment where national identify, geographical borders, religion, or language are no longer an obstacle to TOC police need to be skilled, flexible, and agile enough to respond without the bureaucracy of the past.[18] Unfortunately, some forces have yet to acknowledge the need to evolve and adapt.

To meet these changing demands, law enforcement needs the requisite powers and capabilities to conduct investigations, with sufficient power to secure evidence, the logistical resources to support investigations, and the necessary staff equipped with the relevant skills, experience, and expertise.[19] These elements are often missing in many national forces. Many countries do not have the financial ability to invest properly in tackling TOC. Furthermore, expertise and skills are not always appropriate or present within forces and many law enforcement agencies have not spent time studying the

[13] Le, Bell, and Lauchs, 'Elements of best practice', cited in note 3 above. [14] Ibid.
[15] UNODC, *Globalization of Crime*, cited in note 2 above.
[16] Le, Bell, and Lauchs, 'Elements of best practice', cited in note 3 above.
[17] Ngor and Donald, 'The Nigerian perspective', cited in note 10 above.
[18] Ohr, 'Effective methods to combat TOC', cited in note 8 above.
[19] Le, Bell, Lauchs, 'Elements of best practice', cited in note 3 above.

changing environment of TOC to know how to respond effectively. While some countries do not have the money to invest, others often choose not to invest. A lack of political will to tackle TOC can pose an obstacle to law enforcement in many countries and corruption is often implicit in TOC.[20] Additionally, there can be political, economic, religious, and cultural differences influencing how countries respond.[21] While these factors can collectively, or individually, provide the impetus for states to build and continue to strengthen their own capacity, they can also provide the environment for TOC to develop and flourish.[22] Without a shared commitment at the national level to tackle TOC, criminals will exploit any sign of weakness and/or vulnerabilities within the official structures to enhance their own activities, often infiltrating the very institutions built to tackle TOC.

22.3 Positive Approaches to Tackling TOC from the National Perspective

Law enforcement responses to TOC must evolve and in many cases are evolving in an effort to meet the expanding needs of national security.[23] There appears to be a growing collective acceptance in the developed world that there needs to be increased improvement at the national level in regard to intelligence gathering, information sharing, targeting of the criminals at play and the economies in which they are active, improved investigation, prosecution, and management of offenders, and the use of preventative partnerships. While less-developed nations often share the same view, capacity and competence can be lacking in how they tackle TOC. The use of informants and whistle blowers is becoming more common, as is the use of special investigative techniques. Furthermore, many countries are writing national strategies to tackle TOC domestically. For example, the UK's strategy follows the four 'p's: 'pursue, prevent, protect, and prepare', while the Scottish underpin their strategy with four 'd's: 'divert, disrupt, deter, and detect'.[24] It has been accepted, and is evident within these strategies, amongst others, that for law enforcement to effectively tackle TOC a multipronged approach is required, including reactive and proactive strategies. 'Reactive' strategies are best described as policing responses that take place after the act, when a criminal act comes to the attention of law enforcement. Conversely, 'proactive' policies are those initiated before an act has even been committed in order to reduce opportunities for TOC to take hold.

Proactive approaches are imperative to policing TOC. Although TOC is often viewed as violent serious crime, citizens rarely make formal complaints about it and,

[20] UNODC, *Globalization of Crime*, cited in note 2 above.

[21] Ngor and Donald, 'The Nigerian perspective', cited in note 10 above.

[22] Kramer, 'Witness protection as a key tool', cited in note 12 above.

[23] Peter Drennan, 'National security: implications for law enforcement', speech given at the University of Canberra Lecture Series, 30 April 2010, available at: http://www.afp.gov.au/media-centre/speeches/2010/national-security-implications-for-law-enforcement, accessed 5 September 2015.

[24] National Crime Agency, *National Strategic Assessment of Serious and Organised Crime*, 2014 and Scottish Government, *Letting our Communities flourish; A Strategy for Tackling Serious Organised Crime in Scotland*, 2009.

because many of its victims are often seen as perpetrators, it can often be seen as victimless. As a result, cases of TOC and the extent to which it is endemic in communities often only come to the fore when police proactively investigate such crimes.[25] This makes reactive policies limited in their ability to tackle TOC. Nonetheless such responses need to be strong, to clearly demonstrate to offenders that there will be an effective and efficient response if one is suspected of committing such an act. That being said, effective policing of TOC requires a higher level of proactivity. This involves law enforcement actively seeking out criminality that has yet to come to their notice. Such an approach can require a range of tools, resources, and expert skills to be truly effective. These can include electronic surveillance, undercover operations, the use of informants, etc. Furthermore, as technology and communications methods change, so too has the need for evolution in the tools used by law enforcement. While the use of such tools is paramount to tackling TOC, there are some inherent risks with using them. Some of these tools will be discussed in the next section of this chapter. It should be noted that the order in which these tools are presented in no way reflects their priority or effectiveness in controlling TOC.

22.4 The Law Enforcement Toolkit to Tackle TOC

22.4.1 Legislation and statute

TOC is primarily controlled via the legislation, statute, and procedural codes of each respective nation. An example of such a statute is the USA Racketeer Influenced and Corrupt Organisations (RICO) statute, which is said to be one of the most important single pieces of legislation enacted in the USA against OC. Such legislation provides the cornerstone for criminal investigations in many developed countries. Interestingly, while this type of statute defines the offences of OC and provides for the necessary proofs to secure a conviction, the law also provides protections against abuse of power, and in many cases provides offenders and suspected offenders with safeguards against wrongful arrest and/or conviction; for example, the right to remain silent, the right to legal counsel, the right to be tried in good time and in a fair and impartial court; some require that this is done by a jury of one's peers, while other courts are managed by a judge.[26] With such powers comes room for abuse, if they are not monitored correctly. For example, as the need for intercepting information becomes more apparent owing to the increased role of technology and telecommunications in TOC, the law needs to provide rules and restrictions on when and how such technology can be used by law enforcement. This can result in the imposition of restrictions and limitations, providing what some might see as giving more rights to the suspect than to the victim. However, because of reported cases of misuse and abuse of power by law enforcement across the globe, such restrictions are required to ensure people's rights are upheld.

All that said, there is a growing recognition within law enforcement that criminal legislation does not go far enough to fight TOC effectively, and as a result should not

[25] UNODC, *Globalization of Crime*, cited in note 2 above.

[26] Howard Abadinsky, *Organised Crime*, 7th edn, Belmont, California, Thomson Wadsworth, 2003.

be the only legislation used against TOC. History has showed that successful convictions can illustrate the benefits of using other forms of legislation and regulation against suspected offenders, when the criminal law is not sufficient for the purpose. Such legislation and regulations often have different evidential proofs than criminal law and therefore can be useful when evidence of criminal activity is difficult to attain. This, however, requires law enforcement to be innovative, to think outside the box, to know and understand a broader range of law other than purely criminal. A good example of a case in which this approach was used is that of Al Capone. Whilst wanted for OC-related offences, he was convicted for non-payment of taxes, after he could not account for more than $100,000 annual expenditure through his legitimate income. This resulted in his being convicted of failing to pay taxes on $1 million illegally acquired income.[27] While he was not convicted of organised crime, the proceeds of his crimes were confiscated. This type of approach is becoming more popular. The use of taxation laws, financial accounting procedure, etc. are now being used to proactively identify irregularities in what would appear to be licit business in an effort to identify where the licit and illicit worlds meet. This requires a high level of expertise that often goes beyond that of traditional law enforcement. For example, investigating a suspect offender's tax liabilities, to examine their reported earnings *vis-à-vis* their net worth and spending power, can help provide insight into possible irregularities, but such investigation requires a high level of accounting and tax knowledge. This type of knowledge has not traditionally been available within law enforcement agencies and, accordingly, they have had to look outside for skills. This demonstrates the need to be flexible, a prerequisite when tackling TOC, but it also highlights the need for upskilling, training, and greater interconnectivity between law enforcement and other government departments.

22.4.2 National strategies

Many countries have developed national strategies to provide the framework for tackling TOC from the national law-enforcement perspective. These documents are largely written to support and complement the country's commitments and obligations to the international fight against TOC,[28] thereby acknowledging the need for a two-pronged approach. More interesting still, many of these strategies look beyond a traditional law-enforcement approach to tackling TOC and include a 'whole government approach' as a result of a growing recognition that law enforcement alone cannot fight TOC. Strategies are increasingly looking outwards to the role of and partnership with other governmental organisations and private sector companies, to more effectively manage TOC. Law enforcement agencies are increasingly tapping into such opportunities. While it is understood that private companies do not have a mandate to deal with criminality, the vulnerability of their markets can make them susceptible to infiltration by criminal activities, and as a result, they can be incentivized to play a

[27] Department of Justice, *Assessing the Effectiveness of Organised Crime Control Strategies: A review of the Literature*, Canada, Research and Statistics Division, 2003.

[28] Australian Government, Commonwealth OC Strategic Framework, cited in note 7 above.

part in the fight against TOC, or pay the price of indirect involvement. For example, banks and financial institutions can be incentivized to report anomalies if the cost of not reporting them and being found complicit far exceeds the benefits of keeping such practices quiet. Although not mandated they can have a key role to play in ensuring that loopholes for TOC to exploit in the licit world are closed, thereby influencing the design and implementation of appropriate regulations and policies.[29] Furthermore, these partnerships can often help tackle the market forces influencing TOC, which law enforcement has yet to become experienced at. In addition, such partnerships can assist in limiting the ability of criminals to launder money and impact their ability to do business, resulting in a less favourable criminal environment, whilst also identifying and monitoring suspicious activities before they come to law enforcement knowledge. Overall this helps reduce opportunities for TOC to infiltrate the licit environment and minimize its growth whilst also providing the impetus for partners outside law enforcement to take a role in tackling TOC.

22.4.3 Intelligence gathering

Law enforcement across the world gathers information/intelligence, but what differs is the manner in which it collects, records, assesses, and uses the intelligence received. Intelligence is information that goes through a process of evaluation, collation, analysis, reporting, and dissemination. This process is laborious and requires skilled personnel and data management systems.[30] Intelligence is required to increase knowledge about a particular person, activities, or groups that can inform a response, be it for law enforcement or policy. Intelligence can be tactical or strategic. 'Tactical' refers to intelligence that leads to immediate law-enforcement priorities and 'strategic' intelligence is longer-term in nature, providing material for evidence-based and -grounded response and policy development.[31] Intelligence can be gathered overtly or covertly. Examples of covert intelligence-gathering may include electronic surveillance, undercover operations, and confidential informants, while overt intelligence may be gathered via court reports, document assessment, business records, and media reports.[32] All that said, theory and practice are two different things. Not all law enforcement agencies have the resources to create, run, and develop a full-scale intelligence operation.[33] A lack of a robust system of collection can result in or influence the level of illegal gathering of intelligence; while valuable information might be gathered, such practices can jeopardize court cases, even if the information gained is true.

A functioning intelligence cell can bring great rewards, but requires a thorough understanding of what intelligence is and how to manage it. Intelligence is critical for decision making, planning, targeting, and in the prevention of TOC. As a result, as the use of technology and communications systems evolves, intelligence-gathering tools have had to adapt to make better use of information being spread via

[29] Ibid. [30] Abadinsky, *Organised Crime*, cited in note 26 above. [31] Ibid.

[32] Marilyn Peterson, 'Intelligence-led policing: the new intelligence architecture', Washington, DC, Bureau of Justice Assistance, 2005.

[33] Ibid.

the internet, telephones, and wider social media. This places a demand on law enforcement to ensure their tools and techniques are best designed and placed to maximize the changing TOC techniques and practices. Such evolution is not always fast enough, because the use of intelligence is heavily constrained by legislation and policy in many countries, which as mentioned above is usually slow to change. This gap in matching tools with practices can provide criminals with an enabling environment outside the view of the police.

There are a number of other concerns or issues that must be borne in mind when law enforcement uses intelligence. First, given that intelligence-gathering techniques are often intrusive, strict controls for use need to be put in place. Such techniques often breach privacy and civil liberties laws and as a result law enforcement is required to be respectful of people's rights as far as possible.[34] In some countries, restrictions of use may be provided for in legislation. While some countries have legal exemptions from the applicability of this law to intelligence, they usually provide strict guidelines with regard to data management, and collection and retention rules. Whilst having the information is one thing, sharing the information with other agencies is another. The ability to share intelligence or any form of data held has been a major obstacle in the international fight against TOC but is also evident at the national level. Where exchanges are allowed, informal exchange is often preferred by law enforcement, given that it is often quicker and more efficient. However, that being said, such practices can render evidence inadmissible in court, because the checks, balances, and safeguards in place to protect the data were not used.[35] While intelligence can and does play a significant role in the fight against TOC, national police forces must have the resources to structure and manage their intelligence-gathering system effectively, must be able to change quickly as offenders use different methods and practices, and must have the ability to share and receive intelligence quickly where necessary for the proper investigation of TOC, whilst also accepting the need for proper protocols to be put in place to protect citizens and prevent abuse. Furthermore, intelligence is often unproven allegation rather than fact, and therefore the security surrounding the management and storage of this information is of paramount importance. This requires a high level of physical and technical security, from the perspective of safeguarding files, limiting access, and control of the environment in which they are stored. Many police forces have very restricted access protocols to reduce the opportunity for misuse or wrongful circulation of intelligence, while others do not.

22.4.4 Electronic surveillance

Electronic surveillance includes audio surveillance, visual surveillance, tracking, and data surveillance.[36] Many might argue that electronic surveillance is one of the most important, if not, *the* most important tool against TOC, but it is not a new tool.[37]

[34] Ibid. [35] UNODC, *Globalization of Crime*, cited in note 2 above.

[36] UNODC, 'Current practices in electronic surveillance in the investigation of serious and organised crime', New York, United Nations, 2009.

[37] Ohr, 'Effective methods to combat TOC', cited in note 8 above.

Electronic surveillance has been used in some countries for nearly a century, while for other countries it is a more recent phenomenon. Nonetheless, some countries still do not utilize it to maximum effect.[38] All that said, the increased use of technology, the internet, and improved telecommunications methods has resulted in a greater need for sophisticated and broader-ranging use of electronic surveillance methods. As mentioned above, laws and regulations often lag behind developments in tackling TOC, something which is often apparent with regard to electronic surveillance. As technology develops, so does the need for higher-level electronic surveillance capacity. However, this need for change is not always acknowledged and managed by law enforcement.

Like other tools mentioned above, the use of electronic evidence-gathering techniques is usually regulated by legislation and, in most countries, through the use of a warrant-based system.[39] This legally protects law enforcement if and when they use surveillance data in a situation in which the person being monitored could have normally expected privacy, such as interception of a telephone call. Electronic surveillance in public places is often allowed without the issuance of a warrant, but is often supported by procedural rules and guidelines, while its use in private places is nearly always restricted by use only with a warrant. Once again, this demonstrates the restrictive nature of many of these tools. Nonetheless, it has also been argued that electronic surveillance should only be used when less intrusive means have been exhausted with limited effect, as there are numerous concerns over its use, especially as they relate to people's privacy. A more balanced approach to the use of electronic surveillance has been recommended, one which takes into consideration the protection of citizens' rights, the cost to implement such a system, benefit of the evidence gathered, and the public benefit from a related conviction. While it can be very effective, electronic surveillance can be costly. Surveillance usually has two phases: recording or surveillance, be it digital or manpower; and analysis. Depending on the quantity or duration of the recordings/surveillance both phases can require significant resources. This requires considerable skills for law enforcement, something that is not always present. Furthermore, there are considerable training costs associated with using electronic surveillance, for those conducting and analysing the surveillance, those gathering the data, and for prosecutorial teams and judges presenting and assessing their value. Training is required in regard to the laws and regulations pertaining to the use and misuse of electronic surveillance and to the operational procedures.

22.4.5 Undercover operations

Undercover operations are often perceived to be the second most powerful tool against TOC. Such operations are usually conducted where police officers infiltrate criminal organisations or where they proactively obtain information on criminal operations. They can provide reliable, objective evidence of crimes and criminality, to enable law enforcement to proactively monitor plans to commit crimes, and can be very effective

[38] UNODC, 'Current practices in electronic surveillance', cited in note 36 above. [39] Ibid.

in providing a detailed, insider view of those involved in TOC and the markets in which they operate.[40] As a result, undercover operations often require sophisticated, complex planning as operations can last long periods of time. Without clear goals for such operations, they can go on indefinitely. This can be costly, both financially and in terms of manpower requirements.

In addition, undercover operations are dangerous, especially for those officers embedded within criminal groups. If their identity is found out, they can be violently harmed or in some cases killed and their families put at risk. There is often little supervision in the field, which can easily lead to officers acting beyond their powers and authority. It can be difficult for officers to know exactly where to draw the line. It has not been unheard-of for officers to move from observing to partaking in criminality, either to demonstrate their loyalty to the group or because they start to identify with the criminals and their goals. In other cases, access to cash or drugs can be too difficult to resist. Furthermore, some undercover operations have resulted in undercover operatives entrapping, encouraging, and/or providing incentives for criminals to act. This can be motivated by a desire to speed up the investigation and/or to demonstrate their role and influence in the group to their senior officers. While undercover operations appear to provide a unique insight into the world of TOC, the flexible nature of the networks involved, the diversity of crimes, and the array of communication and technology being used can make it more difficult for such operations to really provide clarity into what is going on. That being said, as TOC attempts to infiltrate the legal world, less risky undercover operations may be possible; if there is suspicion of illegal activities within licit business the presence of law enforcement to monitor activities may be useful. While the need for undercover law-enforcement operations is unlikely to go away, it is likely that they too will evolve in nature, design, and objective.

22.4.6 Undercover operations using the web

Owing to an increased reliance on information and communication technologies (ICT) globally and with regard to TOC, undercover operations have taken on a new guise in many law enforcement agencies, namely undercover cyber operations. As the world becomes more reliant on ICT, it becomes more vulnerable to the inherent threats of these technologies.[41] As offenders exploit the opportunities available through improved ICT, law enforcement needs to respond accordingly. Not only has this required greater law-enforcement knowledge of ICT systems, it has also required officers to identity how such technologies can provide offenders with increased opportunities to evolve traditional crimes, such as fraud and child pornography. The cross-border dimension of TOC can become very apparent when conducting undercover operations online, and as a result legislation and regulations must incorporate

[40] Department of Justice, *Assessing the Effectiveness of OC Control Strategies*, cited in note 27 above.

[41] European Union/Council of Europe, 'Specialised cybercrime units—good practice study', EU/COE Joint Paper on Regional Cooperation against Cybercrime, 2011, available at: http://www.coe.int/en/web/cybercrime/all-reports, accessed 27 August 2015.

a cross-border dimension to allow for easy exchange of data to ensure national law-enforcement efforts are not thwarted by jurisdictional issues.

There are very few differences between traditional undercover operations and online undercover operations. Online officers can easily assume an identity online, be it of another offender or of a potential victim. In many ways, online identities are easier to create, so reduce some of the risk. For example, officers often assume the identity of a child in an effort to communicate with potential offenders looking to groom or meet a child. While the actual actions of the officers might be similar, the environment in which they are working is very different and requires considerable training and expertise. For example, whilst illegal activity is often conducted on the web, many use what is commonly referred to as the 'darkweb' for greater privacy. This requires deeper access for officers. Many people hide their IP address to avoid detection, which makes it more difficult for law enforcement to fully know whether those they are investigating are actually within their jurisdiction or not. As in the offline world, officers often use informants and facilitators to access groups or closed networks where there is a need for someone to vouch for a person before accessing the group. Informants are largely motivated by the same factors in the online world as they are in the offline one.

22.4.7 Forfeiture and seizure of assets

Law enforcement agencies have widely agreed that money is the lifeblood of TOC criminals, and that following the money is central to disrupting their activities.[42] The seizure of assets gained by illegal means arguably discourages many from engaging in such behaviour. Such assets can take the form of cash, buildings, land, vehicles, aeroplanes, or financial securities and does not just refer to property held in the name of the criminal. Assets held by family members can also be investigated if suspected of being funded by the proceeds of crime. Investigations for such seizures are complex as they typically must trace the property or funding for such property back to criminal activity of the offender under investigation. This is a difficult and timely process but has been made easier by the introduction of legislation in a number of countries that moves the burden of proof from law enforcement to the suspect. The state has only to prove probable cause that such assets were acquired by illegal means, while requiring the owner to show evidence of how they acquired the property legally. This has reduced the level of detail to which law enforcement must go to prepare for such a seizure application.

Many countries have incentivized such seizures by law enforcement through providing in legislation that monies returned to the exchequer from such seizures can be used to fund law enforcement's responses or harm-reduction strategies.[43] This has enabled law enforcement agencies to fund other aspects of their TOC policies, which has been shown to be costly. However, this incentivized approach is not without its critics. It has been suggested that such a practice has the potential to motivate law enforcement

[42] Department of Justice, *Assessing the Effectiveness of OC Control Strategies*, cited in note 27 above.
[43] Abadinsky, *Organised Crime*, cited in note 26 above.

to target the wealthiest rather than the most dangerous criminal actors to ensure they receive more financing.[44] That said, and although the seizure of assets has been found to be very useful in the fight against TOC, a number of barriers and obstacles have been identified. These include institutional issues and general barriers, legal barriers and requirements that delay assistance, operational barriers, and communication issues.[45] These all contribute to making the process difficult, protracted, and complex. The degree to which these barriers influence the process differs between countries and jurisdictions. Internationally, the obstacles have been evident. Inconsistencies between countries' policies and protocols can make orders made in one jurisdiction difficult to enforce in another. This has resulted in a growing need for mutual cooperation between countries of concern. While such law enforcement cooperation is easier at the national level, cooperation and information sharing with agencies and organisations outside law enforcement proves to be difficult. Other specific law-enforcement issues that are often highlighted include that the seizure of assets is not a core function of law enforcement, which often requires cooperation between other agencies that is not often forthcoming. The necessary expertise for law enforcement to fully engage in the process is often limited, which can also impact the success of such processes.[46] As a result, it is evident that the use of asset seizure is often more complex than law enforcement can deal with, requiring, for the most part, increased cross-agency work and a level of expertise and information exchange not always readily available.

22.4.8 Use of informants and whistle blowers

Informants are usually viewed in two guises, the good citizen and the criminal. It is rare that citizens provide extensive information about TOC, given the clandestine nature of such crimes and, as a result, much of the literature and reports on TOC informants refers to criminal informants.[47] Given their own criminal activities, such informants usually provide information to law enforcement to serve their own ends, be they for financial reward, vengeance, security, lenience in criminal prosecutions, or to attempt to draw attention away from their criminality.[48] Irrespective of what motivates them to talk, they have to be handled with care and sensitivity. Although the information that a criminal informant can provide is often very useful, the reliability, authenticity, and validity of the information given can often be called into question, particularly as the informant might provide information with the aim of removing their rivals from the criminal environment. Furthermore, the use of informants often raises ethical concerns, especially surrounding the possibility that the desire to take out another offender might lead to their being granted immunity for their own criminality. This often leaves victims or the public looking on bewildered.

44 Department of Justice, *Assessing the Effectiveness of OC Control Strategies*, cited in note 27 above.

45 Gay Mitchel, 'Asset confiscation as an instrument to deprive criminal organisations of the proceeds of their activities', Thematic Paper on Organised Crime, Special Committee on Organised Crime, Corruption, and Money Laundering, 2013, available at: http://www.europarl.europa.eu/document/activities/cont/201210/20121016ATT53712/20121016ATT53712EN.pdf, accessed 27 August 2015.

46 Department of Justice, *Assessing the Effectiveness of OC Control Strategies*, cited in note 27 above.

47 Abadinsky, *Organised Crime*, cited in note 26 above.

48 Ibid.

The degree to which informants are used differs depending on the type of cases being investigated. Law enforcement often targets lower-level actors as possible informants; however, it is difficult to assess the effectiveness of this approach. In many cases, these low-level actors are not privy to the complete works and structures within networks, and although they may claim to know what is going on, the information they provide often lacks the level of reliability and detail necessary for law enforcement to act against those high up. In fact, over-reliance on this information can result in the arrest of perceived kingpins, who in fact are just cannon fodder and easy pickings, their removal having limited impact on the level of criminality at play. Furthermore, successful use of informants is often based on the principle that the structures are hierarchical and relatively rigid, when in fact, as discussed earlier, it may be more fluid and agile. This is likely to make informant selection more difficult in the future, especially when investigating loosely connected groups with a range of business links and activities.

22.4.9 Witness protection

The violent nature of much TOC and the potential consequences of witness testimony can impact the degree to which individuals are willing to act as witnesses to such criminality, if and when the need arises. However, the successful investigation and prosecution of TOC depends, for a large part, on the information offered by witness statements. As a result, many governments have responded by implementing a witness assistance and protection strategy for witnesses and victims to ensure those willing to provide information can do so in a safe and secure environment. Such strategies need to incorporate protective measures ranging from assistance, support, and security before, during, and after the trial, to the provision of special protection measures, including possible relocation and identity changes, if required.[49] Protection and security measures provided for the person giving evidence can take three broad forms. The first is police protection and target-hardening by law enforcement, which is often used as an initial response once a direct threat is identified. This includes advice about personal safety, the provision of close protection, regular patrolling around the witness's neighbourhood, and can extend to the installation of security devices at their home or in offices to assist in monitoring activities. The second form is procedural protection, which includes the use of anonymous testimony, presence of an accompanying person for support, voice or visual-image distortions, giving testimony from a location outside the court via closed-circuit TV (CCTV) or video conferencing, and/or removal of the defendant or the public from the court during testimony. These elements can be undertaken at the request of the prosecutor and the approval of the judge.[50] The third form is covert witness protection. This is a more complex procedure and requires the highest level of confidentiality to ensure a witness's protection and safety. Witness protection programmes require thorough preparation and in many cases require a memorandum of understanding between the witness and the programme managers,

[49] Kramer, 'Witness protection as a key tool', cited in note 12 above. [50] Ibid.

as this level of programme can involve the provision of a new identity, leaving loved ones behind, and the creation of a new life. Such changes are difficult and must be supported as well as possible, long after the trial has finished. At this level, it must be a tool of last resource.[51]

22.4.10 Anti-corruption measures

Corruption is often implicit in TOC especially in countries with developing governance systems or limited rule of law. There is a greater risk of TOC infiltrating the legal structures in such states because TOC networks have proved successful in mobilizing themselves to provide the goods and services demanded by unregulated markets. They also are adept at using corrupt practices to infiltrate legal authorities. Over time these groups become stronger and in some cases grow to such an extent that they challenge the growth of the legitimate structures. Interestingly, in 1986 the US President's Commission on Organised Crime concluded that 'corruption linked to drug trafficking is a widespread phenomenon among political and military leaders, police and other authorities in virtually every country touched by the drug trade. The easily available and enormous amounts of money generated through drug transactions present a temptation too great for many in positions of authority to resist.'[52] As a result, many countries have implemented anti-corruption measures in an attempt to protect their organisation's security as well as the nation's. While law enforcement often assists in implementing such measures, independent oversight bodies often conduct most of the investigation and monitoring to add a level of transparency to such investigations.

22.4.11 Financial monitoring

For decades criminals have sought to legitimize money earned illegally through a process referred to as money laundering. Systems by which this process is conducted can vary in complexity and therefore require significant expertise to investigate and follow the money trail. Such expertise is not always available within law enforcement and, even where it is, access to private banking and businesses is often restricted. As a result, there became a clear need for financial institutions to take on a greater role in monitoring financial dealings. This reduces the opportunity for banks to be complicit in criminality, whether consciously or unconsciously, and also provides another level of monitoring for the possible identification of criminal irregularities. In an effort to detect such irregularities, many countries placed a legal requirement on banking institutions to report transactions of $10,000 or above and to report suspicious activities on accounts.[53] While this has reduced opportunities on some level, some groups have responded by moving money in smaller denominations. The true extent of the impact of anti-money laundering legislation has yet to be assessed, with many studies showing

[51] Ibid. [52] Abadinsky, *Organised Crime*, cited in note 26 above.
[53] Department of Justice, *Assessing the Effectiveness of OC Control Strategies*, cited in note 27 above.

limited successes in comparison with the associated costs of monitoring widespread financial transactions. Unlike the anti-corruption measures, law enforcement usually plays an active role in such investigations, in conjunction with other agencies.

22.5 Use and Types of Technology

While some of the tools available to law enforcement have not changed over the last fifty years, the means and methods by which they are utilized have gone through considerable evolution. Technological advances have changed how many law enforcement agencies conduct their activities, in both proactive and reactive responses to crime. From the reactive perspective, advances in the area of crime scene investigation have made significant contributions not only to solving crimes but also to linking crimes that were not considered connected before. Analysis of telephone data has enabled many law enforcement agencies to place offenders at particular locations at particular times, or linked them to other offenders or victims, which might not have been possible before with physical evidence. Analysing online social networks, mapping routes travelled by offenders, linking telephone network data, etc. has been facilitated by improvements in software and high-powered processing ability. This has enabled crime mapping and geographical information systems analysis, which has helped in a better understanding of patterns, trends, and in assessing the impact of response strategies. Furthermore, forensic accounting software has enabled better analysis of illegal transactions within a seemingly licit trade or business. From the proactive perspective technological improvements, some of which are not specifically targeted at law enforcement, have significantly contributed to greater intelligence on TOC activities. These technologies include drones, thermal imaging, GPS tracking, CCTV cameras, and robotic cameras and tools. These provide valuable perspectives on criminality, in such activities as monitoring, overt and covert surveillance, and tracking. Such technologies have greatly reduced the risk of gathering much of this information, given that they can be monitored remotely now, owing to further improvements in the technology managing these systems.

Other technological advances include in-car or remote technology that can allow officers access to real-time data and intelligence, language translators, and automatic licence-plate recognition. Access to real-time information, such as speed violation or a public order incident, can enable a quicker arrest of a wanted TOC offender. Online surveillance has been made easier by improved systems that can monitor, collect, and analyse small- to large-scale data, whilst also allowing another realm in which law enforcement can navigate undercover to collect more intelligence. Some other technologies include gunshot detection systems (GDS) (which use electronic sensors to help pinpoint the exact location of gunfire), biometrics, improvements in body armour, and less lethal weapons, which all contribute to improving the fight against TOC, whilst reducing the risk to law enforcement personnel.

All that said, access to and proper use of technology requires finances, training, and expertise. Law enforcement must evolve with changes within their environment to reduce the opportunities presented to offenders by technological advances. Being left behind makes it impossible for law enforcement to effectively manage TOC. As new technology comes to the market there is always someone ready to exploit it for illegal, opportunistic ends, so law enforcement needs to be proactive in identifying vulnerabilities and closing them off before TOC can be allowed to manifest. It is clear to see that failures by governments and law enforcement agencies to invest in such technology will provide an enabling environment for TOC to flourish, making the job much more difficult for those actively tackling TOC.

22.6 Policing TOC

As seen above, national law enforcement agencies have a wide array of tools at their disposal. How they actually use these is often led by the strategies and tactics they have developed to target the criminality they want to tackle. Although TOC is largely international in operation, national law enforcement often comes into contact with it at the street level.[54] Some countries have big data hubs that allow them to monitor data at the national and local level, for others the responsibility for data collection is devolved to the local level. As a result, national coordinators need to be mindful that local forces might be able to provide the missing piece of information to their case and therefore should be outward-looking in their approach. These street-level displays of TOC could provide an extra piece of clarity to the puzzle. Conversely, coordinators also need to look at the factors of globalization that influence the international dimensions of TOC, which may also influence the level and type of TOC before them. As a result, there is a need for tactical and strategic approach at a higher level when it comes to national policing of TOC than may have been needed for more traditional OC. To enable officers to devote the much needed time and concentration to TOC and related operations some national-law enforcement agencies have developed specialized units with the sole or primary responsibility of monitoring and tackling TOC. This approach is appropriate given the dynamics of TOC. Dedicated units, for example cybercrime units or fraud units, enable forces to commit manpower for long periods and provide an environment in which detailed and far-reaching analysis can be conducted and acted upon. As TOC requires law enforcement to be proactive, having dedicated units, resources, and expertise allows for continuity in approach and learning case-on-case within the unit. That being said, such units need to be self-driven and to work on their own initiative, developing information and intelligence on possible patterns of criminality, and from this developing strategies to suppress it. This requires consistent use of the tools available to them, whilst also looking for new, innovative ways of gathering intelligence. Policing TOC outside this dedicated structure or in the absence of a dedicated approach can result in inexperienced officers being left to investigate highly technical crimes without the proper skills or know-how. Furthermore, law enforcement agencies often see a quick turnover of staff, meaning experts are often moved on just as they are fully developed and ready for the purpose they were trained for.

A common tactic or tool used by these units to support their activities is 'intelligence-led policing', which is defined as a 'collaboration enterprise based on

[54] Caliber Associates, *State and Local Law Enforcement Response*, cited in note 1 above.

improved intelligence operations and community-oriented policing and problem solving'.[55] To implement this, law enforcement needs to re-evaluate its policies and procedures, whilst incorporating intelligence into the planning process to reflect evidence-based identification of problems and issues. This requires active information sharing, the development of partnerships and cohesive practices, and is underpinned by a strong level of analytical capacity. Additionally, it demands a balanced approach, a dissection of the threats and risks, whilst also looking at the opportunities to suppress these. Furthermore, such units need to break down exactly what TOC is and what it looks like. It has been suggested that, apart from the motivation of profit, TOC criminal markets are very different from each other and, as such, require different approaches.[56] That said, some may overlap at one or more points which need to be identified and understood. Dedicated units also need to be able to work with other units to better understand issues they come across.

22.7 Obstacles and Limitations in the Fight against TOC

The list of law enforcement tools presented in section 22.5 of this chapter is not exhaustive, but presents the broad range of present-day tools used by national law enforcement agencies in the fight against TOC. While it is clearly evident that they all contribute to the fight against TOC, and have evolved to some extent with the influences of globalization, there are still many obstacles in place that make it difficult to maintain a flexible, diverse, and committed law-enforcement response to TOC. First, as TOC permeates a wide range of activities, countries, and commodities the need for an efficient response agile enough to react to the ever-evolving TOC is beyond the realm of enforcement alone. No one ever has the full picture of what is going on, gaps in information will always exists, although increased partnerships will assist greatly in reducing these gaps, thereby enhancing the available picture.[57] That being said, there are still a range of issues within law enforcement specifically that inhibit the growing need for flexibility, innovation, and agility to respond. The lack of sufficient financial resources can greatly restrict the ability of law enforcement to tackle TOC, irrespective of the level of will. Inadequately trained and skilled law enforcement personnel with the right level of experience and know-how can also inhibit the ability of law enforcement to properly preform and respond. Furthermore, not all law enforcement agencies have a comprehensive strategy to tackle TOC and therefore responses can be piecemeal. Where such a strategy is in place, the ability or inability to develop cross-agency support and information exchange can greatly inhibit collecting a holistic picture of where TOC actually manifests itself, country-to-country, or state-to-state. Greater partnerships between law enforcement and other public and private agencies can be very useful in getting different perspectives on TOC given that they

[55] Peterson, 'Intelligence-led policing', cited in note 32 above.

[56] Margaret Beare, 'Structure, strategies and tactics of transnational criminal organisations: critical issues for law enforcement', paper presented at the Transnational Crime Conference, Canberra, Australia, 9–10 March 2000.

[57] UNODC, *Globalization of Crime*, cited in note 2 above.

often have better checks and balances in place to identify suspicious activity or blatant criminality, either way enhancing the picture of the level of TOC.

Second, and as was alluded to earlier, the presence or absence of political will to address TOC can be a challenge. While the majority of developed countries clearly demonstrate their willingness to tackle TOC through legislative changes, the production of comprehensive strategies, and the level of investment they are willing to allocate to the fight against TOC, many countries either do not have the willingness, the financial resources, or the increased capacity necessary to tackle TOC. In a large proportion of developing nations, governments often prioritize issues such as development, peace, security, and upholding human rights over TOC.[58] While such an approach is understandable, ignoring or de-prioritizing TOC may not be the right choices, given that TOC can have negative impacts on the factors that have been given priority. Economic and social stability or development is threatened by TOC, yet many vulnerable and weak nations often fail to place importance on tackling TOC. More worrying still, such nations are particularly vulnerable to the effects of TOC as TOC has proven to have the ability to take hold and even permeate official structures, impeding the development of the rule of law. Unfortunately, this is often compounded by the high level of corruption in many developing countries, resulting in law enforcement having limited, if any, ability to tackle TOC.[59]

Third, an inadequate organisational structure and policy within law enforcement can hinder effectively tackling TOC. In some cases the performance assessment of enforcement officers does not correlate to the complex nature of TOC. The performance of a law enforcement officer is often assessed based on the number of arrests made, charges conferred, tickets written, and summons entered. The complexity of investigation can be largely irrelevant when such assessments are made. This can incentivize officers to go for the less complicated cases, where possible, to ensure they meet their requirements. Without the proper management, this practice can be allowed to continue, as there is little, if no, incentive to go after the more difficult cases. Furthermore, officers can be quite territorial and can hesitate to share information across local law enforcement units, to prevent others from solving the case. This comes as a benefit to the criminals. While such activities are clearly destructive, it can often be difficult to identify such practices given that it is hard to get a true assessment of the size, scope, and scale of TOC in any country.

The final obstacle that limits the ability of law enforcement to engage with TOC relates to statistics and analysis. While nations report statistics to international bodies such as Interpol and the United Nations Office on Drugs and Crime (UNODC), many countries do not use the same data to inform their national picture or policies; or, where they do, they do little to analyse the impact of arrests and operations on such figures. This requires considerable analytical skill, something often not available given its

[58] Thematic Debate of the 66th session of the United Nations General Assembly on Drugs and Crime as a Threat to Development: On the occasion of the UN International Day against Drug Abuse and Illicit Trafficking, 26 June 2012—New York, available at: http://www.un.org/en/ga/president/66/Issues/drugs/drugs-crime.shtml, accessed 2 September 2015.

[59] Ibid.

cost. As mentioned above, law enforcement agencies often use common forms of success measurement that include, but are not limited to, counts of cases, arrests, prosecutions, convictions, and prison terms imposed, size of illicit market such as volume, size, and scope of group, efficiency of police response, harm caused, and/or quantities of assets seized, to measure their own impact against the level of criminality.[60] However, these measures often fail to assess the level of TOC that goes unreported or unnoticed and this results in the use of estimated figures. As a result, figures are often skewed in favour of the police and indicate what would appear to be effective TOC responses, when in fact the level of criminality is far greater and more embedded in society that truly understood, which brings its own risks. Internal oversight and review procedures within law enforcement needs not only to look at performance indicators, but also to look to more innovative measurement approaches to measure in great depth the actual level of criminality in an area. Knowing this will make it easier to assess the impact of law enforcement intervention and arrests more accurately.

22.8 Conclusion

Globalization has transformed communications, technology, trade, and travel and, in so doing, has provided a favourable environment for TOC to grow and flourish, the opportunities for which are being exploited by criminals to build increasingly sustainable criminal markets. While international responses have been implemented to try to reduce these opportunities, national responses have not evolved at the same pace, leaving nations increasingly vulnerable to TOC. A number of factors have contributed to national responses being somewhat limited, such as lack of political will, limited resources, skills deficit, corruption, and lack of suitable legislation. Interestingly, structural difference between OC and TOC has also been highlighted as a factor inhibiting the tackling of TOC. Traditionally, OC structures were hierarchical, while TOC structures are less rigid and are more often driven by markets and profit than by people and geography. This has resulted in traditional policing methods not always being appropriate in tackling TOC. However, as TOC increasingly straddles the illicit and licit worlds of many nations, national responses have become more important.

Many law enforcement agencies have acknowledged the need for a more strategic and proactive national response, to complement the existing international responses. Furthermore, the risk of TOC permeating and weakening a country's political, economic, social, and security structures has made many see TOC as a national security threat, thereby requiring a greater national response. As a result, positive changes are increasingly evident across the globe. Many agencies are taking a strategic and practical approach to tackling TOC, and are looking beyond the traditional law-enforcement response. Better use of proactive policing tools, through surveillance, use of informants, and witness protection, amongst others, is being complemented by the increased use of technology and software to provide law enforcement with a more holistic approach to tackling TOC. That being said, a greater law-enforcement presence in the

[60] Department of Justice, *Assessing the Effectiveness of OC Control Strategies*, cited in note 27 above.

online world is requiring a new level of knowledge, skills, and legislative protection. In conjunction with these improvements and developments, law enforcement is more frequently looking outwards to other government agencies and the private sector for new partners in the fight against TOC. Areas of law beyond the criminal code are also increasingly being used to secure convictions, prosecutions, and fines against criminals. This has all culminated in an improved national response to TOC, but the obstacles mentioned above continue to prevent some nations, by choice or by design, from effectively tackling TOC. This is allowing TOC infiltrate vulnerable nations and provides safe havens for it to grow. As a result, TOC is likely to pose both a national and an international challenge for many years to come.

23

Policing Transnational Organised Crime—The International Perspective

Frank G. Madsen

23.1 Introduction

International law enforcement has developed rapidly since its inception at the end of the nineteenth century, but, spurred on by globalization, it has picked up in speed over recent decades.[1] International cooperation against transnational organised crime is, by definition, a necessity. Indeed, the then Secretary-General of Interpol, Mr André Bossard, defined transnational organised crime as crime necessitating the cooperation of two or more countries to solve, either because the crime itself is transnational insofar as it implies crossing at least one border before, during, or after the fact, e.g. international drug trafficking, or by the consequences or the transnational character of the crime.[2] He notes that the constitutive elements of transnational crime are two, (i) the crossing of a border by people (e.g. the criminal), objects (e.g. firearms), or even the intent or will as in computer fraud, when a cybercriminal gives an order from one country, which is transmitted to and executed in another country; (ii) the 'international' recognition of a crime, through international conventions, extradition treaties, or concordant national laws.[3] In other words, he insists on the definitional aspect of *cooperation* as more stimulating and fruitful than a more legalistic approach. The exception to this view, i.e. the one action that involves law enforcement acting internationally, but not cooperation, is 'extra-territorial' seizure of individuals under international law, which will be further considered in section 23.3.4 of this chapter.

This chapter will argue that the recent past constitutes an epistemological rupture in the field of international law-enforcement cooperation against organised crime. The rupture is caused not only by the nature of the organised criminal activities that law enforcement authorities face, nationally and internationally, but also and in particular

[1] For the history and evolution of international cooperation against transnational organised crime, see Chapter 3 in this book, as well as Jude McCulloch and James Martin, 'Policing the globe: international trends and issues in policing', in Bruce A. Arrigo and Heather Y. Bersot (eds), *The Routledge Handbook of International Crime and Justice Studies*, London and New York, Routledge, 2013, p. 94. For US-driven international law enforcement, the fundamental work is Ethan A. Nadelmann, *Cops across Borders: The Internationalization of US Criminal Law Enforcement*, University Park, Pennsylvania State University Press, 1993.

[2] E.g. gangs of professional pickpockets, who ply their trade for a couple of days in one country and then move on to another before law enforcement authorities realize that an organised crime is in execution. See—for the matter of definition—Ch. 2 of this book, sections 2.1.1 and 2.3.2, and Ch. 21.

[3] André Bossard, *Transnational Crime and Criminal Law*, Chicago, Illinois, Office of International Criminal Justice, 1990.

by the introduction of investigative methodologies that, to the extent they were technologically possible in the past, were within the remit of the security services only. The present chapter will consider these aspects of international law enforcement as linked to a development in law enforcement that many, scholars or not, regard as highly deplorable, namely its militarization and its close links with the security services.

The chapter consists of three parts, of which the first two examine the actors and the acts. A third part constitutes a critical analysis of modern forms of international cooperation in law enforcement, in particular the recent epistemological rupture in international law enforcement.

23.2 Principal International Law-Enforcement Authorities

While there is no international police force in existence with powers of search, arrest, etc., in jurisdictions other than the one from which they come, nevertheless there are agencies with international reach.[4] With the one exception of the United Nations Police acting in countries for which the United Nations has been entrusted with 'transitional administration functions', in all other cases supranational law enforcement agencies must act through the police authority of the jurisdiction in which they wish action to be taken. Such action is therefore dependent on at least two major conditions, namely the willingness to act of the police authority being solicited and the legality of the requested act under the laws and regulations of the country.

23.2.1 Interpol

The International Criminal Police Organization, better known as Interpol, consists in a General Secretariat, located in Lyons, France; a National Central Bureau (NCB) in each of the 190 member countries; seven regional offices; and representation offices at the United Nations, New York, and at the European Union, Brussels, Belgium.[5] It is the only global criminal police organisation in the world.

The main activity of the organisation is expressed in its 'motto', 'Connecting police for a safer world'. From its very inception, indeed, the main role of Interpol was to assist criminal police forces in member countries to cooperate, to exchange information, and to profit from Interpol's large data banks, then consisting of nominative and fingerprint files. Member countries have direct access to the Interpol databases; in the year 2014, for example, 4.7 million searches of Interpol databases were executed every day or in excess of 1.8 billion searches per year.[6] These centralized duties served two purposes and served them well, namely the identification of persons arrested and information exchange regarding such persons' previous criminal records in other

[4] In the present chapter, the exercise of arrest, search, and seizure powers in war or civil conflict areas by foreign military units are not considered. For peacekeeping situations, see section 23.2.5. For the suggestion of the creation of an international police force, see Theodore Roosevelt, 'Fourth Annual Message to Congress', 6 December 1904.

[5] The reader is referred to the excellent Interpol website: www.interpol.int.

[6] Interpol, *Annual Report 2014*. Lyon, France: Interpol-General Secretariat, p. 14, see www.interpol.int.

countries, including their possibly being subjects of arrest warrants elsewhere. Since the organisation's re-establishment in Paris, France, after the Second World War, Interpol has consistently expanded the range of services it offers to member countries. Among the best known of such activities is the colour-coded 'Notice' system, within the parameters of which the Interpol General Secretariat transmits information concurrently to the total membership. Among the most used notices are the following: the red notice is the equivalent of an international arrest warrant issued against a suspected criminal and based on a national arrest warrant in one of the member countries. The black notice, typically containing photos and a fingerprint set, concerns an unidentified cadaver, a yellow notice a missing person. A relatively recent development is the Interpol-United Nations Security Council Special Notice, which is directed at groups and individuals of interest to the UN Security Council Sanctions Committees.

One of the most efficient activities of the organisation is the hosting of so-called working meetings, where investigating officers from a number of countries come together to examine each other's evidence at that precise moment of a complex international investigation and to determine a strategy for further investigative steps. Likewise, over the years, Interpol has undertaken an increasingly important educational role, now perhaps best exemplified by the training provided by the Interpol Digital Crime Centre, which is part of the Interpol Global Complex for Innovation, IGCI, in Singapore.[7]

23.2.2 Europol

Europol is located in The Hague, The Netherlands. The organisation serves to coordinate criminal police operations between countries and, in particular, to act as the criminal intelligence arm on a EU level. The idea of a European police force was put forward in 1991 by Helmut Kohl of Germany, as a sort of European FBI, and it was incorporated in the 1992 Maastricht Treaty, in which 'Justice and Home Affairs' was made the third pillar of the new EU.[8] The following year saw the creation of Europol as the 'Europol Drug Unit', which started functioning in January 1994. A Europol Convention, which formally created Europol under the Maastricht Treaty, was agreed in 1995 and entered into force in 1998. This remained the legal basis for Europol until January 2010, when the police organisation became an EU Agency, funded by the EU Commission.

From a professional and operational point of view, however, one might argue that the most important date in the history of Europol was 1997, when by the so-called Treaty of Amsterdam *the Schengen Agreements* (originating from 1985 and 1990) were incorporated into EU law and entered into force the following year. By these agreements, persons, including criminals and criminal groups, were allowed to circulate freely in the EU—with the exception of the United Kingdom and

[7] For example, 26–30 October 2015, a first training course in the programme ASEAN Cyber Forensic Investigation Capability Project.

[8] From 1992, the organisation is referred to as the European Union; prior to that date it was the European Community (EC).

Ireland—and at the Tampere, Finland, council meeting in 1999 Europol was given a central role in coordinating police activities in the EU. Likewise, the organisation was authorized to create Joint Investigation Teams, in which Europol officials could play a supporting role.

Europol relies heavily on a network of almost two hundred liaison officers (European Liaison Officers, ELOs), placed at the Europol HQ in the Hague, but also at the Interpol General Secretariat. Likewise, Europol is host to liaison officers from non-EU countries such as the United States, which has seconded a number of law enforcement agents to Europol's headquarters in The Hague, for instance from the US Secret Service, the US Postal Service, and the US Drug Enforcement Administration (DEA).

23.2.3 Frontex

Frontex—or more correctly The European Agency for the Management of Operational Cooperation at the External Borders of the Member States of the European Union—has its headquarters in Warsaw, Poland.[9] It was created by a European Union Council Regulation of October 2004.[10] In preamble 1, the document acknowledges that 'a uniform and high level of control and surveillance ... is a necessary corollary to the free movement of persons within the European Union and a fundamental component of an area of freedom, security and justice'. Frontex coordinates the control and surveillance of the external borders, provides expertise and training to external border control forces, is responsible for the development of new technology in the area of border control and surveillance, and manages the joint removal of third-country nationals illegally present in the territories of the member states.

It is in this context that preamble 20 of the same document states that the 'development of the policy and legislation on external border control and surveillance remains a responsibility of the EU institutions, in particular the Council' (with reference to Article 5 on the principle of subsidiarity of the Treaty creating the European Union). A second Regulation of 2007 created 'Rapid Border Intervention Teams'.[11]

There can be little doubt that the control of the external borders of the European Union is one of the most difficult tasks facing the Union. The challenge—considering the length of the land border of the EU, not to mention its maritime borders—is in and by itself formidable. When one furthermore, euphemistically, faces asymmetrical crime assessment, then it becomes quite understandable that the EU policies and legislation governing the external borders may appear tinged with naivety.[12] Control of its external borders linked with the free internal movement of persons may very well become *the* stumbling-block of the European Union or at least a major bone of contention between member states.

[9] Council Decision 2005/358/EC, 26 April 2005.

[10] Council Regulation (EC) 2007/2004 of 26 October 2004.

[11] Council Regulation (EC) 863/2007.

[12] Asymmetrical crime assessment is the situation where countries or departments have different views of the importance of, say, organised crime and therefore adjust their law enforcement priorities differently with a resultant heterogeneous pattern of international enforcement.

23.2.4 The Maritime Analysis and Operations Centre

Another European, albeit not European Union, organisation is the Maritime Analysis and Operations Centre, which was created in 2006 with a headquarters in Lisbon, Portugal. It was set up by a number of European countries and the EU to provide a forum of multinational cooperation to suppress illicit drug trafficking by air and by sea. The Centre is mixed military–law enforcement and it has a large area of operations, namely the Atlantic, from South Africa to the Norwegian Sea. Since its inception, it has been responsible for a number of major drug seizures.

23.2.5 United Nations Police

The civilian police of the United Nations (UNPOL) was first deployed in 1960 and has played a significant role in almost all peacekeeping missions since then. In general, UNPOL assists local police with expertise and coordination, but under particular conditions the force takes on full law enforcement responsibilities, namely when the United Nations has been entrusted with a 'transitional administration function' for a territory. For example, in Kosovo and in Timor-Leste, the UN Security Council conferred arrest, search, and seizure powers on UNPOL.[13]

UNPOL plays an important supporting role in the fight against transnational organised crime in cooperation with the United Nations Office on Drugs and Crime (UNODC) and Interpol. The organisation has identified the fact that criminal elements 'are increasingly fuelling wars by providing belligerents with the resources to finance their expensive military activities ... In these situations, UN police work with host state police to build capacity and enhance their ability to combat serious and organised crime.'[14] In fact, in the *post bellum* situations typical for United Nations peacekeeping missions, criminal organisations use gaps in states' governance capacity to create a competitive advantage.

In these situations, the United Nations civilian police force, backed up by organised crime experts with experience from countries with long traditions in organised crime, in a sense fills the governance gaps invoked by Cockayne.[15]

23.2.6 The liaison officer network

One might consider the world-encompassing liaison officer system a supranational organisation, albeit characterized not by its constitution but rather by its function. It is perhaps the part of international policing that has seen the most rapid development over recent decades.

[13] Respectively by UN SC Res. 1244 (1999) and 1272 (1999). For a recent, important resolution regarding policing in post-conflict situations, see SC Res. 2185 of 20 November 2014.

[14] Statement by Alain Le Roy, Under-Secretary General for Peacekeeping Operations, United Nations. See: www.un.org/en/peacekeeping/sites/police/initiatives/transcrime.shtml, accessed 15 November 2015.

[15] James Cockayne, 'Chasing shadows: strategic responses to organised crime in conflict-afflicted situations', (2013) 158 *RUSI Journal* (2), p. 13.

The expansion of the overseas stationing of law enforcement personnel is most marked by US agents, e.g. in 1967 the DEA had twelve agents stationed in eight countries, while in 1991 it had three hundred agents in seventy countries. As of 2014, the DEA had eighty-five foreign offices (in certain countries more than one office), the Federal Bureau of Investigation seventy-six foreign offices, the US Secret Service twenty foreign offices, the Bureau of Alcohol, Tobacco, Firearms, and Explosives ten foreign offices, and the US Immigration and Customs Enforcement forty-seven foreign offices.[16] Other countries have also stationed liaison officers overseas, albeit to a more modest degree. It should be noted, though, that the network of US agents stationed abroad, being those of the hegemonic power, exerts an influence on law enforcement in host jurisdictions that widely exceeds that of liaison and coordination. The US liaison officer network obtains this power—apart from negotiating from a hegemonic position—by offering training courses in the host countries and thus controlling the methodologies adopted; and by being responsible for drafting the reports subsequently submitted to Congress on issues such as human trafficking and active participation in the 'war on drugs'. A negative notation will lead the US Congress to impose penalties on the countries that allegedly are not up to the standards set by the Congress, including the discontinuance of trade preference treatment and other accommodations offered.[17]

23.2.7 Regional agency

This term refers to several types of reciprocal agreement between two or more countries, for example to allow law enforcement officials from contracting countries to enter the territory of other parties for limited amounts of time and in a limited territory inside and along their common border. The typical example here is 'hot pursuit'. This can be and often is realized through the establishment of joint Customs–police centres located on the borders between the countries concerned.

Likewise, neighbouring countries may have signed data-sharing agreements that are closer and deeper than those they have with supranational agencies such as Europol and Interpol. An example is the cooperation agreement between the Nordic countries, the Nordic Police and Customs Cooperation, which was created in 1984 to deal with drug trafficking, but which as of 1996 covers almost all crime.

Another example is the Memorandum of Understanding (MoU) of 31 May 2003 between Cambodia and Thailand.[18] The MoU first notes that trafficking in children

[16] The website for each individual administration has been consulted although the Central Intelligence Agency has not been included, nor have a number of minor administrations with only a couple of overseas postings, such as the US Postal Inspection Service. Interestingly, the New York Police Department (NYPD) has intelligence analysts stationed in eleven international cities. Police forces throughout the world are well known for the absolute gusto with which they engage in bureaucratic wars with one another. The need felt by the NYPD to station their own overseas rather than relying on assistance from federal agents may very well be a symptom of the war taken overseas.

[17] Alison Siskin and Liana Sun Wyler, *Trafficking in Persons: US Policy and Issues for Congress*, Washington DC, Congressional Research Service, 19 February 2013.

[18] 'Memorandum of Understanding between the Royal Government of the Kingdom of Cambodia and the Royal Government of the Kingdom of Thailand on bilateral cooperation for eliminating trafficking in children and women and assisting victims of trafficking', signed in Siem Reap, Cambodia, on 31 May 2003.

and women is an infringement of human rights and that it impacts negatively on 'the social fabric and value of society'. It then continues to observe 'that transnational criminal groups and organizations are actively involved in trafficking in children and women and that such transnational organized crimes have affected not only Thailand and Cambodia but also the region and the global community at large, ...' In the list of offences, one notes with interest 'sex tourism' as one of the purposes for the traffic in women and children. This is, undoubtedly, related to the important traffic in women and children from Cambodia and Burma (or Myanmar) to houses of pleasure in Thailand, partly, perhaps even mostly, to cover the demand by overseas sex tourists.

23.3 International Investigations

International investigations take several forms. The overwhelming majority of such investigations are dealt with by the requesting country addressing itself to the office coordinating international affairs in the other country, typically the Interpol office or, for example in Belgium, the Commissariat Général created in 1991 for information exchange. The often most effective investigative *modus*, however, is the joint operation, for instance as part of the Interpol network. The main advantage of this investigative form is that it brings together the law enforcement personnel, who have dealt with and will deal with the case in question, offering them an opportunity to exchange very detailed information often of a kind not uploaded to the national databases and therefore not available through the usual channels. Joint investigations of this kind are mostly formal, i.e. take place under the auspices of the relevant judicial or prosecutorial authority of each country participating. There are, however, also informal international investigations. They take place between law enforcement personnel in neighbouring countries, who operate either in direct cooperation or via the liaison officer network, i.e. between a law enforcement agent stationed in the country in question, e.g. a DEA agent, and the operative sector of the host police force. Such cooperation is typically high in trust but, on the negative side, does not lead to results that are directly admissible in court, because of the informal nature of the investigation.

Finally, there are informal international investigations that take place without notifying the law enforcement or judicial authorities of the jurisdiction in which such investigations are executed. Such investigations are frowned upon, quite understandably. Indeed, there are no valid arguments for conducting such investigations except in countries suffering from systemic corruption.

23.3.1 An analogy with epidemics

Regulations, domestic laws, and international conventions are often created but not enforced (perhaps because they cannot be). It is difficult to quantify the cost of such un-enforcement by the means available to criminology or, indeed, international studies scholars. Recent studies in epidemiology, however, may provide an analogy for the pernicious effect of non-enforcement—be it caused by lack of attempt or impossibility to enforce—if we look at epidemic regulations as well as criminal law.[19]

In the first decade of the twenty-first century, 'bird flu' was prevalent in a number of countries in Asia, Africa, and Europe, but only in two did it become endemic, Indonesia and Egypt. In Indonesia, a weak central government was unable to impose the necessary hygienic measures and make them respected. In Egypt, the government launched both the police and the army in an attempt to enforce emergency hygienic measures, but poultry farmers were, nevertheless, able to circumvent the enforcement measures. The result was a relatively elevated death toll. In Indonesia 145 or 82.4 per cent of the 176 cases known were fatal, while in Egypt 45 or 32.8 per cent of the 137 persons infected died.[20] In other words, the strict application of hygiene countermeasures was successful in all countries except two, in which lack of enforcement, based on WHO guidelines, led to a number of avoidable deaths.[21]

Several transnational crimes might constitute an analogy in the sense that un-enforcement leads to very severe, but avoidable consequences, for example commercial sexual exploitation of children.

23.3.2 Exchange of data, information, and evidence

International demands for a physical search-and-seizure procedure, e.g. of residential or commercial premises, follow the hitherto adopted procedure, i.e. that such demands transmitted from a foreign country must be submitted to the local judicial authorities and a warrant issued.

The exchange of 'digital' information, i.e. information held on one or more databases, is subject to a bewildering set of rules and regulations, or none. By way of a generalization, one might say that the authority that has placed information on a database system remains responsible for the information. Therefore, an international law-enforcement user of the system should be referred to the depositing authority by the system itself and should ask the authority to confirm that the information is correct and current. An example here might be the Interpol General Secretariat DNA register, the DNA Gateway, which, as far as one can ascertain from the outside, is an automated system available to participating countries, but that does not contain any nominal information. Instead, if the search is positive, the requesting country must address itself to the depositing country and, respecting the laws and regulation of that country, request full information, e.g. identity, precedents, and current whereabouts, about the person, whose DNA has been tested: 'member countries that use the DNA Gateway retain ownership of their profile data and control its submission, access by other countries and destruction in accordance with their national laws'.[22]

[19] Aline Leboeuf, 'Les états face aux pandémies', in Thierry de Montbrial and Philippe Moreau Defarges (eds), *Ramses 2012*, Paris, Dunod, 2011, pp. 100–103.

[20] WHO, 'Avian influenza—situation in Egypt—Update 49', 6 April 2011. WHO, 'Avian influenza—situation in Indonesia—Update 3', 1 April 2011.

[21] WHO, *International Health Regulations*, 2nd edn, Geneva, Switzerland, WHO, 2008.

[22] See www.interpol.int/Interpol-expertise/forensics/dna.

Within the European Union a number of countries, but not for example the United Kingdom, have agreed to allow other EU countries direct access to their full DNA databases, in accordance with the Prüm Convention of 2005.[23] Fourteen countries have joined and three more have indicated that they wish to join the convention, which allows participating countries to exchange data on DNA, fingerprints, and vehicle registration numbers.

The international transfer of evidence in criminal matters poses a specific problem. Such evidence is either material, for example documentary or ballistic, or witness statements. In Anglo-Saxon countries, witness statements obtained for instance by video-taping the witness interview will normally not be sufficient, since the accused has a right to face the witness and counsel for the defence has the right of cross-examination. Likewise, material evidence must follow a demonstrably perfect chain of evidence also called the golden chain of evidence, proving that the evidence has been secured and protected from contamination from the moment it was collected. Often, by the time officers from an Anglo-Saxon country receive the evidence from their foreign counterpart, the chain has, unwittingly, been broken. Interpol is developing model, uniform procedures of evidence collection, marking, and custody.

The International Criminal Court has taken the view that it should not establish a precise procedure for the obtaining and transfer of evidence. Instead, the evidence may be challenged prior to court proceedings. The court has determined, though, that the Registrar remains responsible for the custody of evidence.[24]

23.3.3 Undercover agents and confidential informants

The use of 'undercover' agents, i.e. law enforcement officials who pretend to be criminals to obtain information or, say, take control of evidence in the form of drugs, stolen goods, or the like, is ruled by internal regulations. The latter concern themselves with the safeguarding of the infiltrated agent by laying down a minimum set of prudent rules for his or her behaviour, but also with ethical concerns regarding the relationship between the agent and the members of the infiltrated group. Thus, for example, in the United Kingdom an infiltrated agent may not go as far—in order to gain confidence—as engaging in an intimate relationship with a member of the group under scrutiny.

'Confidential informants', CIs, are mostly of more use than infiltrated law enforcement officials, since they do not have to attempt to gain the confidence of the group or organisation they are infiltrating—they already have it.[25] It would not be an exaggeration to state that the vast majority of major criminal cases, in particular international cases, have been brought to a successful prosecution because of the work done

[23] 'Convention between the Kingdom of Belgium, the Federal Republic of Germany, the Kingdom of Spain, the French Republic, the Grand Duchy of Luxembourg, the Kingdom of the Netherlands and the Republic of Austria on the stepping up of cross-border cooperation, particularly in combating terrorism, cross-border crime, and illegal migration', 27 May 2005. For the UK, see Oliver Wright, 'France requests access to Britain's DNA database for European police forces', *The Independent*, 18 November 2015, p. 11.

[24] International Criminal Court, *Rules of Procedure and Evidence*, UN Doc. PCNICC/2000/1/Add. 1, 2000.

[25] This section is based on the author's experience, having controlled CIs on an international level.

by CIs. CIs are motivated to undertake their (for the justice system) extremely useful role as double agents for precise reasons, often either monetary compensation, which in major international cases can be substantial, or in order to obtain a full or partial annulment of a criminal procedure engaged against them. There is a third, but less common type of CI, who is motivated by a pleasurable rush or high obtained by playing a dangerous double role.

The use of CIs is fraught with dangers for the controlling law enforcement agent; since CIs survive in their role because of their skills in cunning and manipulation, they quite understandably use the same characteristics against the handling agent. Therefore, in the USA, the Attorney General has laid down a series of guidelines for Department of Justice Law Enforcement Agencies, JLEAs.[26] The guidelines are only binding on JLEAs and therefore not on intelligence or counter-intelligence organisations. Likewise, in section I, article 5, the Attorney General stresses that the guidelines are only binding overseas (outside the United States) 'to the extent that the Confidential Informant is reasonably likely to testify in a domestic case'. Therefore, if a JLEA controls a CI in a foreign country and uses that CI to obtain evidence leading to a prosecution in that country then the guidelines would not seem to apply.

On a European level, the use and conduct of CIs are regulated by each country. It is the unwritten rule, though, that if a European law enforcement agency or a US law enforcement agency in Europe directs a CI into another country, the latter will be notified, out of professional courtesy, certainly, but also more pragmatically—considering the company the CI keeps—in order to guarantee assistance to the CI should they be caught up in, for example, a major arrest operation. In order to protect the identity of the CI, such notification is done typically in a personal communication from one individual official in one country to one in the other, preferably to an official that the former knows personally. A major problem obviously arises when a CI is sent into a country known for a high level of corruption; it might not be possible to protect the CI and concurrently inform local authorities.

Finally, private use of undercover operatives is also common and takes one of two forms. An investigative company, be it local or international in extension, will introduce a person into the workforce of a target company in order to gain access to information, or will attempt to persuade an employee to cooperate, clandestinely. Such use of CIs is not regulated.

23.3.4 Extradition

The possibility that a criminal, who has fled jurisdiction, would be able to live a quiet, but public life in another jurisdiction outside the reach of the law of the offended country has from the time of the Egyptian pharaoh Ramses II been considered unacceptable and has given rise to a network of extradition treaties. It is almost a tautology to state that extradition is of crucial importance to the success of law enforcement

[26] Office of the Attorney General, 'The Attorney General's guidelines regarding the use of confidential informants', Washington DC, 8 January 2001.

in the fight against transnational crimes, since these by definition concern several countries.

Extradition treaties can be bilateral or multilateral, respectively an agreement between two countries and the acceptance of an international instrument that provides for extradition. They are of two kinds, either referring to a list of offences that give rise to extradition, called *thematic* treaties, or *duel criminality* treaties that allow for extradition if the crime is a crime in both countries and if it allows for a custodial sentence of a minimum—typically one year—in both countries. Although extradition procedures are executed continuously throughout the world without giving rise to complications, there are a few issues that sometimes render the extradition process difficult, or occasionally impossible.

Even in the presence of an extradition treaty, however, rendition remains a question of *comity*, i.e. the execution of sovereign discretion, which for example in the UK, remains with the Secretary of State.[27] This serves to explain otherwise unexplainable refusals of extradition in recent times, for example France's refusal to extradite an individual charged with and sentenced in a terrorism case to Italy.

A second difficulty arises if a country is requested to extradite a person to another country in which the extradited individual would not or could not be guaranteed the same human rights as in the extraditing country.[28] Also, if the requested country has a rule or a policy not to extradite if the extradited person risks the capital punishment, then extradition to a country with a federal constitution, as for example the USA, presents a separate set of difficulties since the federal government does not have the authority to guarantee that capital punishment will not be applied on a state level, whence the extradition request often originates.

So-called extra-territorial seizure of individuals is a subject that has given rise to some controversy. The practice is most common in war or war-like situations, when non-state actors from the territory of State B launch military attacks into the territory of State A, and State B is unwilling or unable to prevent repetition. Most scholars accept that such seizure is lawful under international law as self-defence of such attacks.[29]

In non-warlike situations, though, the issue, in the United States, seems to become one of *male captus bene detentus*. In 1886, *Ker v Illinois* determined that an individual having been brought into the jurisdiction by unlawful means does not automatically divest the court of jurisdiction.[30] The best-known recent case is *Sosa v Alvarez-Machin* tried in 2004 by the US Supreme Court,[31] from which scholars draw the conclusion that even if the seizure of the person (*male captus*) is unlawful, but not the result of brutality or fraud, he or she can be presented to the court (*bene detentus*). In the case at hand, the two countries involved were Mexico and the United States, between whom an extradition treaty was in existence. The Supreme Court decided that the availability

[27] Ivor Stanbrook and Clive Stanbrook, *Extradition*, 2nd edn, Oxford, OUP, 2000, paras 8.05 and 9.43.

[28] See *Soering v United Kingdom*, European Court of Human Rights, 7 July 1989, Ser. A, No. 161.

[29] See Yoram Dinstein, *War, Aggression and Self-Defence*, 3rd edn, Cambridge, CUP, 2001; Christian Henderson, 'The extraterritorial seizure of individuals under international law—the case of al-Liby', parts I and II, *EJ IL—Blog*, 6 November 2013 (http://www.ejil.org).

[30] *Ker v Illinois* (1886) No. 119 US 436.

[31] *Sosa v Alvarez-Machin* (2004) No. 542 US 692.

of an extradition treaty did not make the use of same obligatory, unless such was specified in the treaty itself. Also, the court decided that, although the seizure of the person was unlawful, the latter could not sue the country responsible for the seizure, since not the rights of the arrestee were violated, but those of the state in which the arrest took place.

In UK jurisprudence, a person who has been subject to an extra-territorial seizure could not be the subject of the court's jurisdiction if an extradition treaty was in existence between the two countries. In 1986, the courts laid down the principle that the court has no power to enquire into the circumstances under which an individual had been brought into the jurisdiction of the state concerned.[32] Eight years later, however, the House of Lords decided that, where an extradition treaty existed between the UK and the state in which an accused was seized, 'our courts will refuse to try him if he has been forcibly brought within our jurisdiction in disregard of those procedures by a process to which our own police, prosecuting or other executive authorities have been a knowing party'.[33]

Within the EU, the European Arrest Warrant (EAW) was adopted on 13 January 2002 by European Council Framework Decision and came into force on 1 January 2004.[34] It was introduced in order to minimize the political and administrative burdens that had rendered extradition proceedings slow *inter alia* because requests were to be transmitted through diplomatic channels.

23.3.5 Use of covert technological investigative techniques

The astonishing advances in communications and data-treatment technologies have led, as one might have expected, to a modernized version of the sword–shield dichotomy: a larger sword leads to a stronger shield, which leads to an even stronger sword, and so on. In other words, the new technologies provided criminals with new means of committing and hiding their criminal activities, while concurrently offering new investigative methodologies to law enforcement. Although it is probably not possible to determine who is ahead of the game at a precise moment, the sword or the shield, a number of main issues seem to surface, which need careful but immediate attention.

Law enforcement (including the security services in many countries) has used these technologies without proper judicial supervision. Such use may or may not be illegal, but the point is not, one might argue, the legality but the lack of democratic accountability. For example, only recently have two major investigative systems collecting random information been disclosed. From December 2008, the US DEA has installed cameras along roads, but in particular near stop lights throughout the United States, in order to register the licence plates, but also to obtain photos of the occupants of cars, mostly in order to be able to launch *in rem* proceedings against the vehicles. Each vehicle transaction has the ability to store up to ten photos, including four occupant photos.

32 *R v Plymouth Justices, ex p Driver* (1986) Q B 95.

33 *R v Horseferry Road Magistrates' Court* (1994) AC 42.

34 2002/584/JHA, OJ L 190, 18/07/2002 P. 0001-0020 on the EAW and on the surrender procedures between member states.

The latter can then be linked to facial recognition systems.[35] Likewise, since 2007 the US Marshal Service has been using aeroplanes equipped to mimic a cell phone tower, thus causing cell phones to connect to it, and allowing communications interception.[36]

Concurrently, however, Cyrus R. Vance, Manhattan District Attorney, has issued a White Paper arguing that his office was unable to execute 111 search warrants for smartphones between 17 September 2014 and 1 October 2015 because the devices employed Apple's 'full disk' encryption. That technology prohibits anyone, except the iPhone's owner, from accessing a device's content without a user's password. In the new Apple encryption system, which became operational a year ago, Apple does not have the keys to unlock customers' communications if a court order is received—only the customers themselves do.[37] Likewise, strong encryption makes it difficult and often impossible to access the hard disks of individuals suspected of trading child pornography.[38]

23.4 International Law Enforcement Cooperation: A Critical Appraisal

'Modern policing, with its characteristic mixture of informational and supervisory aspects of surveillance, was both made possible and seen to be necessary by the wholesale transferal of populations from rural to urban environments.'[39] The surveillance, of course, was the core of the surveillance society leading to today's security society, in the Foucauldian tripartite system.[40] This section of this chapter consists of three parts, of which the first considers the epistemological rupture postulated above, and the second the unholy triangle of law enforcement, militarization, and the security services. The third part postulates that international law enforcement is slowly directing its efforts towards a series of issues that now present themselves as potentially detrimental to humanity.

23.4.1 The epistemological rupture

The introduction to this chapter maintained that the recent past in international police cooperation against transnational organised crime constituted an *epistemological*

[35] Letter of 31 March 2014 from DEA to the American Civil Liberties Union, New York, pp. 5–6. See also American Civil Liberties Union, *You are Being Tracked*, New York, ACLU, July 2013.

[36] Devlin Barrett, 'Americans' cellphones targeted in secret US spy program', *Wall Street Journal*, 13 November 2014.

[37] District Attorney, New York County, Report of the Manhattan District Attorney's Office on Smartphone Encryption and Public Safety, 18 November 2015, p. 9.

[38] See *United States v Charles Burt*, US CA, 7th Cir., 2007, No. 06-3415 and *United States District Court Eastern District of Wisconsin, United States v Jeffrey W. Feldman*, complaint deposited 13 August 2013, case 13-892M.

[39] Lord Anthony Giddens, *The Nation-State and Violence*, Berkeley, University of California Press, 1992, p. 190.

[40] See Frank G. Madsen, 'Transnational criminal networks', in Thomas G. Weiss and Rorden Wilkinson (eds), *International Organization and Global Governance*, Abingdon and New York, Routledge, 2014, Ch. 29. David Lyon, *The Electronic Eye: The Rise of Surveillance Society*, Minneapolis, Minnesota, University of Minnesota Press, 1994.

rupture, a change fundamental to law enforcement cooperation so that one must accept that there is a rupture in our understanding of international law enforcement, a before and an after. This deep rupture is *random* or *bulk data collection*, which is closely linked with the militarization of law enforcement and the increasing and, in this author's view, unhealthy blurring of the boundary between law enforcement and the intelligence services.

The use of undercover agents and of CIs gave rise, in the 1990s, to scholarly studies that questioned the necessity for such methods, their legality, and pointed out the possible excesses on the part of law enforcement.[41] In a seminal work, Nadelmann opined: 'the internationalization of crime and law enforcement also created a new set of problems, mostly related to the trespassing on national sovereignty. The "Americanization" of police methods and strategies in West European states led to the unsolicited import of American undercover agents and to unsupervised interventions no central authority could account for.'[42]

In the twenty years since Nadelmann's work, preoccupations would seem to have changed, however. On one side, the demand for absolute security—in the sense of *sine cura*—that subtended developed countries is now seen perhaps not to be realistic and populations realize that to arrive at a high level of personal security, albeit not absolute, a number of cherished principles must be surrendered or toned down, in particular privacy rights.[43] The question that faces populations at this stage is to what degree they would allow their governments to intrude on their privacy for security reasons.

On one side of the debate one finds total refusal, for example Giorgio Agamben, in a lecture on Destituent Power, and, on the other, appeals for almost total electronic access to our (digital) lives.[44] The recent terrorist attacks in Paris, France, Antalya, Turkey, Sousse, Tunisia, and Bamako, Mali, act as a sobering background to the observation by law enforcement and security services that strong encryption has made it impossible for them to execute court orders (warrants) giving them access to data or, indeed, to use communications interception to prevent terror attacks. A proposed amendment of the so-called Rule 41 (Federal Rules of Criminal Procedure), which is the regulation of the FBI's use of communication and data intercept, is by some scholars considered very invasive.[45] The proposal is of import in itself, but is particularly thought-provoking since, if accepted, it would give federal judges in the United States the right to issue warrants for the hacking of computers in other jurisdictions. This is possible—not to say unavoidable—because network investigative techniques (NITs) operate by sending surveillance software over the internet seeking the target computer or computers. These, however, may very well be in a foreign jurisdiction. One might obviously oppose the civil liberty preoccupations by pointing out that the target computers from which illegal activity is organised have themselves done everything to

[41] Cyrille Fijnaut and Gary T. Marx, *Undercover: Police Surveillance in Comparative Perspective*, Amsterdam, Martinus Nijhoff Publishers, 1995.

[42] Nadelmann, *Cops Across Borders*, cited in note 1 above.

[43] *Sine cura*: without care.

[44] Giorgio Agamben, 'For a theory of destituent power', public lecture, Athens, 16 November 2013.

[45] Ed Pinkington, 'FBI demands new powers to hack into computers and carry out surveillance', *The Guardian*, 29 October 2014.

be anonymous, including using software concealing the computers' location, thereby leaving law enforcement little choice.[46]

In reality, the introduction of anti-money laundering regulations with an obligation on banks to notify the authorities of suspicious transactions caused an epistemological rupture first in the Western world and then, by coercive imposition of the same on developing countries, in the rest of the world. Without any reference to probable cause that the information concerned a suspect criminal and without needing a court order, the authorities assigned to themselves the right to avail themselves of hitherto confidential banking information.

The development of digital technologies provides the authorities with relatively easy access to information that has so far been considered private and protected as such, for example medical files and, say, listings of books and material one might have borrowed at public libraries. As regards the latter, one clearly sees the dilemma: on one hand, the disagreeable spectre of an opinion police and, on the other, the identification of a person's reading habits to prevent a terror attack; the same dichotomy obtains regarding the use of the internet: not only the monitoring of messaging and communications services, but also of websites accessed might lead to the discovery of terrorists planning an action. One would submit that it is an ethical matter to determine which of the two valid points of views here outlined should be preferred, the philosopher's complete rejection or the practitioner's full acceptance, considering that the former might entail avoidable deaths, the latter a severe loss of citizens' privacy rights.[47]

23.4.2 Militarization

Although both Foucault and Giddens predicted the militarization of law enforcement as a characteristic of post-modernism or high modernism, the equipment of police forces with military-strength weaponry and the creation and excessive use of so-called SWAT teams have had a detrimental effect on policing in a broad sense.[48] In fact, police should be and should be seen to be citizens among citizens; instead, the rapidly increasing militarization of the police creates an 'us–them' dichotomy, which is unhelpful for criminal investigations. It is also directly dangerous for public order enforcement, since the responding officers, of whom many furthermore are ex-military, see the population as a kind of enemy. Weaponry, uniforms, and technical terms ('tactical unit' for example) characterize modern policing leading to military-style responses.

Likewise, law enforcement has developed close links with the security services, the personnel of which often is also mainly former or serving military. This leads to a variety of problems and to a clear lack of accountability, to which law enforcement

[46] Ahmed Ghappour, 'Justice Department proposal would massively expand FBI extraterritorial surveillance', 16 September 2014, available at: http://www.justsecurity.org, accessed 15 February 2016.

[47] Elias Groll, 'Paris attacks reopen crypto wars', *Foreign Policy*, 17 November 2015.

[48] Victor E. Kappeler and Peter B. Kraska, 'Normalising police militarisation, living in denial', (2013) *Policing and Society*; Giddens, *The Nation-State and Violence*, cited in note 39 above; Peter B. Kraska, 'Militarization and policing: its relevance to 21st century policing', (2007) *Policing*, 1.

previously was used, being part of the judicial system. All major countries have established listening posts around the world, where they intercept satellite-born digital traffic, be it voice, text, or images. If such traffic originates from the services' home jurisdiction, one has a situation where they are intercepting a citizen's communications without a court order (warrant), albeit outside the jurisdiction. Also in this respect, modern technology, through the use of NITs, makes it possible and perhaps unavoidable that large-scale interception outside of jurisdiction will, by necessity, involve a number of citizens in the home jurisdiction.

Globalization works towards uniform procedures and uniform legislation, but often, with respect to developing countries, with nefarious consequences through coercive policy making. An example is the imposition of anti-money laundering regulations in South Africa, with the result that many could not open bank accounts, but were forced into the arms of organised crime banks.[49]

23.4.3 Scope of international investigations

Not only investigative techniques, but also the scope of international investigations, have changed over the last couple of decades, albeit not enough. The investigative services are beginning to concentrate their efforts on international traffics that only relatively recently have been identified as posing severe threats not only to individual countries, but to humanity. Among such traffics, managed by organised crime, are the trade in toxic waste, in plundered archaeological remains, in forest products, and in protected animals or parts thereof, all of which, in different ways and to different degrees, diminish humanity. Also, a series of crimes that are offensive to human dignity is beginning to attract more international law-enforcement attention, namely commercial sexual exploitation of children, including child pornography, and human trafficking, including forced labour.

23.5 Conclusion

As noted at the end of section 23.4.3, the present day sees international law enforcement engaged in a series of highly laudable endeavours, targeting criminal conduct that is detrimental, one might say, to humanity rather than to individual countries. The period also sees the highest political levels of the United Nations co-involving international policing in its important work, for instance through the use of the Interpol network to monitor individuals and commercial entities that are under Security Council scrutiny. This is of the utmost importance because the world is seeing the reappearance of destruction of heritage and the vandalizing of culture. In February 2015, the Security Council called upon Interpol, UNESCO, and other partners to assist UN member countries to prevent the trade in stolen Iraqi and Syrian cultural items. At a subsequent UNESCO meeting, the Director-General Irina Bokova referred to the

[49] Zakhele, Hlophe, 'Regulating money laundering in developing countries', PhD thesis, 2012, King's College, London. Unpublished.

Security Council Resolution and stressed that 'violent extremists are showing fierce determination to destroy heritage, to vandalize culture, ...'[50] Every time heritage is destroyed, culture vandalized or made to disappear, and organised crime succeeds in abusing the environment, a bit of humanity dies.

Now, however, more than at any other time to try to draw conclusions is fraught with difficulties. On one hand, it seems clear that transnational organised crime not only is controlling a large commercial empire, stretching from counterfeit toys to arms, but it is very much attuned to societal changes and the opportunities offered for illicit rents. On the other, the prevalence of organised crime and the worrying presence of terrorism have led internal and external security forces in the Western world to adopt investigative methodologies that may be legal, but are not legitimate without democratic approval. In other words, populations around the world will have to decide how much of their privacy rights they are willing to forsake in exchange for security that can never be absolute. This, however, is a purely political question; it can be raised here, but it needs to be answered in a political, not an academic arena.

[50] UN SC Res. 2199, 12 February 2015. UNESCO meeting, 1 April 2015.

Select Bibliography

Abadinsky, Howard. *Organised Crime*, 7th edn, Belmont, California, Thomson Wadsworth, 2003.

Abbott, Kenneth W., Keohane, Robert O., Moravcsik, Andrew, Slaughter, Anne-Marie, and Snidal, Duncan. 'The concept of legalization', (2000) 54 *International Organization* (3), 401.

Abtahi, Hirad. 'The protection of cultural property in times of armed conflict: the practice of the International Criminal Tribunal for the Former Yugoslavia', (2001) 14 *Harvard Human Rights Journal*, 1.

Acharya, Upendra D. 'War on terror or terror on wars, the problem in defining terrorism', (2008–9) 37 *Denver Journal of International Law & Policy*, 653.

Agamben, Giorgio. 'For a theory of destituent power', public lecture, Athens, 16 November 2013, available at http://www.chronosmag.eu/index.php/g-agamben-for-a-theory-of-destituent-power.html, accessed 03 May 2016.

Agence France-Presse. 'Eritrean refugees kidnapped, killed: UNHCR chief', 12 January 2012.

AIDP, International Association of Penal Law. 'Resolutions of the XIXth International Congress of Penal Law. Information Society and Penal Law', (2014) 85 *Revue International de Droit Pénal* (3–4), 607 (French), 629 (English), 649 (Spanish).

Akdeniz, Yaman (ed.). *Internet Child Pornography and the Law, National and International Response*, Aldershot, Ashgate, 2008.

Akinsha, Konstantin *et al. Beautiful Loot, The Soviet Plunder of Europe's Art Treasures*, New York, Random House, 1995.

Albrecht, Hans-Jörg. 'Terrorismus und Organisierte Kriminalität—Beziehungen, Zusammenhänge und Konvergenz', in Arnold, Harald *et al.* (eds), *Terrorismus und organisierte Kriminalität*, Berlin, 2014, pp. 17–31.

Albrecht, Hans-Jörg. 'The UN Transnational Crime Convention', in Albrecht, Hans-Jörg and Fijnaut, Cyrille (eds), *The Containment of Transnational Organized Crime*, Freiburg im Breisgau, Edition Iuscrim, 2002, pp. 1–18.

Albrecht, Hans-Jörg and Fijnaut, Cyrille (eds). *The Containment of Transnational Organised Crime: Comments on the UN Convention of December 2000*, Freiburg im Breisgau, Edition Iuscrim, 2002.

Albrecht, Peter-Alexis. *Kriminologie*, 3rd edn, Munich, C. H. Beck, 2005.

Alford, Kenneth D. *The Spoils of World War II: The American Military's Role in the Stealing of Europe's Treasures*, New York, Birch Lane Press, 1994.

Allum, Felia. 'Italian organised crime in the UK', (2012) 6 *Policing* (4), 354.

Alston, Philip (ed.). *Non-State Actors and Human Rights, Collected Courses of the Academy of European Law*, Vol. 13/3, Oxford, New York, OUP, 2005.

Alston, Philip. 'The "not-a-cat" syndrome: can the international human rights regime accommodate non-state actors?', in Alston, Philip (ed.), *Non-State Actors and Human Rights*, Oxford, OUP, 2005, pp. 3–36.

Ambagtsheer, Frederike and Weimar, Willem. 'A criminological perspective: why prohibition of organ trade is not effective and how the Declaration of Istanbul can move forward', (2012) 12 *American Journal of Transplantation*, 571.

Ambos, Kai. *Treatise on International Criminal Law, Vol. II, The Crimes and Sentencing*, Oxford, OUP, 2014.

Ambos, Kai. *Internationales Strafrecht, Strafanwendungsrecht, Völkerstrafrecht, Europäisches Strafrecht, Rechtshilfe*, 4th edn, Munich, C.H. Beck, 2014.

Ambos, Kai. 'Judicial creativity at the Special Tribunal for Lebanon: is there a crime of terrorism under international law?', (2011) 24 *Leiden Journal of International Law (LJIL)*, 655.

Ambos, Kai. 'International criminal law at the crossroads: From ad hoc imposition to treaty-based universal jurisdiction', in Stahn, Carsten and van den Herik, Larissa (eds), *Future Perspectives on International Criminal Justice*, The Hague, 2010, Ch. 7.

Ambos, Kai. 'What does "intent to destroy" in genocide mean?', (2009) 91 *International Review of the Red Cross (IRRC)* (876), 833.

Ambos, Kai and Timmermann, Anina. 'Terrorism and customary international law', in Saul, Ben (ed.), *Research Handbook on International Law and Terrorism*, Camberley, Edward Elgar, 2014, pp. 20–38.

American Civil Liberties Union. *You are Being Tracked*, New York, ACLU, July 2013.

Amnesty International. 'Kosovo (Serbia and Montenegro), so does that mean I have rights?', 6 May 2004.

Andersen, James H. and Bowers, Stephen R. 'Terrorism and crime: critical linkages', (2009) *Liberty University, Faculty Publications and Presentations*, Paper 19.

Andreas, Peter. 'The rise of the American crimefare state', (1997) 14 *World Policy Journal* (3), 37.

Andreas, Peter and Nadelmann, Ethan. *Policing the Globe, Criminalization and Crime Control in International Relations*, Oxford and New York, OUP, 2006.

Anon. 'Delegates protest over arms pact, diluted small-arms accord accepted', *Toronto Star*, 22 July 2001.

Anon. 'Tourists massacred at temple', *BBC News*, 17 November 1997.

Anton, Michael. *Handbuch Kulturgüterschutz und Kunstrestitutionsrecht*, Vols I–III, Berlin/New York, De Gruyter, 2010.

Anton, Michael. 'Neuer Schutz archäologischer Kulturgüter', in Wittinger, Michaela, Wendt, Rudolf, and Ress, Georg (eds), *Verfassung—Völkerrecht—Kulturgüterschutz. Festschrift für Wilfried Fiedler zum 70. Geburtstag*, Berlin, 2011, pp. 319–51.

APEC. *Pathfinder Dialogue with ASEAN & PIF Partners Combating Corruption and Illicit Trade across the Asia-Pacific Region*, available at: http://www.apec.org/~/media/Files/Groups/ACT/20131027_PathfinderDialogue_ChairsSummary_FINAL.pdf, accessed 29 October 2015.

Argandoña, Antonio. 'The United Nations Convention against Corruption and its impact on international companies', (2007) 74 *Journal of Business Ethics*, 481.

Argandoña, Antonio. 'Corruption and companies: the use of facilitating payments', (2005) 60 *Journal of Business Ethics*, 251.

Arieff, Irwin. 'Paris backs away from mandatory arms marking plan', *Reuters News*, 13 July 2001.

Arlacchi, Pino. 'After the Palermo Convention, new international prospects in the fight against organised crime', in Betti, Stefano (ed.), *Symposium: The United Nations Convention against Transnational Organised Crime, Requirements for Effective Implementation*, Turin, UNICRI *et al.*, 2002, p. 15.

Arnau, Frank. *Kunst der Fälscher, Fälscher der Kunst*, 2nd edn, Düsseldorf/Vienna, Econ, 1969.

Arnauld, Andreas von. *Völkerrecht*, 2nd edn, Heidelberg, C. F. Müller, 2014.

ASEAN. *ASEAN Statement on CITES on the Occasion of the Thirteenth Meeting of the Conference of the Parties to CITES*, 11 October 2004, Bangkok, available at: http://www.asean.org/communities/asean-economic-community/item/asean-statement-on-cites, accessed 29 October 2015.

ASEAN. *What is ASEAN-WEN?*, available at: http://www.asean-wen.org/index.php/about-us/what-is-asean-wen, accessed 29 October 2015.

Associated Press. 'Number of US heroin users rose 300,000 over a decade', 7 July 2015.

Aust, Anthony. *Handbook of International Law*, Cambridge, CUP, 2005.

Aust, Helmut Philipp. 'The normative environment for peace—on the contribution of the ILC's Articles on State Responsibility', in Nolte, Georg (ed.), *Peace through International Law, The Role of the International Law Commission*, Dordrecht, Springer, 2009, pp. 13–46.

Australian Government. *Commonwealth Organised Crime Strategic Framework*, Overview, 2009, available at: https://www.ag.gov.au/CrimeAndCorruption/OrganisedCrime/Documents/OrganisedCrimeStrategicFrameworkOverview.pdf, accessed 29 October 2015.

Ayling, Julie and Broadhurst, Roderic. 'Organized crime control in Australia and New Zealand', in Paoli, Letizia (ed.), *The Oxford Handbook of Organized Crime*, Oxford, OUP, 2014, p. 612.

Babu, Rajesh. *The United Nations Convention Against Corruption*, Calcutta, Indian Institute of Management, 2006.

Backers-Morrison, John and Backers-Morrison, Sharone. 'The dark side of globalisation, the criminalisation of refugees', (2001) 43 *Race & Class* (1), 71.

Bagley, Bruce M. *Drug Trafficking and Organized Crime in the Americas*, Washington DC, Woodrow Wilson Center, 2012.

Bagley, Bruce M. and Rosen, Jonathan D. *Drug Trafficking, Organized Crime, and Violence in the Americas Today*, Gainesville, University Press of Florida, 2015.

Baier, Helmut. 'Die Bekämpfung der Kinderpornografie auf der Ebene von Europäischer Union und Europarat', (2004) 1 *Zeitschrift für Urheber- und Medienrecht*, 39–51.

Bailes, Robert. 'Facilitation payments, culturally acceptable or unacceptable corrupt?', (2006) 15 *Business Ethics, A European Review*, 293.

Baimu, Evarist. 'Children, international protection', in Wolfrum, Rüdiger (ed.), *Max Planck Encyclopaedia of Public International Law*, available at: http://www.mpepil.com, accessed 29 October 2015.

Bantekas, Ilias, Nash, Susan, and Mackerel, Mark. *International Criminal Law*, 4th edn, London, Routledge-Cavendish, 2010.

Barberet, Rosemary. 'Measuring and researching transnational crime', in Reichel, Philip and Albanese, Jay (eds), *Handbook of Transnational Crime and Justice*, 2nd edn, Thousand Oaks, California, SAGE Publications, 2014, pp. 47–62.

Barberini, Roberta. 'Italy and the international community in the fight against organized crime', in Betti, Stefano (ed.), *Symposium: The United Nations Convention against Transnational Organised Crime, Requirements for Effective Implementation*, Turin, UNICRI *et al.*, 2002, p. 25.

Barker, J. Craig. *International Law and International Relations*, London, Bloomsbury, 2000.

Barnes, Richard. 'Criminal jurisdiction on board a foreign ship', in Proelss, Alexander (ed.), *United Nations Convention on the Law of the Sea—A Commentary*, Oxford, Hart Publishing; Munich, C. H. Beck and Nomos, 2016), Art. 27.

Barrett, Damon. *Reflections on Human Rights and International Drug Control*, London, London School of Economics, 2012.

Barrett, Devlin. '"Americans" cellphones targeted in secret US spy program', *Wall Street Journal*, 13 November 2014.

Bartlett, Brent L. *The Negative Effects of Money Laundering on Economic Development*, The Asian Development Bank, Regional Technical Assistance Project No. 5967, 2002.

Basel Committee on Banking Supervision. *Sound Management of Risks related to Money Laundering and Financing of Terrorism*, Bank for International Settlements, 2014.

Bassiouni, Mahmoud Cherif (ed.). *International Criminal Law*, 2nd edn, Vols 1–3, Ardsley, New York, Transaction Publishing, 1999.

Bassiouni, Mahmoud Cherif. *Crimes against Humanity in International Law*, The Hague, Martinus Nijhoff Publishers, 1999.

Bassiouni, Mahmoud Cherif. 'Critical reflections on international and national control of drugs', (1989) 18 *Denver Journal of International Law and Policy* (3), 311.

Bassiouni, Mahmoud Cherif. 'The new wars and the crisis of compliance with the law of armed conflict by non-state actors', (2008) 98 *JCLC* (3), 711.

Bassiouni, Mahmoud Cherif and Vetere, Eduardo (eds). *Organized Crime, a Compilation of UN Documents, 1975–1998*, Ardsley, New York, Transnational, 1998.

Beare, Margaret. 'Structure, strategies and tactics of transnational criminal organisations, critical issues for law enforcement', paper presented at the Transnational Crime Conference, Canberra, Australia, 9–10 March 2000.

Beare, Margaret. 'Shifting boundaries—between states, enforcement agencies, and priorities', in Albrecht, Hans-Jörg and Fijnaut, Cyrille (eds), *The Containment of Transnational Organised Crime, Comments on the UN Convention of December 2000*, Freiburg im Breisgau, Edition Iuscrim, 2002, p. 171.

Beare, Margaret and Woodiwiss, Michael. 'US organized crime control policies exported abroad', in Paoli, Letizia (ed.), *The Oxford Handbook of Organized Crime*, Oxford, OUP, 2014, p. 545.

Beck, Ulrich. *World at Risk*, Bristol, Polity Press, 2009.

Begorre-Bret, Cyrille. 'The definition of terrorism and the challenge of relativism', (2005–6) 27 *Cardozo Law Review*, 1987.

Beltracchi, Helene and Wolfgang. *Selbstporträt*, Reinbek, Rowohlt, 2014.

Benjamin, Barry M. 'Note: unilateral humanitarian intervention, legalizing the use of force to prevent human rights atrocities', (1992–3) 16 *Fordham International Law Journal (Fordham Intl LJ)* (1), 120.

Benson, Bruce L., Rasmussen, David W., and, Sollars, David L. 'Police bureaucracies, their incentives, and the war on drugs', (1995) 83 *Public Choice* (1–2), 21.

Bergal, Carina. 'The Mexican drug war: the case for a non-international armed conflict', (2011) *Fordham Intl Law J* (34), 1042.

Berghoff, Hartmut. 'From the Watergate scandal to the compliance revolution. The fight against corporate corruption in the United States and Germany, 1972–2012', (2013) 53 *Bulletin German Historical Institute*, 6.

Bernick, Lauren. 'Art and antiquities theft', (1998) 4 *Transnational Organized Crime*, 91.

Betti, Stefano (ed.). *Symposium: The United Nations Convention against Transnational Organised Crime, requirements for effective implementation*, Turin, UNICRI *et al.*, 2002.

Bewley-Taylor, David and Jelsma, Martin. 'Regime change: re-visiting the 1961 Single Convention on Narcotic Drugs', (2012) 23 *International Journal of Drug Policy* (1), 72.

Bezotti, Mario. 'Organisierte Kriminalität, zur sozialen Konstruktion einer Gefahr', (2002) 22 *Angewandte Sozialforschung* (3–4), 136.

Bhaba, Jacqueline and Zard, Monette. 'Smuggled or trafficked?', (2006) 25 *Forced Migration Review*, 6.

Biagioli, Antonello. 'Financial crime as a threat to the wealth of nations, a cost-effectiveness approach', (2008) 11 *Journal of Money Laundering Control* (1), 88.

Böhm, Michael. 'Das neue europäische Haftbefehlsgesetz', (2006) 36 *Neue Juristische Wochenschrift*, 2592.

Boister, Neil. 'The (Un-) systematic nature of the UN criminal justice system: The (non) relationship between the draft illicit tobacco trade protocol and the UN convention against transnational organised crime', (2010) 21 *Criminal Law Forum*, 361–397.

Boister, Neil. 'Transnational criminal law?', (2003) 14 *EJIL* (5), 953.

Boister, Neil. 'The exclusion of treaty crimes from the jurisdiction of the proposed International Criminal Court, law, pragmatism, politics', (1998) 3 *Journal of Conflict and Security Law* (1), 27.

Bonner, Raymond. 'US joins 20 nations in urging controls on spread of small arms', *New York Times*, 15 July 1998, p. A7.

Bonner, Raymond. '21 nations seek to limit the traffic in light weapons', *New York Times*, 12 July 1998, p. A3.

Bonner, Raymond. 'Nations endorse moves to eradicate plague of small arms', *New York Times*, 2 April 1998, p. 113.

Boothby, Bill. '"And for such time as", the time dimension to direct participation in hostilities', (2010) 42 *International Law and Politics*, 741.

Bos, Adriaan. 'From the International Law Commission to the Rome Conference (1994–1998)', in Cassese, Antonio, Gaeta, Paola, and Jones, John R. W. D. (eds), *The Rome Statute of the International Criminal Court. A Commentary*, Vol. 1, Oxford, OUP, 2002, Ch. 2.2.

Böse, Martin. *Der Grundsatz der Verfügbarkeit von Informationen in der strafrechtlichen Zusammenarbeit der EU*, Bonn, V&R Unipress, 2007.

Böse, Martin. 'Drogenhandel', in Sieber, Ulrich, Satzger, Helmut, and v. Heintschel-Heinegg, Bernd (eds), *Europäisches Strafrecht*, 2nd edn, Baden-Baden, Nomos, 2014, para. 20.

Böse, Martin. 'Kompetenzen der Union auf dem Gebiet des Straf- und Strafverfahrens', in Böse, Martin (ed.), *Europäisches Strafrecht*, Baden-Baden, Nomos, 2013, para. 4.

Bossard, André. *Transnational Crime and Criminal Law*, Chicago, Illinois, Office of International Criminal Justice, 1990.

Bossert, Oliver and Korte, Guido. *Organisierte Kriminalität und Ausländerextremismus/Terrorismus*, Brühl, Statistisches Bundesamt Zweigstelle Bonn, 2004.

Bourne, Mike. 'Transnational trafficking in weapons', in Reichel, Philip and Albanese, Jay (eds), *Handbook of Transnational Crime and Justice*, 2nd edn, Thousand Oaks, California, SAGE Publications, 2014, pp. 85–100.

Bovenkerk, Frank and Abou Chakra, Bashir. 'Terrorism and organized crime', (2004) 4 *Forum on Crime and Society*, 3.

Bovenkerk, Frank and Abou Chakra, Bashir. 'Terrorism and organised crime', in Leslie Holmes (ed.), *Terrorism, Organised Crime and Corruption*, Camberley, Edward Elgar, 2007, pp. 29–41.

Bowman, Michael, Davies, Peter, and Redgwell, Catherine. *Lyster's International Wildlife Law*, 2nd edn, CUP, 2010.

Business Day. 'Plan B needed to save rhinos', 2 September 2015 (Review & Opinion).

Brand, Sam and Price, Richard. *The Economic and Social Costs of Crime*, London, Home Office Research Study 217, 2000.

Branson, Douglas M. 'Holding multinational corporations accountable—Achilles' heels in Alien Tort Claims Act litigation', (2011) 9 *Santa Clara Journal of International Law*, 227.

Braum, Stefan. 'Europäisches Strafrecht im Fokus konfligierender Verfassungsmodelle. Stoppt das Bundesverfassungsgericht die europäische Strafrechtsentwicklung?', (2009) 4 *Zeitschrift für Internationale Strafrechtsdogmatik* (8–9), 418, available at: http://www.zis-online.com/dat/artikel/2009_8-9_348.pdf, accessed 29 January 2016.

Brenner, Susan W. 'Organized cybercrime? How cyberspace may affect the structure of criminal relationships', (2002) 4 *North Carolina Journal of Law & Technology*, 1.

Breuil, Brenda, Siegel, Diana, van Reenen, Piet, Beljer, Annemaricke, and Roos, Linda. 'Human trafficking revisited: legal, enforcement and ethnographic narratives on sex trafficking to Western Europe', (2011) *Trends in Organized Crime*, 30.

Broadhurst, Roderic and Farrelly, Nicholas. 'Organized crime "control" in Asia: experiences from India, China and the Golden Triangle', in Paoli, Letizia (ed.), *The Oxford Handbook of Organized Crime*, Oxford, OUP, 2014, p. 634.

Broadhurst, Roderic, Grabosky, Peter, Alazab, Mamoun, and Chon, Steve. 'Organizations and cyber crime: an analysis of the nature of groups engaged in cyber crime', (2014) 8 *International Journal of Cyber Criminology* (1), 1.

Brodie, Neil and Doyle, Jennifer. 'Illicit antiquities', in Neil Brodie *et al.* (eds), *Trade in Illicit Antiquities: The Destruction of the World's Archaeological Heritage*, Cambridge, McDonald Institute, 2001, pp. 1–6.

Brodowski, Dominik. 'Preparatory colloquium for the XIXth International Congress of Penal Law (Moscow, 24–27 April 2013)', (2013) 1 *Russian Law Review*, 94.

Brodowski, Dominik. 'Strafrechtsrelevante Entwicklungen in der Europäischen Union—ein Überblick', (2015) *Zeitschrift für Internationale Strafrechtsdogmatik*, 79.

Brodowski, Dominik and Freiling, Felix. *Cyberkriminalität, Computerstrafrecht und die digitale Schattenwirtschaft*, Berlin, Forschungsforum Öffentliche Sicherheit, 2011.

Brolan, Claire. 'An analysis of the human smuggling trade and the Protocol against the Smuggling of Migrants by Land, Air and Sea (2000) from a refugee protection perspective', (2002) 14 *International Journal of Refugee Law* (4), 561.

Brownlie, Ian and Crawford, James. *Principles of Public International Law*, 8th edn, Oxford, OUP, 2012.

Bruch, Elizabeth M. 'Models wanted: the search for an effective response to human trafficking', (2004) 40 *Journal of International Law*, 1.

Bruggeman, Willy. 'The fight against organised crime, possibilities, problems and opportunities, with a special focus on the EU', in Albrecht, Hans-Jörg and Fijnaut, Cyrille (eds), *The Containment of Transnational Organised Crime: Comments on the UN Convention of December 2000*, Freiburg im Breisgau, Edition Iuscrim, 2002, p. 67.

Brunst, Phillip W. *Anonymität im Internet—rechtliche und tatsächliche Rahmenbedingungen, zum Spannungsfeld zwischen einem Recht auf Anonymität bei der elektronischen Kommunikation und den Möglichkeiten zur Identifizierung und Strafverfolgung*, Berlin, Duncker & Humblot, 2009.

Buck, Trevor (ed.). *International Child Law*, 3rd edn, New York, Routledge, 2014.

Budiani-Saberi, Debra A. and Delmonico, Francis L. 'Organ trafficking and transplant tourism: a commentary on the global realities', (2008) 8 *American Journal of Transplantation*, 925.

Buergenthal, Thomas. 'Human rights', in Wolfrum, Rüdiger (ed.), *Max Planck Encyclopaedia of Public International Law*, available at: http://www.mpepil.com, accessed 30 October 2015.

Buergenthal, Thomas. 'The normative and institutional evolution of international human rights', (1997) 19 *Human Rights Quarterly* (4), 703.

Bühler, Alexander. 'Antiken für die Kriegskasse, Antiquities for the war chest', (2015) 1 *SPK-Magazin* (1), 38.

Bundeskriminalamt. *Bundeslagebild Organisierte Kriminalität*, Hamburg, Bundeskriminalamt, 2012.

Burghardt, Tom. 'Drugs, terror and the militarization of Mexican society', *Global Research*, 4 May 2012, available at: http://www.globalresearch.ca/drugs-terror-and-the-militarization-of-mexican-society, accessed 30 October 2015.

Burke, Karin M. and De Leo, Deborah A. 'Innocent passage and transit passage in the United Nations Convention on the Law of the Seas', (1982–3) 9 *Yale Journal of World Public Order*, 389.

Burke-White, William W. 'The domestic influence of International Criminal Tribunals: the International Criminal Tribunal for the Former Yugoslavia and the creation of the state court of Bosnia & Herzegovina', (2008) 46 *Columbia Journal of Transnational Law (CJTL)*, 279.

Buscaglia, Edgardo and van Dijk, Jan. 'Controlling organized crime and corruption in the public sector', *United Nations Office on Drugs and Crime, Forum on Crime and Society*, Vol. 3, Nos 1 and 2, Geneva, United Nations Publication, 2003.

Busuioc, Elena Madalina. 'Defining money laundering', in Unger, Brigitte (ed.), *The Scale and Impacts of Money Laundering*, Camberley, Edward Elgar, 2007, p. 15.

Byers, Michael. 'Terrorism, the use of force and international law after 11 September 2001', (2002) 51 *ICLQ* (2), 401.

Byers, Michael. *Custom, Power and the Power of Rules. International Relations and Customary International Law*, Cambridge, CUP, 1999.

Calder, Martin C. 'The internet: potential, problems and pathways to hands-on sexual offending', in Calder, Martin C. (ed.), *Child Sexual Abuse and the Internet: Tackling the New Frontier*, Lyme Regis, Dorset, Russell House, 2004, pp. 1–23.

Calderoni, Francesco. *Organized Crime Legislation in the European Union: Harmonization and Approximation of Criminal Law, National Legislations and The EU Framework Decision on the Fight against Organized Crime*, Heidelberg, Springer, 2010.

Calderoni, Francesco. '"A definition that does not work": the impact of the EU Framework Decision on the Fight against Organized Crime', (2012) 49 *Common Market Law Review*, 1365.

Caliber Associates. *State and Local Law Enforcement Response to Transnational Crime*, 2005, available at: https://www.ncjrs.gov/pdffiles1/nij/grants/209521.pdf, accessed 30 October 2015.

Campana, Paolo. 'Governing vs. trading: the functional diversification of Mafia activities across territories', in Töttel, Ursula, Bulanova-Hristova, Gregana, and Büchler, Heinz (eds), *Research Conference on Organised Crime at the Bundeskriminalamt in Germany, Vol. II, Organised Crime—Research and Practice in Western and Northern Europe 2011–2012*, Polizei + Forschung 45, Wiesbaden, Luchterhand Verlag, pp. 37–54.

Campana, Paolo. 'Understanding then responding to Italian organized crime operations across territories', (2013) 7 *Policing* (3), 316.

Campbell, Denis and Davison, Nicola. 'Illegal kidney trade booms as new organ is "sold every hour"', *The Guardian*, 27 May 2012.

Caparrós, Martín and Reid, Jasper. *Valfierno: The Man Who Stole the Mona Lisa*, New York, Atria, 2008.

Carl, Michael H. *et al.* (eds). *Kunstdiebstahl vor Gericht. City of Gotha v Sotheby's/Cobert Finance SA*, Berlin/New York, Schriften zum Kulturgüterschutz, 2001.

Carrapiço, Helena. 'Transnational organized crime as a security concept', in Allum, Felia and Gilmour, Stan (eds), *Routledge Handbook of Transnational Organized Crime*, London, Routledge, 2012, pp. 19–35.

Carter, Jimmy. 'Call off the drug war', *New York Times*, 16 June 2011.

Cassese, Antonio *et al. International Criminal Law*, 3rd edn, Oxford, OUP, 2013; 2nd edn, Oxford, OUP, 2008.

Cassese, Antonio. 'International criminal law', in Evans, Malcolm D. (ed.), *International Law*, 1st edn, Oxford, OUP, 2003, pp. 721–56.

Cassese, Antonio. 'The *Nicaragua* and *Tadić* tests revisited in light of the ICJ judgment on genocide in Bosnia', (2007) 18 *European Journal of International Law (EJIL)* (4), 649.

Cassese, Antonio. 'The multifaceted criminal notion of terrorism in international law', (2006) 4 *Journal of International Criminal Justice (JICJ)*, 933.

Cassese, Antonio. 'Is the bell tolling for universality? A plea for a sensible notion of universal jurisdiction', (2003) 1 *JICJ* (3), 589.

Castle, Allan. 'Transnational organized crime and international security', Institute of International Relations, University of British Columbia, Working Paper No. 19, 1997.

Catarious Jr, David M. and Russell, Alison. *Counternarcotics Efforts and Afghan Poppy Farmers: Finding the Right Approach*, Washington DC, Environmental Law Institute and United Nations Environment Programme, 2012.

Cenic, Sonja. 'State responsibility and self-defence in international law post 9/11: has the scope of Article 51 of the United Nations Charter been widened as a result of the US response to 9/11?', (2007) 14 *Australian International Law Journal (Aust ILJ)*, 201.

Center for Advanced Defense Studies. *Out of Africa: Mapping the Global Trade in Illicit Elephant Ivory*, Washington DC, Center for Advanced Defense Studies, 2014.

Center for Strategic and International Studies. *Wildlife Poaching and Insecurity in Africa*, 2015, available at: http://csis.org, accessed 30 October 2015.

Center for the Study of Democracy. *Examining the Links between Organized Crime and Corruption*, Irvine, California, 2010.

Chalmers, Damian, Davies, Gareth, and Monti, Giorgio (eds). *European Union Law*, 2nd edn, Cambridge, CUP, 2010.

Charney, Noah. *The Art of Forgery: The Minds, Motives and Methods of the Master Forgers*, London, Phaidon, 2015.

Chatwin, Caroline. *Mixed Messages from Europe on Drug Policy Reform: The Cases of Sweden and the Netherlands*, Washington DC, Brookings Institution, 2015.

Chawki, Mohamed, Darwish, Ashraf, Khan, Mohammad Ayoub, and Tyagi, Sapna. *Cybercrime, Digital Forensics and Jurisdiction*, Cham, Springer, 2015.

Cheng, Bin. 'United Nations Resolutions on Outer Space: "instant" international customary law', (1965) 5 *Indian Journal of International Law*, 23.

Chester, Lewis. *Watergate: The Full Inside Story*, 1st edn, New York, Ballante Books, 1973.

Chuang, Janie. 'Exploitation creep and the unmaking of human trafficking law', (2014) 108 *American Journal of International Law (AJIL)*, 609.

Churchill, Robin R. and Lowe, Vaughan A. *The Law of the Sea*, 3rd edn, Manchester, Manchester University Press, 1999.

CITES, *National Laws for Implementing the Convention*, available at: https://cites.org/eng/legislation, accessed 1 October 2015.

CITES, *The International Consortium on Combating Wildlife Crime*, available at: http://www.cites.org/eng/prog/ICCWC.php, accessed 16 October 2015.

Clapham, Andrew. *Human Rights Obligations of Non-State Actors*, Oxford, OUP, 2006.

Clapham, Andrew. 'The role of the individual in international law', (2010) 21 *EJIL* (1), 25.

Clapham, Andrew. 'The question of jurisdiction under international criminal law over legal persons: lessons from the Rome Conference on an International Criminal Court', in

Kamminga, Menno T. and Zia-Zarifi, Saman (eds), *Liability of Multinational Corporations under International Law*, The Hague, Kluwer Law International, 2000.
Clark, Roger S. 'The United Nations Convention against Transnational Organized Crime', (2004) 50 *Wayne Law Review* 161.
Clinton, Bill. 'Bill Clinton apologizes to Mexico for war on drugs', *Huffington Post*, 13 February 2015.
Coalition for Organ-Failure Solutions. *Sudanese Victims of Organ Trafficking in Egypt. A Preliminary Evidence-Based, Victim-Centred Report*, Bethesda, Maryland, UNODC, December 2011.
Cockayne, James. 'Chasing shadows. Strategic responses to organised crime in conflict-affected situations', (2013) 158 *RUSI Journal* (2), 10.
Cockayne, James and Lupel, Ada. 'From iron fist to invisible hand: peace operations, organized crime and intelligent international law enforcement', in Cockayne, James and Lupel, Ada (eds), *Peace Operations and Organised Crime: Enemies or Allies?*, London, Routledge, 2011, pp. 190–208.
Cockayne, James and Lupel, Ada (eds), *Peace Operations and Organised Crime: Enemies or Allies?*, London, Routledge, 2011.
Coignard, Jérôme. *Une femme disparaît. Le vol de La Joconde au Louvre en 1911*, Paris/New York, LePassage, 2010.
Coignard, Jérôme. *On a vole la Joconde*, Paris, A. Biro, Pol'Art, 1990.
Cole, Simon A. *Suspect Identities: A History of Fingerprints and Criminal Identification*, Cambridge, Massachusetts, Harvard University Press, 2001.
Costa, Antonio Maria. 'The economics of crime: a discipline to be invented and a Nobel Prize to be awarded', (2010) 32 *Journal of Policy Modeling* (5), 648–661.
Count the Costs of the War on Drugs. *Alternative World Drug Report*, 2012, available at: http://www.countthecosts.org/alternative-world-drug-report, accessed 2 February 2016.
Crandall, Russel. *Driven by Drugs: US Policy toward Colombia*, Boulder, Colorado, Lynne Rienner Publishers, 2002.
Crawford, James. *State Responsibility: The General Part*, Cambridge, CUP, 2013.
Crawford, James. *Brownlie's Principles of Public International Law*, 8th edn, Oxford, OUP, 2012.
Crawford, James. *The International Law Commission's Articles on State Responsibility: Introduction, Text, and Commentaries*, Cambridge, CUP, 2005.
Crawford, James. 'The criteria for statehood in international law', (1978) 48 *British Yearbook of International Law (BYBIL)*, 93.
Cressy, Donald R. *The Theft of the Nation*, New York, Harper and Row, 1969.
Crick, Emily. 'Drugs as an existential threat: an analysis of the international securitization of drugs', (2012) 23 *International Journal of Drug Policy* (5), 407.
Cuellar, Mariano-Florentino. 'The tenuous relationship between the fight against money laundering and the disruption of criminal finance', (2002) 93 *Journal of Criminal Law and Criminology* (2–3), 311.
Cullen, Anthony. 'The definition of non-international armed conflict in the Rome Statute of the International Criminal Court: an analysis of the threshold of application of Article 8(2)(f)', (2008) 12 *Journal of Conflict & Security Law* (3), 419.
Czabanski, Jacek. *Estimates of Cost of Crime: History, Methodologies, and Implications*, Berlin, Springer, 2008.
Daniel, Tim and Maton, James. 'Is the UNCAC an effective deterrent to grand corruption?' in Horder, Jeremy and Alldridge, Peter (eds), *Modern Bribery Law—Comparative Perspectives*, 2013, p. 293.
Dannecker, Gerhard. 'Einführung von Tatbeständen mit supranationaler Schutzrichtung (Europadelikte)', in Böse, Martin (ed.), *Europäisches Strafrecht*, Baden-Baden, Nomos, 2013, para. 8.
Dannecker, Gerhard and Leitner, Roman (eds). *Handbuch Korruption*, Vienna, Boorberg unter Zusammenarbeit mit Linde Verlag, 2012.
Dauvergne, Catherine. *And Yet We Are Not Saved: Hegemony and the Global War on Human Trafficking*, Toronto, Faculty of Law, University of Toronto, 2005.

Davis, Robert C. *Christian Slaves, Muslim Masters: White Slavery in the Mediterranean, the Barbary Coast, and Italy 1500–1800*, New York, Palgrave, 2003.

De Brabandere, Eric. 'Human rights and transnational corporations: the limits of direct corporate responsibility', (2010) 4 *Human Rights & International Legal Discourse*, 66.

De Koker, Louis. 'The FATF's customer identification framework: fit for purpose?', (2014) 17 *Journal of Money Laundering Control* (3), 281.

De Koker, Louis. 'Aligning anti-money laundering, combating of financing of terror and financial inclusion: questions to consider when FATF Standards are clarified', (2011) 14 *Journal of Financial Crime* (4), 361.

De Koker, Louis. 'Applying anti-money laundering laws to fight corruption', in Graycar, Adam and Smith, Russell G. (eds), *Handbook of Global Research and Practice in Corruption*, Camberley, Edward Elgar, 2011, p. 340.

De Koker, Louis. 'Money laundering control and suppression of financing of terrorism: some thoughts on the impact of customer due diligence measures on financial exclusion', (2006) 13 *Journal of Financial Crime* (1), 26.

De Koker, Louis and Pretorius, Loot. 'Confiscation orders in terms of the Proceeds of Crime Act: some constitutional perspectives', (1998) *Journal of South African Law* 39.

De Koker, Louis and Turkington, Mark. 'Anti-money laundering measures and the effectiveness question', in Barry Rider (ed.), *Research Handbook on International Financial Crime*, Cheltenham, Edward Elgar, 2015, pp. 520–31.

De Londras, Fiona. 'Terrorism as an international crime', in Schabas, William and Bernaz, Nadia (eds), *Routledge Handbook of International Criminal Law*, Abingdon, Routledge, 2013, pp. 169–80.

Decroos, Matthieu J. L. 'Criminal jurisdiction over transnational speech offences', (2005) 13 *European Journal of Crime, Criminal Law and Criminal Justice (EJCCLCJ)* (30), 365.

DeFeo, Michael. 'Depriving international narcotics traffickers and other organized criminals of illegal proceeds and combatting money laundering', (1989) 18 *Denver Journal of International Law and Policy*, 405.

Deflem, Mathieu. *Policing World Society: Historical Foundations of International Police Cooperation*, New York, OUP, 2003.

Deflem, Mathieu. 'International police cooperation, history of', in Wright, Richard A. and Miller, J. Mitchell (eds), *The Encyclopedia of Criminology*, New York, Routledge, 2005, p. 796.

Deflem, Mathieu. 'Technology and the internationalization of policing', (2002) 19 *Justice Quarterly* (3), 453.

Degan, Vladimir D. 'Internal waters', (1986) 17 *Netherlands Yearbook of International Law (NYIL)*, 3.

Delston, Ross and Walls, Stephen. 'Reaching beyond banks: how to target trade-based money laundering and terrorist financing outside the financial sector', (2009) 41 *Case Western Reserve Journal of International Law* (8), 85.

Deming, Stuart. *The Foreign Corrupt Practices Act and the New International Norms*, Washington DC, American Bar Association, 2005.

Demleitner, Nora V. 'Organized crime and prohibition: what difference does legalization make?', (1994) 15 *Whittier Law Review*, 613.

Department of Justice. *Assessing the Effectiveness of Organised Crime Control Strategies: A Review of the Literature*, Ottawa, Ontario, Canada, Research and Statistics Division, 2003.

Derby, Daniel H. 'Symposium: International Criminal Law: An International Criminal Court for the Future', (1995) 5 *Transnational Law & Contemporary Problems* (2), 307.

Detotto, Claudio and Otranto, Edoardo. 'Does crime affect economic growth?', (2010) 63 *Kyklos* (3), 330.

Detrick, Sharon (ed.). *A Commentary on the United Nations Convention on the Rights of the Child*, The Hague, Kluwer Law International, 1999.

Di Filippo, Marcello. 'The definition(s) of terrorism in international law', in Saul, Ben (ed.), *Research Handbook on International Law and Terrorism*, Camberley, Edward Elgar Publishing, 2014, pp 3–19.

Diener, Alexander C. and Hagen, Joshua. *Borders*, Oxford, OUP, 2012.

Dikötter, Frank and Laamann, Lars, *et al*. 'Narcotic culture. A social history of drug consumption in China', (2002) 42 *British Journal of Criminology* (2), 317.

Dinstein, Yoram. 'Aggression', in Wolfrum, Rüdiger (ed.), *Max Planck Encyclopedia of Public International Law*. Last updated May 2009, available at: http://opil.ouplaw.com/view/10.1093/law:epil/9780199231690/law-9780199231690-e236?prd=EPIL, accessed 30 October 2015.

Dinstein, Yoram. *War, Aggression and Self-Defence*, 3rd edn, Cambridge, CUP, 2001.

District Attorney, New York County. Report of the Manhattan District Attorney's Office on Smartphone Encryption and Public Safety, 18 November 2015.

Dixon, Martin. *Textbook on International Law*, 5th edn, Oxford, OUP, 2005.

Doig, Alan and Theobald, Robin. *Corruption and Democratization*, Abingdon, Psychology Press, 2000.

Donlon, Fidelma. 'Hybrid tribunals', in Schabas, William A. and Bernaz, Nadia (eds), *Routledge Handbook of International Criminal Law*, London, Routledge, 2011, Ch. 7.

Donnelly, Jack. 'The United Nations and the global drug control regime', in Smith, Peter H. (ed.), *Drug Policy in the Americas*, Boulder, Colorado, Westview Press, 1992.

Đorđević, Saša. 'Understanding transnational organised crime as a security threat and security theories', (2009) 13 *Western Balkans Security Observer*, 29.

Dörr, Oliver. 'Gewalt und Gewaltverbot im modernen Völkerrecht', (2004) 43 *Aus Politik und Zeitgeschichte (APuZ)*, 14.

Dörrmann, Knut. 'The legal situation of unlawful/unprivileged combatants', (2003) 85 *IRRC* (848), 45.

Drennan, Peter. 'National security: implications for law enforcement', speech given at the University of Canberra Lecture Series, 30 April 2010, available at: http://www.afp.gov.au/media-centre/speeches/2010/national-security-implications-for-law-enforcement, accessed 30 October 2015.

Drescher, Seymour. *Abolition: A History of Slavery and Antislavery*, Cambridge, CUP, 2009.

Dromgoole, Sarah. *The Protection of the Underwater Cultural Heritage*, 2nd edn, Leiden/Boston, Martinus Nijhoff Publishers, 2006.

Dubois, Judith. 'Media coverage of organized crime—police managers survey', (2002) 7 *Trends in Organized Crime*, 29.

Duffy, Helen. *The 'War on Terror' and the Framework of International Law*, 2nd edn, Cambridge, CUP, 2015.

Dugard, John. 'Obstacles in the way of an International Criminal Court', (1997) 56 *Cambridge Law Journal* (2), 329.

Economic and Social Council, Commission on Human Rights. 'Report of the Special Rapporteur on Violence against Women, its Causes and Consequences, submitted in accordance with Commission on Human Rights Resolution 1997/44', UN Doc. E/CN.4/2000/68, 29 February 2000.

Economic and Social Council, Commission on Human Rights. 'Report of the Special Rapporteur on Violence against Women, its Causes and Consequences', UN Doc. E/CN.4/1997/47/Add.1, 10 December 1996.

The Economist. 'Return of the hired gun', 10 January 2015, 75.

Egmont Group of Financial Intelligence Units. 'Remarks by the Chair of Egmont Group of Financial Intelligence Units at FATF Plenary', Egmont Group, 2015, available at: http,//www.egmontgroup.org/news-and-events/news/2015/02/27/remarks-by-the-chair-of-egmont-group-of-financial-intelligence, accessed 4 November 2015.

EIA. *Addressing ASEAN's Regional Rosewood Crisis: A Urgent Call to Action*, 2015, available at: https://drive.google.com/viewerng/viewer?url=https://eia-international.org/wp-content/uploads/ASEAN-rosewood-briefing-English-FINAL.pdf, accessed 4 November 2015.

Eisele, Jörg. 'Jurisdiktionskonflikte in der Europäischen Union—Vom nationalen Strafanwendungsrecht zum Europäischen Kollisionsrecht?', (2013) 125 *Zeitschrift für die gesamte Strafrechtswissenschaft (ZStW)*, 1.

Eisenberg, Ulrich. *Kriminologie*, 6th edn, Munich, C. H. Beck, 2005.

Elberling, Björn. 'The *ultra vires* character of legislative action by the Security Council', (2005) 2 *International Organizations Law Review* (2), 337.

Enck, Jennifer L. 'The United Nations Convention Against Transnational Organized Crime: is it all that it is cracked up to be? Problems posed by the Russian mafia in the trafficking of humans', (2003) 30 *Syracuse Journal of International Law and Commerce* (2), 369.

Erickson, Patricia G., Riley, Diane M, *et al. Harm Reduction: A New Direction for Drug Policies and Programs*, Toronto, University of Toronto Press, 2015.

ESCWA, Economic and Social Commission for Western Asia. *Policy Recommendations on Cybersafety and Combating Cybercrime in the Arab Region, Summary*, New York, United Nations, 2015, available at: http://www.escwa.un.org/information/publications/edit/upload/E_ESCWA_TDD_15_1_SUMMARY_E.pdf, accessed 4 November 2015.

Eser, Albin and Kubiciel, Michael. *Institutions Against Corruption*, Baden-Baden, Nomos, 2005.

Essen, Jonte van. '*De facto* regimes in international law', (2012) 28 *Utrecht Journal of International and European Law* (74), 31.

Esser, Robert. 'Die Europäische Staatsanwaltschaft: Eine Herausforderung für die Strafverteidigung', (2014) *Strafverteidiger*, 494.

Esser, Robert. 'Die Rolle von Europol und Eurojust bei der Bekämpfung von Terrorismus und OK', in Sinn, Arndt and Zöller, Mark (eds), *Neujustierung des Strafrechts durch Terrorismus und Organisierte Kriminalität*, Heidelberg, C.F. Müller, 2013, pp. 61–89.

Essig, Rolf-Bernhard and Schury, Gudrun. *Schlimme Finger, Eine Kriminalgeschichte der Künste von Villon bis Beltracchi*, Munich, C. H. Beck, 2015.

European Commission. 'European Parliament backs stronger rules to combat money laundering and terrorism financing', press release, Brussels, 20 May 2015.

European Council. 'Special meeting of the European Council, 23 April 2015—statement', 23 April 2015, available at: http://www.consilium.europa.eu/en/press/press-releases/2015/04/23-special-euco-statement/, last accessed 4 November 2015.

European Criminal Policy Initiative. 'Manifest for the European Criminal Law', (2013) *Zeitschrift für Internationale Strafrechtsdogmatik*, 412 (English version in (2011) *European Criminal Law Review*, 86).

European Parliament, Directorate-General for Internal Policies. 'Europe's crime–terror nexus: links between terrorist and organised crime groups in the European Union', 2012, available at: http://www.europarl.europa.eu/document/activities/cont/201211/20121127ATT56707/20121127ATT56707EN.pdf, last accessed 4 November 2015.

European Parliament. 'Equipping the EU to tackle the Mafia', 15 October 2012.

Europol. *EU Organized Crime Threat Assessment, OCTA 2011*, The Hague, Europol Police Office, 2011, available at: http://www.europol.europa.eu/content/press/europol-organised-crime-threat-assessment-2011-429, accessed 4 November 2015.

Europol, *SOCTA, EU Serious and Organised Crime Threat Assessment, 2013*, available at: http://www.europol.europa.eu, accessed 29 October 2015.

Europol. *The Internet Organised Crime Threat Assessment (iOCTA)*, The Hague, Europol Police Office, 2014, available at: https://www.europol.europa.eu/content/internet-organised-crime-threat-assesment-iocta, accessed 4 November 2015.

Europol. *Why is cash still king? a strategic report on the use of cash by criminal groups as a facilitator for money laundering*, The Hague, European Police Office, 2015.

Europol. *Exploring Tomorrow's Organised Crime*, 2015, available at: http://www.europol.europa.eu/content/exploring-tomorrow's-organised-crime, accessed 4 November 2015.

European Treaty Service. *Explanatory Report on the Convention on Cybercrime*, ETS No. 185, available at http://conventions.coe.int/Treaty/EN/Reports/Html/185.htm, accessed 4 November 2015.

Ezeilo, Joy. 'Achievements of the Trafficking Protocol: perspectives from the former UN Special Rapporteur on Trafficking in Persons', (2015) 4 *Anti-Trafficking Review*, 144.

Fassbender, Bardo (ed.). *Menschenrechteerklärung*, Munich, Sellier European Law Publishers, 2009.

Felch, Jason. 'Case studies involving antiquities trafficking networks', in Manacorda, Stefano and Visconti, Arianna (eds), *Protecting Cultural Heritage as a Common Good of Humanity: A Challenge for Criminal Justice*, Milan, ISPAC, 2014, pp. 177–88.

Feliciano, Hector. *The Lost Museum: The Nazi Conspiracy to Steal the World's Greatest Works of Art*, New York, Basic Books, 1997 (*Das verlorene Museum. Vom Kunstraub der Nazis*, Berlin, Aufbau Verlag, 1998).

Feller, Erika. 'Asylum, migration and refugee protection: realities, myths and the promise of things to come', (2006) 18 *International Journal of Refugee Law* (3–4), 509.

Fellmeth, Aaron. 'The UN Arms Trade Treaty: temporarily holstered', (2012) 16 *ASIL Insights* (30).

Fellmeth, Aaron. 'Cure without a disease: the emerging doctrine of successor liability in international trade regulation', (2006) 31 *Yale J Intl L*, 125.

Feltes, Thomas. 'Organized crime—sleeping with the enemy?', (2007) 2 *Panóptica* (7), 152.

Feltes, Thomas. 'Peacebuilding and police reform in the New Europe: lessons from Kosovo', in Möllers, Martin H. W. and van Ooyen, Robert C. (eds), *Jahrbuch öffentliche Sicherheit 2008/09*, Frankfurt, Verlag für Polizeiwissenschaft, 2008, pp. 439–66.

Feltes, Tilmann. 'Jugend und Demokratie. Die Förderung der Partizipation Jugendlicher durch die internationale Gemeinschaft im Kosovo', (2013) 1 *Südosteuropäische Hefte* (2), 45.

Ferwerda, Joras. 'The economics of crime and money laundering: does anti-money laundering policy reduce crime?', (2009) 5 *Review of Law and Economics* (2), 903.

Ferwerda, Joras, Kattenberg, Mark, Chang, Han-Hsin, Unger, Brigitte, Groot, Loek, and Bikker, Jacob A. 'Gravity models of trade based money laundering?', (2013) 45 *Applied Economics* (22), 3170.

Fichtelberg, Aaron. 'Adjudicating international crimes', in Reichel, Philip and Albanese, Jay (eds), *Handbook of Transnational Crime & Justice*, 2nd edn, Thousand Oaks, California, SAGE Publications, 2014, pp. 310–46.

Fichtner, Ullrich, Popp, Maximilian, Schult, Christoph Schult, and Smoltczyk, Alexander. 'Migration crisis: the EU's shipwrecked refugee plan', *Der Spiegel Online*, 23 June 2015, available at: http://www.spiegel.de/international/europe/how-eu-promises-to-introduce-refugee-quotas-failed-a-1040226.html, accessed 4 November 2015.

Fijnaut, Cyrille. 'Organised crime in Europe and beyond: some general considerations', in Robertson-von Trotha, Caroline (ed.), *Organised Crime: Dark Sides of Globalisation*, Interdisciplinary Studies on Culture and Society 8, Nomos, Baden-Baden, 2013, pp. 11–24.

Fijnaut, Cyrille. 'The UN Convention and the global problem of organized crime', in Albrecht, Hans-Jörg and Fijnaut, Cyrille (eds), *The Containment of Transnational Organized Crime Comments on the UN Convention of December 2000*, Freiburg im Breisgau, Edition Iuscrim, 2002, pp. 55–65.

Fijnaut, Cyrille. 'Transnational crime and the role of the United Nations in its containment through international cooperation: a challenge for the 21st Century', (2000) 8 *EJCCLCJ* (2), 119.

Fijnaut, Cyrille. 'Organisierte Kriminalität in Nordwesteuropa', in Sieber, Ulrich (ed.), *Internationale Organisierte Kriminalität*, Cologne, Springer, 1997, pp. 4–39.

Fijnaut, Cyrille and Paoli, Letizia. 'Transnational organized crime', in Wolfrum, Rüdiger (ed.), *Max Planck Encyclopedia of Public International Law*, Vol. IX, Oxford, OUP, 2012, pp. 1049–56.

Fijnaut, Cyrille and Marx, Gary T. *Undercover: Police Surveillance in Comparative Perspective*, Amsterdam, Martinus Nijhoff Publishers, 1995.

Financial Action Task Force. 'Drivers for "de-risking" go beyond anti-money laundering/terrorist financing', press statement, 26 June 2015, Brisbane, available at: http://www.fatf-gafi.org/documents/news/derisking-goes-beyond-amlcft.html, accessed 4 November 2015.

Financial Action Task Force. 'Financing of the terrorist organization Islamic State in Iraq and the Levant (ISIL)' (February 2015), available at: http://www.fatf-gafi.org/media/fatf/documents/reports/Financing-of-the-terrorist-organization-ISIL.pdf, accessed 26 July 2015.

Financial Action Task Force. *Mutual Evaluation Report: Australia*, FATF, 2015.

Financial Action Task Force. *Mutual Evaluation Report: Belgium*, FATF, 2015.

Financial Action Task Force. *Methodology for Assessing Technical Compliance with the FATF Recommendations and the Effectiveness of AML/CoFT Systems*, FATF, 2014.

Financial Action Task Force. *Annual Report 2013–2014*, FATF, 2014.

Financial Action Task Force. *Mutual Evaluation Report: Norway*, FATF, 2014.

Financial Action Task Force. *Mutual Evaluation Report: Spain*, FATF, 2014.

Financial Action Task Force. 'FATF clarifies risk-based approach: case-by-case, not wholesale de-risking', press statement, 23 October 2014, Paris, available at: http://www.fatf-gafi.org/documents/news/rba-and-de-risking.html, accessed 4 November 2015.

Financial Action Task Force. *Anti-Money Laundering and Terrorist Financing Measures and Financial Inclusion*, FATF, 2013.

Financial Action Task Force. *International Standards on Combating Money Laundering and the Financing of Terrorism & Proliferation: The FATF Recommendations*, FATF, 2012.

Financial Action Task Force. *Best Practices on Trade-Based Money Laundering*, FATF, 2008.

Financial Action Task Force. 'Terrorist financing' (29 February 2008), available at: http://www.fatf-gafi.org/media/fatf/documents/reports/FATF%20Terrorist%20Financing%20Typologies%20Report.pdf, accessed 26 July 2015.

Financial Action Task Force. *Trade Based Money Laundering*, FATF, 2006.

Financial Action Task Force. *1998–1999 Report on Money Laundering Typologies*, FATF, 1999.

Financial Action Task Force on Money Laundering. *Report*, 1990–91, FATF, 1991 available at: http://www.fatf-gafi.org/media/fatf/documents/reports/1990%20ENG.pdf, accessed 20 July 2015.

Financial Action Task Force on Money Laundering. *The Forty Recommendations of the Financial Action Task Force on Money Laundering*, FATF, 1990; revised edn, *The Forty Recommendations*, FATF, 2003.

FinCEN, 'FATF updates anti-money laundering standards', 28 June 1996, available at: http://www.fincen.gov/news_room/nr/html/19960628.html, accessed 4 November 2015.

Finckenauer, James O. 'Problems of definition: what is organized crime?', (2005) 8 *Trends in Organized Crime* (3), 63.

Finckenauer, James O. and Schrock, Jennifer. 'Human trafficking: a growing criminal market in the US', in Troubnikoff, Anna M. (ed.), *Trafficking in Women and Children: Current Issues and Developments*, New York, Nova Science Publishers, 2003, pp. 31–9.

Fitzmaurice, Sir Gerald. 'Some results of the Geneva Conference on the Law of the Sea', (1959) 8 *ICLQ*, 73.

Fitzpatrick, Joan. 'Speaking law to power: the war against terrorism and human rights', (2003) 14 *EJIL* (2), 241.

Fitzpatrick, Joan. 'Trafficking as a human rights violation: the complex intersection of legal frameworks for conceptualizing and combating trafficking', (2003) 24 *Michigan Journal of International Law*, 1143.

Fleck, Dieter. "The law of non-international armed conflicts", in Fleck, Dieter (ed.), *The Handbook of International Humanitarian Law*, Oxford, OUP, 2008, pp. 605–35.

Fletcher, George. 'The indefinable concept of terrorism', (2006) 4 *JICJ*, 894.

Ford, Brian. 'From mountains to molehills: a comparative analysis of drug policy', (2013) 19 *Annual Survey of International & Comparative Law*, 197.

Fortin, Jane (ed.). *Children's Rights and the Developing Law*, 3rd edn, Cambridge, CUP, 2009.

Fouché, Joseph. *Mémoires de Joseph Fouché, Duc d'Otrante, Ministre de la Police Générale*, Paris, Jean de Bonnot, 1986 (1824).

Francis, Leslie P. and Francis, John G. 'Stateless crimes, legitimacy and international criminal law: the case of organ trafficking', (2010) 4 *Criminal Law and Philosophy*, 283.

Franck, Thomas M. *Recourse to Force, State Action Against Threats and Armed Attacks*, Cambridge, CUP, 2002.

Franck, Thomas M. 'Terrorism and the right to self-defense', (2001) 95 *AJIL* (4), 839.

Freeland, Charles. 'How can sound customer due diligence rules help prevent the misuse of financial institutions in the financing of terrorism?', (2002) 4 *European Journal of Law Reform* (2), 291.

Friedrichs, Jorg. *Fighting Terrorism and Drugs: Europe and International Police Cooperation*, Abingdon, Routledge, 2008.

Friesendorf, Cornelius. 'Pathologies of security governance: efforts against human trafficking in Europe', (2007) 39 *Security Dialogue* (3), 379.

Friman, H. Richard. 'Drug markets and the selective use of violence', (2009) 52 *Crime, Law and Social Change* (3), 285.

Frowein, Jochen A. 'Article 39', in Simma, Bruno and Mosler, Hermann (eds), *The Charter of the United Nations: A Commentary*, 1st edn, Oxford, OUP, 1994, pp. 605–16.

Frowein, Jochen A. '*De facto* regime', in Wolfrum, Rüdiger (ed.), *Max Planck Encyclopedia of Public International Law*, last updated March 2013, available at: http://opil.ouplaw.com/view/10.1093/law:epil/9780199231690/law-9780199231690-e1395?rskey=nUgHc0&result=1&prd=EPIL, accessed 29 October 2015.

G-7 Group of Nations. 'Economic Declaration', Paris Summit, 1989, para. 53, available at: http://www.g8.utoronto.ca/summit/1989paris/communique/drug.html, accessed 29 October 2015.

Galante, Matthias, Wendlandt, Astrid, and Heneghan, Tom. 'France calls for fairer asylum seeker distribution within EU', *Reuters*, 16 May 2015, available at: http://www.uk.reuters.com/article/2015/05/16/uk-france-immigration-idUKKBN0O10Q320150516, accessed 29 October 2015.

Gallagher, Anne. 'Migrant smuggling', in Boister, Neil and Currie, Robert J (eds), *Routledge Handbook on Transnational Criminal Law*, London, Routledge, 2014, pp. 187–210.

Gallagher, Anne. 'Human rights and human trafficking: quagmire or firm ground? A response to James Hathaway', (2009) 49 *Virginia Journal of International Law*, 789.

Gallagher, Anne and David, Fiona. *The International Law of Migrant Smuggling*, Cambridge, CUP, 2014.

Gallahue, Patrick. 'Targeted killing of drug lords: traffickers as members of armed opposition groups and/or direct participants in hostilities', (2010) *International Journal on Human Rights and Drug Policy* 1, 15.

Gambetta, Diego. *The Sicilian Mafia: The Business of Private Protection*, Cambridge, Massachusetts, Harvard University Press, 1996.

Gandara, Fabio H. C. 'New legislation defines "organized criminal group" and related criminal procedures', (2013) 29 *International Law Enforcement Reporter* (11), 429.

Garland, David. 'On the concept of moral panic', (2008) 4 *Crime, Media, Culture* (1), 9.

Gastrow, Peter. 'The origin of the Convention', in Albrecht, Hans-Jörg and Fijnaut, Cyrille (eds), *The Containment of Transnational Organised Crime: Comments on the UN Convention of December 2000*, Freiburg im Breisgau, Edition Iuscrim, 2002, pp. 19–30.

Geary, Patrick J. *Furta Sacra: Thefts of Relics in the Central Middle Ages*, rev. edn, Princeton, New Jersey, Princeton University Press, 1990.

Geiß, Robin and Tams, Christian. 'Non-flag states as guardians of the maritime order: creeping jurisdiction of a different kind?', in Ringbom, Henrik (ed.), *Jurisdiction Over Ships*, Leiden/Boston, Brill, 2015, pp. 17–49.

George, Barbara Crutchfield, Lacey, Kathleen A., and Birmele, Jutta. 'On the threshold of the adoption of global antibribery legislation: a critical analysis of current domestic and international efforts toward the reduction of business corruption', (1999) 32 *Vanderbilt Journal of Transnational Law*, 24.

Gercke, Marco. '10 years Convention on Cybercrime', (2011) 12 *Computer Law Review International* (5), 142.

Gercke, Marco. 'Die Bekämpfung der Internetkriminalität als Herausforderung für die Strafverfolgungsbehörden', (2008) 11 *Multimedia und Recht* (5), 291.

Giddens, Lord Anthony. *The Nation-State and Violence*, Berkeley, California, University of California Press, 1992.

Gil, Alicia Gil. 'Die Tatbestände der Verbrechen gegen die Menschlichkeit und des Völkermordes im Römischen Statut des Internationalen Strafgerichtshofs', (2000) 112 *ZStW* (2), 381.

Gilbert, Geoff. 'Who has jurisdiction for cross-frontier financial crimes?', (1995) 2 *Web Journal of Current Legal Issues*, 85.

Gilfoyle, Timothy J. *City of Eros: New York City, Prostitution, and the Commercialization of Vice 1790–1920*, New York, W. W. Norton, 1992.

Gillett, Matthew and Schuster, Matthias. 'Fast-track justice—the Special Tribunal for Lebanon defines terrorism', (2011) 9 *JICJ*, 989.

Gilmore, William C. *Dirty Money*, 3rd edn, Geneva, Council of Europe, 2004.

Gilmore, William C. *International Efforts to Combat Money Laundering*, Cambridge International Documents Series Vol. 4, Cambridge, Grotius Publications, 1992.

Gilmore, William C. 'Money laundering', in Boister, Neil and Curie, Robert J (eds), *The Routledge Handbook of Transnational Criminal Law*, London, Routledge, 2014, pp. 331–47.

Gilmore, William C. 'The proposed International Criminal Court: recent developments', (1995) 5 *Transnational Law & Contemporary Problems* (2), 263.

Gjerdingen, Erick. 'Suffocation inside a cold storage truck and other problems with trafficking as "exploitation" and smuggling as "choice" along the Thai–Burmese border', (2009) 26 *Arizona Journal of International and Comparative Law*, 699.

Gleß, Sabine. 'Kontrolle über Europol und seine Bedienstete', (1998) *Europarecht*, 748.

Global Commission on Drugs Policy. *The Negative Impact of Drug Control on Public Health: The Global Crisis of Avoidable Pain*, Rio de Janeiro, GCDP, 2015.

Global Commission on Drugs Policy. *Taking Control. Pathways to Drug Policy Reform Around the World*, Rio de Janeiro, GCDP, 2014.

Global Commission on Drugs Policy. *Report on the Global Commission on Drugs Policy*, Rio de Janeiro, GCDP, 2011.

Godson, Roy and Williams, Phil. 'Strengthening cooperation against transnational crime: a new security imperative', in Williams, Phil and Vlassis, Dimitri, *Combating Transnational Crime: Concepts, Activities and Responses*, Oxfordshire, Frank Cass Publishers, 2001, pp. 321–55.

Goode, Erich and Ben-Yehuda, Nachman. 'Moral panics: culture, politics, and social construction', (1994) *Annual Review of Sociology* (20), 149.

Goodman, Ryan. 'Humanitarian intervention and pretexts for war', (2006) 100 *AJIL* (1), 107.

Gosalbo-Bono, Ricardo and Boelaert, Sonja. 'The European Union's comprehensive approach to combating piracy at sea: legal aspects', in Koutrakos, Panos and Skordas, Achilles (eds), *The Law and Practice of Piracy at Sea*, Oxford, Hart Publishing, 2014, pp. 81–166.

Gotzmann, Nora. 'Legal personality of the corporation and international criminal law: globalisation, corporate human rights abuses and the Rome Statute', (2008) 1 *Queensland Law Student Review* (1), 38.

Gozdiak, Elzbieta and Walter, Alissa. 'Misconceptions about human trafficking in a time of crisis', (2014) *Forced Migration Review*, 45.

Grabosky, Peter and Stohl, Michael. *Crime and Terrorism*, Thousand Oaks, California, SAGE Publications, 2010.

Grant, Thomas D. 'Defining statehood: the Montevideo Convention and its discontents', (1999) 37 *CJTL* (2), 403.

Gray, Christine. 'The use of force and the international legal order', in Evans, Malcom D. (ed.), *International Law*, 4th edn, Oxford, OUP, 2014, pp. 618–48.

Green, James A. *The International Court of Justice and Self-Defence in International Law*, Oxford, Hart, 2009.

Green, Jody. '*Hostis humani generis*', (2008) 34 *Critical Inquiry* (4), 673.

Green, Leslie C. 'International crimes and the legal process', (1980) 29 *ICLQ* (4), 567.

Greenwood, Christopher. 'Scope of application of humanitarian law', in Fleck, Dieter (ed.), *The Handbook of International Humanitarian Law*, 2nd edn, Oxford/New York, OUP, 2008, pp. 45–78.

Groll, Elias. 'Paris attacks reopen crypto wars', *Foreign Policy*, 17 November 2015.

Gropp, Walter and Huber, Barbara (eds). *Rechtliche Initiativen gegen organisierte Kriminalität*, Freiburg im Breisgau, Iuscrim MPI, 2001.

Grotz, Michael. 'Eurojust', in Sieber, Ulrich, Satzger, Helmut, and v. Heintschel-Heinegg, Bernd (eds), *Europäisches Strafrecht*, 2nd edn, Baden-Baden, Nomos, 2014, pp. 716–28.

Group of 77. 'Declaration of the Group of 77 South Summit', 10–14 April 2000, available at: http://www.g77.org/summit/Declaration_G77Summit.htm, accessed 29 October 2015.

Group of 77. 'Ministerial Declaration of the Ministers for Foreign Affairs of the Group of 77 at the 23rd Annual Meeting. 24 September 1999', available at: http://www.g77.org/doc/Decl1999.html, accessed 29 October 2015.

Grund, Jean-Paul and Breeksema, Joost. *Coffee Shops and Compromise. Separated Illicit Drug Markets in the Netherlands*, New York, Open Society, 2013.

Guilfoyle, Douglas. *Shipping Interdiction and the Law of the Sea*, Cambridge, CUP, 2009.

Guilfoyle, Douglas. 'Human rights issues and non-flag state boarding of suspect ships', in Symmons, Clive (ed.), *Selected Contemporary Issues in the Law of the Sea*, Leiden/Boston, Martinus Nijhoff Publishers, 2011, pp. 83–104.

Guilfoyle, Douglas. 'Counter-piracy law enforcement and human rights', (2010) 59 *ICLQ*, 141.

Gunaratna, Rohan. *Inside Al Qaeda: Global Network of Terror*, New York, Columbia University Press, 2002.

Guymon, Carrie-Lyn Donigan. 'International legal mechanisms for combating transnational organised crime', (2000) 18 *Berkeley Journal of International Law*, 53.

Haase, Günther. *Kunstraub und Kunstschutz*, Hildesheim, self-published, 1991.

Hagan, Frank E. '"Organized Crime" and "organized crime": indeterminate problems of definition', (2006) 9 *Trends in Organized Crime* (4), 127.

Haines, Steven. 'The nature of war and the character of contemporary armed conflict', in Wilmshurst, Elizabeth (ed.), *International Law and the Classification of Conflicts*, Oxford, OUP, 2012, pp. 9–31.

Haken, Jeremy. *Transnational Crime in the Developing World*, Washington DC, Center for International Policy, 2011.

Hall, Stuart, Critcher, Chas, Jefferson, Tony, Clarke, John, and Roberts, Brian. *Policing the Crisis: Mugging, the State and Law and Order*, 2nd edn, Basingstoke, Palgrave Macmillan, 2013.

Hall, Tim. 'Geographies of the illicit: globalization and organized crime', (2013) 37 *Progress in Human Geography* (3), 366.

Hall, Tim. 'Economic geography and organized crime: a critical review', (2010) *Geoforum* (41), 841.

Halliday, Terrence, Levi, Michael, and Reuter, Peter. *Global Surveillance of Dirty Money: Assessing Assessments of Regimes to Control Money Laundering and Combat the Financing of Terrorism*, Champaign, Illinois, Center on Law and Globalization, 2014.

Happold, Matthew. 'Security Council Resolution 1373 and the Constitution of the United Nations', (2003) 16 *LJIL*, 593.

Hauck, Pierre and Peterke, Sven. 'Organized crime and gang violence in national and international law', (2010) 92 *IRRC*, 407.

Healy, Margaret A. 'Prosecuting child sex tourists at home: do laws in Sweden, Australia, and the United States safeguard the rights of children as mandated by international law?', (1995) 18 *Fordham Intl LJ*, 1852.

Hechler, Hannes, Zinkernagel, Gretta, Koechlin, Lucy, and Morris, Dominic. *Can UNCAC address grand corruption?—A political analysis of the UN Convention against Corruption and its implementation in three countries*, U4-Report, Bergen, Norway, U4 Anti-Corruption Resource Centre, 2011.

Hecker, Bernd. *Europäisches Strafrecht*, 5th edn, Heidelberg, Springer, 2015.

Hecker, Bernd. 'Harmonisierung', in Sieber, Ulrich, Satzger, Helmut, and v. Heintschel-Heinegg, Bernd (eds), *Europäisches Strafrecht*, 2nd edn, Baden-Baden, Nomos, 2014, pp. 272–94.

Hecker, Bernd. 'Die rechtlichen Möglichkeiten der Europäischen Union zur Lösung von Kompetenzkonflikten', in Sinn, Arndt (ed.), *Conflicts of Jurisdiction in Cross-border Crime Situations*, Osnabrück, V&R Unipress, 2012, pp. 85–102.

Hecker, Bernd. 'Die gemeinschaftsrechtlichen Strukturen der Geldwäschestrafbarkeit', in Görgen, Thomas, Hoffmann-Holland, Klaus, Schneider, Hans, and Stock, Jürgen (eds), *Festschrift für Arthur Kreuzer*, Frankfurt am Main, Verlag für Polizeiwissenschaft, 2008, pp. 216–30.

Heilborn, Paul. *Grundbegriffe des Völkerrechts*, Berlin, Kohlhammer, 1912.

Heilmann, Daniel. 'The international control of illegal drugs and the UN treaty regime: preventing or causing human rights violations?', available at: http://works.bepress.com/cgi/viewcontent.cgi?article=1000&context=daniel_heilmann, accessed 26 January 2016.

Heintschel von Heinegg, Wolff. 'Vom *ius ad bellum* zum *ius contra bellum* (Kriegsverbot, Gewaltverbot und Interventionsverbot)', in Ipsen, Knut (ed.), *Völkerrecht*, 6th edn, Munich, C. H. Beck, 2014, pp. 1055–77.

Heintze, Hans-Joachim and Peterke, Sven. 'Inhalt und Bedeutung des VN-Protokolls zur Verhütung, Unterdrückung und Bestrafung des Menschenhandels (2000)', (2008) 1 *Journal for International Law of Peace and Armed Conflict*, 10.

Henderson, Christian. 'The extraterritorial seizure of individuals under international law—the case of al-Liby', parts I and II, *EJIL—Blog*, 6 November 2013.

Herdegen, Matthias (ed.). *Europarecht*, 16th edn, Munich, C. H. Beck, 2014.

Herschinger, Eva. 'The drug *dispositif*: ambivalent materiality and the addiction of the global drug prohibition regime', (2015) 46 *Security Dialogue* (2), 183.

Herzog, Ronald. *Kulturgut unter Wasser: Schatztaucher, das Seevölkerrecht und der Schutz des kulturellen Erbes*, Aachen, Shaker Verlag, 2002.

Hesselroth, Alba. 'Struggles of security in US foreign drug policy towards Andean countries', (2004) *Peace Studies Journal* 5, 1.

Hetzer, Wolfgang. 'Finanzindustrie oder Organisierte Kriminalität?', (2013) *APuZ* (38–9), 16 September 2013, available at: http://www.bpb.de/apuz/168914/finanzindustrie-oder-organisierte-kriminalitaet, accessed 29 October 2015.

Heydenreuter, Reinhard. *Kunstraub. Die Geschichte des Quedlinburger Stiftsschatzes*, Munich, Bechtle, 1993.

Higgins, Andrew. 'In testy debate, EU leaders fail to agree on quotas to spread migrants across bloc', *New York Times*, 26 June 2015, available at: http://www.nytimes.com/2015/06/27/world/europe/european-union-migrant-crisis-quotas-italy-greece.html, accessed 29 October 2015.

Higgins, Rosalyn. 'Conceptual thinking about the individual in international law', (1978) 4 *British Journal of International Studies* (1), 1.

Hignett, Kelly. 'Transnational organized crime and the global village', in Allum, Felia and Gilmour, Stan (eds), *Routledge Handbook of Transnational Organized Crime*, London, Routledge, 2012, pp. 281–93.

Hilgendorf, Eric. 'Tendenzen und Probleme einer Harmonisierung des Internetstrafrechts auf Europäischer Ebene', in Schwarzenegger, Christian, Arter, Oliver, and Jörg, Florian (eds), *Internet-Recht und Strafrecht*, Bern, Stämpfli, 2005, pp. 257–98.

Hirsh, Steve. 'Experts question global counternarcotics strategies', *Jane's Intelligence Review*, 1 November 2005.

Hobbs, Dick. 'Going down the glocal: the local context of organised crime', (1998) 37 *The Howard Journal of Criminal Justice* (4), 407.

Hodgson, Jacqueline and Tadros, Victor. 'The impossibility of defining terrorism', (2013) 16 *New Criminal Law Review*, 494.

Hodgson, Martin. 'The coca leaf war: a report from Colombia', (2000) 56 *Bulletin of the Atomic Scientists* (3), 36.

Hoffman, Bruce. *Inside Terrorism*, 3rd edn, New York, Columbia University Press, 2006.

Honan, William H. *Treasure Hunt. A New York Times Reporter Tracks the Quedlinburg Hoard*, New York, Fromm International, 1997.

Hopgood, Mei-Ling. 'Negotiators struggle to reach small-arms pact: complex politics stall agreement', *Toronto Star*, 21 July 2001.

Hotchkiss, Carolyn. 'The sleeping dog stirs: new signs of life in efforts to end corruption in international business', (1998) 17 *Journal of Public Policy & Marketing*, 108.

Huber, Barbara. *Combatting Corruption in the European Union*, Cologne, Bundesanzeiger, 2002.

Huber, Barbara. 'Menschenhandel', in Sieber, Ulrich, Satzger, Helmut, and v. Heintschel-Heinegg, Bernd (eds), *Europäisches Strafrecht*, 2nd edn, Baden-Baden, Nomos, 2014, pp. 394–403.

Huber, Barbara. 'Schutz von Kindern und Frauen (sexuelle Ausbeutung, Pornografie, Gewalt)', in Sieber, Ulrich, Satzger, Helmut, and v. Heintschel-Heinegg, Bernd (eds), *Europäisches Strafrecht*, 2nd edn, Baden-Baden, Nomos, 2014, pp. 412–34.

Hülsse, Rainer and Kerwer, Dieter. 'Global standards in action: insights from anti-money laundering regulation', (2007) 14 *Organization* (5), 625.

International Monetary Fund. *Anti-Money Laundering and Combating the Financing of Terrorism (AML/CFT)—Report on the Review of the Effectiveness of the Program*, New York, IMF, 2011.

Huntington, Samuel. 'Modernization and corruption', in Heidenheimer, Arnold J. and Johnston, Michael (eds), *Political Corruption*, 3rd edn, New York, Transaction, 2009, pp. 253–63.

Hutchinson, Steven and O'Malley, Pat. 'A crime–terror nexus? Thinking on some of the links between terrorism and criminality', (2007) 30 *Studies in Conflict & Terrorism*, 1095.

ICRC. 'Interpretative guidance on the notion of direct participation in hostilities under international humanitarian law', (2009) 90 *IRRC* (872), 991.

IFAW. *Criminal Nature: The Global Security Implications of the Illegal Wildlife Trade*, IFAW, 2013.

International Criminal Court. *Rules of Procedure and Evidence*. UN Doc. PCNICC/2000/1/Add. 1, 2000.

International Crisis Group. 'Breaking the Kosovo stalemate: Europe's responsibility', (2007) *Europe Report* 185, available at: http://www.crisisgroup.org/~/media/Files/europe/185_breaking_the_kosovo_stalemate___europe_s_responsibility.ashx.

International Federation of Red Cross and Red Crescent Societies. *Out of Harm's Way. Injecting Drug Users and Harm Reduction*, Geneva, IFRC, 2010.

International Labour Office. *Profits and Poverty: the Economics of Forced Labour*, Geneva, ILO, 2014.

International Law Commission. *Yearbook of the International Law Commission*, Vol. II, New York, United Nations, 1966.

International Organization for Migration. 'Migrant boat arrivals in europe top 150,000 in 2015', 10 July 2015, available at: http://www.iom.int/news/migrant-boat-arrivals-europe-top-150000-2015, accessed 29 October 2015.

Irrera, Daniela. 'The EU strategy in tackling organized crime in the framework of multilateralism', (2011) 12 *Perspectives on European Politics and Society* (4), 407.

Irwin, Angela Samantha Maitland, Choo, Kim-Kwang Raymond, and Liu, Lin. 'An analysis of money laundering and terrorism financing typologies', (2011) 15 *Journal of Money Laundering Control* (1), 85.

ITU (International Telecommunication Union) and Gercke, Marco. *Understanding Cybercrime: Phenomena, Challenges and Legal Responses*, ITU, 2012, available at: http://www.itu.int/ITU-D/cyb/cybersecurity/projects/crimeguide.html, accessed 29 October 2015.

IUCN, *Proceedings of the 8th Session of the General Assembly*, Gland, Switzerland, IUCN, 1963.

Jäger, Thomas. 'Transnationale Organisierte Kriminalität', (2013) *APuZ* (38–9), 16 September 2013, available at: http://www.bpb.de/apuz/168912/transnatinale-organisierte-kriminalitaet, accessed 29 October 2015.

Jakobi, Anja P. *Common Goods and Evils? The Formation of Global Crime Governance*, Oxford, OUP, 2013.

Jakobs, Günther. 'Bürgerstrafrecht und Feindstrafrecht', (2004) *HRRS* (3), 88.

Jakobs, Günther. 'Kriminalisierung im Vorfeld einer Rechtsgutsverletzung', (1985) 97 *ZStW*, 751.

James, Mark. 'The other civil society: organised crime in fragile and failing states', (2012) 12 *Defence Studies* (2), 218.

Jamil, Zahid. 'Cybercrime model laws: discussion paper prepared for the Cybercrime Convention Committee, T-CY)', 2014, available at: http://www.coe.int/t/dghl/cooperation/economiccrime/Source/Cybercrime/TCY/2014/3021_model_law_study_v15.pdf, accessed 29 October 2015.

Jane's Intelligence Digest. 'Organ-trafficking: A fast-expanding black market', 7 March 2008.

Jelsma, Martin. *UNGASS 2016: Prospects for Treaty Reform and UN System-Wide Coherence on Drug Policy*, Washington, Brookings Institution, 2015.

Jelsma, Martin. *The Development of International Drug Control: Lessons Learned and Strategic Challenges for the Future*, Amsterdam, Transnational Institute, 2011.

Jenner, Matthew S. 'Drug trafficking as a transnational crime', in Reichel, Philip and Albanese, Jay (eds), *Handbook of Transnational Crime and Justice*, Thousand Oaks, California, SAGE Publications, 2014, pp. 65–85.

Jenner, Matthew S. 'International drug trafficking: a global problem with a domestic solution', (2011) 18 *Indiana Journal of Global Legal Studies* (2), 901.

Jennings, John M. *The Opium Empire: Japanese Imperialism and Drug Trafficking in Asia, 1895–1945*. Westport, Connecticut, Praeger, 1997.

Jennings, Robert. 'The limits of state jurisdiction', (1962) 32 *Nordic Journal of International Law*, 209.

Jennings, Robert and Watts, Arthur. *Oppenheim's International Law*, 9th edn, Oxford, OUP, 1992.

Jensen, Richard. 'Daggers, rifles and dynamite: anarchist terrorism in nineteenth century Europe', (2004) 16 *Terrorism and Political Violence* (1), 116.

Jessen, Henning. 'United States' bilateral shipboarding agreements—upholding law of the sea principles while updating state practice', in Henrik Ringbom (ed.), *Jurisdiction Over Ships*, Leiden/Boston, Brill, 2015, pp. 50–81.

Jessup, Philip C. *The Law of Territorial Waters and Maritime Jurisdiction*, New York, G. A. Jennings, 1927.

Johnston, Peter, Schneider, Stephen *et al. Developing and Applying an Organized Crime Harm Index: A Scoping and Feasibility Study*, Public Safety Canada, Ottawa, 2010.

Jokisch, Jens and Jahnke, Moritz. 'Der Raum der Freiheit, der Sicherheit und des Rechts', in Sieber, Ulrich, Satzger, Helmut, and v. Heintschel-Heinegg, Bernd (eds), *Europäisches Strafrecht*, 2nd edn, Baden-Baden, Nomos, 2014, pp. 124–35.

Jordan, Ann D. 'Annotated guide to the complete UN Trafficking Protocol', May 2012, updated August 2002, Washington DC, International Human Rights Law Group.

Joutsen, Matti. 'International cooperation against transnational organized crime: criminalizing participation in and organized criminal group', (2002) 59 *UNAFEI Resource Materials*, 417.

Joyner, Christopher C. 'Arresting impunity: the case for universal jurisdiction in bringing war criminals to accountability', (1996) 59 *Law and Contemporary Problems*, 153.

Kamminga, Menno T. and Zia-Zarifi, Saman (eds). *Liability of Multinational Corporations under International Law*, Springer Netherlands, 2000.

Kane, June. *Sold for Sex*, Brookfield, Vermont, Arena, 1998.

Kappeler, Victor E. and Kraska, Peter B. 'Normalising police militarisation, living in denial', (2013) *Policing and Society*, 268, doi: 10.1080/10439463.2013.864655.

Kapstein, Ethan B. 'The new global slave trade', (2006) *Foreign Affairs*, November–December, 103.

Karstedt, Susanne. 'Organised crime, democracy, and democratisation: how vulnerable are democracies?', in Robertson-von Trotha, Caroline (ed.) *Organised Crime: Dark Sides of Globalisation*, Interdisciplinary Studies on Culture and Society 8, Baden-Baden, Nomos, 2013, pp. 95–112.

Katz, Karen. 'The enemy within: the outlaw motorcycle gang moral panic', (2011) 36 *American Journal of Criminal Justice* (3), 231.

Kaul, Hans-Peter. 'Preconditions to the exercise of jurisdiction', in Cassese, Antonio, Gaeta, Paola, and Jones, John R. W. D. (eds), *The Rome Statute of the International Criminal Court. A Commentary*, Vol. 1, Oxford, OUP, 2002, pp. 583–618.

Kavemann, Barbara. 'Die praktischen Auswirkungen des deutschen Prostitutionsgesetz', in Benkel, Thorsten (ed.), *Das Frankfurter Bahnhofsviertel: Devianz im öffentlichen Raum*, Wiesbaden, V. S. Verlag für Sozialwissenschaften/G. W. V. Fachverlage, 2010, pp. 211–28.

Kaye, Stuart M. 'The Proliferation Security Initiative in the maritime domain', in Sparks, Thomas McK. and Sulmasy, Glenn M. (eds), *International Law Challenges: Homeland Security and Combating Terrorism*, Newport, Rhode Island, Naval War College, 2006, pp. 141–64.

Keazor, Henry. *Täuschend echt! Eine Geschichte der Kunstfälschung*, Darmstadt, Theiss, 2015.

Keazor, Henry and Öcal, Tina. *Der Fall Beltracchi und die Folgen. Interdisziplinäre Fälschungsforschung heute*, Berlin, De Gruyter, 2014.

Kemp, Gerhard. 'The United Nations Convention against Transnational Organized Crime: a milestone in international criminal law', (2001) 14 *South African Journal of Criminal Justice* 152.

Kempadoo, Kamala. 'The war on human trafficking in the Caribbean', (2007) 49 *Race & Class* (2), 79.

Kilchling, Michael. 'Finance oriented strategies of organized crime control', in Paoli, Letizia (ed.), *The Oxford Handbook of Organized Crime*, Oxford, OUP, 2014, pp. 655–73.

Kilchling, Michael. 'Substantive aspects of the UN Convention against Transnational Organised Crime', in Albrecht, Hans-Jörg and Fijnaut, Cyrille (eds), *The Containment of Transnational Organised Crime: Comments on the UN Convention of December 2000*, Freiburg im Breisgau, Edition Iuscrim, 2002, pp. 83–96.

Kilchling, Michael. 'Geldwäsche', in Sieber, Ulrich, Satzger, Helmut, and v. Heintschel-Heinegg, Bernd (eds), *Europäisches Strafrecht*, 2nd edn, Baden-Baden, Nomos, 2014, pp. 332–42.

Kilchling, Michael and Herz, Annette. 'Schleuserkriminalität', in Sieber, Ulrich, Satzger, Helmut, and v. Heintschel-Heinegg, Bernd (eds), *Europäisches Strafrecht*, 2nd edn, Baden-Baden, Nomos, 2014, pp. 404–11.

Killmann, Bernd-Roland. 'Unbare Zahlungsmittel', in Sieber, Ulrich, Satzger, Helmut, and v. Heintschel-Heinegg, Bernd (eds), *Europäisches Strafrecht*, 2nd edn, Baden-Baden, Nomos, 2014, pp. 328–31.

Kinzig, Jörg. *Die rechtliche Bewältigung von Erscheinungsformen organisierter Kriminalität*, Berlin, Duncker & Humblot, 2004.

Kinzig, Jörg. 'Kunstfälschung—eine Skizze anhand des Falles "Sammlung Werner Jägers"', in Hilgendorf, Eric and Rengier, Rudolf (eds), *Festschrift für Wolfgang Heinz*, Baden-Baden, Nomos, 2012, pp. 124–40.

Kirchner, Andrée and Schiano di Pepe, Lorenzo. 'International attempts to conclude a Convention to combat illegal migration', (1998) 10 *International Journal of Refugee Law*, 662.

Kirgis Jr, Frederick L. 'Custom on a sliding scale', (1987) 81 *AJIL* (1), 146.

Kittichaisaree, Kriangsak. *International Criminal Law*, Oxford, OUP, 2001.

MacNamara, Donald E. J. and Stead, Philip J. *New Dimensions in Transnational Crime*, New York, John Jay Press, 1982.

Kleemans, Edward R. 'Organized crime and the visible hand: a theoretical critique on the economic analysis of organized crime', (2013) 13 *Criminology and Criminal Justice* (5), 615.

Klein, Natalie. *Maritime Security and the Law of the Sea*, Oxford, OUP, 2011.

Knight, Alexandra. 'Global environmental threats: can the Security Council protect our Earth?', (2005) 80 *New York University Law Review* (5), 1549.

Kogelfranz, Siegfried and Korte, Willi A. *Quedlinburg—Texas und zurück. Schwarzhandel mit geraubter Kunst*, Munich, Knaur, 1994.

Kohl, Andreas, Krevert, Peter, and Wittkämper, Gerhard W. *Europa und die innere Sicherheit*, Wiesbaden, BKA, 1996.

Kolb, Robert and Hyde, Richard, *An Introduction to the International Law of Armed Conflicts*, Oxford, Hart Publishing, 2008.

Koldehoff, Stefan and Timm, Tobias. *Falsche Bilder, Echtes Geld*, Berlin, Kiepenheuer & Witsch, 2012.

Kolodkin, Anatolij L, Bobrova, Yulia V., and Shinkaretskaia, Galina G. 'Peaceful uses of the seas in the light of new challenges and threats', in Ndiaye, Tafsir Malik and Wolfrum, Rüdiger (eds), *Law of the Sea, Environmental Law and Settlement of Disputes, Liber Amicorum Judge Thomas M. Mensah*, Leiden/Boston, Martinus Nijhoff Publishers, 2007, pp. 437–42.

König, Doris. *Durchsetzung internationaler Bestands- und Umweltschutzvorschriften auf Hoher See im Interesse der Staatengemeinschaft*, Berlin, Duncker & Humblot, 1990.

Koskenniemi, Martti. 'The future of statehood', (1991) 32 *Harvard International Law Journal* (2), 397.

Kraemer-Mbula, Erika, Tang, Puay, and Rush, Howard. 'The cybercrime ecosystem: online innovation in the shadows?', (2013) 80 *Technological Forecasting & Social Change* (3), 541.

Krajewski, Krzysztof. 'Some legal and criminological aspects of implementation', in Albrecht, Hans-Jörg and Fijnaut, Cyrille (eds), *The Containment of Transnational Organised Crime: Comments on the UN Convention of December 2000*, Freiburg im Breisgau, Edition Iuscrim, 2002, p. 235.

Kramer, Karen. 'Witness protection as a key tool in addressing serious and organised crime', UNAFEI, 2012, available at: http://www.unafei.or.jp/english/pdf/PDF_GG4_Seminar/Fourth_GGSeminar_P3-19.pdf, accessed 29 October 2015.

Kraska, Peter B. 'Militarization and policing: its relevance to 21st century policing', (2007) *Policing*, 1.

Krebs, Brian. *Spam Nation*, Naperville, Illinois, Sourcebooks, 2014.

Kreß, Claus. 'Völkerstrafrecht der dritten Generation gegen transnationale Gewalt Privater?' in Hankel, Gerd (ed.), *Die Macht und das Recht: Beiträge zum Völkerrecht und Völkerstrafrecht zu Beginn des 21. Jahrhunderts*, Hamburg, Hamburger Edition, 2008, pp. 323–413.

Kreß, Claus. 'Das Strafrecht in der Europäischen Union vor der Herausforderung durch organisierte Kriminalität und Terrorismus', (2005) *Juristische Arbeitsblätter*, 220.

Kreß, Claus. 'Die Rettungsoperation der Bundeswehr in Albanien am 14. März 1997 aus völker- und verfassungsrechtlicher Sicht', (1997) 57 *Zeitschrift für ausländisches öffentliches Recht und Völkerrecht*, 329.

Kreß, Claus and Gazeas, Nikolaos. 'Organisierte Kriminalität', in Sieber, Ulrich, Satzger, Helmut, and v. Heintschel-Heinegg, Bernd (eds), *Europäisches Strafrecht*, 2nd edn, Baden-Baden, Nomos, 2014, para. 18.

Kretschmann, Georg. *Faszination Fälschung*, Berlin, Parthas Verlag, 2001.

Kretschmer, Bernhard. *Der Grab- und Leichenfrevel als strafwürdige Missetat*, Baden-Baden, Nomos, 2002.

Kretzmer, David. 'The inherent right to self-defence and proportionality in "*jus ad bellum*"', (2013) 24 *EJIL* (1), 235.

Kretzmer, David. 'Targeted killing of suspected terrorists: extrajudicial executions or legitimate self-defence?', (2005) 16 *EJIL* (2), 171.

Krisch, Nico. 'Article 39', in Simma, Bruno, Nolte, Georg, Khan, Daniel-Erasmus, and Paulus, Andreas (eds), *The Charter of the United Nations: A Commentary*, Vol. II, 3rd edn, Oxford, OUP, 2012, pp. 1272–96.

Kshetri, Nir. *The Global Cybercrime Industry*, Berlin, Springer, 2010.

Kubiciel, Michael. 'Core criminal law provisions in the United Nations Convention Against Corruption', (2009) *International Criminal Law Review* 9, 139.

Kubiciel, Michael. 'Facilitation payments: a crime?', *Cologne Papers on Criminal Law Policy* 2/2015, Cologne, Institute for Criminal Law and Criminal Procedure, 3.

Kubiciel, Michael. 'International legal development and national legal change in the fight against corruption', in Linnan, David K. (ed.), *Legitimacy, Legal Development and Change*, Farnham, Ashgate, 2012, p. 419.

Kuhl, Lothar. 'Geldfälschung', in Sieber, Ulrich, Satzger, Helmut, and v. Heintschel-Heinegg, Bernd (eds), *Europäisches Strafrecht*, 2nd edn, Baden-Baden, Nomos, 2014, para. 14.

Kyriakakis, Joanna. 'International legal personality, collective entities and international crimes', in Gal-Or, Noemi, Ryngaert, Cedric, and Noortmann, Math (eds), *Responsibilities of the Non-State Actor in Armed Conflict and the Market Place*, Heidelberg, Brill, 2015, pp. 79–104.

Kyriakakis, Joanna. 'Corporate criminal liability and the ICC Statute: the comparative law challenge', (2009) 56 *Netherlands International Law Review* (3), 333.

Kyriakos-Saad, Nadim. 'The methodology for assessing compliance with anti-money laundering and combating the financing of terrorism standard', (2005) 3 *Current Developments in Monetary and Financial Law*, 265.

La Rosa, Anne-Marie and Wuerzner, Carolin. 'Armed groups, sanctions and the implementation of international humanitarian law', (2008) 90 *IRRC* (870), 327.

Laczko, Frank. 'Data and research on human trafficking', (2005) 43 *International Migration* (1–2), 6.

Langille, Benjamin. 'It's "instant custom": how the Bush Doctrine became law after the terrorist attacks of September 11, 2001', (2003) 26 *Boston College International and Comparative Law Review (Boston College Intl Comp L Rev)* (1), 145.

Laqueur, Hannah. 'Uses and abuses of drug decriminalization in Portugal', (2015) 40 *Law & Social Inquiry* (3), 746.

Laqueur, Walter. 'Terrorism: a brief history', (2007) *eJournal USA*, 20.

Laqueur, Walter. 'Postmodern terrorism', (1996) 75 *Foreign Affairs*, 24.

Lauterpacht, Hersch. *Recognition in International Law*, Cambridge, CUP, 1947.

Le Billon, Philippe. 'Buying peace or fuelling war: the role of corruption in armed conflicts', (2003) 15 *Journal of International Development* (4), 413.

Le Nguyen, Chat. *International anti-money laundering standards and their implementation by Vietnam*, PhD thesis, Canterbury, Canterbury University, 2014.

Le, Vy, Bell, Peter, and Lauchs, Mark. 'Elements of best practice in policing transnational organized crime: critical success factors for international cooperation', (2013) 2 *International Journal of Management and Administrative Sciences* (3), 24.

Leboeuf, Aline. 'Les états face aux pandémies', in de Montbrial, Thierry and Defarges, Philippe Moreau (eds), *Ramses 2012*, Paris, Dunod, 2011, pp. 100–103.

Lee III, Rensselaer W. 'Transnational organized crime: an overview', in Farer, Tom (ed.), *Transnational Crime in the Americas: An Inter-American Dialogue Book*, New York, Routledge, 1999, pp. 1–38.

Lee, Jyh-An and Liu, Ching-Yi. 'Forbidden City enclosed by the Great Firewall: the law and power of internet filtering in China', (2012) 13 *Minnesota Journal of Law, Science & Technology*, 125.

Lee, Luke T. 'Jurisdiction over foreign merchant ships in the territorial sea: an analysis of the Geneva Convention on the Law of the Sea', (1961) 55 *AJIL*, 77.

Leipold, Klaus, Tsambikakis, Michael, and Zöller, Mark A. *AnwaltKommentar StGB*, 2nd edn, Heidelberg, C. F. Müller, 2015.

Leong, Angela Veng Mei. *The Disruption of International Organised Crime: An Analysis of Legal and Non-Legal Strategies*, Aldershot, Ashgate, 2007.

Lesaffer, Randall. 'Too much history: from war as sanction to the sanctioning of war', in Weller, Marc (ed.), *The Oxford Handbook of the Use of Force in International Law*, Oxford, OUP, 2015, pp. 35–55.

Lesaffer, Randall. 'Kellogg-Briand Pact (1928)', in Wolfrum, Rüdiger (ed.), *Max Planck Encyclopedia of Public International Law*, last updated October 2010, available at: http://opil.ouplaw.com/view/10.1093/law:epil/9780199231690/law-9780199231690-e320?rskey=ADfWXL&result=1&prd=EPIL, accessed 29 October 2015.

Levi, Michael. *Controlling the International Money Trail: A Multi-Level Cross-National Public Policy Review*, Swindon, Economic and Social Research Council, 2003.

Levi, Michael. 'Money laundering', in Paoli, Letizia (ed.), *The Oxford Handbook of Organized Crime*, Oxford, OUP, 2014, p. 419.

Levi, Michael. 'The organization of serious crime for gain', in Maguire, Mike, Morgan, Rod, and Reiner, Robert (eds), *The Oxford Handbook of Criminology*, Oxford, OUP, 2012, p. 595.

Levi, Michael. 'States, frauds, and the threat of transnational organized crime', (2012) 66 *Journal of International Affairs* (1), pp. 37–48.

Levi, Michael. 'Suite revenge?: The shaping of folk devils and moral panics about white-collar crimes', (2009) 49 *British Journal of Criminology* (1), 248.

Levi, Michael. 'Regulating money laundering: the death of bank secrecy in the UK', (1991) 31 *British Journal of Criminology* (2), 109.

Levi, Michael and Maguire, Mike. 'Reducing and preventing organised crime: an evidence-based critique', (2004) 41 *Crime, Law and Social Change*, 397.

Levi, Michael and Reuter, Peter. 'Money laundering: a review of current controls and their consequences', (2006) 34 *Crime and Justice: An Annual Review of Research*, 289.

Levine, Harry G. 'Global drug prohibition: its uses and crises', (2003) 14 *International Journal of Drug Policy* (2), 145.

Liang, Bin. 'Drugs and drug control in the People's Republic of China (1949–present)', in Cao, Liqun, Hebenton, Bill, and Sun, Yvan (eds), *The Routledge Handbook of Chinese Criminology*, New York, Routledge, 2013, pp. 183–96.

Lindee, Kirstin M. 'Love, honor, or control: domestic violence, trafficking, and the question of how to regulate the mail-order bride industry', (2007) 16 *Columbia Journal of Gender and Law* (2), 551.

Linneweber, Edward C. 'To target, or not to target: why 'tis nobler to thwart the Afghan narcotics trade with nonlethal means', (2011) 207 *Military Law Review*, 155.

Livingstone, Grace. *Inside Colombia: Drugs, Democracy, and War*, New Brunswick, New Jersey, Rutgers University Press, 2004.

Löffler, Joachim. 'Künstlersignatur und Kunstfälschung', (1993) *Neue Juristische Wochenschrift*, 1421.

Loree, Don. 'Organized crime: changing concepts and realities for the police', (2002) *Trends in Organized Crime*, 73–8.

Lovell, Julia. *The Opium War*, London, Picador, 2011.

Luban, David. 'The war on terrorism and the end of human rights', Washington DC, Georgetown University Law Center, 2002.

Luft, Gal and Korin, Anne. 'Terrorism goes to sea', (2004) *Foreign Affairs*, November/December, 62.

Lusthaus, Jonathan. 'How organised is organised cybercrime?', (2013) 14 *Global Crime* (1), 52.

Lutz, Brenda and Lutz, James M. *Global Terrorism*, 3rd edn, Abingdon, Routledge, 2013.

Lynch, Gerard E. 'The crime of being a criminal. Parts I and II', (1987) 87 *Columbia Law Review*, 661.

Lyon, David. *The Electronic Eye: The Rise of Surveillance Society*, Minneapolis, Minnesota, University of Minnesota Press, 1994.

Macedo, Stephen (ed.). *The Princeton Principles on Universal Jurisdiction*, Princeton, New Jersey, Princeton University Press, 2001.

Mackarel, Mark 'Procedural aspects of the Convention against Transnational Organised Crime', in Albrecht, Hans-Jörg and Fijnaut, Cyrille (eds), *The Containment of Transnational Organised Crime: Comments on the UN Convention of December 2000*, Freiburg im Breisgau, Edition Iuscrim, 2002, p. 145.

Mackenzie, Simon and Davis, Tess. 'Cambodian statue trafficking networks: an empirical report from regional case study fieldwork', in Manacorda, Stefano and Visconti, Arianna (eds), *Protecting Cultural Heritage as a Common Good of Humanity: A Challenge for Criminal Justice*, Milan, ISPAC, 2014, pp. 149–64.

Maddox, Alexia, Barratt, Monica J., *et al.* 'Constructive activism in the dark web: cryptomarkets and illicit drugs in the digital "demimonde"', (2015) *Information, Communication & Society*, 1.

Madsen, Frank G. *Transnational Organized Crime*, London and New York, Routledge, 2009.

Madsen, Frank G. 'Trafficking crimes', in Rider, Barry A. K. (ed.), *Research Handbook on International Financial Crimes*, Cheltenham, Gloucestershire, Edward Elgar Publishing, 2015.

Madsen, Frank G. 'Transnational criminal networks', in Weiss, Thomas G. and Wilkinson, Rorden (eds), *International Organization and Global Governance*, Abingdon and New York, Routledge, 2014, Ch. 29.

Madsen, Frank G. 'International narcotics law enforcement: a study in irrationality', (2012) 66 *Journal of International Affairs* (1), 1.

Madsen, Frank G. 'Transnational organized crime', in Weiss, Thomas G. and Daws, Sam (eds), *The Oxford Handbook on the United Nations*, Oxford, OUP, 2007, pp. 611–9.

Maihold, Günther. 'Der Mensch als Ware. Konzepte und Handlungsansätze zur Bekämpfung des globalen Menschenhandels', Berlin, SWP Research Paper S24, 2011.

Mair, Stefan. 'The world of privatized violence', in Pfaller, Alfred and Lerch, Marika (eds), *Challenges of Globalization: New Trends in International Politics and Society*, New Brunswick, Transaction Publishers, 2005, pp. 47–61.

Makarenko, Tamara. 'Foundations and evolution of the crime–terror nexus', in Allum, Felia and Gilmour, Stan (eds), *Routledge Handbook of Transnational Organized Crime*, Abingdon, Routledge, 2012, pp. 234–49.

Makarenko, Tamara. 'Criminal and terrorist networks: gauging interaction and the resultant impact on counter-terrorism', in Brimmer, Esther (ed.), *Five Dimensions of Homeland and International Security*, Washington DC, Center for Transatlantic Relations, 2008, pp. 57–72.

Makarenko, Tamara. 'The crime–terror continuum: tracing the interplay between transnational organised crime and terrorism', (2004) 6 *Global Crime*, 129.

Malanczuk, Peter (ed.). *Studies and Materials on the Settlement of International Disputes*, Vol. 7, The Hague, Kluwer Law International, 2000.

Malanczuk, Peter. *Akehurst's Modern Introduction to International Law*, 7th edn, London, Routledge, 1997.

Maljević, Almir. *Participation in a Criminal Organisation and Conspiracy; Different Legal Models and Criminal Collectives*, Berlin, Duncker and Humblot, 2011.

Mallia, Patricia. *Migrant Smuggling by Sea: Combating a Current Threat to Maritime Security through the Creation of a Cooperative Framework*, Leiden/Boston, Martinus Nijhoff Publishers, 2010.

Mann, Frederick A. 'The doctrine of jurisdiction in international law', (1964) 111 *Recueil de Cours* I, 9.

Marauhn, Thilo. 'Schutz von Kindern gegen sexuelle Ausbeutung und Gewalt: Das Fakultativprotokoll zum Übereinkommen über die Rechte des Kindes betreffend den Verkauf von Kindern, die Kinderprostitution und die Kinderpornographie', in von Schorlemer, Sabine and Schulte-Herbrüggen, Elena (eds), 1989–2009: 20 Jahre UN-Kinderrechtskonvention Erfahrungen und Perspektiven, Dresdner Schriften zu Recht und Politik der Vereinten Nationen, Frankfurt/am Main, Peter Lang, 2010, pp. 143–57.

Marischka, Christoph. 'Rüsten für den globalen Bürgerkrieg' [Arming for the global civil war], IMI Paper No. 2007/08, Informationsstelle Militarisierung, 6 October 2007.

Martin, Augustus. 'Terrorism and transnational organized crime', in Reichel, Philip and Albanese, Jay (eds), *Transnational Crime and Justice*, 2nd edn, Thousand Oaks, California, SAGE Publications, 2014, pp. 243–61.

Martin, Claudia. 'Terrorism as a crime in international and domestic law: open issues', in van den Herik, Larissa and Schrijver, Nico (eds), *Counter-Terrorism Strategies in a Fragmented International Legal Order*, Cambridge, CUP, 2013, pp. 639–66.

Martin, Gus. *Understanding Terrorism. Challenges, Perspectives and Issues*, 3rd edn, Thousand Oaks, California, SAGE Publications, 2010.

Martin, Susan. 'Global migration trends and asylum', *New Issues in Refugee Research*, UNHCR Working Paper 41, 30 April 2001.

Mayr, Walter. 'Elefanten vor dem Wasserloch', (2008) 17 *Der Spiegel*, 128.

Maywald, Jörg. 'UN-Kinderechtskonvention: Bilanz und Ausblick', (2010) 38 *APuZ*, 8.

McClean, David. *Transnational Organized Crime: A Commentary on the UN Convention and its Protocols*, Oxford, OUP, 2007.

McCoy, Alfred. *The Politics of Heroin, CIA Complicity in the Global Drug Trade, Afghanistan, Southeast Asia, Central America*, Chicago, Lawrence Hill, 2003.

McCulloch, Jude and Martin, James. 'Policing the globe: international trends and issues in policing', in Arrigo, Bruce A. and Bersot, Heather Y. (eds), *The Routledge Handbook of International Crime and Justice Studies*, London and New York, Routledge, 2013, pp. 98–121.

McDougal, Myres S. and Burke, William T. *The Public Order of the Oceans*, Montreal, McGill University Press, 1962.

McFadden, Michael, O'Flaherty, Martin, Boreham, Paul, and Hayne, Michele. *Targeting the Profits of Illicit Drug Trafficking through Proceeds of Crime Action*, Canberra, Monograph series 52, National Drug Law Enforcement Research Fund, 2014.

McFate, Sean. *The Modern Mercenary: Private Armies and What They Mean for World Order*, Oxford, OUP, 2015.

McGallaghy, Joseph and McKeganey, Neil. 'The impact of drug seizure on local communities', in Töttel, Ursula, Bulanova-Hristova, Gergana and Büchler, Heinz (eds), Research Conferences on Organised Crime at the Bundeskriminalamt in Germany, Vol. II, *Organised Crime—Research and Practice in Western and Northern Europe, 2011–2012*, Polizei & Forschung Bd. 45, Wiesbaden, Luchterhand Verlag, (2013), pp. 81–105.

McIntosh, Mary. *The Organisation of Crime*. London, Macmillan, 1975.

McSkimming, Samuel. 'Trade-based money laundering: responding to an emerging threat', (2009) 15 *Deakin Law Review* (1), 37.

Meagher, Douglas. *Organised Crime*: Papers presented by Mr Douglas Meagher, QC, to the 53rd ANZAAS Congress, Perth, Western Australia, 16–20 May 1983, Canberra, 1983.

Melzer, Milton. *Slavery: A World History*, Boston, Massachusetts, Da Capo Press, 1993.

Melzer, Nils. *Targeted Killing in International Law*, Oxford/New York, OUP, 2008.

Meron, Theodor. 'International criminalization of internal atrocities', (1995) 89 *AJIL* (3), 554.

Metaal, Pien and Youngers, Coletta. *Systems Overload. Drug Laws and Prisons in Latin America*, Washington DC, Washington Office on Latin America, 2011.

Mettraux, Guénael. 'The United Nations Special Tribunal for Lebanon: prosecuting terrorism', in Saul, Ben (ed.), *Research Handbook on International Law and Terrorism*, Camberley, Edward Elgar Publishing, 2014, pp. 651–65.

Meyer, Frank. 'Titel V Der Raum der Freiheit, der Sicherheit und des Rechts', in, v. d. Groeben, Hans, Schwarze, Jürgen, and Hatje, Armin (eds), *Europäisches Unionsrecht*, 7th edn, Baden-Baden, Nomos, 2015, pp. 169–95.

Meyers, Reinhard. 'Krieg und Kriegsentwicklung in der wissenschaftlichen Diskussion', in Varwick, Johannes (ed.), *Krieg und Frieden*, Schwalbuch/Ts., Wochenschau Verlag, 2014, pp. 41–71.

Miko, Francis T. 'Trafficking in women and children: the US and international response', in Troubnikoff, Anna M. (ed.), *Trafficking in Women and Children: Current Issues and Developments*, New York, Nova Science Publishers, 2003, pp. 1–30.

Milanovic, Marko. *Extraterritorial Application of Human Rights Treaties: Law, Principles, and Policy*, Oxford, OUP, 2011.

Milanovic, Marko. 'From compromise to principle: clarifying the concept of state jurisdiction in human rights treaties', (2008) 8 *Human Rights Law Review (HRLR)*, 411.

Militello, Vincenzo. 'Participation in an organised criminal group as international offence', in Albrecht, Hans-Jörg and Fijnaut, Cyrille (eds), *The Containment of Transnational Organised Crime: Comments on the UN Convention of December 2000*, Freiburg im Breisgau, Edition Iuscrim, 2002, p. 97.

Mitchel, Gay. 'Asset confiscation as an instrument to deprive criminal organisations of the proceeds of their activities', Thematic Paper on Organised Crime, Special Committee on Organised Crime, Corruption, and Money Laundering, 2013, available at: http://www.europarl.europa.eu/document/activities/cont/201210/20121016ATT53712/20121016ATT53712EN.pdf, accessed 29 October 2015.

Minnesota Advocates for Human Rights, Stop Violence against Women, 'Trafficking in women—law and policy', available at: http://www1.umn.edu/humanrts/svaw/trafficking/law/, accessed 3 February 2016.

Mladenovic, Nemanja. 'Transnational organised crime: the failed divorce of Serbia's government and organised crime', (2012) 66 *Journal of International Affairs* (1), 195.

Möhn, Heinz-Josef. *Organisierte Kriminalität—Terminologische Darstellung und Begriffsbestimmung*, Trier, Verlag Dr Kovac, 2006.

Moir, Lindsay. *The Law of Internal Armed Conflict*, Cambridge, CUP, 2002.

Molloy, Molly. 'The Mexican undead: toward a new history of the "drug war" killing fields', (2013) *Small Wars Journal*, August 21.

Moran, Clare Frances. 'Human trafficking and the Rome Statute of the International Criminal Court', (2014) 3 *The Age of Human Rights Journal*, 32.

Morris, Stephen D. 'Corruption, drug trafficking, and violence in Mexico', (2012) *Brown Journal of World Affairs* (11), 29.

Mudde, Cas (ed.). *Racist Extremism in Central and Eastern Europe*, Abingdon, Routledge, 2005.

Mueller, Gerhard. 'Transnational crime: definitions and Concepts', in Williams, Phil and Vlassis, Dimitri (eds), *Combating Transnational Crime*, Milan/London, ISPAC/Frank Cass, 2001, p. 13.

Müller-Graff, Peter-Christian (ed.). *Europäische Zusammenarbeit in den Bereichen Justiz und Inneres—Der dritte Pfeiler der Europäischen Union*, Baden-Baden, Nomos, 1996.

Munk School of Global Affairs, Consulting Team Elad Dvash-Banks, Elizabeth Severinovskaya, Megan Strachan, Perizat Sarsenbayeva. 'Gap analysis & stakeholder engagement report for the Egmont Group of Financial Intelligence Units', Toronto, Univeristy of Toronto, Munk School of Global Affairs, 2014.

Muntarbhorn, Vitit. 'Article 34: sexual exploitation and sexual abuse of children', in Alen, André, Lanotte, Johan Vande, Verhellen, Eugeen, Ang, Fiona, Berghmans, Eva, and Verheyde, Mieke (eds), *A Commentary on the United Nations Convention on the Rights of the Child*, Leiden, Martinus Njhoff, 2007.

Murphy, John F. 'Is US adherence to the rule of law in international affairs feasible?', in Schmitt, Michael N. and Pejic, Jelena (eds), *International Law and Armed Conflict: Exploring the Faultlines. Essays in Honour of Yoram Dinstein*, Leiden/Boston, Martinus Nijhoff Publishers, 2007, pp. 197–227.

Nadelmann, Ethan A. *Cops Across Borders: The Internationalization of US Criminal Law Enforcement,* University Park, Pennsylvania State University Press, 1993.

Nadelmann, Ethan A. 'Global prohibition regimes: the evolution of norms in international society', (1990) 44 *International Organization* (4), 479.

Nadelmann, Ethan A. 'Unlaundering dirty money abroad: US foreign policy and financial secrecy jurisdictions', (1986) 18 *University of Miami Inter-American Law Review* (1), 33.

Napoleoni, Loretta. 'The new economy of terror: how terrorism is financed', (2004) 4 *Forum on Crime and Society*, 31.

National Crime Agency. *National Strategic Assessment of Serious and Organised Crime*, 2014.

Naylor, R. Thomas. 'Wash-out: a critique of follow-the-money methods in crime control policy', (1999) 32 *Crime, Law and Social Change* (1), 1.

Naylor, R. Thomas. 'Violence and illegal economic activity: a deconstruction', (2009) 52 *Crime, Law & Social Change*, 231–42.

Naylor, R. Thomas. 'The underworld of art', (2008) 50 *Crime, Law and Social Change*, 263.

Neff, Stephen C. *War and the Law of Nations: A General History*, Cambridge, CUP, 2005.

Nellemann, Christian, Henriksen, Rune, Baxter, Patricia, Ash, Neville, and Mrema, Elizabeth (eds). *The Environmental Crime Crisis: Threats to Sustainable Development from Illegal exploitation and Trade in Wildlife and Forest Resources*, Geneva, UNICRI, 2014.

Nelles, Ursula. 'Europäisierung des Strafverfahrens—Strafprozessrecht für Europa?', (1997) 109 *ZStW*, 727.

Népote, Jean. 'Interpol et le crime organisé', (1974) 282 *Revue Internationale de Police Criminelle*, 230.

Neske, Matthias. 'Human smuggling to and through Germany', (2006) 44 *International Migration* (4), 121.

Neumann, Dietrich. 'Europol', in Sieber, Ulrich, Satzger, Helmut, and v. Heintschel-Heinegg, Bernd (eds), *Europäisches Strafrecht*, 2nd edn, Baden-Baden, Nomos, 2014, para. 44.

Ngoo, Irene. 'US wins out but irks 160 nations', *Straits Times*, 23 July 2001.

Ngor, Ngor and Awunah, Donald. 'Effective methods to combat transnational organised crime in criminal justice processes: the Nigerian perspective', Resource Material Series No. 58, 116th International Training Course visiting expert papers, UNAFEI, 2001, pp. 171–82.

Nicholas, Lynn H. *The Rape of Europa. The Fate of Europe's Treasures in the Third Reich and the Second World War*, New York, Vintage, 1994 (*Der Raub der Europa*, Munich, Kindler Verlag, 1995).

Nicita, Antonio and Rizzoli, Matteo. 'The economics of art thefts: too much screaming over Munch's *The Scream*?', (2009) 28 *Economic Papers, A Journal of Applied Economics and Policy*, 291.

Nolte, Georg. 'Article 2(7)', in Bruno Simma, Georg Nolte, Daniel-Erasmus Khan, and Andreas Paulus (eds), *The Charter of the United Nations: A Commentary*, Vol. I, 3rd edn, Oxford, OUP, 2012, pp. 280–311.

Noortmann, Math. *Enforcing International Law: From Self-Help to Self-Contained Regimes*, Aldershot, Ashgate, 2005.

Nowak, Manfred (ed.). *UN Covenant on Civil and Political Rights Commentary*, Kehl, Engel Publishers, 1993.

O'Brien, John. *International Law*, London, Cavendish, 2002.

O'Connell, Daniel Patrick. *The International Law of the Sea*, Vol. II, Oxford, Clarendon Press, 1984.

O'Keefe, Roger. 'Universal jurisdiction. Clarifying the basic concept', (2004) 2 *JICJ* (3), 735. doi: 10.1093/jicj/2.3.735.

O'Manique, Sophie. *From prohibition to decriminalization: interrogating the emerging international paradigm shift in the war on drugs discourse*, MA thesis, Ottawa, Carleton University, 2014.

Obokata, Tom. *Transnational Organised Crime in International Law*, Oxford, Hart, 2010.

Obokata, Tom. 'Smuggling of human beings from a human rights perspective: obligations of non-state and state actors under international human rights law', (2005) 17 *International Journal of Refugee Law* 394.

Obokata, Tom. 'The legal framework on immigration control at sea', in Ryan, Bernard and Mitsilegas, Valsamis (eds), *Extraterritorial Immigration Control: Legal Challenges*, Leiden/ Boston, Martinus Nijhoff Publishers, 2010, p. 151.

O'Connor, Anne-Marie and Leeds, Jeff. 'US agents seize smuggled arms', *Los Angeles Times*, 15 March 1997, p. 19.

OECD (Organisation for Economic Development). *OECD Factbook 2013: Economic, Environmental and Social Statistics*, Paris, OECD Publishing, 2013.

OECD. *Corruption—A Glossary of International Standards in Criminal Law*, Paris, OECD Publishing, 2008.

OECD. 'FATF mandate renewed for eight years', press release, Paris, 14 May 2004.

Oegel, Wolfgang. 'Die Internationalität der Schleuserkriminalität', in Gehl, Günter (ed.), *Europa im Griff der organisierten Kriminalität*, Weimar, Bertuch, 2006, p. 39.

Oehmichen, Anna. *Terrorism and Anti-Terror Legislation: The Terrorised Legislator?*, Mortsel, Belgium, Intersentia, 2009.

Office of the Attorney General. 'The Attorney General's guidelines regarding the use of confidential informants', Washington DC, 8 January 2001.

Ohr, Bruce. 'Effective methods to combat transnational organised crime in criminal justice processes', Resource Material Series No. 58, 116th International Training Course visiting expert papers, UNAFEI, 2001, pp. 40–60.

O'Neill, Maria. 'Trafficking in human beings and the European Neighbourhood Policy: new challenges for the EU Justice and Law Enforcement Framework', in O'Neill, Maria, Swinton, Ken, and Winter, Aaron (eds), *New Challenges for the EU Internal Security Strategy*, Cambridge, Cambridge Scholars Publishing, 2013, pp. 188–216.

Orlova, Alexandra V. and Moore, James W. '"Umbrellas" or "building blocks"?, Defining international terrorism and transnational organized crime in international law', (2005) 27 *Houston Journal of International Law* (2), 267.

Oswald, Bruce and Finnin, Sarah. 'Combatting the trafficking of persons on peace operations', in Langholtz, Harvey, Kondoch, Boris, and Wells, Alan (eds), *International Peacekeeping: The Yearbook of International Peace Operations*, Vol. 10, Dordrecht, Brill/Nijhoff, 2006, p. 32.

Otto, Roland. *Targeted Killings and International Law*, Heidelberg, Springer, 2011.

Oxman, Bernard. 'Jurisdiction of states', in Wolfrum, Rüdiger (ed.), *Max Planck Encyclopedia of Public International Law*, Vol. VI, Oxford, OUP, 2012, pp. 546–57.

Paoli, Letizia. 'Implementation: concepts and actors', in Albrecht, Hans-Jörg and Fijnaut, Cyrille (eds), *The Containment of Transnational Organized Crime*, Freiburg im Breisgau, edition Iuscrim, 2002, pp. 207–34.

Paoli, Letizia and Vander Beken, Tom. 'Organized crime: a contested concept', in Paoli, Letizia (ed.), *The Oxford Handbook of Organized Crime*, Oxford, OUP, 2014, p. 13.

Papastavridis, Efthymios. *The Interception of Vessels on the High Seas*, Oxford and Portland, Hart Publishing, 2013.

Parliamentary Committee of Inquiry into Mafia-related and Other Criminal Organisations. 'Report of the Italian Presidency of the EU on the fight against mafia-related crime in Europe and outside Europe', 2014.

Passas, Nikos (ed.). *Transnational Crime*, Aldershot, Dartmouth, 1999.

Paulus, Manfred. 'Sexual slavery and trafficking in women—a summary of current developments in Europe', in Robertson-von Trotha, Caroline (ed.), *Organised Crime: Dark Sides of Globalisation*, Interdisciplinary Studies on Culture and Society 8, Baden-Baden, Nomos, 2013, pp. 127–36.

Payne, Valerie. 'On the road to victory in America's war on human trafficking: landmarks, landmines, and the need for centralized strategy', paper presented at the First Annual Interdisciplinary Conference on Human Trafficking, 2009.

Peet, Thomas Eric. *The Great Tomb-Robberies of the Twentieth Egyptian Dynasty*, Oxford, Clarendon Press, 1930.

Perlroth, Nicole and Sanger, David E. 'FBI Director repeats call that ability to read encrypted messages is crucial', *New York Times*, 19 November 2015.

Peterke, Sven. *Rio de Janeiros 'Drogenkrieg' im Lichte der Konfliktforschung und des Völkerrechts: Eine Fallstudie zur Behandlung organisierter bewaffneter Gewalt*, Berlin, Berliner Wissenschafts-Verlag, 2009.

Peterke, Sven. 'Völkerrechtliche Selbstverteidigung gegen transnationales organisiertes Verbrechen?', (2011) 24 *Humanitäres Völkerrecht Informationsschriften* (4), 202.

Peterke, Sven. 'Urban insurgency, "drug war" and international humanitarian law: the case of Rio de Janeiro', (2010) 1 *Journal of International Humanitarian Legal Studies* (1), 165.

Peterke, Sven and Noortmann, Math. 'Transnationale kriminelle Organisationen im Völkerrecht: mehr als Outlaws?', (2015) 53 *Archive des Völkerrechts*, 1–34.

Peterson, Marilyn. 'Intelligence-led policing: the new intelligence architecture', Washington DC, Bureau of Justice Assistance, 2005.

Pickering, Sharon. 'Transnational crime and refugee protection', (2007) 34 *Social Justice* (2), 47.

Pictet, Jean S. *The Geneva Conventions of 12 August 1949, Commentary*, Vol. I, Geneva, ICRC, 1952.

Pieth, Mark. 'The harmonisation of law against economic crime', (1999) 1 *European Journal of Law Reform*, 527.

Pieth, Mark. 'Der Beitrag der UN Konvention zur Bekämpfung der transnationalen Korruption', in Balmelli, Tiziano and Jaggy, Bernard (ed.), *Les traités internationaux contre la corruption*, Lausanne, 2004, p. 7.

Pieth, Mark and Aiolfi, Gemma. 'The private sector becomes active: the Wolfsberg process', (2003) 10 *Journal of Financial Crime* (4), 359.

Pieth, Mark, Low, Lucinda, and Bonucci, Nicola (ed.). *The OECD Convention on Bribery—A Commentary*, 2nd edn, Cambridge, CUP, 2014.

Pinkington, Ed. 'FBI demands new powers to hack into computers and carry out surveillance', *The Guardian*, 29 October 2014.

Piotrowicz, Ryszard. 'The legal nature of trafficking in human beings', (2009) 4 *Intercultural Human Rights Law Review*, 179.

Plachta, Michael. 'First meeting of Council of Europe's Special Group of Experts on Organized Crime', (2013) 29 *International Law Enforcement Reporter* (10), 387.

Polk, Milbry and Schuster, Angela M. H. *The Looting of the Iraq Museum, Baghdad: The Lost Legacy of Ancient Mesopotamia*, New York, Harry N. Abrams, 2005.

Pomorski, Stanislaw. 'Conspiracy and criminal organization', in Ginsburgs, George and Kudriavtsev, Vladimir N. (eds), *The Nuremberg Trial and International Law*, Dordrecht, Martinus Nijhoff Publishers, 1990, p. 213.

Portmann, Roland. *Legal Personality in International Law*, Cambridge, CUP, 2010.

Potier, Chloé, Laprévote, Vincent, *et al.* 'Supervised injection services: what has been demonstrated? A systematic literature review', (2014) 145 *Drug and Alcohol Dependence*, 48.

Potts, LeRoy G. 'Global trafficking in human beings: assessing the success of the United Nations Protocol to Prevent Trafficking in Persons', (2003) *George Washington International Law Review* 35.

Pounds, Norman J. G. *An Historical Geography of Europe*, Cambridge, CUP, 1985.

Pretorius, Loot and Strydom, Hennie. 'The constitutionality of civil forfeiture', (1998) 13 *South African Public Law* 385.

Pries, Ludger. *Die Transnationalisierung der sozialen Welt*, Frankfurt am Main, Suhrkamp, 2008.

Proelss, Alexander. 'Piracy and the use of force', in Koutrakos, Panos and Skordas, Achilles (eds), *The Law and Practice of Piracy at Sea*, Oxford, Hart Publishing, 2014, pp. 53–66.

Proelss, Alexander. 'The law on the Exclusive Economic Zone in perspective: legal status and resolution of user conflicts revisited', (2012) 26 *Ocean Yearbook*, 87.

Projekt ALPhA, available at: http://www.alpha.uni-osnabrueck.de/, accessed 29 October 2015.

Prott, Lyndel. 'The UNIDROIT Convention on Stolen or Illegally Exported Cultural Objects—Ten Years On', (2009) *Uniform Law Review*, 215.

Prott, Lyndel. 'UNESCO and UNIDROIT: a partnership against trafficking in cultural objects', in Palmer, Norman (ed.), *The Recovery of Stolen Art*, London, Kluwer Law International, 1998, pp. 205–15.

Proulx, Vincent-Joël. *Transnational Terrorism and State Accountability: A New Theory of Prevention*, Oxford, Hart Publishing, 2012.

Quillen, Jeffrey L. 'The international attack on money laundering: European initiatives', (1991) *Duke Journal of Comparative and International Law* 213.

Ragazzi, Maurizio. *The Concept of International Obligations Erga Omnes*, Oxford, Clarendon Press, 2000.

Ram, Christopher. 'The United Nations Convention Against Transnational Organized Crime and its Protocols', (2001) 1 *Forum on Crime and Society* (2), 135.

Ramthun, Christian. 'OECD, Deutschland versagt im Kampf gegen Geldwäsche', *Wirtschaftswoche*, 26 April 2014, available at: http://www.wiwo.de/politik/deutschland/geldwaesche-oecd-deutschland-versagt-im-kampf-gegen-geldwäsche/9804692.html, accessed 29 October 2015.

Randall, Kenneth C. 'Universal jurisdiction under international law', (1988) 66 *Texas Law Review*, 785.

Randelzhofer, Albrecht and Dörr, Oliver. 'Article 2(4)', in Simma, Bruno, Nolte, Georg, Khan, Daniel-Erasmus, and Paulus, Andreas (eds), *The Charter of the United Nations: A Commentary*, Vol. I, 3rd edn, Oxford, OUP, 2012, pp. 200–234.

Randelzhofer, Albrecht and Nolte, Georg. 'Article 51', in Simma, Bruno, Nolte, Georg, Khan, Daniel-Erasmus, and Paulus, Andreas (eds), *The Charter of the United Nations: A Commentary*, Vol. II, 3rd edn, Oxford, OUP, 2012, pp. 1397–1428.

Rapoport, David. 'The four waves of modern terrorism', in Chermak, Steven M. and Freilich, Joshua D. (eds), *Transnational Terrorism*, Farnham, Ashgate, 2013, pp. 46–73.

Ratcliffe, James. 'The Art Loss Register and due diligence in the trade in cultural property' in Manacorda, Stefano and Visconti, Arianna (eds), *Protecting Cultural Heritage as a Common Good of Humanity: A Challenge for Criminal Justice*, Milan, ISPAC, 2014, pp. 191–201.

Rawlinson, Paddy. 'Transnational organized crime: media, myths and moralities', in Allum, Felia and Gilmour, Stan (eds), *Routledge Handbook of Transnational Organized Crime*, London, Routledge, 2012, pp. 294–306.

Rehman, Javaid. 'Islam, terrorism and international law', in Saul, Ben (ed.), *Research Handbook on International Law and Terrorism*, Cheltenham, Edward Elgar Publishing, 2014, pp. 177–91.

Reichel, Philip and Albanese, Jay (eds). *Handbook of Transnational Crime & Justice*, 2nd edn, Thousand Oaks, California, SAGE Publications, 2014.

Reindl-Krauskopf, Susanne and Grafl, Christian. *Kriminalität nicht integrierter Ausländer — eine vielfältige Herausforderung für das Strafrecht*, Verhandlungen des Siebzehnten Österreichischen Juristentages Vienna 2009, Manzsche Verlags- und Universitätsbuchhandlung, 2009.

Reinisch, August. 'The changing international legal framework for dealing with non-state actors', in Alston, Philip (ed.), *Non-State Actors and Human Rights*, Vol. 9, Oxford and New York, OUP, 2005, p. 387.

Reitan, Ruth. 'Human rights in US policy: a casualty of the "war on terrorism"?', (2003) 7 *International Journal of Human Rights* (4), 51.

Reitz, Manfred. *Die geraubte Mona Lisa*, Frankfurt/Leipzig, Suhrkamp, 2001.

Revue Internationale de Police Criminelle, Special Cinquantenaire (1923–73), No. 267, April–May 1973, 98–102.

Rothfield, Lawrence. *The Rape of Mesopotamia behind the Looting of the Iraq Museum*, Chicago, University of Chicago Press, 2009.

Reno, William. 'Understanding criminality in West African conflicts', (2009) *International Peacekeeping*, 16.

Report of the Expert Group on the Democratic Republic of the Congo UN Doc. S/2014/42, 23 January 2014.

Report to the Committee on Foreign Relations, United States Senate. 'Afghanistan's narco war: breaking the link between drug traffickers and insurgents', 10 August 2009, Washington DC, US Government Printing, 2009.

Reuter, Peter and Truman, Edwin M. *Chasing Dirty Money: The Fight Against Money Laundering*, Washington DC, Institute for International Economics, 2004.

Revaz, Cris R. 'An introduction to the UN Convention on the Rights of the Child', in Todres, Jonathan, Wojcik, Mark E., and Revaz, Cris R. (eds) *The UN Convention on the Rights of the Child*, Ardsley, New York, Transnational Publishers, 2006, pp. 9–18.

Richani, Nazih. *The Peace Process in Colombia and US Foreign Policy: Plan Colombia II*, 2013, available at: https://nacla.blog/2013/6/3/peace-process-colombia-and-us-foreign-policy-plan-colombia-II.

Richter-White, Holly. 'The direct and indirect impacts of organized crime on youth, as offenders and victims', (2002) *Trends in Organized Crime*, 79–111.

Rider, Barry. 'Taking the profit out of crime', in Rider, Barry (ed.), *Money Laundering Control*, Dublin, Round Hall Sweet and Maxwell, 1996, p. 1.

Riedel, Eibe. 'International Covenant on Economic, Social, Cultural Rights', in Wolfrum, Rüdiger (ed.), *Max Planck Encyclopaedia on Public International Law*, available at: http://www.mpepil.com, accessed 29 October 2015.

Rink, Cornelia. '*Leges sine moribus vanae*', (2016) 17 *German Law Journal* 19.

Ríos, Viridiana. 'Why did Mexico become so violent? A self-reinforcing violent equilibrium caused by competition and enforcement', (2013) 16 *Trends in Organized Crime* (2), 138.

Roberts, Adam. 'Countering terrorism: a historical perspective', in Samuel, Katja L. H. and White, Nigel D. (eds), *Counter-Terrorism and International Law*, Farnham, Ashgate, 2012, pp. 3–41.

Robertson-von Trotha, Caroline. *Organised Crime: Dark Sides of Globalisation*, Interdisciplinary Studies on Culture and Society 8, Baden-Baden, Nomos, 2013.

Robinson, Patrick. 'The missing crimes', in Cassese, Antonio, Gaeta, Paola, and Jones, John R. W. D. (eds), *The Rome Statute of the International Criminal Court. A Commentary*, Vol. 1, Oxford, OUP, 2002, Ch. 11.7.

Rollins, John, Wyler, Liana Sun, and Rosen, Seth. 'International terrorism and transnational crime', Congressional Research Service, Report for Congress, (2010), available at: http://fas.org/sgp/crs/terror/R41004-2010.pdf, accessed 29 October 2015.

Room, Robin. 'Reform by subtraction: the path of denunciation of international drug treaties and reaccession with reservations', (2012) 23 *International Journal of Drug Policy* (5), 401.

Room, Robin. 'Harm reduction, human rights and the WHO Expert Committee on Drug Dependence', in Erickson, Patricia G., Riley, Diane M., Cheung, Yuet W., O'Hare, Patrick A. (eds), *Harm Reduction: A New Direction for Drug Policies and Programs*, Toronto, University of Toronto Press, 1997, pp. 119–30.

Room, Robin and Reuter, Peter. 'How well do international drug conventions protect public health?', (2012) 379 *The Lancet* (9810), 84.

Roosevelt, Theodore. 'Fourth Annual Message to Congress', 6 December 1904.

Rosa, Solange and Dutschke, Mira. 'Child rights at the core: the use of international law in South African cases on children's socio-economic rights', (2006) *South African Journal on Human Rights (SAJHR)*, 224.

Rosser, Alison R. and Haywood, Mandy J. *Guidance for CITES Scientific Authorities: Checklist to assist in making non-detriment findings for Appendix II exports*, Cambridge, IUCN, 2002.

Roth, Michael P. 'Historical overview over transnational crime', in Reichel, Philip and Albanese, Jay (eds), *Transnational Crime and Justice*, 2nd edn, Thousand Oaks, California, SAGE Publications, 2014, pp. 5–22.

Ruggiero, Vincenzo. 'Legal pre-requisites and socio-economic structures for a successful implementation of the Palermo Convention', in Betti, Stefano (ed.), *Symposium: The United Nations Convention against Transnational Organised Crime, requirements for effective implementation*, Turin, UNICRI *et al.*, 2002, p. 149.

Ruys, Tom. *'Armed Attack' and Article 51 of the UN Charter, Evolutions in Customary Law and Practice*, Cambridge, CUP, 2010.

Ryngaert, Cedric. *Jurisdiction in International Law*, Oxford, OUP, 2008.

Salbu, Steven. 'Bribery in the global market: a critical analysis of the Foreign Corrupt Practices Act', (1997) 54 *Washington and Lee Law Review*, 230.

Salt, John. 'Trafficking and human smuggling: a European perspective', (2000) 1 *International Migration* 38 (3), 31.

Salvador, W. Joseph. 'Dismantling the internet mafia: RICO's applicability to cyber crime', (2015) 41 *Rutgers Computer and Technology Law Journal*, 268.

Samosseiko, Dmitry. 'The *partnerka*—what is it, and why should you care?', Technical Paper, SophosLabs Canada, 2009, available at: https://www.sophos.com/security/technical-papers/samosseiko-vb2009-paper.pdf, accessed 29 October 2015.

Sand, Peter H. 'Whither CITES? The evolution of a treaty regime in the borderland of trade and environment', (1997) 1 *EJIL*, 29.

Sandoz, Yves, Swinarski, Christophe, and Zimmermann, Bruno (eds). *Commentary on the Additional Protocols of 8 June 1977 to the Geneva Conventions of 12 August 1949*, Dordrecht, Martinus Nijhoff Publishers, 1987.

Sands, Philippe and Peel, Jaqueline. *Principles of International Environmental Law*, Cambridge, CUP, 2012.

Sanyal, Rajib. 'Determinants of Bribery in International Business: The Cultural and Economic Factors', (2005) 59 *Journal of Business Ethics*, 139.

Sassòli, Marc. 'State responsibility for violations of international humanitarian law', (2002) 84 *IRRC* (846), 401.

Satzger, Helmut. *International and European Criminal Law*, Munich, C. H. Beck, 2012.

Saul, Ben. *Defining Terrorism in International Law*, Oxford, OUP, 2006.

Saul, Ben. 'Criminality and terrorism', in Salinas de Frias, Ana Maria, Samuel, Katja L. H., and White, Nigel D. (eds), *Counter Terrorism. International Law and Practices*, Oxford, OUP, 2012, pp. 133–70.

Saul, Ben. 'Legislating from a Radical Hague: The United Nations Special Tribunal for Lebanon Invents an International Crime of Transnational Terrorism', (2011) 24 *LJIL*, 677.

Savona, Ernesto U. and Vettori, Barbara. 'Evaluating the cost of organised crime from a comparative perspective', (2009) 15 *European Journal on Criminal Policy and Research* (4), 379.

Savoy, Bénédicte. *Kunstraub. Napoleons Konfiszierungen in Deutschland und die europäischen Folgen*, Cologne/Weimar/Vienna, Böhlau, 2010.

Savoy, Bénédicte. *Patrimoine annexé. Les biens culturels saisis par la France en Allemagne autour de 1800*, Paris, Éditions de la Maison des Sciences de l'Homme, 2003.

Scarpinato, Roberto. 'Organised crime in the third millenium', in *Organised Crime: Dark Sides of Globalisation*, Robertson-von Trotha, Caroline (ed.), Interdisciplinary Studies on Culture and Society 8, Baden-Baden, Nomos, 2013, pp. 81–94.

Scharf, Michael P. 'International criminal jurisdiction', (1993) 87 *AJIL*, 604.

Schjolberg, Stein. *The History of Cybercrime, 1976–2014*, Norderstedt, Books on Demand, 2014.

Schloenhardt, Andreas. *Palermo in the Pacific: Organised Crime Offences in the Asia Pacific Region*, Leiden/Boston, Martinus Nijhoff Publishers, 2009.

Schloenhardt, Andreas. *Migrant Smuggling: Illegal Migration and Organized Crime in Australia and the Asia Pacific Region*, Leiden/Boston, Martinus Nijhoff Publishers, 2003.

Schloenhardt, Andreas. 'Transnational organised crime', in Boister, Neil and Currie, Robert J. (eds), *The Routledge Handbook of Transnational Criminal Law*, London, Routledge, 2014, pp. 409–33.

Schloenhardt, Andreas. 'Transnational organised crime and the International Criminal Court. Towards global criminal justice', in *Crime in Australia: International Connections, Australian Institute of Criminology International Conference*, Hilton on the Park, Melbourne, Australia, 29–30 November 2004, available at: http://www.aic.gov.au/media_library/conferences/2004/schloenhardt.pdf, accessed 29 October 2015.

Schloenhardt, Andreas and Jolly, Jarrod M. *Trafficking in Persons in Australia: Myths and Realities*, Chatswood, New South Wales, LexisNexis, 2013.

Schloenhardt, Andreas and Dale, Jessica E. 'Twelve years on: revisiting the UN Protocol against the Smuggling of Migrants by Land, Sea and Air', (2012) 67 *Zeitschrift für öffentliches Recht* (1), 127.

Schloenhardt, Andreas and Davies, Connor. 'Smugglers and Samaritans: defences to people smuggling in Australia', (2013) 36 *University of New South Wales Law Journal* (3), 954.

Schloenhardt, Andreas and Hickson, Hadley. 'Non-criminalization of smuggled migrants: rights, obligations, and Australian practice under Article 5 of the Protocol against the Smuggling of Migrants by Land, Sea, and Air', (2013) 25 *International Journal of Refugee Law* (1), 39.

Schloenhardt, Andreas and Macdonald, Hamish. 'Barriers to ratification of the United Nations Protocol against the Smuggling of Migrants', Research Paper, The University of Queensland Migrant Smuggling Working Group, February 2015, available at: http://www.law.uq.edu.au/migrantsmuggling, accessed 29 October 2015.

Schloenhardt, Andreas and Stacey, Kate L. 'Assistance and protection of smuggled migrants: international law and Australian practice', (2013) 35 *Sydney Law Review*, 53.

Schmid, Alex P. 'The links between transnational organized crime and terrorist crimes', (1996) 2 *Transnational Organized Crime*, 40.

Schmitt, Michael N. *Essays on Law and War at the Fault Lines*, The Hague, T. M. C. Asser Press, 2012.

Schmitt, Michael N. 'The interpretative guidance on the notion of direct participation in hostilities: a critical analysis', (2010) 1 *Harvard National Security Journal*, 5.

Schneckener, Ulrich. *Transnationaler Terrorismus: Charakter und Hintergründe des 'neuen' Terrorismus*, Frankfurt am Main, Suhrkamp, 2006.

Schönke, Adolf and Schröder, Horst. *Strafgesetzbuch Kommentar*, 29th edn, Munich, C. H. Beck, 2014.

Schott, Paul Allan. *Reference Guide to Anti-Money Laundering and Combating the Financing of Terrorism*, 2nd edn, New York, World Bank, 2006.

Schramm, Edward. 'Auf dem Weg zur Europäischen Staatsanwaltschaft', (2014) *Juristenzeitung*, 749.

Schrijver, Nico. 'The ban on the use of force in the UN Charter', in Weller, Marc (ed.), *The Oxford Handbook of the Use of Force in International Law*, Oxford, OUP, 2015, pp. 465–87.

Schünemann, Bernd. 'Die sog. Finanzkrise-Systemversagen oder global organisierte Kriminalität?', in Schünemann, Bernd (ed.), *Die sogenannte Finanzkrise- Systemversagen oder global organisierte Kriminalität*, Berlin, Berliner Wissenschafts-Verlag, 2010, pp. 71–105.

Schutter, Olivier de. *International Human Rights Law*, Cambridge, CUP, 2010.

Scottish Government, *Letting our Communities flourish; A Strategy for Tackling Serious Organised Crime in Scotland*, 2009.

Selle, Claudia and Dirk von. 'Illegaler Kunsthandel—Teil 1', in Unverzagt, Alexander and Röckrath, Gereon (eds), *Kultur & Recht*, 2nd edn, Düsseldorf, Raabe Verlag, 2008, L 3.7.

Selter, Christian. *Gewaltanwendung unter und neben der UN-Charta*, Berlin, Duncker & Humblot, 2007.

Shams, Heba. *Legal Globalisation: Money Laundering Law and Other Cases*, London, British Institute of International and Comparative Law, 2004.

Shaw, Malcolm N. *International Law*, 6th edn, Cambridge, CUP, 2008 and 7th edn, Cambridge, CUP, 2014.

Shearer, Ivan A. 'Problems of jurisdiction and law enforcement against delinquent vessels', (1986) 35 *ICLQ*, 320.

Shelley, Louise I. *Dirty Entanglements. Corruption, Crime and Terrorism*, Cambridge, CUP, 2014.

Shelley, Louise I. *Human Trafficking: A Global Perspective*, New York, CUP, 2010.

Shelley, Louise. 'The crime of human trafficking', (2008) 4 *Global Studies Review* (2), available at: http://www.globality-gmu.net/archives/622, accessed 29 October 2015.

Shelley, Louise and Melzer, Sharon. 'The nexus of organised crime and terrorism: two case studies in cigarette smuggling', (2008) 32 *International Journal of Comparative and Applied Criminal Justice*, 1.

Shelley, Louise and Picarelli, John T. 'Methods and motives: exploring links between transnational organized crime and international terrorism', (2005) 9 *Trends in Organized Crime*, 52.

Sheptycki, James. 'Transnational crime: an interdisciplinary perspective', in Boister, Neil and Currie, Robert J. (eds), *The Routledge Handook of Transnational Criminal Law*, London, Routledge, 2014, p. 41.

Sheptycki, James. 'Against transnational organized crime', in Beare, Margaret E. (ed.), *Critical Reflection on Transnational Organized Crime, Money Laundering, and Corruption*, Toronto, University of Toronto Press, 2003, p. 124.

Sheptycki, James. 'The governance of organised crime in Canada', (2003) 28 *Canadian Journal of Sociology* (4), 489.

Sheptycki, James, Ben Jaffel, Hager, and Bigo, Didier. 'International organised crime in the European Union', in *Directorate General for internal Policies. Policy Department C: Citizens' Rights and Constitutional Affairs*, Civil Liberties, Justice and Home Affairs, 2011.

Sieber, Ulrich. *Straftaten und Strafverfolgung im Internet, Gutachten C zum 69. Deutschen Juristentag*, Munich, C. H. Beck, 2012.

Sieber, Ulrich. 'Computerkriminalität', in Sieber, Ulrich, Satzger, Helmut, and v. Heintschel-Heinegg, Bernd (eds), *Europäisches Strafrecht*, 2nd edn, Baden-Baden, Nomos, 2014, para. 24.

Sieber, Ulrich. 'Legal order in a global world', in v. Bogdandy, Armin and Wolfrum, Rüdiger (eds), *Max Planck Yearbook of United Nations Law*, Vol. 14, Leiden/Boston, Martinus Nijhoff Publishers, 2010.

Sieber, Ulrich. 'Die Zukunft des europäischen Strafrechts', (2009) 121 *ZStW*, 1.

Sieber, Ulrich. 'Mastering complexity in the global cyberspace', in Delmas-Marty, Miereille, Pieth, Mark, and Sieber, Ulrich (eds), *Les chemins de l'harmonisation pénale*, Paris, Société de Législation Comparée, 2008, pp. 127–202.

Sieber, Ulrich. 'Organisierte Kriminalität in der Bundesrepublik Deutschland', in Sieber, Ulrich (ed.), *Internationale Organisierte Kriminalität*, Cologne, Springer, 1997, pp. 43–85.

Siehr, Kurt. 'Das UNIDROIT-Übereinkommen von 1995 und Staatseigentum an archäologischen Kulturgütern', in Ligustro, Aldo and Sacerdoti, Giorgio (eds), *Problemi e tendenze del diritto internazionale dell'economia. Liber amicorum in onore di Paolo Picone In evidenza*, Naples, Editoriale Scientifica, 2011, pp. 983–97.

Siehr, Kurt. 'Die UN-Konvention über den Schutz des kulturellen Erbes unter Wasser und das Internationale Sachenrecht', in Wittinger, Michaela, Wendt, Rudolf, and Ress, Georg (eds), *Verfassung—Völkerrecht—Kulturgüterschutz. Festschrift für Wilfried Fiedler zum 70. Geburtstag*, Berlin, Duncker & Humblot, 2011, pp. 447–60.

Siehr, Kurt. 'The Protection of Cultural Property: the 1995 UNIDROIT Convention and the EEC Instruments of 1992/93 Compared', (1998) *Uniform Law Review* (2–3), 671.

Silverman, Craig. 'An appeal to the United Nations: terrorism must come within the jurisdiction of an International Criminal Court', (1998) *New England International and Comparative Law Annual*, 4.

Simon, Hannah. 'Human trafficking from an international protection perspective: probing the meaning of anti-trafficking measures for the protection of trafficking victims, with special regard to the United Kingdom', (2010) 28 *Pennsylvania State International Law Review*, 633.

Sinha, Jay. *The History and Development of the Leading International Drug Control Conventions*, Ottawa, Parliamentary Research Branch, 2001.

Sinn, Arndt. Organisierte Kriminalität 3.0, Heidelberg, Springer, 2016, due: June 3, 2016.

Sinn, Arndt. 'Jurisdictional law as the key to resolving conflicts: comparative-law observations', in Arndt Sinn (ed.), *Conflicts of Jurisdiction in Cross-border Crime Situations*, Osnabrück, V&R Unipress, 2012, pp. 531–54.

Sinn, Arndt. 'The influence of power on the criminal justice system', in Sinn, Arndt (ed.), *Straffreistellung aufgrund von Drittverhalten*, Tübingen, Mohr Siebeck, 2007.

Sinn, Arndt. 'Das Lagebild der Organisierten Kriminalität in der EU-Tendenzen, rechtliche Initiativen und Perspektiven einer wirksamen OK-Bekämpfung', in Gropp, Walter and Sinn, Arndt (eds), *Organisierte Kriminalität und kriminelle Organisationen*, Baden-Baden, Nomos, 2006, p. 503.

Sinn, Arndt. 'Europäische Gemeinschaften', in Gropp, Walter and Huber, Barbara (eds), *Rechtliche Initiativen gegen organisierte Kriminalität*, Freiburg im Breisgau, Iuscrim MPI, 2001, p. 291.

Siskin, Alison and Wyler, Liana Sun. *Trafficking in Persons: US Policy and Issues for Congress*, Washington DC, Congressional Research Service, 19 February 2013.

Sivakumaran, Sandesh. *The Law of Non-International Armed Conflict*, Oxford, OUP, 2012.

Skaperdas, Stergios. 'The political economy of organized crime: providing protection when the state does not', (2001) *Economics of Governance*, 173–202.

Smagadi, Aphrodite (ed.). *Sourcebook of International Human Rights Materials*, London, British Institute of International and Comparative Law, 2008.

Smith, Peter H. 'The political economy of drugs: conceptual issues and policy options', in Smith, Peter H. (ed.), *Drug Policy in the Americas*, Boulder, Colorado, Westview Press, 1992.

Smolin, David M. 'Child laundering and the Hague Convention on Intercountry Adoption: the future and past of intercountry adoption', (2010) 48 *University of Louisville Law Review [Online]* (3), 441, available at: http://works.bepress.com/david_smolin/8/, accessed 29 October 2015.

Smolin, David M. 'Child laundering: how the intercountry adoption system legitimizes and incentivizes the practices of buying, trafficking, kidnapping, and stealing children', (2006) 52 *Wayne Law Review* [Online] (1), 113, available at: http://works.bepress.com/david_smolin/1/, accessed 29 October 2015.

Sobocinski, Aurélie. 'En dépit des lois, les condamnations pour tourisme sexuel restent rares', *Le Monde*, 10 September 2004.

Sofaer, Abraham D. and Goodman, Seymour E. (ed.). *The Transnational Dimension of Cyber Crime and Terrorism*, Stanford, California, Hoover Institution Press, 2001.

Solis, Gary D. *The Law of Armed Conflict. International Humanitarian Law in War*, Cambridge, CUP, 2010.

Soska, Kyle and Christin, Nicolas. 'Measuring the longitudinal evolution of the online anonymous marketplace ecosystem', in *Proceedings of the 24nd USENIX Security Symposium*, USENIX Association, 2015, 33–48, available at: https://www.usenix.org/conference/usenixsecurity15/technical-sessions/presentation/soska, accessed 29 October 2015.

Soudijn, Melvin. 'A critical approach to trade-based money laundering', (2014) 17 *Journal of Money Laundering Control* (2), 230.

Spannbrucker, Christian. 'Convention on Cybercrime (ETS 185): ein Vergleich mit dem deutschen Computerstrafrecht im materiell- und verfahrensrechtlicher Hinsicht', university dissertation, Regensburg, 2004.

Spillane, Joseph and McAllister, William B. 'Keeping the lid on: a century of drug regulation and control', (2003) 70 *Drug and Alcohol Dependence* (3, Supplement), S5.

Spoenle, Jan. 'Underground economy', in Bellini, Marcello, Brunst, Phillip, and Jähnke, Jochen (eds), *Current Issues in IT Security*, Berlin, Duncker & Humblot, 2010, pp. 67–79.

Sproat, Peter. 'Payback time? To what extent has the new policing of assets provided new assets for policing?', (2009) 12 *Journal of Money Laundering Control* (4), 392.

Squire Patton Boggs. *Maritime Alert: Protecting Crews and Ships from Piracy by Arming Merchant Vessels for Self Defense*. Squire Patton Boggs Online, May 2009, available at: http://www.squiresanders.com, accessed 29 October 2015.

Srinivasan, Murugesan, Raja Pandian, Solomon, and Enoch, Arockiasamy. 'International crimes: cyber crime, crimes against cultural heritage, environmental crimes, and money laundering', in Kethineni, Sesha (ed.), *Comparative and Internatiional Policing, Justice, and Transnational Crime*, Durham, North Carolina, Carolina Academic Press, 2010, pp. 390–408.

Staker, Christopher. 'Jurisdiction', in Evans, Malcolm (ed.), *International Law*, 4th edn, Oxford, OUP, 2014, p. 309.

Stanbrook, Ivor and Stanbrook, Clive. *Extradition*, 2nd edn, Oxford, OUP, 2000.

Stannard, David. *American Holocaust: The Conquest of the Modern World*, Oxford, OUP, 1992.

Steenberghe, Raphaël van. 'Self-defence in response to attacks by non-state actors in the light of recent state practice: a step forward?', (2010) 23 *LJIL* (1), 183.

Steer, Cassandra. 'Non-state actors in international criminal law', in d'Aspremont, Jean (ed.), *Participants in the International Legal System: Multiple Perspectives on Non-State Actors in International Law*, Abingdon, Routledge, 2011.

Steinbrenner, Christian. *Zur Verurteilungspraxis deutscher Gerichte auf dem Gebiet der Schleuserkriminalität*, Wiesbaden, Kriminologische Zentralstelle, 2005.

Stessens, Guy. 'Corporate criminal liability: a comparative perspective', (1994) 43 *ICLQ* (3), 493.

Stewart, David. 'Internationalizing the war on drugs: the UN Convention against Illicit Traffic in Narcotic Drugs and Psychotropic Substances', (1989) *Denver Journal of International Law and Policy* 18, 387.

Stewart, Gwyneth G. 'Enforcement problems in the endangered species conventions: reservations regarding the reservation clauses', (1981) 14 *Cornell International Law Journal*, 429.

Stiglitz, Joseph. *Globalization and its Discontents*, Harmondsworth, Penguin Books, 2002.

Sullivan, Clare and Smith, Evan. *Trade-Based Money Laundering: Risks and Regulatory Responses*, Canberra, Australian Institute of Criminology, 2011.

Streinz, Rudolf (ed.). *Europarecht*, 9th edn, Heidelberg, Müller, 2012.

Suhr, Oliver. 'Titel V. Der Raum der Freiheit, der Sicherheit und des Rechts', in Calliess, Christian and Ruffert, Matthias (eds), *EUV/AEUV, Das Verfassungsrecht der Europäischen Union mit Europäischer Grundrechtecharta*, 4th edn, Munich, C. H. Beck, 2011.

Sulk, Jan Rolf. 'Internationalisierung Innerer Sicherheit auf völkerrechtlicher Ebene', (2010) *JURA*, 683.

Sutherland, Edwin H. *The Professional Thief.* Chicago, University of Chicago Press, 1937.

Swaleheen, Mushfiq and Stansel, Dean. 'Economic freedom, corruption and growth', (2007) *Cato Journal*, 343.

Syrigos, Angelos. 'Interdiction of vessels on the high seas', in Strati, Anastasia, Gavouneli, Maria, and Skourtos, Nikos (eds), *Unresolved Issues and New Challenges to the Law of the Sea*, Leiden/Boston, Martinus Nijhoff Publishers, 2006, pp. 149–201.

Talmon, Stefan. 'The responsibility of outside powers for acts of secessionist entities', (2009) 58 *ICLQ* (3), 493.

Talmon, Stefan. 'The Security Council as world legislature', (2005) 99 *AJIL*, 175.

Tanaka, Yoshifumi. *The International Law of the Sea*, 2nd edn, Cambridge, CUP, 2015.

Tao, Dominick. 'Worldwide markets fuel illegal traffic in organs', *New York Times*, 29 July 2009.

The Global Initiative against Transnational Organized Crime. 'Reinforcing multilateral approaches to transnational organized crime by strengthening local ownership and accountability', available at: http://www.globalinitiative.net/download/global-initiative/Global%20Initiative%20-%20Input%20to%20the%20High%20Level%20Panel%20on%20Peacekeeping%20Operations%20-%20Feb%202015.pdf, accessed 29 October 2015.

Thomas, Chantal. 'Disciplining globalization: international law, illegal trade, and the case of narcotics', (2002) 24 *Michigan Journal of International Law*, 549.

Thomas, Kevin V., Bijlsma, Lubertus, *et al.* 'Comparing illicit drug use in 19 European cities through sewage analysis', (2012) *Science of the Total Environment*, 432–9.

Thomson, Janice E. *Mercenaries, Pirates, and Sovereigns. State-building and Extra-territorial Violence in Early Modern Europe*, Princeton, New Jersey, Princeton University Press, 1994.

Thorn, Bettina. *Internationaler Kulturgüterschutz nach der UNIDROIT-Konvention*, Berlin, De Gruyter, 2005.

Thoumi, Francisco. 'The international drug control regime's straight jacket: are there any policy options?', (2010) 13 *Trends in Organized Crime* (1), 75.

Thoumi, Francisco. E. 'Colombian organized crime: from drug trafficking to parastatal bands and widespread corruption', in Siegel, Dina and van de Bunt, Henk (eds), *Traditional Organized Crime in the Modern World: Responses to Socioeconomic Change*, New York, Springer, 2012, pp. 131–148.

Tijhuis, Antonius J. G. *Transnational Crime and the Interface between Legal and Illegal Actors: The Case of the Illicit Art and Antiquities Trade*, Nijmwegen, Wolf Legal Publishers, 2006.

Tilly, Charles. 'War making and state making as organised crime', in Evans, Peter B. *et al.* (eds), *From Bringing the State Back In*, Cambridge, CUP, 1985, pp. 169–91.

Tonry, Michael. 'Transnational organised crime—prospects for success of the UN Convention', in Albrecht, Hans-Jörg and Fijnaut, Cyrille (eds), *The Containment of Transnational Organised Crime: Comments on the UN Convention of December 2000*, Freiburg im Breisgau, Edition Iuscrim, 2002, p. 253.

Trapp, Kimberley N. 'Back to basics: necessity, proportionality, and the right of self-defence against non-state terrorist actors', (2007) 56 *ICLQ* (1), 141.

Traynor, Ian. 'EU draws up plans for military attacks on Libya targets to stop migrant boats', *The Guardian*, 10 May 2015, available at: http://www.theguardian.com/world/2015/may/10/eu-considers-military-attacks-on-targets-in-libya-to-stop-migrant-boats, accessed 29 October 2015.

Traynor, Ian. 'Germany presses for quota system for EU migrant distribution', *The Guardian*, 29 April 2015, available at: http://www.theguardian.com/world/2015/apr/29/germany-quota-system-eu-migrant-distribution, accessed 29 October 2015.

Treves, Tullio. 'Human rights and the law of the sea', (2010) 28 *Berkeley Journal of International Law*, 1.

Treves, Tullio. 'Piracy, law of the sea, and use of force: developments off the coast of Somalia', (2009) 20 *EJIL*, 399.

Trocki, Carl A. *Opium, Empire and the Global Political Economy. A Study of the Asian Opium Trade 1750–1950*, London, Routledge, 1999.

Tsingou, Eleni. 'Global governance and transnational financial crime: opportunities and tensions in the global anti-money laundering regime', Centre for the Study of Globalisation and Regionalisation, Working Paper 161/05, 2005.

Turner, Mark and Hulme, David. *Governance, Administration & Development: Making the State Work*, Basingstoke, Palgrave Macmillan, 1997.

US Department of Justice. 'Overview of the Law Enforcement Strategy to Combat International Organised Crime', Washington DC, 2008, available at: http://www.justice.gov/criminal/icitap/pr/2008/04-23-08combat-intl-crime-overview.pdf, accessed 29 October 2015.

UNCTAD, United Nations Conference on Trade and Development. *Review of e-commerce legislation harmonization in the Economic Community of West African States*, United Nations, 2015, available at: https://tft.unctad.org/wp-content/uploads/2014/03/ECOWAS-study-on-cyberlaws.pdf, accessed 29 October 2015.

Unger, Brigitte. 'Can money laundering decrease?', (2013) 41 *Public Finance Review*, 658.

United Nations Children's Fund (UNICEF). *Handbook on the Optional Protocol on the Sale of Children, Child Prostitution and Child Pornography*, Geneva, Innocenti Research Centre, 2009.

United Nations General Assembly. 'Report of the Special Rapporteur on the sale of children, child prostitution and child pornography', Najat Maalla M'jid, 23 December 2013, A/HRC/25/48.

United Nations General Assembly. 'Report of the Special Rapporteur on the sale of children, child prostitution and child pornography', Juan Miguel Petit, 12 January 2006, E/CN.4/2006/67.

UNHCR and Save the Children UK (eds). *Sexual Violence and Exploitation: The Experience of Refugee Children in Guinea, Liberia and Sierra Leone Based on Findings and Recommendations from Assessment Mission 22.10.–30.11.2001*, London, UNHCR and Save the Children UK, 2002.

United Nations High-level Panel on Threats, Challenges and Change. 'A more secure world: our shared responsibility', New York, United Nations, 2004, available at: http://www.un.org/en/peacebuilding/pdf/historical/hlp_more_secure_world.pdf, accessed 29 October 2015.

United Nations Office on Drugs and Crime. *Comprehensive Study on Cybercrime*, New York, United Nations, 2013.

United Nations Office on Drugs and Crime. *The Compendium of International Legal Instruments of Corruption*, 2nd edn, Vienna, 2005.

United Nations Office on Drugs and Crime. *United Nations Convention Against Transnational Organized Crime and the Protocols Thereto*, New York, UNODC, 2004.

United Nations Office on Drugs and Crime. 'World Drug Report 2015', 2015, available at: http://www.unodc.org/documents/wdr2015/World_Drug_Report_2015.pdf, accessed 29 October 2015.

United Nations Office on Drugs and Crime. *ICCWC*, available at: https://www.unodc.org/unodc/en/wildlife-and-forest-crime/iccwc.html, accessed 29 October 2015.

United Nations Office on Drugs and Crime. 'UN General Assembly: cooperation vital to combating organized wildlife crime', 6 March 2015, available at: https://www.unodc.org/unodc/en/frontpage/2015/March/un-general-assembly-cooperation-vital-to-combating-organized-wildlife-crime.html, accessed 29 October 2015.

United Nations Office on Drugs and Crime. *United Nations World Drug Report 2014*, Vienna, UNODC, 2014.

United Nations Office on Drugs and Crime. 'Wildlife and forest crime analytic toolkit', 2012, available at: https://www.unodc.org/documents/Wildlife/Toolkit_e.pdf, accessed 29 October 2015.

United Nations Office on Drugs and Crime. *Global Report on Trafficking in Persons 2012*, New York, United Nations Publications, 2012.

United Nations Office on Drugs and Crime. *Legislative guide for the implementation of the United Nations Convention against Corruption*, 2nd revised edn, Vienna, UNODC, 2012.

United Nations Office on Drugs and Crime. *World Drug Report*, Vienna, UNODC, 2012.

United Nations Office on Drugs and Crime. *Model law against the illicit manufacturing of and trafficking in firearms, their parts and components and ammunition*, 2011, UN Pub. No. E.11.V.9.

United Nations Office on Drugs and Crime. *The Globalization of Crime. A Transnational Organized Crime Threat Assessment*, Vienna, UNODC, 2010.

United Nations Office on Drugs and Crime. *Crime and Instability: Case Studies of Transnational Threats*, Vienna, UNODC, 2010.

United Nations Office on Drugs and Crime. *Anti-Human Trafficking Manual for Criminal Justice Practitioners*, New York, United Nations Publications, 2009.

United Nations Office on Drugs and Crime. 'Making drug control "fit for purpose": building on the UNGASS decade', Vienna, UNODC, 2008.

United Nations Office on Drugs and Crime. 'An introduction to human trafficking: vulnerability, impact and action', background paper, Vienna, UNODC, 2008.

United Nations Office on Drugs and Crime. *Assistance for the Implementation of the ECOWAS Plan of Action against Trafficking in Persons*, New York, United Nations Press, 2006.

United Nations Office on Drugs and Crime. *Travaux Préparatoires of the negotiations for the elaboration of the United Nations Convention against Transnational Organized Crime and the Protocols thereto*, UN Pub. No. E.06.V.5, 2006.

United Nations Office on Drugs and Crime. *Legislative Guides for the Implementation of the United Nations Convention Against Transnational Organized Crime and the Protocols Thereto*, Vienna, UNODC, 2004.

United Nations Office on Drugs and Crime. 'Global Programme against Transnational Organized Crime: results of a pilot survey of forty selected organized criminal groups in sixteen countries', Geneva, United Nations, 2002.

United Press International. 'Illegal organ trafficking up in Egypt', 12 December 2011.

USAID, 'LMI: Asia's regional response to endangered species trafficking', available at: https://www.usaid.gov/asia-regional/fact-sheets/lmi-asias-regional-response-endangered-species-trafficking-arrest, accessed 29 October 2015.

van Bueren, Geraldine. 'The United Nations Convention on the Rights of the Child: an evolutionary revolution', in, Davel, C. J. (ed.), *Introduction to Child Law in South Africa*, Claremont, Juta, 2000.

van der Wilt, Harmen. 'Corporate criminal responsibility for international crimes: exploring the possibilities', (2013) 12 *Chinese Journal of International Law* (1), 43.

van Dijk, Jan. 'Mafia markers: assessing organized crime and its impact on societies', (2007) 10 *Trends in Organized Crime*, 39.

van Dijk, Jan and Spapens, Toine. 'Transnational organized crime networks across the world', in Albanese, Jay and Reichel, Philip (eds), *Transnational Organized Crime, A View from Six Continents*, 2nd edn, Thousand Oaks, California, SAGE Publications, 2014, pp. 213–26.

van Duyne, Petrus. 'Organized crime, corruption and power', (1997) 26 *Crime, Law & Social Change*, 201.

Velasco, Cristos. 'Cybercrime jurisdiction: past, present and future', *ERA Forum*, 24 June 2015.

Veno, Arthur. *The Mammoth Book of Bikers*, New York, Carroll & Graf Publishers, 2007.

Verbruggen, Frank. 'On containing organized crime using "container offences": some reflections on substantive criminal law issues', in Albrecht, Hans-Jörg and Fijnaut, Cyrille (eds), *The Containment of Transnational Organised Crime: Comments on the UN Convention of December 2000*, Freiburg im Breisgau, Edition Iuscrim, 2002, pp. 113–34.

Vettori, Barbara. 'Comparing data sources on organised crime across the EU: a first step towards an EU statistical apparatus', in van Duyne, Petrus, Maljevic, Almir, van Dijk, Maarten, Lampe, Klaus von, and Newell, James (eds), *The Organisation of Crime for Profit: Conduct, Law and Measurement*, Nijmwegen, Wolf Legal Publishers, 2006, pp. 43–67.

Vietti, M. G. 'The Palermo Convention: Italy's ratification and the need to adapt national legislation', in Betti, Stefano (ed.), *Symposium: The United Nations Convention against Transnational Organised Crime: requirements for effective implementation*, Turin, UNICRI *et al.*, 2002, p. 39.

Villalpando, Santiago and Condorelli, Luigi. 'Can the Security Council extend the ICC's jurisdiction?', in Cassese, Antonio, Gaeta, Paola, and Jones, John R. W. D. (eds), *The Rome Statute of the International Criminal Court. A Commentary*, Vol. 1, Oxford, OUP, 2002, Ch. 15.

Vlassis, Dimitri. 'The United Nations Convention against Transnational Organized Crime and its protocols: a new era in international cooperation', in International Centre for Criminal Law Reform and Criminal Justice Policy (eds), *The Changing Face of International Criminal Law*, Vancouver, BC, International Centre for Criminal Law Reform and Criminal Justice, 2002, p. 75.

Vogel, Joachim. 'Towards a global Convention against cybercrime', (2008) *Revue électronique de l'AIDP* C-07,1–10, available at: http://www.penal.org/sites/default/files/files/Guadalajara-Vogel.pdf, accessed 29 October 2015.

Vogel, Joachim. 'Geldwäsche—ein europaweit harmonisierter Straftatbestand?', (1997) 109 *ZStW*, 335.

Vogel, Joachim. 'Kapitel 4 Justizielle Zusammenarbeit in Strafsachen', 55. Ergänzungslieferung, in Grabitz, Eberhard, Hilf, Meinhard, and Nettesheim, Martin (eds), *Das Recht der Europäischen Union*, Munich, C. H. Beck, 2015.

von Clausewitz, Carl. *On War* (first published 1832), Oxford, OUP, 2007.

von Heinegg, Wolff Heintschel. 'Repressing piracy and armed robbery at sea—towards a new international regime?', (2010) 40 *Israel Yearbook of Human Rights*, 219.

von Lampe, Klaus. *Organized Crime*, Frankfurt am Main, Peter Lang, 1999.

von Lampe, Klaus. 'Transnational organized crime challenges for future research', (2009) 58 *Crime, Law and Social Change* (2), 179.

von Lampe, Klaus. 'Definitions of organized crime', available at: http://www.organized-crime.de/organizedcrimedefinitions.htm, accessed 29 October 2015.

von Lampe, Klaus. 'Organized crime in Europe: conceptions and realities', (2008) 2 *Policing* (1), 7.

von Lampe, Klaus. 'Making the second step before the first: assessing organized crime', (2005) 42 *Crime, Law and Social Change* (4–5), 227.

Waldmann, Peter. 'Is there a culture of violence in Colombia?', (2007) 1 *International Journal of Politics* (1), 61.

Wall, David S. *Cybercrime: the Transformation of Crime in the Information Age*, Cambridge, Polity Press, 2007.

Wall, David S. 'The organization of cybercrime and organized cybercrime', in Bellini, Marcello, Brunst, Phillip, and Jähnke, Jochen (eds), *Current Issues in IT Security*, Berlin, Duncker & Humblot, 2010, pp. 51–66.

Wannenburg, Gail. 'Organized crime and terrorism', (2003) 10 *South African Institute of International Affairs Journal* (2), 77–90.

Wassenaar Arrangement. 'Best practices to prevent destabilising transfers of small arms and light weapons (SALW) through air transport', adopted at the Plenary Meeting of 11–12 December 2002, revised in December 2007.

Watson, Calinka. 'The organised crime of organ trafficking', *Magister Legum* dissertation, Faculty of Law, University of the Free State, Bloemfontein, 2006, RSA. Unpublished.

Watson, Peter and Todeschini, Cecial. *The Medici Conspiracy: the Illicit Journey of Looted Antiquities from Italy's Tomb Raiders to the World's Greatest Museums*, New York, Public Affairs, 2006.

Webster, Daniel. 'Letter from Daniel Webster to Henry Stephen Fox', 24 April 1841, available at: http://avalon.law.yale.edu/19th_century/br-1842d.asp, accessed 29 October 2015.

Webster, Peter. 'Learning from history: a review of David Bewley-Taylor's *The United States and International Drug Control, 1909–1997*', (2003) 14 *International Journal of Drug Policy* (4), 343.

Wedgewood, Ruth. 'Responding to terrorism: the strikes against bin Laden', (1999) 24 *Yale J Intl L* (2), 559.

Weenink, Anton. 'The Russian mafiya: a private actor in international relations', in Arts, Bas, Noortmann, Math, and Reinalda, Bob (eds), *Non-State Actors in International Relations*, Aldershot, Ashgate, 2001, pp. 179–98.

Wehinger, Frank. 'Illegale Märkte', MPlfG Working Paper 11/6, Max Planck Institute for the Study of Societies, Cologne, 2011.

Weigend, Thomas. 'The universal terrorist. The international community grappling with a definition', (2006) 4 *JICJ*, 912.

Weissbrodt, David and Anti-Slavery International. *Abolishing Slavery and its Contemporary Forms*, New York/Geneva, OHCHR, 2002.

Weißer, Bettina. 'Angleichung von Strafvorschriften zur grenzüberschreitenden (organisierten) Kriminalität', in Böse, Martin (ed.), *Europäisches Strafrecht mit polizeilicher Zusammenarbeit*, Baden-Baden, Nomos, 2013, para. 9, pp. 337–78.

Wells, Celia and Elias, Juanita. 'Catching the conscience of the king: corporate players on the international stage', in Alston, Philip (ed.), *Non-State Actors and Human Rights*, Oxford and New York, OUP, 2005, pp. 141–75.

Werle, Gerhard and Jeßberger, Florian. *Principles of International Criminal Law*, Oxford, OUP, 2014.

Weschke, Eugen and Heine-Heiß, Karla. *Organisierte Kriminalität als Netzstrukturkriminalität*, Berlin, Fachhochschule für Verwaltung und Rechtspflege, 1990.

Wheatley, Joseph. 'Transnational organized crime: a survey of laws, policies and international conventions', in Allum, Felia and Gilmour, Stan (eds), *Routledge Handbook of Transnational Organized Crime*, London, Routledge, 2012, pp. 65–79.

WHO, *International Health Regulations*, 2nd edn, Geneva, Switzerland, WHO, 2008.

WHO, 'Avian influenza—situation in Egypt—Update 49', 6 April 2011.

WHO, 'Avian influenza—situation in Indonesia—Update 3', 1 April 2011.

Wicker, Magda. 'Durchsuchung in der Cloud. Nutzung von Cloud-Speichern und der strafprozessuale Zugriff deutscher Ermittlungsbehörden', (2013) 16 *Multimedia und Recht* (12), 765.

Wijnstekers, Willem. *The Evolution of CITES*, 9th edn, Budapest, CIC—International Council for Game and Wildlife Conservation, 2011.

Williams, Phil. 'Terrorist financing and organized crime. Nexus, appropriation, or transformation?', in Biersteker, Thomas J. and Eckert, Sue E. (eds), *Countering the Financing of Terrorism*, Abingdon, Routledge, 2008, pp. 126–49.

Williams, Phil. 'Transnational criminal networks', in Aquilla, John and Ronfeld, David F. (eds), *Netwars and Networks: The Future of Terror, Crime and Militancy*, Santa Monica, California, RAND, 2001.

Williams, Phil and Savona, Ernesto. 'Problems and dangers posed by organized transnational crime in the various regions of the world', in Williams, Phil and Savona, Ernesto (eds), *The United Nations and Transnational Organized Crime*, London, Frank Cass, 1996, p. 1.

Williams, Sharon A. 'Article 12. Preconditions to the exercise of jurisdiction', in Triffterer, Otto (ed.), *Commentary on the Rome Statute of the International Criminal Court, Observers' Notes, Article by Article*, 2nd edn, Oxford/Baden-Baden, Nomos, 2008.

Witt, John Fabian. *Lincoln's Code: The Laws of War in American History*, New York, Free Press, 2012.

Witten, Samuel. 'The International Convention for the Suppression of Terrorist Bombings', in Ben Saul (ed.), *Research Handbook on International Law and Terrorism*, Cheltenham, Edward Elgar Publishing, 2014, pp. 136–62.

Wodak, Alex. 'The international drug treaties: "paper tigers" or dangerous behemoths?', (2003) 14 *International Journal of Drug Policy* (2), 221.

Wolfrum, Rüdiger. 'Freedom of navigation: new challenges', in Nordquist, Myron H., Koh, Tommy T. B., and Norton Moore, John (eds), *Freedoms of the Sea, Passage Rights and the 1982 Law of the Sea Convention*, Leiden, Brill, 2009, pp. 79–102.

Wolfrum, Rüdiger. 'The attack of September 11, 2001, the wars against the Taliban and Iraq: is there a need to reconsider international law on the recourse to force and the rules in armed conflict?', (2003) 7 *Max Planck Ybk UN L*, 1.

Wood, Michael. 'United Nations, Security Council', in Wolfrum, Rüdiger (ed.), *Max Planck Encyclopedia of Public International Law*, last updated July 2007, available at: http://opil.ouplaw.com/view/10.1093/law,epil/9780199231690/law-9780199231690-e561?rskey=vL1T1x&result=1&prd=EPIL, accessed 29 October 2015.

Woodiwiss, Michael and Hobbs, Dick. 'Organized evil and the Atlantic Alliance: moral panics and the rhetoric of organized crime policing in America and Britain', (2009) 49 *British Journal of Criminology* (1), 106.

World Bank and Eastern and Southern Africa Anti-Money Laundering Group. *Mutual Evaluation Report: The Federal Democratic Republic of Ethiopia*, ESAAMLG, 2015.

Wouters, Jan, Ryngart, Cedric, and Cloots, Ann Sofie. 'The international legal framework against corruption: achievements and challenges', (2013) *Melbourne Journal of International Law*, 1.

Wright, Alan. *Organised Crime*, Portland, Oregon, Willian Publishing, 2006.

Wright, Oliver. 'France requests access to Britain's DNA database for European police forces', *The Independent*, 18 November 2015.

Wünschel, Jörg. 'Die Datenbank kritischer Werke im Lichte des Datenschutzes', (2015) *Kunst und Recht*, 49.

Würtenberger, Thomas. *Der Kampf gegen das Kunstfälschertum in der deutschen und schweizerischen Strafrechtspflege*, Wiesbaden, Franz Steiner Verlag, 1951.

Yang, Haijiang. *Jurisdiction of the Coastal State over Foreign Merchant Ships in Internal Waters and the Territorial Sea*, Berlin, Springer, 2005.

Yepes, Concepcion Verdugu. 'Compliance with the AML/CFT International Standard: lessons from a cross-country analysis', IMF Working Paper, WP/11/177, New York, IMF, 2011.

Yoo, John C. and Ho, James C. 'International law and the war on terrorism', (2003) *Yoo NYU Combatants.Doc*, 1.

Young, Mary A. 'The smuggling and trafficking of refugees and asylum seekers: is the international community neglecting the duty to protect the persecuted in the pursuit of transnational organized crime?', (2003) 27 *Suffolk Transnational Law Review* (1), 101.

Young, Reuven. 'Defining terrorism: the evolution of terrorism as a legal concept in international law and its influence on definitions in domestic legislation', (2006) 29 *Boston College Intl Comp L Rev*, 23.

Zagaris, Bruce. 'EU committee recommends action to combat transnational organised crime', (2013) 29 *International Law Enforcement Reporter* (1), 501.

Zakhele, Hlophe. 'Regulating money laundering in developing countries', PhD thesis, 2012, King's College, London. Unpublished.

Zaremba, Maciej. 'Koloni Kosovo. Part 1: Report from Unmikistan, land of the future', available at: http://www.dn.se/kultur-noje/kulturdebatt/part-1-report-from-unmikistan-land-of-the-future/; 'Koloni Kosovo. Part 2: The UN state and the seven robbers', available at: http://www.dn.se/kultur-noje/kulturdebatt/part-2-the-un-state-and-the-seven-robbers/; 'Koloni Kosovo. Part 3: Complain in Azerbaijan', available at: http://www.dn.se/kultur-noje/kulturdebatt/part-3-complain-in-azerbaijan/; 'Koloni Kosovo: Part 4: Prowess, courage and plastic socks', available at: http://www.dn.se/kultur-noje/kulturdebatt/part-4-prowess-courage-and-plastic-socks/, all in *Dagens Nyheter*, 25 June 2007, all accessed 29 October 2015.

Zdanowicz, John. 'Trade-based money laundering and terrorist financing', (2009) 5 *Review of Law and Economics* (2), 858.

Zeder, Fritz. 'Europastrafrecht, Vertrag von Lissabon und Stockholmer Programm "Mehr Grundrechtsschutz?"', (2012) *Europarecht*, 34.

Ziegler, Katja S. 'Domaine réservé', in *Max Planck Encyclopedia of Public International Law*, available at: http://opil.ouplaw.com/search?sfam=&q=Domaine+r%C3%A9serv%C3%A9&prd=EPIL&searchBtn=Search, accessed 29 October 2015.

Zimmerman, Mara E. 'The black market for wildlife: combating transnational organized crime in the illegal wildlife trade', (2003) 36 *Vanderbilt Journal of Transnational Law*, 1657.

Zimmermann, Andreas. 'Article 5. Crimes within the jurisdiction of the Court', in Triffterer, Otto (ed.), *Commentary on the Rome Statute of the International Criminal Court, Observers' Notes, Article by Article*, Oxford and Baden-Baden, Nomos, 2008.

Zimmermann, Andreas. 'The creation of a permanent International Criminal Court', (1998) 2 *Max Planck Ybk UN L*, 169.

Zimmermann, Sarah. *Die Strafbarkeit des Menschenhandels im Lichte internationaler und europarechtlicher Rechtsakte*, Baden-Baden, Nomos, 2010.

Zöller, Mark A. 'Verschwimmende Grenzen zwischen Terrorismus und Organisierter Kriminalität', in Sinn, Arndt and Zöller, Mark A. (eds), *Neujustierung des Strafrechts durch Terrorismus und Organisierte Kriminalität*, Heidelberg, C. F. Müller, 2013, pp. 1–14.

Zöller, Mark A. 'Europäische Strafgesetzgebung', (2009) *Zeitschrift für internationale Strafrechtsdogmatik*, 340.

Index

The manufacturer's authorised representative in the EU for product safety is Oxford University Press España S.A. of el Parque Empresarial San Fernando de Henares, Avenida de Castilla, 2 – 28830 Madrid (www.oup.es/en or product.safety@oup.com). OUP España S.A. also acts as importer into Spain of products made by the manufacturer.

www.ingramcontent.com/pod-product-compliance
Lightning Source LLC
LaVergne TN
LVHW062202200926
848484LV00006B/1302
9780198733737